T0212678

Lecture Notes in Computer Science 9281

Commenced Publication in 1973
Founding and Former Series Editors:
Gerhard Goos, Juris Hartmanis, and Jan van Leeuwen

More information about this series at http://www.springer.com/series/7412

Vittorio Murino · Enrico Puppo
Diego Sona · Marco Cristani
Carlo Sansone (Eds.)

New Trends in Image Analysis and Processing – ICIAP 2015 Workshops

ICIAP 2015 International Workshops
BioFor, CTMR, RHEUMA, ISCA, MADiMa
SBMI, and QoEM
Genoa, Italy, September 7–8, 2015
Proceedings

Springer

Editors
Vittorio Murino
Istituto Italiano di Tecnologia (IIT)
Genoa
Italy

Enrico Puppo
University of Genoa
Genoa
Italy

Diego Sona
Istituto Italiano di Tecnologia (IIT)
Genoa
Italy

Marco Cristani
University of Verona
Verona
Italy

Carlo Sansone
University of Napoli Federico II
Napoli
Italy

ISSN 0302-9743   ISSN 1611-3349   (electronic)
Lecture Notes in Computer Science
ISBN 978-3-319-23221-8   ISBN 978-3-319-23222-5   (eBook)
DOI 10.1007/978-3-319-23222-5

Library of Congress Control Number: 2015947119

LNCS Sublibrary: SL6 – Image Processing, Computer Vision, Pattern Recognition, and Graphics

Springer International Publishing AG Switzerland is part of Springer Science+Business Media
(www.springer.com)

Preface

This volume contains the 71 papers accepted for presentation at the workshops hosted by the 18th International Conference on Image Analysis and Processing, held in Genova, Italy, September 7–11, 2015, organized by the Istituto Italiano di Tecnologia (IIT).

The International Conference on Image Analysis and Processing (ICIAP) is a conference organized every two years by the GIRPR, the Italian group of researchers affiliated with the IAPR. The aim of these conferences is to bring together researchers working on image analysis, image processing, and pattern recognition from around the world.

Seven individual workshops — three one-day and four half-day — were selected by the workshop chiars, Marco Cristani and Carlo Sansone, to complement ICIAP 2015 in Genova:

- BioFor 2015, International Workshop on Recent Advances in Digital Security: Biometrics and Forensics
- CTMR 2015, Color in Texture And Material Recognition
- RHEUMA 2015, Medical Imaging in Rheumatology: Advanced Applications for the Analysis of Inflammation and Damage in the Rheumatoid Joint
- ISCA 2015, Image-Based Smart City Application
- MADiMa 2015, First International Workshop on Multimedia Assisted Dietary Management
- SBMI 2015, Scene Background Modeling and Initialization
- QoEM 2015, Workshop on Image and Video Processing for Quality of Multimedia Experience

The International Workshop on Recent Advances in Digital Security: Biometrics and Forensics (BioFor 2015) organized by Modesto Castrillón Santana, from Universidad de Las Palmas de Gran Canaria, Spain, Matthias Kirchner, from Binghamton University, USA, Daniel Riccio and Luisa Verdoliva, both from Università Federico II di Napoli, Italy, provides a forum for researchers from academia and industry to develop and foster synergies between biometrics and forensics. Attacks to biometrics systems are also becoming very frequent, and ever more sophisticated, aiming both at committing commercial frauds and acts of terrorism. A similar scenario involves the world of digital media, by now pervasive in our daily life, where images and videos can be manipulated for various evil purposes, including both crimes against intellectual property and against national security. Although the goals of biometrics and media forensics are different, they have strong similarities in purposes and tools. They both aim at supporting law enforcement and investigation, and both draw on methodologies and technologies that change and evolve on a daily basis. Increasingly, new scenarios arise where techniques designed for biometrics can be utilized for forensic purposes or vice versa. The eight papers accepted for presentation to BioFor reflect a good scenario of the field from both the scientific and applicative point of view.

The study of texture and material recognition have a long history in image analysis and computer vision. Recent works that deal with large collections of images taken from the Internet or that exploit large-scale machine learning techniques have renewed the interest in these topics. The most relevant intuition is that features from other domains, such as object recognition, may achieve comparable or at times better performance than those achieved with features specially designed for texture and material classification. Moreover, while for some artificial materials color and texture are independent properties, for natural materials they are strongly related. Whether or not color information is useful for texture and material classification is still an open issue especially "in the wild" where imaging conditions such as lighting color and direction, orientation, sensor type, etc., are unpredictable. The Color in Texture and Material Recognition (CTMR 2015) workshop, organized by Claudio Cusano - University of Pavia, Italy, Paolo Napoletano and Raimondo Schettini - University of Milan- Bicocca, Italy, and Joost Van De Weijer - Autonomous University of Barcelona, Spain, explores these topics by providing new insights for understanding color in texture and material recognition. The seven accepted papers cover different areas, including color science, computer vision, computer graphics, and machine learning.

The aim of the RHEUMA 2015 workshop — Medical Imaging in Rheumatology: Advanced applications for the analysis of inflammation and damage in the rheumatoid Joint — is to provide an overview on the development of new medical imaging methods for the early diagnosis and therapeutic control of rheumatic musculo-skeletal diseases. The goal of the RHEUMA organizers, Silvana Dellepiane and Marco A. Cimmino - University of Genova, Italy, and Gianni Viano - Softeco Sismat S.R.L., is to promote the use of alternative techniques such as MRI and US, which can even be used in a combined manner. The workshop focuses on the development of appropriate techniques for data analysis and 2D/3D visualization, in order to increase and improve the information available to the doctor during the diagnostic process and follow-up. The results of the research can also be verified at the workshop through the presentation of experimental demonstrators and database collections of case studies that can be used as a reference for training and validation sessions. The technical program featured six accepted research papers and two invited speakers, Mikael Boesen, from the Department of Radiology and Parker Institute, Bispebjerg and Frederiksberg Hospital, Copenhagen (Denmark) and Zbisaw Taborm from the Faculty of Physics, Mathematics and Computer Science, Cracow University of Technology, Cracow (Poland).

The term "smart city" is generally used to conceptualize an urban space in which digital technologies are used to enhance quality of life while saving resource consumption. The main characteristics of a smart city are participation, cooperation, and inclusiveness of citizens, which must be engaged more effectively and actively. For this purpose, a strong integration between human, collective, and artificial intelligence is necessary in a smart city, in order to improve city performance and well-being, reducing resource consumption. Of course, ICT represent a critical aspect for smart city design and implementation and innovative solutions are necessary to monitor and improve many aspects of a city life in real time, and hence to make possible the development of knowledge-intensive collaborative activities capable of adapting themselves to manage uncertainty and maximize the problem-solving capability of the city. The ISCA 2015 — Image- Based Smart City Application — workshop focuses on the innovative image-based applications for smart city that of course involve a wide range of key sectors including intelligent mobility, health care and active aging, energy saving, e-government, tourism, e-justice, urban safety, etc. Featuring 16 accepted papers, ISCA 2015 was organized by Giuseppe Pirlo, from the University of Bari, Italy, Donato Impedovo from Dyrectalab, Italy, and Byron Leite Dantas Bezerra from the University of Pernambuco, Brazil.

The prevention of onset and progression of diet-related acute and chronic diseases requires reliable and intuitive dietary management. The need for accurate, automatic, real-time, and personalized dietary advice has been recently complemented by the advances in computer vision and smartphone technologies, permitting the development of the first mobile food multimedia content analysis applications. The proposed solutions rely on the analysis of multimedia content captured by wearable sensors, smartphone cameras, barcode scanners, RFID readers and IR sensors, along with already established nutritional databases and often require some user input. In the field of nutritional management, multimedia not only bridges diverse information and communication technologies, but also computer science with medicine, nutrition, and dietetics. This congruence brings new challenges and opportunities on dietary management. MADiMa2015, organized by Stavroula Mougiakakou - University of Bern, Switzerland, Giovani Maria Farinella - University of Catania, Italy, and Keiji Yanai - The University of Electro-Communications, Tokyo, Japan, aimed to bring together researchers from the diverse fields of engineering, computer science, and nutrition who investigate the use of information and communication technologies for better monitoring and management of food intake. The technical program featured 19 papers, carefully selected by the Program Committee, as well as two invited speakers, Prof. Edward Sazonov from the University of Alabama (USA) and Gerald Cultot, Research Programme Officer of the European Commission.

In scene analysis, the availability of an initial background model that describes the scene without foreground objects is the prerequisite, or at least can be of help, for many applications video surveillance, video segmentation, video compression, video in-painting, privacy protection for videos, and computational photography. The aim of the Scene Background and Modeling Initialization — SBMI 2015 — Workshop is to bring together researchers interested in scene background modeling and initialization (also known as bootstrapping, background estimation, background reconstruction, initial background extraction, or background generation) in different application areas, in order to disseminate their most recent research results, to advocate and promote the research into scene background modeling and initialization, to discuss rigorously and systematically potential solutions and challenges, to promote new collaborations among researchers working in different application areas, and to share innovative ideas and solutions for exploiting the potential synergies emerging from the integration of different application domains. Jointly organized by Lucia Maddalena, from the National Research Council, Italy, and Thierry Bouwmans, from the Université De La Rochelle, France, SBMI 2015 featured nine accepted papers and an invited presentation, titled "Motion Detection: Unsolved Issues and [Potential] Solutions," by Pierre-Marc Jodoin from the University of Sherbrooke, Canada.

Tremendous technological advances in the area of video compression and communication made image/video over the Internet and wireless mobile networks an inevitable part of our lives. Indeed, video traffic is exploding over the Internet, and is becoming a dominant application over 3G/4G mobile systems. The necessity for seamless access and exchange of a large amount of multimedia content anytime and anywhere by mobile users is driving intensive research within this field as it provides a number of business opportunities through commercial multimedia application provisioning. High user satisfaction with multimedia services is the most meaningful quality evaluation criterion. For this reason the set of issues encompassed by the term quality of experience (QoE), i.e., the quality perceived subjectively by the end-user, is key to service providers, network and software engineers, developers, and scientists. To address the ever-increasing consumer requirements, the emerging solutions for multimedia delivery over next-generation networks have to rely on the state of the art in multimedia processing and communications. The goal of the workshop on Image and Video Processing for Quality of Multimedia Experience — QoEM 2015, organized by Nicu Sebe - University of Trento, Italy, Ben Herbst - Stellenbosch University, South Africa, and Dubravko Culibrk - University of Trento, Italy / University of Novi Sad, Serbia — is to give an overview of the recent technologies and system solutions, as well as create a forum to exchange ideas and address challenges emerging in this field. The technical program featured oral presentations of all six accepted regular papers.

On the whole, the addressed topics constituted a good mix between current trends in computer vision and the fundamentals of image analysis and pattern recognition.

September 2015   Vittorio Murino
                                                                 Enrico Puppo
                                                                 Diego Sona
                                                                 Marco Cristani
                                                                 Carlo Sansone

Organization

Organizing Institution

Pattern Analysis and Computer Vision (PAVIS)
Istituto Italiano di Tecnologia (IIT), Genova, Italy
http://www.iit.it/pavis

General Chair

Vittorio Murino   Istituto Italiano di Tecnologia, Italy
University of Verona, Italy

Program Chairs

Enrico Puppo   University of Genova, Italy
Gianni Vernazza   University of Genova, Italy

Workshop Chairs

Marco Cristani   University of Verona, Italy
Carlo Sansone   University of Napoli Federico II, Italy

Tutorial Chair

Alessio Del Bue   Istituto Italiano di Tecnologia, Italy

Special Sessions Chairs

Giuseppe Boccignone   University of Milano, Italy
Giorgio Giacinto   University of Cagliari, Italy

Finance and Industrial Chairs

Sebastiano Battiato   University of Catania, Italy
Luigi Di Stefano   University of Bologna, Italy

Publicity/Web Chair

Manuele Bicego   University of Verona, Italy
Umberto Castellani   University of Verona, Italy

Publications Chairs

Ryad Chellali   Istituto Italiano di Tecnologia, Italy
Diego Sona   Istituto Italiano di Tecnologia, Italy

US Liaison Chair

Silvio Savarese   Stanford University, USA

Asia Liaison Chair

Hideo Saito   Keio University, Japan

Steering Committee

Virginio Cantoni   University of Pavia, Italy
Luigi Cordella   University of Napoli Federico II, Italy
Alberto Del Bimbo   University of Firenze, Italy
Marco Ferretti   University of Pavia, Italy
Fabio Roli   University of Cagliari, Italy
Gabriella Sanniti di   ICIB-CNR, Italy
   Baja

Area Chairs

Video Analysis and Understanding:

Rita Cucchiara   University of Modena and Reggio Emilia, Italy
Jordi Gonzàlez   Universitat Autònoma de Barcelona, Spain

Multiview Geometry and 3D Computer Vision:

Andrea Fusiello   University of Udine, Italy
Michael Goesele   TU Darmstadt, Germany

Pattern Recognition and Machine Learning:

Marcello Pelillo   University of Venezia, Italy
Tiberio Caetano   NICTA, Australia

Image Analysis, Detection and Recognition:

Raimondo Schettini   University of Milano-Bicocca, Italy
Theo Gevers   University of Amsterdam, The Netherlands

Shape Analysis and Modeling:

Leila De Floriani   University of Genova, Italy
Gunilla Borgefors   Uppsala University, Sweden

Multimedia:

Nicu Sebe   University of Trento, Italy
Cees Snoek   University of Amsterdam, The Netherlands

Biomedical Applications:

Silvana Dellepiane   University of Genova, Italy
Dimitri Van De Ville   EPFL and University of Genève, Switzerland

Local Committee

Sara Curreli   Istituto Italiano di Tecnologia, Italy
Matteo Bustreo   Istituto Italiano di Tecnologia, Italy
Nicholas Dring   Istituto Italiano di Tecnologia, Italy
Carlos Beltran   Istituto Italiano di Tecnologia, Italy

Endorsing Institutions

International Association for Pattern Recognition (IAPR)
Italian Group of Researchers in Pattern Recognition (GIRPR)
IEEE Computer Society's Technical Committee on Pattern Analysis
    and Machine Intelligence (IEEE-TCPAMI)

Institutional Patronage

Istituto Italiano di Tecnologia
University of Genova
University of Verona
Regione Liguria
Comune di Genova

Sponsoring and Supporting Institutions

Istituto Italiano di Tecnologia, Italy
Datalogic, Italy
Google Inc., USA
Centro Studi Gruppo Orizzonti Holding, Italy
EBIT Esaote, Italy
Ansaldo Energia, Italy
Softeco, Italy
eVS embedded Vision Systems S.r.l., Italy
3DFlow S.r.l., Italy
Camelot Biomedical Systems S.r.l.

University of Genova, Italy
University of Verona, Italy
Camera di Commercio di Genova, Italy

Acknowledgments

We kindly acknowledge Camera di Commercio of Genova for the availability of the conference location of "Sala delle Urla" in the Stock Exchange building, and for related services.

BioFor 2015 Organization

Organizers

Modesto Castrillón Santana	Universidad de Las Palmas de Gran Canaria, Spain
Matthias Kirchner	Binghamton University, USA
Daniel Riccio	Università Federico II di Napoli, Italy
Luisa Verdoliva	Università Federico II di Napoli, Italy

Program Committee

Pradeep Atrey, Canada
Mauro Barni, Italy
Sebastiano Battiato, Italy
Luis Baumela, Spain
Tiziano Bianchi, Italy
Giulia Boato, Italy
Pedro Comesaña Alfaro, Spain
Maria De Marsico, Italy
Óscar Déniz-Suárez, Spain
Julián Fiérrez, Spain
Maria Frucci, Italy
Ajay Kumar, Hong Kong
Marco La Cascia, Italy

Shujun Li, UK
Gianluca Marcialis, Italy
Heydi Méndez -Vázquez, Cuba
Michele Nappi, Italy
Tian Tsong Ng, Singapore
Christian Riess, Germany
Kaushik Roy, USA
Gabriella Sanniti di Baja, Italy
Riccardo Satta, Italy
Taha Sencar, Turkey
Matthew Stamm, USA
Massimo Tistarelli, Italy
Harry Wechsler, USA

CTMR 2015 Organization

Organizers

Claudio Cusano	University of Pavia, Italy
Paolo Napoletano	University of Milan-Bicocca, Italy
Raimondo Schettini	University of Milan-Bicocca Italy
Joost van de Weijer	Autonomous University of Barcelona, Spain

Program Committee

André Backes, Brazil
Simone Bianco, Italy
Francesco Bianconi, Italy
Simone Calderara, Italy
Barbara Caputo, Italy
Antonio Fernández, Spain
Rocco Furferi, Italy
Giovanni Gallo, Italy
Ovidiu Ghita, Ireland
Adilson Gonzaga, Brazil

Elena González, Spain
Richard Harvey, UK
Fahad Khan, Sweden
Jussi Parkkinen, Finland
Nol Richard, France
Christian Riess, Germany
Xiaoyang Tan, China
Shoji Tominaga, Japan
Alain Tremeau, France

RHEUMA 2015 Organization

Organizers

Marco A. Cimmino   Università degli Studi di Genova, Italy
Silvana Dellepiane   Università degli Studi di Genova, Italy
Gianni Viano   Softeco Sismat S.r.l., Italy

Program Committee

Xin Chen, UK
Luigi Satragno, Italy
Bianca Falcideno, Italy
Matteo Santoro, Italy

Additional Reviewers

Zbislaw Tabor, Poland
Roberta Ferretti, Italy
Giulia Troglio, Italy
Marios Pitikakis, Italy

ISCA 2015 Organization

Organizers

Giuseppe Pirlo	University of Bari, Italy
Donato Impedovo	DyrectaLab, Italy
Byron Leite Dantas Bezerra	University of Pernambuco, Brazil

Program Committee

Ignacio Aedo Cuevas, Spain
Andrea Alberici, Italy
André L.L. Aquino, Brazil
Giovanni Attolico, Italy
Donato Barbuzzi, Italy
Roberto Bellotti, Italy
Micheal Blumenstein, Australia
Mohamed Cheriet, Canada
Matteo D'Aloia, Italy
Tiziana D'Orazio, Italy
Moises Diaz, Spain
Monica Divitini, Norway
Jihad El-Sana, Israel
Michael Fairhurst, UK
Miguel A. Ferrer, Spain
Angelika Garz, Germany
Mei Han, USA

Mohamed Jemni, Tunisia
Zhenhong Jia, China
Irman Malik, Germany
Angelo Marcelli, Italy
Alke Martens, Germany
Giuseppe Mastronardi, Italy
Carlos A.B. Mello, Brazil
Luiz E.S. Oliveira, Brazil
Umapada Pal, India
Ioannis Pratikakis, Greece
Maria Rizzi, Italy
Kozeta Sevrani, Albania
Tea Tavanxhiu, Italy
Kurban Ubul, China
Seiichi Uchida, Japan
Tuergin Yibulayin, China

MADiMa 2015 Organization

Organizers

Stavroula Mougiakakou	University of Bern, Switzerland
Giovanni Maria Farinella	University of Catania, Italy
Keiji Yanai	The University of Electro-Communications, Japan

Program Committee

Antonella Agodi, Italy
Kiyoharu Aizawa, Japan
Oliver Amft, Germany
Marios Anthimopoulos, Switzerland
Andreas Arens, Luxembourg
Sebastiano Battiato, Italy
Edward J. Delp, USA
Ajay Divakaran, USA
David Duke, USA
Xian-Hua Han, Japan

Wanqing Li, Australia
Alessandro Mazzei, Italy
Patrick Olivier, UK
Vikas Ramachandra, USA
Daniele Ravi, London
Sergey Shevchik, Switzerland
Shervin Shirmohammadi, Canada
Jindong Tan, USA
Guang-Zhong Yang, London

SBMI 2015 Organization

Organizers

Lucia Maddalena   National Research Council, Italy
Thierry Bouwmans   Université de La Rochelle, France

Program Committee

Walid Barhoumi, Tunisia
Harish Bhaskar, UAE
Rita Cucchiara, Italy
Soon Ki Jung, Korea
Janusz Konrad, USA
Paul Miller, UK
Alfredo Petrosino, Italy

Fatih Porikli, Australia
Caifeng Shan, The Netherlands
Antoine Vacavant, France
Sergio A. Velastin, Chile
Brendt Wohlberg, USA
Shengping Zhang, China

QoEM 2015 Organization

Organizers

Niculae Sebe   University of Trento, Italy
Ben Herbst   Stellenbosch University, South Africa
Dubravko Culibrk   University of Trento, Italy/University of Novi Sad, Serbia

Program Committee

Gustavo Benvenutti Borba, Brazil
Willie Brink, South Africa
Jacob Chakareski, USA
Samuel Cheng, USA
Lai-Tee Cheok, Samsung Telecom
America, USA
Gene Cheung, Japan
Vladimir Crnojevic, Serbia
Keiko Verônica Ono Fonseca, Brazil
Borko Furht, USA
Hari Kalva, USA
Thomas Maugey, France

Rodrigo Minetto, Brazil
Milan Mirkovic, Serbia
Richard Demo Souza, Brazil
Lina Stankovic, UK
Vladimir Stankovic, UK
Nikolaos Thomos, UK
Laura Toni, Switzerland
Vladan Velisavljevic, UK
Dejan Vukobratović, Serbia
Riaan Wolhuter, South Africa
Zixiang Xiong, USA

Contents

**RHEUMA 2015 – Medical Imaging in Rheumatology:
Advanced Applications for the Analysis of Inflammation
and Damage in the Rheumatoid Joint**

ISCA 2015 - Image-Based Smart City Application

MADiMa 2015 - First International Workshop on Multimedia Assisted Dietary Management

SBMI 2015 - Scene Background Modeling and Initialization

**QoEM 2015 - Workshop on Image and Video Processing for Quality
of Multimedia Experience**

BioFor 2015 - International Workshop on Recent Advances in Digital Security: Biometrics and Forensics

Reflectance Normalization in Illumination-Based Image Manipulation Detection

Christian Riess[✉], Sven Pfaller, and Elli Angelopoulou

Pattern Recognition Lab, Friedrich-Alexander University, Erlangen, Germany
christian.riess@fau.de
http://www5.cs.fau.de/~riess

Abstract. One approach to detect spliced images is to compare the lighting environment of suspicious objects or persons in the scene. The original method, proposed by Johnson and Farid, requires an investigator to mark occluding contours of multiple objects, from which the distribution of the incident light intensity is estimated. Unfortunately, this method imposes relatively strict constraints on the user and on the scene under investigation.

In this work, we propose a color-normalization approach to relax one important constraint. With our modification, a user is able to select the contours from multiple different materials (instead of having to use a single material). The proposed method will automatically compensate the differences in the reflected intensities. We demonstrate the robustness of the method with a carefully designed ground-truth dataset, consisting of 10 subjects, each of them under 3 controlled lighting environments. With the proposed method, lighting direction as a forensic cue becomes applicable to a much wider range of natural images.

1 Introduction

The goal of blind image forensics is to verify the authenticity and origin of an image without the support from an embedded security scheme. With the increasing availability of digital imagery and image processing software, researchers developed a family of forensic algorithms that either a) detect traces of manipulation in an image or b) verify characteristic scene or imaging properties to determine its authenticity. For an overview of existing methods, please refer to [3,10].

Several forensic algorithms aim to exploit the physics of geometry in the scene. For instance, to verify the consistency of a scene containing people, Johnson and Farid [7] proposed to exploit the position of specular highlights in the eyes. Zhang *et al.* [12] investigated the shadows of objects on planar surfaces for detecting spliced images. Also based on geometry, Conotter *et al.* [1] proposed an algorithm for verifying ballistic motion in video captures. For a more complete overview on physics-based approaches, please refer, e.g., to [3].

One potentially powerful approach, based on illumination geometry, has been proposed by Johnson and Farid [6]. A user has to annotate the contour of persons

© Springer International Publishing Switzerland 2015
V. Murino et al. (Eds.): ICIAP 2015 Workshops, LNCS 9281, pp. 3–10, 2015.
DOI: 10.1007/978-3-319-23222-5_1

of interest (or objects, respectively[1]). Based on the intensity distribution along the contours, the brightness distribution of the incident light can be estimated as a function of the angle of incidence. This distribution is computed in the image plane, i. e. in two dimensions. It acts as a descriptor for the lighting environment of a person. Thus, if a spliced image contains persons from two different source images, it is likely that their illumination environments also differ. In [8], this approach is extended to three dimensions. However, in three dimensions, this method requires known 3D geometry of the persons under investigation. This leads to another estimation step (for fitting a 3D model), adding complexity and potential sources of error. Recently, Fan *et al.* [2] proposed an alternative to this approach by replacing the estimation of a 3D surface model with a shade-from-shading algorithm.

For humans, assessing lighting environments is a difficult task [9]. Computers can quantify the perceived deviation, or even detect differences that are imperceptible for humans. Additionally, concealing illumination differences in spliced images might force a forger to manually repaint parts of the image, which raises the effort to create a plausible forgery.

In spite these encouraging prospects, these algorithms are not straightforward to apply in practice. The lighting environment can only be estimated from solid, purely diffuse materials. The surface normals of the regions under investigation must exhibit a large variety of directions. Additionally, all marked regions must consist of the same material.

In this paper, we propose a straightforward approach to relax the last constraint, i. e., to be able to estimate lighting environments on mixed materials. We focus on the 2D algorithm by Johnson and Farid [6] to avoid the additional requirement of 3D object geometry. We restate the baseline algorithm in Sec. 2. In Sec. 3, we present the proposed algorithm, which we call *Intrinsic Contour Estimation*. In Sec. 4, we first present our evaluation dataset, and then provide the results of our algorithm. We conclude our work in Sec. 5.

2   Forensic Exploitation of Lighting Environments

We restate the algorithm by Johnson and Farid (for additional details and a full derivation of the equations, please refer to the original work [6]).

Assume that an image contain two persons of interest. A user marks the contours of these persons, satisfying several constraints. The 2D contour in the image must correspond to a (true) 3D contour in the scene. Then, surface normals on this contour approximately lie in the image plane. Contours can be piecewise defined, and must everywhere be exposed to the environment light (i. e., regions of locally cast shadows are not admissible). For estimating the direction of the surface normals along these contours, it suffices to fit a 2D polynomial to the contour. The intensity of each point along the contour is extrapolated from the surrounding pixels (for details, confer [6]).

---

[1] Without loss of generality, we assume in this paper that persons are in the focus of interest.

The lighting environment is modelled as a weighted sum of spherical harmonics. In 2D, using spherical harmonics of up to order 2, only five coefficients need to be estimated. Let

$$
\begin{aligned}
Y_{0,0}(\boldsymbol{\nu}) &= \tfrac{1}{\sqrt{4\pi}} \\
Y_{1,-1}(\boldsymbol{\nu}) &= \sqrt{\tfrac{3}{4\pi}}\, y \qquad & Y_{1,1}(\boldsymbol{\nu}) &= \sqrt{\tfrac{3}{4\pi}}\, x \\
Y_{2,-2}(\boldsymbol{\nu}) &= 3\sqrt{\tfrac{5}{4\pi}}\, xy \qquad & Y_{2,2}(\boldsymbol{\nu}) &= \tfrac{3}{2}\sqrt{\tfrac{5}{12\pi}}(x^2 - y^2)
\end{aligned}
\tag{1}
$$

denote the five spherical harmonics basis functions $Y_{0,0}$ through $Y_{2,2}$ that are required to model a lighting environment in 2D, depending on a normal vector in the image plane $\boldsymbol{\nu} = (x\ \ y)^{\mathrm{T}}$. If the reflectance of an object material is purely diffuse (Lambertian), an intensity along an object boundary corresponds simply to a linear combination of the basis functions. Thus, for a contour of n points, the basis functions can be evaluated in a matrix $\boldsymbol{M} \in \mathbb{R}^{n \times 5}$. The unknown weighting factors $\boldsymbol{h} \in \mathbb{R}^5$ must then satisfy

$$
\boldsymbol{M}\boldsymbol{h} = \boldsymbol{b} \ ,
\tag{2}
$$

where $\boldsymbol{b} \in \mathbb{R}^n$ contains the (grayscale) intensities along the contour. Instead of solving Eqn. 2 directly for $\boldsymbol{h}$, an energy function $E(\boldsymbol{h})$ is defined to incorporate a regularization term $\boldsymbol{C} \in \mathbb{R}^{5 \times 5}$, $\boldsymbol{C} = \mathrm{diag}(1\ 2\ 2\ 3\ 3)$:

$$
E(\boldsymbol{h}) = \|\boldsymbol{M}\boldsymbol{h} - \boldsymbol{b}\|^2 + \lambda_1 \|\boldsymbol{C}\boldsymbol{h}\|^2 \ ,
\tag{3}
$$

where the strength of the influence of $\boldsymbol{C}$ is determined by a parameter λ_1. Minimizing Eqn. 3 for $\boldsymbol{h}$ yields

$$
\boldsymbol{h} = (\boldsymbol{M}^{\mathrm{T}}\boldsymbol{M} + \lambda_1 \boldsymbol{C}^{\mathrm{T}}\boldsymbol{C})^{-1}\boldsymbol{M}^{\mathrm{T}}\boldsymbol{b} \ .
\tag{4}
$$

Equations 2 and 4 transfer the intensity distribution along the object boundary to a basis of spherical harmonics. In Eqn. 2, differences in contour brightness are assumed to result from differences in the incident illumination. If contours of highly contrasting surface materials, e.g. a black T-shirt and light skin, are both used in Eqn. 2, the computation is severely biased. An example for such a situation is shown in Fig. 1.

3   Reflectance Normalization as a Preprocessing Step

We investigated methods to normalize material brightnesses prior to the estimation of the lighting environment. The separation of object texture and shading is commonly referred to as intrinsic image decomposition. For our task, the shading component is the ideal input for Eqn. 2. We experimented with the recent algorithms by Gehler *et al.* [5] and Shen and Yeo [11]. Although these methods showed encouraging performances on laboratory images, we failed to transfer this performance to real-world images. In particular for large brightness differences, we were not able to obtain satisfying shading components.

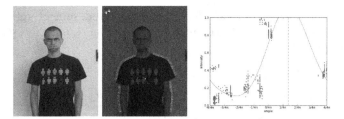

Fig. 1. Illustration of mixed-material contours: the brightness contrast between the black T-shirt and bright skin prevents cross-material estimation of the lighting environment.

However, this particular forensic application offers additional constraints compared to what is typically assumed in intrinsic image decomposition: we only need to operate along user-annotated object contours. Thus, the surface normals along our pixels of interest are known. We exploit this fact in a novel algorithm, which we call *intrinsic contour estimation*. Figure 2 illustrates the basic idea. On the left, one of our evaluation subjects is shown. We marked the contour across the black T-shirt, as well as the bright skin. On the right, we plotted the contours of skin regions in green, and shirt regions in red as a function of the normal direction of the contour point. We can reasonably demand that contour points that are pointing in the same direction should exhibit the same brightness. Thus, we search a neutralization factor r that best equalize the intensities of both clusters for points that face in *the same normal direction*. In Fig. 2 (right), this means that multiplication by r should lead to equality of the intensities in the matching blue circles.

The details of the algorithm are outlined below. Assuming purely diffuse (Lambertian) reflectance, let

$$p = \int_{\lambda \in \Omega} \rho(\lambda) e(\lambda) c(\lambda) d\lambda \tag{5}$$

denote the captured color in a pixel p, where Ω denotes the visible spectrum of light waves λ, $\rho(\lambda)$ the object color (albedo), $e(\lambda)$ the intensity of the light source, and $c(\lambda)$ a three-component vector of color matching functions of the camera (which ultimately yield the red, green and blue color channels). Assuming that $c(\lambda)$ are linear functions, a change in the material $\rho(\lambda)$ affects the observed colors in p multiplicatively. Thus, to neutralize the distorting effect of different surface materials, we are seeking a multiplicative correction term r_j for each surface material.

Given a contour of k materials, we extend the existing algorithm with a brightness normalizing factor. The colors of the contour pixels are clustered into multiple materials, either automatically using, e. g., the k-means algorithm [4, page315] or manually by the operator while the contours are marked.

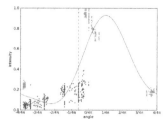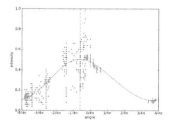

Fig. 2. Idea of intrinsic contour decomposition: contours of different materials (marked in red and blue) can be jointly used by adjusting the reflectance contributions. Left: input image. Middle: uncorrected intensity distribution estimates light to be coming from the right. Right: corrected intensity distributions estimates light to be coming from top.

For two intensities $p_u(\boldsymbol{\nu})$, $p_v(\boldsymbol{\nu})$ from different clusters u, v with the same normal direction $\boldsymbol{\nu}$, we seek $\boldsymbol{r}$, such that the condition

$$(p_u(\boldsymbol{\nu}) - p_v(\boldsymbol{\nu})) \cdot \boldsymbol{r} = 0 \tag{6}$$

is satisfied. For increased numerical robustness, we relax the constraint of identical normals to just *similar* normals. To account for the angular difference, we compute for each pair of points a weighting factor w,

$$w(\boldsymbol{\nu}_1, \boldsymbol{\nu}_2) = \begin{cases} \exp\left(\frac{\delta^2}{\sigma^2}\right) & \text{if } \delta \le 2\sigma \\ 0 & \text{otherwise} \end{cases} \tag{7}$$

Here, $p_u(\boldsymbol{\nu}_1)$ and $p_v(\boldsymbol{\nu}_2)$ denote points from clusters u, v with similar normals $\boldsymbol{\nu}_1$ and $\boldsymbol{\nu}_2$, and $\delta = \arccos(\boldsymbol{\nu}_1^T \boldsymbol{\nu}_2)$. In our implementation, we empirically set σ to $18.75°$. The threshold for $w = 0$ is derived from a Gaussian filter[2]. Hence, the generalized constraint for $\boldsymbol{r}$ using m pairs of data points on k clusters is

$$\boldsymbol{W}\boldsymbol{r} = \boldsymbol{0} \ , \tag{8}$$

where $W \in \mathbb{R}^{m \times k}$. Let the j-th pair of points $p(\boldsymbol{\nu}_1)$ and $q(\boldsymbol{\nu}_2)$ be from clusters i_1, i_2. Then,

$$W_{j,i_1} = w(\boldsymbol{\nu}_1, \boldsymbol{\nu}_2)p(\boldsymbol{\nu}_1) \ , \tag{9}$$
$$W_{j,i_2} = w(\boldsymbol{\nu}_1, \boldsymbol{\nu}_2)q(\boldsymbol{\nu}_2) \ . \tag{10}$$

All other entries of W are set to 0. To avoid the trivial solution $\boldsymbol{r} = \boldsymbol{0}$, we set $r_1 = 1$, which yields the final solution

$$\boldsymbol{W}'\boldsymbol{r}' = -\boldsymbol{l} \ , \tag{11}$$

where $\boldsymbol{W} = (\boldsymbol{l} \ \boldsymbol{W}')$ and $\boldsymbol{r} = \left(\begin{smallmatrix} 1 \\ \boldsymbol{r}' \end{smallmatrix}\right)$. Equation 11 is solved via singular value decomposition (SVD).

---

[2] Integrating the tails of a Gaussian with standard deviation σ outside a range of 2σ yields about 5% of the overall area under the curve.

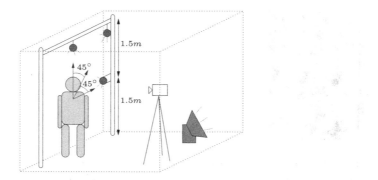

Fig. 3. Experimental setup. Ambient light is provided by the brown background lamp. Direct illumination (red) on the subjects (yellow) comes from $0°$, $45°$ and $90°$, measured $1.5m$ above the floor.

4   Evaluation

To demonstrate the feasibility of the proposed approach, we captured a benchmark dataset where the direction of the dominant illuminant is known[3]. This enables us in the quantitative evaluation to compare the angles of the maximum incident light.

4.1   Data

Figure 3 shows our experimental setup. We captured 30 images consisting of ten subjects under three lighting conditions. In a closed room without windows, one light source was set up for scattered background illumination. Further light sources were fixated at angles of roughly $0°$, $45°$ and $90°$ to the person in the scene. These lights act as "dominant" light sources, with a distance of only about $1.5m$ from the person. Note that such a close light violates the assumption of the original method [6] of an infinitely distant light source. Indeed, when validating the performance of our re-implementation of the algorithm by Johnson and Farid, we noticed a worse performance than reported in [6], which may partly be due to the violation of this constraint. However, we consider a light source at finite distance to be a reasonable compromise between the theoretical requirements of the algorithm and a practical setup, e.g., for indoor applications.

4.2   Experiments

In our evaluation, we compared three methods. First, denoted as "Original", we used the method by Johnson and Farid [6] (cf. Sec. 2). Second, denoted as "Gehler", we used the input images to compute intrinsic images with the method by Gehler *et al.* [5], which, in theory, should isolate the shading component.

---

[3] The dataset is publicly available at http://www5.cs.fau.de/

Table 1. Median and mean angular error on the lighting environment database, and the number images for which the estimation error of the dominant light direction was less than 22° degrees. In the left columns, the best single-colored contour per image is used, in the right columns, mixed-color contours are used.

	Single-colored contour				Multi-colored contour		
	Median	Mean	Within 22.5°		Median	Mean	Within 22.5°
Original	10.7	13.6	25/30 (83%)	Original	40.2	56.5	10/30 (33%)
Gehler	9.1	12.5	**26/30 (86%)**	Gehler	33.0	50.7	13/30 (43%)
ICE	10.9	14.1	24/30 (80%)	ICE	12.6	13.0	**26/30 (86%)**

We then applied the method by Johnson and Farid on the shading component. Finally, denoted as "ICE" (intrinsic contour estimation), we evaluated the proposed algorithm. Table 1 shows the results of this evaluation. In the first three rows, we report results when selecting only the best, single-material contour of our database subjects. Per method, the median and mean angular error of the estimated dominant light direction are shown. We also (somewhat arbitrarily) set a binary threshold of 22.5° (one eighth of a circle), and counted for how many test cases the dominant light direction was estimated within 22.5° degrees of the ground truth.

For single-colored contours, all methods achieve similar performance, with a median angular deviation between 9.1° (Gehler) and 10.9° (ICE). Note that, in theory, Gehler's intrinsic image decomposition should not change a single-colored contour at all. Yet, it affects to some degree the estimated shading image, which leads to a slightly better result for this method.

The situation is quite different in case that we select multi-colored contours. While (expectedly) the method by Johnson and Farid can not deal with this situation, it turns out that also the Gehler's intrinsic image decomposition is not really able to produce a shading image that yields good results. Only the proposed intrinsic contour estimation (ICE) is able to maintain the performance of the single-colored contour case.

5   Conclusion

Johnson and Farid proposed a pioneering method for exploiting inconsistencies in the lighting direction for forensic applications. Unfortunately, the original method imposes a number of relatively strict constraints to the user. Particularly, in order for the method to be applicable, it is necessary that the objects under examination exhibit a wide angular range of a same-material occluding contour. In practice, such a contour oftentimes does not exist.

In this work, we propose a slight extension to the original method, which relaxes the requirement on the contour material. We use a ground-truth dataset containing people, where illuminants were located at 0°, 45° and 90° in the scene. On this ground-truth data, we demonstrate that the proposed intrinsic contour estimation method can reliably compensate multi-material contours.

Acknowledgments. The authors gratefully acknowledge support of the Erlangen Graduate School of Heterogeneous Image Systems (HBS) by the German National Science Foundation (DFG).

References

1. Conotter, V., O'Brien, J.F., Farid, H.: Exposing Digital Forgeries in Ballistic Motion. IEEE Transactions on Information Forensics and Security **7**(1), 283–296 (2012)
2. Fan, W., Wang, K., Cayre, F., Xiong, Z.: 3D lighting-based image forgery detection using shape-from-shading. In: Proceedings of the 20th European Signal Processing Conference (EUSIPCO-2012), pp. 1777–1781, Bucarest, Romania, August 2012
3. Farid, H.: Digital Image Forensics, June 2011. http://www.cs.dartmouth.edu/farid/downloads/tutorials/digitalimageforensics.pdf
4. Forsyth, D.A., Ponce, J.: Computer Vision – A Modern Approach. Pearson Education Inc. (2003)
5. Gehler, P.V., Rother, C., Kiefel, M., Zhang, L., Schölkopf, B.: Recovering intrinsic images with a global sparsity prior on reflectance. In: Advances in Neural Information Processing Systems (NIPS 2011), vol. 24, pp. 765–773, Granada, Spain, December 2011
6. Johnson, M., Farid, H.: Exposing Digital Forgeries in Complex Lighting Environments. IEEE Transactions on Information Forensics and Security **2**(3), 450–461 (2007)
7. Johnson, M.K., Farid, H.: Exposing digital forgeries through specular highlights on the eye. In: Furon, T., Cayre, F., Doërr, G., Bas, P. (eds.) IH 2007. LNCS, vol. 4567, pp. 311–325. Springer, Heidelberg (2008)
8. Kee, E., Farid, H.: Exposing digital forgeries from 3-d lighting environments. In: Proceedings of the 2nd IEEE International Workshop on Information Forensics and Security (WIFS 2010), Seattle, WA, USA, December 2010
9. Ostrovsky, Y., Cavanagh, P., Sinha, P.: Perceiving Illumination Inconsistencies in Scenes. Perception **34**(11), 1301–1314 (2005)
10. Redi, J., Taktak, W., Dugelay, J.L.: Digital Image Forensics: A Booklet for Beginners. Multimedia Tools and Applications **51**(1), 133–162 (2011)
11. Shen, L., Yeo, C.: Intrinsic images decomposition using a local and global sparse representation of reflectance. In: Proceedings of the 24th IEEE Computer Society Conference on Computer Vision and Pattern Recognition (CVPR 2011), pp. 697–704, Colorado Springs, CO, USA, June 2011
12. Zhang, W., Cao, X., Qu, Y., Hou, Y., Zhang, C.: Detecting and Extracting the Photo Composites Using Planar Homography and Graph Cut. IEEE Transactions on Information Forensics and Security **5**(3), 544–555 (2010)

Evaluation of Residual-Based Local Features for Camera Model Identification

Francesco Marra, Giovanni Poggi, Carlo Sansone, and Luisa Verdoliva$^{(\boxtimes)}$

DIETI, University Federico II of Naples, Naples, Italy
{francesco.marra,poggi,carlosan,verdoliv}@unina.it

Abstract. Camera model identification is of interest for many applications. In-camera processes, specific of each model, leave traces that can be captured by features designed *ad hoc*, and used for reliable classification. In this work we investigate on the use of *blind* features based on the analysis of image residuals. In particular, features are extracted locally based on co-occurrence matrices of selected neighbors and then used to train an SVM classifier. Experiments on the well-known Dresden database show this approach to provide state-of-the-art performances.

Keywords: Camera model identification · Local features · Residuals

1 Introduction

Identifying which camera took a given photo can be of great interest in many instances [1]. Law enforcement agencies may be interested to trace back the origin of some unlawful or dangerous images. Likewise, linking a photo to a given camera may represent evidence before a court of law. On the other hand, someone may be interested in proving that a photo was taken by his/her camera to claim intellectual property. The growing interest towards this task is a direct consequence of the huge growth in the acquisition and diffusion of digital images, therefore it is bound to increase further.

On the technical side, a great impulse to research in this field came with the pioneering work of Lukàš et al. [2] proposing a simple and effective tool for source identification. The photo-response non uniformity (PRNU) pattern, also known as sensor pattern noise, is a distinctive pattern, unique for each camera and stable in time, originated by the unavoidable imperfections occurring during the sensor manufacturing process. Each photo taken by a given camera contains traces of the PRNU, which represents, therefore, sort of a camera fingerprint, which can be used for reliable identification. However, even these very promising methods have their drawbacks, which limit their field of application. In particular, to extract a camera's PRNU pattern, a large number of images taken by that camera are necessary. This is often not possible without the collaboration of the camera owner and, in any case, is extremely time-consuming. A more viable intermediate step is the identification of the camera model. Finding the model may significantly narrow the search, which can be completed also by more conventional methods.

© Springer International Publishing Switzerland 2015
V. Murino et al. (Eds.): ICIAP 2015 Workshops, LNCS 9281, pp. 11–18, 2015.
DOI: 10.1007/978-3-319-23222-5_2

Camera model identification is made possible by the distinctive traces left in images as a result of the unique combination of in-camera processing steps. In fact, in modern digital cameras, the final image is produced through a number of algorithms, each characterized by several free parameters. Popular examples are demosaicing, based often on complex adaptive nonlinear interpolation, and JPEG compression, where the quantization matrix can be defined by the user. It is highly unlikely that different camera models use the very same set of algorithms and parameters and, therefore, very likely that their traces allow reliable identification.

Indeed, in the very same literature on PRNU-based identification, the appearance of model-based artifacts in the estimated PRNU pattern was observed [3], and used to identify the camera model. However, this path was followed before by other researchers. In [4], inspired by the work of Popescu and Farid for image forgery detection [5], traces of different interpolation algorithms where sought and used as distinctive model features. In fact, each pixel is strongly correlated with its neighbors (both spatial and across color channels). The weights of the interpolation kernel are estimated and used as features for camera identification combined with frequency domain features, that take into account the periodic artifacts caused by the CFA pattern. The strong dependencies among pixels has been also explored in [6] [7]. In [6], in particular, and also in [8], weight estimation is conducted locally on each color band, and a different procedure is used based on the content of the region. This reflects the fact that often adaptive demosaicing techniques are used to reduce blurring artifacts. In [7], instead, partial second-order derivative correlation models are proposed to detect both the intrachannel and the cross-channel dependence due to demosaicing. Other methods seek to characterize JPEG compression artifacts [9], DCT coefficients statistics [10], or lens distortion artifacts like chromatic aberration [11]. A different approach is proposed in [12] where the heteroscedastic noise model valid for raw images and characterized by two parameters is used to identify camera models.

The majority of the methods look for artifacts related to some specific in-camera processing step, trying to estimate its unknown parameters. A "blind" approach is also possible, however, where no hypotheses is made on the origin of camera-specific marks, and the identification task is regarded simply as a texture classification problem. With this approach, the focus shifts on the definition of the most discriminative features, irrespective of their meaning. Both global and local features can be considered, drawing often from the vast literature of closely related fields, such as material classification or steganalysis. The aim of this paper is to evaluate a class of such features, based on co-occurrences of image residuals, and show their potential for the camera model identification task.

In the next Section we review "blind" feature-based methods, then the residual-based local features are described in Section 3, and evaluated experimentally in Section 4.

2   Related Work

The use of generic features was first considered in the work of Kharrazi et al. [13]. The Authors propose to use various global statistics, extracted from each individual color band, based on the correlation of couples of color bands, and also extracted from some wavelet subbands. In addition, some Image Quality Metrics (IQM), used in [14] for steganalysis, are evaluated on all the color bands, both in the spatial and transform domain. It is worth noting that these last features are computed on residual images (high-pass filtered versions of the original data).

Indeed, computing features on image residuals is common to the majority of methods proposed in the literature. This way, results become independent of the image content, and artifacts are more easily detected. In [15] IQM features are extracted from high-pass residuals of each color band. These features are then combined with BSM (Binary Similarity Measures), i.e., LBP (Local Binary Pattern) extracted from the least-significant bit planes, and with an enlarged set of features computed in the wavelet domain. Besides the features used in [13], other first-order statistics are computed, as well as some inter-band correlation indexes, inspired by [16]. Instead in [17] Gloe proposes to add some color features to the ones used in [13]. Experiments on the Dresden Image Database [18] prove this combination to guarantee a performance gain w.r.t. both [13] and [15].

The majority of the features recalled thus far are evaluated globally on the whole image (both original and high-pass filtered) or a decimated version of it, if wavelet subbands are considered. However, in order to capture subtle image patterns which may correspond to discriminative features, it is important to consider local features, extracted from a small neighborhood of each pixel of the image, as it happens for LBP. This is the main focus of the work of Xu et al. [19], where LBP features are evaluated both on the original image and on some residuals. Note that LBP is computed on two-pixel supports, and hence encodes only first-order spatial variations. However, combining it with a preliminary high-pass filter amounts to considering a larger support, and evaluating higher-order statistics [20]. We mention briefly other approaches [21] which look at the statistical differences in the DCT domain by computing Markovian transition probabilities. Also in this case, similar features had been already considered in steganalysis [22].

3   Residual-Based Local Features

The analysis of the state of the art shows that local descriptors can provide precious clues for camera model identification. Moreover, since such clues, related to the camera processing chain, are contained in the image micro-patterns and not in the scene content, it makes sense to remove the latter and work on image residuals. Even in this framework, however, two main open issues remain about *i)* how to extract informative image residuals and *ii)* how to process them in order to obtain an expressive camera-related feature. Given the complexity and variety of the in-camera processes involved, no conclusive answer can be hoped for. However, we will show that co-occurrence based local features, computed on image residuals and proposed originally in [23] for steganalysis, may represent a valuable tool for this task. A similar path was used successfully in digital image forensics [24] [25].

The feature vector associated with the image under test is extracted through the following steps:

- computation of residuals through high-pass filtering;
- quantization and truncation of the residuals;
- computation of the histogram of co-occurrences.

In [23] a number of linear and non-linear high-pass filters have been used for the computation of residuals, combining all resulting feature vectors by means of an ensemble classifier. In [25], instead, a few filters have been selected based on a preliminary performance analysis on the training set. In particular, the third order linear filter defined as

$$r_{i,j} = x_{i,j-1} - 3\,x_{i,j} + 3\,x_{i,j+1} - x_{i,j+2} \tag{1}$$

with x and r indicating original and residual images, and (i,j) the spatial coordinates, has been found to provide good and stable results. When filters are not row-column symmetric, they are applied also on the image transpose to augment data.

A further alternative, that will be explored in this paper is the use of an image denoising algorithm to compute residuals. In fact, if the aim of this process is to remove the scene content from the image, keeping all the noise, this is best achieved by resorting to specialized filters that abound in the literature. In particular we will consider the nonlocal BM3D filter, among the best and well-known denoiser, already used for residual computation [26] in PRNU-based image forensics. The residual image will be therefore obtained as the difference between the original image x and its denoised version $\widehat{x} = f(x)$, with $f(\cdot)$ the denoising filter.

Co-occurrences are then evaluated on these residuals, which provide information on higher-order phenomena and involve a relatively large number of image pixels. In order to obtain a manageable co-occurrence matrix, residuals are quantized/truncated to a small number of values as:

$$\widehat{r}_{i,j} = \mathrm{trunc}_T(\mathrm{round}(r_{i,j}/q)) \tag{2}$$

with q the quantization step and T the truncation value. To limit the matrix size we consider only $T = 1$ or $T = 2$, leading to uniform mid-thread quantizers with 3 and 5 bins, respectively. At this point co-occurrences on four pixels along the filter direction (say, rows) are computed, that is

$$C_1(k_0, k_1, k_2, k_3) =$$
$$\sum_{i,j} I(\widehat{r}_{i,j} = k_0, \widehat{r}_{i,j+1} = k_1, \widehat{r}_{i,j+2} = k_2, \widehat{r}_{i,j+3} = k_3) \tag{3}$$

where $I(A)$ is the indicator function of event A, equal to 1 if A holds and 0 otherwise, and all k indexes take values in $\{-T, \ldots, +T\}$. Another co-occurrence matrix is then computed working across the filter direction (say, columns)

Table 1. Performance comparison for various spam descriptors (512 × 512 cropping).

filter name	deriv. order	accuracy T=1 length 50	T=2 length 338
spam1_14hv	1	95.14	96.66
spam2_12hv	2	97.08	97.31
spam3_14hv	3	96.83	**98.99**
spam11(3x3)	2	95.80	98.23
spam11(5x5)	4	96.07	96.71

$$C_2(k_0, k_1, k_2, k_3) =$$
$$\sum_{i,j} I(\widehat{r}_{i,j} = k_0, \widehat{r}_{i+1,j} = k_1, \widehat{r}_{i+2,j} = k_2, \widehat{r}_{i+3,j} = k_3) \qquad (4)$$

Invoking left-right and positive-negative symmetries, the original $(2T + 1)^4$ features can be reduced through pooling to just 338 and 50 for $T = 2$ and $T = 1$, respectively. The extracted features are eventually used to train an SVM classifier.

4 Experimental Results

To assess the performance of the features under analysis we carried out experiments on the Dresden database [18]. This is one of the most widespread databases in this field, used in many recent papers. In the Dresden database, 26 different camera models are available, each with several individual devices and hundreds or thousands photos. However, to speed up the experimental phase, we used a smaller version of this database, as done in [17], comprising only 10 models. We trained an SVM with linear kernel using all the images coming from one single device for each camera model. We run 20 times this procedure, each time randomly choosing the devices used for training, and averaged results. Notice that the images are not cropped, therefore they keep the original camera resolution, going from about 5 to about 15 Mpixels.

For comparison we implemented the features proposed in Celiktutan-2008 [15], Gloe-2012 [17] and Xu-2012 [19]. As for the features based on co-occurrences, some preliminary experiments are carried out to select the best configuration. In Table 1 we report results obtained on the selected database using linear high-pass filters computing derivatives of first to fourth order, called of type *spam* [23]. The residual are then quantized to 3 or 5 levels, changing the quantization step q accordingly. Since these features are relatively short, 50 or 338 components, they can be estimated reliably also on a portion of the image, so we worked on a 512 × 512 section to expedite the process. Results show that it is worth using longer features, associated with 5-level quantization,

Table 2. Performance of various descriptors on the 10-model Dresden subset. Note that the wavelet-based features used in Celiktutan-2008 cannot be extracted from very small images, like 64 × 64.

Feature	length	whole image	accuracy		
			512 × 512	128 × 128	64 × 64
Celiktutan-2008	592	96.89	91.29	73.16	-
Gloe-2012	82	97.60	82.32	64.25	55.60
Xu-2012	354	98.87	97.96	89.82	74.82
co-occurrences (BM3D)	338	99.06	97.03	84.03	68.12
co-occurrences (best spam)	338	**99.44**	**98.99**	**94.82**	**85.07**

while indication on the filter are more controversial. In any case, we used the best performing filter, spam3_14hv, in the rest of the experiments.

Table 2 shows results for the 10-model identification experiment. The co-occurrence based local feature with the best spam filter provides a 99.44% accuracy, better than both Gloe-2012 and than Xu-2012. When residuals are computed through denoising, the performance is slightly worse. Table 3 provides detailed model-by-model results for the co-occurrence based feature. The latter provides perfect on near-perfect accuracy in all cases, except for the Nikon D200 images, associated sometimes with the Kodak M1063 camera. It is worth pointing out that also in other investigations, including [17], this particular camera model has been found hard to identify, which raises interest on the in-camera processes it adopts.

In Table 2 we show also results obtained after cropping images to much smaller sizes. As expected, a 512 × 512 section allows one to obtain almost the same results as on the full image. With much smaller sections, even 64 × 64

Table 3. Mis-Classification matrix for the best co-occurrence feature.

device	identified as									
	I70	Z150	M10	S710	D200	μ	DCZ	7325	L74	NV
I70	100	-	-	-	-	-	-	-	-	-
Z150	0.6	98.6	-	-	-	0.8	-	-	-	-
M10	-	-	99.7	-	-	-	0.1	0.1	-	0.1
S710	-	-	-	100	-	-	-	-	-	-
D200	-	-	4.1	-	95.1	-	0.4	0.2	-	0.2
μ	-	-	-	-	-	100	-	-	-	-
DCZ	-	0.4	-	-	-	-	99.6	-	-	-
7325	-	-	-	-	-	-	-	100	-	-
L74	-	-	-	-	-	-	-	-	100	-
NV	-	-	0.4	0.4	-	-	-	-	-	99.2

pixels, only the co-occurrence features based on the best spam filter keep being reliable. If confirmed in other experiments, this might be a valuable property, not only for reducing analysis time when computational power is limited, but also for dealing with situations in which only a fragment is available, for example in image forgery localization.

5   Conclusions

Our analyses confirm for camera model identification the excellent performance exhibited in other domains by co-occurrence based features. Improved features can be certainly designed, for example by taking into account individually the three color bands. In any case, this is only a preliminary exploration, and much work remains to be done. Among the most important issues: more comprehensive experiments are necessary, with the full Dresden database, as well as other datasets; robustness to various forms of post-processing should be studied; the open set scenario should be also considered, dealing with unknown models.

Acknowledgments. This work was partially funded by the Italian Ministry of Education, University and Research (MIUR) within the framework of the project PAC02L1_00050 AETERNUUM.

References

1. Kirchner, M., Gloe, T.: Forensic camera model identification. In: Ho, T., Li, S. (eds.) Handbook of Digital Forensics of Multimedia Data and Devices. Wiley-IEEE Press (2015)
2. Lukàš, J., Fridrich, J., Goljan, M.: Digital camera identification from sensor pattern noise. IEEE Transactions on Information Forensics and Security **1**(2), 205–214 (2006)
3. Filler, T., Fridrich, J., Goljan, M.: Using sensor pattern noise for camera model identification. In: IEEE International Conference on Image Processing, pp. 1296–1299 (2008)
4. Bayram, S., Sencar, H., Memon, N., Avcibas, I.: Source camera identification based on CFA interpolation. In: IEEE Int. Conference on Image Processing, pp. 69–72 (2005)
5. Popescu, A., Farid, H.: Exposing digital forgeries by detecting traces of resampling. IEEE Transactions on Signal Processing **53**(2), 758–767 (2005)
6. Swaminathan, A., Wu, M., Liu, K.J.R.: Rich models for steganalysis of digital images. IEEE Transactions on Information Forensics and Security **2**(1), 91–105 (2007)
7. Cao, H., Kot, A.: Accurate detection of demosaicing regularity for digital image forensics. IEEE Trans. on Information Forensics and Security **4**(4), 899–910 (2009)
8. Bayram, S., Sencar, H., Memon, N.: Improvements on source camera-model identification based on CFA. In: Advances in Digital Forensics II, IFIP International Conference on Digital Forensics, pp. 289–299 (2006)

9. Fan, N., Jin, C., Huang, Y.: Source Camera identification by JPEG compression statistics for image forensics. In: TENCON, pp. 1–4 (2006)

10. Thai, T., Retraint, F., Cogranne, R.: Camera model identification based on dct coefficient statistics. Digital Signal Processing **4**, 88–100 (2015)

11. Van, L., Emmanuel, S., Kankanhalli, M.: Identifying source cell phone using chromatic aberration. In: IEEE International Conference on Multimedia and Expo, pp. 883–886 (2007)

12. Thai, T., Cogranne, R., Retraint, F.: Camera model identification based on the heteroscedastic noise model. IEEE Transactions on Image Processing **23**(1), 250–263 (2014)

13. Kharrazi, M., Sencar, H., Memon, N.: Blind source camera identification. In: IEEE International Conference on Image Processing, pp. 709–712 (2004)

14. Avcibaş, I., Memon, N., Sankur, B.: Steganalysis using image quality metrics. IEEE Transactions on Image Processing **12**(2), 221–229 (2003)

15. Çeliktutan, O., Sankur, B., Avcibaş, I.: Blind identification of source cell-phone model. IEEE Transactions on Information Forensics and Security **3**(3), 553–566 (2008)

16. Lyu, S., Farid, H.: Steganalysis using higher-order image statistics. IEEE Transactions on Information Forensics and Security **1**(1), 111–119 (2006)

17. Gloe, T.: Feature-based forensic camera model identification. In: Shi, Y.Q., Katzenbeisser, S. (eds.) Transactions on DHMS VIII. LNCS, vol. 7228, pp. 42–62. Springer, Heidelberg (2012)

18. Gloe, T., Böhme, R.: The Dresden image database for benchmarking digital image forensics. Journal of Digital Forensic Practice **3**(2–4), 150–159 (2010)

19. Xu, G., Shi, Y.: Camera model identification using local binary patterns. In: IEEE International Conference on Multimedia and Expo, pp. 392–397 (2012)

20. Gragnaniello, D., Poggi, G., Sansone, C., Verdoliva, L.: An investigation of local descriptors for biometric spoofing detection. IEEE Transactions on Information Forensics and Security **10**(4), 849–863 (2015)

21. Xu, G., Gao, S., Shi, Y.Q., Hu, R.M., Su, W.: Camera-model identification using markovian transition probability matrix. In: Ho, A.T.S., Shi, Y.Q., Kim, H.J., Barni, M. (eds.) IWDW 2009. LNCS, vol. 5703, pp. 294–307. Springer, Heidelberg (2009)

22. Shi, Y.Q., Chen, C.-H., Chen, W.: A markov process based approach to effective attacking JPEG steganography. In: Camenisch, J.L., Collberg, C.S., Johnson, N.F., Sallee, P. (eds.) IH 2006. LNCS, vol. 4437, pp. 249–264. Springer, Heidelberg (2007)

23. Fridrich, J., Kodovsky, J.: Rich models for steganalysis of digital images. IEEE Transactions on Information Forensics and Security **7**, 868–882 (2012)

24. Kirchner, M., Fridrich, J.: On detection of median filtering in images. In: SPIE, Electronic Imaging, Media Forensics and Security XII, pp. 101–112 (2010)

25. Verdoliva, L., Cozzolino, D., Poggi, G.: A feature-based approach for image tampering detection and localization. In: IEEE Workshop on Information Forensics and Security, pp. 149–154 (2014)

26. Chierchia, G., Parrilli, S., Poggi, G., Sansone, C., Verdoliva, L.: On the influence of denoising in PRNU based forgery detection. In: 2nd ACM workshop on Multimedia in Forensics, Security and Intelligence, pp. 117–122 (2010)

Biometric Walk Recognizer

Maria De Marsico[✉] and Alessio Mecca

Sapienza University of Rome, Via Salaria 113, 00198 Rome, Italy
demarsico@di.uniroma1.it, alessio.mecca@hotmail.com

Abstract. In this paper we present a comparative test of different approaches to gait recognition by smartphone accelerometer. Our work provides a twofold contribution. The first one is related to the use of low-cost, built-in sensors that nowadays equip most mobile devices. The second one is related to the use of our system in identification mode. Instead of being used to just verify the identity of the device owner, it can also be used for identification among a set of enrolled subjects. Whether the identification is carried out remotely or even if its results are transmitted to a server, the system can also be exploited in a multibiometric setting. Its results can be fused with those from computer-vision based gait recognition, as well as other biometric modalities, to enforce identification for accessing critical locations/services. We obtained the best results by matching complete walk captures (Recognition Rate 0.95), but the implicit limitation is represented by the fixed number of steps in the walks. Therefore we also investigated methods based on first dividing the signal into steps. The best of these achieved a Recognition Rate of 0.88.

Keywords: Biometrics · Gait recognition · Accelerometer · Mobile devices

1 Introduction

Biometric recognition is attracting increasing interest, since in many environments it can provide efficient means of identity recognition. Some biometric traits can be considered as *strong*, since they allow robust authentication especially in controlled settings. Examples are face, iris, and fingerprints. Strong biometrics often concern physical traits. Other traits, mostly *behavioral* ones, can be less reliable, for example because they can be affected by emotional conditions. At present, gait recognition, i.e. recognizing people from the way they walk, is often classified in the latter category. It can be used to complement other strong or soft traits in a multibiometric approach, and is one of the recent attractive topics in biometric research. Gait recognition modalities can be categorized into three groups based on the technological setting they require: a) machine vision-based: these approaches suffer from typical image processing issues, e.g., occlusions and illumination variations; b) floor sensor-based: these approaches require specific ambient equipment, therefore cannot be used everywhere and require a preliminary complex set-up; c) wearable sensor-based: these approaches can be further distinguished according to the number and kind of sensors exploited (more accelerometers, accelerometers plus gyroscopes, etc.).

© Springer International Publishing Switzerland 2015
V. Murino et al. (Eds.): ICIAP 2015 Workshops, LNCS 9281, pp. 19–26, 2015.
DOI: 10.1007/978-3-319-23222-5_3

Given the limitations of the first two groups of techniques in terms of feasibility and ready availability, we will focus on the third group. Even in this case, we aim at exploiting the simplest possible set-up. It is easy to assume that such set-up should use off-the-shelf, widespread equipment, and possibly exploit only one sensor of one kind, to keep the method feasible on a wide range of devices. Moreover, it would be desirable to exploit the least computationally demanding procedure.

We present the results obtained using the accelerometer built in the OnePlus One mobile phone, and compare different matching algorithms to evaluate the better compromise between accuracy and computational cost. The latter would allow performing recognition both locally, e.g., on a smartphone, or remotely on a computer receiving gait data. Moreover, we will test these techniques in identification modality (no identity is claimed by the user). This also allows combination with other biometrics to secure the access not only to personal devices but also to locations or services. On the contrary, most approaches in literature use (implicit) verification: the identity claim is implicit in the preliminary enrollment of a single user, namely the owner of the device, and the algorithms aim at verifying if the user keeping the device is the owner. In identification, assuming open set mode (probe user may not be known to the system), a template distance threshold regulates acceptance as in verification; in addition the right subject has not only to be close enough, but also to be the closest one.

2 State of the Art for Accelerometer-Based Gait Recognition

During the last years, among the approaches mentioned above, the gait recognition based on wearable sensors is becoming increasingly popular in respect to the others. This is because, on one hand, the related techniques used for recognition are less computationally expensive, and wearable sensors have a cost much lower than cameras and floor sensors; on the other hand achieved results are similar or even better. Wearable sensors do not suffer from the problems normally raised by computer vision-related techniques, e.g., occlusion, and illumination. In addition, differently from approaches based on floor sensors, the subject can be followed in any place without the need to equipping the environment. Last but not least, nowadays the most common wearable sensor used for gait recognition, the accelerometer, is practically built in most portable devices such as mobile phones and tablets. This avoids the use of expensive ad-hoc equipment. The reader can find in [1] a comprehensive survey on present approaches to gait recognition divided into the three mentioned main groups; [2] provides a review of present vision-based technique, the most used so far.

In most papers about gait recognition by accelerometer, the aim is to identify the owner of the phone. The recognition modality is verification: the identity claim is implicit, since only the owner is enrolled. Performances are usually measured by computing all-against-all matching results in a set of subjects. For verification, the performance measures are False Acceptance Rate (FAR), False Reject Rate (FRR) and Equal Error Rate (EER) given by the acceptance threshold were FAR=FRR.

In [3] the authors use the low sampling rate accelerometer that is built-in in Google G1 phone. Their system achieves an EER of 20% with a dataset of 51 volunteers. The algorithm uses cycle detection, computes average cycle and uses Dynamic Time

Warping for matching. The EER is not that low, however this is also due to the very low quality of the used accelerometer. As a matter of fact, in [4] a pair of the same authors improve their previous results using a better accelerometer, Motion Recording 100, which is not built in a mobile personal device. They perform some preprocessing operations, such us outlier steps removal, before matching performed by Dynamic Time Warping (DTW). The dataset size is increased to 60 users and the achieved EER is 5.7%. In comparison with this approach, we compute the average cycle to discard outliers, but we do not use it for matching. In addition, we also test our system in identification mode, which in some cases might be more challenging. While verification just requires sufficient similarity with the claimed identity, in identification one also has to avoid confusion between candidate identities, i.e., the right subject must not only be close enough, but also be the closest one. For both verification and identification the degree of similarity must be very high to obtain a correct answer of the system. However, consider a person that in identification modality is close enough but is not the closest one to the right one, and hence is not erroneously identified, e.g., as the owner of the device. This person, in verification modality, could be erroneously interpreted as the owner of the device if the similarity is just sufficiently good.

The recognition technique presented in [5] uses an accelerometer which is a standard in nowadays mobile devices, with sampling rate of 100 samples/second. They achieve a 5% of EER using histogram similarity and a 9% of EER using cycle group matching. However, though using the same accelerometer as in the preceding work, they use a smaller dataset (21 users). They do not report results for identification.

The work in [6] presents a framework for gait recognition using an Android mobile phone to get the accelerometer and gyroscope raw data. Verification is carried out on a desktop computer to recognize if the person who is walking with the phone is the enrolled user. The framework uses continuous wavelet transform time frequency spectrogram analysis for feature extraction and ciclostationarity analysis for matching. The tests achieve a 99.4% of verification rate at 0.1% of FAR for pace walk VS pace walk, 96.8% for fast walk VS fast walk, and a 61.1% for pace walk VS fast walk on a dataset of 36 users. This work achieves good results but uses the gyroscope too. In [7] the authors use Hidden Markov Model (HMM). They achieve a 10.42% of False Non Match Rate and a 10.29% of False Match Rate on a dataset of 48 users. The system uses only one enrolled user for training the HMM. All the registrations for all users are used as probe to test performance of verification. The performances achieved by this method are not competitive with the above ones.

The work in [8] exploits a signature point based method for identification. The user is recognized among a set of enrolled subjects. The system exploits five accelerometers attached in various parts of the body. This method does not use the cycle division as the others discussed above. It achieves a high recognition rate (96.7%) with a dataset of 30 users. In [9] an evolution of the previous method is proposed, and is used for both identification and verification modalities. It uses clustering to preliminarily group the signature points. The authors have also created a huge dataset (with 175 different subjects) of raw acceleration data, which is publicly available for non-commercial use[1]. On this dataset they achieve a Recognition Rate (RR) of 95.7% for identification and a 2.2% of EER for verification. This method achieves the best results among the mentioned ones, but uses a very complex equipment.

3   The Approaches We Tested

We now describe the different approaches we tested, starting from the best performing yet more constrained one, and releasing constraints afterwards. As for most papers in Section 2, the matching algorithm exploits DTW (in its basic version).

In order to capture the gait information, we chose 3-axis accelerometer as other related works. This sensor seems to better monitor the exact movement of a subject in the space, and nowadays is widespread and simple to set up, being built in most normal Android phones. The components exploited by our system are a OnePlus smartphone equipped with a 3-axis accelerometer and a desktop computer with Java Virtual Machine. We have not addressed interoperability issues yet, therefore the devices for enrollment and testing need to be of the same model.

Among the apps for monitoring and recording the accelerometer data, we chose Physics Toolbox Accelerometer, available on Google Play[2]. This application has a number of advantages among which the instant saving of data in Comma Separated Values (CSV) format. Moreover, the app is light, very fast, and compatible with any device with an accelerometer, including less recent versions of Android or less performing devices. Android captures accelerometer information automatically in an intelligent way: once the designer has set a minimum threshold of time to acquire the information, the data capture along the three axes is done according to a sampling density that depends on the displacement of the device relative to the previous position, i.e., the lower the variation the sparser the sampling and vice versa. Many approaches include time interpolation to obtain fixed intervals, but we avoid this step.

3.1   Enrollment Phase

In enrollment phase, our goal is to obtain a uniform enough data capture, which is quite usual in most applications. Therefore we decided to standardize the movements for each recording according to the following procedure: 1) the subject is asked to put the phone in the belt, either on the right hip or on the left one, in vertical position with the screen facing out (because recording is ended by tapping on the screen), in about the same position for all users; 2) the subject is then asked to keep feet together and start walking by the leg opposite to phone location; 3) the system records 10 steps along a straight line in the most natural way. For each enrolled user a folder is created on the desktop computer, where data is transferred (manually by now), and results of possible processing are stored. At the moment, we acquire data for three different user walks that during tests are used from time to time as probe or as gallery (during identification, probe data

---

[1] http://www.ytzhang.net/datasets/zju-gaitacc
[2] https://play.google.com/store/apps/details?id=com.chrystianviey
ra.android.physicstoolboxaccelerometer&hl=it

is matched with data from two different instances of walk). However, all approaches can handle a different number of templates per enrolled user. At present the dataset has 26 users, wearing different shoes (but no high heels).

In order to have each walk signal starting from a relevant point, we discard all initial local maxima created by noise. To do this, we use a threshold experimentally set at 1.05 on y axis (this value is device dependent). After the procedure finds the first value greater than the threshold, the system searches for the first relative maximum from that point. Once this has been identified, it is saved and will be the starting point of the vector that will be used by matching. A similar procedure is used to identify the useful end of the signal. As for now, the same threshold is used.

The system uses the DTW separately for each axis. In order to investigate an effective fusion of the three results for each comparison into a final similarity, we preliminarily studied the plots returned and performed some tests. In most cases, and considering that axes depend from the device position, our y-axis is the most important for recognition, followed by z-axis. The resulting weights are very similar to those used in other works in literature. The x-axis of our device has very little impact on the recognition. All walks achieve a very similar value on that axis, mainly because it assumes specific meanings only in case of strong jerks or jumps, that are generally absent in natural walking. We perform a linear combination of the three values using experimentally determined weights that depend on the processing method (see below).

3.2   Testing Phase and Experimental Results

As for testing, we investigated different possibilities, that we will denote according to the way walk data is pre-processed and to the way matching is performed: Walk, Best Step and Best Step VS All, AllSteps VS All, and Steps Sliding Window. The pre-processing described above applies to all. We apply essentially two strategies. The first one exploits the overall signal for matching, and is implemented only in the Walk method. All the others rely on a preliminary segmentation of the walk signal into steps, and on the possible discarding of outliers. This further pre-processing phase is applied to both gallery templates and to the probe. We first identify the starting and ending points of the useful portion of the signal using the thresholds mentioned above. Afterwards, for each walk belonging to the same user, maxima are extracted and ordered by amplitude. We underline that, thanks to the way we ask the user to walk, we can assume a certain distribution of maxima within the signal. In particular, each step is generally characterized by a first higher peak, corresponding to moving the leg with the accelerometer, and a second higher peak corresponding to moving the other leg. Moreover, it contains many further local maxima corresponding to noise. For each walk in the gallery, local maxima are extracted and ordered. In doing this, we consider the #walks sequences captured for a user all together. The value of the local maximum in position 10*#walks of this ordered list is taken as the threshold for step segmentation for the user at hand. Maxima higher than such threshold are taken as the starting points of new steps. In this way, we obtain on average 10 steps per walk for each user, unless some error happens. Moreover, we discard outliers. After dividing the walk into steps, we use DTW to compute pairwise differences and discard steps showing a distance from the others higher than the average distance plus the variance. In our case, we have an average of 20 steps per registered user. For each user, the threshold identified for step segmentation is stored together with the whole walk as well as the identified steps, with and without the outliers. At present, we assume closed set identification (the user is in the database) but setting a threshold is sufficient to pass to open set identification (the user might be unknown).

Walk. In Walk method, it is assumed that the probe contains the same number of steps as the gallery templates. The probe walk is matched against all stored walks (at present, two for each enrolled user). The system returns the labels of the candidates ordered by decreasing distance of each walk from the probe (the two walks for the same user are not necessarily close in the returned list). We use the following weights to combine results from the axes: x-axis=0, y-axis=0.8, z-axis=0.2.

Notwithstanding the simple approach, Walk modality achieves very interesting identification results. Notice that Recognition Rate (RR) is above 0.95 in the best test. However, the limitations given by the strictly controlled acquisition, especially the fixed number of steps, make this method not much appealing for real-world settings.

Best Step and Best Step VS All. These methods are a first attempt to overcome the limitations of Walk. They use step segmentation and outlier elimination, also for the probe. A further information is stored during the enrolling phase: the centroid of steps for each enrolled user is computed using DTW-based distances, and is saved in the gallery. It should represent the *average* user's step. During testing by Best Step, this *centroid step* of each user in the gallery is matched against the *centroid step* of the probe. For each matching operation, the probe is segmented into steps using the segmentation threshold stored in the gallery for the user to match. This algorithm achieves much lower performances with respect to Walk, with a RR of only 38.5%. It is reasonable to assume that this is due to the reduced size of the matched signal (a single step) which is the only information used to determine the final distance. We also tried to match the centroid step of each enrolled user to all steps of the probe, to take the minimum distance as result (Best Step VS All). However, this achieved the worst result of all algorithms we tried (a very poor RR of 23.1% in the best test).

AllSteps VS All. In AllSteps VS All method (AllSteps for short), we perform segmentation as described above and discard outliers, also for the probe. The identification phase is more articulated in this modality. For each gallery user, we divide the probe walk according to the user-specific threshold. For each step so obtained, we compute the minimum distance from the steps of that user. The final distance will be the average of all probe step minimum distances. The linear combination of results from the three axes is performed using the following weights: x-axis=0.1, y-axis=0.7, z-axis=0.2 (yet with very little performance decrease with the same Walk weights).

The reverse of the medal for all methods allowing much more freedom in the probe walk, i.e., that avoid setting in advance any number of steps in testing operations, is a decrease in performance, which is lower for this one, i.e., a RR of above 0.88 is achieved in the best test that corresponds in any case to a very promising result.

Steps Sliding Window. This method tries to recover some of the accuracy achieved by Walk. It uses segmentation just to compute the number of steps in the signal to match, and of course does not discard outliers, since matching is performed on sequential portions of the signals. We consider a window of x steps, where x is the minimum between the total number of steps of the probe and the total number of steps for the enrolled user being matched. The method applies DTW by sliding the shortest window over the longest one, and returning the minimum distance found. The weights assigned to axes are: x-axis= 0, y-axis=0.6, z-axis=0.4. This is the computationally most expensive among the tested algorithms and achieves a RR of 84.6% in the best test. In fact, it is slightly worse than AllSteps and also more onerous.

Figure 1 summarizes the achieved results in terms of Cumulative Match Curves (CMCs) in the best test. Since Walk returns ordered walks, while the others return ordered identities, the plot for Walk spans more ranks. We also performed   a kind of 3-fold validation, with each gallery template playing in turn the role of probe. To stress the Walk experimental setting, we did not repeat it three times with a balanced number of templates between the identity corresponding to the probe and those of the others: in each experiment we picked one template per user as probe (so that only two were left in the gallery) and matched it against all three templates of the other users. Results were only slightly worse, with similar relative performance of methods.

We tested the system for verification too using an all-against-all procedure. We assigned to each probe the identity of all enrolled users in turn (claim). Impostors were obviously much more than genuine users (|probe|*|gallery-1| impostors and |probe| genuines). The results confirm the relative performance for the different methods. We achieved the following ERR values: 7.69% for Walk, 30.46% for Best Step, 30.92% for Best Step VS All, 10.46% for AllSteps, and 15.38% for StepSlidingWindow. This confirms that the use of the centroid step is the worst strategy for verification too. Walk confirms to be the best method while the two methods with less restriction, i.e., AllSteps and StepSlidingWindow, achieve an acceptable result.

3.3   Discussion and Conclusions

This work presented a preliminary investigation on biometric identification by gait recognition via smartphone accelerometer. We tested different methods, starting from Walk that requires a fixed number of steps, but achieved the best results (RR above 0.95, EER 7.69%). The best compromise between low constraints and good accuracy is AllSteps (RR above 0.88, EER 10.46%). Identification results are confirmed in a kind of 3-fold validation. Methods achieving better results for verification used a more complex equipment and/or more expensive computational methods.

The only method in related work achieving better results in identification modality (RR 95.5% with no limitation on walk length) uses 5 accelerometers, therefore it is not suited for use with personal mobile devices. Moreover, the reported results using only the accelerometer located on pelvis, which is the same setting as our, only reach an RR of 73.4%, yet with a larger gallery. We will test further modalities and future work will address a number of issues. We will study how to make the method interoperable, by devising a kind of signal normalization procedure allowing to match signals from different accelerometers. We will also extend the database in less controlled or adverse conditions, i.e., by shoes with heels, and at different walking pace.

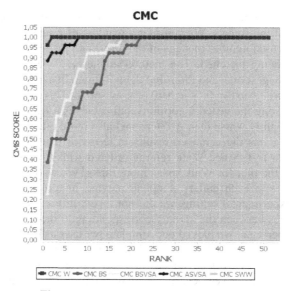

Fig. 1. CMCs for best tests in all modalities

References

1. Gafurov, D.: A survey of biometric gait recognition: approaches, security and challenges. In: Annual Norwegian Computer Science Conference, pp. 19–21 (2007)
2. Lee, T.K., Belkhatir, M., Sanei, S.: A comprehensive review of past and present vision-based techniques for gait recognition. MTAP **72**(3), 2833–2869 (2014)
3. Derawi, M.O., Nickel, C., Bours, P., Busch, C.: Unobtrusive user-authentication on mobile phones using biometric gait recognition. In: 2010 Sixth Int. Conf. on Intelligent Information Hiding and Multimedia Signal Processing (IIH-MSP), pp. 306–311 (2010)
4. Derawi, M.O., Bours, P., Holien, K.: Improved cycle detection for accelerometer based gait authentication. In: 2010 Sixth International Conference on Intelligent Information Hiding and Multimedia Signal Processing (IIH-MSP), pp. 312–317. IEEE (2010)
5. Gafurov, D., Helkala, K., Søndrol, T.: Biometric gait authentication using accelerometer sensor. Journal of Computers **1**(7), 51–59 (2006)
6. Juefei-Xu, F., Bhagavatula, C., Jaech, A., Prasad, U., Savvides, M.: Gait-ID on the move: pace independent human identification using cell phone accelerometer dynamics. In: IEEE BTAS 2012, pp. 8–15. IEEE (2012)
7. Nickel, C., Busch, C., Rangarajan, S., Mobius, M.: Using hidden markov models for accelerometer-based biometric gait recognition. In: 2011 IEEE 7th International Colloquium on Signal Processing and its Applications (CSPA), pp. 58–63. IEEE (2011)
8. Pan, G., Zhang, Y., Wu, Z.: Accelerometer-based gait recognition via voting by signature points. Electronics Letters **45**(22), 1116–1118 (2009)
9. Zhang, Y., Pan, G., Jia, K., Lu, M., Wang, Y., Wu, Z.: Accelerometer-based gait recognition by sparse representation of signature points with clusters. IEEE Transactions on Cybernetics, November 2014. doi:10.1109/TCYB.2014.2361287, http://ieeexplore.ieee.org/xpls/abs_all.jsp?arnumber=6963443&tag=1

Touchstroke: Smartphone User Authentication Based on Touch-Typing Biometrics

Attaullah Buriro[1]([✉]), Bruno Crispo[1,2], Filippo Del Frari[1], and Konrad Wrona[3]

[1] Department of Information Engineering and Computer Science,
University of Trento, Trento, Italy
{attaullah.buriro,bruno.crispo,filippo.delFrari}@unitn.it
[2] DistrNet, KU Leuven, Leuven, Belgium
bruno.crispo@cs.kuleuven.be
[3] NATO Communications and Information Agency, The Hague, Netherlands
konrad.wrona@ncia.nato.int

Abstract. Smartphones are becoming pervasive and widely used for a large variety of activities from social networking to online shopping, from message exchanging to mobile gaming, to mention just a few. Many of these activities generate private information or require storing on the phone user credentials and payment details. In spite of being so security and privacy critical, smartphones are still widely protected by traditional authentication mechanisms such as PINs and passwords, whose limitations and drawbacks are well known and documented in the security community. New accurate, user-friendly and effective authentication mechanisms are required. To this end, behavior-based authentication has recently attracted a significant amount of interest in both commercial and academic contexts.

This paper proposes a new bi-modal biometric authentication solution, *Touchstroke*, which makes use of the user's hand movements while holding the device, and the timing of touch-typing(Touch-typing is the act of typing input on the touchscreen of a smartphone.) when the user enters a *text-independent* 4-digit PIN/password. We implemented and tested the new biometrics in real smartphones. Preliminary results are encouraging, showing high accuracy. Thus, our solution is a plausible alternative to traditional authentication mechanisms.

Keywords: Smartphone · Behavioral biometrics · Keystroke · Transparent

1 Introduction

Smartphones and tablets have become essential devices in the lives of many people. A key factor of such success is their ability to offer mobility, computing power, storage capacity and an easy-to-use interface. This combined with the availability of millions of mobile applications explains the huge popularity of such devices.

© Springer International Publishing Switzerland 2015
V. Murino et al. (Eds.): ICIAP 2015 Workshops, LNCS 9281, pp. 27–34, 2015.
DOI: 10.1007/978-3-319-23222-5_4

Access to modern smartphones is still protected by old-fashioned mechanisms such as passwords and PINs. These methods are not only a burden to use, they are also not very secure (susceptible to guessing, shoulder surfing and smudge attacks [1]). Users often leave devices without any protection or choose too-easy-to-guess passwords (e.g. all zeros).

Recently, researchers proposed the use of behavior-based authentication means such as gait, phone movement, touch and keystroke as a replacement for passwords. Behavioral biometrics require minimal interaction during the authentication process, resulting in a significant increase in user acceptability.

This paper presents a new behavior-based authentication scheme called *Touchstroke*, which takes into account two human behaviors: how the phone is held and how a 4-*digit text-independent* PIN/password is entered. Our experiments confirmed that every user has a unique phone movement behavior and a different way of touch-typing a PIN/password on the smartphone. *Touchstroke* computes the phone-holding behavior with 7 built-in smartphone sensors, for: the orientation, the gravity, the magnetometer, the gyroscope and 3 variants of the accelerometer. Sensors are started at the time of the first touch-type and stopped after the fourth and final touch-type. Users are allowed to input any combination of 4-digit numbers and/or alphabets, hence they are expected to be able to use this authentication mechanism quite comfortably.

We extracted 4 statistical features from each data stream from all the physical sensors (a total of 16 from each sensor) and 14 features related with *n-graph*, related with dwell time and flight time (see Figure 1), from each typing pattern. In [2] authors show that these time-based features are the most widely used features in keystroke dynamics. In order to check the usability of our proposed method, we collected 30 observations from 12 users in six significantly different activities. As user authentication is essentially a binary class classification problem, we tested our dataset using two state-of-the art binary classifiers, BayesNET and Random Forest. The reason behind this selection is that they have shorter computation time and resistance against over-fitting.

The remainder of the paper is as follows. Section 2 covers related work. Section 3 explains the sensors and classifiers used. In section 4, we present an initial assessment of our intuition. Section 5 presents the experimental setup, data collection and feature extraction and discusses obtained results. Section 7 presents planned future work and concludes the paper.

2   Related Work

Keystroke-based user authentication is the most evaluated and tested behavioral biometric method for user authentication on PCs and smartphones using hardware and software keyboards. Since we have implemented text-independent touch-typing dynamics using Android software-keyboards, we consider software-keyboard-based work as our related work.

2.1   Software Keyboard-Based User Authentication

Keystroke-based recognition systems use the measurement of user's typing behavior on digital input devices such as smartphones and tablets. A digital signature is prepared on the basis of a user's interactions with these devices. Specifically, a user is asked to provide an alpha-numeric PIN/password to the system for creating a template for training and later for testing. [2,3] suggest that this fingerprinting is fairly unique from person to person thus can be used as a base for user identification.

A study conducted by Huang et al. [4] explored software-based-keyboard user authentication on mobile phones. Users were asked to enter their names and passwords 6 times for training. Based on the keystroke latency and key-hold-time features, the study reported an Equal Error Rate (EER) of 7.5%.

Saevancee and Bhattarakosol [5] reported an EER of 1% using the K-Nearest Neighbor (KNN) algorithm and reported similar results using neural networks [6]. However, they conducted their experiments only using a notebook touchpad. A recent study conducted by Saira et al. [7], on smartphones, revealed that the keystroke pressure might not be unique and reported an EER of 8.4% when used in conjunction with classical keystroke features (timings).

2.2   Sensor-Assisted Keystroke-Based User Authentication

Recent literature reports the feasibility of using sensor data in combination with keystrokes for user authentication.

Several projects have been conducted to study the use of accelerometers and gyroscopes. For example, Giuffrida et al. [3] introduced *UNAGI*, a *fixed-text* and sensor-enhanced authentication mechanism for Android phones. They evaluated their method with 20 subjects and achieved an EER of 4.97% for passwords, and 0.08% for only sensor data. Miluzzo et al. [8] used sensor data to infer the icon activated by the user of iOS devices and reported 90% accuracy.

Similarly, Aviv et al. [9] present a method that relies on accelerometer data and keystroke timings to infer 4-digit PINs for unlocking smartphones. Specifically, they demonstrated the use of accelerometer data for learning user tapping and gesture-based inputs as these methods are required to unlock smartphones using PIN/password and graphical password patterns. Additionally, they collected data in two situations, *sitting* and *walking*.

Touchstroke is different from the previous solutions in terms of features (for sensors), classification strategies, number of sensors, sensor-data-acquisition and constraints on the input.

3   Background

3.1   Considered Sensors and Classifiers

Modern smartphones are equipped with multiple sensors with the capability to detect and compute device/user movement. Accelerometer and orientation

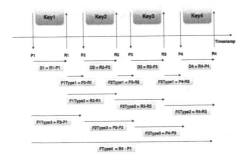

Fig. 1. Touchstroke features used in this paper, adapted from [2].

sensors are the most used sensors for movement recognition. Our solution uses seven three-dimensional sensors, for: three variants of the accelerometer; the gravity; the magnetic field or magnetometer; the gyroscope; and the orientation. All these physical sensors generate a continuous stream in 3 dimensions. We also added a fourth dimension to all of these sensors and name it magnitude, e.g. this dimension for the accelerometer is calculated as follows:

$$S_M = \sqrt{(a_x^2 + a_y^2 + a_z^2)} \tag{1}$$

where a_x, a_y and a_z are the readings from the accelerometer sensor along the X, Y, Z dimensions, respectively.

Classification is a way of comparing an unknown query input sample with the stored templates. Classifier selection depends on type and size of the dataset. We selected two classifiers by considering their short computation time and their resistance against over-fitting. Normally, Bayesian classifiers work well on small datasets and a random forest classifier is equally good for small and large datasets. We have applied these classifiers (with default parameters) in portable GUI-based Weka Experimenter Workbench.

3.2 Performance Metric

- True Acceptance Rate (TAR): The fraction of correctly accepted attempts of a real user.
- False Acceptance Rate (FAR: The fraction of incorrectly accepted attempts of an adversary.
- False Rejection Rate (FRR): The fraction of incorrectly rejected real users.
- Receiver Operating Characteristics (ROC): A parameter for the measurement of classifier performance. Specifically, a graphical representation of FAR vs FRR.

4   Intuition Assessment

It is our intuition that each user has a different way of holding and moving the phone when entering his PIN/password. If a user is holding a phone in his

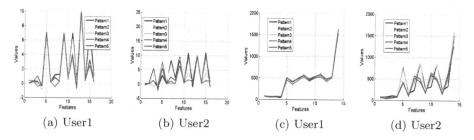

(a) User1   (b) User2   (c) User1   (d) User2

Fig. 2. Comparison of 5 patterns of accelerometer (a and b) and touchstroke data (c and d), in *sitting* position for two users.

hand, it is very challenging for others to generate exactly the same movement pattern. Even in case of a successful mimicry, the movement pattern will still be different due to the differences in the structure of the human body (e.g., the height and exact orientation of the phone). Physical sensors can compute these minute differences. Similarly every user has a unique way of inputting data on a smartphone. An adversary can spoof and copy what is being written but it is very difficult to copy the exact timings of touch-types. Our assumption holds true if the patterns of the same user are similar enough and different enough from other users.

We argue (see Figure 2) that the patterns of the same user are very similar to each other and patterns of two users are different enough. Owing to space limitations, we show the patterns of raw accelerometer and touchstroke sensors for a single situation: when the user is sitting.

5   Experimental Evaluations

In order to validate our initial intuition we ran a set of experiments, described in the sections below.

5.1   Data Collection

We implemented *Touchstroke* as an Android application that triggers all physical sensors from the first touch-type and stops them after the last touch-type. At this moment the app is designed for only four touch-types with the possibility to be extended. We recruited 12 volunteers for our experiment; most of them are either MSc or PhD students but not security experts. In order to check the usability of our proposed mechanism, we collected data in six different user positions, i.e., *sitting, standing, walking, lying on sofa, walking upstairs* and *walking downstairs*. We used Google Nexus 5 running KitKat 4.4.2 for data collection. We collected 30 patterns from each user in each activity. In total, we collected 180 samples (in all 6 activities) from each user, making a total of 2160 samples from 12 users.

After registering the sensor with registerlistener(), data can be collected in both fixed and customized user-defined intervals. Android supports four fixed delivery rates, termed Sensor Delay Modes, namely, SENSOR_DELAY_FASTEST with a fixed delay of 0 sec, SENSOR_DELAY_GAME with a fixed delay of 0.02 sec, SENSOR_DELAY_UI with a fixed delay of 0.06 sec and the last one,
SENSOR_DELAY_NORMAL with a fixed delay of 0.2 seconds.

Touchstroke collects sensor data in SENSOR_DELAY_GAME mode.

5.2 Feature Extraction

We have four data streams from every three-dimensional sensor. We chose statistical features because it is computationally cheaper to compute them. We extracted 4 statistical features, namely mean, standard deviation, skewness and kurtosis from each data stream. In this way data from every sensor is transformed into a 4 by 4 feature matrix. Thus we have 16 features from all four dimensions of each sensor. Similarly, we extracted 14 features (see Figure 1), based on touch-typing timing, from the *text-independent* 4-digit PIN/password entered by the user.

Table 1. BayesNET classifier results for fused data for *standing, walking, lying on sofa, walking upstairs* and *walking downstairs*(averaged over all 12 users).

Sensors	Standing			Sofa			Walking			Upstairs			Downstairs		
	TAR	FRR	FAR	TAR	FRR	FAR	TAR	FRR	FAR	TAR	FRR	FAR	TAR	FRR	FAR
Raw + Touch	0.98	0.02	0.02	0.98	0.02	0.02	0.99	0.01	0.01	0.97	0.03	0.03	0.98	0.02	0.03
LPF + Touch	0.98	0.02	0.02	0.98	0.02	0.01	0.99	0.01	0.01	0.97	0.03	0.03	0.97	0.03	0.03
HPF + Touch	0.97	0.03	0.03	0.96	0.04	0.04	0.97	0.03	0.03	0.96	0.04	0.04	0.96	0.04	0.04
Grav + Touch	0.98	0.02	0.02	0.98	0.02	0.02	0.98	0.02	0.02	0.97	0.03	0.03	0.97	0.03	0.03
Gyro+Touch	0.97	0.03	0.03	0.96	0.04	0.04	0.98	0.02	0.02	0.96	0.04	0.04	0.97	0.03	0.03
Mag + Touch	0.97	0.01	0.01	0.99	0.01	0.01	0.96	0.04	0.04	0.95	0.05	0.05	0.96	0.04	0.04
Orient + Touch	0.98	0.02	0.02	0.97	0.03	0.03	0.98	0.02	0.02	0.96	0.04	0.03	0.97	0.03	0.03

5.3 Data Fusion

Data fusion can be done at the sensor level, feature level, match score level, rank level and decision level. Data fusion at an early stage may be more productive. However, sensor level fusion is not the best choice because of the presence of noise during data acquisition. Since feature representation shows much more relevant information corresponding to the class, the fusion at feature level is expected to provide better results. Thus, we fused data at feature level, in order to provide maximum relevant information to our recognition system. We fused the feature vector of each sensor with the touch-type feature vector, making a feature vector of 30 features. The reason for fusing only two sensors is to prevent over-fitting. Larger feature vectors may end up with over-fitting of the classifier.

5.4 Analysis

We used Weka Experimenter Workbench for the classification of these patterns. Data files were converted to ARFF files and later these ARFF files and two classifiers were added to the Weka Experimenter Workbench. We collected 30 observations for each activity from each user. We performed stratified cross-validation for training and testing of both classifiers for two reasons; firstly, because of equal number of patterns from each class assuming that it will arrange the data such that in each fold, each class comprises around half the instances. Secondly to test the classifiers with maximum possible user patterns. We present our results in terms of TAR, FRR, FAR and ROC curves.

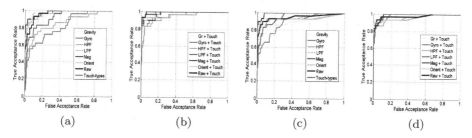

Fig. 3. ROC curve for BayesNET (a) for Individual and (b) for fused sensors and random forest (c) Individual and (d) fused sensors.

6 Discussion of Results

We achieved acceptable authentication rates for all the activities from individual sensors especially variants of accelerometers. As it can be very difficult to type while *walking, going downstairs* and *upstairs*, we can expect a little increase in error rates in those situations. However, *Touchstroke* performed well even in these positions, yielding acceptable authentication results (see Table 1).

The purpose of fusion of each sensor with touchstroke data is twofold. Firstly, to improve authentication accuracy; ROC curves for both the classifiers show an improvement in accuracy for fused data (see Figures 3b and 3d). Secondly, to make the system more secure; it is comparatively difficult to mimic two behaviors at the same time. Due to space limitations, we present ROC curves for *sitting* activity and authentication results of the BayesNET classifier (see Table 1) for fused data only.

Another important observation is related to the way users hold the phone. Some users use one hand and others use both hands for holding and entering the *text-independent* text. *Touchstroke* works for both types of user. Our experiments are preliminary since we run the tests with a limited number of users who are not representative of the general population, thus we cannot exclude some bias due to the particular composition of our test set.

7   Conclusions and Future Work

We propose a bi-modal biometric system, *Touchstroke*, for smartphone user authentication based on phone movement patterns and *free-text* 4-digit touch-type patterns. We implemented and evaluated the system on Android smartphones. The initial experiments indicate that our solution is highly accurate in each situation. Each sensor can potentially be used with touch-type features for user authentication. Our solution can be implemented in any off-the-shelf smartphone without the need for additional hardware, hence can be used as a stand-alone method or can be complemented by traditional passwords for additional security.

In future work, we will test whether or not the fusion of multiple sensors and/or with touchstrokes has an impact on accuracy. Futher, in order to check the impact of the length of the touch-type, we will investigate whether or not typing a long-digit password/PIN gives different results from those obtained for 4-digit entries.

References

1. Raza, M., Iqbal, M., Sharif, M., Haider, W.: A survey of password attacks and comparative analysis on methods for secure authentication. World Applied Sciences Journal **19**, 439–444 (2012)
2. Teh, P.S, Teoh, A.B.J., Yue, S.: A survey of keystroke dynamics biometrics. The Scientific World Journal, Hindawi Publishing Corporation (2013)
3. Giuffrida, C., Majdanik, K., Conti, M., Bos, H.: I sensed it was you: authenticating mobile users with sensor-enhanced keystroke dynamics. In: Dietrich, S. (ed.) DIMVA 2014. LNCS, vol. 8550, pp. 92–111. Springer, Heidelberg (2014)
4. Huang, X., Lund, G., Sapeluk, A.: Development of a typing behavior recognition mechanism on android. In: Proceeding of the IEEE 11th International Conference on Trust, Security and Privacy in Computing and Communications (TrustCom), pp. 1342–1347. IEEE, Bradford (2012)
5. Saevanee, H., Bhatarakosol, P.: User authentication using combination of behavioral biometrics over the touchpad acting like touch screen of mobile device. In: Proceeding of the International Conference on Computer and Electrical Engineering (ICCEE 2008), pp. 82–86. IEEE, Phuket (2008)
6. Saevanee, H., Bhatarakosol, P.: Authenticating user using keystroke dynamics and finger pressure, In: Proceedings of the 6th IEEE Consumer Communications and Networking Conference (CCNC 2009), pp. 1–2. IEEE, Las Vegas (2009)
7. Zahid, S., Shahzad, M., Khayam, S.A., Farooq, M.: Keystroke-based user identificationon smart phones. In: Kirda, E., Jha, S., Balzarotti, D. (eds.) RAID 2009. LNCS, vol. 5758, pp. 224–243. Springer, Heidelberg (2009)
8. Miluzzo, E., Varshavsky, A., Balakrishnan, S., Choudhury, R.R.: Tapprints: your finger taps have fingerprints, In: Proceedings of the 10th international conference on Mobile systems, applications, and services, pp. 323–336. ACM (2012)
9. Aviv, A.J., Sapp, B., Blaze, M., Smith, J.M.: Practicality of accelerometer side channels on smartphones, In: Proceedings of the 28th Annual Computer Security Applications Conference, pp. 41–50. ACM (2012)

EEG/ECG Signal Fusion Aimed at Biometric Recognition

Silvio Barra[1]([✉]), Andrea Casanova[1], Matteo Fraschini[2], and Michele Nappi[3]

[1] Department of Mathematics and Computer Science,
University of Cagliari, Via Ospedale, 40, 09124 Cagliari, Italy
`silvio.barra@unica.it`
[2] Department of Electrical and Electronic Engineering (DIEE),
University of Cagliari, 09123 Cagliari, Italy
[3] University of Salerno, Via Giovanni Paolo II 132, 84084 Fisciano, Salerno, Italy

Abstract. The recognition of individuals based on behavioral and biological characteristics has made important strides over the past few years. Growing interest has been recently devoted to the study of physiological measures, which include the electrical activity of brain (EEG) and heart (ECG). Even if the use of multimodal approaches overcome several limitations of traditional uni-modal biometric systems, the simultaneous use of EEG and ECG characteristics has been scarcely investigated. In this paper, we present a set of preliminary results derived by the investigation of a biometric system based on the fusion of simple features simultaneously extracted from EEG and ECG signals. The reported results show high performance both from uni-modal approach (higher performance being EER = 11.17 and EER = 3.83 for EEG and ECG respectively) and fusion (EER = 2.94). However, caution should be considered in the interpretation of the reported results mainly beacuse the analysis was performed on a limited set of subjects.

1 Introduction

Biometric systems, which allow to automatically recognize individuals on the basis of their behavioral and biological characteristics, have made important strides over the past few years. These pattern recognition systems will play an increasingly relevant role in the future of highly reliable security systems.

During the last years, the interest in the identification of more robust subject-specific traits has widen the scenario of possible new relevant physical characteristics. In particular, growing interest has been recently devoted to the study of physiological measures, which include the electrical activity of brain and heart. Electroencephalography (EEG) and electrocardiography (ECG) have been indeed extensively investigated as possible markers of biometric traits.

The potential role of brain activity has been highlighted using both simple spectral measures [12] and more complex parameters such as functional connectivity [7] and network topology [5]; for a comprehensive review see [7].

Recently, it has also been shown that some features of ECG signals are very subject-dependent and thus, a high inter-subject variability can be observed [15].

© Springer International Publishing Switzerland 2015
V. Murino et al. (Eds.): ICIAP 2015 Workshops, LNCS 9281, pp. 35–42, 2015.
DOI: 10.1007/978-3-319-23222-5_5

However, up to date there are several issues that hinder a clear interpretation of the reported results for both EEG-based and ECG-based biometric systems. In particular, the current literature is characterized by high variability in experimental protocols, dataset structure, number of subjects, features extracted, frequency components.

Multimodal biometric systems are characterized by the fusion of different biometric traits; in [16] it has been stated that such systems are able to overcome several limitations of traditional uni-modal biometric systems. Nevertheless, the simultaneous use of EEG and ECG characteristics has been scarcely investigated [[14], [15]].

In this paper, we present a set of preliminary results derived from the investigation of a biometric system based on the fusion of simple features simultaneously extracted from EEG and ECG signals. Uni-modal results are also reported. Our thesis is that the contemporary evaluation of such characteristics may represent an important advance towards the development of new efficient and robust authentication systems.

2 Related Works

In the last ten years, fusion of EEG and ECG signals has been extensively used in several fields. Definitely, diagnostic is the most covered purpose by this practice. In [1], the authors fused the signals in order to detect epileptic events in a patient, based on the fact that such events produce some alterations in the cardiac rhythm. In [8] and [9] a seizure detector is presented, which exploits Support Vector Machines for classification of time and frequency features. Further applications lie in the field of BCI (brain computer interface) systems. In [17], a two-stage hybrid BCI has been developed: first, a feature extraction process over the EEG and ECG signals, based on bispectrum, is achieved; then, a classification is applied to the normalized features, by means of the Fisher's Linear Discriminant analysis (LDA).

The simultaneous use of EEG and ECG characteristics for the development of a biometric system has been scarcely investigated. Some interesting and promising approaches are described in [[14], [15]].

However, it must be kept in mind that the physiological signals are always contaminated by several artifacts which strongly affect the recorded electrical activity; therefore, caution should be used in the interpretation of the results. The investigation of possible solutions for automatic artifact removal ([2], [3], [6], [11], [13]) still represents an important challenge.

3 The Proposed Approach

The idea behind our proposal is to construct a biometric system by composing characteristics and subject-specific traits extracted from the EEG and ECG signals.

In the following, we describe the acquisition process of EEG and ECG, the extraction of the corresponding features and finally the definition of the new biometric proposal by fusing the extracted EEG and ECG signals. In Fig. 1 the steps involved in the system are summarized.

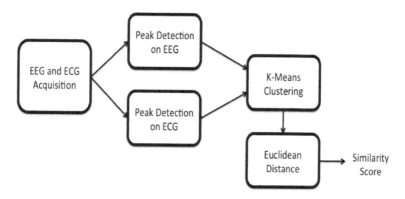

Fig. 1. The process starts with the acquisition of the signals which first are band pass filtered and then given as input to the peak detection method. The detected peaks are represented by a decreasing ordered 48-features vector. Finally, the fusion by clustering is computed. The Euclidean Distance is used to achieve the matching between the centroids of the clusters.

3.1   The Acquisition Process

EEG signals were recorded according to a standard protocol using a 64 channels EEG system. During the EEG recording, the subject involved in the acquisition was instructed to close his/her eyes, stay awake, and reduce eye movements as much as possible, in order to minimize the noise caused by the ocular muscles. The reference electrode was placed in close proximity of the electrode POz, with the ground electrode on the forehead. In Fig. 2, a schematic representation of the position of the electrodes placed on the head of the subject via a soft-helmet is shown.

The acquired signals were digitized with a sampling frequency of 1024 Hz and successively resampled to 256 Hz. Signals were band-pass filtered between 0.5 and 70 Hz. For each subject, five eyes-closed epochs of 16.384 samples (16 s) were selected. In the selection, periods indicating drowsiness were excluded from the analysis.Furthermore, in order to limit as much as possible the contamination of external sources (not neural), we decided to focus the analysis on epochs free from artifacts (blinks and eye movements) which can be visually detected. However, the possible impact of these artifacts on classification performance need investigation.

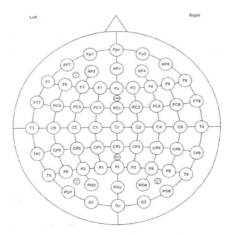

Fig. 2. Electrode position for the 64 channels Micromed system *BrainQuickSystem* by Micromed (Mogliano-Veneto, Italy).

EEG signals were successively band-pass filtered in the classical EEG frequency bands: *theta* (4-8 Hz), *alpha* (8-13 Hz), *beta* (13-30 Hz) and *gamma* (30-50 Hz). The broadband (0.5-50 Hz) signal was also included in the analysis. All the analyses were performed for each band separately.

ECG signals were band-pass filtered in the band 3-15 Hz to avoid noise contamination. Furthermore, since ECG signals show a baseline shift (not representing true amplitude) a detrend procedure based on a low order polynomial fitting was used.

3.2   Feature Extraction

At the end of the acquisition process, for each subject and each epoch, the EEG signals were obtained and represented by a set of 61 vectors, one for each channel, containing 16384 samples of the y-coordinate of the corresponding signal. The ECG signal were represented similarly, by a vector obtained by the potential difference, *ECG+-ECG-*, of the electrodes posed on the wrists. In Fig. 3, the first 61 signals are referred to the EEG, the last one is the *ECG+-ECG-* signal.

The description of the ECG signal has been based on the characterization of the most prominent repeating peaks, which consists of three major components: the Q, R, and S waves (QRS-complex).

The detection of QRS-complex still represents an important challenge. Main problems arise from differences in shape, low signal-to-noise ratio, artifacts and abnormalities. Many detection techniques have been proposed in the literature. These techniques include thresholding, neural networks, hidden Markov model, matched filters, zero-crossing, and singularity techniques. For a more detailed description of these techniques see [4].

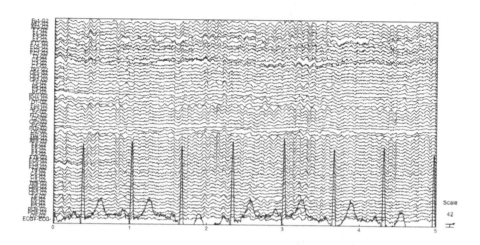

Fig. 3. A typical EEG/ECG acquisition: the first 61 signals are referred to the EEG. The last signal is referred to the ECG.

However, it is important to highlight that the aim of the present study was not develop a novel methods for QRS-complex detection. Therefore, in this study the feature extraction procedure was based on a simple peak detection method which is not accurate for detecting the QRS-complex. The extracted peaks were successively sorted in descending order (based on the peak amplitude) and a fixed set of k elements (most prominent peaks) were selected as features.

In order to avoid any arbitrary selection, the choice of the optimal k threshold was based on the assessment of the possible number of QRS-complex repetitions which could be identified on the selected time interval (16 seconds). All the subsequent analysis is therefore based on a fixed threshold k, with $k = 48$ (sixteen single peaks, one per second, for each of the three waves of the QRS-complex). The impact of the threshold k on the system performance should be further investigated.

The same procedure, with the same k value, was successively used to select the EEG features.

3.3   EEG and ECG Fusion

As for the EEG signal, the previous phase produced 61 vectors of 48 components for each of the five bands *theta* (4-8 Hz), *alpha* (8-13 Hz), *beta* (13-30 Hz) and *gamma* (30-50 Hz) and *broadband*. Analogously, the 62nd vector is obtained for the ECG signal. The fusion process of the two traits is done as follows:

- for each band separately, the 61 vectors for EEG and the one for ECG are clustered, using the well known *k-means* algorithm;
- then, for each cluster the centroid vector is evaluated;
- the biometric is then composed, grouping the centroid vectors of all the clusters.

All the signals share the same feature space and both EEG and ECG waves are band-pass filtered in such a way that the clustering process is done among similar vectors. The centroids of each cluster represent the fused vectors between EEG and ECG signal, as well as the entry point for that cluster. In our study, we considered different numbers of clusters in order to evaluate the better choice fitting our biometric system. Then, given the number of vectors, we evaluated different options, respectively with 4, 8, 16 and 24 clusters for each bandwidth. In a further analysis, we excluded the first option (i.e. 4 clusters) since we observed an excessive loss of information. Each cluster contains a subset of signals such that the intra variability is minimized, and only one of these contains the ECG signal.

4   Experimental Results

In the study, nine healthy (without cardiovascular or neurological complications) volunteer subjects were included in the experimental protocol; their informed consent was obtained. The EEG system used in the experimentation was the *BrainQuickSystem* by Micromed (Mogliano-Veneto, Italy).

The results use the equal error rate (EER), which refers to the intersection point between the false acceptance rate (FAR) and the false rejection rate (FRR) curves.

In Table 1, the results for the uni-modal EEG approach are summarized. Higher results were obtained using the broadband (0.5-50 Hz) EEG signal component.

From the uni-modal ECG approach an EER = 3.83% has been obtained.

Finally, in Table 2, we reported the results (in terms of EER) obtained from the fusion of EEG and ECG features.

Table 1. EEG signal: EER values for each band

Theta (4-8Hz)	Alpha (8-13Hz)	Beta (13-30Hz)	Gamma (30-50Hz)	Broadband (0.5-50 Hz)
16.67%	17.11%	15.83%	15.50%	**11.17%**

Table 2. EER values derived from the fusion of the signals

number of clusters	Theta(4-8Hz)	Alpha(8-13Hz)	Beta(13-30Hz)	Gamma(30-50Hz)	Broadband
8	**2.94%**	4,44%	**2.94%**	**2.94%**	11.11%
16	**2.94%**	8.94%	**2.94%**	4.44%	17.78%
24	**2.94%**	**2.94%**	**2.94%**	6.67%	4.50%

5   Further Works and Considerations

The reported results show good classification performance and then they seem to be promising. Probably the most relevant finding reported in this paper is that by means of a very simple and inexpensive procedure (peak detection and sorting), it is still possible to detect subject-specific traits extracted from both EEG and ECG activities. Furthermore, it seems that from the fusion of these specific traits the system is even more accurate.

However, caution should be used in the interpretation of the reported results, since it is needed to validate the proposed approach on a higher number of subjects. Nevertheless, it is quite interesting that EEG still has the capability to reduce the EER when fused with ECG features.

Moreover, the results obtained from the study of high-frequency (above 30 Hz), which include both gamma band and broadband analysis, should be considered potentially compromised by muscle artifatcs [10].

In conclusion, the results obtained suggest that the fusion of EEG and ECG characteristics show results of potential interest in the development of new biometric systems.

References

1. Bermudez, T., Lowe, D., Arlaud-Lamborelle, A.-M.: EEG/ECG information fusion for epileptic event detection. In: 2009 16th International Conference on Digital Signal Processing (2009)
2. Chaumon, M., Bishop, D.V.M., Busch, N.A.: A practical guide to the selection of independent components of the electroencephalogram for artifact correction. Journal of Neuroscience Methods (2015)
3. Dewan, M.A.A., Hossain, M.J., Hoque, M., Chae, O.: Contaminated ECG artifact detection and elimination from eeg using energy function based transformation. In: International Conference on Information and Communication Technology, ICICT 2007 (2007)
4. Elgendi, M., Eskofier, B., Dokos, S., Abbott, D.: Revisiting qrs detection methodologies for portable, wearable, battery-operated, and wireless ecg systems. PloS One **9**(1) (2014)
5. Fraschini, M., Hillebrand, A., Demuru, M., Didaci, L., Marcialis, G.L.: An EEG-based biometric system using eigenvector centrality in resting state brain networks. Signal Processing Letters. IEEE (2015)
6. Huang, R., Heng, F., Hu, B., Peng, H., Zhao, Q., Shi, Q., Han, J.: Artifacts reduction method in EEG signals with wavelet transform and adaptive filter. In: Ślęzak, D., Tan, A.-H., Peters, J.F., Schwabe, L. (eds.) BIH 2014. LNCS, vol. 8609, pp. 122–131. Springer, Heidelberg (2014)
7. La Rocca, D., Campisi, P., Vegso, B., Cserti, P., Kozmann, G., Babiloni, F.,and De Vico Fallani, F.: Human brain distinctiveness based on eeg spectral coherence connectivity. IEEE Transactions on Biomedical Engineering (2014)
8. Mporas, I., Tsirka, V., Zacharaki, E., Koutroumanidis, M., Megalooikonomou, V.: Evaluation of time and frequency domain features for seizure detection from combined EEG and ECG signals. In: Proceedings of the 7th International Conference on PErvasive Technologies Related to Assistive Environments (2014)

9. Mporas, I., Tsirka, V., Zacharaki, E.I., Koutroumanidis, M., Richardson, M., Megalooikonomou, V.: Seizure detection using EEG and ECG signals for computer-based monitoring, analysis and management of epileptic patients. Expert Systems with Applications (2015)

10. Muthukumaraswamy, S.: High-frequency brain activity and muscle artifacts in meg/eeg: A review and recommendations. Frontiers in Human Neuroscience **7**, 138 (2013)

11. Park, H.-J., Jeong, D.-U., Park, K.-S.: Automated detection and elimination of periodic ECG artifacts in EEG using the energy interval histogram method. IEEE Transactions on Biomedical Engineering (2002)

12. Del Pozo-Banos, M., Alonso, J.B., Ticay-Rivas, J.R., Travieso, C.M.: Electroencephalogram subject identification: A review. Expert Systems with Applications (2014)

13. Raofen, W., Jianhua, Z., Xingyu, W.: Automatic ocular artifact suppression from human operator's eeg based on a combination of independent component analysis and fuzzy c-means clustering techniques. In: 2011 30th Chinese Control Conference (CCC) (2011)

14. Riera, A., Dunne, S., Cester, I., Ruffini, G.: Starfast: a wire-less wearable EEG/ECG biometric system based on the enobio sensor. In: Proceedings of the International Workshop on Wearable Micro and Nanosystems for Personalised Health (2008)

15. Riera, A., Soria-Frisch, A., Caparrini, M., Cester, I., Ruffini, G.: 1 multimodal physiological biometrics authentication. Biometrics: Theory, Methods, and Applications (2009)

16. Ross, A., Jain, A.K.: Multimodal biometrics: an overview. In: 2004 12th European Signal Processing Conference (2004)

17. Shahid, S., Prasad, G., Sinha, R.K.: On fusion of heart and brain signals for hybrid BCI. In: 2011 5th International IEEE/EMBS Conference on Neural Engineering (NER) (2011)

Fusion of Holistic and Part Based Features for Gender Classification in the Wild

Modesto Castrillón-Santana$^{(\boxtimes)}$, Javier Lorenzo-Navarro,
and Enrique Ramón-Balmaseda

Universidad de Las Palmas de Gran Canaria, Las Palmas de Gran Canaria, Spain
{modesto.castrillon,javier.lorenzo}@ulpgc.es
http://berlioz.dis.ulpgc.es/roc-siani

Abstract. Gender classification (GC) in the wild is an active area of current research. In this paper, we focus on the combination of a holistic state of the art approach based on features extracted from the facial pattern, with patch based approaches that focus on inner facial areas. Those regions are selected for being relevant to the human system according to the psychophysics literature: the ocular and the mouth areas. The resulting proposed GC system outperforms previous approaches, reducing the classification error of the holistic approach roughly a 30%.

Keywords: Gender classification · Local descriptors · Score level fusion

1 Introduction

Gender classification (GC) is a growing area of research with different potential applications. This fact has recently been stated by NIST in their 2015 evaluation [20]. That review highlights the difference between GC with constrained or controlled datasets, and unconstrained or *in the wild* datasets. In the first scenario, the most accurate system reached an accuracy up to 96.5% with a dataset containing almost one million samples.

However, the reported results in unconstrained imagery datasets did not present always a similar behavior. Two datasets were selected for that experiment: 1) *The Labeled Faces in the Wild* (LFW) [16], and 2) *The images of Groups* (GROUPS) [11].

Even when both datasets contain variations in terms of pose, illumination, etc., the best Face Recognition Vendor Test (FRVT) participants reported a remarkable difference in accuracy for each. For LFW, the best accuracy reached 95.2%, quite close to the numbers reported for constrained datasets. However, for GROUPS it just reached 90.4%. We can argue that this effect is due to the larger variations in terms of pose exhibited by GROUPS, and the multiple

---

M. Castrillón-Santana—Work partially funded by the Institute of Intelligent Systems and Numerical Applications in Engineering and the Computer Science Department at ULPGC.

V. Murino et al. (Eds.): ICIAP 2015 Workshops, LNCS 9281, pp. 43–50, 2015.
DOI: 10.1007/978-3-319-23222-5_6

samples per identity included in LFW. These results were obtained with a lights-out, black-box testing methodology.

Extending the NIST review, we summarize in Table 1 the most recent results reported in the research literature for both datasets. A fast analysis suggests that GROUPS is the most challenging one. The achieved accuracies are however not comparable to those obtained by commercial systems. The reader must observe that these results were achieved not following a lights-out, black-box testing methodology. Focusing on GROUPS, with the exception of the protocol described by Dago et al. [9], used in [4] too, the adopted protocols are not easily reproducible. The fact that GROUPS is currently the most challenging in the wild dataset, has convinced us to focus on this dataset.

Table 1. GC accuracies in recent literature. The whole dataset is used, i.e. 28000 samples, with the exception of [1] aropund 14000 samples with inter ocular distance > 20, [2] 22778 aut. detected faces, [3] > 12 years old, [4] 7443 of the total 13233 images, [5] BEFIT protocol, and [6] half dataset.

Reference	Dataset	Accuracy (%)
[9]	GROUPS[1]	86.6%
[4]	GROUPS[1]	89.8%
[19]	GROUPS[2]	86.4%
[7]	GROUPS[2]	90.4%
[3]	GROUPS[3]	80.5%
[14]	GROUPS	87.1%
[23]	LFW[4]	94.8%
[25]	LFW[4]	98.0%
[9]	LFW[5]	97.2%
[21]	LFW[6]	98.0%
[3]	LFW	79.5%
[17]	LFW	96.9%
[22]	LFW	94.6%

Two recent results support the approach described in this paper. On the one hand, the extraction of features at different scales may benefit the GC performance [2,4]. In [4] the features are extracted from the face and its local context, thus, the face is analyzed at different resolutions. This fact might introduce redundancy, but the resulting improved performance suggests that an adequate design reports indeed an accuracy improvement.

On the other hand, the fusion of multiple descriptors do not just reports a benefit in GC accuracy, but also diminishes the occurrences of ambiguous cases as demonstrated for a demographics balanced dataset [6].

Therefore, the aim in this paper is to explore whether the additional integration of features extracted from specific areas of the inner face, improves the overall GC accuracy. The contributions of this work are: 1) separately the periocular and the mouth area provide an accuracy greater than 80% for GROUPS, 2) the adequate selection of periocular and mouth features, that are later fused with standard state-of-the-art facial based GC systems, provides a significant augment in terms of GC accuracy.

2 Approach

We therefore assume the ideas described above, i.e. the interest for the GC problem of a proper combination of features and regions of interest. We start from a baseline, given by a state of the art facial based GC system [4], to later explore the fusion with features densely extracted from some specific areas of the inner face [5]. With this concept in mind, we have revisited the analysis of the human visual system for the GC problem using *bubbles* [13], where the authors argue that both the ocular and the mouth areas are discriminant for this task to the human system.

An initial study of the integration of the periocular area [5] has already suggested that this approach may improve the GC performance up to 2 percentage points. Indeed, the use of components for facial analysis is a known idea. The work by Heisele et al. [15] made use of two layers of classifiers, being the second the combination of the first layer scores. The approach obtained better results than just using global features. In this paper, we indeed do not restrict to inner facial patches but also integrate features extracted from the whole facial pattern. To avoid redundancy, we select the best configuration of features, areas and grid configurations.

Summarizing, the considered patterns are presented in Figure 1: the head and shoulders (HS), the face (F), the periocular (P), and the mouth (M) areas. They all are automatically cropped from the original head and shoulders pattern (with a dimension of 155×159 pixels with 26 pixels of inter-eye distance), with the exception of the HS pattern that is down-sampled to 64×64 pixels. The original pattern is obtained after a normalization process guided by the eye locations, that encloses rotation, scaling and translation to fix the normalized eye locations.

Fig. 1. From left to right, head and shoulders (HS) (64×64 pixels), face (F) (59×65 pixels), periocular (P) (37×31 pixels), and mouth (M) (19×49 pixels) regions. Sample taken from GROUPS.

After selecting the patterns to be used, we proceed with a number of steps with the final goal of evaluating the fusion or combination of multiple experts. We analyze the periocular (P) and mouth (M) areas as follows:

1. Explore the features and grid resolutions for both P and M.
2. Select the most discriminant features and grids using P and M.
3. Evaluate the combination of the state of the art GC system with the best P and M descriptors separately.
4. Evaluate the combination of the state of the art GC system with the best P and M descriptors jointly.

Based on current literature and our background related to GC, we use as features different local descriptors. Local descriptors are currently being applied for facial analysis, based on a grid configuration to avoid the loss of spatial information produced by a single based histogram representation [1].

A grid configuration is defined by its number of horizontal and vertical cells, respectively cx and cy, making a total of $cx \times cy$ cells. For a given feature, a histogram is computed in each cell, h_i, where the bins indicate the number of occurrences of the different codes. The final feature vector, $\mathbf{x}$, is composed by the concatenation of $cx \times cy$ histograms, i.e. $\mathbf{x} = \{h_1, h_2, ..., h_{cx \times cy}\}$.

In few words, each expert is designed with a particular feature and grid configuration. For P we have analyzed grid configurations in the range $cx \in [1, 8]$ and $cy \in [1, 6]$, while for M we have covered the range $cx \in [1, 8]$ and $cy \in [1, 8]$. That makes respectively a total of 48 and 64 variants per descriptor. As descriptors we have considered 8 different alternatives:

- Histogram of Oriented Gradients (HOG) [10].
- Local Binary Patterns (LBP) and uniform Local Binary Patterns (LBP^{u2}) [1].
- Local Gradient Patterns (LGP) [18].
- Local Ternary Patterns (LTP) [24].
- Local Phase Quantization (LPQ) [26].
- Weber Local Descriptor (WLD) [8].
- Local Oriented Statistics Information Booster (LOSIB) [12].

For the final fusion analysis, we adopt a score level fusion approach based on SVM classifiers similarly to [4,15]. The first layer is formed by the classifiers after selecting the best descriptors and grid configurations of each pattern for the problem, while the second layer classifier takes as input the first layer scores.

3   Results

As mentioned above, we adopt the Dago's protocol as experimental setup. This protocol defines a 5-fold cross validation for the GROUPS dataset. The dataset is reduced to around 14000 samples as the protocol includes only those faces that present an inter-eye distance larger than 20 pixels in the original source image.

We present in first term the results achieved making use of features extracted only from P and M. Tables 2 and 3 summarize the best results achieved for the first fold of the Dago's protocol. Due to the lack of space, only their best accuracy obtained for each descriptor configuration and pattern is included in both tables.

Table 2. Periocular based best single descriptor results in terms of accuracy (%) obtained for the first fold of the Dago's protocol. For each descriptor the best grid setup is indicated. Those descriptors providing an accuracy larger than 77% are highlighted.

	$HOG_{7\times6}$	$LBP^{u2}_{8\times3}$	$LBP_{6\times3}$	$LGP_{6\times6}$	$LTP_{3\times2}$	$LPQ_{2\times2}$	$WLD_{6\times3}$	$LOSIB_{7\times6}$
Periocular	**83.02**	**80.31**	76.24	**77.88**	**80.08**	76.00	**82.20**	76.45

Table 3. Mouth based best single descriptor results in terms of accuracy (%) obtained for the first fold of the Dago's protocol. For each descriptor the best grid setup is indicated. Those descriptors providing an accuracy larger than 75% are highlighted.

	$HOG_{8\times8}$	$LBP^{u2}_{5\times5}$	$LBP_{4\times5}$	$LGP_{7\times6}$	$LTP_{3\times2}$	$LPQ_{2\times2}$	$WLD_{4\times5}$	$LOSIB_{7\times6}$
Mouth	**80.90**	**77.71**	**74.87**	**76.62**	**77.68**	74.43	**78.23**	73.37

Table 4. Mean accuracies for the Dago's protocol with score level fusion based on the face (F), head and shoulders (HS), periocular (P) and mouth (M) areas. Each result is associated with the pattern and features fused.

Pattern(s)	Approach	Features	Acc.
P	Single	P-HOG	81.61
	Fusion	P-HOG + P-LBP^{u2} + P-LBP + P-WLD	82.79
M	Single	M-HOG	80.55
	Fusion	M-HOG + M-LBP + M-WLD + M-LGP	81.43
F+HS	Fusion	F-HOG + F-LBP^{u2} + HS-HOG	**90.49**
F+HS+P	Fusion	F-HOG + F-LBP^{u2} + HS-HOG P-HOG + P-LBP^{u2} + P-LBP + P-WLD + P-LOSIB	92.42
F+HS+M	Fusion	F-HOG + F-LBP^{u2} + HS-HOG M-HOG + M-LBP + M-WLD + M-LGP	91.60
F+HS+P+M	Fusion 1	F-HOG + F-LBP^{u2} + HS-HOG P-HOG + P-LBP^{u2} + M-HOG + M-WLD	**93.22**
	Fusion 2	F-HOG + F-LBP^{u2} + HS-HOG P-HOG + P-LBP^{u2} + P-LGP + M-HOG	93.22
	Fusion 3	F-HOG + F-LBP^{u2} + HS-HOG P-HOG + P-LBP^{u2} + M-LGP + M-HOG	93.15

The accuracies are slightly worse for M compared to P. Being in both cases significantly worse than those reported by recent face based GC systems. For the later fusion analysis, we have selected those descriptors providing an accuracy larger than 77% for P, and larger than 75% for M. Making a total of 11 descriptors.

The next step considers the fusion of the most discriminant descriptor setups with the state of the art approach described in [4]. This approach extracts HOG and LBP features from F (F-HOG and F-LBP), and HOG from HS (HS-HOG). The fusion is evaluated first separately with the best descriptors for P and M, including exhaustive search among all possible combinations. This means that we evaluated all possible combinations with P, 2^5, and M, 2^6.

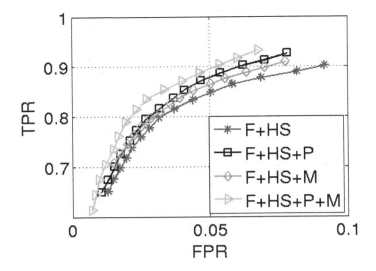

Fig. 2. ROC curves using the Dago's protocol. Comparison of state-of-the-art classification based on F and HS, with the proposed fusion alternatives considering HS and F features respectively with P, M and both.

The final experiment evaluates the fusion with both sets of descriptors, i.e. covering the whole range of possible combinations, i.e. 2^{11} possibilities. The results reported for each approach are summarized in Table 4 indicating the best descriptors combination. The reported results correspond to the 5-folds mean highest accuracy achieved, varying the cost and gamma parameters respectively within the intervals $C = [0.5, 5]$ and $gamma = [0.04, 0.15]$.

As suggested by the table, the best approach fuses descriptors extracted from all the patterns. We have included the top-3 approaches, they report quite similar accuracies, but certainly those using a lower number of features will reduce the processing cost.

A detailed observation indicates that for the Dago's protocol, the improvement in accuracy is close to 3 percentage points. Observing the resulting ROC curves (only the best results for each fusion approach is presented in Figure 2) the fusion with P alone, is better than fusing with M. However, the combination with both P and M reports better performance, in terms of accuracy and AUC, that not using features extracted from any of those inner facial areas.

4   Conclusions

In this paper, we have explored the benefits of combining holistic features with features extracted from specific inner facial regions. In particular we have focused on the ocular and mouth areas, that have evidenced their main importance for this task in the human system.

The achieved results indicate a promising line of research. Indeed the GC performance increased up to 3 percentage points, reducing the gap present in GC accuracy with other simpler datasets. Observing the error for the facial based state of the art approach, 9.5%, the proposed systems reduces the gender classification error in more than 28%.

References

1. Ahonen, T., Hadid, A., Pietikäinen, M.: Face description with local binary patterns: Application to face recognition. IEEE Transactions on Pattern Analysis and Machine Intelligence **28**(12), December 2006
2. Alexandre, L.A.: Gender recognition: A multiscale decision fusion approach. Pattern Recognition Letters **31**(11), 1422–1427 (2010)
3. Bekios-Calfa, J., Buenaposada, J.M., Baumela, L.: Robust gender recognition by exploiting facial attributes dependencies. Pattern Recognition Letters **36**, 228–234 (2014)
4. Castrillón-Santana, M., Lorenzo-Navarro, J., Ramón-Balmaseda, E.: Improving gender classification accuracy in the wild. In: Ruiz-Shulcloper, J., Sanniti di Baja, G. (eds.) CIARP 2013, Part II. LNCS, vol. 8259, pp. 270–277. Springer, Heidelberg (2013)
5. Castrillón-Santana, M., Lorenzo-Navarro, J., Ramn-Balmaseda, E.: Evaluation of periocular over face gender classification in the wild (under review)
6. Castrillón-Santana, M., Marsico, M.D., Nappi, M., Riccio, D.: MEG: Multi-Expert Gender classification in a demographics-balanced dataset. In: 18th International Conference on Image Analysis and Processing (2015)
7. Chen, H., Gallagher, A.C., Girod, B.: The hidden sides of names - face modeling with first name attributes. IEEE Transactions on Pattern Analysis and Machine Intelligence **36**(9), 1860–1873 (2014)
8. Chen, J., Shan, S., He, C., Zhao, G., Pietikainen, M., Chen, X., Gao, W.: WLD: A robust local image descriptor. IEEE Transactions on Pattern Analysis and Machine Intelligence **32**(9), 1705–1720 (2010)
9. Dago-Casas, P., González-Jiménez, D., Long-Yu, L., Alba-Castro, J.L.: Single- and cross- database benchmarks for gender classification under unconstrained settings. In: Proc. First IEEE International Workshop on Benchmarking Facial Image Analysis Technologies (2011)
10. Dalal, N., Triggs, B.: Histograms of oriented gradients for human detection. In: Schmid, C., Soatto, S., Tomasi, C. (eds.) International Conference on Computer Vision & Pattern Recognition, vol. 2, pp. 886–893, June 2005
11. Gallagher, A., Chen, T.: Understanding images of groups of people. In: Proc. CVPR (2009)
12. García-Olalla, O., Alegre, E., Fernández-Robles, L., González-Castro, V.: Local oriented statistics information booster (LOSIB) for texture classification. In: International Conference in Pattern Recognition (ICPR) (2014)
13. Gosselin, F., Schyns, P.G.: Bubbles: a technique to reveal the use of information in recognition tasks. Vision Research, 2261–2271 (2001)
14. Han, H., Jain, A.K.: Age, gender and race estimation from unconstrained face images. Tech. Rep. MSU-CSE-14-5. Michigan State University (2014)
15. Heisele, B., Serre, T., Poggio, T.: A component-based framework for face detection and identification. International Journal of Computer Vision Research **74**(2), August 2007

16. Huang, G.B., Ramesh, M., Berg, T., Learned-Miller, E.: Labeled faces in the wild: A database for studying face recognition in unconstrained environments. Tech. Rep. 07-49. University of Massachusetts, Amherst, October 2007
17. Jia, S., Cristianini, N.: Learning to classify gender from four million images. Pattern Recognition Letters (2015)
18. Jun, B., Kim, D.: Robust face detection using local gradient patterns and evidence accumulation. Pattern Recognition 45(9), 3304-3316 (2012)
19. Kumar, N., Berg, A.C., Belhumeur, P.N., Nayar, S.K.: Describable visual attributes for face verification and image search. IEEE Transactions on Pattern Analysis and Machine Intelligence (PAMI), October 2011
20. Ngan, M., Grother, P.: Face recognition vendor test (frvt) performance of automated gender classification algorithms. Tech. Rep. NIST IR 8052. Narional Institute of Standars and Technology, April 2015
21. Ren, H., Li, Z.N.: Gender recognition using complexity-aware local features. In: International Conference on Pattern Recognition (2014)
22. Shafey, L.E., Khoury, E., Marcel, S.: Audio-visual gender recognition in uncontrolled environment using variability modeling techniques. In: International Joint Conference on Biometrics (2014)
23. Shan, C.: Learning local binary patterns for gender classification on realworld face images. Pattern Recognition Letters 33, 431-437 (2012)
24. Tan, X., Triggs, B.: Enhanced local texture feature sets for face recognition under difficult lighting conditions. IEEE Transactions on Image Processing 19(6), 1635-1650 (2010)
25. Tapia, J.E., Pérez, C.A.: Gender classification based on fusion of different spatial scale features selected by mutual information from histogram of lbp, intensity and shape. IEEE Transactions on Information Forensics and Security 8(3), 488-499 (2013)
26. Ojansivu, V., Heikkilä, J.: Blur insensitive texture classification using local phase quantization. In: Elmoataz, A., Lezoray, O., Nouboud, F., Mammass, D. (eds.) ICISP 2008 2008. LNCS, vol. 5099, pp. 236-243. Springer, Heidelberg (2008)

A Hand Gesture Approach to Biometrics

Nahumi Nugrahaningsih, Marco Porta[✉], and Giuseppe Scarpello

Dip. di Ingegneria Industriale e dell'Informazione,
Università di Pavia, Via Ferrata 5, 27100 Pavia, Italy
{nahumi.nugrahaningsih01,
giuseppe.scarpello01}@universitadipavia.it,
marco.porta@unipv.it

Abstract. In this paper we present a biometric technique based on hand gestures. By means of the Microsoft Kinect sensor, the user's hand is tracked while following a circle moving on the screen. Both 3D data about the position of the hand and 2D data about the position of the screen pointer are provided to different classifiers (SVM, Naive Bayes, Classification Tree, KNN, Random Forest and Neural Networks). Experiments carried out with 20 testers have demonstrated that the method is very promising for both identification and verification (with success rates above 90%), and can be a viable biometric solution, especially for soft biometric applications.

Keywords: Hand gesture biometrics · Soft biometrics · Vision-based biometrics · Microsoft Kinect

1 Introduction

Hand gestures, and the way they are performed, can be exploited for biometric identification and authentication. To date, relatively few biometric approaches exploit this principle (see Section2), in spite of its potentials.

In the general context of hand gesture recognition, an important distinction is that between *explicit* (or *control*) gestures — when their purpose is to provide some form of input to the computer, such as a command — and *implicit* gestures — when they are exploited to obtain indirect information about the user and his or her environment, such as activity recognition. A further distinction is that between *dynamic* gestures (associated with hand movements) and *static* gestures (characterized by specific hand positions and/or postures).

Two main approaches exist to hand gesture recognition, depending on the kind of device employed for data acquisition: techniques which require the user to move some physical object (e.g. an accelerometer) and vision-based methods in which hand shifts are detected by means on one or more cameras. The second case is more complex, but fortunately there are now sensors, such as Microsoft Kinect, which greatly simplify the tasks of hand recognition and tracking. Microsoft Kinect, in particular, can merge 2D with 3D data, thus allowing to work in the "RGBZ" (color + distance) space.

Using Microsoft Kinect, in this paper we propose a novel hand gesture based biometric approach in which the user has to "follow" a circle moving on the screen.

© Springer International Publishing Switzerland 2015
V. Murino et al. (Eds.): ICIAP 2015 Workshops, LNCS 9281, pp. 51–58, 2015.
DOI: 10.1007/978-3-319-23222-5_7

The obtained results are very encouraging (in particular for soft biometric applications), and suggest further research in this direction.

The article is organized as follows. In Section 2 we briefly present some previous works related to hand gestures used for biometric purposes. In Section 3 we describe our approach and the experimental setting. In Section 4 we illustrate the results of our tests. In Section 5, lastly, we draw some conclusions and provide hints for future research.

2   Related Work

In this section we provide a short overview of some relevant works in which dynamic hand gestures have been exploited for biometric purposes.

Okumura et al. [1] collected acceleration data from 22 participants, who were asked to shake an accelerometer. The data were then analyzed using the squared error of Euclidean distance, Error of Angle and DP-matching. Matsuo et al. [2], from the same research group, proposed a template update approach to overcome the long term stability problem from their previous study.

Zaharis et al. [3] used seven features from hand signature gestures obtained using the Nintendo WiiMote remote device to verify four participants. The features were the elapsed time of gesture completion, maximum and minimum acceleration values per axis per time segments, starting and ending sensor positions, and maximum and minimum overall acceleration per axis.

In [4] and [5], Liu et al. developed a verification system called *uWave*. uWave adopted eight predefined simple gestures from a Nokia research study [6], and applied the Dynamic Time Warping (DTW) algorithm on time series data (acquired through Nintendo WiiMote) of each one of the three axes.

Also Guna et al. [7] exploited the Nintendo WiiMote to implement an identification system based on three natural gestures, i.e. making a signature in the air, picking up the device, and shaking the device. The DTW algorithm was applied to the data obtained from 10 participants.

Tian et al. [8] developed an authentication system called *Kin-Write*. This study involved 18 participants. Participants were asked to perform a hand signature in the air. In this case a vision-based approach was used, exploiting the Microsoft Kinect device to capture hand movements, and the DTW algorithm was applied on six features, namely: hand position and position differences between frames, velocity, acceleration, slope angle, path angle, and log radius of curvature.

Other techniques (e.g. [9]) are based on measurements of the user's hand pose (i.e. static gestures) in hand sign language. There are also biometric systems not specifically based on hand movements but which use the Kinect as a source of data. For example, Lai et al. [10] focused on the body silhouette, while Wu et al. [11] and Ball et al. [12] exploited the body skeleton.

3   Methodology

3.1   Apparatus and Participants

Hand movements were captured using a *Kinect for Windows v1* sensor, and the stimuli were displayed on a 30'' monitor with 2048×1536 screen resolution. The sampling rate of the RGB camera was 30 fps. Twenty testers were involved as participants (8 females and 12 males), aged between 14 and 50.

3.2   Procedure and Stimuli

The principle of our biometric approach is as follows. Randomly, a circle appears (sequentially) in five predefined positions of the screen (the four corners and the center, as shown in Fig. 1), where it is displayed for 3.8 seconds. The task of the user is simply to move the hand so that the screen pointer is always over the circle: when the circle disappears from a position and (almost instantaneously) appears in another position, the user has to immediately move the cursor to the new location, as fast as he or she can. All 20 paths between all couples of positions are covered (Fig. 1, bottom), which means that, in total, the circle is displayed in each position four times.

In our experiments, participants stood at a distance of 150 cm from the monitor, over which the Kinect was placed at a height of 120 cm from the floor (Fig. 2). These distances were chosen after some trials to obtain adequate precision. The diameter of the circle was 350 pixels and its color blue (displayed on a white background). Also the display time of 3.8 seconds was selected after preliminary assessments aimed at finding a good compromise between task duration and significance of the acquired data.

Each participant repeated the test 20 times, with the interval between two tests varying between two hours and two weeks. In total, 400 data recordings were therefore collected.

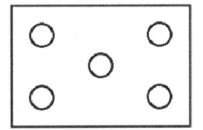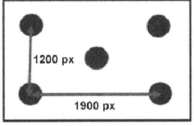

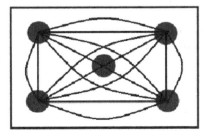

Fig. 1. Stimuli

Fig. 2. Experimental setting

3.3   Data Processing

This study used two kinds of raw data acquired by the Kinect: *hand position* in the 3D space and *pointer position* in the 2D screen space.

From these raw data, 11 features were derived, namely: 1) the average position of the hand (x, y and z coordinates) when the screen pointer is within a circle; 2) the average position of the pointer (x, y coordinates) within a circle; 3) the total time spent by the pointer inside a circle; 4) the user's "reaction time", i.e. the interval between the disappearance of the circle from a position and the time when the hand starts moving to shift the pointer to the new position; 5) the pointer's "travel time", i.e. the interval between the disappearance of the circle from a position and the instant when the pointer enters the circle in the new position; 6) the average speed of the hand (over the 20 paths) when moving the pointer from one position to another; 7) the average speed of the pointer (over the 20 paths) when it is shifted from one position to another; 8) the highest vertical position (y coordinate) reached by the hand; 9) the lowest vertical position reached by the hand; 10) the average vertical position of the hand; and 11) the variance of the pointer position when it is within a circle. After applying the Greedy Backward feature selection method [13], we excluded features 10 and 11, as they were not significant.

3.4   Classifiers

The first nine features described in the previous section became the input to six different classifiers, namely: K-Nearest Neighbors (KNN), Naive Bayes, Support Vector Machines (SVM), Classification Tree, Neural Network, and Random Forest.

Both random sampling and cross validation were used. With random sampling, we tried two different compositions of the training and test sets' data: 1) 70% training and 30% test, and 2) 50% training and 50% test. The final result was calculated from the average of 100 trials. In the cross validation method, we tried with 10- and 20-fold cross validation.

4   Results

In the classification process, the configurations described in Section 3.4 were applied to both the identification and verification cases.

4.1   Identification

As can be seen from Table 1, the accuracy of SVM was higher than that of the other classifiers in all sampling methods (and did not significantly decrease when the training dataset was reduced from 70% to 50%).

Table 1. Results of Identification

| | Classification Accuracy | | | |
	Random sampling 70% : 30%	Random sampling 50% : 50%	Cross validation 10 fold	Cross validation 20 fold
SVM	0.9452	0.9268	0.9475	0.955
Naive Bayes	0.8745	0.8697	0.8725	0.88
Classification Tree	0.7337	0.6976	0.7275	0.715
KNN	0.8321	0.8237	0.8425	0.85
Random Forest	0.9072	0.8922	0.9175	0.9275
Neural Network	0.9201	0.9006	0.92	0.925

4.2   Verification

In the verification scenario, we considered three performance metrics, namely: 1) sensitivity (true positive rate); 2) specificity (true negative rate); and 3) accuracy. From Tables 2 to 5, we can see that the classifiers' performance varied over the sampling methods. Considering as a reference the best performer in each metrics category, we can briefly summarize results as follows.

In random sampling with 70%:30% composition, SVM, Classification Tree, KNN, and Random Forest obtained (similar) good results with accuracy, sensitivity, and specificity. In random sampling with 70%:30% composition, Naive Bayes had generally a good performance, even though it was the lowest in terms of specificity.

In ten-fold cross validation, Random Forest and Neural Network exhibited very low values of specificity; conversely, the other three classifiers were overall comparable. In 20-fold cross validation, KNN showed the best global results, with 0.99, 1, and 0.9895 for accuracy, sensitivity, and specificity, respectively.

Table 2. Results of Verification: random sampling, 70% training and 30% test

	Accuracy	Sensitivity	Specificity
SVM	0.9968	0.9367	1
Naive Bayes	0.8823	1	0.8761
Classification Tree	0.997	0.98	0.9979
KNN	0.9987	0.9733	1
Random Forest	0.9987	0.9333	1
Neural Network	0.9935	0.87	1

Table 3. Results of Verification: random sampling, 50% training and 50% test

	Accuracy	Sensitivity	Specificity
SVM	0.9647	0.474	0.9905
Naive Bayes	0.8351	0.994	0.8267
Classification Tree	0.9434	0.41	0.9715
KNN	0.9566	0.628	0.9739
Random Forest	0.95	0.008	0.9996
Neural Network	0.9449	0.134	0.9876

Table 4. Results of Verification: cross validation, 10-fold

	Accuracy	Sensitivity	Specificity
SVM	0.975	0.9921	0.65
Naive Bayes	0.8275	0.8184	1
Classification Tree	0.97	0.9868	0.65
KNN	0.9625	0.9763	0.7
Random Forest	0.9525	1	0.05
Neural Network	0.9475	0.9842	0.25

Table 5. Results of Verification: cross validation, 20-fold

	Accuracy	Sensitivity	Specificity
SVM	0.995	0.9	1
Naive Bayes	0.8025	1	0.7921
Classification Tree	0.9475	0.35	0.9789
KNN	0.99	1	0.9895
Random Forest	0.97	0.55	0.9921
Neural Network	0.9875	0.75	1

5   Conclusion and Future Work

In this paper we have proposed a biometric approach based on hand gestures. The technique is mainly conceived for soft biometrics, and the encouraging results obtained are surely a spur to continue in this research direction.

In this preliminary study we have considered all 20 paths as the input of the classification system. In a real identification or verification scenario, however, performing so many gestures would probably be too demanding for the user. As a further study, we will therefore consider (random) subsets of the 20 paths, so as to reduce the user's effort and the duration of the procedure. In particular, we will focus on finding the shortest path length that guarantees a good performance.

A further interesting development could be the integration of the proposed verification/authentication method with other approaches (e.g. facial recognition or general body movements), to implement a multimodal biometric system. Moreover, to improve precision, the new Kinect sensor (version $v2$) could be tried, as well as the joint use of two Kinect devices in parallel.

References

1. Okumura, F., Kubota, A., Hatori, Y., Matsuo, K., Hashimoto, M., Koike, A.: A study on biometric authentication based on arm sweep action with acceleration sensor. In: International Symposium on Intelligent Signal Processing and Communications (ISPACS 2006), pp. 219–222 (2006)
2. Matsuo, K., Okumura, F., Hashimoto, M., Sakazawa, S., Hatori, Y.: Arm swing identification method with template update for long term stability. In: Lee, S.-W., Li, S.Z. (eds.) ICB 2007. LNCS, vol. 4642, pp. 211–221. Springer, Heidelberg (2007)
3. Zaharis, A., Martini, A., Kikiras, P., Stamoulis, G.: ``User authentication method and implementation using a three-axis accelerometer''. In: Chatzimisios, P., Verikoukis, C., Santamaría, I., Laddomada, M., Hoffmann, O. (eds.) MobiLight 2010. LNICST, vol. 45, pp. 192–202. Springer, Heidelberg (2010)
4. Liu, J., Wang, Z., Zhong, L., Wickramasuriya, J., Vasudevan, V.: uWave: accelerometer-based personalized gesture recognition and its applications. In: IEEE International Conference on Pervasive Computing and Communications, PerCom 2009, pp. 1–9 (2009)
5. Liu, J., Zhong, L., Wickramasuriya, J., Vasudevan, V.: User evaluation of lightweight user authentication with a single tri-axis accelerometer. In: 11th International Conference on Human-Computer Interaction with Mobile Devices and Services, p. 15 (2009)
6. Kela, J., Korpipää, P., Mäntyjärvi, J., Kallio, S., Savino, G., Jozzo, L., Marca, D.: Accelerometer-based gesture control for a design environment. Pers. Ubiquitous Comput. **10**(5), 285–299 (2005)
7. Guna, J., Humar, I., Pogacnik, M.: Intuitive gesture based user identification system. In: 35th International Conference on Telecommunications and Signal Processing (TSP), pp. 629–633 (2012)
8. Tian, J., Qu, C., Xu, W., Wang, S.: KinWrite: handwriting-based authentication using kinect. In: 20th Annual Network & Distributed System Security Symposium (2013)
9. Fong, S., Zhuang, Y., Fister, I., Fister, I.: A biometric authentication model using hand gesture images. BioMedical Engineering OnLine **12**(1), 111 (2013)

10. Lai, K., Konrad, J., Ishwar, P.: Towards gesture-based user authentication. In: IEEE 9th International Conference on Advanced Video and Signal-Based Surveillance (AVSS), pp. 282–287 (2012)
11. Wu, J., Konrad, J., Ishwar, P.: Dynamic time warping for gesture-based user identification and authentication with kinect. In: IEEE International Conference on Acoustics, Speech and Signal Processing (ICASSP), pp. 2371–2375 (2013)
12. Ball, A., Rye, D., Ramos, F., Velonaki, M: Unsupervised clustering of people from 'skeleton' data. In: 7th ACM/IEEE International Conference on Human-Robot Interaction (HRI), pp. 225–226 (2012)
13. Caruana, R., Freitag, D.: Greedy attribute selection. In: 11th International Conference on Machine Learning, pp. 26–36 (1994)

Quis-Campi: Extending *in the Wild* Biometric Recognition to Surveillance Environments

João C. Neves[1], Gil Santos[1(✉)], Sílvio Filipe[1], Emanuel Grancho[1],
Silvio Barra[2], Fabio Narducci[3], and Hugo Proença[1]

[1] Department of Computer Science, IT - Instituto de Telecomunicações,
University of Beira Interior, Covilhã, Portugal
gmelfe@ubi.pt
[2] DMI - Dipartimento di Matematica e Informatica,
University of Cagliari, Cagliary, Italy
[3] DISTRA-MIT, University of Salerno, Fisciano, Salerno, Italy

Abstract. Efforts in biometrics are being held into extending robust recognition techniques to *in the wild* scenarios. Nonetheless, and despite being a very attractive goal, human identification in the surveillance context remains an open problem. In this paper, we introduce a novel biometric system – *Quis-Campi* – that effectively bridges the gap between surveillance and biometric recognition while having a minimum amount of operational restrictions. We propose a fully automated surveillance system for human recognition purposes, attained by combining human detection and tracking, further enhanced by a PTZ camera that delivers data with enough quality to perform biometric recognition. Along with the system concept, implementation details for both hardware and software modules are provided, as well as preliminary results over a real scenario.

1 Introduction

Biometrics is one of the most active fields in the area of computer vision, which is justified by our societies' increasing concern about security. Biometric systems significantly rely on the accurate extraction of individuals' distinctive features, which is conditioned by the acquisition environment and constraints. As such, the most reliable systems are deployed on controlled scenarios and count on subject cooperation. On the other hand, surveillance cameras are widely deployed and can constitute a good source of input for biometric systems. Filling the gap between biometrics and visual surveillance is quite a desirable goal, allowing to produce *automata* capable of recognizing human beings *in the wild*, without their cooperation and, possibly, even without their awareness.

When moving to *in the wild* scenarios the acquisition constraints are substantially lowered and, most of the time, subject cooperation is not even expectable. In order to deal with such challenging conditions, alternatives are sought over three axes [6]: 1) improve the existing algorithms so they can handle more degraded data; 2) resort to multi-modal biometric systems so that the usage of multiple traits can compensate for their lack of "quality"; 3) explore new

V. Murino et al. (Eds.): ICIAP 2015 Workshops, LNCS 9281, pp. 59–68, 2015.
DOI: 10.1007/978-3-319-23222-5_8

biometric traits that could better cope with this new reality. Despite the recent efforts, no system yet exists capable of dealing effectively with all the issues introduced by *in the wild* biometrics, and even those systems able to cope with less constrained conditions (e.g. the Iris On The Move project [11]) still lack an ideal level of user abstraction. Most of existing surveillance systems are focused on activity recognition (e.g. W^4 project [5]), and not that many of them are prepared to handle surveillance scenarios by a watchlist approach (e.g. Kamgar-Parsi *et al.* [8]). In this paper, we present a novel biometric recognition system, designed to work covertly in a non-habituated and non-attended fashion, over non-standard environments. Our main goal is to conceive a system that links together both biometrics and visual surveillance, being able to conduct biometric recognition over typical surveillance scenarios, with the minimum possible amount of operational restrictions.

The remainder of this paper is organized as follows: in Sect. 2 we detail the three layers of the recognition system, its operation premises and devised modules; in Sect. 3 we present the exploited techniques for each module, along with preliminary results of our system over a real surveillance scenario and, finally, Sect. 4 states some final considerations.

2   The QUIS-CAMPI System

The optimal recognition system would operate in any environment, thus minimizing the amount of operational restrictions. Aiming at bridging biometrics with the visual surveillance, we have developed our system in a typical surveillance scenario – a parking lot (Fig. 3(a)) – particularly harsh for recognition purposes: 1) it is a non-standard environment with irregular lighting that changes during the day and accordingly to weather conditions, reflections, etc.; 2) complex background regions and the varying resolution of humans poses increasing challenges for both detection and recognition phases; 3) subjects can come from

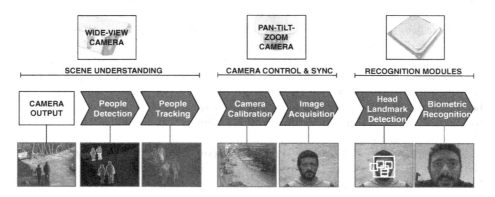

Fig. 1. Working diagram of the proposed system, and the three-layer architecture: scene understanding, camera control/synchronization and recognition modules.

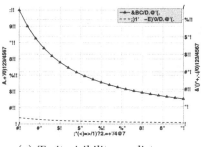 

(a) Trait visibility *vs* distance   (b) Illustration of the acquired data

Fig. 2. Visible face and periocular width, in pixels, as function of the system's working distance (a), and illustration of the acquired data for both cameras (b).

any direction, and they are rarely facing the camera which is typically placed on an upper position.

To develop such a system we combine a PTZ with a typical surveillance camera in a master-slave configuration. We believe that this architecture is able to provide enough quality for biometric recognition at-a-distances (15 to 35 meters), since the mechanical properties of the PTZ camera allow to acquire high-resolution imagery of arbitrary locations in the scene. The advantages of using PTZ cameras for biometric recognition are further evidenced by Fig. 2, where the resolution differences between using a wide-view camera and using a PTZ device are evident.

The proposed system is thus devised over three main layers (Fig. 1): scene understanding, camera control/synchronization, and recognition modules. Scene understanding refers to the detection and tracking of human beings. This phase should be supported by the wide-view camera so that it provides head location of persons in the scene, allowing the PTZ camera to zoom-in on those regions. Following the PTZ image acquisition, the recognition modules are responsible to infer the identify of the subject.

2.1 Scene Understanding

The scene understanding layer has two main modules: people detection and tracking. The first module locates persons as they enter the scene and tracks them until they are no longer visible, taking as input the video feed from the wide-view camera, and has three main steps: background subtraction, upper-body detection and tracking – Fig. 3.

2.2 Camera Control and Synchronization

Considering that the wide-view and the PTZ can be disposed arbitrarily in the scene, a calibration algorithm is required to relate the image coordinates of both

(a) Wide-view feed   (b) Background subtraction   (c) People tracking

Fig. 3. Illustration of the preliminary results obtained by the people detection and tracking module: a) sample image acquired with the wide-view camera; b) foreground regions attained by background subtraction; c) people tracking module results.

devices. However, due to the lack of depth information, this problem is ill-defined and thus several approximations have been proposed to alleviate the innacuracies of 2D-based methods. With a view to determine a precise mapping the devices, different solutions have been proposed to infer 3D information from the scene. In our system, we rely on [15] where the subjects height is inferred and used as an ancillary measure to define a precise mapping between the cameras.

Additionally, it is necessary to plan, in real-time, the sequence of PTZ observations when multiple subjects are in the scene. Despite a random walk could be adopted, this strategy would lead to failures in the observation of some targets as the number of subjects increases. For this purpose, we rely on [16] where an algorithm for maximizing the observed number of targets has been devised.

2.3   Recognition Modules

After a successful acquisition of a PTZ shot, the recognition module should be supported by a head landmark detection phase. This strategy improves recognition performance since it determines which facial landmarks are visible, and thus decides the weight of each recognition module. Being able to describe which facial traits are visible and where, is far more important than actually getting a close estimation of the head's pose, as we can tell to which extent the trait is reliable or not. For recognition purposes, the proposed system relies on a multi-modal biometric approach that combines face, iris, periocular, ear shape and gait information.

The face is not only one of the most common and widely used biometric trait, but also one of the most successful applications of image analysis and understanding, with a lot of techniques available [20]. As the "great variability in head rotation and tilt, lighting intensity and angle, facial expression and aging" make face recognition an extremely hard challenge [2], it is mandatory to rely on robust approaches (e.g. [19]). Face recognition algorithms are based either on the global analysis of the whole image, or the relation between facial elements, their location and shape. The main drawbacks are: the 3D structure of the face, which leads to altered appearance accordingly to subject's pose; the occlusion of large portions of non-orthogonal data acquisition; the changes in appearance introduced by facial expressions; and the easiness in disguise. These factors become more evident *in the wild*, or with uncooperative subjects trying to avoid detection.

The ocular region is one of the most explored in biometrics. Iris in particular is a very popular biometric trait, delivering very high recognition accuracy under controlled environments. Although iris performance as a biometric trait being severely impacted in non-ideal setups, due essentially to its reduced size and moving profile, researchers are putting efforts in overcoming those limitations. The periocular region represents a good trade-off between the whole face and the iris alone, being easy to acquire without user cooperation, and not requiring a constrained close capturing, being one of the strongest candidates for the purposes of our system.

The shape of the ear can also be used as a biometric trait, as the structure of its cartilage is unique for each individual and its patterns can be imaged on the visible wavelength (VIS) with regular cameras. Despite all ear recognition methods traditionally require some degree of user cooperation, if proper alignment estimation can be established it can be used as biometric trait *in the wild*.

Gait is the only trait that will be imaged from the wide-view cam. Acquiring data about the way a person walks is non-invasive, and can be done at-a-distance. The majority of the gait recognition methods in the literature do not require high-resolution data, so they can run over surveillance camera data.

3   Experimental Results

This section details the exploited techniques for each module, along with preliminary results over the selected surveillance scenario. In our experiments a wide-view camera (Canon VB-H710F) and a PTZ camera (Hikvision DS-2DE5286-AEL) were mounted on the exterior of a building at a first-floor level (approximately 5m above the ground) pointing towards a parking lot.

3.1   People Detection and Tracking

For the background subtraction step, SOBS [10] and Mixture of Gaussians [14] were used. This option was taken after visually inspecting multiple state-of-the-art techniques' performance over test data. Using the output from the background subtraction, we filtered the most consisted regions with human presence by exploiting an upper body detector based on Haar feature-based cascade classifiers [18].

The tracking phase is then initialized, exploiting motion and appearance features. Using the omega-shape (head and shoulder region) as the primary source of key-points, the Kanade-Lucas-Tomasi (KLT) algorithm [13] tracks the initial set of features accordingly to motion and appearance constraints. Since some features may be lost during the process, re-initialization of the features is ensured by the detection phase – Fig. 3(c). The KLT algorithm was preferred since it assumes that a set of discriminant points of the object move with a constant

Table 1. Tracking performance in our surveillance scenario, when using KLT. Performance metrics are Multiple Object Tracking Accuracy (MOTA), Multiple Object Tracking Precision (MOTP), True Positive Rate (TPR), False Positive Rate (FPR) and mismatch (MIS).

Scenario	MOTA	MOTP	TPR	FPR	MIS
S1	0.940	0.600	0.970	0.030	0
S2	0.800	0.590	0.900	0.100	0
S3	0.745	0.336	0.862	0.138	0
S4	0.589	0.288	0.792	0.202	3

speed and maintain a constant appearance. Based on the set of previous locations provided by the tracking module, a Kalman filter [7] is used to provide a coarse estimation of the future position. We observed that although maintaining their exterior looking while passing through the scene, dynamic lighting and shadow interference perturb persons' appearance. On the contrary, people moving at constant speed provide higher confidence on motion features.

To assess the reliability of the proposed method for tracking, we considered four different scenarios with increasing level of difficulties: *S1*- single person, moving away from the camera, noiseless background subtraction, no significant changes in lighting; *S2*- single person, moving away from the camera at a higher speed, some noise in the background subtraction, no significant changes in lighting; *S3*- single person, walking towards the camera, significant noise in the background subtraction, significant lighting changes; *S4*- three persons, moving away from the camera, little noise in background subtraction, one of the subjects crosses the path of the other two.

Results are presented in Table 1, using the CLEAR-MOT metrics (Multiple Object Tracking Accuracy (MOTA), Multiple Object Tracking Precision (MOTP), True Positive Rate (TPR), False Positive Rate (FPR) and mismatch (MIS)), a standard metric for evaluating multiple target tracking algorithms [9].

High levels of accuracy (MOTA) and precision (MOTP) were obtained for the first scenario, with a negligible FPR, mostly due to the high quality mask from background subtraction which led to a very precise tracking. Regarding scenarios *S2* and *S3*, all MOTA, FPR and TPR confirm encouraging levels of performance of the tracking algorithm. The significant change in precision observed in *S3* comparatively to *S2* is related to the distance that the subject enters the scene: at long walking distances the number of pixels representing a person is very small, leading to a failure of the upper body detector. In the most challenging scenario (*S4*) the FPR increases, along with some mismatches related essentially to the path crossing between persons. Nonetheless, we can assert that the tracking method achieves good level of performances. Although the omega shape at long distance being hard to detect, the whole body shape should be a better alternative, and once a tracker detects the shape of a person, the head will appear on the top of the selected area.

3.2 Biometric Recognition

To have a preliminary assessment of the recognition performance of our system, 20 participants were imaged between distances 15 to 35 meters. These working distances ensure regions with widths between 500 px and 200 px in the face, and approximately 220 px to 100 px for the periocular region. Facial region was determined using a cascade object detector based on Viola and Jones algorithm [18], and facial features encoded using the Principal Component Analysis (PCA) approach [17]. Prior to encoding the periocular features, a second Region of Interest (ROI) containing the periocular region was defined still using a Viola and Jones based cascade object detector, trained for the detection of the right eye using Haar features to encode the details [3]. Upon that region, five different descriptors were extracted, based on the works of Park *et al.* [12] and Bharadwaj *et al.* [1]: Histogram of Oriented Gradients (HOG), Local Binary Patterns (LBP), Scale-Invariant Feature Transform (SIFT), Uniform Local Binary Patterns (ULBP) and GIST. The HOG, LBP and ULBP descriptors deliver a distribution-based analysis, and were computed over 35 non-overlapping patches of the periocular ROI, evenly distributed on a 7×5 grid. Each descriptor was computed sequentially, forming a global 1-D array storing both shape and texture information.

Finally, two score-level fusion were also stressed: one combining the scores from the individual periocular recognition methods; and a second one combining them with the PCA results. Score fusion was achieved training a Neural-Network (NN) with two hidden layers using back-propagation. NN based methods are widely applied in classification problems, for their learning abilities and good generalization capabilities. The architecture of the used NN consisted on a first hidden layer with the number of neurons equalling the number of scores to be fused, and a second hidden layer of three neurons. The final (output) layer had one neuron, since we were dealing with a binary classification problem. The NNss were trained with a smaller partition of the data, not included on the test phase.

Three metrics were used to assess recognition modules' performance: Decidability (DEC) [4], Area Under Curve (AUC) and Equal Error Rate (EER). The evaluation of the stressed feature encoding techniques for the different working distances and traits is registered in Table 2. For a better interpretation of their performance, the Receiver Operating Characteristic (ROC) curves are also presented in Fig. 4. Results refer to a total of 69960 comparisons, performed in a 1:N fashion.

As we can see from Table 2, top recognition performance was attained at closer working distances (15m to 25m), with an AUC of 0.835. However, widening the working range to the whole driveway (15m to 35m), a considerable good performance is still achieved (AUC = 0.779). We must have in mind that results come from a fully automated system, operating on an adverse surveillance scenario. Furthermore, matches were not performed against a separate dataset of good registration images, but between different Pan-Tilt-Zoom (PTZ) images acquired during system operation.

Table 2. Performance for each one of the exploited methods, traits and working distances. Metrics are Decidability (DEC), Area Under Curve (AUC) and Equal Error Rate (EER).

Trait →		Periocular						Face	Global
Method →		LBP	HOG	SIFT	ULBP	GIST	Fusion	PCA	Fusion
15m - 25m	DEC	0.802	0.699	0.404	1.090	0.918	1.162	1.171	1.407
	AUC	0.753	0.703	0.617	0.786	0.772	0.805	0.779	0.835
	EER	0.302	0.358	0.416	0.281	0.304	0.287	0.307	0.246
25m - 35m	DEC	0.677	0.641	0.341	0.972	0.808	1.033	1.173	1.267
	AUC	0.697	0.674	0.598	0.744	0.755	0.771	0.772	0.810
	EER	0.376	0.380	0.431	0.334	0.321	0.303	0.328	0.254
15m - 35m	DEC	0.529	0.520	0.310	0.830	0.747	0.891	0.676	1.025
	AUC	0.663	0.640	0.591	0.710	0.721	0.754	0.674	0.779
	EER	0.396	0.409	0.435	0.360	0.348	0.317	0.395	0.293

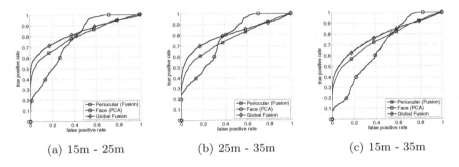

(a) 15m - 25m   (b) 25m - 35m   (c) 15m - 35m

Fig. 4. Receiver Operating Characteristic (ROC) curves for the periocular recognition, face recognition and global fusion, at different working distances.

As for the differences between the different exploited traits, the periocular region seems to be less affected by changes in distance, although further facial recognition techniques should be stressed. Also from the ROC curves at Fig. 4, we can see how the PCA applied to the face alone delivers lower true positive rate while introducing higher amounts of false positives, when compared to the fusion of methods operating on the periocular region. Nonetheless, fusing that information with the periocular methods scores produces a considerable improvement on the latter. Thus, if considering deploying a more restrictive system with higher security constraints, the face trait should not be used alone, but can be a powerful ally to further improve its final outcome.

4   Final Considerations

In this paper, we present the concept of a fully automated surveillance and biometric recognition system, able to complement human detection and tracking with biometric recognition over *in the wild* surveillance environments. Although further state-of-the-art techniques can be stressed for each module, we give evidence for the feasibility of such system, providing both tracking performance and biometric recognition results over a real surveillance scenario.

Although a functional system is presented, further work should be considered over three axes: 1) a larger dataset should be acquired, not only with a larger number of subjects going through the scene, but also with the system running over different environments (e.g. indoor lounge); 2) some modules are still to be developed, that would increase the recognition performance even further (e.g. head landmark detector); 3) additional state-of-the-art techniques should be tested for each module, and results cross-validated over the different scenarios. In particular, different face recognition techniques should be stressed, along with ear shape and iris biometrics and gait recognition.

Acknowledgments. The authors would like to acknowledge the financial support provided by *FCT - Fundação para a Ciência e Tecnologia* through the research grants SFRH/BD/72575/2010, SFRH/ BD/80182/2011 and SFRH/BD/92520/2013, and the funding from 'FEDER - QREN - Type 4.1 - *Formação Avançada*', subsidized by the European Social Fund and by Portuguese funds through 'MCTES'.

References

1. Bharadwaj, S., Bhatt, H., Vatsa, M., Singh, R.: Periocular biometrics: when iris recognition fails. In: 4th IEEE Int'l Conf. on Biometrics: Theory Applications and Systems (BTAS), 2010, pp. 1–6, September 2010
2. Bledsoe, W.W.: The model method in facial recognition. Tech. Report PRI 15, Panoramic Research Inc, Palo Alto, California (1964)
3. Castrillón, M., Dénis, O., Guerra, C., Hernández, M.: Encara2: Real-time detection of multiple faces at different resolutions in video streams. Journal of Visual Communication and Image Representation **18**(2), 130–140 (2007)
4. Daugman, J.: High confidence visual recognition of persons by a test of statistical independence. Pattern Analysis and Machine Intelligence **15**(11), 1148–1161 (1993)
5. Haritaoglu, I., Harwood, D., Davis, L.: W4: Real-time surveillance of people and their activities. Pattern Analysis and Machine Intelligence **22**(8), 809–830 (2000)
6. Jain, A., Pankanti, S., Prabhakar, S., Hong, L., Ross, A.: Biometrics: a grand challenge. In: Proc. of the 17th Int'l Conf. on Pattern Recognition (ICPR), vol. 2, pp. 935–942 (2004)
7. Kalman, R.E.: A New Approach to Linear Filtering and Prediction Problems. Trans. of the ASME - Journal of Basic Engineering, (82 (Series D)), 35–45 (1960)
8. Kamgar-Parsi, B., Lawson, W., Kamgar-Parsi, B.: Toward development of a face recognition system for watchlist surveillance. Pattern Analysis and Machine Intelligence **33**(10), 1925–1933 (2011)
9. Keni, B., Rainer, S.: Evaluating multiple object tracking performance: the clear mot metrics. EURASIP Journal on Image and Video Processing (2008)
10. Maddalena, L., Petrosino, A.: A self-organizing approach to background subtraction for visual surveillance applications. IEEE Trans. on Image Processing **17**(7), 1168–1177 (2008)

11. Matey, J., Naroditsky, O., Hanna, K., Kolczynski, R., LoIacono, D., Mangru, S., Tinker, M., Zappia, T., Zhao, W.: Iris on the move: Acquisition of images for iris recognition in less constrained environments. Proc. of the IEEE **94**, 1936–1947 (2006)
12. Park, U., Ross, A., Jain, A.: Periocular biometrics in the visible spectrum: a feasibility study. In: IEEE 3rd Int'l Conf. on Biometrics: Theory, Applications, and Systems (BTAS), pp. 1–6, September 2009
13. Shi, J., Tomasi, C.: Good features to track. In: IEEE Computer Society Conf. on Computer Vision and Pattern Recognition, pp. 593–600. IEEE (1994)
14. Stauffer, C., Grimson, W.E.L.: Adaptive background mixture models for real-time tracking. IEEE Comp. Soc. Conf. on Computer Vision and Pattern Recognition **2**, 252 (1999)
15. Neves, J.C., Moreno, J.C., Barra, S., Proença, H.: A calibration algorithm for multi-camera visual surveillance systems based on single-view metrology. In: Paredes, R., Cardoso, J.S., Pardo, X.M. (eds.) IbPRIA 2015. LNCS, vol. 9117, pp. 552–559. Springer, Heidelberg (2015)
16. Neves, J.C., Proença, H.: Dynamic camera scheduling for visual surveillance in crowded scenes using Markov random fields. In: Proc. of the 12th IEEE Int'l Conf. on Advanced Video and Signal based Surveillance (AVSS) (2015)
17. Turk, M., Pentland, A.: Face recognition using eigenfaces. In: IEEE Computer Society Conf. on Computer Vision and Pattern Recognition. Proc. CVPR 1991, pp. 586–591 (1991)
18. Viola, P., Jones, M.: Rapid object detection using a boosted cascade of simple features. In: Proc. of the 2001 IEEE Computer Society Conf. on Computer Vision and Pattern Recognition, vol. 1, pp. 511–518 (2001)
19. Wagner, A., Wright, J., Ganesh, A., Zhou, Z., Mobahi, H., Ma, Y.: Toward a practical face recognition system: Robust alignment and illumination by sparse representation. Pattern Analysis and Machine Intelligence **34**(2), 372–386 (2012)
20. Zhao, W., Chellappa, R., Phillips, P., Rosenfeld, A.: Face recognition: A literature survey. ACM Computing Surveys **35**(4), 399–458 (2000)

CTMR 2015 - Color in Texture and Material Recognition

On Comparing Colour Spaces
From a Performance Perspective:
Application to Automated Classification
of Polished Natural Stones

Francesco Bianconi[1](✉), Raquel Bello[2], Antonio Fernández[2],
and Elena González[2]

[1] Department of Engineering, Università degli Studi di Perugia,
Via G. Duranti, 93, 06125 Perugia, Italy
bianco@ieee.org
[2] School of Industrial Engineering, Universidade de Vigo,
Campus Universitario, Rúa Maxwell s/n, 36310 Vigo, Spain
bellocerezo@gmail.com, {antfdez,elena}@uvigo.es

Abstract. In this paper we investigate the problem of choosing the adequate colour representation for automated surface grading. Specifically, we discuss the pros and cons of different colour spaces, point out some common misconceptions about their use, and propose a number of 'best practices' for colour conversion. To put the discussion into practice we generated a new dataset of 25 classes of natural stone products which we used to systematically compare and evaluate the performance of seven device-dependent and three device-independent colour spaces through two classification strategies. With the nearest neighbour classifiers no significant difference emerged among the colour spaces considered, whereas with the linear classifier it was found that device-independent Lab and Luv spaces performed significantly better than the others.

Keywords: Soft colour descriptors · Colour spaces · Visual appearance · Natural stones

1 Introduction

The evaluation and comparison of the visual appearance of real-world materials plays a pivotal role in many applications such as defect detection, surface grading, creation of batches of similar appearance and image-based material recognition. For a wide range of products including natural stones, ceramic tiles, parquet, leather and the like such tasks are of primary importance. Among them natural stones play an important part with a net worldwide production of finished products in excess of 76.000 tons/year [12]. Since natural stones are typically used for cladding and tiling areas which are supposed to be uniform in appearance, one of the major problems is to guarantee the uniformity of the visual aspect within

© Springer International Publishing Switzerland 2015
V. Murino et al. (Eds.): ICIAP 2015 Workshops, LNCS 9281, pp. 71–78, 2015.
DOI: 10.1007/978-3-319-23222-5_9

the same lot. In the stone industry this task is usually carried out manually by skilled and experienced workers. Consequently, the process is intrinsically subjective, and the results may suffer from significant intra- and inter-observer variability. The use of automated computer vision systems either in replacement of or as an aid for human operators could in principle offer higher quality standards, better reproducibility, and more reliable product records. In this context the objective of this work is to propose a theoretically well-founded procedure to compare colour spaces and determine the most appropriate for this task.

In the remainder of the paper, after a brief review of the relevant literature (Sec. 2), we describe the materials (Sec. 3) and methods (Sec. 4) used in this study. We present the experimental set-up and the results in Sec. 5 and conclude the paper with final considerations and ideas for future studies in Sec. 6.

2   Related Research

Performance analysis of colour spaces in computer vision has generated considerable research interest since early on. One could reasonably expect that device-dependent, uniform colour spaces should be superior to the others, but the results available in the literature are rather inconclusive in this regard. On the one side Adel *et al.* [1] compared five colour spaces for wood defect detection and found that device-independent spaces (CIE Luv and CIE Lab) outperformed device-dependent spaces (Ohta's I1I2I3, HSI and RGB). Likewise, Paschos [15] determined that in most cases perceptually uniform/approximately uniform colour spaces (CIE Lab and HSV) outperformed RGB. Similar findings were later on reported also by Rajadell and García-Sevilla [18]. On the other hand, Drimbarean and Whelan [7] found that none of the RGB, HSI, CIE XYZ, CIE Lab and YIQ spaces was significantly superior in classifying colour texture, whereas Qazi *et al.* [17] observed that for pure colour features RGB and IHLS colour spaces gave slightly better results than CIE Lab, but the trend was just the opposite for colour textures. More recently Bianconi *et al.* [6] compared the performance of colour descriptors and spaces for automated sorting of parquet slabs and noticed very little difference among the performance of RGB, HSV and CIE Lab.

The lack of agreement among the results available in the literature also parallels with the fact that in most cases data and/or code are not available to the public, making it difficult (if not impossible) to reproduce the experiments and carry on further comparisons and evaluations. It is also important to point out that, regrettably, in most studies the experimental configuration was far from optimal: it is not uncommon that conversion from device-dependent to device-independent colour spaces be performed in a sloppy way using pre-defined formulas regardless of the acquisition system and the lighting conditions, an approach which is likely to produce biased results [16, Chap. 7.3].

3   Materials

One hundred tiles representing 25 classes (four tiles for each class) of polished natural stone products (marble and granite) were kindly provided to the authors

Azul Capixaba	Acquamarina	Bianco Cristal	Kashmir Gold	Bianco Sardo
Giallo Napoletano	Rosa Porriño	Rosa Monçao	Giallo S. Cecilia	Giallo Veneziano
Azul Platino	Verde Marino	Rosso Multicolor	Giallo Antico	Violetta
Sky Brown	Paradiso Bash	Paradiso Classico	Verde Ming	Baltic Brown
Verde Oliva	Dakota Mahogany	Blue Pearl	Nero Africa	Verde Bahía

Fig. 1. The 25 classes of MondialMarmi 2.0. The images are column-wise ordered by decreasing average luminance (brightest → top-left, darkest → bottom-right).

by Mondial Marmi S.r.l., a stone manufacturing company based near Perugia, Italy. The dataset, which we refer to as MondialMarmi 2.0 (Fig. 1), extends the previous version 1.1 (see also [4]) by adding 13 more classes; it also provides a higher image resolution and avoids the JPEG compression artifacts that affected version 1.1 [9].

Image acquisition was based on the system described in [5], which is composed of a dome-shaped illuminator, a slot to accommodate the object to be acquired and a camera mounted on a rotatable device placed at the top of the dome. The acquisition process was carried out as follows: each tile was placed in the image acquisition slot and 10 images were taken at different rotation angles from 0° to 90° by steps of 10°. Diffuse illumination with an average level of ≈600lx measured at the top surface of the tile was guaranteed by white leds with colour temperature in the range 5700K-6000K. The illumination conditions were kept constant throughout the whole acquisition process. The images were captured through a CMOS camera (Edmund Optics EO-5012C LE) equipped with a 6mm fixed-focal lens (Pentax H614-MQ-KP) at the natural resolution of the sensor (2560px × 1920px), and were finally cropped to a central part of size 1500px × 1500px corresponding to an area of ≈21cm × 21cm. Image encoding was linear with no gamma correction. An X-Rite Digital SG colour checker (140 colour targets) was also put in place with the aim of enabling the colour calibration procedure as described in Sec. 4.5. The RGB values of the 140 colour targets were acquired using the same settings adopted for the tiles; the corresponding device-independent CIE XYZ coordinates (under illuminant D65) were measured through a Minolta CR-200 Chroma Meter. The whole dataset is freely available to the public for future evaluations and comparisons [11].

4   Methods

4.1   Colour Descriptors

Soft colour descriptors as defined by López *et al.* [10] are sets of global statistics describing colour and texture properties of the material. Soft colour descriptors are particularly appealing since they are easy to implement, computationally fast, and produce low-dimensional feature vectors. Based on the good results provided in previous studies [6,10] herein we considered the following five descriptors: mean, mean + standard deviation, mean + moments from 2nd to 5th, quartiles and quintiles of each colour channel.

4.2   Colour Spaces

Colour spaces may be either device-dependent or device-independent. The data encoded by device-dependent spaces such as RGB and HSV are device-specific, since they depend on the characteristics of the imaging system. Among them RGB plays a pivotal role, for most imaging devices provide their output in this space. By contrast, data encoded by device independent spaces such as CIE XYZ (also referred to as *colorimetric* spaces) represent the response of an ideal standard observer, hence they do not depend on the acquisition device. The kernel of the device-independent spaces is CIE XYZ: any other device-independent space is a space which can be converted to or obtained from CIE XYZ with no additional information. Perceptual uniformity is another important feature of colour spaces: in a perceptually uniform space the difference between two colour stimuli as perceived by the human eye is expected to be proportional to the Euclidean distance between the corresponding points in the space. In this sense RGB is not perceptually uniform; CIE Lab and CIE Luv are locally uniform, whereas HSV is approximately uniform.

4.3   Device-Dependent Spaces

In the experiments we considered the following device-dependent spaces: RGB, HSV, YUV, YIQ, YCbCr, Ohta's I1I2I3 and the opponent colour space RG-YeB-WhBl. Conversion from the original RGB data to the other device-dependent spaces was carried out using the standard formulas for which references are given hereafter.

HSV is a colour space in which colour information is decomposed into three intuitive and perceptually relevant coordinates: hue (H), saturation (S) and intensity (V). Unfortunately, conversion from RGB to HSV requires a non-linear transform [8, Sec. 7.2] which generates non-removable singularities. YIQ, YUV and YCbCr are obtained from RGB through simple linear transforms of the colour channels [14, Secs. 4.3.1–4.3.3]. Their common feature is to separate luminance (Y) from chrominance; they are also known as *television* colour spaces, since they have been used for encoding and broadcasting television signals. Ohta's I1I2I3 colour space aims at separating colour information into three approximately orthogonal (decorrelated) components [13]. Conversion from RGB is carried out through a simple linear transform [14, Sec. 4.5]. Finally, the RG-YeB-WhBl space derives from Hering's theory of opponent colour vision: the conversion formula [14, Sec. 4.4] is again a linear transform of the RGB space.

4.4   Device-Independent Spaces

The following device-independent spaces were included in this study: CIE XYZ, CIE Lab and CIE Luv. The original RGB data were first converted to CIE XYZ trough colour calibration (see Sec. 4.5), then from CIE XYZ to CIE Lab and CIE Luv through the standard non-linear transforms [8, Secs. 5.2–5.3].

4.5   Colour Calibration and Gamut Mapping

Conversion from RGB to CIE XYZ was performed under the assumption of a linear transformation model between device-dependent and device-independent data. Thought other approaches are also possible [2], the linear model was chosen on the basis on the ease of implementation, low computational demand and the good results provided in previous work [3]. In formulas we have:

$$
\left\{ \begin{array}{c} X \\ Y \\ Z \end{array} \right\} = \left[\begin{array}{ccc} M_{11} & M_{12} & M_{13} \\ M_{21} & M_{22} & M_{23} \\ M_{31} & M_{32} & M_{33} \end{array} \right] \left[\begin{array}{c} R \\ G \\ B \end{array} \right] + \left\{ \begin{array}{c} T_1 \\ T_2 \\ T_3 \end{array} \right\} \tag{1}
$$

The conversion requires estimating the 12 parameters of the model (i.e.: the $M_{i,j}$ and the T_i; where $i, j \in \{1, \ldots, 3\}$), operation which was carried out by solving the resulting overdetermined linear system (12 unknowns and $3 \times 140 = 420$ equations) through least-square estimation based on the 140 colour targets of the calibration rig (Sec. 3). Gamut mapping was obtained by projecting the eight vertices of the RGB cube into each of the other colour spaces considered in the experiments. The transformed gamuts were used to normalise the data in each of the destination colour spaces. For comparison purposes we also performed the transformation from RGB to XYZ using the approximate method based on the general-purpose approximated formula [10] instead of colour calibration. In the remainder we indicate as Lab_f and Luv_f the corresponding Lab and Luv coordinates obtained this way.

Table 1. Overall accuracy (1-NN and linear classifier).

Col. space	Mean	Mean+Std	Mean+Mom.	Quartiles	Quintiles	Col. space	Mean	Mean+Std	Mean+Mom.	Quartiles	Quintiles
			Descriptors						Descriptors		
	Classifier: *1-NN*						Classifier: *Linear*				
CIE XYZ	82.3	90.0	85.7	90.9	91.1	CIE XYZ	82.3	92.6	91.3	88.6	89.0
CIE Lab	89.8	93.5	91.8	93.5	93.6	CIE Lab	**94.8**	**98.6**	**98.3**	**95.7**	**96.0**
CIE Luv	**90.4**	94.0	**92.4**	93.9	94.0	CIE Luv	**94.8**	98.1	97.6	**95.7**	95.8
CIE Lab$_f$	88.0	93.8	91.0	93.0	93.3	CIE Lab$_f$	92.4	95.7	96.5	93.8	94.4
CIE Luv$_f$	89.1	94.1	91.8	93.8	94.1	CIE Luv$_f$	88.9	92.4	89.7	94.7	95.0
RGB	89.1	**94.9**	91.2	94.4	**94.7**	RGB	85.2	94.9	93.7	90.4	90.8
HSV	90.0	94.1	90.0	91.7	91.3	HSV	91.3	97.2	93.7	91.7	91.6
YUV	89.1	94.1	91.6	93.5	93.7	YUV	93.0	95.6	96.4	94.5	94.3
YIQ	88.5	93.8	91.2	93.1	93.4	YIQ	93.3	95.6	96.5	94.5	95.0
YCbCr	89.1	94.0	91.6	93.5	93.7	YCbCr	93.0	95.6	96.3	94.2	94.4
I1I2I3	89.8	**94.9**	92.3	**94.2**	94.5	I1I2I3	93.1	95.9	96.8	94.5	95.2
RG-YeB-WhBl	89.8	**94.9**	89.8	94.1	94.4	RG-YeB-WhBl	93.4	96.1	95.5	94.8	95.2

5   Experiments and Results

To evaluate the performance of the colour spaces presented in Sec. 4.2 we run a supervised classification experiment using two different classification strategies: nearest-neighbour (1-NN) rule with Euclidean distance and linear classifier with diagonal covariance matrix. The experimental basis included the 25 classes described in Sec. 3 where each image was subdivided into four non-overlapping sub-images giving 16 samples for each class. Accuracy estimation was based on 100-fold validation with stratified sampling and a train ratio of $1/4$. To assess the robustness against rotation of the descriptors the train images were always picked from the $0°$-group; the test images from each of the $\theta°$-group (including the $0°$-group). For each rotation angle the accuracy was the percentage of test images correctly classified; finally, the overall accuracy values were averaged over the rotation angles of each dataset to give a global accuracy measure (Tab. 1). To estimate the effect of the colour space we computed, for each of them, the average accuracy over all the colour descriptors considered in the experiment and estimated the 95% confidence interval assuming a normal distribution (Tab. 2).

Table 2. Average overall accuracy by colour space (confidence intervals for the mean).

Colour space	C.I. for the mean	Colour space	C.I. for the mean
Classifier: *1-NN*		Classifier: *Linear*	
CIE XYZ	87.8 - 88.1	CIE XYZ	88.6 - 88.9
CIE Lab	92.4 - 92.5	CIE Lab	**96.6 - 96.7**
CIE Luv	92.9 - 93.0	CIE Luv	**96.4 - 96.5**
CIE Lab$_f$	91.7 - 91.9	CIE Lab$_f$	94.5 - 94.6
CIE Luv$_f$	92.5 - 92.7	CIE Luv$_f$	92.0 - 92.2
RGB	92.8 - 93.0	RGB	90.8 - 91.1
HSV	91.3 - 91.5	HSV	93.0 - 93.2
YUV	92.3 - 92.5	YUV	94.7 - 94.8
YIQ	91.9 - 92.1	YIQ	94.9 - 95.0
YCbCr	92.3 - 92.5	YCbCr	94.6 - 94.8
I1I2I3	93.0 - 93.2	I1I2I3	95.0 - 95.2
RG-YeB-WhBl	92.5 - 92.7	RG-YeB-WhBl	95.0 - 95.1

6   Conclusions and Future Work

In this paper we have presented a rigorous procedure for comparing colour spaces from a performance perspective, and have applied it to the problem of automated grading polished natural stones. The results show that under controlled illumination conditions simple and computationally cheap colour descriptors are quite effective for the task, with overall accuracy beyond 97%. With the nearest neighbour classifier no colour space emerged as significantly superior to the others. This finding parallels with the results reported by Drimbarean and Whelan [7] and by Bianconi et al. [5]. With the linear classifier, however, the perceptually-uniform spaces CIE Lab and CIE Luv outperformed the others. With both classifiers the conversion from device-dependent to device-independent spaces gave better results when performed through colour calibration than through the approximated formula. In future it would be interesting to validate these results in a larger cohort of materials. Another important question for future research is the extension of this study to the case of variable illumination conditions.

Acknowledgments. This work was partially supported by the European Commission under project LIFE12 ENV/IT/000411 and by the Spanish Government under project AGL2014-56017-R.

References

1. Adel, M., Wolf, D., Vogrig, R., Husson, R.: Evaluation of colour spaces in computer vision. In: Proc. of the International Conference on Systems, Man and Cybernetics, vol. 2, pp. 499–504. Le Touquet, France, October 1993
2. Bianco, S., Gasparini, F., Russo, A., Schettini, R.: A new method for RGB to XYZ transformation based on pattern search optimization. IEEE Transactions on Consumer Electronics **53**(3), 1020–1028 (2007)
3. Bianconi, F., Saetta, S.A., Sacchi, G., Asdrubali, F., Baldinelli, G.: Colour calibration of an artificial vision system for industrial applications: comparison of different polynomial models. In: Rossi, M. (ed.) Colour and Colorimetry Multidisciplinary Contributions. Optics and Photonics Series Notebooks, no. 21, pp. 18–25. Maggioli Editore (2011)

4. Bianconi, F., González, E., Fernández, A., Saetta, S.A.: Automatic classification of granite tiles through colour and texture features. Expert Systems with Applications **39**(12), 11212–11218 (2012)

5. Bianconi, F., González, E., Fernández, A., Saetta, S.A.: Apparato per acquisire una pluralità di immagini di almeno un corpo e relativo metodo (Apparatus to acquire a plurality of superficial images of at least one body and related method), 2015. IT patent no. 0001413266. Filed on July 25, 2012; granted on January 16, 2015

6. Bianconi, F., Fernández, A., González, E., Saetta, S.A.: Performance analysis of colour descriptors for parquet sorting. Expert Systems with Applications **40**(5), 1636–1644 (2013)

7. Drimbarean, A., Whelan, P.F.: Experiments in colour texture analysis. Pattern Recognition Letters **22**(10), 1161–1167 (2001)

8. Kang, H.R.: Computational Color Technology. Spie Press (2006)

9. Kylberg, G., Sintorn, I.-M.: Evaluation of noise robustness for local binary pattern descriptors in texture classification. EURASIP Journal on Image and Video Processing **2013**(17) (2013)

10. López, F., Valiente, J.M., Prats, J.M., Ferrer, A.: Performance evaluation of soft color texture descriptors for surface grading using experimental design and logistic regression. Pattern Recognition **41**(5), 1744–1755 (2008)

11. Marmi, M.: A collection of images of polished natural stones for colour and texture analysis. version 2.0 (2015). http://dismac.dii.unipg.it/mm. (last accessed on May 7, 2015)

12. Montani, C.: XXV World Marble and Stone Report. Aldus Casa di Edizioni, Carrara (2014)

13. Ohta, Y., Kanade, T., Sakai, T.: Color information for region segmentation. Computer Graphics and Image Processing **13**(3), 222–241 (1980)

14. Palus, H.: Representations of colour images in different colour spaces. In: Sangwine, S.J., Horne, R.E.N. (eds.) The Colour Image Processing Handbook, pp. 67–90. Springer (1998)

15. Paschos, G.: Perceptually uniform color spaces for color texture analysis: An empirical evaluation. IEEE transactions on Image Processing **10**(6), 932–937 (2001)

16. Petrou, M., Petrou, C.: Image Processing: The Fundamentals. John Wiley & Sons Ltd (2010)

17. Qazi, I.U.H., Alata, O., Burie, J.C., Moussa, A., Fernández Maloigne, C.: Choice of a pertinent color space for color texture characterization using parametric spectral analysis. Pattern Recognition **44**(1), 16–31 (2011)

18. Rajadell, O., García-Sevilla, P.: Influence of color spaces over texture characterization. In: Medina Barrera, M.G., Ramírez Cruz, J.F., Sossa Azuela, J.H. (eds.) Advances in Intelligent and Information Technologies. Research in Computing Science, vol. 38, pp. 273–281. Instituto Politécnico Nacional, Centro de Investigación en Computación, México (2008)

Methods for Predicting Spectral Response of Fibers Blends

Rocco Furferi$^{(\boxtimes)}$, Lapo Governi, and Yary Volpe

Department of Industrial Engineering of Florence, University of Florence,
Via di Santa Marta 3, 50139 Firenze, Italy
{rocco.furferi,lapo.governi,yary.volpe}@unifi.it
http://www.dief.unifi.it

Abstract. Textile companies usually manufacture fabrics using a mix of pre-colored fibers according to a traditional recipe based on their own experience. Unfortunately, mainly due to the fibers dyeing process, the colorimetric distance between the obtained fabric and the desired one results unsatisfactory with respect to a colorimetric threshold established by the technicians. In such cases, colorists are required to slightly change the original recipe in order to reduce the colorimetric distance. This trial and error process is time-consuming and requires the work of highly skilled operators. Computer-based color recipe assessment methods have been proposed so far in scientific literature to address this issue. Unlikely, many methods are still far to be reliably predictive when the fabric is composed by a high number of components. Accordingly, the present work proposes two alternative methods based on Kubelka-Munk and subtractive mixing able to perform a reliable prediction of the spectrophotometric response of a fabric obtained by means of any variation of a recipe. The assessment performed on a prototypal implementation of the two methods demonstrates that they are suitable for reliable prediction of fabric blends spectral response.

Keywords: Computer-based color assessment · Kubelka-Munk theory · Spectro-photometer · Fabric blend

1 Introduction

One of the key phases in producing textile fabrics of a desired color is the so called "recipe-based mixing" i.e. the process of mixing together a number of differently colored fibers in different percentages stated by textile companies on the basis of their know-how. Unfortunately, whichever the dyeing process, the result obtained by mixing the fibers may be very different, in terms of color, from the reference, even using the same consolidated recipe. In most cases, color differences between the recipe-based reflectance factors and the spectrophotometric response of the reference, in terms of CIELAB and CMC(2:1) distances [1] under several standard illuminants [2], may be higher than 0.8 when measured using a spectrophotometer. As a consequence, companies are required to slightly change

© Springer International Publishing Switzerland 2015
V. Murino et al. (Eds.): ICIAP 2015 Workshops, LNCS 9281, pp. 79–86, 2015.
DOI: 10.1007/978-3-319-23222-5_10

the original recipe on the basis of their experience and to produce several samples in order to reduce the gap between the color of the final product and the desired one. This trial and error approach constitutes a bottleneck of the entire fabric production process since each trial is usually performed in, at least, 40 minutes. To speed-up this process several computer-based approaches have been proposed in literature dealing with the assessment of the color matching of dyed fibers. Most of them are based on the Kubelka-Munk (K-M) theory [3,4] that is widely used for predicting the spectral reflectance for a mixture of components (colorants) that have been characterized by absorption K and scattering S coefficients. Unfortunately, the Kubelka-Munk function leads to problems in practical use due to the fact that fiber blends are not obtained by adding colorants on a substrate but, as already stated, by mixing together fibers [5,6] . To overcome these limitations, several studies, related to the tristimulus-matching algorithm based on the Stearns-Noechel (S-N) model [7] (and its implementations [8–11]), have been proposed so far. However S-N model provides reliable results only for blends composed by maximum $5 - 6$ differently colored fibers thus limiting the approach to a lower number of cases since most companies mix together up to $15 - 20$ elements. As a consequence, further experimentations and studies have been carried out with the aim of integrating traditional theories with more practical methods. In fact, since textile companies always create a first-attempt fabric using their recipe it is possible to have, as an additional information, the actual spectrophotometric response of at least one blend (whose reflectance values are often "near" to the reference ones). This allows to introduce, by a way of example, both theoretical approaches (using comparison between expected and actual blend reflectance values [12]), and non-deterministic models such as Artificial Neural Networks (ANNs)[13]. On the basis of considerations presented above, the present work aims to propose two alternative methods able to perform a reliable prediction of the spectrophotometric response of a fabric obtained by means of any variation of an original formula without the need of implementing trained systems such as ANNs.

2   Methods

2.1   Statement of the Problem

Let $\mathbf{p}_i(\lambda)(i = 1, 2, , n)$ be the spectral reflectance factors of the ith component of a fabric (being n the total number of components and λ indicates the wavelength). Now, let $\mathbf{R}_F(\lambda)$ be the spectral reflectance factors of the fabric obtained by mixing the components $\mathbf{p}_i(\lambda)$ according to a given recipe $A = [\alpha_1, \alpha_2, \ldots, \alpha_n]$ with $\sum_{i=1}^{n} \alpha = 1$. The general relationship between $\mathbf{R}_F(\lambda)$ and the vectors $\mathbf{p}_i(\lambda)$ may be stated by the following formula:

$$\mathbf{R}_F(\lambda) = \mathcal{F}(A, \mathbf{p}_i(\lambda)) \qquad (1)$$

Varying the wavelength in the range [400 700 nm] and with a 10 nm step, the size of vectors $\mathbf{p}_i(\lambda)$ and $\mathbf{R}(\lambda, \alpha_i)$ is 1 x 31. According to Eq. 1, if a method for evaluating the transfer function $\mathcal{F}$ is established, it is possible to evaluate the spectral reflectance factors of a fabric $\mathbf{R}_F(\lambda)$ given the parameters α_i and the vectors $\mathbf{p}_i(\lambda)$. As mentioned in the introductory section, the determination of the transfer function is not straightforward, especially for blends composed by more than $5 - 6$ components (i.e. for $n > 6$) when theoretical approached such as K-M and S-N have been demonstrated to provide inaccurate results.

2.2 K-M-Based Approach

K-M theory states a correlation between the K-S ratio of a blend (mix) and the K-S ratio of singular components to be mixed together plus the substrate according to the following equation:

$$\left(\frac{K}{S}\right)_{\lambda,mix} = \left(\frac{k_{\lambda,t}}{s_{\lambda,t}}\right) + \alpha_1 \left(\frac{k_{\lambda,1}}{s_{\lambda,1}}\right) + \ldots + \alpha_n \left(\frac{k_{\lambda,n}}{s_{\lambda,n}}\right) \qquad (2)$$

Where the term $\mathbf{\Psi}_S(\lambda) = \left(\frac{k_{\lambda,t}}{s_{\lambda,t}}\right)$ is the ratio between absorption and scattering of the substrate. In blends obtained by mixing fibers, the definition of "substrate" is quite weak since unlike fabrics dipped in dye bath (where a "monochrome" substrate is dyed) the final product is obtained using pre-colored fibers. As a consequence the scattering and absorption coefficients of the substrate are not evaluable. For this reason the K-M approach is not suitable for predicting the color of such blends. Fortunately, since colorists working in textile companies always create a first-attempt blend using their historical recipe, the actual reflectance factors of the blend are known together with the recipe and the spectra of each component. This additional information may be used to evaluate a K-S ratio $\mathbf{\Psi}_S^*(\lambda)$ by using Eq. 2.

$$\mathbf{\Psi}_S^*(\lambda) = \left(\frac{K}{S}\right)_{\lambda,mix} - \left\{\alpha_1 \left(\frac{k_{\lambda,1}}{s_{\lambda,1}}\right) + \ldots + \alpha_n \left(\frac{k_{\lambda,n}}{s_{\lambda,n}}\right)\right\} = \mathbf{\Psi}_F(\lambda) - \mathbf{\Psi}_C(\lambda) \quad (3)$$

Even if $\mathbf{\Psi}_S^*(\lambda)$, in the present work named "K-S ratio of an equivalent fabric substrate", has not a physical meaning, it describes the K-M ratio of an ideal equivalent fabric having the same reflectance values of the actual ones but obtained using a dye dipping process. Since, as already mentioned, such a term is defined in a theoretical way, and no physical counterpart actually exists, it may consist also of negative values in the 400-700 nm wavelength range. In Fig. 1 the terms $\mathbf{\Psi}_F$, $\mathbf{\Psi}_S^*$ and $\mathbf{\Psi}_C$ of Eq. 3 for 4 fabric samples are shown.

Under the hypothesis that the turbid mixing mechanism of fibers only slightly changes by varying the original recipe (i.e. by changing the values α_i), it can be assumed that $\mathbf{\Psi}_S^*$ is constant for a given fabric. As a consequence the K-S ratio for any given variation of recipe $\mathbf{\Psi}_{Fnew}$ can be evaluated as follows:

$$\mathbf{\Psi}_{Fnew} = \mathbf{\Psi}_S^*(\lambda) + \overline{\mathbf{\Psi}}_C(\lambda) \qquad (4)$$

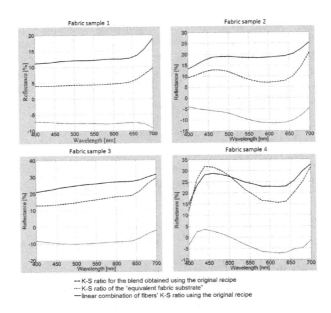

Fig. 1. Terms $\mathbf{\Psi}_F$, $\mathbf{\Psi}_S^*$ and $\mathbf{\Psi}_C$ of Eq. 3 for 4 fabric samples

where $\overline{\mathbf{\Psi}}_C(\lambda)$ is the linear combination of fibers' K-S ratio using the modified recipe. Once $\mathbf{\Psi}_{Fnew}$ is calculated using Eq. 4, it is straightforward to evaluate the spectral response $\mathbf{R}_F^*(\lambda)$, constituting the best prediction of actual $\mathbf{R}_F(\lambda)$, by using the following equation [5]:

$$\mathbf{\Psi}_{Fnew}(\lambda) = \frac{(1 - \mathbf{R}_F^*(\lambda))^2}{2\mathbf{R}_F^*(\lambda)} \tag{5}$$

The correctness of Eq. 5 is validated in Section 3.

2.3   Subtractive Mixing-Based Approach

As widely known, in case pigments are mixed together, the subtractive color mixing model is reliable in predicting the spectrophotometric response of the blend [14]. The density of the pigments $\mathbf{d}_i(\lambda)$ (for any given wavelength) are approximately additive and can be expressed as follows:

$$\mathbf{d}_i(\lambda) = -\log_{10}(\mathbf{p}_i(\lambda)) \tag{6}$$

Accordingly, it is possible to define a subtractive color mixing spectrum $\mathbf{R}_S(\lambda, \alpha_i)$ as:

$$\mathbf{R}_S(\lambda, \alpha_i) = exp\left(\sum_{i=1}^n \alpha_i \mathbf{d}_i(\lambda)\right) \tag{7}$$

As stated in the scientific literature, and further demonstrated in the industrial practice, Eq. 7 is not appropriate for the evaluation of the spectral reflectance factors of fabrics. Actually, unlike - for instance - mixtures of paints, it is not possible to obtain a complete homogenization of textile fibers because they remain separate entities on a macroscopic scale. The difference between reflectance values $\mathbf{R}_S(\lambda, \alpha_i)$ and $\mathbf{R}_F(\lambda)$ for 4 fabrics with different compositions are depicted in Fig. 2, showing that the color subtractive model is not suitable as it stands for predicting the fabric reflectance values.

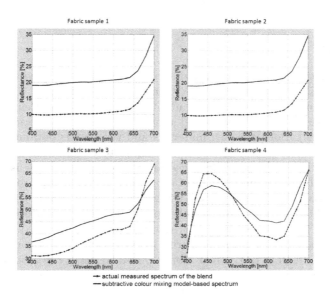

Fig. 2. Difference between actual measured spectrum and subtractive color mixing model-based estimation for the 4 fabric blends of Fig. 1

However, the definition of $\mathbf{R}_S(\lambda, \alpha_i)$ can be considered a very rough approximation of the real blend spectrum, to be corrected using an appropriate wavelength-dependant function $\mathbf{\Phi}(\lambda)$ in order to evaluate a predicted $\mathbf{R}_F^{**}(\lambda)$ of $\mathbf{R}_F(\lambda)$ as follows:

$$\mathbf{R}_F^{**}(\lambda) = \mathbf{\Phi}(\lambda) \cdot \mathbf{R}_S(\lambda, \alpha_i) \tag{8}$$

Since, as already stated, in the industrial practice a first-attempt fabric is physically realized using the standard recipe, it is possible to know for such a blend both the vectors $\mathbf{R}_F(\lambda)$ - measured using a spectrophotometer - and $\mathbf{R}_S(\lambda, \alpha_i)$. This additional information allows the determination of the transfer function $\mathbf{\Phi}(\lambda)$ as follows:

$$\mathbf{\Phi}(\lambda) = \frac{\mathbf{R}_F(\lambda)}{\mathbf{R}_S(\lambda, \alpha_i)} \tag{9}$$

Under the hypothesis that the transfer function $\Phi(\lambda)$ remains unchanged once the recipe is changed, the spectral response $\mathbf{R}^{**}_{Fnew}(\lambda)$ of a fabric obtained by changing the original recipe is provided by:

$$\mathbf{R}^{**}_{Fnew}(\lambda) = \frac{\mathbf{R}_F(\lambda)}{\mathbf{R}_S(\lambda, \alpha_i)} \cdot \mathbf{R}_{Snew}(\lambda, \alpha_i) \tag{10}$$

Where $\mathbf{R}_{Snew}(\lambda, \alpha_i)$ is the subtractive colour mixing spectrum obtained by changing the weights α_i according to the new recipe and the $\mathbf{R}^{**}_{Fnew}(\lambda)$ is the best prediction of actual $\mathbf{R}_F(\lambda)$ for modified recipe. The correctness of the Eq. 10 is validated in Section 3.

3   Results

The two prediction methods described above have been validated thanks to the collaboration of the staff of the Textile Company New Mill s.p.a. - Prato (Italy) by using a set of 80 fabrics obtained adopting their standard recipe (40 fabrics used to evaluate $\mathbf{\Psi}^*_S(\lambda)$ and $\mathbf{\Phi}(\lambda)$) and a modified version (40 fabrics to evaluate the two methods). Both the raw materials and the blends obtained by mixing them were processed by using an acquisition system consisting of a bench on which a Hunterlab Ultrascan VIS reflectance spectrophotometer is placed and connected to a PC. The final results of this experimental setup are: the spectral responses of the 40 samples obtained using the standard recipe; the 40 spectral responses for the modified recipe and the spectra of each raw material composing the blends. The predicted spectra ($\mathbf{R}_F(\lambda)$ and $\mathbf{R}^{**}_{Fnew}(\lambda)$) obtained using the two proposed approaches are then compared in terms of CMC(2:1) distance with the actual measurement of the real fabrics obtained using the modified recipes. Moreover a comparison between the results obtained using the two approaches provided by [12] and [13] is proposed. In Table 1 the aggregate results of the comparison for the 40 samples are shown.

In Fig. 3 the predicted spectra obtained using respectively the K-M-based approach, the Subtractive mixing-based approach, the theoretical method provided in [12] and the ANN-based method provided in [13] are plotted for the 4 exemplificative samples.

Table 1. Aggregate results obtained by comparing the two proposed methods with tho once described in [12] and [13]

	CMC(2:1) distance from reference			
	K-M-based approach	Subtractive mixing-based approach	Theoretical approach [12]	ANN-based approach [13]
Mean value	0.5633	0.5260	0.7886	0.4761
Median value	0.5080	0.4738	0.7589	0.4438
Max value	1.0924	1.0280	1.4272	0.9982
Min value	0.1283	0.1285	0.4231	0.1058
Variance	0.047	0.045	0.054	0.041

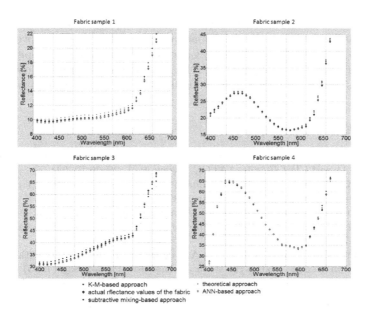

Fig. 3. Predicted spectra obtained using respectively the K-M-based approach, the Subtractive mixing-based approach, the theoretical method provided in [12] and the ANN-based method provided in [13]

4   Conclusions

The present paper described two methods for predicting the spectral response of a fabric obtained by mixing pre-colored fibers. The first method implements a simplified version of the Kubelka-Munk two constant approach by introducing a term named "K-S ratio of an equivalent fabric substrate" used to provide a robust prediction once a first-attempt fabric (blend) is physically realized. The second method uses a rough prediction based on a subtractive color mixing model to build a transfer function between the spectral responses of the raw materials composing the blend and the expected reflectance factors of the blend. Results of validation test show that, as expected, the ANN-based method is the one that generally provides better results in predicting the actual color of the blend (average CMC(2:1) distance less than 0.48) but the two proposed methods perform well with a color distance averagely equal to 0.5633 and 0.5260 respectively for K-M-based and subtractive mixing-based methods. This is a noticeable result since the two proposed methods does not requires training phases as is the case for ANN-based ones. The prediction errors, i.e. the color distance, increases for blends characterized by high number of raw materials (i.e. ¿16). However, a prediction error lower than 1.2 for such cases has been measured; this is acceptable for many companies. Both in terms of mean and median values, subtractive mixing-based method performs slightly better than the K-M-based ones; both methods, in any case, provide a closer prediction when compared with theoretical approach proposed in [12]. Future work will be addressed to increase the validation set and to further increase the performance especially for recipes characterized by a high number of differently colored fibers and in assessing the influence of the roughness of fibers composing the blend.

References

1. Aspland, R., Shanbhag, P.: Comparison of color difference equations for textiles. CMC (2: 1) and CIEDE2000. AATCC review **4**(6), 26–30 (2004)
2. Furferi, R., Governi, L., Volpe, Y.: Image processing-based method for glass tiles color matching. Imaging Science Journal **61**(2), 183–194 (2013)
3. Amirshahi, S.H., Pailthorpe, M.T.: Applying the Kubelka-Munk equation to explain the color of blends prepared from precolored fibers. Textile research journal **64**(6), 357–364 (1994)
4. Amirshahi, S.H., Pailthorpe, M.T.: An algorithm for the optimization of color prediction in blends. Textile Research Journal **65**(11), 632–637 (1995)
5. Burlone, D.A.: Effect of Fibre Translucency on the Color of Blends of Precolored Fibres. Textile Research Journal **60**(3), 162–167 (1990)
6. Hongying, Y., Zhu, S., Pan, N.: On the Kubelka-Munk Single-Constant/Two-Constant Theory. Textile Research Journal **80**(3), 263–270 (2010)
7. Steams, E.I., Noechel, F.: Spectrophotometric Prediction of Color Wool Blends. Am. Dyest **33**(9), 177–180 (1944)
8. Rong, L.I., Feng, G.U.: Tristimulus algorithm of colour matching for precoloured fibre blends based on the Stearns- Noechel model. Coloration Technology **122**(2), 74–81 (2006)
9. Thompson, B., Hammersley, M.J.: Prediction of the colour of scoured-wool blends. Journal of the Textile Institute **69**(1), 1–7 (1978)
10. Kazmi, S.Z., Grady, P.L., Mock, G.N., Hodge, G.L.: On-line color monitoring in continuous textile dyeing. ISA Transactions **35**(1), 33–43 (1996)
11. Philips-Invernizzi, B., Dupont, D., Jolly-Desodt, A.M., Caze, C.: Color formulation by fiber blending using the Stearns -oechel model. Color Research and Application **27**(2), 100–107 (2002)
12. Furferi, R., Carfagni, M.: Colour mixing modelling and simulation: Optimization of colour recipe for carded fibres. Modelling and Simulation in Engineering, vol. 2010, Article ID 487678, 9 p. (2010)
13. Furferi, R., Governi, L.: Prediction of the spectrophotometric response of a carded fiber composed by different kinds of coloured raw materials: An artificial neural network-based approach. Color Research and Application **36**(3), 179–191 (2011)
14. Hawkyard, C.J.: Synthetic reflectance curves by subtractive colour mixing. Journal of the Society of Dyers and Colourists **109**(78), 246–251 (1993)

Texture Classification Using Rotation Invariant LBP Based on Digital Polygons

Juan Pardo-Balado[1], Antonio Fernández[1($\boxtimes$)], and Francesco Bianconi[2]

[1] Universidade de Vigo, School of Industrial Engineering,
Campus Universitario, Rúa Maxwell s/n, 36310 Vigo, Spain
jpardo@alumnos.uvigo.es, antfdez@uvigo.es
[2] Department of Engineering, Università degli Studi di Perugia,
Via G. Duranti, 93, 06125 Perugia, Italy
bianco@ieee.org

Abstract. This paper investigates the use of digital polygons as a replacement for circular interpolated neighbourhoods for extracting texture features through Local Binary Patterns. The use of digital polygons has two main advantages: reduces the computational cost, and avoids the high-frequency loss resulting from pixel interpolation. The solution proposed in this work employs a sub-sampling scheme over Andres' digital circles. The effectiveness of the method was evaluated in a supervised texture classification experiment over eight different datasets. The results showed that digital polygons outperformed interpolated circular neighbourhoods in most cases.

Keywords: Local Binary Patterns · Texture classification · Digital circles · Digital polygons · Rotation invariance

1 Introduction

Texture analysis plays a pivotal role in many machine vision applications including, among many others, material recognition, surface inspection and grading, remote sensing, computer-assisted diagnosis and content-based image retrieval. No surprise, then, that texture analysis has been attracting increasing research interest over the last four decades, and that many texture descriptors have appeared in the literature [14]. Among them, Local Binary Patterns (LBP) has emerged as one of the most successful methods due to the high descriptive capability, ease of implementation and low computational cost. In many applications it is mandatory that texture description be invariant to image rotation, for real world textures can occur at any orientation. In the case of LBP the usual way to achieve robustness against rotation consists of using circular neighbourhoods and grouping together all the binary patterns that can be transformed into each other through a discrete rotation around the central pixel. Since exact circular neighbourhoods are not possible on the square lattice of digital images, the common solution involves estimating the intensities of the points that do not

© Springer International Publishing Switzerland 2015
V. Murino et al. (Eds.): ICIAP 2015 Workshops, LNCS 9281, pp. 87–94, 2015.
DOI: 10.1007/978-3-319-23222-5_11

coincide with image pixels through bilinear interpolation [8]. Yet this approach has two main drawbacks: on the one hand, interpolation is time-consuming hence impractical in those applications where real-time processing is required; on the other, it is well-known that interpolation smooths the image and therefore alters the high-frequency content of the original signal producing artifacts and/or significant loss of information [4]. In this paper we propose a solution to overcome these problems. Our approach consists of replacing the interpolated circular neighbourhood by digital polygons. The vertices of the polygons perfectly overlap the image's pixels making interpolation unnecessary. To ensure robustness against rotation, the resemblance of digital polygons to the approximated circle is measured through one quantitative index, namely the circularity. From a set of image classification experiments we conclude that LBP features based on digital polygons are at least as good (and in general better) at discriminating textures than those based on the traditional circular neighbourhoods.

The remainder of the paper is organized as follows. After a brief review of the relevant literature we introduce the proposed method in Sec. 2, and describe the experimental set-up in Sec. 3. We summarise and discuss the results in Sec. 4, then conclude the paper with some final considerations and ideas for future research (Sec. 5).

2   Methodology

The problem of approximating circles on square lattices has long been a relevant topic in digital geometry and computer graphics, and studies on this subject can be traced as far back as to Gauss [7, Sec. 2.3.1]. The Bresenham's algorithm is one of the most common approaches to trace circles on raster devices, and has also been applied to image processing tasks such as circle extraction using Hough transform [13]. It can be shown that Bresenham's algorithm is the solution to the minimum residual distance displacement approximation problem for integer radius [9]. More recently, Andres' circles [1] were used to compute rotation invariant texture features from grey level co-occurrence matrices [2,12]. In the general form an Andres' circle of radius R and center $C \equiv (x_C, y_C) \in \mathbb{Z}^2$ is defined as follows:

$$\mathcal{C}_R = \{(x,y) \in \mathbb{Z}^2 \mid R - \frac{1}{2} \le \sqrt{(x - x_C)^2 + (y - y_C)^2} < R + \frac{1}{2}\} \qquad (1)$$

Compared with Bresenham's a potential advantage of Andres' circles is that for a given center any pixel of the plane belongs to one and only one Andres' circle, a property which does not hold for Bresenham's. This is the reason why the approach presented herein is based on Andres' solution. In either case both Bresenham's and Andres' methods are unsuitable for computing rotation invariant LBP texture features since the number of pixels of the resulting circular neighbourhood grows rapidly as the radius of the digital circle increases, therefore producing excessively long feature vectors. To avoid this issue we propose a

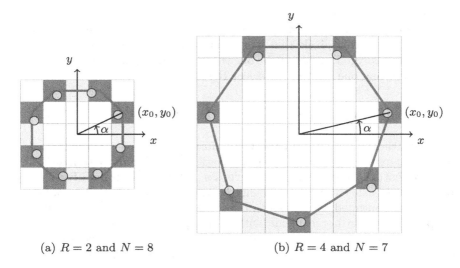

(a) $R = 2$ and $N = 8$ (b) $R = 4$ and $N = 7$

Fig. 1. Examples of digital polygons $\mathcal{P}_{R,N}$ of different number of vertices (N) obtained from digital circles of different radii (R). Shaded squares represent the pixels that make up Andres' circles. A subset of this set of pixels (shown in blue) are used as vertices of the polygons. The yellow dots depict the coordinates that Eq. 2 would yield if we removed the function $\| \cdot \|$ from the formulas.

sub-sampling scheme which retains a subset of N pixels of Andres' circle. This way we approximate the digital circle $\mathcal{C}_R$ trough a digital polygon $\mathcal{P}_{R,N}$ of N vertices, where $\mathcal{P}_{R,N} = \{(x_n, y_n) \in \mathbb{Z}^2 \mid n = 0, 1, \ldots N - 1\} \subseteq \mathcal{C}_R$. The construction of such a digital polygon is summarised in Fig. 1. As a first step we select a starting pixel $(x_0, y_0) \in \mathcal{C}_R$ which represents the starting vertex of the polygon. Note that, in principle, any pixel of the Andres' circle could be chosen as the starting vertex, but, due to symmetry reasons, we can conveniently limit the choice to just one octant of the digital circle, i.e.: we assume $0 \leq \alpha \leq \pi/4$, where α is the counter-clockwise angle formed by the radius through the point (x_0, y_0) and the horizontal axis x. The coordinates of the remaining vertices are calculated through the following formulas:

$$
\begin{aligned}
x_n &= x_C + \| R \cos(2\pi n/N + \alpha) \| \\
y_n &= y_C + \| R \sin(2\pi n/N + \alpha) \|
\end{aligned}
\tag{2}
$$

where $\| \cdot \|$ stands for the 'nearest integer'. If the decimal part of the argument of the function $\| \cdot \|$ is exactly $1/2$ the returned value is the integer number farthest away from zero. Ideally the digital polygon should resemble a circle as closely as possible. As measure of the goodness-of-fit we consider the concept of *circularity*, also known as roundness or isoperimetric quotient [3]:

$$
f_{\text{circ}} = \frac{4\pi A}{P^2}
\tag{3}
$$

where A and P denote the area and the perimeter of the digital polygon, respectively. The circularity of a circle is 1, whereas for any other shape is less than 1. Among the possible pixels that can be chosen as the starting vertex of the approximating polygon, we select the one that gives the highest circularity; when there is more than one solution we select the pixel with lowest α.

3   Experiments

To validate the proposed approach we performed a set of supervised texture classification experiments using rotation-invariant local binary patterns (LBP^{ri}) as texture features. For comparison purposes, rotation invariant LBP features were computed using the proposed digital polygons as well as the traditional circular neighbourhood. In the second case the intensities of those neighbourhood points that do not coincide with image pixels were estimated through bilinear interpolation as recommended in [8]. We tested both methods over eight datasets (Tab. 1) derived from publicly available texture databases: ALOT, Brodatz, HeLa 2D, Kylberg-Sintorn, MondialMarmi, Outex 00045, Pap Smear and Vectorial (see Refs. [6,11] for further details). The resulting benchmark includes a large number of images and a broad variety of textures. In order to determine the influence of the radius of the digital circle and the number of vertices of the polygon we considered all possible pairs of whole numbers $(R, N) \in [1, 7] \times [5, 16]$ that are compatible with the existence of a digital polygon of the type described in Sec. 2. The circularity values of the considered polygons are shown in Table 2. The reader will notice that some of the cells of the table are empty. This is due to the following reasons: 1) the number of vertices of the approximating polygon cannot exceed the number of pixels of Andres' circle (for instance a polygon approximating a digital circle of radius $R = 2$ cannot have more than $N = 12$ vertices); 2) for some pairs of values, such as $R = 3$ and $N = 15$, Eq. 2 returns pixels coordinates that do not belong to the Andres' circle.

Table 1. Datasets used in the experiments: summary table

Dataset	No. of classes	No. of samples per class	Rotation angles
ALOT	80	16	$0°, 60°, 120°, 180°$
Brodatz	13	16	$0°, 10°, 20°, 30°, 40°, 50°, 60°, 70°, 80°, 90°$
HeLa 2D	10	20	N/A
Kylberg-Sintorn	25	16	$0°, 40°, 80°, 120°, 160°, 200°, 240°, 280°, 320°$
MondialMarmi	12	16	$0°, 5°, 10°, 15°, 30°, 45°, 60°, 75°, 90°$
Outex 00045	45	20	$0°, 5°, 10°, 15°, 30°, 45°, 60°, 75°, 90°$
Pap Smear	2	204	N/A
Vectorial	20	16	$0°, 10°, 20°, 30°, 40°, 50°, 60°, 70°, 80°, 90°$

Table 2. Circularity (in percentage) as a function of N and R. Number of features indicates the dimension of the $LBP_{N,R}^{ri}$ histogram.

Number of vertices	Number of features	Radius						
		1	2	3	4	5	6	7
5	8	80.85	84.41	85.82	86.00	86.19	86.45	86.41
6	14	80.85	90.00	90.00	90.64	90.41	90.64	90.64
7	20	80.01	90.00	92.26	92.53	93.00	92.87	93.10
8	36	78.54	94.33	94.33	94.25	94.79	94.36	94.79
9	60	–	92.34	94.43	94.37	–	95.25	95.60
10	108	–	94.33	94.43	95.90	96.15	96.26	96.49
11	188	–	94.33	94.41	95.22	96.51	96.63	96.80
12	352	–	94.33	94.33	97.50	96.61	97.50	97.48
13	632	–	–	94.41	93.75	96.74	96.53	97.41
14	1182	–	–	94.33	96.68	96.61	96.24	97.99
15	2192	–	–	–	95.62	–	96.32	97.61
16	4116	–	–	94.33	95.90	98.50	98.06	98.50

The texture samples were classified using a nearest-neighbourhood (1-NN) classifier with Euclidean distance. It is reasonable to expect that classifiers such as SVM or SOM might perform better. However, we avoided such classifiers owing to the fact their performance strongly depends on a number of parameters which are notoriously difficult to determine [5]. The overall accuracy was estimated through split-half validation with stratified sampling: in each classification problem each dataset was randomly subdivided into two equal parts (train and test set) in which the proportion of samples of each class was the same as in the whole dataset. For each problem the accuracy was estimated as the proportion of samples of the test set classified correctly. In each dataset the process was repeated for all the rotation angles available in that dataset in the following way: the train samples were always picked from the unrotated textures (images taken at $0°$), while the test samples were taken from textures rotated by θ_k degrees, $k \in \{0, \ldots, K-1\}$ where K is the number of rotation angles provided by that dataset (see Tab.1). The accuracy was the average of the classification rates obtained for each rotation angle. For a stable estimation the classification accuracy was averaged over 100 random partitions of the database into train and test set.

4   Results and Discussion

The main effects on the overall classification accuracy resulting from using digital polygons or interpolated circular neighbourhoods are summarised in Tab. 3. For each dataset and rotation angle the table reports the classification accuracy averaged over all the combinations of (N, R) considered in the experiments (see Tab. 2). The figures show that, on average, digital polygons outperformed interpolated circles (the reverse occurred with the Brodatz dataset only). To validate these findings a statistical test (Student's t-test, significance level 5%) was also performed on each combination of (N, R) to determine whether the difference

Table 3. Average classification accuracy obtained using digital polygons (p) and interpolated circular neighbourhoods (c).

	Dataset											
	ALOT		Brodatz		Kylberg-Sintorn		Mondial Marmi		Outex 00045		Vectorial	
Angle	p	c	p	c	p	c	p	c	p	c	p	c
0°	74.8	67.4	97.4	97.2	99.2	98.8	81.9	81.1	72.1	65.5	85.3	85.0
5°							81.8	80.4	72.2	65.7		
10°			90.1	89.5			81.8	80.9	72.0	65.1	78.0	77.3
15°							82.0	80.8	71.8	64.7		
20°			87.1	88.2							79.6	78.0
30°			88.1	90.1			80.5	80.3	72.9	65.8	80.0	78.3
40°			87.9	89.6	88.1	86.2					80.1	77.8
45°							81.6	81.7	72.7	65.8		
50°			87.7	90.2							80.0	77.9
60°	72.4	65.7	88.0	90.4			82.7	83.2	71.8	65.1	81.4	79.5
70°			87.7	90.3							80.5	79.1
75°							84.2	84.7	70.7	64.3		
80°			86.7	88.8	87.5	85.8					79.0	78.3
90°			88.9	89.1			85.5	86.1	70.4	64.1	87.2	86.7
120°	69.7	63.1			89.6	88.3						
160°					91.0	88.8						
180°	72.7	65.3										
200°					92.0	90.2						
240°					91.8	90.6						
280°					82.8	80.6						
320°					89.7	87.8						
Avg	**72.4**	65.4	89.0	**90.3**	**90.2**	88.6	**82.4**	82.1	**71.8**	65.1	**81.1**	79.8
Std	2.1	**1.8**	3.1	**2.5**	4.4	4.9	**1.5**	2.1	0.8	**0.6**	**2.9**	3.3

	Dataset			
	HeLa 2D		Pap Smear	
Angle	p	c	p	c
N/A	**54.3**	53.9	**72.8**	72.3

between the performance of the two methods was statistically significant. The outcome of this analysis is summarised in Fig. 2. For each combination the figure reports the number of datasets where digital polygons performed significantly better than interpolated circles (left matrix) and vice-versa (right matrix). Again the results show that digital polygons outperformed interpolated circular neighbourhoods in most cases (average value of left matrix = 5.7; average value of right matrix = 1.8). As for robustness against rotation (herein estimated through the standard deviation of the average accuracy over the angles of each dataset – last line of Tab. 3) we can see that none of the two methods clearly outperformed the other.

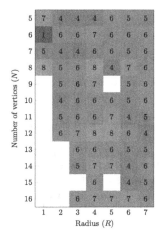 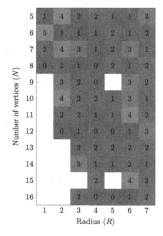

Fig. 2. Number of datasets where digital polygons performed significantly better than interpolated circles (left) and number of datasets where interpolated circles performed significantly better than digital polygons (right).

5   Conclusions and Future Work

The definition of approximately circular domains over digital images is a fundamental step for obtaining rotation-invariant texture descriptors. In this work we have proposed and investigated the use of digital polygons as a replacement for interpolated circular neighbourhoods for computing rotation-invariant features from Local Binary Patterns. Our approach employs a sub-sampling scheme over Andres' digital circles and aims at obtaining polygons with the highest circularity. The proposed method was tested on a large texture classification experiment including 69 combinations radius/number-of-pixels and eight image datasets). The results showed that LBP features computed using digital polygons were at least as accurate than those computed through interpolated circular neighbourhoods: actually, in our experiments the former outperformed the latter in most cases. As for future extensions of the present paper, we are currently working along three lines: 1) inclusion of more texture descriptors of the class Histograms of Equivalent Patterns [5] such as Improved Local Binary Patterns, Local ternary Patterns, Binary Gradient Contours, etc.; 2) extension of the analysis to multiresolution neighbourhoods (i.e.: concentric polygons), and 3) investigation and comparison of other approaches for defining digital circles based on different neighbourhood sequences [10].

Acknowledgments. This work was supported by the Spanish Government under grant TIN2014-56919-C3-2-R and by the European Commission under project LIFE12 ENV / IT / 000411.

References

1. Andres, E., Roussillon, T.: Analytical description of digital circles. In: Debled-Rennesson, I., Domenjoud, E., Kerautret, B., Even, P. (eds.) DGCI 2011. LNCS, vol. 6607, pp. 235–246. Springer, Heidelberg (2011)
2. Bianconi, F., Fernández, A.: Rotation invariant co-occurrence features based on digital circles and discrete Fourier transform. Pattern Recognition Letters **48**, 34–41 (2014)
3. Burger, W., Burge, M.J.: Principles of Digital Image Processing: Core Algorithms. Springer (2009)
4. Fernández, A., Ghita, O., González, E., Bianconi, F., Whelan, P.F.: Evaluation of robustness against rotation of LBP, CCR and ILBP features in granite texture classification. Machine Vision and Applications **22**(6), 913–926 (2011)
5. Fernández, A., Álvarez, M.X., Bianconi, F.: Texture description through histograms of equivalent patterns. Journal of Mathematical Imaging and Vision **45**(1), 76–102 (2013)
6. González, E., Bianconi, F., Fernández, A.: General framework for rotation invariant texture classification through co-occurrence of patterns. Journal of Mathematical Imaging and Vision **50**, 300–313 (2014)
7. Klette, R., Rosenfeld, A.: Digital Geometry. Geometric Methods for Digital Picture Analysis. Morgan Kaufmann (2004)
8. Mäenpää, T., Pietikäinen, M.: Texture analysis with local binary patterns. In: Chen, C.H., Wang, P.S.P. (eds.) Handbook of Pattern Recognition and Computer Vision, 3rd edn, pp. 197–216. World Scientific Publishing (2005)
9. McIlroy, M.D.: Best approximate circles on integer grids. ACM Transactions on Graphics **2**(4), 237–263 (1983)
10. Mukherjee, J., Das, P.P., Aswatha Kumar, M., Chatterji, B.N.: On approximating Euclidean metrics by digital distances in 2D and 3D. Pattern Recognition Letters **21**(6–7), 573–582 (2000)
11. Nanni, L., Brahnam, S., Lumini, A.: Survey on LBP based texture descriptors for image classification. Expert Systems with Applications **39**(3), 3634–3641 (2012)
12. Petrou, M., García Sevilla, P.: Image Processing. Dealing with Texture. Wiley Interscience (2006)
13. Prakash, J., Rajesh, K.: A novel approach for coin identification using eigenvalues of covariance matrix, Hough transform and raster scan algorithms. World Academy of Science, Engineering and Technology **2**(8), 170–176 (2008)
14. Xie, X., Mirmehdi, M.: A galaxy of texture features. In: Mirmehdi, M., Xie, X., Suri, J. (eds.) Handbook of texture analysis, pp. 375–406. Imperial College Press (2008)

Analysis of Albedo Influence on Surface Urban Heat Island by Spaceborne Detection and Airborne Thermography

Giorgio Baldinelli[✉] and Stefania Bonafoni

Department of Engineering, University of Perugia, Perugia, Italy
{giorgio.baldinelli,stefania.bonafoni}@unipg.it

Abstract. Urban environment overheating is gaining growing importance for its consequences on citizens comfort and energy consumption. The surface albedo represents one of the most influencing parameters on the local temperature, therefore, its punctual and large scale detection could give a significant contribution to the urban microclimate assessment. A comparison of satellite data with airborne infrared thermography images is proposed for the city of Florence, starting from temperature analyses and moving to surface albedo assessments. It is shown that, despite the aircraft surveys higher resolution, their area covering limitation, sporadic availability, and high cost make the satellite retrieved data competitive, considering that the current 30 m pixel size of the Landsat images seems to be already suitable for the construction material classification.

Keywords: Albedo · Urban heat island · Infrared thermography · Satellite observations

1 Introduction

The urban overheating during summer months may constitute a public health threat, with people living in cities having more elevated health risks when temperature and humidity increase [1]. A relation seems arising between the discomfort due to climate conditions during the summer heat wave and an overall increase in human mortality, especially amongst the elderly.

The metropolitan heating effect is mainly due to the increase of the urbanization process, with a reduction of the vegetation, together with the raise of city air pollution and anthropogenic heat sources. The urbanization process replaced natural land cover with artificial construction materials and building structures that trap solar radiation during the day, releasing the energy slowly at night. For these reasons, especially on summer, this effect could be dangerous for human health.

The detection of the surface urban heat island (SUHI) and the identification of the surface thermal and optical properties (albedo, in particular, which is a measure of a surface capacity to reflect solar radiation, and it is consequently connected with the surface temperatures) play therefore a crucial role on the definition of city microclimate, together with the monitoring of their evolution. Satellite data fulfill the

© Springer International Publishing Switzerland 2015
V. Murino et al. (Eds.): ICIAP 2015 Workshops, LNCS 9281, pp. 95–102, 2015.
DOI: 10.1007/978-3-319-23222-5_12

requirements of wide territory covering and availability of information relative to different periods; on the other hand, the resolution for the bands necessary for thermal analyses is around 100 m. This circumstance opens the theme of the detailed recognition and classification of materials constituting the urban texture.

The paper proposes a comparison of satellite data with airborne infrared thermography images, characterized by a higher resolution (up to 1 m); the strengths and weaknesses of both methods are analyzed, and the correlation between the satellite retrieved surface albedo and the SUHI is finally investigated.

2   Description of Data Recovery

2.1   Landsat Data

The Landsat Thematic Mapper (TM) sensor is composed by seven bands, six of them (TM1-5, TM7) in the visible, near infrared (NIR) and short-wavelength infrared (SWIR), and one band (TM6) in the thermal infrared (TIR) region.

TM has a native spatial resolution of 30 m for the six reflective bands and 120 m for the thermal band. TM6 is also delivered at 30 m, resampled with a cubic convolution by the US Geological Survey (USGS) Center. In this study, observations of the TM instrument onboard Landsat-5 platform were used (16-day revisit interval), passing over Florence at 11:50 CEST (Central European Summer Time), projected in the Universal Transverse Mercator (UTM) WGS84 coordinate system (meter). Landsat TM data were processed and calibrated in order to convert digital number values to at-sensor spectral radiance values and then to at-sensor reflectances for the reflective bands [2]. Finally, an atmospheric correction was carried out to obtain at-surface reflectivities [3].

2.2   Airborne Data

The airborne measurements were carried out by a Sky Arrow 650 TCNS ERA research aircraft, with a FLIR A40-M thermal camera installed onboard, producing images of brightness temperature in the TIR region (7.5-13.0 μm), with a thermal resolution of 0.08° and an IFOV of 1.3 mrad. Visible images were also acquired during the aircraft flight by means of a Canon EOS-20D camera, allowing a direct comparison between the thermographic and the visible images.

The flight was carried out on July 18, 2010, at around 13:30 CEST, at an average altitude of 1370 m above sea level. Each thermal image has a resolution of 320 × 240 pixels with a nadir pixel size of about 1 m. The area covered by the aerial survey approximately corresponds to the yellow box shown in Fig. 1. The raw thermal images were analyzed by the ThermaCam Researcher Software and then geometrically corrected by Ground Control Points (GCP) and Digital Elevation Model (DEM) before applying the mosaicking tool of Geomatica PCI software.

2.3   LST Recovery from Landsat and Airborne

Land surface temperature (LST) can be obtained from the channel located in the thermal infrared region by inversion of the radiative transfer equation according to the following expression:

$$L_{sens,\lambda} = [\varepsilon_\lambda \, B_\lambda(T_s) + (1 - \varepsilon_\lambda) \, L_\lambda^{\downarrow}] \, \tau_\lambda + L_\lambda^{\uparrow} \qquad (1)$$

Where $L_{sens,\lambda}$ is the at-sensor radiance, ε_λ is the surface emissivity, $B_\lambda(T_s)$ is the Planck's law where T_s is the LST, $L_\lambda^{\downarrow}$ is the downwelling atmospheric radiance, τ_λ is the total atmospheric transmissivity and $L_\lambda^{\uparrow}$ is the upwelling atmospheric radiance. The atmospheric parameters τ_λ, $L_\lambda^{\downarrow}$ and $L_\lambda^{\uparrow}$ can be calculated by a web-based tool [4] able to calculate these atmospheric-correction parameters for the thermal band for a given site and date.

The knowledge of land surface emissivity ε_λ is necessary for the inversion of Eq. (1): a method based on the Normalized Difference Vegetation Index (NDVI) using the at-surface reflectivity values was applied [5].

Fig. 1. Area covered by the aircraft flight for the infrared thermography measurements

3   Surface Urban Heat Island Assessment

Land surface temperature (LST) is a fundamental parameter controlling the surface energy balance of the Earth. In urban areas, LST allows the assessment of the SUHI effect [6]. The SUHI describes the changes in temperature at the urban surface and is strongly linked with the material type and orientation of the surface respect to the sun. Since decades, with the advent of earth observation satellites, remote sensing technology has been widely utilized to measure LST and SUHI: compared to the traditional meteorological observation methods measuring air temperature, spaceborne sensors have the advantages of providing information completely covering large areas at the same time, while conventional data registered *in situ* are typically un-evenly distributed in space.

The SUHI intensity is a parameter used to quantify the urban heating effects: it is defined as the difference in surface temperature between the urban pixels and the surrounding rural areas, used as an average reference, within a given time period:

$$SUHI = LST_{urban} - LST_{rural} \qquad (2)$$

In order to have a rural reference taking into account all the possible scenarios (countryside or suburbs) of the areas surrounding Florence, T_{rural} has been computed as the average among the air temperatures measured by the three rural stations.

The retrieved SUHI images of Florence study area observed by the spaceborne and airborne sensors are shown in Fig. 2. For comparison purposes, the images are gridded with a resolution of 30 m. Beyond the two Landsat images acquired on 10th and 26th July 2010, it is also shown the image obtained averaging the two ones.

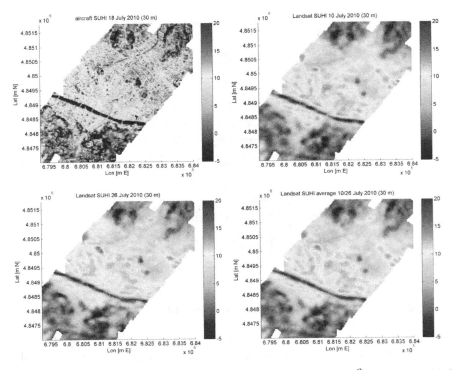

Fig. 2. From top to bottom: SUHI [°C] full image from airborne data (18th July 2010) with 30 m averaged pixels; SUHI [°C] from Landsat TM (10th July 2010); SUHI [°C] from Landsat TM (26th July, 2010); SUHI [°C] from Landsat TM (average of 10th and 26th July). Landsat TM pixels are 30 x 30 m (resampled from thermal observation at 120 m). Lat/lon are in UTM [m], 32 T zone

Despite the clear difference in detailing the spatial features, the trends of the surface urban heat island pattern result similar: negative SUHI values are registered in water bodies and vegetation areas, while higher values are located in the central urbanized areas, as expected. The SUHI, with values higher than 10 K, reaches the maximum impact on the urban in the early afternoon (the airborne flight was made on July 18, 2010, at around 13:30 CEST, while the Landsat passed over Florence on July 10 and July 26, 2010, both at 11:50 CEST).

However, clear differences emerge in the detailed definition due to the different spatial resolution of the Landsat TM and airborne sensor acquisitions, where the former (TM6) has a native 120 m spatial resolution resampled at 30 m by the USGS Center, while the latter is obtained by block-averaging at 30 m the original acquisition at 1 m.

These results suggest that LST from the Landsat TM thermal channel can be considered reliable to evaluate, for instance, the presence and the pattern of the SUHI over a wide urban area: however, it smoothes the heat discontinuities at a finer scale and it is not adequate to resolve details over a complex urban texture.

4   Albedo

Since the Landsat Thematic Mapper sensor provides data on seven bands, it is possible to use five of them (TM1: 0.452–0.518 µm, TM3: 0.626–0.693 µm, TM4: 0.776–0.904 µm, TM5: 1.567–1.784 µm, TM7: 2.097–2.349 µm) to retrieve the shortwave albedo, as described by Liang relation [7]:

$$\alpha = 0.356\alpha_1 + 0.130\alpha_3 + 0.373\alpha_4 + 0.085\alpha_5 + 0.072\alpha_7 - 0.0018 \qquad (3)$$

All of the above mentioned bands have a spatial resolution of 30 m.

Surface albedo is defined as the ratio between the reflected flux density and the incident flux density (irradiance) at the surface level [8]. It represents one of the most influent input parameters in the regulation of the city environment thermal balance. As a matter of fact, the presence of wide surfaces characterized by a high level of solar radiation absorption (low albedo) within city textures, seems linked to the SUHI effect increase [9].

Hence, it results interesting to compare the maps of SUHI (both the Landsat and the airborne ones) with albedo maps, looking for eventual correlations.

Figure 3 reports the full albedo map, next to the SUHI full image from Landsat; since the focus is now directed on the artificial materials, the vegetation and water pixels were excluded from the albedo image, on the basis of two indices: the NDVI and the NDWI (Normalized Difference Water Index) [10].

The patterns result quite correlated (low albedo means higher temperature), confirming the influence of the albedo on SUHI, mainly because of the large presence in highly urbanized towns of absorptive roofs and impervious surfaces, such as asphalt parking lots, roads, squares and pavements.

If the spaceborne detected albedo map is compared with the high definition (1 m) airborne infrared thermography, it emerges that, despite the lower resolution of satellite data, the latter show an effective potential for the assessment of the albedo of single roofs or single streets, with an impressive level of accuracy. Figures 4 and 5 show the detail of two sub-areas of interest: one of the main road of the city (Viale Lavagnini), and the platform roof of Santa Maria Novella railway station.

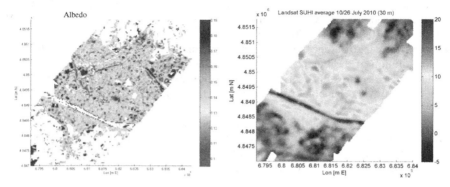

Fig. 3. Comparison between albedo and SUHI [°C] maps retrieved from satellite observations

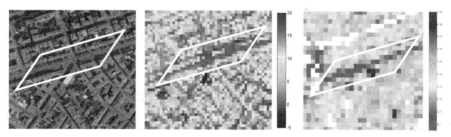

Fig. 4. Detail of an asphalt road: visible image, SUHI (°C) from airborne IR thermography (pixel 1 x 1 m) and Landsat TM albedo (pixel 30 x 30 m)

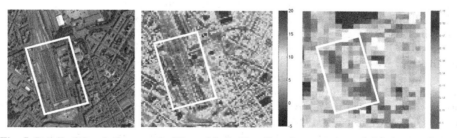

Fig. 5. Detail of the platform roof of Santa Maria Novella railway station: visible image, SUHI (°C) from airborne IR thermography (pixel 1 x 1 m) and Landsat TM albedo (pixel 30 x 30 m)

Figure 4 demonstrates how the low albedo of road asphalt turns into high temperature levels (when the road is not shadowed from the neighbouring buildings); Fig. 5 focuses on roofs with highly absorptive external surface, which produce again the effect of raising the temperature of the surrounding area.

It results interesting to note that the satellite albedo succeeds on detecting these noteworthy wide parts of the urban texture, as well as the high resolution IR thermography [11]. Overall, to recognize the thermal details within a urban environment the airborne image is obviously better than the Landsat one, even though the spaceborne detection has already proven as un useful tool to detect large scale SUHI. Also, the future availability of spaceborne observations with higher spatial resolution at the visible, NIR and SWIR bands would allow to perform albedo analysis at a finer spatial scale. It will be therefore possible to provide details that today are not distinguishable at the 30 m TM resolution, detailing up to the single roof.

5   Conclusions

The use of remote sensing instruments like onboard both satellite and aircraft platforms provide a global monitoring of extended areas and, using suitable recovery algorithms, an inspection of different surface properties: the analysis detail depends on the spatial resolution of the sensors. Peculiar surface properties, such as the surface temperature and albedo, occupy a key position in the material classification and recognition in a urban texture. In particular, this work points out the possibility to detect construction materials and building structures absorbing solar radiation (low albedo) and exposed to thermal effects highlighted by a SUHI increase. The availability of an airborne thermal image and of both thermal and reflective images from Landsat TM over Florence allowed to correlate the absorption and thermal characteristics of particular areas within a urban texture, and to analyze the role of the sensor spatial resolution. Examples of impervious surfaces characterized by low albedo producing the effect of raising their temperature were shown, and even if the current 30 m pixel size of the Landsat data seems to be suitable for the construction material classification, the hoped-for availability of observations with higher spatial resolution would allow to perform albedo recognition at a finer scale. In fact, although aircraft surveys ensure a pixel size of about 1 m, and in some cases provide both thermal and reflective data, they result sporadic, area-limited and expensive.

Acknowledgments. Authors wish to thank Beniamino Gioli and Piero Toscano (CNR IBIMET) for the airborne data processing, Roberta Anniballe for the software support, Claudio Belli for the flight coordination and airborne data acquisition provided by Terrasystem (www.terrasystem.it). Airborne surveys were made in the frame of the EC project BRIDGE (www.bridge-fp7.eu).

References

1. Tan, J., Zheng, Y., Tang, X., Guo, C., Li, L., Song, G., Zhen, X., Yuan, D., Kalkstein, A.J., Li, F., Chen, H.: The heat island and its impact on heat waves and human health in Shanghai. International Journal of Biometeorology **54**(1), 75–84 (2010)
2. Chander, G., Markham, B.L., Helder, D.L.: Summary of Current Radiometric Calibration Coefficients for Landsat MSS, TM, ETM+, and EO-1 ALI sensors. Remote Sensing of Environment **113**, 893–903 (2009)
3. Chavez, P.S.: Image-based atmospheric correction—revisited and improved. Photogrammetric Engineering and Remote Sensing **62**, 1025–1036 (1996)
4. National Aeronautics and Space Administration. http://atmcorr.gsfc.nasa.gov
5. Stathopoulou, M., Cartalis, C.: Downscaling AVHRR land surface temperatures for improved surface urban heat island intensity estimation. Remote Sens. Environ. **113**(15), 2592–2605 (2009)
6. Voogt, J.A.: Urban Heat Island: Hotter Cities - America Institute of Biological Sciences (2004). http://www.actionbioscience.org/environment/voogt.html
7. Liang, S.: Narrowband to broadband conversions of land surface albedo – I Algorithms. Remote Sens. Environ. **76**(2), 213–238 (2000)
8. Schaepman-Strub, G., Martonchik, J., Schaaf, C., Schaepman, M.: What's in a satellite albedo product? In: IGARSS 2006, pp. 2848–2851. IEEE Press, Denver (2006)
9. Santamouris, M., Synnefa, A., Karlessi, T.: Using advanced cool materials in the urban built environment to mitigate heat islands and improve thermal comfort conditions. Sol. Energy **85**(12), 3085–3102 (2011)
10. Xu, H.: Extraction of urban built-up land features from Landsat imagery using a thematic-oriented index combination technique. Photogrammetric Engineering & Remote Sensing **73**(12), 1381–1391 (2007)
11. Baldinelli, G., Bonafoni, S., Anniballe, R., Presciutti, A., Gioli, B., Magliulo, V.: Space-borne detection of roof and impervious surface albedo: Potentialities and comparison with airborne thermography measurements. Solar Energy **113**, 281–294 (2015)

An Interactive Tool for Speed up the Analysis of UV Images of Stradivari Violins

Piercarlo Dondi[1,2]([⊠]), Luca Lombardi[2], Marco Malagodi[1,3],
Maurizio Licchelli[1,3], Tommaso Rovetta[1], and Claudia Invernizzi[1]

[1] Arvedi Laboratory of Non-Invasive Diagnostics, University of Pavia,
via Bell'Aspa 3, 26100 Cremona, Italy
{piercarlo.dondi,marco.malagodi,maurizio.licchelli,tommaso.rovetta,
claudia.invernizzi}@unipv.it
[2] Department of Electrical, Computer and Biomedical Engineering,
University of Pavia, via Ferrata 5, 27100 Pavia, Italy
luca.lombardi@unipv.it
[3] Department of Chemistry, University of Pavia, via Taramelli 12, 27100 Pavia, Italy

Abstract. UV fluorescence photography is widely use in the study of artworks, in particular for the analysis of historical musical instruments. This technique allows seeing important details which cannot be observed with visible light, such as retouching, different paints coats or worn areas. The complexity of the interpretation of the surface of a violin is proportional to its state of preservation: more alterations correspond to a more wide range of colors. We designed an interactive tool able to help the scientist to understand the composition of the surface and in particular the distribution of the colors on the entire instrument, avoiding perception illusion. The result is achieved using a quantized histogram in HSV color space. The tests were performed on UV imagery of the Stradivari violins collection stored by "Museo del Violino" in Cremona.

Keywords: Cultural heritage · Violin · UV fluorescence · Histogram analysis

1 Introduction

UV (Ultraviolet) fluorescence photography is widely use in the study of artworks, in particular for the analysis of historical musical instruments. This technique allows seeing important details which cannot be observed with visible light, such as retouching, different paints coats or worn areas. UV radiation penetrates only superficial levels, so underlying paint coats are not detected; however the analysis of UV fluorescence images gives some clues to apply more precise not destructive techniques, such as XRF (X-Ray Fluorescence spectroscopy)[1] and FTIR (Fourier Transform Infrared spectroscopy)[2], that allow to get information respectively about chemical elements presence and organic and inorganic compounds. Different substances interact in different ways with UV illumination, showing different and typical fluorescence colors, for example a yellow fluorescence

© Springer International Publishing Switzerland 2015
V. Murino et al. (Eds.): ICIAP 2015 Workshops, LNCS 9281, pp. 103–110, 2015.
DOI: 10.1007/978-3-319-23222-5_13

means oils, a green one protein substances such as casein, and so on (complete overview of this technique is in [3]). However it is not so simple analyze an UV photo of a historical violin. The complexity of the interpretation is proportional to the state of preservation of the instrument: more alterations correspond to a more wide range of hues and to possible overlapping ranges of colors.

For this reason we designed an automatic tool, based on the analysis of the image in HSV color space, able to help the scientist to understand the composition of the surface and in particular the distribution of the colors on the entire instrument.

The previous version of this tool [4] works in a semi-automatic way and it was planned for helping expert users to achieve a precise detection on regions of interest avoiding perception illusion (the standard way to analyze such data is in fact based only on human visual interpretation). The tool was able to highlight all the areas of the surface with the same color starting from a sample chosen by the user. The detection is precise and allows a great level of flexibility due to several tolerance thresholds (default values was computed by statistical analysis on a sample dataset). However the user needs a good expertize of the problem for reaching quickly good results, since it is important to choose a valid input area and good thresholds. So the tool is useful for helping the users in analyzing the images, but it can not produce an objective classification due the dependence to subjective choices. Its main goal is to find the occurrence of specific details/colors not clearly visible with the naked eye, but it is not designed for a classification of the entire surface, that can need a long time also for expert people.

This paper presents a new and more general solution able to overcome these constraints. For obtaining a more objective detection of the colors the analysis considers multiple images at a time. A quantized histogram of the entire surface of the instrument is computed, and starting from these data the exact distribution of all colors/materials present on a violin is retrieved. The histogram uses the HSV color space and its quantization is designed to compensate small alterations in saturation and brightness, so it can be used also for studying the occurrence of particular hues on different instruments photographed in different times.

All the tests were performed on UV imagery of the Stradivari violins collection preserved by "Museo del Violino" in Cremona.

The paper is organized as follow: section 2 describes the photographic set used; section 3 describes the proposed method of surface analysis; section 4 shows the results of the tests performed on four Stradivari violins; finally section 5 draws some conclusions.

2   Photographic Setup

A dedicated photographic set (Fig. 1) was prepared following the protocol for the UV induced fluorescence photography created by British Museum as part of CHARISMA project[5]. In particular we used a Nikon D4 camera with 50mm lens, two wood lamps of 40 Watt for providing the UV illumination, and a Kodak 2e gelatin filter, as an alternative to the Schott KV418 currently dismissed.

The backdrop is black for maximize the quality of the UV photos. For each main views of each instrument (front, back, left side and right side) a visible and a UV photo was taken. It is important to guarantee a perfect overlapping between the two kind of images in order to simplify following analysis. A rotating platform, controlled by a computer, was used for moving the violin in order to maintain always the same angles of rotation during different photographic sessions. All the photo was acquired at the same distance, so the proportion of the instrument is always respected.

Fig. 1. The photographic set used for acquisition.

Visible images were acquired with an aperture size of f/10, ISO 100 and an exposure time computed in function of the camera light meter. The illumination in this case was provided by two softbox leds (T = 5400K). UV fluoresce images were acquired with an aperture size of f/10, as for visible, but with ISO 400 and an exposure time of 30 seconds to compensate the low illumination power of the UV lamps.

3   Surface Analysis

Color histogram quantization is a standard and very effective way to retrieve similar images in large databases [6]. This technique can be apply to any kind of color space, depending on the needs; in particular the use of HSV color space, a model closer to human perception, proves to be very efficient [7]. The basic idea of the histogram quantization is to group the wide range of colors of each image

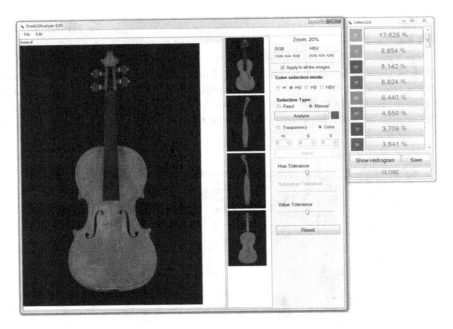

Fig. 2. Execution of the program on Stradivari Hellier (1679)

into a small set of main colors, in order to speed up the research and compare the data in a more objective way.

This approach can be very useful also in our case. As said in the previous sections, historical violins have undergone many modifications and repairs during the centuries, so their surface in UV fluorescence can show a large range of small color variations, that can mix up the interpretation of their composition. Using a well designed quantized histogram in HSV space it is possible to minimize these differences and extract the main colors distribution on the entire instrument.

3.1 HSV Histogram Quantization

For understanding the correct way to subdivide the color space we made a series of statistical analysis on a set of UV images of Stradivari violins. As expected, the more important component is the Hue, while Saturation and Value are less crucial. This behavior is coherent with the characteristic of the fluorescence technique and of the analyzed objects: variations of the pure hues mark directly variation in substances or materials, while variations in saturation and in value are less correlated with them, but can be useful refinements factors. Moreover these two channels are also more influenced by ambient changes so it is better to reduce their contribution in the detection. In fact, even if the photographic set is a controlled environment, some variations between photos are possible due to slight differences in the size of the instruments, or small changes in the angle of incidence of the lamps, or the presence of very reflective paint coats.

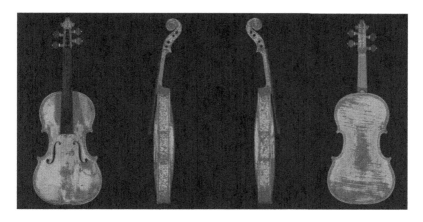

Fig. 3. Quantized histogram of Stradivari Hellier mapped on its surface.

So the chosen quantization of the color space is the follow: 16 bins of Hue; 3 of Saturation (high, medium and low); 3 of Value (high, medium and low). Hues ranges are equals because, even if there are less frequent colors in our testing photos, the current sample set is yet too small to generalize this kind of consideration. Since we want to keep the possibility to analyze different instruments at the same time, we choose to maintain this distribution. However, even if is out of main topic of this work, we consider the possibility to use an irregular quantization scheme for better handle cases in which there is a high concentration of hues in a small range.

Finally, to overcome the possible presence of salt & pepper noise introduced by the high exposure time needed for UV photography and by the presence of the Wratten Filter, a median filter is applied to all the images before the computation of the quantized histogram. At the same time the background, always of the same known color, is excluded a priori from the analysis.

3.2 User Interaction

Our goal is to supply to the researchers an intuitive instrument to quickly analyze and visualize the regions of interest on the surface of the violins. Figure 2 shows the user interface of the tool and the result of the execution on the Stradivari Hellier. The analysis was performed on the four main views (front, back, left side, right side), so all the surface was considered. The right menu shows all the colors in descending frequency order, with their percentage respect to the total. Selecting a color it is possible to see where is placed on one or on all the sides (see the main windows of the interface) and also in what view is more diffused. Two kind of visualizations are available: highlight a single color at a time (Fig. 2) or directly map the entire histogram (or part of it) on the surface (Fig. 3).

The output can be saved as a series of images and then used as a sort of guide for subsequent analysis with more precise technique, like XRF and FTIR, on the

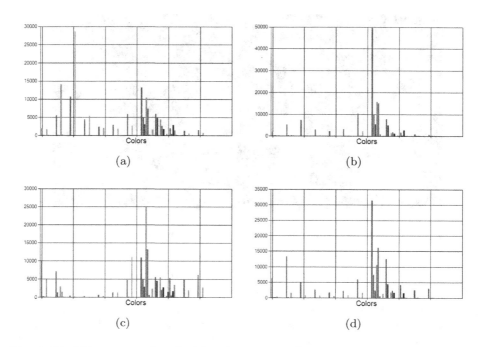

Fig. 4. Final histograms of studied Stradivari violins (on X-axis hues are ordered from red to violet tonalities): (a) Hellier (1679); (b) Cremonese (1715); (c) Vesuvius (1727); (d) Scotland (1734).

real instrument. Historical violins, as art works, must generally be conserved on stable conditions of humidity and temperature so their availability for deep studies is very limited. Highlighting zones with the same hue it is possible to avoid the repetition of tests on similar areas, and so speed up the analysis.

The original detection version [4], based on manual selection of input samples, is still available (see central menu on Fig. 2) in case the user needs to retrieve some specific details present only on one side of the instrument, that obviously will be lost in a global analysis of the surface.

4   Results

This section shows the overall analysis of the tests made on four Stradivari violins of the historical collection of Museo del Violino: Hellier (1679), Cremonese (1715), Vesuvius (1727) and Scotland University (1734).

The four quantized histograms can be seen in Fig. 4. It is interesting to notice that each of them has a unique distribution of colors depending by its state on conservation. The Hellier in particular presents a concentration of brown and yellows hues higher than the other three instruments, that instead show a higher frequency of blue and green colors. This discrepancy is probably related to the

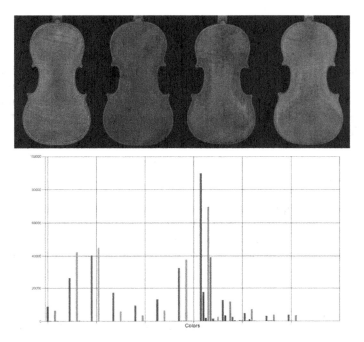

Fig. 5. Combined histogram of the four Stradivari's back plates

fact that the Hellier is the least used and best conserved violin of the four, so it has a more high levels of original paint coats.

The study of these histograms can be very useful for the point of view of preservation. Each of them freezes the actual state of an instrument. So, repeating the experiments periodically, it is possible to evaluate how it evolves in time. At difference of other art objects in fact, historical violins are not only preserved but also actually played, so they can be undergone heavy structural modifications and then need of repairs.

Figure 5 shows an example of the combined histogram obtained analyzing four back plates of different violins instead of four views of the same one. This kind of analysis permits the user to find the most frequent colors on a set of instruments, such information can mark the presence of recurrent substances.

The quantized histogram compensates the discrepancy in illumination between photos taken in different times and shows an objective distribution of the colors on the surfaces. The analysis of the data allows to the restorer to check if a particular color is placed in the same position on all the backs, a clue of a possible original paint coats or of a recurrent element in instrument of different times. A more refined analysis of the backs able to discriminates the distribution and a quantitative measure of the warn areas is actually under study.

5   Conclusions

Currently a common task for researchers and restorers is the analysis of UV images of historical instruments. Up to now the are only tools that use false color visualization or image enhancement techniques, but at the end the analysis is demanded to a pure visual interpretation. This paper describes a new interactive solution to speed up this kind of work. The chosen approach exploits the use of quantized histogram, a well known techniques generally adopted in the field of image retrieval.

Tests made on four Stradivari violins, show that the proposed method is able to give clear and objective information about the color distribution on the surface, avoiding perceptual illusions.

Refinements of the quantization process, adjusting the range distribution, will be made at growing of sample set of UV images. The limited time of availability of the instruments involves a long period to achieve a large set of data.

A comparative analysis between colors detected by the UV analysis and the presence of organic materials detected with FTIR technique is currently under study.

Acknowledgments. We would like to thank the "Fondazione Antonio Stradivari Museo del Violino" of Cremona for the collaboration and availability to improve this research. We are grateful to the "Fondazione Cariplo" for the financing of the research activities.

References

1. Echard, J.P.: In situ multi-element analyses by energy-dispersive X-ray fluorescence on varnishes of historical violins. Spectrochimica Acta Part B **59**, 1663–1667 (2004)
2. Bertrand, L., Robinet, L., Cohen, S., Sandt, C., Le Ho, A., Soulier, B., Lattuati-Derieux, A., Echard, J.P.: Identification of the finishing technique of an early eighteenth century musical instrument using FTIR spectromicroscopy. Analytical and Bioanalytical Chemistry **399**(9), 3025–3032 (2010)
3. Bitossi, G., Giorgi, R., Mauro, M., Salvadori, B., Dei, L.: Spectroscopic Techniques in Cultural Heritage Conservation: A Survey. Applied Spectroscopy Reviews **40**(3), 187–228 (2005)
4. Dondi, P., Lombardi, L., Malagodi, M., Licchelli, M., Rovetta, T., Invernizzi, C.: Semi automatic system for UV images analysis of historical musical instruments.In: Proc. SPIE 9527, Optics for Arts, Architecture, and Archaeology V, 95270H (2015)
5. Dyer, J., Verri, G., Cupitt, J.: Multispectral Imaging in Reflectance and Photo-induced Luminescence modes: A User Manual. The British Museum, Charisma Project, pp. 81–85 (2013)
6. Meskaldji, K.; Boucherkha, S.; Chikhi, S.: Color quantization and its impact on color histogram based image retrieval accuracy. In: Proc. of First International Conference on The Networked Digital Technologies, NDT 2009, pp. 515–517 (2009)
7. Hsueh S.; Wu, H.: Building Specified Web-Searching Image Database Using Quantization-Color-Size Histogram, In: Proc. of International Symposium on Computer, Consumer and Control (IS3C), pp. 694–697 (2012)

Local Angular Patterns
for Color Texture Classification

Claudio Cusano[1], Paolo Napoletano[2], and Raimondo Schettini[2]($\boxtimes$)

[1] Università degli Studi di Pavia, via Ferrata 1, 27100 Pavia, Italy
claudio.cusano@unipv.it
[2] DISCo (Dipartimento di Informatica, Sistemistica E Comunicazione),
Università degli Studi di Milano-Bicocca, Viale Sarca 336, 20126 Milano, Italy
{napoletano,schettini}@disco.unimib.it

Abstract. The description of color texture under varying lighting conditions is still an open issue. We defined a new color texture descriptor, that we called Local Angular Patterns, specially designed to be robust to changes in the color of the illuminant. The results show that our descriptor outperforms the state-of-the-art on a dataset of food textures.

1 Introduction

The role of color in texture classification has been widely debated in the literature. Despite the number and the depth of the experimental verifications, it is still not completely clear how much and under what circumstances color information is beneficial. Notable examples of this kind of analysis are the work by Mäenpää and Pietikäinen [14], and that by Bianconi *et al.* [4]. They observed how color can be effective, but only in those cases where illumination conditions do not vary too much between training and test sets. In fact, methods that exploit color information greatly suffer variations in the lighting conditions. A possible strategy to exploit color in texture classification consists in the extraction of image features that are invariant with respect to changes in the illumination. Khan *et al.* [13], for instance, considered a diagonal/offset model for illumination variations, deduced from it an image normalization transformation, and finally extracted Gabor features from the normalized images. Other color normalization techniques can be used for this purpose. Finlayson *et al.* proposed rank-based features obtained from invariant color representations [10]. Seifi *et al.*, instead, proposed to characterize color textures by analyzing the rank correlation between pixels located in the same neighborhood. They obtained a correlation measure which is related to the colors of the pixels, and is not sensitive to illumination changes [16]. The reader can also refer to [3,5–7,9,12]. In this paper we propose a new texture descriptor that has been specially designed to deal with variations of the color of the illuminant. We will show how the proposed descriptor, that we call Local Angular Patterns, outperforms all the other approaches considered.

© Springer International Publishing Switzerland 2015
V. Murino et al. (Eds.): ICIAP 2015 Workshops, LNCS 9281, pp. 111–118, 2015.
DOI: 10.1007/978-3-319-23222-5_14

2 Proposed Descriptor

Many descriptors have been proposed to encode color and texture information at the same time. Several of them consist just in the replication to multiple color channels of known techniques that have been originally designed for intensity images. The introduction of color information into a texture descriptor improves its capability in discriminating certain types of classes. However, it also increases its sensitivity to changes in the lighting conditions in general and in the illuminant color in particular. If we assume a simplified illumination model, some descriptors are capable of exploiting color information while, at the same time, staying invariant to illumination changes. For instance, Finlayson *et al.* demonstrated how, under a diagonal illumination model in the RGB color space, the relative order of pixels values is preserved [10] (e.g. redder pixels stay redder independently on the color of the illuminant). Therefore descriptors based on the relative order among pixels (Local Binary Patterns, for instance) should be invariant with respect to the illumination color. However, in practice this is far for the truth, as we will show in the section on the experimental results. In fact, illumination changes do not follow the diagonal illumination model because of the presence of acquisition noise and of non-linear interactions between the illuminant, the sample and the camera [1,2,4].

The luminance value L, computed from the RGB components as $L = 0.299R + 0.587G + 0.114B$, has been demonstrated to be very robust to illumination changes. Part of its robustness, that is due to the weighted averaging of the color channels, is paid in terms of the amount of information lost during the conversion process. We propose the use of a new color space that keeps part of the advantages of using the luminance, while preserving the color information. The conversion from RGB to this new color space consists in two steps: first the RGB coordinates are projected to the RG, RB and GB planes, then luminance is computed for the three projections. We call this, the P3 color space since it is obtained through three different projections. The transformation from RGB is linear, and corresponds to the following equation:

$$\begin{pmatrix} P_1 \\ P_2 \\ P_3 \end{pmatrix} = \begin{bmatrix} 0 & 0.587 & 0.114 \\ 0.299 & 0 & 0.114 \\ 0.299 & 0.587 & 0 \end{bmatrix} \times \begin{pmatrix} R \\ G \\ B \end{pmatrix}, \tag{1}$$

where P_1, P_2 and P_3 are the components of the new space.

Equation (1) defines a full-rank transformation, therefore it preserves all the color information. Moreover, since none of the coefficients is negative the transformed values enjoy the order-preserving property of RGB under the diagonal illumination model. We will show how the simple substitution of RGB with P3 brings significant improvements in the classification of color textures under varying illumination conditions.

2.1 Local Angular Patterns

Original LBPs are invariant with respect to scalings of the color channels, that is, they are invariant with respect to the diagonal illumination model. We propose a descriptor which is invariant with respect to other kind of transformations of the color space. Interpreting colors as three-dimensional vectors, we may notice how the angle between two of them is invariant with respect to similarity transformations (i.e. rotations, reflections, uniform scalings, and their combinations). Angular information is encoded by the proposed descriptor in a way which is very similar to that used by standard LBPs for the encoding of the pixels' values. Therefore, we call it LAP, since it represents information about Local Angular Patterns.

LAP is computed as follows: for each pixel p a circular neighborhood $c_1, \ldots, c_n$ is considered and the average color $\mu = \left(\sum_{i=1}^{n} c_i \right) / n$ is computed. The angle α between p and μ is computed:

$$\alpha = \cos^{-1} \left(\frac{p \cdot \mu}{\|p\| \|\mu\|} \right), \tag{2}$$

and similar angles $\beta_1, \ldots, \beta_n$ are computed for each of the neighbors of p:

$$\beta_i = \cos^{-1} \left(\frac{c_i \cdot \mu}{\|c_i\| \|\mu\|} \right), \quad i \in \{1, \ldots n\}. \tag{3}$$

A pattern of n bits is formed as a results of the comparison between α and $\beta_1, \ldots, \beta_n$. In practice, each bit tells whether or not the corresponding neighbor is more far away from the average than the central pixel. After their computation, the angular patterns are treated as standard LBPs: a histogram of occurrences is formed, possibly by counting in the same bin all the non-uniform (i.e. irregular) patterns.

To combine the advantages of the P3 color space with those of LAP, we adopted the following strategy: we projected the pixels on the RG, RB and GB planes, and we computed three LAP histograms (one for each projection). The final descriptor is formed by concatenating the three histograms with the three obtained by computing standard LBPs on the three components of the P3 space. In this way the descriptor contains parts that are invariant to scalings of the color channels, and parts that are invariant to similarity transformations in the color space. Their combination is thus expected to be robust to a variety of transformations of the color space.

3 Experiments

For the experiments we used the Raw Food Texture database (RawFooT), that has been specially designed to investigate the robustness of descriptors and classification methods with respect to variations in the lighting conditions [8]. Classes correspond to 68 samples of raw food, including various kind of meat, fish, cereals, fruit etc. Samples taken under D65 at light direction $\theta = 24°$ are showed in Fig. 1. The database includes images of 68 samples of textures, acquired under 46 lighting conditions which may differ in:

1. the light direction: 24, 30, 36, 42, 48,54, 60, 66, and 90 degrees;

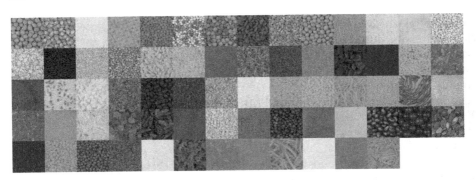

Fig. 1. Overview of the 68 classes included in the Raw Food Texture database. For each class it is shown the image taken under D65 at direction $\theta=24°$.

2. illuminant color: 9 outdoor illuminants: D40, D45, ..., D95; 6 indoor illuminants: 2700 K, 3000 K, 4000 K, 5000 K, 5700 K and 6500 K, we will refer to these as L27, L30, ..., L65;
3. intensity: 100%, 75%, 50% and 25% of the maximum achievable level;
4. combination of these factors.

For each of the 68 classes we considered 16 patches obtained by dividing the original texture image, that is of size 800×800 pixels, in 16 non-overlapping squares of size 200×200 pixels. For each class we selected eight patches for training and eight for testing by following a chessboard pattern. We form subsets of $68 \times (8 + 8) = 1088$ patches by taking the training and test patches from images taken under different lighting conditions. In this way we defined 364 subsets, grouped in six texture classification tasks.

1. *No variations*: 46 image subsets. Each subset is composed of training and test images taken under the same lighting condition.
2. *Light intensity*: 12 image subsets obtained by combining the 4 intensity variations. Each subset is composed of training and test images with different light intensity values.
3. *Daylight temperature*: 132 image subsets obtained by combining all the 12 daylight temperature variations. Each subset is composed of training and test images with different light temperatures.
4. *LED temperature*: 30 image subsets obtained by combining all the 6 LED temperature variations. Each subset is composed of training and test images with different light temperatures.
5. *Daylight vs. LED*: 72 image subsets obtained by combining 12 daylight temperatures with 6 LED temperatures.
6. *Color directions*: 72 image subsets obtained by combining all the 9 combinations of color temperatures and light directions. Each subset is composed of training and test images with different lighting conditions.

In all the experiments we used the nearest neighbor classification strategy: given a patch in the test set, its distance with respect to all the training patches is computed. The prediction of the classifier is the class of closest element in the training set. For this purpose , after some preliminary tests with several descriptors in which we evaluated the most common distance measures, we decided to use the $L1$ distance: $d(\mathbf{x}, \mathbf{y}) = \sum_{i=1}^{N} |\mathbf{x_i} - \mathbf{y_i}|$, where $\mathbf{x}$ and $\mathbf{y}$ are two feature vectors. All the experiments have been conducted under the *maximum ignorance* assumption, that is, no information about the lighting conditions of the test patches is available for the classification method and for the descriptors. Performance is reported as classification rate (i.e., the ratio between the number of correctly classified images and the number of test images).

For the comparison we selected a number of descriptors from several classes of approaches [4,15]: color based, statistical, spectral, structural and hybrid. Most of the considered descriptors have been applied to both color and gray-scale images. The gray-scale image is the luminance of the image and is obtained by using the standard formula: $L = 0.299R + 0.587G + 0.114B$.

The descriptors evaluated are:
- a single 256-dimensional gray level histogram as well as 512- and 768-dimensional color histograms (computed on different color spaces);
- A set of 10 normalized *chromaticity moments* as defined in [4];
- contrast, correlation, energy, entropy and homogeneity features extracted from *co-occurrence matrices*, so obtaining 5 components for each color channel;
- *Gabor* features computed as the mean and standard deviation of four orientations extracted at four frequencies, 96 components for each color channel;
- *opponent Gabor* features extracted from several inter/intra channel combinations;
- *Dual Tree Complex Wavelet Transform* (DT-CWT) features with four scales, two features (mean and standard deviation), and three color channels, so obtaining 24 components;
- morphological features (*granulometries*) to each color channel separately. The number of components used is 78;
- *Gist* features with eight orientations and four scales for each channel, for a total of 1536 components;
- *Histogram of Oriented Gradients* (HOG), in the version described in [11].We considered nine histograms with nine bins that is concatenated to make a 81-dimensional feature vector [11];
- gray *Local Binary Patterns* (LBP) and its color variants applied to different color spaces such as, the RGB, CIE-Lab and Ohta's $I_1I_2I_3$ [14]. We considered 243 LPBs for each color channel;
- combination of LBP computed on pairs of color channels, namely the *Opponent Color LBP* (OCLBP). We considered 243 LPBs for each color channel;
- Local Color Contrast, as defined in [7], with 499 components.

Table 1 reports the performance obtained by the considered and proposed descriptors in each single classification task as *average* and *minimum accuracy*. The last column of the table represents the *average rank* over the six tasks for each descriptor. It is clear that color information is very useful when training and test images are taken under the *same illumination*. In fact, the histogram

Table 1. Evaluation of several texture descriptors. For each classification task, the best result is reported in bold.

Features	No variations avg (min)	Light intensity avg (min)	Daylight temp. avg (min)	LED temp. avg (min)	Daylight vs LED avg (min)	Temp. & Dir. avg (min)	Rank avg
Hist. L	78.32 (60.66)	6.77 (1.47)	49.94 (11.95)	27.18 (5.88)	38.05 (6.43)	10.45 (1.29)	19.67
Hist. H V	96.38 (84.56)	31.45 (14.52)	49.11 (9.93)	51.56 (23.35)	44.39 (9.19)	16.47 (4.23)	12.33
Hist. RGB	94.93 (87.13)	15.89 (3.12)	56.45 (18.20)	37.51 (12.68)	43.44 (8.00)	15.53 (2.76)	14.83
Hist. rgb	**97.24** (92.46)	67.08 (36.95)	37.35 (6.43)	17.38 (3.31)	25.71 (5.15)	20.16 (2.39)	14.17
Chrom. mom.	82.54 (58.46)	68.43 (48.90)	33.41 (4.96)	18.66 (3.68)	24.16 (5.06)	17.03 (2.21)	17.00
Coocc. matr.	35.33 (9.93)	7.20 (2.02)	23.02 (9.74)	19.01 (6.62)	19.88 (5.61)	3.30 (0.18)	22.50
Coocc. matr. L	18.68 (1.47)	3.32 (0.00)	16.99 (6.99)	9.49 (3.31)	12.94 (2.85)	2.49 (0.00)	24.00
DT-CWT	92.26 (81.62)	21.68 (1.65)	66.29 (25.92)	42.31 (14.34)	49.77 (15.44)	19.23 (3.12)	12.83
DT-CWT L	72.85 (58.09)	10.65 (1.29)	60.13 (27.39)	32.70 (4.04)	44.06 (5.06)	14.70 (1.47)	18.00
Gabor RGB	93.02 (61.76)	66.96 (32.35)	64.81 (20.77)	38.13 (12.13)	48.03 (12.59)	27.18 (3.49)	10.00
Gabor L	72.91 (70.04)	46.57 (18.75)	68.94 (59.56)	67.62 (58.82)	66.86 (53.40)	27.58 (2.57)	9.50
Opp. Gabor	96.15 (59.38)	21.51 (3.49)	67.75 (22.98)	41.78 (14.34)	50.80 (15.07)	20.22 (3.86)	11.17
Gist RGB	66.20 (62.50)	55.06 (31.99)	55.49 (28.31)	36.78 (13.24)	43.41 (13.79)	25.13 (2.76)	15.17
Granulometry	91.98 (51.65)	63.73 (27.76)	69.80 (21.51)	33.58 (6.80)	48.79 (6.34)	22.20 (1.65)	11.67
HoG	46.74 (43.20)	37.52 (24.82)	41.14 (29.60)	35.29 (22.24)	36.30 (19.30)	16.99 (3.49)	18.00
LBP L	80.37 (77.02)	51.15 (17.83)	77.76 (72.24)	70.77 (54.60)	73.15 (55.06)	29.54 (5.51)	7.67
LBP RGB	93.55 (90.81)	68.87 (33.46)	72.40 (24.63)	48.39 (15.07)	56.08 (16.82)	23.72 (0.55)	7.00
LBP Lab	92.90 (88.42)	71.88 (32.54)	70.61 (24.08)	51.56 (21.69)	56.00 (19.49)	27.55 (3.31)	6.33
LBP $I_1I_2I_3$	91.40 (82.90)	66.28 (28.12)	70.58 (25.92)	49.90 (18.38)	54.76 (17.00)	27.05 (1.10)	8.67
OCLBP	95.92 (92.28)	**78.75** (51.47)	67.92 (19.67)	49.94 (15.81)	53.93 (15.81)	25.73 (1.65)	6.83
LCC	92.92 (88.60)	62.64 (26.84)	88.78 (73.71)	74.25 (46.88)	78.82 (50.64)	31.13 (5.15)	5.00
Proposed							
LBP P3	88.59 (85.85)	56.22 (16.36)	86.37 (79.60)	76.53 (53.49)	79.84 (54.14)	31.50 (4.60)	5.67
LAP	93.76 (89.71)	65.59 (24.26)	**90.02** (75.74)	**76.86** (49.63)	**80.74** (50.46)	**33.11** (3.12)	3.00

Table 2. Accuracy of selected color descriptors combined with different preprocessing methods.

Features	No variations avg (min)	Light intensity avg (min)	Daylight temp. avg (min)	LED temp. avg (min)	Daylight vs LED avg (min)	Temp. & Dir. avg (min)
Histogram rgb (Hrgb)	97.24 (92.46)	67.08 (36.95)	37.35 (6.43)	17.38 (3.31)	25.71 (5.15)	20.16 (2.39)
Hrgb + McCann	98.66 (95.77)	65.40 (38.60)	32.79 (7.17)	17.54 (2.76)	23.76 (5.70)	16.22 (2.21)
Hrgb + Frankle	**98.82** (95.77)	66.42 (39.52)	34.81 (6.99)	17.95 (3.12)	24.45 (5.24)	16.73 (2.76)
Hrgb + Gray-World	98.81 (96.32)	47.87 (19.30)	51.90 (10.48)	22.42 (1.10)	35.12 (0.46)	13.41 (0.00)
Hrgb + Gray-Edge	98.36 (96.32)	**78.80** (59.38)	64.46 (17.10)	37.95 (8.46)	46.55 (9.47)	**33.42** (6.25)
Hrgb + W. Gray-Edge	98.16 (84.01)	75.97 (55.15)	**64.62** (18.38)	**38.65** (9.74)	**46.90** (8.46)	33.08 (6.99)
Hrgb + Compr.Norm.	91.16 (80.88)	52.63 (21.32)	49.06 (10.11)	19.06 (4.04)	31.95 (4.50)	16.35 (0.74)
LBP-RGB (LBP)	93.55 (90.81)	68.87 (33.46)	72.40 (24.63)	48.39 (15.07)	56.08 (16.82)	23.72 (0.55)
LBP + McCann	94.07 (91.18)	69.61 (38.24)	76.21 (31.80)	**56.59** (26.47)	**61.71** (23.71)	**28.42** (2.94)
LBP + Frankle	**94.21** (90.62)	68.37 (33.64)	71.99 (24.45)	47.73 (16.54)	55.40 (16.54)	24.71 (2.21)
LBP + Gray-World	93.63 (90.81)	**80.01** (62.68)	**77.88** (37.68)	47.09 (12.68)	58.19 (13.51)	27.10 (0.74)
LBP + Gray-Edge	94.03 (91.18)	62.96 (27.02)	72.79 (30.33)	44.01 (10.66)	54.02 (13.60)	22.75 (0.37)
LBP + W. Gray-Edge	93.93 (81.62)	63.45 (26.65)	72.83 (27.76)	44.09 (10.85)	53.98 (14.25)	22.95 (0.55)
LBP + Compr. Norm.	93.85 (87.32)	57.63 (17.28)	55.29 (3.12)	20.70 (1.47)	35.02 (1.47)	18.16 (0.00)
LAP	93.76 (89.71)	65.59 (24.26)	**90.02** (75.74)	**76.86** (49.63)	**80.74** (50.46)	33.11 (3.12)
LAP + McCann	91.47 (87.87)	66.82 (30.33)	88.11 (76.65)	72.18 (42.10)	77.34 (44.12)	**34.61** (7.54)
LAP + Frankle	91.86 (86.95)	65.75 (31.07)	88.03 (73.16)	69.18 (38.24)	75.09 (38.97)	32.84 (7.90)
LAP + Gray-World	90.38 (85.66)	**76.18** (54.96)	79.69 (49.82)	49.20 (10.11)	59.58 (10.48)	27.50 (4.78)
LAP + Gray-Edge	92.48 (88.60)	56.57 (18.93)	85.01 (62.13)	58.75 (19.12)	67.87 (22.52)	26.78 (4.04)
LAP + W. Gray-Edge	92.39 (82.35)	56.77 (20.59)	85.07 (61.95)	59.28 (22.43)	68.11 (23.44)	26.84 (4.04)
LAP + Compr. Norm.	**95.86** (90.07)	57.80 (17.28)	61.15 (6.62)	24.83 (0.18)	39.63 (1.93)	20.86 (1.10)

rgb descriptor achieves the best accuracy rate of 97.24% with a minimum value of 92.46%. In this case, also other histogram schemes achieve good performance. The best LBP scheme is the OCLBP with a classification rate of 95.92%. The proposed LAP achieves 93.76% thus occupying the 6th position in this task with a distance of 3.5% from the best. When the light intensity changes, the most robust descriptor is the OCLBP with a classification accuracy of 78.75% and a minimum value of 51.47%. Several color descriptors achieve a classification rate of about 65% (that is about 10% less than the best) with the LAP occupying the 8th position. In contrast, descriptors computed on gray-scale images struggle to deal with such a variability. In the remaining classification tasks, that are the focus of this work, it is clear that both LAP and LBP P3 achieve the best performance. The closest descriptors are: LCC, LBP L, LBP RGB, GABOR L and LBP Lab. In the case of *Daylight temperature* variations, the LBP L achieves a classification rate of about 13% less than the LAP. In both cases of *LED temperature* variations and *Daylight vs LED*, the LBP L achieves a classification rate of about 7% less than the LAP. It is important to point out that all the evaluated descriptors achieve poor performance in the *Temperature and Direction* task (about 30% on average and with a lowest performance below to the 1%). Overall, looking at the average rank column, the proposed LAP is better than existing descriptors.

Illumination variations can be also compensated by preprocessing images with a color normalization method. Color normalization methods try to assign a constant color to objects even under different illumination conditions [7]. In order to evaluate this strategy, we have preprocessed the database by using several existing normalization methods and next we have extracted features by using the best color descriptors from the set of descriptors evaluated in table 1. More precisely, we considered two implementations of the Retinex method: the *McCann99* and the *Frankle-McCann*. Furthermore, we considered the Gray World, two variants of edge based algorithm, the Gray-Edge and the weighted Gray-Edge method, and the Comprehensive Normalization. Table 2 reports the performance obtained by these color normalization methods combined with the selected descriptors. It is clear that color normalization helps to improve performance in the case of *no variations* and *light intensity* variations. In the remaining tasks, histogram *rgb* and LBP RGB achieve better performance, while LAP is negatively influenced by the use of preprocessing.

4   Conclusions

We focused, here, on texture classification under variable light color. To this purpose, we proposed a new descriptor that exploits a novel color space transformation and a novel descriptor based on Local Angular Patterns. Such a descriptor, that has been designed to be robust with respect to scalings of the color channels and to similarity transformations in the color space, significantly outperformed the state of the art.

References

1. Bianco, S., Bruna, A., Naccari, F., Schettini, R.: Color space transformations for digital photography exploiting information about the illuminant estimation process. JOSA A **29**(3), 374–384 (2012)
2. Bianco, S., Bruna, A.R., Naccari, F., Schettini, R.: Color correction pipeline optimization for digital cameras. Journal of Electronic Imaging **22**(2), 023014–023014 (2013)

3. Bianco, S., Cusano, C., Napoletano, P., Schettini, R.: On the robustness of color texture descriptors across illuminants. In: Petrosino, A. (ed.) ICIAP 2013, Part II. LNCS, vol. 8157, pp. 652–662. Springer, Heidelberg (2013)

4. Bianconi, F., Harvey, R., Southam, P., Fernández, A.: Theoretical and experimental comparison of different approaches for color texture classification. J. of Electronic Imaging **20**(4), 043006–043006 (2011)

5. Cusano, C., Napoletano, P., Schettini, R.: Illuminant invariant descriptors for color texture classification. In: Tominaga, S., Schettini, R., Trémeau, A. (eds.) CCIW 2013. LNCS, vol. 7786, pp. 239–249. Springer, Heidelberg (2013)

6. Cusano, C., Napoletano, P., Schettini, R.: Intensity and color descriptors for texture classification. IS&T/SPIE Electronic Imaging, 866113–866113 (2013)

7. Cusano, C., Napoletano, P., Schettini, R.: Combining local binary patterns and local color contrast for texture classification under varying illumination. JOSA A **31**(7), 1453–1461 (2014)

8. Cusano, C., Napoletano, P., Schettini, R.: Evaluating color texture descriptors under large variations of controlled lighting conditions. IEEE Transaction in Image Processing (2015, submitted)

9. Drbohlav, O., Leonardis, A.: Towards correct and informative evaluation methodology for texture classification under varying viewpoint and illumination. Computer Vision and Image Understanding **114**(4), 439–449 (2010)

10. Finlayson, G., Hordley, S., Schaefer, G., Yun Tian, G.: Illuminant and device invariant colour using histogram equalisation. Pattern recognition **38**(2), 179–190 (2005)

11. Junior, O.L., Delgado, D., Gonçalves, V., Nunes, U.: Trainable classifier-fusion schemes: an application to pedestrian detection. In: Intelligent Transportation Systems (2009)

12. Kandaswamy, U., Schuckers, S.A., Adjeroh, D.: Comparison of texture analysis schemes under nonideal conditions. IEEE Transactions on Image Processing **20**(8), 2260–2275 (2011)

13. Khan, R., Muselet, D., Trémeau, A.: Classical texture features and illumination color variations. In: Proc. third Int'l Conf. on Machine Vision, pp. 280–285 (2010)

14. Mäenpää, T., Pietikäinen, M.: Classification with color and texture: jointly or separately? Pattern Recognition **37**(8), 1629–1640 (2004)

15. Mirmehdi, M., Xie, X., Suri, J.: Handbook of Texture Analysis. Imperial College Press, London (2008)

16. Seifi, M., Song, X., Muselet, D., Tremeau, A.: Color texture classification across illumination changes. In: Conf. on Colour in Graphics, Imaging, and Vision, pp. 332–337 (2010)

Complexity Perception of Texture Images

Gianluigi Ciocca[1,2], Silvia Corchs[1,2(✉)], and Francesca Gasparini[1,2]

[1] Dipartimento di Informatica, Sistemistica e Comunicazione,
University of Milano-Bicocca, Viale Sarca 336, 20126 Milano, Italy
{ciocca,corchs,gasparini}@disco.unimib.it
[2] NeuroMi - Milan Center for Neuroscience, Milan, Italy

Abstract. Visual complexity perception plays an important role in the fields of both psychology and computer vision: it can be useful not only to investigate human perception but also to better understand the properties of the objects being perceived. In this paper we investigate the complexity perception of texture images. To this end we perform a psycho-physical experiment on real texture patches. The complexity of each image is assessed on a continuous scale. At the end of the evaluation, each observer indicates the criteria used to assess texture complexity. The most frequent criteria used are regularity, understandability, familiarity and edge density. As candidate complexity measures we consider thirteen image features and we correlate each of them with the subjective scores collected during the experiment. The performance of these correlations are evaluated in terms of Pearson correlation coefficients. The four measures that show the highest correlations are energy, edge density, compression ratio and a visual clutter measure, in accordance with the verbal descriptions collected by the questionnaire.

Keywords: Image complexity · Psycho-physical experiment · Color image features · Texture

1 Introduction

Visual scenes are composed of numerous textures, objects, and colors. Texture helps us to understand the visual world. It provides a cue to the shape and orientation of a surface, to segmenting an image into meaningful regions, and to classifying those regions in terms of material properties [1]. Human texture processing has not yet been fully understood given its complexity and the involvement of mechanisms at different levels. Researches have addressed the problem of texture processing using both artificial and natural materials [2]. Investigating the complexity of real texture images can provide new insights in understanding how humans perceive texture and if the material recognition influences such process. Some studies of visual complexity perception deal with real world images [3] but little research has been carried out into the visual complexity of texture images.

Depending on the specific task and the application domain, different definitions of image complexity are possible. From a purely mathematical point of view,

© Springer International Publishing Switzerland 2015
V. Murino et al. (Eds.): ICIAP 2015 Workshops, LNCS 9281, pp. 119–126, 2015.
DOI: 10.1007/978-3-319-23222-5_15

Kolmogorov [4] defines the complexity of an object as the length of the shortest program that can construct the object from basic elements, or description language. Snodgrass et al. [5] refer to the visual complexity as the amount of detail or intricacy in an image. Birkhoff [6] relates the image complexity to visual aesthetics. Heaps and Hande [7] define complexity as the degree of difficulty in providing a verbal description of an image. Visual complexity is in general represented by a multi-dimensional space, where according to Oliva et al. [3], quantity of objects, clutter, openness, symmetry, organization and variety of colors modulate the shape of the complexity space for the case of real-world scenes.

In a previous work [8] we have studied the image complexity perception of real world images. In particular we have investigated how different image features, based both on color and spatial properties, correlate with the collected subjective data. We have found that features that work on grayscale values better correlate with subjective data than features developed to measure color properties, suggesting that color does not influence significantly the perception of image complexity when real world scenes are considered. In this kind of images, in fact the lightness component provides enough information about the semantic content.

Recently, Guo et al. [9,10] have considered the perception of texture complexity. They identified five low-level characteristics that are used by humans to perceive the visual complexity of textures: regularity, roughness, directionality, density, and understandability. Visual complexity is a function of not only each individual characteristic but also of interactions between them. The authors conclude that visual complexity perception is related to the objective characteristics of a texture as well as respondents subjective knowledge.

In this paper we investigate the complexity perception of texture images. To this end we perform a psycho-physical experiment on real texture patches. During the experiment no explicit definition of *complexity* was provided to the observers. The complexity of each image is assessed on a continuous scale. At the end of the evaluation, each observer was asked to fill out a questionnaire indicating the criteria used to assess texture complexity. To find out if objective measure can predict subjective scores, we here consider thirteen image features that measure colors as well as other spatial properties of the images. We correlate each of them with the subjective scores collected during the experiment and we evaluate the performance of these correlations in terms of Pearson correlation coefficients. In Section 2 the experimental set up is described, while in Section 3 the thirteen objective measures are listed. Finally in Section 4 we report the correlation results and the analysis of the verbal descriptions.

2   Subjective Experiment

The aim of this experiment is to assess the complexity perception of real texture images. In this evaluation, both bottom-up and top-down cognitive mechanisms may be active. In our experiment we intentionally gave as little guidance as possible about the definition of complexity with the aim to elucidate if some common criteria in perceiving complexity can be extracted from the experimental data.

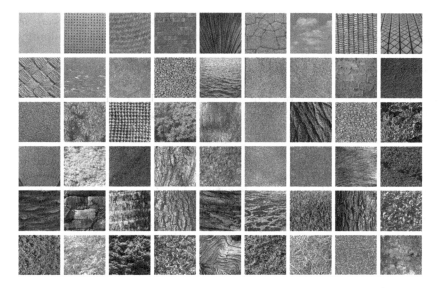

Fig. 1. Thumbnails of the texture images chosen to sample each of the 54 classes in the VisTex data set, ordered from the less complex (top left) to the most complex (bottom right), according to the subjective scores.

Participants and Stimuli

A group of 17 observers with normal or corrected-to-normal visual acuity and normal color vision took part in the experimental session. All the observers were recruited in the Department of Informatics System and Communication of the University of Milano Bicocca. Their ages ranged from 23 to 50 years old.

The 54 images used as stimuli belong to the VisTex25 data set [11]. This data set consists of 864 images representing 54 classes of natural objects or scenes captured under non-controlled conditions with a variety of devices. From each of the 54 classes, one image has been chosen.

Experimental Setup

The images are individually shown on a web-interface. They are shown in a random order, different for each subject. The subjects report their complexity judgments (scores) by dragging a slider onto a continuous scale in the range [0-100]. They can look at the stimuli for an unlimited time. The position of the slider is automatically reset after each evaluation. A grayscale chart is shown to calibrate the brightness and the contrast of the monitor. Ishihara color test have been preliminarily presented to the observers for estimating color vision deficiency. Nine training images are presented to the observers prior to the 54 test ones. These images have been used to train the subjects about the range of complexity to be evaluated. The corresponding data has been discarded and not considered as experimental data. At the end of the test, the observers were asked to verbally describe the characteristics of textures that affect their evaluation of visual complexity perception.

We have applied Z-score and outliers detection to obtain the final Mean Opinion Scores (MOS) of each image. The raw complexity score r_{ij} for the i-th subject ($i = 1, ...14$ in case of color images or $i = 1, ...17$ in case of grayscale images) and j-th image ($j = 1, ...29$) was converted into Z scores:

$$z_{ij} = \frac{r_{ij} - \bar{r}_i}{\sigma_i} \tag{1}$$

where $\bar{r}_i$ is the average of the complexity scores over all images evaluated by the subject, and σ_i is the standard deviation. The Z scores were then averaged across subjects after the removal of the outlier scores. A score for an image was considered to be an outlier, and thus removed from the average computation, if it was outside an interval of width two standard deviations about the average score for that image.

3   Objective Measures

In what follows we list and briefly describe the candidate complexity measures here considered. The first four of them work on grayscale images. They measure properties of the Grey Level Co-occurrence Matrix (GLCM), which is one of the earliest techniques used for image texture analysis. In particular GLCM is capable of identifying the repetition, uniformity, disorder, contrast, and heterogeneity within images. In this work the MATLAB function *graycoprops* is used:

$\mathcal{M}_1$: Contrast, it is a measure of the intensity contrast between a pixel and its neighbor over the whole image.

$\mathcal{M}_2$: Correlation, it is a measure of how correlated a pixel is to its neighbor over the whole image.

$\mathcal{M}_3$: Energy, it is the sum of squared elements in the GLCM.

$\mathcal{M}_4$: Homogeneity, it measures the closeness of the distribution of elements in the GLCM with respect to the GLCM diagonal.

Measures from $\mathcal{M}_5$ to $\mathcal{M}_8$ describe image features associated to frequency, edge density, compression and number of regions:

$\mathcal{M}_5$: Frequency factor, it is the ratio between the frequency corresponding to the 99% of the image energy and the Nyquist frequency.

$\mathcal{M}_6$: Edge density [12], it is obtained applying the Canny edge detector to the grayscale image.

$\mathcal{M}_7$: Compression Ratio, it is here evaluated as the ratio of the image JPEG compressed with Q factor = 100 and the full size uncompressed image.

$\mathcal{M}_8$: Number of regions calculated using the mean shift algorithm [13].

Measures from $\mathcal{M}_9$ to $\mathcal{M}_{11}$ evaluate mainly color image properties:

$\mathcal{M}_9$: Colorfullness : it is the simplified version of the metric proposed by [14], that consists in a linear combination of the mean and standard deviation of the pixel cloud in the color plane.

$\mathcal{M}_{10}$: Number of colors [15]: measures the number of distinct color in the image. RGB values are first quantized by removing the least significant bits, then these values are indexed and the number of unique index values are counted.

$\mathcal{M}_{11}$: Color harmony [15,16]: it is based on the perceived harmony of color combinations. It is composed of three parts: the chromatic effect, the luminance effect, and the hue effect.

We underline that these measures were not specifically developed to predict subjective complexity. However some of them have shown to successfully predict image complexity for particular set of stimuli or tasks.

We also consider two clutter measures developed by Rosenholtz et al. [17]. They attempt to measure the efficiency with which the image can be encoded while maintaining perceptual image quality. The MATLAB implementation provided by the authors has been used:

$\mathcal{M}_{12}$: Feature Congestion: three clutter maps for the image, representing color, texture and orientation congestion are evaluated across scales and properly combined to get a single measure.

$\mathcal{M}_{13}$: Subband Entropy: it is related to the number of bits required for subband image coding: the less cluttered an image is, the more it is redundant and the more efficiently it can be encoded.

4   Results

In Figure 1 the 54 stimuli are shown in increasing order of complexity, according to MOS. We can notice that images with regular pattern and symmetries have been judge as less complex, while images with more details and less ordered structures have been judged as more complex.

In Table 1 the verbal descriptions of the observers, are summarized in terms of the most frequent criteria used to assess texture complexity. We underline that each observer could have used more than one criteria. Table 1 shows that the major texture characteristics considered are regularity, understandability, familiarity and edge density. While regularity and edge density can be associated to bottom-up cognitive mechanisms, understandability and familiarity are related to top-down processes. Moreover, several observers have reported both types of criteria, confirming that bottom-up and top-down mechanisms interfere in perception.

To find out how the objective metrics described in Section 3 predict subjective scores, we have correlated each of them to the MOS using a logistic regression function. The correlation performance is expressed in terms of Pearson Correlation Coefficient (PCC), reported in Table 2. We observe that in general the

Table 1. Summary of verbal description

Criterium	Frequency
Regularity	60%
Understandability	47%
Edge Density	33%
Familiarity	13%

Table 2. PCC of the 13 objective metrics

	$\mathcal{M}_1$	$\mathcal{M}_2$	$\mathcal{M}_3$	$\mathcal{M}_4$	$\mathcal{M}_5$	$\mathcal{M}_6$	$\mathcal{M}_7$	$\mathcal{M}_8$	$\mathcal{M}_9$	$\mathcal{M}_{10}$	$\mathcal{M}_{11}$	$\mathcal{M}_{12}$	$\mathcal{M}_{13}$
PCC	0.43	-	0.53	0.42	0.35	0.58	0.50	0.47	0.24	0.44	-	0.55	0.44

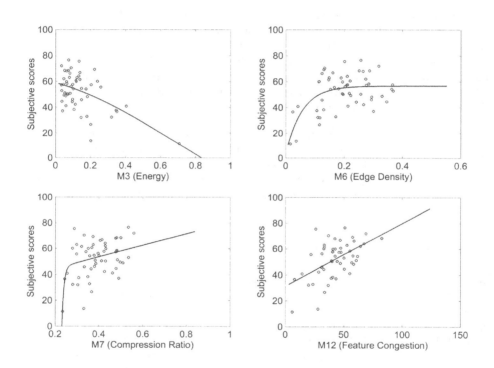

Fig. 2. Logistic correlations of the four metrics with the highest PCC.

metrics do not perform very well. For measures $\mathcal{M}_2$ (Correlation) and $\mathcal{M}_{11}$ (Color harmony) we were not able to find a significant correlation and thus we do not report in Table 2 the corresponding PCCs. Only four of them show PCC greater or equal to 0.5. These four metrics are: $\mathcal{M}_3$ (Energy), $\mathcal{M}_6$ (Edge density), $\mathcal{M}_7$ (Compression ratio) and $\mathcal{M}_{12}$ (Feature Congestion). We plot in Figure 2 the corresponding logistic correlation functions.

Taking into account the criteria that came out from the observers (Table 1), we can easily associate the verbal description *edge density* with the metric $\mathcal{M}_6$. The description *regularity* could be described by $\mathcal{M}_3$ and $\mathcal{M}_6$ but also by the measure of visual clutter $\mathcal{M}_{12}$. We recall that this measure combines color, luminance contrast, and orientation energy. With respect to the *understandability* and *familiarity* criteria, none of the considered metric is able to capture these top-down concepts. This fact could partially explain the low correlations found.

5   Conclusions

In this work we provide insight into the texture complexity perception, with the aim to underline if some common criteria in perceiving complexity can be extracted from the experimental data. The results of our analysis give a hint about the main aspects that should be considered when formulating a model to predict texture complexity. In particular we have identified some low level features (such as edge density) that play an important role. However how to integrate them within a model that also take into account top down mechanisms is still an open problem. As future research we will investigate if a combining of several single measures is able to predict the subjective perception of texture images. Moreover another important issue that will be address is to evaluate the role of color in texture complexity perception. To this end we plan to perform a further experiment with the same stimuli here considered, but in their gray-scale version to compare the results.

References

1. Tuceryan, M., Jain, A.K.: Texture analysis. The handbook of pattern recognition and computer vision **2**, 207–248 (1998)
2. Cusano, C., Napoletano, P., Raimondo, S.: Intensity and color descriptors for texture classification. In: SPIE Electronic Imaging International Society for Optics and Photonics, pp. 866113–866113 (2013)
3. Oliva, A., Mack, M.L., Shrestha, M.: Identifying the perceptual dimensions of visual complexity of scenes. In: Proc. 26th Annual Meeting of the Cognitive Science Society (2004)
4. Kolmogorov, A.N.: Three approaches to the quantitative definition of information. Problems of information transmission **1**(1), 1–7 (1965)
5. Snodgrass, J.G., Vanderwart, M.: A standardized set of 260 pictures: norms for name agreement, image agreement, familiarity, and visual complexity. Journal of experimental psychology: Human learning and memory **6**(2), 174 (1980)
6. Birkhoff, G.D.: Collected mathematical papers (1950)
7. Heaps, C., Handel, S.: Similarity and features of natural textures. Journal of Experimental Psychology: Human Perception and Performance **25**(2), 299 (1999)
8. Ciocca, G., Corchs, S., Gasparini, F., Bricolo, E., Tebano, R.: Does color influence image complexity perception? In: Trémeau, A., Schettini, R., Tominaga, S. (eds.) CCIW 2015. LNCS, vol. 9016, pp. 139–148. Springer, Heidelberg (2015)

9. Guo, X., Asano, C.M., Asano, A., Kurita, T., Li, L.: Analysis of texture characteristics associated with visual complexity perception. Optical review **19**(5), 306 (2012)
10. Guo, X., Asano, C.M., Asano, A., Kurita, T.: Visual complexity perception and texture image characteristics. In: IEEE International Conference on Biometrics and Kansei Engineering, pp. 260–265 (2011)
11. MIT Media Lab, Vision texture homepage. http://vismod.media.mit.edu/vismod/imagery/VisionTexture/
12. Mack, M.L., Oliva, A.: Computational estimation of visual complexity. In: the 12th Annual Object, Perception, Attention, and Memory Conference (2004)
13. Comaniciu, D., Meer, P.: Mean shift: A robust approach toward feature space analysis and the edge detection algorithm. IEEE Transactions on Pattern Analysis and Machine Intelligence **24**, 603–619 (2002)
14. Hasler, D., Suesstrunk, S.E.: Measuring colorfulness in natural images. In: Electronic Imaging 2003, pp. 87–95 (2003)
15. Artese, M.T., Ciocca, G., Gagliardi, I.: Good 50x70 project: a portal for cultural and social campaigns. In: Final Program and Proceedings of the IS&T Archiving 2014 Conference, pp. 213–218 (2014)
16. Solli, M., Lenz, R.: Color harmony for image indexing. In: IEEE 12th International Conference on Computer Vision Workshops, pp. 1885–1892 (2009)
17. Rosenholtz, R., Li, Y., Nakano, L.: Measuring visual clutter. Journal of Vision **7**(2), 17 (2007)

RHEUMA 2015 – Medical Imaging in Rheumatology: Advanced Applications for the Analysis of Inflammation and Damage in the Rheumatoid Joint

An MRI Study of Bone Erosions Healing in the Wrist and Metacarpophalangeal Joints of Patients with Rheumatoid Arthritis

Francesca Barbieri[1(✉)], Veronica Tomatis[1], Giuseppe Zampogna[1], Elena Aleo[2], Valentina Prono[2], Stefania Migone[2], Patrizia Parascandolo[3], Lorenzo Cesario[3], Gianni Viano[3], and Marco Amedeo Cimmino[1]

[1] Dipartimento di Medicina Interna, Clinica Reumatologica, Genoa, Italy
{francesca.barbieri,cimmino}@unige.it,
veronicatomatis@alice.it, gzampogna@libero.it
[2] Divisione di Radiologia, Università di Genova, Genoa, Italy
{elena.aleo,stefania.migone}@libero.it,
valentina.prono@gmail.com
[3] Softeco Sismat S.r.l., Via de Marini 1, Genoa, Italy
{patrizia.parascandolo,lorenzo.cesario,gianni.viano}@softeco.it

Abstract. Bone erosions, considered the hallmark of rheumatoid arthritis (RA), are shown more accurately by MRI than by conventional radiography (CR). Erosions healing is exceptional when studied by CR. This study is concerned with an extremity-dedicated MRI evaluation of erosion changes in patients with RA followed over time. Wrist and metacarpo-phalangeal (MCP) joints of 57 RA patients were imaged with a dedicated-extremity, 0.2 T MRI at baseline and follow up. A decrease of the RAMRIS erosion score indicating erosion healing, calculated both by conventional visual judgement and by a semi-automated method, was seen in 7 (12.3%) patients at the wrist and in 3 (5.3%) at the MCPs. In the same locations, RAMRIS was unchanged in 17 (29.8%) and 31 (54.4%) patients, and worsened in 33 (57.9%) and 17 (29.8%), respectively. Healing of erosions occurs, although rarely, in patients with RA when studied with sensitive imaging techniques, such as MRI.

Keywords: Rheumatoid arthritis · Magnetic resonance imaging · Erosion · Bone · Bone segmentation · Rheumascore

1   Introduction

Bone erosions have been always considered the hallmark of rheumatoid arthritis (RA) [1]. Advanced imaging techniques, such as computed tomography, MRI, and, at least in several joint areas, ultrasonography have shown increased sensitivity for demonstration of erosions in comparison with conventional radiography [2]. In addition, modern follow-up of erosions requires high sensitivity to change in view of the increased capability of new therapeutic strategies to promote their improvement [3]. Erosions healing in patients with RA is considered exceptional when studied by conventional radiology [4]. Modern and sensitive imaging techniques can appreciate

V. Murino et al. (Eds.): ICIAP 2015 Workshops, LNCS 9281, pp. 129–134, 2015.
DOI: 10.1007/978-3-319-23222-5_16

more subtle changes of bone morphology due to their multiplanar capacity. The calculation of the volume of erosions is traditionally performed in a semiquantitative way based on the subjective evaluation of the reader. A more reproducible method based on automated bone segmentation could be of help in this task. This study is concerned with an extremity-dedicated MRI evaluation of erosion changes in patients with RA followed over time. A comparison between the traditional erosion score and a novel automated one is also described.

2   Patients and Methods

Fifty-seven patients affected by RA (42 women, median age 52 years, range 20-73 years, median disease duration 22 months, range 1-420 months) diagnosed according to the 1987 revised ACR criteria [5] were studied. Disease activity was evaluated by calculating the disease activity score based on 28 joints (DAS 28) [6]. The following laboratory investigations were performed at the time of MRI examinations: erythrocyte sedimentation rate (ESR), C-reactive protein (CRP), IgM rheumatoid factor (RF), and anti citrullinated peptide antibodies (APCA). In the interval between the two MRI examinations, the patients underwent standard antirheumatic treatment, including glucocorticoids, synthetic disease modifying antirheumatic drugs (DMARDs), and biological drugs. The detailed description of these therapies and of their efficacy is beyond the scope of this paper, which is concerned with the evaluation of the changes of bone lesions.

Wrist and metacarpophalangeal (MCP) joints were imaged with a dedicated-extremity, 0.2 T MRI (Artoscan, Esaote, Genova, Italy) at baseline and after a median of 15 months (range 6-121 months). A turbo T1-weighted three dimensional sequence (T3-D T1) in the coronal plane, with subsequent multiplanar reconstructions on the axial and sagittal planes was used; slice thickness was 0.6 mm, TR 860 ms, TE 26 ms, and number of excitations (NEX) 1. Bone studied included the 2nd to 5th MCPs, the 1st to 5th metacarpal bases, the 8 wrist bones, and the distal radius and ulna. Erosions were scored according to the RAMRIS [7]. Each bone was scored from 0 to 10 where 0 corresponded to a normal bone and scores from 1 to 10 were attributed by deciles of percentage of articular bone eroded. As an example, a bone with an erosion involving 10% of it is given a score of 1. They were evaluated in 23 regions in the hand and wrist, for a total score of 0–230.

A semi-automated 3D reconstruction was performed using a tool for computer-aided diagnosis (RheumaSCORE, Softeco Sismat Srl, Genova, Italy) for the segmentation of wrist/hand bones, 3D reconstruction and automatic calculation of the bone volume [8]. The user "paints" some "clues" in the anatomical element to segment, with all parameters automatically adjusted by the software. Starting from the reconstructed bones, the program calculates bones' volume, erosion's volume and the RAMRIS for erosions.

3   Results

Thirty/57 (52.6%) patients were RF positive and 34/57 (59.6%) APCA positive. Median ESR was 40 mm/h (range 7-120 mm/h) and median CRP was 6.9 mg/dL (range 0.6-128 mg/dL).

A decrease of the RAMRIS erosion score of at least one point, indicating erosion healing, was seen in 7 (12.3%) patients at the wrist and in 3 (5.3%) at the MCPs.

Two examples of erosion healings are shown in Figures 1 and 2. In Fig. 1, it is more correct to define the structural change of the bone with the generic term of lesion, because at least part of it may be due to bone marrow edema (osteitis) rather than to a true erosion. This is suggested by the complete disappearance of the large lesion of the metacarpal basis, an uncommon event for true erosions. An unchanged RAMRIS was seen in 17 (29.8%) patients at the wrist and in 31 (54.4%) at the MCPs, and a worsened one was observed in 33 (57.9%) and 17 (29.8%) patients, respectively. Altogether 1288 bones were evaluated (840 wrist and 448 MCP bones). A decrease of at least one point in the RAMRIS for erosions was observed in 32 (3.8%) wrist bones and in 7 (1.6%) MCPs. The bones with more frequent healing were 2nd metacarpal basis (0.7%), triquetrum (0.6%), 2nd (0.5%) and 5th (0.74%) metacarpal heads. Fig. 3 shows a scheme of the more frequent sites of erosion healing ordered on a color map with at the opposite ends green, indicating a high frequency of healing, and red indicating that healing is less frequent, although present. Three patients with improved global RAMRIS had, however, worsening of the erosions in at least one wrist bone. Three patients with unchanged RAMRIS and 7 with worsening RAMRIS had erosion healing in at least one wrist bone. The same finding was observed at the MCPs level in 2 and 1 patients, respectively. Finally 5 patients with unchanged RAMRIS had worsening of the erosions at the wrist and 2 patients at the MCPs.

The bones with erosion healing were given a RAMRIS value by both traditional visual evaluation and by using the RheumaSCORE. The correlation between the methods is reported in Fig. 4, where concordance is shown in green and discordance in red for the 25 patients in whom erosion changes were seen. The x axis reports the different bones studied. Concordance was present if the reader and RheumaSCORE gave the identical RAMRIS score to the erosion. Discordance occurred in all remaining cases.

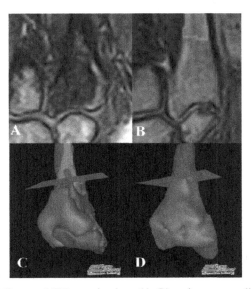

Fig. 1. Baseline and follow up MRI examinations (A, B) and corresponding 3D models (C, D) for the 2nd metacarpal basis. The bone lesion is shown in red, the normal bone in blue.

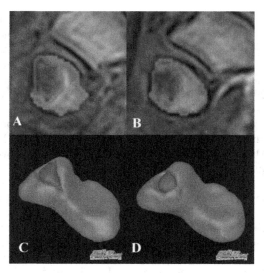

Fig. 2. Baseline and follow up MRI examinations (A, B) and corresponding 3D models (C, D) for the scaphoid. Erosion in red, bone in blue.

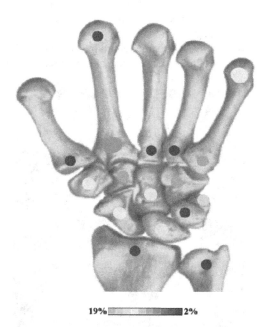

Fig. 3. Color map of the locations where RAMRIS erosion score improvement was seen. Green dots correspond to the highest frequency of lesion improvement, red ones to the lowest frequency.

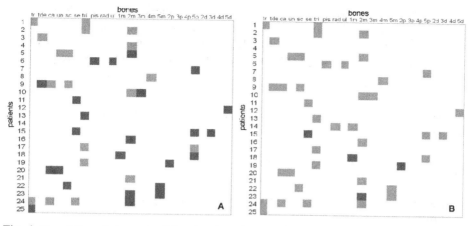

Fig. 4. Correlations between traditional and semi-automated RAMRIS erosions score at baseline (A, 45.2% concordance) and at follow up (B, 92.9% concordance). Agreement is shown in green, disagreement in red.

4   Discussion

Detection of erosions in RA and quantification of their extent are important for both diagnosis and clinical management [9]. Current anti-rheumatic therapy has the goal of retarding or even arresting the progression of bone erosions through suppression of inflammation. This event induces a transformation of the bone microenvironment towards bone anabolism, a situation shown to be central for the induction of erosion repair in experimental models of arthritis. In RA patients, erosion repair can occur under certain circumstances, such as sustained pharmacological TNF inhibition [3].

Our results confirm that healing of erosions occurs, although rarely, in patients with RA when studied with sensitive imaging techniques, such as MRI. The percentages of improved bones was higher in our study than the 1.8% observed with MRI by Møller Døhn et al in a trial where RA patients were treated with adalimumab [3]. This difference may be ascribed to the different population of RA patients studied.

A new finding is the coexistence of erosion's healing and deterioration in the same hand or even in the same bone. This was a frequent observation, which supports the view that not only general disease activity but also localized inflammatory and mechanical stress-associated mechanisms are probably at work.

The agreement between the traditional and semi-automated RAMRIS evaluations was good only for the follow up MRI, after patient treatment (Fig. 4). This discrepancy is apparently difficult to justify because the observers and the techniques were identical at both time points. A possible explanation is the concomitant decrease of bone marrow edema that could have occurred after successful treatment. The experienced reader is in most cases able to differentiate bone marrow edema from real erosions, whereas the automated method may be not. As a consequence, a human supervision to correct possible imprecisions of the automated procedure is still necessary.

In conclusion, we have shown that the study of the volume of bone erosions reveals that healing of the erosions occurs in a limited percentage of RA patients. This information is useful for the clinicians in order to tailor the treatment to the individual patient. The use of a dedicated software may further facilitate the procedure of erosion staging.

Acknowledgements. Supported in part by a grant from the Univerity of Genova (Progetti di Ateneo 2013).

References

1. Scott, D.L., Wolfe, F., Huizinga, T.W.: Rheumatoid arthritis. Lancet **376**, 1094–1108 (2010)
2. McQueen, F.M., Stewart, N., Crabbe, J., et al.: Magnetic resonance imaging of the wrist in early rheumatoid arthritis reveals a high prevalence of erosions at four months after symptoms onset. Ann. Rheum. Dis. **57**, 350–356 (1998)
3. Møller Døhn, U., Boonen, A., Hetland, M.L., et al.: Erosive progression is minimal, but erosion healing rare, in patients with rheumatoid arthritis treated with adalimumab. A 1-year investigator-initiated follow-up study using high-resolution computed tomography as primary outcome measure. Ann. Rheum. Dis. **68**, 1585–1590 (2009)
4. Rau, R., Herborn, G., Wassenberg, S.: Healing of erosive changes in rheumatoid arthritis. Clin. Exp. Rheumatol. **22**, S44–S49 (2004)
5. Arnett, F.C., Edworthy, S.M., Bloch, D.A., McShane, D.J., Fries, J.F., Cooper, N.S., et al.: The American Rheumatism Association 1987 revised criteria for the classification of rheumatoid arthritis. Arthritis Rheum. **1988**(31), 315–324 (1987)
6. van Gestel, A.M., Haagsma, C.J., van Riel, P.L.: Validation of rheumatoid arthritis improvement criteria that include simplified joint counts. Arthritis Rheum. **41**, 1845–1850 (1998)
7. Bird, P., Conaghan, P., Ejbjerg, B., McQueen, F., Lassere, M., Peterfy, C., Edmonds, J., Shnier, R., O'Connor, P., Haavardsholm, E., Emery, P., Genant, H., Ostergaard, M.: The development of the EULAR-OMERACT rheumatoid arthritis MRI reference image atlas. Ann. Rheum. Dis. **64**(Suppl 1), i8–i10 (2005)
8. Catalano, C.E., Robbiano, F., Parascandolo, P., Cesario, L., Vosilla, L., Barbieri, F., Spagnuolo, M., Viano, G., Cimmino, M.A.: Exploiting 3D part-based analysis, description and indexing to support medical applications. In: Greenspan, H., Müller, H., Syeda-Mahmood, T. (eds.) MCBR-CDS 2012. LNCS, vol. 7723, pp. 21–32. Springer, Heidelberg (2013)
9. Haavardsholm, E.A., Ostergaard, M., Hammer, H.B., et al.: Monitoring anti-TNFalpha treatment in rheumatoid arthritis: responsiveness of magnetic resonance imaging and ultrasonography of the dominant wrist joint compared with conventional measures of disease activity and structural damage. Ann. Rheum. Dis. **68**, 1572–1579 (2009)

RheumaSCORE: A CAD System for Rheumatoid Arthritis Diagnosis and Follow-Up

Patrizia Parascandolo, Lorenzo Cesario[✉], Loris Vosilla, and Gianni Viano

Softeco Sismat S.r.l., Via de Marini 1, Genoa, Italy
{patrizia.parascandolo,lorenzo.cesario,
loris.vosilla,gianni.viano}@softeco.it

Abstract. Recently, computer-aided diagnosis (CAD) has become one of the major research subjects in medical imaging and diagnostic radiology. The goal of a CAD is to improve the quality and productivity of physicians' job by improving the accuracy and consistency of radiological diagnosis. This paper describes RheumaSCORE, a CAD system specialized for the diagnosis and treatment of patients affected by bone erosions, as a consequence of one of the most common and serious forms of arthritis, the Rheumatoid Arthritis (RA), and gives an overview of its main features.

Keywords: Computer aided diagnosis (CAD) · Rheumatoid arthritis · Medical imaging · Erosion scoring · Rheumascore

1 Introduction

With the rapid advances in computing and electronic imaging technology, there has been an increasing interest in developing *Computer Aided Diagnosis* (CAD) systems to improve the medical service. CAD is emerging as an advanced interdisciplinary technology which combines fundamental elements of different areas such as digital image processing, image analysis, pattern recognition, medical information processing and management. This technology can be applied to all imaging modalities, including projection radiography, computed tomography (CT), magnetic resonance imaging (MRI), ultrasound (US) and nuclear medicine imaging (PET, SPECT), used for all body parts and for all kinds of examinations.

Although current CAD systems cannot fully replace human doctors for medical detection/diagnosis in clinical practice, the analytical results will assist doctors in providing functionalities for diagnosis, treatment, adequate follow-up, and timely monitoring of disease indicators [1,2,3,4,5].

This paper provides an overview of the main functionalities of the RheumaSCORE CAD system [11], specialized for the diagnosis, quantification and monitoring of one of the most common consequence of musculoskeletal diseases (MSD) like the Rheumatoid Arthritis (RA), the bone erosions of the wrist and hand district, through their automatic quantification using the OMERACT-RAMRIS method [30].

RA is one of the most common and serious forms of arthritis. It can lead to long-term joint damage, resulting in chronic pain, loss of function and disability. This chronic

© Springer International Publishing Switzerland 2015
V. Murino et al. (Eds.): ICIAP 2015 Workshops, LNCS 9281, pp. 135–142, 2015.
DOI: 10.1007/978-3-319-23222-5_17

disease affects about 2.9 million people in Europe [24,25]. An early diagnosis, the continuous monitoring of disease activity and the constant evaluation of therapy effects can improve patients' quality of life and may reduce related social costs. MRI has been demonstrated to be two to ten times more sensitive than conventional radiography in detecting wrist erosions in RA, especially in its early phases [26]. In general, erosions detectable on MRI may become visible in x-ray images only 2-6 years later [26,27,28,29].

The wide use of MRI in the assessment of joints in RA patients in the last years emphasizes the need for an objective and reproducible scoring system of RA lesions. An international working group developed a MRI scoring system to assess both inflammation (activity) and bone lesions (damage) in RA patients based on the Outcome Measures in Rheumatology Clinical Trials (OMERACT) [30].

Manual evaluation of bone erosions volume is however tedious, time consuming and not fully repeatable (especially for inexperienced users). Considering the big amount of patients suffering from RA, this is a critical task. The *RheumaSCORE* software was developed by Softeco Sismat S.r.l. to face the RA problem [11,12], [31].

The paper is organized as follows. In Section 2, the state of the art of CAD systems will be described with focus on segmentation and erosion evaluation techniques in literature. In Section 3, RheumaSCORE and its main functionalities will be presented and some clinical trials will be discussed.

2   State of the Art

2.1   CAD Systems

Early studies on quantitative analysis of medical images by computers [15,16,17,18,19,20] were reported in the 1960s. At that time, it was generally assumed that computers could replace radiologists in detecting abnormalities, because computers and machines are better at performing certain tasks than human beings.

In the medical subspecialty of hematology, R.L. Engle [21] stated in the conclusion of his review article on 30 years' experience in using computers as diagnostic aids in medical decision making, that the computers cannot replace the physicians, but only support them during the diagnostic process. This awareness was already confirmed in the 1980s, when another approach emerged which assumed that the computer output could be utilized by radiologists, but not replace them. This concept is currently known as computer aided diagnosis, which has spread widely and quickly.

A large number of CAD systems has been employed for assisting physicians in the early detection of cancer (breast tumors in mammograms [6], lung nodules in chest radiographs/CT [7], colorectal polyps in CT colonography [8]) and intracranial aneurysms in magnetic resonance angiography (MRA) [9].

In the context of RA, Kubassova et al. [10] developed a CAD software for semi-automated and automated quantitative analysis of dynamic contract-enhanced MRI (DCE-MRI) data, DYNAMIKA. This CAD incorporates algorithms for the estimation of various inflammation such as the one related to the synovial activity in RA. Peloschek et al. [22] developed a software that allows a fast, accurate, and reliable documentation of erosive and degenerative changes on radiographs of hands, wrists, and feet in RA.

The current trend of the research in this field is the development of CAD systems assembled as packages, associated with some specific imaging modalities such as digital mammography, CT, and MRI, and implemented as a part of PACS (Picture Archiving and Communication Systems). For example, one of the potential advantages in packaging a CAD in the PACS environment is the comparison between images and related measured data acquired in different times (follow-up). Another potential advantage is the use of similar cases in practical clinical situations: a unique database that includes a large number of cases which can be used as a tool for finding cases similar to an unknown one (knowledge management). In that sense, a first result for MSD application is the RheumaSCORE software [11,12], a specific CAD for RA.

2.2   Segmentation

The most important functionality of the CAD systems for supporting evaluation of RA within the wrist/hand joints is the segmentation. Segmentation is an important task in medical imaging, in order to recognize anatomical or pathological structures and determine their relevant characteristics such as size, shape, and volume. Moreover, image segmentation is the prerequisite for many interaction techniques to explore data and to carry out treatment planning.

In the context of RA, there is relatively few work on segmentation of wrist bones in 3-D MRI sequences. Sebastian et al. [13] describe an approach to segment carpal bones from computed tomography (CT) sequences using skeletally coupled deformable models. Similarly Duryea et al.[14] describe their semi-automated approach using CT data. Koch et al. [32] and Włodarczyk et al. [33] developed wrist segmentation framework on 3D MRI images. However, to the best of our knowledge, there is no commercial framework for wrist/hand segmentation designed for MR images.

2.3   Erosion Evaluation

Although a diagnostic standard for assessing RA in MR images of wrist/hand is used for almost a decade, there is currently no commercial tool supporting automated evaluation of erosions within the wrist/hand joints. In fact, no comprehensive framework for automated evaluation of these lesions has been even published. Although recently there have been some efforts to develop quantitative methods of assessing RA-related changes and comparing them with RAMRIS outcomes [34,35], these efforts were essentially based on manual outlining of wrist bones or joints borders in 3D MRI of wrist. Although based on manual outlining, the results of Crowley et al. [34] and Chand et al. [35] demonstrated that RAMRIS-based assessment of RA can be possibly replaced with a computer-aided detection (CAD) tool for estimating the volumes of lesions.

3   RheumaSCORE

3.1   Main Functionalities

RheumaSCORE is a CAD that supports the user (e.g. radiologist or rheumatologist) during the diagnostic process and the management of RA progression, by means of analysis, visualization, measurement and comparison of MRI acquisitions of different patients. This application offers to the physician the most common features that a CAD system must offer to the user:

1. image processing/clinical data storage for detection, visualization and qualitative/quantitative evaluation of abnormalities;
2. comparisons among images and clinical data of the same patient;
3. quantitative evaluation and retrieval of cases similar to those of unknown lesions.

3.2   Bones Segmentation

In RheumaSCORE the bones segmentation is performed using a semi-automatic segmentation algorithm based on level-set method [36]. The level-set method developed evolves a surface implicitly by manipulating a higher dimensional function, called the level-set function $\phi(x,t)$. The evolving surface can be extracted from the zero level-set $\Gamma(x,t) = \{(x,t)| \phi(x,t)=0\}$ with $\phi:R^n \rightarrow R$. In the level-set framework, one can execute a wide variety of deformations by introducing an appropriate motion function $\upsilon(x,t)$ of the surface. For segmentation, the $\upsilon(x,t)$ often consists of a combination of two terms [37]

$$\frac{\partial \phi}{\partial t} = |\nabla \phi| \left[\alpha D(x) + (1-\alpha)\nabla \cdot \frac{\nabla \phi}{|\nabla \phi|} \right] \tag{1}$$

where D is a data term that forces the model toward desirable features in the input data, the term $\nabla \cdot (\nabla \phi / |\nabla \phi|)$ is the mean curvature of the surface, which forces the surface to have a smaller area (and to remain smooth) and $\alpha \in [0,1]$ is a free parameter that controls the degree of smoothness in the solution.

The data function D (speed function) acts as the principal "force" that drives the segmentation. In our implementation, the speed function at any one voxel x is the result of the combination between two terms: $D_{intensity}$ and D_{fuzzy}. The first term $D_{intensity}$, based on the input gray value of the voxel x, is given by

$$D_{intensity} = \varepsilon - |I - T| \tag{2}$$

where T describes the dominant intensity of the region to be segmented and ε describes the range of grayscale values around T that could be considered inside the object. Thus, for a voxel x, the level-set propagation front will expand if the voxel intensity $I \in \{T \pm \varepsilon\}$, otherwise it will contract.

The second term D_{fuzzy} describes the fuzzy affinity between contiguous voxels. Affinity is intended to be a relation between every two image elements c and d. That is, if c and d are far apart, the strength of this relationship is intended to be zero. If the elements are nearby, the strength of their affinity, lying between 0 and 1, depends on the distance between them, on the homogeneity of the intensities surrounding them, and on the closeness of their intensity-based features to the feature values expected for the object. The strength of this relation, denoted μ(c, d), is given by

$$\mu(c, d) = k(c,d)\sqrt{g_1(f(c), f(d))g_2(f(c)f(d))}$$ (3)

where k(c,d) has 0 or 1 value depending on c and d adjacency, g_1 and g_2 are Gaussian functions of (f(c)+f(d))/2 and (f(c)-f(d))/2, respectively. In this equation, g_1 is a Gaussian with mean and variance that are related to the mean and variance of the intensity of the object we wish to segment in the scene. That is, this affinity component takes a high value when c and d are both close to an expected intensity value for the object. g_2 is a 0-mean Gaussian, the underlying idea being to capture the degree of local hanging togetherness of c and d based on intensity homogeneity. For each voxel x, the term D_{fuzzy} is the mean value between the fuzzy affinity evaluated on the neighborhood of the voxel x. This term helps the level-set propagation front to evolve also in areas with different homogeneity intensity. Segmentation results are reconstructed in 3D and displayed using the Marching Cube algorithm [23]. More details and results of our segmentation method are described in [36].

3.3   Evaluation of RA Status and Progression

RheumaSCORE allows for the analysis of the bones in the hand and the wrist to assess the RA status through erosions scoring and progression monitoring. This evaluation is performed after segmentation using the same method proposed by OMERACT RAMRIS (see Fig. 1).

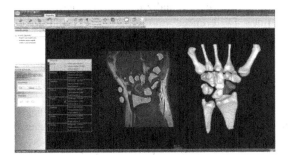

Fig. 1. Erosion Scoring in the RheumaSCORE software.

This method identifies and measures bone erosions, not segmenting directly the erosion, i.e. the missing part of the bone, but through the segmentation of the bone of interest and then the reconstruction of its original shape. RheumaSCORE uses a statistical shape model extracted from a collection of training samples of healthy bone. The resulting model consists of the mean shape and a number of modes of variation obtained with a Principal Component Analysis (PCA). Every healthy bone can be obtained as a linear combination of the mean shape with these modes. The reconstruction of the original shape of the bone of interest is performed finding the best coefficients of this linear combination.

The difference between the segmented bone and the reconstructed bone is the erosion of which it is possible to calculate the volume and then the scoring. Processing takes a few minutes for all wrist bones (or hand bones), which leads to a substantial reduction of diagnosis time and costs.

3.4   RheumaSCORE in Clinical Applications

A preliminary clinical test has been carried out at DIMI[1]. 57 patients (42 women, median age 52 years, range 20-73 years, median disease duration 22 months, range 1-420 months) diagnosed with early RA according to the 1987 ACR criteria were studied. The wrists were imaged in an extremity-dedicated MRI device (Artoscan C, Esaote, Genova, Italy) using a turbo T1-weighted sequence. Some experts evaluated the erosion scores using the manual RAMRIS method and the RheumaSCORE software: perfect concordance was 45.2% at baseline, and 92.9% at follow up. Detailed informations can be found on the paper "An MRI study of bone erosions healing in the wrist and metacarpophalangeal joints of patients with Rheumatoid Arthritis".

Moreover, the framework permits the management and storage of clinical data (like C-reactive protein), useful for measurement and monitoring the disease activity of RA. Physicians can also add annotations, possibly using the system ontology, in order to highlight lessons learnt or critical issues linked to specific features of the current patient. All the information related to the patient's examination (e.g. acquired DICOM images, anatomical 3D segmented elements, 3D features, user annotations) are stored in the system database and are available for retrieval. The patient disease follow-up is supported by storing, visualizing and comparing several sets of data acquired at different times. Differences among parameters and trends can be computed and visualized.

References

1. Doi, K., Giger, M.L., MacMahon, H., et al.: Computer-aided diagnosis: development of automated schemes for quantitative analysis of radiographic images. Sem. Ultrasound CT MR **13**, 140–152 (1992)
2. Doi, K., Giger, M.L., Nishikawa, R.M., Hoffmann, K.R., MacMahon, H., Schmidt, R.A., et al.: Digital radiography: a useful clinical tool for computer-aided diagnosis by quantitative analysis of radiographic images. Acta. Radiol. **34**, 426–439 (1993)
3. Giger, M.L., Huo, Z., Kupinski, M.A., Vyborny, C.J.: Computer aided diagnosis in mammography. In: Fitzpatrick, J.M., Sonka, M. (eds.) The Handbook of Medical Imaging: Medical Imaging Processing and Analysis, vol. 2, pp. 915–1004. SPIE, Bellingham (2000)
4. Li, Q., Li, F., Armato III, S.G., Suzuki, K., Shiraishi, J., Abe, H., et al.: Computer-aided diagnosis in thoracic CT. Seminars in Ultrasound. CT MRI **26**, 357–363 (2005)

---

[1] *DIMI -Dipartimento di Medicina Interna, Clinica Reumatologica, Università degli Studi di Genova.*

5. Yoshida, H., Dachman, A.H.: Computer-aided diagnosis for CT colonography. Seminars in Ultrasound, CT MRI **25**, 404–410 (2004)
6. Moberg, K., Bjurstam, N., Wilczek, B., Rostgard, L., Egge, E., Muren, C.: Computer assisted detection of interval breast cancers. Eur. J. Radiol. **39**, 104–110 (2001)
7. Arimura, H., Katsuragawa, S., Suzuki, K., Li, F., Shiraishi, J., Doi, K.: Computerized scheme for automated detection of lung nodules in low-dose CT images for lung cancer screening. Acad. Radiol. **11**, 617–629 (2004)
8. Summers, R.M., et al.: Automated polyp detection at CT colonography: Feasibility assessment in the human population. Radiology **219**, 51–59 (2001)
9. White, P.M., Teasdale, E.M., Wardlaw, J.M., Easton, V.: Intracranial aneurysms: CT angiography andMRangiography for detection—prospective blinded comparison in a large patient cohort. Radiology **219**, 739–749 (2001)
10. Kubassova, O., Boesen, M., Cimmino, M.A., Bliddal, H.: A computer-aided detection system for rheumatoid arthritis MRI data interpretation and quantification of synovial activity. European Journal of Radiology **74**(3), 67–72 (2010)
11. RheumaSCORE. http://www.research.softeco.it/rheumascore.aspx
12. Barbieri, F., Parascandolo, P., Vosilla, L., Cesario, L., Viano, G., Cimmino, M.A.: Assessing MRI erosions in the rheumatoid wrist: a comparison between RAMRIS and a semiautomated segmentation software. Ann. Rheum. Dis. **71**(Suppl 3) (2012)
13. Sebastian, T.B., Tek, H., Crisco, J.J., Kimia, B.B.: Segmentation of carpal bones from CT images using skeletally coupled deformable models. Medical Image Analysis **7**(1), 21–45 (2003)
14. Duryea, J., Magalnick, M., Alli, S., Yao, L., Wilson, M., Goldbach-Mansky, R.: Semiautomated three-dimensional segmentation software to quantify carpal bone volume changes on wrist CT scans for arthritis assessment. Medical Physics **36** (2008)
15. Lodwick, G.S., Haun, C.L., Smith, W.E., et al.: Computer diagnosis of primary bone tumor. Radiology **80**, 273–275 (1963)
16. Myers, P.H., Nice, C.M., Becker, H.C., et al.: Automated computer analysis of radiographic images. Radiology **83**, 1029–1033 (1964)
17. Winsberg, F., Elkin, M., May, J., et al.: Detection of radiographic abnormalities in mammograms by means of optical scanning and computer analysis. Radiology **89**, 211–215 (1967)
18. Kruger, R.P., Towns, J.R., Hall, D.L., et al.: Automated radiographic diagnosis via feature extraction and classification of cardiac size and shape descriptors. IEEE Trans. Biomed. Eng. **19**, 174–186 (1972)
19. Kruger, R.P., Thompson, W.B., Turner, A.F.: Computer diagnosis of pneumoconiosis. IEEE Transactions on Systems, Man, and Cybernetics **4** (1974)
20. Toriwaki, J., Suenaga, Y., Negoro, T., et al.: Pattern recognition of chest x-ray images. Computer Graphics and Image Processing **2**, 252–271 (1973)
21. Engle, R.L.: Attempt to use computers as diagnostic aids in medical decision making: a thirty-year experience. Perspect. Biol. Med. **35**, 207–219 (1992)
22. Peloschek, P.L., Langs, G., Bischof, H., Kainberger, F., Kropatsch, W., Imhof, H.: Computer aided diagnosis (CAD) in rheumatoid arthritis : automated joint localization, estimation of the bone contour and consecutive detection of defects of the bone contour in metacarpal bones. In: Proceedings of the Annual Meeting of the Radiological Society of North America RSNA (2003)
23. Lorensen, W.E., Cline, H.E.: Marching cubes: a high resolution 3D surface construction algorithm. In: Proc. of ACM SIGGRAPH, pp. 163–169 (1987)

24. Markenson, J.A.: Worldwide trends in the socioeconomic impact and long-term prognosis of rheumatoid arthritis. Semin. Arthritis Rheum. **21**, 4–12 (1991)
25. Weinblatt, M.E.: Rheumatoid arthritis: treat now, not later [editorial]. Ann. Intern. Med. **124**, 773–774 (1996)
26. Østergaard, M., Hansen, M., Stoltenberg, M., Jensen, K.E., Szkudlarek, M., Pedersen-Zbinden, B., Lorenzen, I.: New radiographic bone erosions in the wrists of patients with rheumatoid arthritis are detectable with magnetic resonance imaging a median of two years earlier. Arthritis Rheum. **48**, 2128–2131 (2003)
27. Benton, N., Stewart, N., Crabbe, J., Robinson, E., Yeoman, S., McQueen, F.M.: MRI of the wrist in early rheumatoid arthritis can be used to predict functional outcome at 6 years. Ann. Rheum. Dis. **63**, 555–561 (2004)
28. McQueen, F.M., Benton, N., Perry, D., Crabbe, J., Robinson, E., Yeoman, S., McLean, L., Stewart, N.: Bone edema scored on magnetic resonance imaging scans of the dominant carpus at presentation predicts radiologic joint damage of the hands and feet six years later in patients with rheumatoid arthritis. Arthritis Rheum. **48**, 1814–1827 (2003)
29. Østergaard, M., Hansen, M., Stoltenberg, M., Jensen, K.E., Szkudlarek, M., Klarlund, M., Pedersen-Zbinden, M.: MRI bone erosions in radiographically non-eroded rheumatoid arthritis wrist joint bones give a 4-fold increased risk of radiographic erosions five years later. Arthritis Rheum. **46**(Suppl.), S526–S527 (2002)
30. Ejbjerg, B., McQueen, F., Lassere, M., Haavardsholm, E., Conaghan, P., O'Connor, P., Bird, P., Peterfy, C., Edmonds, J., Szkudlarek, M., Genant, H., Emery, P., Ostergaard, M.: The EULAR-OMERACT rheumatoid arthritis MRI reference image atlas: the wrist joint. Ann. Rheum. Dis. **64**(Suppl 1), 23–47 (2005)
31. Catalano, C.E., Robbiano, F., Parascandolo, P., Cesario, L., Vosilla, L., Barbieri, F., Spagnuolo, M., Viano, G., Cimmino, M.A.: Exploiting 3D part-based analysis, description and indexing to support medical applications. In: Greenspan, H., Müller, H., Syeda-Mahmood, T. (eds.) MCBR-CDS 2012. LNCS, vol. 7723, pp. 21–32. Springer, Heidelberg (2013)
32. Koch, M., Schwing, A.G., Comaniciu, D., Pollefeys, M.: Fully automatic segmentation of wrist bones for arthritis patients. In: Proceedings of the 8th IEEE International Symposium on Biomedical Imaging, from Nano to Macro, ISBI, Chicago, Illinois, USA, pp 636–640
33. Włodarczyk, J., Czaplicka, K., Tabor, Z., Wojciechowski, W., Urbanik, A.: Segmentation of bones in magnetic resonance images of the wrist. International Journal of Computer Assisted Radiology and Surgery **10**(4), 419–431 (2015)
34. Crowley, A.R., Dong, J., McHaffie, A., Clarke, A.W., Reeves, Q., Williams, M., et al.: Measuring bone erosion and oedema in rheumatoid arthritis: a comparison of manual segmentation and RAMRIS methods. J. Magn. Reson. Imaging **33**, 364–371 (2011)
35. Chand, A.S., McHaffie, A., Clarke, A.W., Reeves, Q., Tan, Y.M., Dalbeth, N., et al.: Quantifying synovitis in rheumatoid arthritis using computer-assisted manual segmentation with 3 Tesla MRI scanning. J. Magn. Reson. Imaging **33**, 1106–1113 (2011)
36. Parascandolo, P., Cesario, L.,Vosilla, L., Pitikakis, M., Viano, G.: Smart brush: a real time segmentation tool for 3D medical images. In: 8th International Symposium on Presented at Image and Signal Processing and Analysis (ISPA), pp. 689–694 (2013)
37. Caselles, V., Kimmel, R., Sapiro, G.: Geodesic active contours. In: International Conference on Computer Vision, pp. 694–699. IEEE Computer Society Press (1995)

A Database of Segmented MRI Images of the Wrist and the Hand in Patients with Rheumatic Diseases

Veronica Tomatis[1], Marco A. Cimmino[1], Francesca Barbieri[1], Giulia Troglio[2],
Patrizia Parascandolo[2], Lorenzo Cesario[2(✉)], Gianni Viano[2], Loris Vosilla[2],
Marios Pitikakis[2], Andrea Schiappacasse[3], Michela Moraldo[3], and Matteo Santoro[3]

[1] Dipartimento di Medicina Interna, Clinica Reumatologica, Università di Genova, Genoa, Italy
`veronicatomatis@alice.it`, `{cimmino,francesca.barbieri}@unige.it`
[2] Softeco Sismat S.r.l, Genoa, Italy
`{giulia.troglio,patrizia.parascandolo,lorenzo.cesario,gianni.via`
`no,loris.vosilla}@softeco.it`, `marios.pitikakis@gmail.com`
[3] Camelot Biomedical Systems S.r.l., Genoa, Italy
`{andrea.schiappacasse,michela.moraldo,`
`matteo.santoro}@camelotbio.com`

Abstract. This paper is concerned with the ideation, organization and distribution of a database of segmented MRI images - and associated clinical parameters - of the wrist and the hand in patients affected by a variety of the most frequent rheumatic diseases. The final goal is empowering future biomedical research thanks to the completeness of details and cases. MRI Images were analyzed by means of the software RheumaSCORE (Softeco Sismat Srl), which performs semi-automatic segmentation of the bones, returns the volume of bones and erosions, as well as their tri-dimensional reconstruction. In order to favor its exploitation, the database of segmented images, along with many relevant clinical anthropometric parameters, are available online through the Patient Browser platform (Softeco Sismat Srl). Moreover, the original images and their clinical parameters are accessible online through the dedicated DICOM viewer QuantaView (CAMELOT Biomedical Systems Srl).

Keywords: Database · Image segmentation · MRI · Arthritis · DICOM viewer · Rheumascore · Patient browser · Quantaview

1 Introduction

Rheumatic diseases, in particular erosive arthritides, represent the most common cause of severe long-term pain and physical disability [1]. In order to minimize them, an early diagnosis, the choice of the most appropriate therapy, and the control of its efficacy are crucial items. In the management of these diseases, the rheumatologist is helped by radiology, which offers different imaging techniques. Even if conventional radiography is traditionally considered the gold standard for assessing structural joint damage [2], it does not visualize the earliest stage of erosive damage and identify the predictor of aggressive disease. Magnetic resonance imaging (MRI) is more effective

© Springer International Publishing Switzerland 2015
V. Murino et al. (Eds.): ICIAP 2015 Workshops, LNCS 9281, pp. 143–150, 2015.
DOI: 10.1007/978-3-319-23222-5_18

than conventional radiology for detection of bone erosions [3]. At the same time, it allows to depict synovitis and bone oedema, which represent important predictors of bone damage [4]. Articular MRI is highly sensitive to the anatomical changes due to its different sequences [5]; all components of the joint, including soft tissues, articular cartilages, and bones, can be evaluated on a single examination. Moreover, MRI is a non-invasive imaging technique, which does not use ionizing radiation. For all this features it is increasing used in clinical trials, becoming the standard for the follow up of arthritis [6].

In order to standardize this evaluation, the OMERACT (Outcome Measure in Rheumatoid Arthritis Clinical Trials) MRI working group has developed a MRI scoring system called RAMRIS (Rheumatoid Arthritis Magnetic Resonance Imaging Score). The focus is set on the semi quantitative assessment of wrist and metacarpophalangeal joints and three parameters are considered: bone erosion, bone oedema and synovitis [7].

The RAMRIS system has demonstrated good reliability and high levels of reader agreement for all the parameters analyzed, but reliability is less satisfactory in discriminating between two time points. In addition, the feasibility represents a problem, especially for the time necessary for scoring [8].

In order to support the diagnostic process, MRI images can be analyzed and segmented. Segmentation is an important task that allows recognizing anatomical or pathological structures and determining their relevant characteristics such as size, shape, and volume. Moreover, image segmentation is the prerequisite for many interaction techniques to explore data and facilitate treatment planning. Mc Queen et al. have recently shown that a computer-assisted manual segmentation technique for measuring bone erosions significantly correlates with the RAMRIS score with good reliability of the former method [9].

The spectrum of segmentation techniques available in the literature is broad, ranging from manual slice-by-slice outlining to fully automatic techniques. Among them are interactive approaches, which combine the high accuracy, efficiency, and repeatability of automatic methods with the expertise and quality control obtained through human supervision. Interactive segmentation can be based, e.g., on thresholding techniques [10], region growing approaches [11], and level set methods [12,13]. Computer-Aided Diagnosis (CAD) systems, which offer semi-automatic segmentation tools, are being developed.

The aim of this study is to create a database of segmented MRI images in patients affected by the most frequent rheumatic diseases and to provide an automatic score of bone erosions. Rheumatologists collected MRI images of the wrist and hand in patients affected by rheumatic disorders and used a CAD system (RheumaSCORE) to segment these images and to supervise the automatic scoring of bone erosions. The segmented database is available online through the Patient Browser website (Softeco Sismat Srl) and the QuantaView DICOM Viewer (Camelot Biomedical Systems Srl).

The paper is organized as follows. In Section 2, rheumatic diseases will be introduced. Section 3 will describe the collection of the database, including image acquisition, image segmentation, and sharing of the results. Finally, in Section 4 results will be assessed and in Section 5 conclusions will be drawn.

2   Rheumatic Diseases

Erosive arthritides are the most disabling rheumatic diseases. Bone erosions are considered the central feature of Rheumatoid Arthritis (RA) [14] even if they can be found in other rheumatic diseases, such as Psoriatic Arthritis (PSA), gout, Palindromic Rheumatism (PR), Systemic SClerosis (SSC), OsteoArthritis (OA), septic arthritis, systemic lupus erythematosus and other less frequent conditions. In particular, the most frequent erosive arthritides are analyzed: each of them has several distinctive features, both in clinical manifestations and in the pattern of bone damage.

RA is a chronic systemic inflammatory disease characterized by recurrent, poliarticular and symmetrical episodes of arthritis. The chronic inflammation is responsible for the formation of the synovial pannus with bone eroding capacity. In RA, erosions are marginal and localized at the "bare area", the bone surface within the synovial space, which is not protected by cartilage [15]. PSA is an inflammatory disorder characterized by the association of cutaneous psoriasis and inflammatory arthritis. Different type of PSA are described: a symmetrical polyarthritis similar to RA, an oligoarticular form, a spondylitic form characterized by axial involvement and a mutilans form. In PSA, episodes of dactylitis and enthesitis are frequent. Bone erosions, unlike the ones observed in RA, are not in the marginal but in the central area of the articular surface [16].

Gout is a metabolic disease correlated with hyperuricemia, and characterized by recurring acute arthritis, usually monoarticular, and later by chronic deforming arthritis. The characteristic lesion of the chronic stage is the tophus, a nodular deposit of monosodium urate monohydrate crystals that can be found in cartilage, and subcutaneous, articular and periarticular tissues. Characteristic of gout are well-defined, punched-out erosion with overhanging edges [17]. The erosions are often adjacent to the tophus [18].

PR is a form of inflammatory arthritis characterized by sudden and rapidly developing arthritis episodes leaving no residual or radiographic change. In the long term, some patients will develop RA. The risk of progression to RA is associated with serum Rheumatoid Factor (RF) and AntiCitrullinated Peptides Antibodies (ACPA) [19].

Bone erosion can also be found in SSC, a chronic systemic connective tissue disorder characterized by diffuse fibrosis of the skin and internal organs. Joint involvement is frequent and the possible radiological features are distal phalange resorption, demineralization, joint space narrowing and erosions [20].

3   Database Collection

MRI images of patients followed in the Academic Division of Rheumatology of the University of Genoa are available. MRI is performed with a 0.2T extremity dedicated machine (Artoscan, Esaote) using 3D T1 weighted sequences with reconstruction on the axial and sagittal plane. Low field extremity-dedicated MRI machines provide similar information on bone damage as high field MRI machines, and the low cost added to better patient compliance explains the emerging role of this technique in the diagnosis and follow-up of rheumatoid arthritis [21].

Image segmentation is carried out by the clinical experts through the support of a CAD system, RheumaSCORE [22,23], developed by Softeco Sismat S.r.l. RheumaSCORE supports the rheumatologist during the segmentation process, by providing a semi-automatic tool for the detection of bones (based on level sets [24]) volume measurement, three-dimensional reconstruction of the segmented structures and automatic evaluation of bone erosions [25,26]. The system provides a GUI for the visualization of MRI images and the selection of the anatomical structures to be segmented. The segmentation feature allows the radiologist to select a starting region, to interactively correct the segmented region during the process and to edit the results. During the segmentation process, the bone surface is automatically reconstructed using the marching cubes algorithm [27]. Once the segmentation has been completed, the system provides automatic scoring of bone erosions.

The collected images and segmentation results are available online, through a DICOM Viewer (QuantaView) and a web browsing application (Patient Browser). These two applications are described in the following paragraphs.

3.1   QuantaView DICOM Viewer

The QuantaView DICOM image viewer, designed and developed by Camelot Biomedical Systems, is completely based on web technologies and is accessible through a web browser, also on mobile devices, at www.quantaviewpolo.camelotbio.com upon registration. The user interface is implemented in HTML5/CSS3/JS. The image display is based on WebGL standard, that is supported by all major modern browsers and also by iOS since version 8.

QuantaView main functionalities are the following:

- PACS connection via DICOM standard, in order to explore and see its contents (query/retrieval commands through C-FIND, C-MOVE and C-STORE are allowed operations).
- Local archive on file-system, directly accessible from the server. DICOM objects can be imported from any physical support (USB, CD, DVD) from the operating system hosting the frontend.
- User management, through authentication. Users are assigned to one or more groups, defining the data and users visibility. Each group has a role, defining a certain configuration of permissions (e.g. writing or reading) on accessible data.
- Browsing data. The user can navigate through the data on all accessible sources. Data are displayed according to the DICOM hierarchy patient/study/series.
- DICOM metadata editing, guaranteed only to a narrow class of users (e.g., data owner, group administrator, etc.).
- Insertion of non-DICOM metadata, such as tags and notes in free text, to objects in each level of the hierarchy (patient, study, series). Permission is guaranteed only to a narrow class of users (e.g., data owner, group administrator, etc.).

- DICOM visualization, which includes: navigation among the series slices, play-back of multi-frame, changing windowing parameters, pan, zoom and reset win-dowing, saving the current slice in jpeg format.
- Image graphical annotations that can be added to the individual slices of a DICOM series. Permission, which can be configured, to view/remove the annotations is guaranteed only to a narrow class of users.

3.2   Patient Browser Web Application

Patient Browser is a web application that has been developed by Softeco Sismat S.r.l., in order to assist and support the user in the diagnosis and follow-up processes of rheumatic diseases. The idea is to provide a web-based framework for storing, search-ing and visualizing MRI images and medical data, as well as to retrieve and display different kinds of diagnostic measurements.

In this context, the Patient browser application is intended to share and retrieve visual data (MRI exams, segmentations and 3D mesh models generated by RheumaSCORE), to compare clinical data (inserted by the radiologists) and diagnos-tic measurements (e.g. bone volume, erosion volume, erosion scoring, etc., calculated through RheumaSCORE), and to assist the radiologists in the diagnostic procedure. The users interaction with the system may differ depending on the user profile and access rights.

The basic functionalities include:

- Sharing the data analyzed through RheumaSCORE both in terms of meshes and in terms of segmented data.
- Uploading and storing patient studies exported from RheumaSCORE.
- Browsing and visualizing the analysis results of different patient studies.
- Display diagnostic measurements and compare them.
- Downloading the original images, segmentation results and diagnostic measure-ments.

Access will be provided upon request (please, contact the authors for detailed access instructions).

4   Assessment of the Results

The database comprises 100 MRI examinations performed between August 2014 and January 2015. Each examination includes the hand and the wrist districts. Among the 100 MRI images examined, 10 belong to healthy controls, 30 belong to patients af-fected by RA, 15 belong to patients affected by PSA, 15 to patients affected by gout, 15 to patients affected by PR and 15 to patients affected by SSC. The patients affected by RA are divided into three groups according to disease duration, eight patients for each group. The patients of the first group have disease duration less than 6 months, those of the second group between 6 and 36 months, and those of third group have disease duration longer than 36 months. For six patients a follow up examination is available.

Overall, about 2800 bones are segmented and bone erosions are analyzed and scored. Through the software RheumaSCORE, a tridimensional reconstruction of the bones is obtained, together with the bone and erosion volumes.

The images are segmented and the automatic bone-erosion score is analyzed and corrected, pixel-by-pixel, by a clinical expert. The entire work is supervised by another clinical expert. The time necessary to analyze the segmentation differs, depending on the severity of the disease and ranges from 340 minutes (100 minutes for the district of the hand and 240 minutes for the district of the wrist) to 460 (130 minutes for the district of the hand and 330 minutes for the district of the wrist).

Additionally, for each patient, a set of clinical and laboratory parameters are included within the database, which allow to better understand the severity and the course of diseases. Some of these parameters are common among all diseases and others are specific for each disease. The common parameters are gender, age, disease duration, inflammatory indexes (ESR and CRP), number of tender joints (NTJ), number of swollen joints (NSJ) and the visual analogue scale of pain (a subjective grading of pain).

The disease specific parameters are the same for RA and PR, including RF, ACPA, and DAS28 (Disease Activity Score on 28 joints). High titers of RF and ACPA, in patients affected by RA, are indicators aggressive diseases and correlate with the risk of bone damage [28] The DAS28 is a quantitative measure of disease activity used to monitor the trend of RA and to monitor the efficacy of therapy. DAS28 provides a number on a scale from 0 to 10 indicating current RA disease activity (Remission: DAS28 ≤ 2.6 • Low Disease activity: 2.6 < DAS28 ≤ 3.2 • Moderate Disease Activity: 3.2 < DAS28 ≤ 5.1 • High Disease Activity: DAS28 >5.1). A high score of DAS28 is associated with the risk of bone damage and its progression. The serum positivity of RF and ACPA in patients affected by PR predicts the subsequent development of RA and, therefore, a potentially erosive disease [19].

The DAS28 is also analyzed in patients affected by PSA, where the subtype of PSA is also specified. The parameters considered in gout are serum uric acid, the number of acute arthritis episodes and the presence of tophi. Levels of serum uric acid are considered an index of disease activity; high levels promote urate crystal deposition and acute arthritis attacks. A high number of acute episodes is a forerunner of the chronic stadium of the disease, where joint damage is most likely found [29]. Finally, the presence of tophi correlate with the risk of bone erosions [18].

The parameters considered in SSC are nailfold videocapillaroscopy (NCV) score and patterns, and two serum autoantibodies, anticentromer (ACA) and antitopoisomerase I (anti-Scl70). In a large number of patients affected by SSC there are three distinct NCV pattern that are the early, active and late patterns. The NCV pattern is correlated with disease severity, particularly skin and pulmonary involvement [30]. The presence of Scl70 antibodies is related to a more rapid progression of the microangiopathy, whereas ACA positivity is related to a slower progression.

5   Conclusions

The segmentation process and the automatic analysis of bone erosions represent two important tools for rheumatologist to visualize and interpret medical images and offer a powerful tool to support the diagnostic process. However, at the time being, the analysis of the automatic-segmentation results is very time-consuming. An increasing automation of the segmentation process is continuously pursued and, hopefully, progresses will be achieved.

The high number of images analyzed, the different diseases considered, their characterization in terms of disease duration and activity, and their online availability make this database interesting for future challenges in image segmentation. Interoperator reliability and comparison of different segmentation methods could be investigated. Additionally, RAMRIS scoring could be used as a reference for comparison.

In future the database will be extended, in order to include other diseases such as osteoarthritis. Moreover, more MRI examinations of the same patient will be available to the clinicians and will be included in the database, in order to provide more follow-up cases. Finally, in order to create new databases, segmentation of other joints may be investigated.

References

1. Woolf, A.D., Pfleger, B.: Burden of major musculoskeletal conditions. Bulletin of the World Health Organization **81**(9) (2003)
2. American college of rheumatology subcommittee on rheumatoid arthritis: 2002 update. Guidelines for the management of Rheumatoid arthritis: 2002 update. Arthritis Rheum. **46**(2), 328–346, February 2002
3. Baillet, A., Viala, C.G., Mouterde, G., et al.: Comparison of the efficacy of sonography, magnetic resonance imaging and conventional radiography for the detection of bone erosions in rheumatoid arthritis patients: a systematic review and meta-analysis. Rheumatology (Oxford) **50**(6), 1137–1147 (2011)
4. McQueen, F.M.: Bone marrow edema and osteitis in rheumatoid arthritis: the imaging perspective. Arthritis Res Ther. **14**(5), 224 (2012). doi:10.1186/ar4035
5. Haavardsholm, E.A., Ostergaard, M., et al.: Reliability and sensitivity to change of the OMERACT Rheumatoid Arthritis Magnetic Resonance Imaging Score in a Multireader, longitudinal setting. Arthritis and Rheumatism **52**(12), 3860–3867 (2005)
6. Cimmino, M.A.: Does magnetic resonance represent the gold-standard of imaging for the follow-up of arthritis? Reumatismo **58**(4), 245–252 (2006)
7. Østergaard, M., Edmonds, J., McQueen, F., et al.: An introduction to the EULAR-OMERACT Rheumatoid Arthritis MRI reference image atlas. Ann. Rheum. Dis. **64**, i3–i7 (2005). doi:10.1136/ard.2004.031773
8. McQueen, F., Lassere, M., Edmonds, J., et al.: OMERACT rheumatoid arthritis magnetic resonance imaging studies. Summary of OMERACT 6 MRImaging module. J. Rheumatol. **30**(6), 1387–1392 (2003)
9. Crowley, A.R., Dong, J.: A. McHaffie et all. Measuring bone erosion and edema in rheumatoid arthritis: a comparison of manual segmentation and RAMRIS methods. J. Magn. Reson. Imaging **33**(2), 364–371 (2011). doi:10.1002/jmri.22425

10. Huang, D., Wang, C.: Optimal multi-level thresholding using a two-stage Otsu optimization approach. Pattern Recognition Letters **30**, 275–284 (2009)

11. Adams, R., Bischof, L.: Seeded region growing. IEEE Trans. Pattern Anal. Machine Intell. **16**, 641–647 (1994). doi:10.1109/34.295913

12. Caselles, V., Kimmel, R., Sapiro, G.: Geodesic Active Contours. ICCV, 694–699 (1995)

13. Chan, T., Vese, L.: Active Contours without Edges. IEEE TIP (2001)

14. American college of rheumatology subcommittee on rheumatoid arthritis. Guidelines for the management of Rheumatoid arthritis: 2002 update. Arthritis Rheum **46**(2), 328–346, February 2002

15. Resnick, D.: Early abnormalities of pisiform and triquetrum in rheumatoid arthritis. Ann. Rheum. Dis. **35**(1), 46–50 (1976)

16. Lange. Mc Graw Hill Education. Current medical diagnosis & treatement 2015

17. Gentili, A.: Advanced imaging of gout. Semin. muscoloskelet Raiol. **7**(3), 165–174 (2003)

18. Dalbeth, N., et al.: Mechanisms of bone erosion in gout: a quantitative analysis using plain radiography and computed tomography. Ann. Rheum. Dis. **68**(8), 1290–1295 (2009)

19. Gonzalez-Lopez, L., Gamez-Nava, J.I., Jhangri, G.S., Ramos-Remus, C., Russell, A.S., Suarez-Almazor, M.E.: Prognostic factors for the development of rheumatoid arthritis and other connective tissue diseases in patients with palindromic rheumatism. J. Rheumatol. **26**(3), 540–545 (1999)

20. Avouac, J., Guerrini, H., Wipff, J., et al.: Radiological hand involvement in systemic sclerosis. Ann. Rheum. Dis. **65**(8), 1088–1092 (2006)

21. Ejbjerg, B., Narvestad, E., Jacobsen, S., et al.: Optimized low cost, low field dedicated extremity MRI is highly specific and sensitive for synovitis and bone erosions in rheumatoid arthritis wrist and finger joints: comparison with conventional high field MRI and radiography. Ann. Rheum. Dis. **64**, 1280–1287 (2005)

22. RheumaSCORE. http://www.research.softeco.it/rheumascore.aspx

23. Parascandolo, P., Cesario, L., Vosilla, L., Viano, G.: Computer aided diagnosis: state-of-the-art and application to musculoskeletal diseases. In: 3D Multiscale Physiological Human, pp. 277–296. Springer London (2014)

24. Parascandolo, P., Cesario, L., Vosilla, L., Pitikakis, M., Viano, G.: Smart brush: a real time segmentation tool for 3D medical images. In: 2013 8th International Symposium on Image and Signal Processing and Analysis (ISPA), pp. 689–694, September 4–6, 2013

25. Barbieri, F., Parascandolo, P., Vosilla, L., Cesario, L., Viano, G., Cimmino, M.A.: Assessing MRI erosions in the rheumatoid wrist: a comparison between RAMRIS and a semiautomated segmentation software. Ann. Rheum. Dis. **71**(Suppl 3) (2012)

26. Catalano, C.E., Robbiano, F., Parascandolo, P., Cesario, L., Vosilla, L., Barbieri, F., Spagnuolo, M., Viano, G., Cimmino, M.A.: Exploiting 3D part-based analysis, description and indexing to support medical applications. In: Greenspan, H., Müller, H., Syeda-Mahmood, T. (eds.) MCBR-CDS 2012. LNCS, vol. 7723, pp. 21–32. Springer, Heidelberg (2013)

27. Lorensen, W.E., Cline, H.E.: Marching cubes: a high resolution 3D surface construction algorithm. In: Proc. of ACM SIGGRAPH, pp. 163–169 (1987)

28. Kocijan, R., Harre, U., Schett, G.: ACPA and bone loss in rheumatoid arthritis. Curr. Rheumatol. Rep. **15**(10), 366 (2013). doi:10.1007/s11926-013-0366-7

29. Doghramji, P.P., Wortmann, R.L.: Hyperuricemia and gout: new concepts in diagnosis and management. Postgrad. Med. **124**(6), 98–109 (2012). doi:10.3810/pgm.2012.11.2616

30. Sulli, A., Ruaro, B., Alessandri, E., et al.: Correlations between nailfold microangiopathy severity, finger dermal thickness and fingertip blood perfusion in systemic sclerosis patients. Ann. Rheum. Dis. **73**(1), 247–251 (2014)

Novel Automatic Tool for Magnetic Resonance Imaging Quantification of Bone Erosion Scoring in Rheumatoid Arthritis

Patrizia Parascandolo[1], Lorenzo Cesario[1(✉)], Loris Vosilla[2], Francesca Barbieri[1], Marco Amedeo Cimmino[2], and Gianni Viano[1]

[1] Softeco Sismat S.r.l., Via de Marini 1, Genoa, Italy
{patrizia.parascandolo,lorenzo.cesario,
gianni.viano}@softeco.it, francesca.barbieri@unige.it
[2] DIMI, Dipartimento di Medicina Interna, Clinica Reumatologica,
Università degli Studi di Genova, Genoa, Italy
loris.vosilla@softeco.it, cimmino@unige.it

Abstract. Rheumatoid arthritis (RA) is a systemic disease that affects the synovial joints. Currently, the gold standard measurement for tracking the progression of the disease involves a semi-quantitative assessment of bone erosion, bone marrow edema and synovitis, as seen in magnetic resonance images (MRI). The work presented in this paper identifies how computer automation can be used to quantify bone erosion volumes in MRI without expert and time consuming interventions. This tool is fully integrated in a computer aided diagnosis (CAD) system named RheumaSCORE (Softeco Sismat Srl). Preliminary results of qualitative and quantitative validation are presented and discussed at the end of the paper.

Keywords: Computer aided diagnosis (CAD) · Erosion scoring · Image processing · Principal component analysis (PCA) · Shape reconstruction · Rheumascore · Rheumatoid arthritis

1 Introduction

Rheumatoid arthritis (RA) is a chronic inflammatory autoimmune disease that affects synovial joints and leads to the destruction of periarticular bone. Bone erosions are localized lesions with a break in the cortical shell. Since bone erosions are closely related to disease activity, they are an early prognostic indicator and an important clinical parameter for monitoring treatment efficacy [1,2,3]. It is therefore desirable to detect them as early as possible with high precision in order to quantify small changes. Currently, the gold-standard measurement for tracking the progression of the disease involves a semi-quantitative assessment of bone erosion, bone marrow edema and synovitis, as seen in magnetic resonance images (MRI), by a musculoskeletal radiologist.

The work presented in this paper shows how computer automation can be used to quantify bone erosion volumes in MRI without a radiologists' expert and time

V. Murino et al. (Eds.): ICIAP 2015 Workshops, LNCS 9281, pp. 151–158, 2015.
DOI: 10.1007/978-3-319-23222-5_19

consuming intervention. A new automatic 3D tool for quantification of bone erosion scoring is described and evaluated for use in a clinical setting. The effectiveness of this approach is demonstrated by presenting both qualitative and quantitative results of wrist bones considering both normal and pathological RA cases. For this purpose, the tool is fully integrated in a CAD system named RheumaSCORE [19,20,21,22].

The paper is organized as follows. Section 2 gives an overview of the existing techniques and tools for RA scoring on MRI. Section 3 provides the description of the diagnostic tool implemented. Section 4 describes the integration of the tool in the RheumaSCORE software and provides an evaluation of the performance of the approach. Qualitative results on various datasets and preliminary quantitative analysis of the performance of the method for wrist bone scoring are presented.

2   Background and Previous Work

Historically, conventional radiographs (CRs) are used to semi-quantitatively assess bone erosions in patients with RA. However, due to their projectional character, the use of CRs results in an underestimation of the number and size of erosions and therefore, probably, disease activity [4].

Other imaging modalities have emerged as methods for more sensitive detection of early bone erosions. MRI has been demonstrated to be more sensitive than radiography in detecting erosive bone changes in RA, especially the subtle changes that occur in early disease [5,6,7]. The Outcome Measures in Rheumatology (OMERACT) Rheumatoid Arthritis MRI Scoring System (RAMRIS) has been developed [10,11] with data from iterative multicenter studies [10,12,13].

Some methods for the semi-automated quantification of erosions have also been developed on MRI datasets. The studies performed by Crowley et al. [8], using MRI data, relied on manual outlining of the erosions slice by slice. While a trained operator may produce reliable results, manual outlining can be very time consuming. Moreover, a slice-wise approach does not take the true 3D erosion structure into account. In contrast, Emond et al. [9] employed a true three-dimensional (3D) segmentation of erosions in MRI data. Only the placement of a seed point and the selection of five parameter were required. Moreover, this approach has the complexity related to the choice of the parameter to segment the erosion.

In addition, to the best of our knowledge, there is no commercial framework for wrist/hand erosion scoring designed for MR images. In that sense, a first result is the tool described in this paper and fully integrated in RheumaSCORE software [19,20], a specific CAD for RA. This tool identifies and measures bone erosions, not segmenting directly the erosion, i.e. the missing part of the bone, but through the segmentation of the bone of interest and then the reconstruction of its original shape. It uses a statistical shape model extracted from a collection of training samples of healthy bone. The resulting model consists of the mean shape and a number of modes of variation obtained with a Principal Component Analysis (PCA). Every healthy bone can be obtained as a linear combination of the mean shape with these modes. The reconstruction of the original shape of the bone of interest is performed finding the best coefficients of this linear combination. The difference between the segmented bone and the reconstructed bone is the erosion of which it is possible to calculate the volume and then the scoring. Processing takes a few minutes for all wrist bones (or hand bones), which leads to a substantial reduction of diagnosis time and costs.

3   Automatic Bone Erosion Scoring

3.1   Construction of the Statistical Shape Model

Constructing a statistical shape model (SSM) basically consists of extracting the mean shape and a number of modes of variation from a collection of training samples.

Shape is defined as a property which does not change under similarity transformations, i.e. it is invariant to translation, rotation and scaling. In general, shape changes induced by these global transformations should not be modeled by an SSM in order to keep the model as specific as possible. Thus, the first step is to align all training samples in a common coordinate frame. For our application, we are interested in aligning binary images since that is how we encode the training shapes. We use a rigid-based image registration algorithm to align our training set.

The original images for the training set consists of 40 MRI volumes acquired using an Esaote C-Scan, a scanner dedicated for imaging of extremities. The sequence was a sagittal Turbo 3D T1 and the resolution was 0.55 mm x 0.55 mm in each slice with a slice thickenss between 0.60 mm and 0.80 mm (with no gap slices). Each slice is 256x256 pixels and a scan has around 105 slices. All the images are manually segmented by an expert. We choose an Euclidean signed distance function as our representation for shape. So, each registered data set $\tilde{I}$ is transferred into structure specific signed distance maps $D_a^{(i)}$, where a represents the structure of interest, and i the i-th registered image sample of the training set (Fig. 1). In these distance maps negative values are assigned to voxels within the boundary of the object, while positive values indicate voxels outside the object.

By taking the average over all these distance maps $D_a^{(i)}$ we define the mean distance map

$$\overline{D_a} = \frac{1}{n}\Sigma_i^n D_a^i \tag{1}$$

where n is the size of the training set, and the mean corrected signed distance maps

$$\tilde{D}_a^i = D_a^{(i)} - \overline{D_a} \tag{2}$$

These mean-offset functions are then used to capture the variabilities of the training shapes through the Principle Component Analysis (PCA) [15]. The PCA allows to reduce the dimensionality of the training set, i.e. to find a small set of modes that best describes the observed variation. Then, it is possible to approximate every valid shape by a linear combination of the first c modes

$$D = \overline{D} + \Sigma_{m=1}^c b_m \, \phi_m \tag{3}$$

where b_m are the weights associated with the eigenvectors ϕ_m.

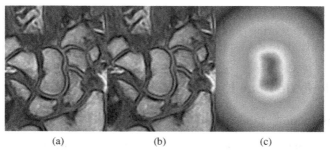

(a)   (b)   (c)

Fig. 1. Distance map of the registered capitate. In (a) the coronal slice of the original MRI volume, in (b) the segmentation of the capitate overlaid on the grayscale image and in (c) the registered distance map.

3.2   Bone Reconstruction

The reconstruction of the healthy bone of interest starting from its eroded shape and from the PCA describing the variability within the training set of corresponding healthy shapes of the bone is done in two steps as follows:

1. *First adjustment of the real bone and the model.* In this step the registration between the coordinates system of the mean binary shape of the PCA and the eroded bone is performed using a rigid transformation (rotation + translation). The resulting parameters of the transform are used during the next step.
2. *Reconstruction by successive optimizations.* An evaluation function which represents the error between the transformed model by the parameters computed in the previous step and the real bone is calculated. By repeating the optimization process, this evaluation function is minimized by changing the initial model (Fig. 2). Modifying the initial model consists in changing the c shape parameters defined by the PCA (i.e. changing the vector of parameters' weights b defined in formula (3)). The evaluation function chosen for this optimization process is the Dice's Coefficient [18] that is a statistic used for comparing the similarity of two samples. In the bone reconstruction algorithm the similarity is between the binary image of the eroded bone and the binary image made by the modified initial healthy model.

3.3   Volume Evaluation

Volumetric measurements are essential to evaluate the success of a therapy. As an example, the reduction of bone erosion's volume determines the success of the treatment. Once we have selected all voxels of a target structure, the volume represented by these voxels can be approximated for volumetry. In this work we follow the Voxel Counting with Edge Resampling method (VCER) [16].

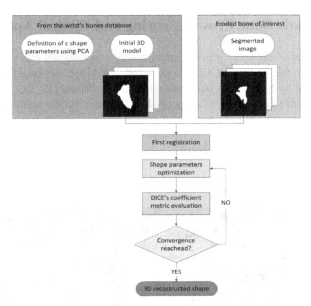

Fig. 2. Overall method for the 3D reconstruction.

After reconstructing the shape of the healthy bone, we make the difference between the original eroded segmented bone and the reconstructed bone. The resulting volume is the erosion. Then, using the voxel counting with edge resampling algorithm, we evaluate the volume and the OMERACT RAMRIS score.

Some preliminary tests have been carried on using real wrist MRI. In order to evaluate both the qualitative performance of the bone reconstruction algorithm and the quantitative reliability of the volume evaluation algorithm, described in the previous section, we simulated some erosions on healthy bones, previously segmented. In this way, it has been possible to make a visual inspection and to understand if the algorithm could fill those missing part manually deleted and reconstruct them taking the bone to its original shape.   Fig. 3 shows the erosion identification *via* bone reconstruction on healthy bones segmented in order to simulate some erosions.

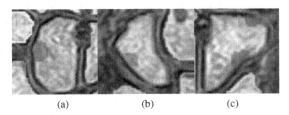

(a)   (b)   (c)

Fig. 3. Bone reconstruction of simulated eroded bones. Some erosions have been simulated on the capitate   bone (a), the scaphoid bone (b) and the hamate bone (c). In all the figures the blue area overlaid the MRI corresponds to the segmentation having holes inserted manually. The red part is the reconstructed part of the bone, i.e. the erosion, obtained using our algorithm

4   Automatic Bone Erosion Scoring and Clinical Applications

As the test results of our scoring procedure are very encouraging, this pipeline has been fully integrated in the RheumaSCORE application, a CAD (Computer-Aided Diagnosis) system developed by Softeco Sismat to address the RA disease [19,20,21,22]. Processing takes a few minutes for all wrist bones (or hand bones), which leads to a remarkable reduction of diagnosis time and costs.

Fig. 4 shows the Diagnostic environment of RheumaSCORE after the bones erosions measurement.

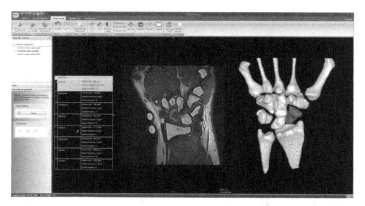

Fig. 4. RheumaSCORE: Diagnostic environment. The selected bone is the scaphoid. This bone is eroded and the missing part is shown in red.

A study comparing traditional RAMRIS score and semi-automated score by RheumaSCORE was performed. 57 patients affected by RA (42 women, median age 52 years, range 20-73 years, median disease duration 22 months, range 1-420 months) diagnosed according to the 1987 revised ACR criteria were studied. Wrist and meta-carpophalangeal (MCP) joints were imaged with a dedicated-extremity, 0.2 T MRI (Artoscan, Esaote, Genova, Italy) at baseline and after a median of 15 months (range 6-121 months). Erosions were scored according to the RAMRIS.

The study was concerned on changes in RAMRIS score (single bone and total score). We found that, comparing traditional and semi-automated RAMRIS' erosions score, perfect concordance was 45.2% at baseline and 92.9% at follow up. Further detailed information about traditional and semi-automated score's comparison can be found on the paper "An MRI study of bone erosions healing in the wrist and metacar-pophalangeal joints of patients with Rheumatoid Arthritis".

Studies for intra and inter-reader operators evaluation and for comparing the standard RAMRIS and the RheumaSCORE methods were performed: seven patients affected by RA according to the 1987 ACR criteria were studied with two MRIs with a 0.2 T dedicated machine (Artoscan, ESAOTE, Genova, Italy) using a turbo T1-weighted three dimensional sequence (T3-D T1) in the coronal plane, with subsequent multiplanar reconstructions on other planes, of the hand and wrist (baseline and follow-up 17 months apart, range 8-36 months).

The RAMRIS for erosions was calculated in agreement by two experienced readers (FB, MAC). An experienced reader (FB) and 6 inexperienced readers evaluated the 3D reconstructions of MRIs using RheumaSCORE software.

In the evaluation of bones' volumes, the intraclass correlation ICC for FB in 8 consecutive readings, 2 weeks apart, was 0.99. The ICC for the inexperienced readers was also 0.99, independently from the RAMRIS for erosions. The inter-rater agreement (k) between FB and the inexperienced readers varied between 0.77 and 0.86 (mean 0.81) for patients with a low RAMRIS for erosions of 3, and between 0.49 and 0.77 (mean 0.65) for patients with higher RAMRIS of 9. During follow up, the median RAMRIS score for erosions remained unchanged (p=0.12); accordingly, also bone and erosion volume measured by RheumaSCORE did not change (p=0.19).

The semi-automated calculation of bone and erosion volumes in MRI images of the hand and wrist of RA patients is feasible and has a good reliability. Concordance between traditional and automated RAMRIS was modest at baseline but became almost complete in the second examination (follow-up). This finding may be ascribed to a decrease of the possible interference exerted by bone marrow edema on automatic readings.

References

1. Tan, Y.K., Conaghan, P.G.: Imaging in rheumatoid arthritis. Best Pract. Res. Clin. Rheumatol. **25**(4), 569–584 (2011)
2. Schett, G., Redlich, K., Smolen, J.S.: Inflammation-induced bone loss in the rheumatic diseases. In: Primer on the Metabolic Bone Diseases and Disorders of Mineral Metabolism, 2nd edn., pp. 482–488. John Wiley & Sons, USA (2013)
3. Farrant, J.M., Grainger, A.J., O'Connor, P.J.: Advanced imaging in rheumatoid arthritis: part 2: erosions. Skeletal Radiol. **36**, 381–389 (2007)
4. Sokka, T.: Radiographic scoring in rheumatoid arthritis: a short introduction to the methods. Bull. NYU Hosp. Jt. Dis. **66**, 166–168 (2008)
5. McQueen, F.M., Stewart, N., Crabbe, J., Robinson, E., Yeoman, S., Tan, P.L., McLean, L.: Magnetic resonance imaging of the wrist in early rheumatoid arthritis reveals a high prevalence of erosions at four months after symptom onset. Ann. Rheum. Dis. **57**, 350–356 (1998)
6. Conaghan, P., O'Connor, P., McGonagle, D., Astin, P., Wakefield, R.J., Gibbon, W.W., Quinn, M., Karim, Z., Green, M.J., Proudman, S., Isaacs, J., Emery, P.: Elucidation of the relationship between synovitis and bone damage: a randomized magnetic resonance imaging study of individual joints in patients with early rheumatoid arthritis. Arthritis Rheum. **48**, 64–71 (2003)
7. Lindegaard, H.M., Vallø, J., Hørslev-Petersen, K., Junker, P., Østergaard, M.: Low-cost, low-field dedicated extremity magnetic resonance imaging in early rheumatoid arthritis: a 1-year follow-up study. Ann. Rheum. Dis. **65**, 1208–1212 (2006)
8. Crowley, A.R., Dong, J., McHaffie, A., Clarke, A.W., Reeves, Q., Williams, M., Robinson, E., Dalbeth, N., McQueen, F.M.: Measuring bone erosion and edema in rheumatoid arthritis: a comparison of manual segmentation and RAMRIS methods. J. Magn. Reson. Imaging **33**, 364–371 (2011)
9. Emond, P.D., Inglis, D., Choi, A., Tricta, J., Adachi, J.D., Gordon, C.L.: Volume measurement of bone erosions in magnetic resonance images of patients with rheumatoid arthritis. Magn. Reson. Med. **67**, 814–823 (2012)

10. Østergaard, M., Peterfy, C., Conaghan, P., McQueen, F., Bird, P., Ejbjerg, B., Shnier, R., O'Connor, P., Klarlund, M., Emery, P., Genant, H., Lasser, M., Edmonds, J.: OMERACT Rheumatoid Arthritis Magnetic Resonance Imaging Studies. Core set of MRI acquisitions, joint pathology definitions, and the OMERACT RA-MRI scoring system. J. Rheumatol. **30**, 1385–1386 (2003)
11. Lassere, M., McQueen, F., Østergaard, M., Conaghan, P., Shnier, R., Peterfy, C., Klarlund, M., Bird, P., O'Connor, P., Stewart, N., Emery, P., Genant, H., Edmonds, J.: OMERACT Rheumatoid Arthritis Magnetic Resonance Imaging Studies. Exercise 3: an international multicenter reliability study using the RA-MRI score. J. Rheumatol. **30**, 1366–1375 (2003)
12. Østergaard, M., Klarlund, M., Lassere, M., Conaghan, P., Peterfy, C., McQueen, F., O'Connor, P., Shnier, R., Stewart, N., McGonagle, D., Emery, P., Genant, H., Edmonds, J.: Interreader agreement in the assessment of magnetic resonance images of rheumatoid arthritis wrist and finger joints – an international multicenter study. J. Rheumatol. **28**, 1143–1150 (2001)
13. Conaghan, P., Lassere, M., Østergaard, M., Peterfy, C., McQueen, F., O'Connor, P., Bird, P., Ejbjerg, B., Klarlund, M., Shnier, R., Genant, H., Emery, P., Edmonds, J.: OMERACT Rheumatoid Arthritis Magnetic Resonance Imaging Studies. Exercise 4: an international multicenter longitudinal study using the RA-MRI score. J. Rheumatol. **30**, 1376–1379 (2003)
14. Parascandolo, P., Cesario, L., Vosilla, L., Pitikakis, M., Viano, G.: Smart brush: a real time segmentation tool for 3D medical images. In: 8th International Symposium on Presented at Image and Signal Processing and Analysis (ISPA), pp. 689–694 (2013)
15. Cootes, T.F., Taylor, C.J., Graham, J.: Active shape models- their training and application. Comput. Vis. Image Underst. **61**, 38–59 (1995)
16. Bartz, D., Orman, J., Gürvit, Ö.: Accurate volumetric measurements of anatomical cavities. Methods of Information in Medicine **43**(4), 331–335 (2004)
17. Lorensen, W.E., Cline, H.E.: Marching cubes: a high resolution 3D surface construction algorithm. In: Proc. of ACM SIGGRAPH, pp. 163–169 (1987)
18. Dice, L.R.: Measures of the Amount of Ecologic Association Between Species. Ecology **26**(3), 297–302 (1945)
19. RheumaSCORE. http://www.research.softeco.it/rheumascore.aspx
20. Barbieri, F., Parascandolo, P., Vosilla, L., Cesario, L., Viano, G., Cimmino, M.A.: Assessing MRI erosions in the rheumatoid wrist: a comparison between RAMRIS and a semiautomated segmentation software. Ann. Rheum. Dis. **71**(Suppl 3) (2012)
21. Catalano, C.E., Robbiano, F., Parascandolo, P., Cesario, L., Vosilla, L., Barbieri, F., Spagnuolo, M., Viano, G., Cimmino, M.A.: Exploiting 3D part-based analysis, description and indexing to support medical applications. In: Greenspan, H., Müller, H., Syeda-Mahmood, T. (eds.) MCBR-CDS 2012. LNCS, vol. 7723, pp. 21–32. Springer, Heidelberg (2013)
22. Parascandolo, P., Cesario, L., Vosilla, L., Viano, G.: Computer aided diagnosis: state-of-the-art and application to musculoskeletal diseases. In: 3D Multiscale Physiological Human, pp. 277–296. Springer London (2014)

Optimizing and Evaluating a Graph-Based Segmentation of MRI Wrist Bones

Sonia Nardotto, Roberta Ferretti, Laura Gemme$^{(\boxtimes)}$, and Silvana Dellepiane

DITEN, Università degli Studi di Genova, Genova, Italy
{sonia.nardotto,roberta.ferretti,laura.gemme}@edu.unige.it,
silvana.dellepiane@unige.it

Abstract. In this paper, a quantitative evaluation of the graph-based segmentation method presented in a previous work is performed. The algorithm, starting from a single source element belonging to a region of interest, aims at finding the optimal path minimizing a new cost function for all elements of a digital volume. The method is an adaptive, unsupervised, and semi-automatic approach.

For the assessment, a training phase and a testing phase are considered. The system is able to learn and adapt to the ground truth. The performance of the method is estimated by computing classical indices from the confusion matrix, similarity measures, and distance measures.

Our work is based on the segmentation and 3D reconstructions of carpal bones derived from Magnetic Resonance Imaging (MRI) volumetric data of patients affected by rheumatic diseases.

Keywords: Quantitative evaluation · 3D graph-based segmentation · Carpal bones · MRI volumes

1   Introduction

Rheumatic musculoskeletal diseases are among the most common chronic conditions affecting the European population. Some of these diseases, such as osteoarthritis, are the result of wear and tear; others, such as Rheumatoid Arthritis (RA), are autoimmune diseases. In some cases, chronic inflammation leads to the destruction of cartilage, bone, and ligaments, causing deformity of the joints.

Recent research works have proven that through the analysis of Magnetic Resonance Imaging (MRI) erosive change due to rheumatoid arthritis can be detected with greater sensitivity than by using conventional radiography, particularly in the early stages of the disease [2]. In addition, MRI allows the visualization of the three main signs of RA: synovitis, bone oedema and bone erosion [3].

For these reasons, it is important to perform a quantitative or semi-quantitative analysis, and novel scoring systems have recently been proposed such as the OMERACT rheumatoid arthritis scoring system (RAMRIS), which is based on MRI acquisitions [4].

In this context, volume segmentation plays an important role because it makes it possible to extract every single bone and analyze it to evaluate the disease progression.

© Springer International Publishing Switzerland 2015
V. Murino et al. (Eds.): ICIAP 2015 Workshops, LNCS 9281, pp. 159–166, 2015.
DOI: 10.1007/978-3-319-23222-5_20

The aim of this work is to optimize and evaluate the graph-based segmentation method presented in [1] against the available ground truth, which is representative of the user needs and requirements. A training phase is executed to allow the method to learn and adapt itself to the given data set characteristics and to the user desiderata. Due to the noise, extremely low contrast, and bone conformation, the preliminary segmentation results achieved with no a priori knowledge show some differences from the proposed training results. For instance, in the ground-truth volumes, internal holes are often considered as belonging to the bone tissue.

The training phase evaluates some simple post-processing steps that allow improving the segmented volumes and achieving the best result. To this end, a few Mathematical Morphology (MM) operators are proposed to regularize the shape, fill holes, and make the result more robust to noise. In this step, the Receiving Operating Characteristic curve (ROC) and some similarity measures are taken into account.

In a subsequent phase, the testing data set is processed, and all of the obtained results are tested by applying similarity measures and distance metrics between the real and achieved volume surfaces.

The paper is organized as follows. In Section 2, the proposed segmentation approach is briefly introduced, together with a brief description of the database and its use in the training and testing phases. In Section 3, the parameters used for quantitative evaluation are described and discussed. The application of the method to MRI volumes of the hand district and the performance evaluation are presented in Section 4.

2   Proposed Method

This work focuses on applying the segmentation approach presented in [1] to MRI wrist volumes, a training phase for its optimization, and a subsequent quantitative evaluation. The employed database consists of hand and wrist district MRI volumes whose ground truth is based on a segmentation process accomplished by expert physicians in this medical field.

After giving the main idea of the method and after introducing the reference database (DB), the two phases of training and testing are described.

Despite the very low contrast of the wrist bones with respect to the surrounding tissues, the presence of noise, and the lack of shape and smoothness information in the proposed segmentation method, the extracted Region of Interest (ROI) volumes are quite accurate and well separated from nearby similar structures.

The segmentation method is very sensitive to inhomogeneities, so that fine details and internal holes are tracked even when they are of no interest to the medical expert.

By comparing the results obtained by the proposed segmentation approach with the ground truth, one can appreciate how the detected volumes and surfaces can significantly benefit from simple post-processing steps. Simple mathematical morphology operators greatly improve the result accuracy.

2.1   Segmentation

The proposed method is a 3D seed-based algorithm that applies a graph-based segmentation driven by research into the minimum cost paths for the analysis of digital volumes. Starting from a single seed point belonging to the ROI chosen by the user, an optimal aggregation algorithm selects the best paths and finds a spanning tree that is minimum with respect to the following cost function [1]:

$$f_{w_s}(v_i) = \min_{\pi(s,v_i)}[\max_{x \in \pi(s,v_i)} w_s(x)] \tag{1}$$

where w is the weight associated with the graph vertices, and $\pi(s, v_i)$ is the path from the seed s to a generic vertex v_i.

The proposed cost criterion is comparable to the single-source shortest path problem for a graph with non-negative vertex weights, producing a Minimum Path Spanning Tree (MPST) in routing problems [1].

It is a non-iterative mechanism adaptive to the image content that takes into account the contextual information. The main advantages are that the segmentation can be obtained in one shot. As opposed to other graph-based methods, this algorithm considers only a single seed point (usually in the literature, two seeds are given: one for the foreground and one for the background), and its growth mechanism produces results that are also optimal from the computational point of view.

To obtain a binary volume from the MPST, it is necessary to apply a graph cut. Because the present paper is devoted to the study of the efficiency of the method in separating single wrist bone tissues, the threshold is chosen in a semi-interactive way corresponding to the maximum graph-cut that does not generate leakage problems. As a consequence, one can prove that the optimal result is encompassed in the MPST, from where it can be extracted.

The elapsed processing time is approximately 30 seconds for each bone when running on an Intel Core i7-4700MQ (2.4 GHz, 6 MB cache, 4 core).

2.2   Database: Training and Testing Phases

The database (DB) used is described in paper [7] and is made of 100 MRI T1-weighted volumes acquired by the 0.2 Tesla ARTOSCAN (Esaote Spa, Genova, Italy). Each volume is made of approximately 120 images of size 256×256 pixels. A sample coronal slice is shown in Fig. 1.

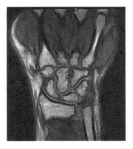

Fig. 1. Coronal MRI slice of the wrist.

A wrist is a complex joint between the distal forearm and the hand, composed of 15 bones: the distal parts of the radius and ulna, eight carpal bones, and the proximal parts of five metacarpal bones.

The bone volumes have been segmented by medical experts with RheumaSCORE Software, implemented by Softeco Sismat srl (Genova, Italy) [8]. The segmentation method takes into account bone and erosion; areas of oedema are considered to belong to the bone tissue.

After the preliminary segmentation step applied without any a priori or model information, the training phase is started where the binary segmented volumes are compared with the ground truth. In this phase, the training of the proposed method is executed to decide which type of post-processing gives the best results. As said before, the approach is an adaptive system that learns from the volumes present in the database.

For all of the binary volumes of the analyzed patients, we considered the following operations of mathematical morphology: a 3D dilation applied one time and two times (with a circular structural element) and a 3D dilation with hole filling. After the application of these processing steps, the results are evaluated by means of the classical parameters (sensitivity and precision) and similarity measure (Dice coefficient). This analysis provides the best post-processing segmentation result, which drives the subsequent testing phase. During the testing phase, all of the test cases are evaluated by the above mentioned measures.

Various measures exist to evaluate the quality of a segmentation; the most common are metrics based on volumetric overlap and surface distance. Depending on the application, one parameter may be favoured over another. In this work, various metrics are employed to allow a global quality evaluation.

3   Quantitative Evaluation

In this section, the already mentioned metrics used for the performance evaluation are described in detail, starting from the similarity measure and followed by distance measures.

The basic indices Precision (PR), Sensitivity (SENS) and DICE are given by these formulae:

$$PR = \frac{TP}{TP+FP}, \quad SENS = \frac{TP}{TP+FN} \tag{2}$$

$$DICE = \frac{2\,TP}{(TP+FP)+(TP+FN)} \tag{3}$$

where TP are the True Positives, FP are the False Positives, and FN are the False Negatives. Precision (or positive predictive value) is the proportion of the predicted positive cases that are correct; Sensitivity tells how many voxels are correctly classified positive of the total positive observations. The values of 1-precision (on the x axis) and sensitivity (on the y axis) are usually plotted in a ROC graph.

The Dice coefficient is similarity index that measures the overlap between two sets; a value of 0 indicates no overlap and a value of 1 indicates perfect agreement.

Higher numbers note better agreement between the sets, so when we apply these indices to evaluate the agreement between the segmentation results, the goal is to get as close to 1 as possible.

After some simple operations, the Dice coefficient can be reformulated by these expressions:

$$DICE = \frac{2}{PR^{-1}+SENS^{-1}} = \frac{2}{2+\frac{err}{TP}} \tag{4}$$

where *err* is the overall segmentation error.

Formula (4) shows the relationship between the Dice coefficient and precision and sensitivity, particularly with the inverse of these two parameters. It may be noted that the Dice coefficient have nonlinear correspondences with the error [5].

The evaluation metrics based on distances [6] perform a comparison of the surface voxels of two segmentations A and B. For each surface voxel of A, the Euclidean distance to the closest surface voxel of B is measured.

Let $S(A)$ be the set of surface voxels of A. The shortest distance of an arbitrary voxel v to $S(A)$ is defined as $d(v, S(A)) = \min_{s_A \in S(A)} \|v - s_A\|$, where $\|\cdot\|$ denotes the Euclidean distance.

The Average Symmetric Surface Distance (ASD) is given by

$$ASD(A, B) = \frac{1}{|S(A)|+|S(B)|} \left(\sum_{s_A \in S(A)} d(s_A, S(B)) + \sum_{s_B \in S(B)} d(s_B, S(A)) \right) \tag{5}$$

The Root Mean Square Symmetric Surface Distance (RMSD) is

$$RMSD(A, B) = \sqrt{\frac{1}{|S(A)|+|S(B)|} \cdot \left(\sum_{s_A \in S(A)} d^2(s_A, S(B)) + \sum_{s_B \in S(B)} d^2(s_B, S(A)) \right)} \tag{6}$$

These two distances are strongly correlated, with RMSD giving a large penalty for large deviations from the true contour.

The Maximum Symmetric Surface Distance (Hausdorff distance) is defined as

$$MSD(A, B) = \max\{\max_{s_A \in S(A)} d(s_A, S(B)), \max_{s_B \in S(B)} d(s_B, S(A))\} \tag{7}$$

This last metric is sensitive to outliers and returns the true maximum error. By the definition of the formulae, the distance is 0 for a perfect segmentation, and greater the value of the distance, the worse the segmentation is.

4   Results and Discussion

For the experiments, 43 patients are analyzed and evaluated; 10 of these cases are non-pathological. In particular, in the training phase, 20 pathological and 4 non-pathological cases are studied. In the testing phase, 13 pathological and 6 non- pathological cases are considered. For the present application, the carpal bones are taken into account: the scaphoid, lunate, triquetrum, pisiform, trapezium, trapezoid, capitate and hamate.

Training Phase. After the segmentation, a binary volume is obtained for each bone. To regularize the results and improve the accuracy with respect to the ground truth, some mathematical morphology steps can be applied to each bone volume. This phase allows the determination of the best MM operator to apply and the corresponding structural element. The considered expansions are 3D dilation, 3D dilation applied twice and 3D dilation with filling holes.

In Fig. 2, it is possible to observe, for the triquetrum bone, the trend of the Dice coefficient in the different patients analyzed for all three dilations. In almost all cases, the best result is the 3D dilation with hole filling.

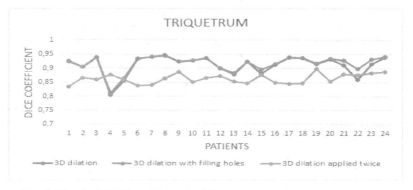

Fig. 2. Trend of DICE coefficient in different patients for all three dilations.

Fig. 3 shows the 3D visualization of all bones obtained using the 3D dilation with hole filling (on the left) and the ground truth (on the right).

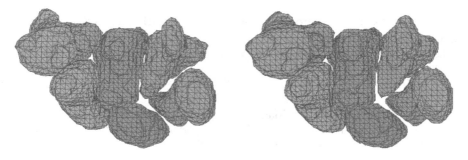

Fig. 3. 3D visualization of results retrieved by our method (on the left) and by the database (on the right)

Testing Phase. Once the 3D dilation with hole filling is defined as the best procedure, 19 patients are evaluated. A first analysis is performed using the Dice coefficient. As shown in Tab.1 (Testing phase), the mean, minimum and maximum values are computed for each bone. The value 1 corresponds to the two coincident volumes. In our cases, the Dice coefficient takes values of approximately 0.91, so the results obtained are good. By analysing the minimum and maximum values, one can note that they are distributed within a limited range.

By comparing the training and testing phases, it results that the mean values are similar. This underlines the validity of the testing phase.

Table 1. Dice coefficients in the Training and Testing phases for each carpal bone.

TRANING PHASE				TESTING PHASE			
DICE COEFFICIENT				DICE COEFFICIENT			
	Mean	Minimum	Maximum		Mean	Minimum	Maximum
CAPITATE	0.9323	0.8128	0.9626	CAPITATE	0.9189	0.8430	0.9620
TRIQUETRUM	0.8967	0.7573	0.9435	TRIQUETRUM	0.8921	0.6818	0.9411
PISIFORM	0.9142	0.8298	0.9515	PISIFORM	0.9214	0.8494	0.9463
SCAPHOID	0.9346	0.8324	0.9603	SCAPHOID	0.9308	0.8571	0.9603
LUNATE	0.8994	0.7098	0.9539	LUNATE	0.8893	0.6203	0.9464
TRAPEZIUM	0.9016	0.7858	0.9456	TRAPEZIUM	0.9036	0.7817	0.9477
TRAPEZOID	0.9165	0.8116	0.9463	TRAPEZOID	0.9002	0.7241	0.9509
HAMATE	0.8938	0.6484	0.9569	HAMATE	0.9014	0.7622	0.9448
MEAN	0.9111	0.7735	0.9526	MEAN	0.9072	0.7650	0.9499

A second analysis applied to the volumes is based on the distances ASD, RMSD, and MSD. The results obtained for each bone and the mean values are shown in Tab.2 (Testing phase). The results are also good for these parameters. In fact, for ASD and RMSD, the obtained values are on an average under unity. The values of MSD are larger than the previous ones because they are not normalized over the total surface and they take into account the worst case. However, on an average, the results are close to 4 voxels. Also in this case the mean values in the two phases are similar.

Table 2. Distance measure in the Training and Testing phases for each carpal bone.

TRAINING PHASE				TESTING PHASE			
	ASD	RMSD	MSD		ASD	RMSD	MSD
CAPITATE	0.6038	0.9283	4.9703	CAPITATE	0.6468	0.9566	4.8575
TRIQUETRUM	0.6810	1.0198	4.6848	TRIQUETRUM	0.8259	1.2548	5.1991
PISIFORM	0.5321	0.7981	3.2313	PISIFORM	0.5325	0.8062	3.1545
SCAPHOID	0.4920	0.7677	3.5450	SCAPHOID	0.5471	0.8289	3.4033
LUNATE	0.6645	0.9913	4.2234	LUNATE	0.6945	1.0275	4.3575
TRAPEZIUM	0.6699	0.9854	4.1040	TRAPEZIUM	0.7062	1.0335	4.1369
TRAPEZOID	0.5288	0.7994	3.3465	TRAPEZOID	0.6020	0.9163	3.7777
HAMATE	0.7309	1.0788	4.9428	HAMATE	0.6665	0.9798	4.7162
MEAN	0,6129	0,9211	4.1310	MEAN	0.6527	0.9754	4.2003

5   Conclusions

In this work, a quantitative evaluation of the graph-based segmentation method has been performed. The proposed approach essentially consists of three steps: the segmentation, the training phase, and the testing phase. The segmentation, starting from a single seed and using graph theory, allows the extraction of each bone separately. The training phase has been crucial to defining the best result of our system with respect to the ground truth by computing some common parameters (sensitivity and precision) and similarity measure (Dice coefficient). The testing phase proves the robustness of our method by computing similarity and distance measures (Average Symmetric Surface Distance, Root Mean Square Symmetric Surface Distance, Hausdorff Distance).

The application consists of the extraction of carpal bones from real MRI volumes. It is possible to apply this method to different anatomical districts and different pathologies using appropriate qualitative validation.

The results show the good accuracy and precision of the method with respect to the ground truth. As future work, we intend to automate the optimization process and validate all the data sets.

Acknowledgments. The MRI volumes are available thanks to the Project MEDIARE: "New methodologies of Diagnostic Imaging for Rheumatic Diseases". PAR FAS 2007-2013 Program 4 – Pos. N. 14.

References

1. Gemme, L., Dellepiane, S.: A new graph-based method for automatic segmentation. In: 18th International Conference on Image Analysis and Processing, ICIAP, Genova (in press, 2015)
2. Włodarczyk, J., Czaplicka, K., Tabor, Z., Wojciechowski, W., Urbanik, A.: Segmentation of bones in magnetic resonance images of the wrist. International Journal of Computer Assisted Radiology and Surgery, 1–13 (2014)
3. Cimmino, M.A., Innocenti, S., Livrone, F., Magnaguagno, F., Silvestri, E., Garlaschi, G.: Dynamic gadolinium-enhanced magnetic resonance imaging of the wrist in patients with rheumatoid arthritis can discriminate active from inactive disease. Arthritis & Rheumatism 48(5), 1207–1213 (2003)
4. Boesen, M., Østergaard, M., Cimmino, M.A., Kubassova, O., Jensen, K.E., Bliddal, H.: MRI quantification of rheumatoid arthritis: current knowledge and future perspectives. European Journal of Radiology 71(2), 189–196 (2009)
5. Chang, H.H., Zhuang, A.H., Valentino, D.J., Chu, W.C.: Performance measure characterization for evaluating neuroimage segmentation algorithms. Neuroimage 47(1), 122–135 (2009)
6. Heimann, T., Van Ginneken, B., Styner, M.A., Arzhaeva, Y., Aurich, V., Bauer, C., Wolf, I.: Comparison and evaluation of methods for liver segmentation from CT datasets. IEEE Transactions on Medical Imaging 28(8), 1251–1265 (2009)
7. Tomatis, V., et al.: A database of segmented MRI images of the wrist and the hand in patients with rheumatic diseases. In: Murino, V., Puppo, E., Sona, D., Cristani, M., Sansone, C. (eds.) ICIAP 2015 Workshops. LNCS, vol. 9281, pp. 143–150. Springer, Heidelberg (2015)
8. Parascandolo, P., Cesario, L., Vosilla, L., Viano, G.: Computer aided diagnosis: state-of-the-art and application to musculoskeletal diseases. In: 3D Multiscale Physiological Human, pp. 277–296. Springer, London (2014)

Generation of 3D Canonical Anatomical Models: An Experience on Carpal Bones

Imon Banerjee[1]([⊠]), Hamid Laga[2], Giuseppe Patanè[1], Sebastian Kurtek[3], Anuj Srivastava[4], and Michela Spagnuolo[1]

[1] CNR-IMATI, Genova, Italy
{imon.banerjee,giuseppe.patane,michela.spagnuolo}@ge.imati.cnr.it
[2] University of South Australia, Adelaide, Australia
Hamid.Laga@unisa.edu.au
[3] The Ohio State University, Columbus, USA
kurtek.1@stat.osu.edu
[4] Florida State University, Tallahassee, USA
anuj@stat.fsu.edu

Abstract. The paper discusses the initial results obtained for the generation of canonical 3D models of anatomical parts, built on real patient data. 3D canonical models of anatomy are key elements in a computer-assisted diagnosis; for instance, they can support pathology detection, semantic annotation of patient-specific 3D reconstructions, quantification of pathological markers. Our approach is focused on carpal bones and on the elastic analysis of 3D reconstructions of these bones, which are segmented from MRI scans, represented as 0-genus triangle meshes, and parameterized on the sphere. The original method [8] relies on a set of sparse correspondences, defined as matching vertices. For medical applications, it is desirable to constrain the mean shape generation to set-up the correspondences among a larger set of anatomical landmarks, including vertices, lines, and areas. Preliminary results are discussed and future development directions are sketched.

Keywords: Medical data · Carpal bones · Shape analysis · Mean shape

1 Introduction

Thanks to the widespread availability of medical imaging devices, digital 3D data of patients are more and more used, accurate and massive. Diagnosis, image-guided surgery, prosthesis fitting or legal medicine now heavily rely on the analysis of 3D information, such as data measuring the spatial extent of organs, tissues, cells, and even molecules. While there is an agreement on the importance of patient-specific models of the human body, there is still a huge gap between patient data and actual 3D models able to simulate digitally the specificity of each patient, the complexity of the human body, and its anatomical sub-systems (e.g., cardiovascular, musculoskeletal, gastrointestinal systems).

© Springer International Publishing Switzerland 2015
V. Murino et al. (Eds.): ICIAP 2015 Workshops, LNCS 9281, pp. 167–174, 2015.
DOI: 10.1007/978-3-319-23222-5_21

The shape of anatomical structures is highly important: shape is, indeed, related to function and its deviation from a *normality* might indicate pathological situations. The shape variability, even within healthy situations, is considerable: statistical shape models have been used for guiding 3D image segmentation [11] and cope with the variability of shapes in this phase of medical data analysis. This fact made it difficult until now to exploit fully the usage of 3D reconstructions of anatomical parts for supporting diagnosis or follow-up studies.

In this paper, we explore the suitability of statistical shape analysis to produce 3D *canonical models* of bones, built from homogeneous classes of 3D bone reconstructions, extracted from MRI data. Starting with the method proposed in [8], our aim is to generate a 3D model that captures the variability exhibited by the members of the class, while preserving important anatomical landmarks, which characterize both the function and status of the anatomical part. We argue that 3D canonical models could be used to support diagnosis of musculoskeletal diseases, acting as reference 3D atlases (healthy average shape) based on which important morphometric parameters can be evaluated and quantified.

The paper is organized as follows. First (Sect. 2), we describe the role of 3D canonical models in medicine and give more details on the type and number of anatomical landmarks that are relevant for describing carpal bones. Then (Sect. 3), we introduce the reference framework for the generation of mean shapes, which uses the definition of a shape space constructed from a sparse set of corresponding shape landmarks. The two approaches to 3D mean shape generation, augmented by anatomical landmarks, are described together with the experimental setting. Finally (Sect. 4), our preliminary results are discussed and future work is presented (Sect. 5).

2   3D Canonical Models in the Medical Domain

There is an agreement in medicine that both spatial data (e.g., drawings, 2D/3D image, 3D models) and symbolic information (e.g., texts, taxonomies, biomedical ontologies) have equal importance for describing the human anatomy, and the optimal solution goes in the direction of a tighter integration of the two [2]. Moreover, a comprehensive integration between patient-specific geometric data and symbolic information is required to bring 3D patient-specific models (3D-PSM) fully into clinical practice: this challenging research direction mainly builds on the processes required to (i) extract automatically 3D models from acquisitions (e.g., MRI, CT) and to (ii) characterize the 3D reconstructions according to the needs of the bio-medical domain.

The paper addresses the bridge between (i) and (ii), investigating an approach to define canonical 3D models of anatomy, which encapsulates and integrates medical knowledge (e.g., presence of anatomical landmarks) and shape variability (i.e., statistical variations within an anatomical class). This idea will be discussed focusing on statistical 3D atlases of carpal bones. The wrist joint consists of eight carpal bones-hamate, scaphoid, trapezium, trapezoid, pisiform, triquetrum, capitate. In general, each carpal bone has complex and variable geometry, and knowledge about healthy shape variations is essential for the diagnosis of wrist pathologies, such as osteoarthritis or rheumatoid arthritis.

Today, various digital 3D atlases [3, 10] are available and the access to spatial digital entities tagged with appropriate symbolic information provides an optimal understanding of generic anatomical knowledge. This kind of 3D atlases are used mostly for educational purposes, while computer-assisted diagnosis systems need more specific and statistically-relevant 3D reference shapes to evaluate the regularity of anatomical structures. We target the definition of patient-derived atlases, and we envisage the definition of methods that, using these atlases, might derive automatically morphometric or morphological values for the relevant parameters and descriptors that are considered crucial for the description of the anatomy and its function.

3D reference models of healthy bones are indeed necessary to automatize a number of operations that could help clinicians in their daily practice: these include, for instance, the comparison of a patient-specific 3D reconstructions with the reference healthy models in order to detect anomalies (e.g., fractures, deformations), monitor changes (e.g., pathology evolution), quantify morphometric parameters (e.g., volume, distal area), or compute markers of pathologies (e.g., scores of bone erosion). Anatomical landmarks are defined as any anatomical feature (e.g., fold, prominence, duct, vessel) consistently presents in a tissue (e.g., bone, muscle) that serves to indicate a specific structure or position, and that helps to determine homologous parts of an organism. For carpal bones, anatomical landmarks can be, for instance, contact area, pressure points, or ligament insertion sites that are located on the boundary of the 3D model. Often, these landmarks can be correlated with geometric features, such as grooves or ridges. An interesting study of the capability of geometric reasoning for the extraction of anatomical landmarks of femur is given in [12]. To treat complex injuries or fractures, or in the diagnosis of musculoskeletal pathologies, such as osteoarthritis or rheumatoid arthritis, clinicians need to have a clear idea about the 3D shape of the patient bones, as well as specific positions and characteristics of these landmarks in the patient.

In the present study, we build a taxonomy of landmarks for carpal bones in OWL language, which formalizes a set of landmarks and has been collected by osteological surveys and clinical literatures, and discussed among medical professionals. The landmarks refer to: (i) *areal features*, which are typically used to describe the shape of the bone, and indicate the correlation of the shape with its function within the articulation (e.g., the articular and non-articular facets of the bone, or prominent features, such as the scaphoid tubercle); (ii) *linear features*, which usually delineate the boundaries between the landmark regions; (iii) *point features*, which typically represent either an extremal feature of the bone, such the tip of a protruded facet, or functional sites within the bone, such as ligament insertion sites. It is important to underline that the landmarks have a varying topological dimension and influence the statistical generation of mean shapes. Given the nature of the landmarks, it is clear that their geometric definition is intrinsically vague and their location, or boundaries, is hardly captured by mathematical formulation. Statistical analysis is therefore much more appropriate to locate them.

3 Statistical Shape Analysis

The main steps of the statistical analysis are: elastic registration, landmark-guided refinement of the registration, and statistic analysis.

Elastic Registration. According to [8], we represent anatomical shapes as spherically-parameterized surfaces $f : \mathbb{S}^2 \to \mathbb{R}^3$. Let the set of all such surfaces be $\mathcal{F} = \{f : \mathbb{S}^2 \mapsto \mathbb{R}^3 | \int_{\mathbb{S}^2} |f(\mathbf{s})|^2 ds < \infty$ and f is smooth$\}$, where $\mathbf{s} = (\theta, \phi)$ are the standard spherical coordinates, $ds = \sin(\theta)d\theta d\phi$ the standard Lebesgue measure on $\mathbb{S}^2$, and $|\cdot|$ denotes the standard 2-norm in $\mathbb{R}^3$. Let also Γ be the set of all diffeomorphisms of $\mathbb{S}^2$ to itself. With a slight abuse of notation, we assume that all the surfaces in $\mathcal{F}$ have been normalized for translation and scale. Let each surface of interest be manually annotated by n anatomical landmarks and $\mathbf{s}_1, \mathbf{s}_2, \ldots, \mathbf{s}_n$ are their location on $\mathbb{S}^2$, such that $f(\mathbf{s}_i)$, $i = 1, 2, \ldots, n$, become the given landmarks on a parametrized surface f.

With this representation, the elastic registration of two surfaces f_1 and f_2 can be formulated as the problem of finding the optimal rotation $O \in SO(3)$ and diffeomorphism, or re-parameterization, $\gamma \in \Gamma$, such that the distance between f_1 and $(Of_2, \gamma) = Of_2 \circ \gamma$ is minimized:

$$(O^*, \gamma^*) = \arg \min_{SO(3) \times \Gamma} d(f_1, (Of_2, \gamma)), \tag{1}$$

where $d(\cdot, \cdot)$ is a certain measure of distances between surfaces in $\mathcal{F}$. Kurtek *et al.* [6,7] showed that the Euclidean distance (or $\mathbb{L}^2$ metric) is not suitable for comparing surfaces in $\mathcal{F}$, and thus for solving the registration problem. In fact, the $\mathbb{L}^2$ metric can lead to non-symmetric registration between f_1 and f_2, and more importantly, the re-parameterization group does not act by isometry under this metric, i.e. $\|f_1 \circ \gamma - f_2 \circ \gamma\| \neq \|f_1 - f_2\|$ unless γ is area preserving, which is often not the case, particularly when dealing with elastic deformations.

To overcome these limitations of the $\mathbb{L}^2$ metric, Jermyn *et al.* [5] proposed a simplified elastic metric that quantifies differences between two surfaces f_1 and f_2 as a weighted sum of the amount of bending and stretching that is needed to align one surface onto the other. Furthermore, they showed that by carefully choosing the weights of the two terms, the metric reduces to an Euclidean distance between the *Square Root Normal Fields* (SRNF) representations of the two surfaces. Formally, the SRNF representation of a surface f is a function $q : \mathbb{S}^2 \to \mathbb{R}^3$ defined as $q(\mathbf{s}) = \frac{n(\mathbf{s})}{\sqrt{a(\mathbf{s})}}$, where $n(\mathbf{s}) = \frac{\partial f}{\partial \theta} \times \frac{\partial f}{\partial \phi}$ is the normal to f at $\mathbf{s} = (\theta, \phi)$ and $a(\mathbf{s}) = |\mathbf{n}(\mathbf{s})|$ is the local surface area at s.

With this representation, the elastic registration problem defined in Eq. (1) can be formulated using the Euclidean metric in the space of SRNFs:

$$(O^*, \gamma^*) = \arg \min_{SO(3) \times \Gamma} \|q_1 - (Oq_2 \gamma)\|^2, \tag{2}$$

where q_i is the SRNF representation of f_i and $(q, \gamma) = \sqrt{J_\gamma} q \circ \gamma$. Here, J_γ is the determinant of the Jacobian of γ. Note that the Euclidean distance in the space of SRNFs corresponds to the geodesic distance in $\mathcal{F}$. We refer the reader to [5] and [7] for the theoretical details of this representation and also for the approach used for solving the optimization of Eq. (2). Then, we rotate f_2 with O^* and re-parameterize it with γ^* to obtain a new surface $\tilde{f}_2$ that is in full correspondence with f_1.

Landmark-guided Refinement of the Registration. While the proposed approach finds plausible elastic registrations between surfaces, in many cases, however, it fails to correctly align the anatomical landmarks (provided by medical experts), particularly when the landmarks are located in feature-less regions. We propose to refine the registration by finding an additional diffeomorphism γ_0 that aligns the landmarks of the two surfaces. Let us assume that the surface f_1 is annotated by a number, n, of anatomical landmarks. Let $s_1, s_2, \ldots, s_n$ be the locations of these landmarks on $\mathbb{S}^2$. Similarly, let $\tilde{s}_1, \tilde{s}_2, \ldots, \tilde{s}_n$ be the locations on $\mathbb{S}^2$ of the landmarks of $\tilde{f}_2$. Let us assume that the corresponding landmark pairs are $\{f_1(s_i), \tilde{f}_2(\tilde{s}_i)\}$. Following [8], we connect each pair of matched landmarks on $\mathbb{S}^2$ with a great circle and sample it uniformly using k steps ($k = 5$, in our implementation). Then, we solve, using [4], for a small deformation that matches the $(k-1)$-st point to the k-th point on this circle for all j. A composition of these k small deformations leads to the larger desired deformation γ_0. Finally, the composition $\gamma^* \circ \gamma_0$ leads to the optimal diffeomorphism that puts f_2 in full correspondence with f_1.

Summary Statistics. Let $F = \{f_1, \ldots, f_N\}$ be a set of N spherically-parameterized carpal bone surfaces of the same type. Let also q_i be the SRNF representation of f_i. We seek to build an atlas that is composed of the average shape μ and its modes of variation. The first step is to register all the surfaces into the same coordinate frame. To this end, we first compute the pairwise distances between every pair of surfaces f_i and f_j in F using the geodesic distance defined in Eq. (2). We then select among all the surfaces in F the one that has the minimum average distance to all the other surfaces. Let us denote it by g and note that g corresponds to the medoid point of the set F.

Next, for every surface $f_i \in F$, we find the optimal rotation O_i^* and diffeomorphism γ_i^* that align f_i onto g. Let $\tilde{f}_i = (Q^* f_i, \gamma_i^*)$. Then, all the surfaces $\tilde{f}_i$ are now fully aligned and one can use standard linear statistics to compute the mean shape and the modes of variation. That is, the mean shape μ is given as: $\mu = \frac{1}{N} \sum_{i=1}^N \tilde{f}_i$.

Finally, the principal modes of variations can be obtained using standard Principal Component Analysis on the surfaces $\tilde{f}_i$ after discretization. Note that it is possible to compute the summary statistics directly on the non-linear manifold $\mathcal{F}$ by computing for example the Karcher mean [8] and studying the modes of variation on the tangent space to $\mathcal{F}$ at the Karcher mean. This approach, however, can be computationally expensive, particularly when dealing with high resolution data sets.

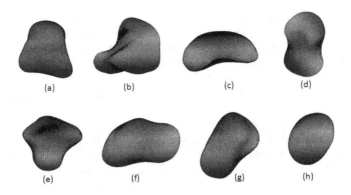

Fig. 1. Mean shape of the bone of the right wrist: (a) capitate, (b) hamate, (c) lunate, (d) scaphoid, (e) trapezium, (f) trapezoid, (g) triquetrum, (h) pisiform.

4   Experiments and Discussion

In this case study, we mainly focus on (i) testing the original elastic 3D shape analysis framework with the carpal bone data set, and assessing the quality of resulting 3D mean shapes and (ii) discussing the hypothesis that guarantees that actual anatomical features can be preserved in the mean shape, by using the anatomical landmark-guided correspondence in the mean shape generation step.

Creation of 3D Carpal Bone Data Set. We have generated and classified a data set that contains two sets of patient-specific carpal bones. The first set contains 49 healthy and pathological subjects segmented from T1 weighted MRI images. On average, for each class of the carpal bone, we have 14 3D surface models for left wrist and 18 surface models for right wrist. Moreover, the data set contains 8 pathological subjects for left wrist and 6 for right wrist. We have augmented this set with the models provided by the Digital database of wrist bone anatomy [9], which contains 30 triangulated 3D models for each carpal bone (healthy) segmented by experts from high-resolution CT images. We manually annotated the 3D models in our training data set [1], using the carpal bone landmark taxonomy, where we have formalized the landmarks mentioned in Sect. 2. Each bone model was annotated with 6-8 landmark regions, where the regions mostly represented the prominent bone features (e.g., hook of the hamate) and articulation facets.

Atlas Generation Without and with Anatomical Landmark Guided Correspondence. In Fig. 1, we show a set of mean shapes computed from the carpal bone training data set (healthy subjects) without anatomical landmark guided correspondence. The generated mean shapes loses some anatomical features with respect to the training data set. According to our preliminary results, we derive the hypothesis that the actual anatomical features can be preserved in the mean

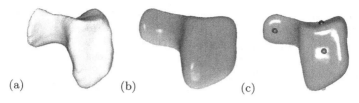

(a)   (b)   (c)

Fig. 2. (a) Input shape (hamate), generated mean shape (b) without and (c) with anatomical landmark guided correspondence.

shape generation process by applying anatomical landmark-guided refinement of the registration. To verify our hypothesis, we performed experiment by generating the mean shape of the healthy hamate bone (right) based on anatomical landmark-guided correspondences. The anatomical landmarks were manually annotated by the experts on the training data set (16 -18 shapes) using the *SemAnatomy3D* [1] tool, which allows interactive annotation of anatomical landmarks on the 3D models. As the shape generation works with vertex correspondences only, we have established the correspondences between healthy bone models considering only the centroid of each annotated region; e.g., the centroid of the hook of hamate region. In Fig. 2, the anatomical features in the mean shape generated with landmark-guided correspondences (c) appear more reliable and similar to the input shape than the ones generated without taking into account the anatomical landmarks (b). Moreover, another advantage is that the generated mean shape contains the canonical landmark positions, which can be further utilize in several applications (Sect 2).

5   Conclusions and Future Work

In this paper, we presented a framework that generates canonical 3D models from the real patient data by using an elastic shape analysis guided by the correspondence of anatomical landmarks. The generated models capture the healthy variability while preserving important anatomical landmarks. It can be used as an average healthy shape for supporting the comparison with patient data to detect anomalies or compute markers of pathologies. We introduced the framework with carpal bone case study, but it can be extended to generate canonical model of other anatomical districts. The results presented are preliminary and several steps are necessary to better evaluate the performance of the method. There is an obvious need for a deeper analysis of the results and a validation framework involving experts. On the technical side, we would like to address shape correspondences defined by fully real landmarks. This step requires to design also a more elaborate parametrization method to properly map these constraints during the parametrization step and then use them to guide the correspondences. Once the method is refined, we are also planning to use the 3D canonical model to automatically identify landmarks and transfer the annotation from the template to the patient-specific reconstructions.

Acknowledgments. This work is supported by the FP7 Marie Curie Initial Training Network "MultiScaleHuman": *Multi-scale Biological Modalities for Physiological Human Articulation* (2011-2015), contract MRTN-CT-2011-289897. This work is also partially supported by the Project FAS-MEDIARE *"Nuove metodologie di Imaging Diagnostico per patologie reumatiche"*.

References

1. Banerjee, I., Agibetov, A., Catalano, C., Patané, G., Spagnuolo, M.: Semantic annotation of patient-specific 3D anatomical models. In: IEEE Proceedings of the International Conference on Cyberworlds (in press, 2015)
2. Banerjee, I., Catalano, C.E., Robbiano, F., Spagnuolo, M.: Accessing and representing knowledge in the medical field: visual and lexical modalities. In: 3D Multiscale Physiological Human, pp. 297–316. Springer, London (2014)
3. Blume, A., Chun, W., Kogan, D., Kokkevis, V., Weber, N., Petterson, R.W., Zeiger, R.: Google body: 3D human anatomy in the browser. In: ACM SIGGRAPH 2011 Talks, p. 19. ACM (2011)
4. Glaunès, J., Vaillant, M., Miller, M.: Landmark matching via large deformation diffeomorphisms on the sphere. Journal of Mathematical Imaging and Vision 20(1–2), 179–200 (2004)
5. Jermyn, I.H., Kurtek, S., Klassen, E., Srivastava, A.: Elastic shape matching of parameterized surfaces using square root normal fields. In: Fitzgibbon, A., Lazebnik, S., Perona, P., Sato, Y., Schmid, C. (eds.) ECCV 2012, Part V. LNCS, vol. 7576, pp. 804–817. Springer, Heidelberg (2012)
6. Kurtek, S., Klassen, E., Ding, Z., Srivastava, A.: A novel Riemannian framework for shape analysis of 3D objects. In: IEEE CVPR, pp. 1625–1632 (2010)
7. Kurtek, S., Klassen, E., Gore, J.C., Ding, Z., Srivastava, A.: Elastic geodesic paths in shape space of parameterized surfaces. IEEE Transactions on Pattern Analysis and Machine Intelligence 34(9), 1717–1730 (2012)
8. Kurtek, S., Srivastava, A., Klassen, E., Laga, H.: Landmark-guided elastic shape analysis of spherically-parameterized surfaces. Comper Graphics Forum 32, 429–438 (2013)
9. Moore, D.C., Crisco, J.J., Trafton, G.T., Leventhal, E.: A digital database of wrist bone anatomy and carpal kinematics. Journal of Biomechanics 40(11), 2537–2542 (2007)
10. Qualter, J., Sculli, F., Oliker, A., Napier, Z., Lee, S., Garcia, J., Frenkel, S., Harnik, V., Triola, M.: The biodigital human: a web-based 3D platform for medical visualization and education. Studies in Health Technology and Informatics 173, 359–361 (2011)
11. Rajamani, T.K., Styner, A.M., Talib, H., Zheng, G., Nolte, L.P., Ballester, A.: Statistical deformable bone models for robust 3d surface extrapolation from sparse data. Medical Image Analysis 11(2), 99–109 (2007)
12. Subburaj, K., Ravi, B., Agarwal, M.: Automated identification of anatomical landmarks on 3d bone models reconstructed from ct scan images. Computerized Medical Imaging and Graphics 33(5), 359–368 (2009)

ISCA 2015 - Image-Based Smart City Application

DicomPrint, an Application
for Managing DICOM Images

Edlira Kalemi[1(✉)], Edlira Martiri[2], Brunela Manaj[3], and Dionis Prifti[3]

[1] GrowIdeas Albania, University of Tirana, Tirana, Albania
e.kalemi@growideas.eu
[2] University of Tirana, Tirana, Albania
edlira.martiri@unitir.edu.al
[3] GrowIdeas Albania, Tirana, Albania
{b.manaj,d.prifti}@growideas.eu

Abstract. Digital Imaging and Communications in Medicine (DICOM) is a standard for handling, storing, printing and transmitting information in medical imaging. It includes: the file format and the networking protocol. The image consists of a list of attributes which contains a) metadata for image like size, dimensions, resolution etc. and b) patient metadata like patient name, sex, ID, age etc. The process of reading and printing the image in itself is difficult because of the adaption between different modalities and devices.

The aim of this work is to develop an application that reads, views and prints DICOM images of a certain user, regardless of the device. The image can be printed with and without the patient metadata and has to be integrated in the DICOMRX (RxScan) software, developed by GrowIdeas Ltd which examines the patient and scans his/her inner parts. The developed application selects a DICOM image from a folder, extracts its metadata and loads these data into a form. The form is then printed according to the needs of the doctor.

Keywords: DICOM format · Metadata · Printing format

1 Introduction

Transmission of images and textual information between health care information systems has always been difficult for two reasons. First, information systems use different computer platforms, and second, images and data are generated from various imaging modalities by different manufacturers. With the emergent health care industry standards, Health Level 7 (HL7) and Digital Imaging and Communications in Medicine (DICOM) [1], it has become feasible to integrate all these heterogeneous, disparate medical images and textual data into an organized system [2]. One of the systems for digital image data management is Picture Archive and Communication System (PACS). The main components of PACS include image acquisition, data management, data transmission, image display, interfaces to printers and portable media, and communication routes to other electronic systems [3]. PACS are usually based on DICOM standards [4]. The following sessions of this paper will give a general description of the module, the logical architecture of the software, a dynamic behavior of functionalities and workflows.

© Springer International Publishing Switzerland 2015
V. Murino et al. (Eds.): ICIAP 2015 Workshops, LNCS 9281, pp. 177–184, 2015.
DOI: 10.1007/978-3-319-23222-5_22

2   System Architecture

2.1   Environment Description

The environment where the application works is a medical laboratory equipped with all the necessary devices such as scanners, sensors, etc. The practitioner (referred here as Doctor), after examining the patient and scanning his/her inner parts can modify the images and apply any of the options which are part of RXScan or RXViewer. The printing option will be added in this interface and the Doctor can choose one of the following:

1. Print the image only.
2. Print the image and the metadata of the patient in landscape view.
3. Print the image and the metadata of the patient in portrait view.

As inputs will serve the events generated by the Doctor (chooses one of the options) and the output will be the printed paper of the patient data (image with/without metadata in landscape/portrait view).

2.2   Architecture Overview and Main Software Components

The main physical components of the project are a computer on which the software runs and a printer. A general picture of the system architecture workflow is shown figure 1. The Doctor examines the patient and captures images or videos with camera. The samples are transmitted to the PACS server and when the operator or doctor wants to examine them, he/she can do so via a computer where the software we have implemented runs. As hardware resources we recommend using a PC with processor over 2.5GHz, and RAM over 1GB of capacity.

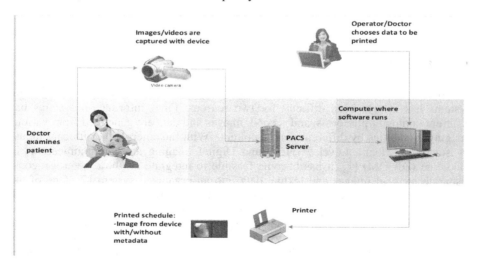

Fig. 1. System architecture workflow

The application is built in Embarcadero Delphi XE6 as a Firemonkey Desktop Application. There are 5 Units, namely: (1) Main Unit, (2) Landscape Unit, (3) Portrait Unit, (4) NoMetadata Unit, (5) PatientMetadata Unit. The relationship between units is described in the diagram in figure 2:

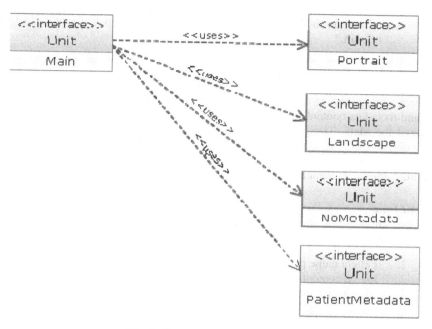

Fig. 2. Unit's relationship diagram

Main Unit Description and Functionalities

The most important unit of the application is Main Unit. It serves as the first interface that the user sees. This interface is divided into 4 components: upper bar, thumbnail bar, image content, and metadata content. The upper bar component is a panel containing:

a. "Load File" button: opens a dialog box where the user first chooses a DICOM image from a set of images stored in a folder.
b. "Include metadata" checkbox: the user chooses to add patient metadata to the image or not.
c. View panel: user has to choose between the two options, whether he/she wants to print the document in portrait or landscape view.
d. Print panel: contains two buttons for the user to set printing preferences and to preview what will be printed.
e. "Print" button: prints what the user has chosen in the previous settings.

The thumbnail viewer is a panel containing a thumbnail of the chosen image. This component is implemented for future situations where a certain user can have more than one DICOM image associated with his name. Whereas the Image content panel displays the extracted image from the DICOM format.

1. In the metadata content panel we have:

    a. Panel containing a grid where metadata are imported from the extracted text file of the DICOM image.

    b. "Show on the right" button changes the position of the metadata content from bottom (default case) to the right of the image.

    c. "Show on the bottom" button changes the position from the right to the bottom.

Landscape Unit Description and Functionalities

If the user chooses to print his patient document in landscape view, what he will see will be a static interface divided into 3 components: patient name panel, image content, and metadata content. The patient name panel contains the patient name from the extracted metadata. The image content panel contains an image viewer component which displays the extracted image from the DICOM format, and the metadata panel contains the following data from the extracted metadata file: ID, Birthdate, Sex, Age, Weight, Address, Telephone, Bodypart, Study ID.

Portrait Unit

If the user chooses to print his patient document in portrait view, what he will see will be a static interface divided into 3 components:

    1. Patient name panel
    2. Image content
    3. Metadata content

NoMetadata Unit

If the user chooses to print his patient document without metadata, the form will be very simple. It will contain only two components:

1. Patient name panel
2. Image content

PatientMetadata Unit Description and Functionalities

If the user chooses to print his patient document with metadata, the main form will add a grid containing the patient data. This unit calls three functions, from which two are private and one is public. The public function extracts the patient metadata from a text file of metadata regardind the Dicom tags [5]. The private functions do string processing over the metadata.

3   Dynamic Behavior of Architecture

The architecture was designed to answer functional requirements. For each function of the system, we will describe the sequences / data flow that occur.

The first case is the way that the user interacts with the GUI. The flow chart is shown in figure 3.

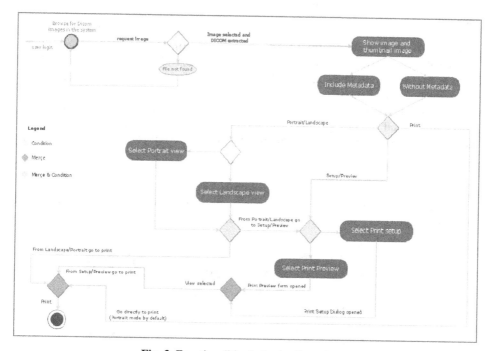

Fig. 3. Functionalities behavior flow chart

3.1   Interaction between Components and Procedures

Firstly the user (doctor) clicks on the Load File button in order to view the DICOM image. This event calls a procedure which executes the open dialog component. After the dialog component is opened the user can choose the image that he wants to view. The user selects the DICOM Image via a procedure which executes CMD in background in order to convert the DICOM image selected into a BMP image using the *dcmj2pnm* command of the preinstalled DCMTK toolkit, It also generates a text file with all the metadata of the DICOM image selected. The image is shown in the main content part and the thumbnail version of the image is also shown.

The user can check the "Include metadata" checkbox. This events makes the pre-filled metadata container visible to the form, below image container. The user has the possibility to choose between portrait mode and landscape mode by clicking the Portrait radio-button or the Landscape radio-button. To preview the selected mode, the user can click on the Print Preview.

This procedure implementation controls if the user has checked the Include Metadata checkbox and the mode the user has clicked and shows another form (portrait form or landscape form) beside the main form with the attributes that the user has selected.

If the user clicks the Print Setup button, a procedure opens the Print Setup Dialog.

The user can click on the Print button in order to print the DICOM image with or without the patient data. This implementation controls if the user has checked the Include Metadata checkbox and the Portrait or Landscape radio-button selected in which the user wants the image to be printed.

According to the mode selected the Print Dialog is opened. The image and the metadata are printed in correspondence to the printer specification [6] and the print dialog box settings, maximizing the print quality and the layout for a better view.

3.2   Software Screenshots

The following figures represent the screen shots of the application. Fig. 4 shows a DICOM image in the main form of the application.

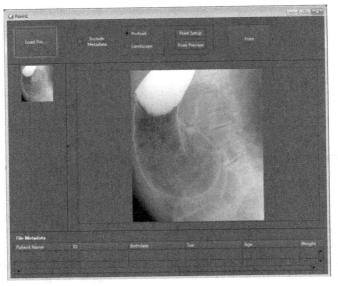

Fig. 4. Image in the main form

Figure 5 shows the DICOM image with its metadata in portrait view while figure 6 shows it in landscape view.

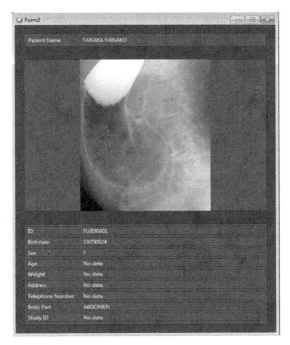

Fig. 5. Image with metadata in portrait view

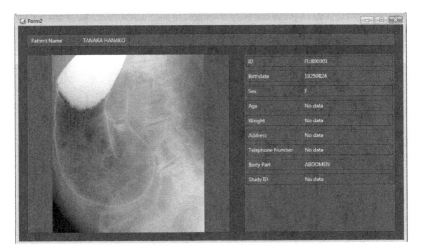

Fig. 6. Image with metadata in landscape view

4   Discussion and Further Work

DicomPrinting application will first support the dentistry clinics in managing the process of printing this image format. It is efficient and easy to use from the user's perspective. It works in Windows and OS X operating system. This module is part of the system named RXScan and in the future GrowIdeas Albania. As a future work we will focus on the medical video management and its integration to the whole system.

References

1. Huang, K.H.: Industrial Standards (HL7 and DICOM) and Work Flow Protocols (IHE). PACS and Imaging Informatics, Chapter 6, ISBN: 0471251232. Wiley (2004)
2. Huang, K.H.: Industrial Standards (HL7 and DICOM) and Work Flow Protocols (IHE). PACS and Imaging Informatics, Chapter 7, ISBN: 0471251232. Wiley (2004)
3. Hood, N.M., Scott, H.: Introduction to Picture Archive and Communication Systems. Journal of Radiology Nursing **26**(3) (2006). Elsevier
4. NEMA Standards Publications PS3.1 2015b, Digital Imaging and Communications in Medicine (DICOM), Part 1: Introduction and Overview (2015), National Electrical Manufacturers Association (2015). http://www.dclunie.com/dicom-status/status.html#BaseStandard2015b
5. NEMA Standards Publications PS3.5 2015b, Digital Imaging and Communications in Medicine (DICOM), Part 5: Data Structures and Encoding (2015), National Electrical Manufacturers Association (2015). http://www.dclunie.com/dicom-status/status.html#BaseStandard2015b
6. Eichelberg, M., Kleber, K., Riesmeier, J.: Test Plan for Print Composers (2003-12-01), Integrating the Healthcare Enterprise (2003)

Accurate Positioning and Orientation Estimation in Urban Environment Based on 3D Models

Giorgio Ghinamo[1(✉)], Cecilia Corbi[1], Piero Lovisolo[1],
Andrea Lingua[2], Irene Aicardi[2], and Nives Grasso[2]

[1] Telecom Italia, Torino, Italy
{giorgio.ghinamo,cecilia.corbi,piero.lovisolo}@telecomitalia.it
[2] Department of Environment, Land and Infrastructure Engineering (DIATI),
Politecnico di Torino, Torino, Italy
{andrea.lingua,irene.aicardi,nives.grasso}@polito.it

Abstract. This paper describes a positioning algorithm for mobile phones based on image recognition. The use of image recognition based (IRB) positioning in mobile applications is characterized by the availability of a single camera for estimate the camera position and orientation. A prior knowledge of 3D environment is needed in the form of a database of images with associated spatial information that can be built projecting the 3D model on a set of synthetic solid images (range + RGB images). The IRB procedure proposed by the authors can be divided in two steps: the selection from the database of the most similar image to the query image used to locate the camera and the estimation of the position and orientation of the camera based on available 3D data on the reference image. The MPEG standard Compact Descriptors for Visual Search (CDVS) has been used to reduce hugely the processing time. Some practical results of the location methodology in outdoor environment have been described in terms of processing time and accuracy of position and attitude.

Keywords: Image recognition based location · Visual search · Positioning · Smartphones · Low cost

1   Introduction

As known, the positioning in indoor environments and within urban canyon is difficult and with poor accuracy through the use of common sensors GPS/GNSS. In recent years there has been evaluated the possibility of using alternative sensors that allow the positioning in these areas; among these image [1], optical [2], radio [3], magnetic [4], RFID [5] and acoustic [6] sensors were analyzed and tested.

The improvement of the sensors for image acquisitions included inside smartphones makes it possible to use these tools, more and more common, for navigation based on images; furthermore a challenge of this approach is to achieve real-time capability.

Kitanov et al. [7] compare image lines, that have been detected in images of a robot mounted camera, with a 3D vector model. Jason Zhi Liang generated a sparse

© Springer International Publishing Switzerland 2015
V. Murino et al. (Eds.): ICIAP 2015 Workshops, LNCS 9281, pp. 185–192, 2015.
DOI: 10.1007/978-3-319-23222-5_23

2.5D georeferenced image database using an ambulatory backpack-mounted system with two 2D laser scanners, two fish-eye cameras and one orientation sensor originally developed for 3D modeling of indoor environments.

In this paper we propose an innovative approach for positioning/navigation using a single camera of a mobile phone based on image recognition, exploiting 3D environment models in form of a set of 3D solid images (range+RGB data) and the new MPEG standard Compact Descriptors for Visual Search (CDVS). IRB positioning represents a good opportunity for Location Based Services (LBS), for example in the case of GNSS/Pseudolites denied environments as dense urban scenarios. Moreover, an advantage of IRB technology is the availability of 3D orientation of the used device (smartphone), information not available or not reliable using alternative positioning technologies.

A Terrestrial LiDAR Survey (TLS) with an associated camera can be used to acquire the 3D model of urban environment and to generate the database of reference images, a set of synthetic 3D images produced projecting the clouds of points over synthetic image plans. In this context MPEG algorithms for visual search play an important role in defining light and interoperable solution for processing and comparing the query and database images. This location procedure can be used for accurate navigation and augmented reality in urban scenarios for smart phones applications. In these use cases, to optimize battery consumption and compensating latencies of few seconds, the IRB procedure can be used jointly with inertial system, in particular with PDR (Pedestrian Dead Reckoning) technology.

The proposed procedure has already demonstrated excellent results in indoor environment [8], [9], then the purpose of this article is to validate the procedure also for the outdoor case.

2   The Positioning Procedure

The proposed procedure can be divided in two steps. As first step, a reference image is selected out of the database of images synthetically generated from the 3D environment model; this selection procedure exploits MPEG CDVS [10] visual search technology. The second step of the positioning procedure is the estimation of the camera parameters (position and orientation) based on available 3D information on the previously selected reference image according to the collinearity equations [11]. Key points and related features are extracted from query and reference images and matched for the selected set of key-points pairs.

In this section the positioning procedure is described in terms of functional steps (Image DB set up, reference image extraction, camera parameter estimation for the query image camera); the section 3 describes the test site, the image based positioning procedure and the related set up procedure; section 4 presents the performance results in terms of achieved accuracy and processing time gain.

2.1   High Level Functional Steps

The proposed location methodology consists of the following parts (Fig. 1):

- acquisition of a 3D model of the area where the positioning service is offered: the model is used to generate a synthetic images database with related 3D information. Due to the properties of image recognition algorithms based on local descriptors, whose performances rely on the similar perspective of details (i.e. key points), the database should provide an exhaustive coverage of the area where the service is offered, in terms of a grid of camera positions, orientations and focal length;

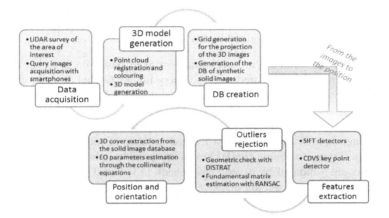

Fig. 1. Workflow of the Image Recognition Based procedure

- mobile phone takes a query picture used for locating the camera: a reference image, that is the most similar to the query one, is extracted from the database. For this task, the MPEG CSVS technology is used, with a minor changes regarding the distribution of selected most significant key points;
- using 3D information available for the selected reference image, external orientation parameters of camera (3D position and attitude angles) are estimated.

2.2   The 3D Model and the Synthetic Images Database

All the images of the database with related 3D information are created processing a colored 3D model of the environment. The 3D model can be generated with a TLS system, that also allows the image acquisitions with an integrated camera. The acquired point cloud are colored using the camera associated to the LiDAR instrument.

Numerous different scans are acquired and all of them are mounted in a single model and reported in used coordinates system (Fig. 2 left). As a result of the process, a geo-referenced RGB point cloud of the environment is made, on which you can directly read 3D coordinates/color of object points.

From the 3D model of the environment, a database of Solid Images (SIs) is created. SIs are synthetic RGB color images with the additional information about the distance from the camera center of the spatial point represented in each pixel [12]. Combining the camera parameters information together with the distance of object represented in the pixel from the camera, the 3D position of points is estimated, in terms of 3D coordinates of key points in the model reference system.

2.3   The Retrieval of Reference Image out of the Reference Database

The goal of the retrieval procedure is to select a reference image out of the images database with the highest level of similarity with the query image acquired by the terminal camera. To quickly select out of a database the most similar image, the following operations have been defined by MPEG CDVS:

- the images of the database are preliminary ranked based on a global descriptors similarity score when compared with the query image. Global descriptors provide a statistical representation of a set of most significant local descriptors extracted from the two images;
- for the images selected in previous step, the pairwise matching procedure with query image is executed between a limited number of most significant extracted key points. Trying to couple similar key points present in both images, the matched key points are validated by a geometric check [13] based on the concept that the statistical properties of the log distance ratio for pairs of incorrect matches are distinctly different from the properties of that for correct matches.

2.4   The Estimation Procedure of Camera Parameters

The second step of the location procedure, EO (External Orientation) parameters estimation (position and orientation), is based on the resolution of collinearity equations where key points of the query image are associated with 3D position information available in the reference image extracted from the database, with related spatial information (see 2.2). The 3D information is stored in construction of the solid images where for each pixel the distance (range) of the obstacle depicted in the image is reported, together with internal/external orientation parameters of SI in terms of orientation, focal length and sensor position.

The information that should be estimated in the location procedure are the EO parameters of the query image camera. The procedure to estimate these parameters from a solid image consists of the following steps:

1. features extraction from query and reference images using SIFT detector [14] or CDVS key point detector [10];
2. CDVS geometric check (DISTRAT) [13] is used for a coarse preliminary rejection of matched outliers; the use of DISTRAT is required to speed up outliers rejection procedure. However, the DISTRAT output still contains few percentiles of outliers in the selected set of paired features;

3. given the set of common features selected out of DISTRAT geometric check, the fundamental matrix is estimated with a RANSAC procedure, where the fundamental matrix is a representation of the rototraslation of the camera between query image and reference image [15]. This step allows to exclude remaining outliers out of DISTRAT check. In fact, the preliminary use of DISTRAT reduces the percentage of outliers from 30-70% order to few percentiles, this allows to strongly reduce the RANSAC execution time, approximately of 100 times (at this stage focal length is assumed to be similar in both images out of retrieval step and the camera distortion model are not taking into account);
4. the spatial information (3D coordinates) of the common features between query and reference image is retrieved using the solid image information available for the reference images of the DB, derived from the 3D model of the scene;
5. using the collinearity equations the EO parameters are estimated ([15], [16]), as this step is implemented through a non-linear Least Square estimation, as starting solution the EO parameters of the selected SI out of step 2.3 are considered.

3   The Test Site

An outdoor test has been done to validate the procedure analyzing the result accuracy. The defined area is along three blocks of via Garibaldi, an historical central pedestrian road, in Torino (Piedmont, Italy). A Faro laser scanner (series Cam2 Focus 3D) has been used for a TLS survey composed by six scans for a length of about 150 m. Examples of used scans are presented, as spherical images, in fig. 2 (right). However, if the interest area is larger, it is possible to acquire the colored point cloud and to generate the 3D model of the environment using Mobile Mapping Systems techniques (MMS), that allows to get information over a large area in a short time [17].

Fig. 2. Example of spherical image in pedestrian downtown road

In order to generate a reference images database characterized by an exhaustive cove-rage of all the possible perspective of the environment, a grid of points have been taken into account. Points are spaced 2 meters on the direction orthogonal to buildings front and 3 meter on the direction parallel to building front. For each points 16 different headings on the horizontal plane and 4 different inclination of the vertical axe (0, 5, 10 and 15 degrees) have been considered for a total of 64 images (Fig. 3, left), 1826 images for a single laser scanner position [18]. Fig. 3 (right) shows a snapshot of some synthetic images of the DB.

4   Trial Results

The proposed location procedure has been tested in terms of processing load benefit and the accuracy of the approach. For accuracy estimation we have considered a set of 20 smartphone images geo-located with photogrammetric techniques, in terms of position and attitude, as described in Section 2.

Fig. 3. The schema for the synthetic images generation (left) and examples of a part of the database of synthetic images (right)

4.1   Accuracy

Twenty images captured with a Samsung S4 smartphone have been considered in the test. The true positions and EOs of S4 have been acquired using an "ad hoc" calibrated system (the butterfly, Fig. 4) that consists on a car support for mobile phone mounted on a plate with 4 colored spheres (red, blu, yellow and grey). The system can be placed on a tripod that allows rotations for vertical and horizontal camera images. Thus, the spheres have been measured in a carthographic reference frame with high accuracy (mm) using surveying techniques.

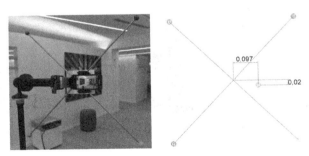

Fig. 4. The butterfly system, in green the camera projection center

Table 1 summarizes the accuracy results in terms of discrepancies from ground truth and estimated values in case of good level of similarity between the query image and the reference one extracted out of the database. The standard deviations of discrepancies are about 30 cm in position and about 0.15 radians in attitude. No systematic errors are present.

Fig. 5 describes an examples of results of key points detection, matching and outliers rejection in a couple of query and reference images. Query images and TLS are acquired in not ideal condition including people and cars randomly present in the scene, good level of similarity is detected between the two images. A maximum number of 2000 key points have been selected, ranked by the absolute value in descending order of the response of the keypoint to the Laplacian of Guassian filtering (peak), bring benefit in terms of reduction of number of key points.

Table 1. Accuracy results in outdoor trial for position (ΔX ΔY ΔZ) and attitude ($\Delta \omega$ $\Delta \varphi$ Δk)

Param	ΔX [m]	ΔY [m]	ΔZ [m]	$\Delta \omega$ [rad]	$\Delta \varphi$ [rad]	Δk [rad]
|Max|	0.420	0.500	0.320	0.139	0.037	0.118
Mean	0.059	-0.023	0.045	0.035	-0.012	-0.081
Dev.St.	0.249	0.383	0.191	0.098	0.047	0.093

Fig. 5. Example of query and reference images key points matching results.

4.2 Processing Load

The tests have shown that the use of geometric check in pairwise matches outliers rejection allows to reduce processing time of a factor of 10 times or more with respect of pure RANSAC procedure, in case of medium degree of similarity between the query and the reference image, guaranteeing at the meantime an good accuracy.

Table 2 describes the processing load results of outlier rejection procedure for pure RANSAC procedure versus the hybrid DISTRAT and RANSAC approach, for an Intel Core 2 T7500 processor. When the similarity between query and reference image is not so high (the rate of good matches is around 30%) the hybrid approach provide strong benefit. Otherwise the processing load for the 2 approaches is similar.

Table 2. Processing load gain: hybrid DISTRAT and RANSAC vs RANSAC

Rate of inliers	RANSAC only	DISTART+RANSAC
35%	10 sec	0.6 sec
70%	0.5 sec	0.6 sec

5 Conclusions

The proposed location procedure offer a good level of accuracy with a standard error of few decimeters in the described scenarios. It is a very good results if we remember that the approach is based on a single camera available on the smartphones, whose characteristics are significantly different respect to the cameras used for photogrammetric purpose. In the collinearity equations the focal length and the principal point are assumed known (it is also possible to take the nominal focal length, but it was not used in these tests). The proposed technique can be a component of image based navigation that we are now analyzing introducing the integration of the internal sensors data acquired from the smartphones or video odometry for consumer camera.

References

1. Nishkam, R., Pravin, S., Andrew, F., Ahmed, E., Liviu, I.: Indoor localization using camera phones. In: Mobile Computing Systems and Applications (2006)
2. Mautz, R., Tilch, S.: Survey of optical indoor positioning systems. In: International Conference on Indoor Positioning and Indoor Navigation (IPIN), September 21-23, 2011
3. Biswas, J., Veloso, M.: WiFi localization and navigation for autonomous indoor mobile robots. In: International Conference on Robotics and Automation (2010)
4. Chung, L., Donahoe, M., Schmandt, C., Kim, I., Razavai, P., Wiseman, M.: Indoor location sensing using geomagnetism. In: Proceedings of the 9th International Conference on Mobile Systems, Applications, and Services, pp. 141–154 (2011)
5. Schneegans, S., Vorst, P., Zell, A.: Using RFID snapshots for mobile robot self-localization. In: European Conference on Mobile Robots (2007)
6. Hong-Shik, K., Jong-Suk, C.: Advanced indoor localization using ultrasonic sensor and digital compass. In: International Conference on Control, Automation and Systems (2008)
7. Kitanov, A., Biševac, S., Petrović, I.: Mobile robot self-localization in complex indoor environments using monocular vision and 3D model. In: IEEE/ASME International Conference on Advanced Intelligent Mechatronics, Zürich, Switzerland (2007)
8. Piras, M., Dabove, P., Lingua, A.M., Aicardi, I.: Indoor navigation using smartphone technology: a future challenge or an actual possibility? In: IEEE/ION Position, Location Proceedings of the and Navigation Symposium, May 5-8, 2014
9. Lingua, A.M., Aicardi, I., Ghinamo, G., Francini, G., Lepsoy, S.: The MPEG7 visual search solution for image recognition based positioning using 3D models. In: Proceedings of the 27th International Technical Meeting of the Satellite Division of the Institute of Navigation (ION GNSS+ 2014), September 8-12, 2014
10. CDVS. ISO/IEC DIS 15938-13 Compact Descriptors for Visual Search (2014)
11. McGlone, C. (ed.): Manual of Photogrammetry, 5th edn., pp. 280–281. ASPRS
12. Bornaz, L., Dequal, S.: A new concept: the solid image. In: CIPA 2003 Proceedings of XIXth International Symposium, pp. 169–174 (2003)
13. PCT/EP2011/050994 Method and system for comparing images
14. Lowe, D.: Distinctive image features from scale-invariant keypoints. International, Journal of Computer Vision **60**(2), 91–110 (2004)
15. Hartley, R., Zisserman, A.: Multiple View Geometry in Computer Vision, 2nd edn. Cambridge University Press, March 2004
16. Karara, H.M. (ed.): Non Topography Photogrammetry, 2nd edn., pp. 46–48. ASPRS
17. De Agostino, M., Lingua, A., Marenchino, D., Nex, F., Piras, M.: GIMPHI: a new integration approach for early impact assessment. Applied Geomatics **3**(4), 241–249. ISSN 1866-9298
18. Fusiello, A.: Visione computazionale. Tecniche di ricostruzione tridimensionale (2013)

An Hippocampal Segmentation Tool Within an Open Cloud Infrastructure

Nicola Amoroso[1,2]([✉]), Sabina Tangaro[1], Rosangela Errico[2,3], Elena Garuccio[4],
Anna Monda[2], Francesco Sensi[3], Andrea Tateo[2],
and Roberto Bellotti[1,2]
for the Alzheimer's Disease Neuroimaging Initiative

[1] Istituto Nazionale di Fisica Nucleare, Sezione di Bari, Bari, Italy
nicola.amoroso@ba.infn.it
[2] Dipartimento Interateneo di Fisica, Università Degli Studi di Bari, Bari, Italy
[3] Istituto Nazionale di Fisica Nucleare, Sezione di Genova, Genova, Italy
[4] Dipartimento di Fisica, Università Degli Studi di Siena, Siena, Italy

Abstract. This study presents a fully automated algorithm for the segmentation of the hippocampus in structural Magnetic Resonance Imaging (MRI) and its deployment as a service on an open cloud infrastructure. Optimal atlases strategies for multi-atlas learning are combined with a voxel-wise classification approach. The method efficiency is optimized as training atlases are previously registered to a data driven template, accordingly for each test MRI scan only a registration is needed. The selected optimal atlases are used to train dedicated random forest classifiers whose labels are fused by majority voting. The method performances were tested on a set of 100 MRI scans provided by the Alzheimer's Disease Neuroimaging Initiative (ADNI). Leave-one-out results (Dice = 0.910 ± 0.004) show the presented method compares well with other state-of-the-art techniques and a benchmark segmentation tool as FreeSurfer. The proposed strategy significantly improves a standard multi-atlas approach ($p < .001$).

Keywords: Segmentation · Quantitative image analysis · Imaging biomarkers · Magnetic resonance imaging · Machine learning

1 Introduction

The "Smart cities and communities and social innovations" national operative programs have outlined the need for an efficient reorganization of health-care

Data used in preparation of this article were obtained from the Alzheimers Disease Neuroimaging Initiative (ADNI) database (adni.loni.usc.edu). As such, the investigators within the ADNI contributed to the design and implementation of ADNI and/or provided data but did not participate in analysis or writing of this report. A complete listing of ADNI investigators can be found at: http://adni.loni.usc.edu/wp-content/uploads/how_to_apply/ADNI_Acknowledgement_List.pdf

© Springer International Publishing Switzerland 2015
V. Murino et al. (Eds.): ICIAP 2015 Workshops, LNCS 9281, pp. 193–200, 2015.
DOI: 10.1007/978-3-319-23222-5_24

both to ensure higher standards in terms of quality of life for patients and to rationalize the economic resources to be allocated. Accordingly, the connected health and the e-health technologies can be considered pillars of an innovative smart thinking of cities and communities. Hippocampal atrophy is an established bio-marker for several neurodegenerative diseases, such as the Alzheimer's disease [7], a disease characterized by an impressive social and economic impact. However, no segmentation tool is currently employed in clinical practice, especially because computational requirements of best performing algorithms such as [10,11] are difficult to fulfill.

With this aim, in this paper we present a novel machine learning tool for hippocampal segmentation which has been proven to yield consistent improvements with respect of recent studies [12]. In particular, the proposed segmentation workflow for the human hippocampus and its deployment *as a Service*, on the PRISMA cloud[1] which exploits the Bari ReCaS [2] computer center, are described. Both PRISMA and ReCaS are national operative programs, the first in particular is a smart city program dealing with the development of Open Source platforms for computing solutions dedicated to e-Health or e-Government, just to mention a few.

The proposed approach efficiently exploits the cloud computational resources requiring only a linear registration followed by a warp to segment a test image. After registration optimal atlases are adaptively selected. First, a shape analysis algorithm is used to detect peri-hippocampal volumes of interest (VOIs). Then, the optimal atlases are selected by measuring the pairwise Pearson's correlation and they are used to train supervised classifiers. The leave-one-out performances of the methodology are compared with the publicly available segmentation tool FreeSurfer [8] and a basic multi-atlas pipeline, *i. e.* consisting of registration and label fusion, showing a significant improvement.

2   Materials and Methods

A data set of 100 T1 MRI scans from the ADNI database, including 29 normal controls (NC), 34 mild cognitive impairment (MCI) and 37 Alzheimer's disease (AD) subjects, has been used in preparation of this article. The set is composed by male and female subjects aged between 60 and 90 years old. The relative hippocampal labelings were provided by the EADC-ADNI harmonized segmentation protocol[3] [4,5]. The ADNI set consists of MPRAGE MRI brain scans with a resolution of $1 \times 1 \times 1$ mm^3. According to this, in the following, voxels or mm^3 will be interchangeably used without further specifications.

2.1   Increasing Inter-subject Similarity

Registration processes are sensitive to initial conditions, accordingly the intensities of MRI scans are normalized and the bias field removed with the improved

---

[1] http://www.ponsmartcities-prisma.it

[2] http://www.pon-recas.it

[3] www.hippocampal-protocol.net

N3 MRI bias field correction algorithm [14]. The MRI scans are co-registered with the MNI152 template with the FSL libraries [9] and the warp fields $\mathcal{F}_i$ are stored for later use. The goal of this processing is to maximize inter-subject similarity in order to help the classifiers to learn the disease patterns. The proposed algorithm is schematically represented in Fig. 1.

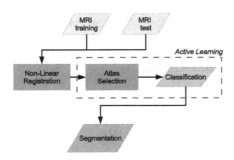

Fig. 1. A schematic overview of the proposed method: 1) non-linear registration, 2) Atlas selection and 3) classification with the latter two phases encompassed in a unique active learning framework.

After registration a gross peri-hippocampal region $\omega(VOI)_i$ is extracted with FAPoD [1], a fully automated hippocamapal shape analysis algorithm, from each scan. The $\omega(VOI)_i$ extracted by FAPoD contains a probable hippocampal region of about 17000 voxels distributed in a rectangular volume of interest of dimensions $50 \times 70 \times 70$ voxels. $\omega(VOI)_i$ are used for the atlas selection.

At this point, the data set is divided into a training subset $\mathcal{D}_t$ and a validation MRI scan a_v to perform a leave-one-out analysis. We use the Pearson's correlation to directly measure the similarity between the peri-hippocampal regions $\omega(VOI)_i$ of $\mathcal{D}_t$ and the $\omega(VOI)_v$ of the validation scan a_v. Pearson's correlation is then used as a ranking score to detect the first k optimal atlases. Machine learning approaches usually use training examples to build a shared base of knowledge and then learn a generalized model, on the contrary we adopt a substantial change of perspective. We try to learn different patterns from each $\omega(VOI)_i$, then, through image processing, we make the validation scan as similar as possible to training examples. Finally, we actively select the k most representative examples and use them for prediction, thus requiring the validation sample to reproduce these training patterns.

2.2   Classification and Segmentation

Each hippocampal $\omega(VOI)_i$ undergoes a voxel-wise feature extraction process which assigns to each voxel a set of 315 features [13]. Each voxel is represented as a vector whose elements represent information about position, intensity and texture. Texture information (contrast, uniformity, rugosity, regularity, etc.) is expressed using Haar-like and some Haralick features. With this set of features, we train N random forest classifiers $\mathcal{C}_{\{1,...,N\}}$, the labels for each training scan being the manual tracings of expert neuroradiologists.

For each validation scan we perform atlas selection as previously described in 2.1, then we pick the k models $\mathcal{C}_i$ of the optimal atlases and perform a voxel-wise prediction. For each voxel of the $\omega(VOI)_v$ the relative label is calculated as a weighted average of the k predicted v_k labels, the weight being the pairwise distance between the selected atlases and the target image. Finally, the inverse warps $\mathcal{F}_v^{-1}$ is applied and a 0.5 threshold is adopted to obtain a binary segmentation. The classification performances are measured in terms of Dice similarity index D and standard error ϵ defined as:

$$D = \frac{2\,|A \cap B|}{|A| + |B|} \tag{1}$$

$$\epsilon = \frac{\sigma}{N} \tag{2}$$

where A and B represent the regions being compared, cardinalities $|A|$, $|B|$ are intended as the measured volumes, σ being the standard deviation of the Dice distribution and $N = 100$ is the sample size.

2.3   Cloud Deployment as a Service

The field of medical imaging has seen in recent years an enormous development. Image databases, made of thousands of medical images, are currently available to supply clinical diagnosis, this is particularly true for brain diseases [2]. Medical image processing applications would greatly take advantage from open clouds deployment: run-time reduction, sharing of data collections and platform-hardware independent configurations are just a few examples.

The proposed algorithm requires an overall CPU time of 40 ± 10 minutes per scan. When dealing with large data sets this can represent a too much expensive computational cost to afford. Accordingly, cloud technology can tackle these computational issues by providing a user dedicated computing environment. Besides, offering the segmentation tool as a service (submitting images to be segmented to the related web portal[4]) can help its clinical adoption as no technical background is required to use it.

With this purpose the segmentation pipeline presented in this work has been encased within a virtualized wrapping framework, to fully automate not only the job submission and monitoring, but also the resource exploitation. In this way the segmentation pipeline can be accessed as a pure Software as a Service.

Once the end user proceeds to upload a brain scan to be segmented, a job management tool JST (Job Submission Tool) manages the submission and monitoring of the application. JST monitors the submission of all of jobs required by a given application thus hiding to the end user the complexity of operating in a heterogeneous and distributed computational environment. Moreover, JST is

---

[4] https://recasgateway.ba.infn.it

portable on different infrastructures like the EGI grid infrastructure, dedicated servers, local batch farms, IaaS/SaaS based cloud resources and as a consequence it allows to efficiently exploits the computational resources needed by the application.

3   Results

Active learning performances are stable, in fact they are not affected by the number of chosen atlases (no significant $p > .05$ difference can be found using $10 \sim 15$ atlases or more) as shown in Fig. 2. Statistical significance is assessed by means of non parametric Kruskal-Wallis test.

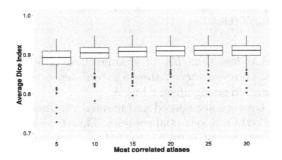

Fig. 2. The figure shows the Dice distribution obtained by averaging the corresponding left and right hippocampal performances and varying the number of selected atlases. Performances reach a plateau beyond $10 \sim 15$ atlases.

An analogous result shows that even basic multi-atlas performances reach a plateau when using ~ 10 atlases and beyond. Accordingly, to assess whether active learning can improve basic multi-atlas performance, with a fair comparison, we use 15 atlases for both cases. The proposed method improves the overall performances obtained by basic multi-atlas and FreeSurfer (see Fig. 3).

In fact, for left hippocampi median Dice index with the relative standard error is 0.908 ± 0.004, for right hippocampi 0.912 ± 0.003. Basic multi-atlas and FreeSurfer respectively achieve 0.845 ± 0.005 and 0.728 ± 0.005 for left hippocampi and 0.851 ± 0.004 and 0.733 ± 0.004 for right hippocampi. A Kruskal-Wallis test demonstrates the three Dice distributions are significantly different ($p < .001$).

Dice metric has an important drawback, in fact, it does not distinguish between false positive and false negative errors. As a consequence, two distinct segmentations can obtain the same Dice index performance, even if reproducing the manual tracing in one case with an excess of false positives, in the other with false negatives. This is why it is also important to perform an "agreement" measure, for example with a Bland-Altman analysis [3].

For the present work, we perform a Bland Altman analysis of the standardized manual and segmentation volumes, for both left and right hippocampi. The

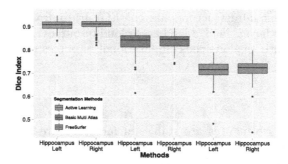

Fig. 3. The figure shows the Dice index performances varying with the different segmentation methods for both left and right hippocampi. Active learning performances (red) are significantly higher than those obtained through basic multi-atlas (green) or FreeSurfer segmentations (blue).

analysis confirms that less than 5% of standardized differences between segmented and manual volumes exceed the 95% confidence bounds, so that they can be considered statistical significant Fig. 4.

The correlation between segmented and manual volumes is 0.80 and 0.84 for respectively left and right hippocampal volumes. Therefore, active learning seems also to improve the agreement between manual and automated segmentations.

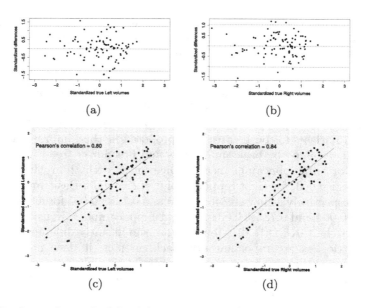

Fig. 4. The figure shows the Bland Altman analysis (measure agreement and correlation) for standardized volumes. Results for both left (a,c) and right (b,d) hippocampi are separately shown.

4   Conclusion and Future Work

In this study we present a novel segmentation algorithm based on a combined multi-atlas and machine learning strategy. A key role on the method is played by atlas selection. We select optimal atlases according to Pearson's correlation measurements between VOIs automatically detected to specifically contain the hippocampus. The performances obtained respectively for left and right hippocampi are 0.908 ± 0.004 and 0.912 ± 0.003.

This work demonstrates how active learning strategies, such as those presented, can bring substantial performance improvements. Nevertheless, which similarity metric to use should be further investigated. In fact, other similarity measurements, especially non linear techniques, such as Locally Linear embedding and Laplacian Eigenmaps, could be adopted for atlas selection. Besides, recent works suggest the use of warping fields for similarity measurements, accordingly a fair comparison should be performed.

It is worth noting that the method is computationally efficient, requiring a processing time of about 10 minutes per test scan. Moreover, the exploitation of cloud infrastructures potentially suggest it could be adopted for large clinical trials. With this regard, a limitation of the study is due to the absence of a clinical evaluation, even if the goal of this work lies far from this aspect. Future work will investigate how structural hippocampal properties obtained with this method can improve Alzheimer's disease diagnosis [6].

Acknowledgments. Nicola Amoroso, Rosangela Errico and Andrea Tateo acknowledge funding by the Italian MIUR grant PON PRISMA Cod. PON04a2_A from Università degli Studi di Bari, Italy. This research was also supported by Istituto Nazionale di Fisica Nucleare (INFN), Italy.

References

1. Amoroso, N., Bellotti, R., Bruno, S., Chincarini, A., Logroscino, G., Tangaro, S., Tateo, A.: Automated Shape analysis landmarks detection for medical image processing. In: Proceedings of the International Symposium, CompIMAGE (2012)
2. Bellotti, R., Pascazio, S.: Editorial: Advanced physical methods in brain research. The European Physical Journal Plus **127**(11), 145 (2012)
3. Bland, J.M., Altman, D.G.: Comparing methods of measurement: why plotting difference against standard method is misleading. The Lancet **346**(8982), 1085–1087 (1995)
4. Boccardi, M., Bocchetta, M., Apostolova, L.G., Barnes, J., Bartzokis, G., Corbetta, G., DeCarli, C., Firbank, M., Ganzola, R., Gerritsen, L., et al.: Delphi definition of the EADC-ADNI Harmonized Protocol for hippocampal segmentation on magnetic resonance. Alzheimer's & Dementia **11**(2), 126–138 (2015)
5. Boccardi, M., Bocchetta, M., Morency, F.C., Collins, D.L., Nishikawa, M., Ganzola, R., Grothe, M.J., Wolf, D., Redolfi, A., Pievani, M., et al.: Training labels for hippocampal segmentation based on the eadc-adni harmonized hippocampal protocol. Alzheimer's & Dementia **11**(2), 183–191 (2015)

6. Bron, E.E., Smits, M., van der Flier, W.M., Vrenken, H., Barkhof, F., Scheltens, P., Papma, J.M., Steketee, R.M.E., Orellana Méndez, C., Meijboom, R., Pinto, M., Meireles, J.R., Garrett, C., Bastos-Leite, A.J., Abdulkadir, A., Ronneberger, O., Amoroso, N., Bellotti, R., Cárdenas-Peña, D., Álvarez Meza, A.M., Dolph, C.V., Iftekharuddin, K.M., Eskildsen, S.F., Coupé, P., Fonov, V.S., Franke, K., Gaser, C., Ledig, C., Guerrero, R., Tong, T., Gray, K.R., Moradi, E., Tohka, J., Routier, A., Durrleman, S., Sarica, A., Di Fatta, G., Sensi, F., Chincarini, A., Smith, G.M., Stoyanov, Z.V., Sørensen, L., Nielsen, M., Tangaro, S., Inglese, P., Wachinger, C., Reuter, M., van Swieten, J.C., Niessen, W.J., Klein, S.: Standardized evaluation of methods for computer-aided diagnosis of dementia based on structural MRI: the CADDementia challenge. NeuroImage (in press)

7. Chincarini, A., Bosco, P., Gemme, G., Esposito, M., Rei, L., Squarcia, S., Bellotti, R., Minthon, L., Frisoni, G., Scheltens, P., et al.: Automatic temporal lobe atrophy assessment in prodromal ad: Data from the descripa study. Alzheimer & Dementia 1, 12 (2013)

8. Fischl, B.: FreeSurfer. NeuroImage **62**(2), 774–781 (2012)

9. Jenkinson, M., Beckmann, C.F., Behrens, T.E., Woolrich, M.W., Smith, S.M.: Fsl. NeuroImage **62**(2), 782–790 (2012)

10. Kim, M., Wu, G., Li, W., Wang, L., Son, Y.D., Cho, Z.H., Shen, D.: Automatic hippocampus segmentation of 7.0 Tesla MR images by combining multiple atlases and auto-context models. NeuroImage **83**, 335–345 (2013)

11. Lotjonen, J.M.P., Wolz, R., Koikkalainen, J.R., Thurfjell, L., Waldemar, G., Soininen, H., Rueckert, D.: Fast and robust multi-atlas segmentation of brain magnetic resonance images. NeuroImage **49**(3), 2352–2365 (2010)

12. Tangaro, S., Amoroso, N., Boccardi, M., Bruno, S., Chincarini, A., Ferraro, G., Frisoni, G., Maglietta, R., Redolfi, A., Rei, L., Bellotti, R.: Automated voxel-by-voxel tissue classification for hippocampal segmentation: Methods and validation. Physica Medica **30**(8), 878–887 (2014)

13. Tangaro, S., Amoroso, N., Brescia, M., Cavuoti, S., Chincarini, A., Errico, R., Inglese, P., Longo, G., Maglietta, R., Tateo, A., Riccio, G., Bellotti, R.: Feature Selection Based on Machine Learning in MRIs for Hippocampal Segmentation. Computational and Mathematical Methods in Medicine, Article ID(814104) (in press)

14. Tustison, N.J., Avants, B.B., Cook, P.A., Zheng, Y., Egan, A., Yushkevich, P.A., Gee, J.C.: N4itk: improved n3 bias correction. IEEE Transactions on Medical Imaging **29**(6), 1310–1320 (2010)

A Survey on Traffic Light Detection

Moises Diaz[1]([✉]), Pietro Cerri[2], Giuseppe Pirlo[3], Miguel A. Ferrer[1],
and Donato Impedovo[4]

[1] Instituto Universitario para el Desarrollo Tecnológico y la Innovación en
Comunicaciones, Universidad de las Palmas de Gran Canaria, Las Palmas, Spain
{mdiaz,mferrer}@idetic.eu
[2] VisLab, University of Parma, Parma, Italy
cerri@vislab.it
[3] Dipartimento di Informatica, Universitá degli Studi di Bari Aldo Moro,
Via Orabona, 4, 70125 Bari, Italy
giuseppe.pirlo@uniba.it
[4] DyrectaLab, Conversano, Italy
impedovo@gmail.com

Abstract. Traffic light detection is an important matter in urban environments during the transition to fully autonomous driving. Many literature has been generated in the recent years approaching different pattern recognition strategies. In this paper we present a survey summarizing relevant works in the field of detection of both suspended and supported traffic light. This survey organizes different methods highlighting main reasearch areas in the computer vision field.

Keywords: Traffic light detection survey · Advanced driver assistance systems · Intelligent transportation systems · Image recognition · Intelligent vehicles

1 Introduction

Although fully autonomous driving is a possible scenario in the future, traffic lights are active tools used to control the traffic in both urban and motorway scenarios. However, both for the current advances in autonomous vehicle and a support for the human-driving, the traffic light detection still remain an active challenge.

Another use of traffic light recognition, is to help blind pedestrian or people with some visual impairment: these systems are often developed on mobile device. In [1] is presented a system architecture based on a mobile-cloud computing. In such a paper, the authors shared promising results obtained with the system working at real-time. Another work is shown in [27]. Authors focused their work on pedestrian lights and they developed a prototype implemented on a Nokia N95 mobile phone. Finally, in [14] a software developed in a similar mobile phone was prototyped in order to be used by blind people. Authors claim that the system was tested with blind volunteer, which guarantee the successful of such method.

© Springer International Publishing Switzerland 2015
V. Murino et al. (Eds.): ICIAP 2015 Workshops, LNCS 9281, pp. 201–208, 2015.
DOI: 10.1007/978-3-319-23222-5_25

Additional I2V communication can also be considered. In [19] a wireless network that periodically braodcasts traffic lights scheduling information is proposed. Traffic lights lamps can also be used as a light road-to-vehicle communication device. In [26] an high speed camera is used to allow communication between traffic lights and vehicles.

However traffic light detection has been traditionally solved with cameras, so many interesting approaches have been published in the pattern recognition field. Issues related to interpretation of suspended and supported traffic lights are the same, but suspended traffic lights detection is slightly more affected by lighting problems. Some of the most novel contributions have been summarized along this paper. This paper classifies the different works into the following issues: features extraction according to color or shape properties, classifiers and prior information through digital maps. An analysis of these phases to deal with traffic light recognition problems is presented in the following sections.

2   Feature Extraction

2.1   Color Segmentation

RGB-cameras are widely used to detect the scenario where the traffic light are present due to the utility of the color properties [35] [25] [24] [28] [31] [15] [30] [17] [20]. Different authors study the more properly combination of color. A determined color spaces or a combination of several ones are used in a same approach in order to cluster the color.

The clustering leads to analyze the color properties of different lights: while the red color luminosity from a LED spot lights have a brighter component, traditional light bulb color component are less prominent. This situation leads to systems able to integrate both sort of lamps, specially in not very modern urban environments.

Different color spaces are used in the literature. In [35] [16] a simple RGB color space is supposed to support a preliminary information of the state color. Also the normalized RGB is a color space which seems to be more robust against illumination variations or different lighting conditions [11] [25] [24] [9]. Other authors prefer a cylindrical representation of the RGB color space: we could find approaches in [31] [15] which are based on the Hue, Saturation and Value/Lightness (HSV/HLS) color space. This color thresholding model is focused on human vision and it is usually a substitution of RGB color space. Another used color space is the so called YUV color space which highlights the luminance (Y) and chrominance (UV) of images. For instance, in [28], an equalization of the image was performed by the luminance (channel Y). Then, a combination between the hue and the chorminance was carried out for the color segmentation. The LAB color space is also used for this issue in [30] [17]. In [30] a method called Fast Radial Symmetry Transform is proposed to elaborate an image that is composed by the maximum of a and b channel of LAB, reaching a good classification rate for red traffic light. In [17] a novel feature space (called V) is computed, by computing the product of the normalized gray scale, the A channel of LAB and the S channel of HSV: two different approaches are proposed for day and night, both based on Convolutional Neural Network and Saliency Map. Also in [23] the HSV color space was uased. Finally, the convenience of the YCbCr color space is discussed in [2], where authors shows a system able to work at real-time.

The color properties are often exploited by using a set of sequential rules. On the one hand, it could be seen in [25] [24] [33] [9] a simple sequential procedure for this kind of clustering. On the other hand, the integration of a fuzzy clustering combined with sequential rules in [8] seems to enhance the procedure. Another similar approach was shown in [6] where traffic lights detection was based on combination of the hue and intensity image with lighting data, then possible traffic lights were obtained by fuzzification of all this values.

Additionally, the systems should be robust to the whether (rain, fog, snow) as well as the daily hours (morning, evening or night): the color properties in such atmospheric conditions changes, this matter is also widely studied in the literature in [9] [35] [8] [7] [10].

In any case, with no additional I2V information, the current tendency to identify traffic lights and establish their state is carried out by means of a color components approach.

2.2   Shape Properties

Traffic light lamps present particular features which could be studied separately in the image. Looking for this particular features in the image is a good practice to remove whose candidates which are clearly not a traffic light. Such features are frequently based on the shape, aspect ratio, texture and size of detected objects. After studying how these features are in the real traffic lights, rules delimiting features properties is a possibility to extract the correct traffic lights, removing the false candidates.

For instance, authors proposed a straightforward approach in [35] with a concurrent set of rules based on common sense. Although promising results were obtained during the day test, the success rate was quite low during the night.

The contribution [29] presents a system composed by a low cost camera and a robust algorithm written in Matlab. Once, the traffic light parameters are learned using a 2D Gaussian distribution, authors modeled the hue and saturation parameters by using a set of training images. The strongest part of this work is the recognition stage based on the traffic light shape. A weak part of this procedure is both the high computation time and the low frame rate (about 1.4 fps).

An algorithm carried out in this kind of issues is the Hough Transform, since it is able to recognize pattern and forms in an image like the circular shapes. In order to save computation time, an edge detector, commonly a Canny filter, is usually applied to grayscale images at the first stage. Thus, the search is based on detecting parameterized curve circles in the frames. In [34] a discussion about the edge detector is carried out working on traffic light detection. Then, Omachi et. al have worked with traffic lights with lenses mounted in a row. They can be typically found in countries like Japan or in cities like Miami, among others.

In their approach, authors have modified the classical Hough Transform achieving a computation time of 0.15 s and an accuracy rate of 89 %. A classical Hough Transform is used in their initial work [24] and their last approach is discussed in [25]; this new method is used after the clustering and the edge detection process.

Additionally, Circular Hough Transform (CHT) is an acceptable approach to compute the center of a circle object as well [18]. For instance, CHT is used in several traffic signs recognition, such as [13] or [3]. The weakness of this kind of techniques is the computation time, which should be carefully taken into account.

3   Classifiers

The structure of a traffic light is quite standard in many countries. It is composed mainly by a vertical structure and three circular lenses with the colors green - amber - red. Some approaches are based on cascade classifiers to detect this structures.

R. de Charette et al worked on this topic. Several classifiers, based on AdaBoost learning processes, are developed. An interesting and customized Adaptative Templates Matching helped to assay traffic lights from different countries. In their first publication [4] the method is tested in urban roads. Then, in their second publication [5], the method is evidenced in China, France and USA, where 640×480 images were processed with a 2.9 GHz single core desktop computer in real-time. The precision achieved is 95 %.

On one hand, a large set of traffic light images is used in [10] to train the proposed ADAS. In this work, two out three traffic light states were considered: red and green. On the other hand, although not in real-time, a challenging detection results are obtained by using a cascade classifier is used in [22].

The histogram of oriented gradients (HOG) features and support vector machine (SVM) are also recognizer used in this field. Their convenience was evaluated in [23]. Hence, a nearest neighbor classifier is also adopted as recognizer in [2] and a Hidden Markov Models (HMM) in [12].

3.1   Distance Estimation

Estimating the distance between vehicle and detected traffic light is an additional value for any ADAS. In some reviewed works, we could find different approaches. For instance, in [31] authors label traffic lights, their size (radius), number of lenses and height. Labelling traffic lights in a city supports robustness to computer vision system performance.

While in [9] authors dealt with the distance estimation from visual detected candidate properties, in an extension of such work in [8] the distance was computed through Bayesian filters.

Moreover, the distance could be approximated assuming a permanent diameter for the traffic lights lenses [10]. The traffic light location is also estimated through record tracking, back-projection, and triangulation combined with

Bayesian filters in the tracking stage of the algorithm [21]. In [22] [33] the maximum distance at which it is possible to detect traffic lights is presented as well.

State estimation and tracking is as well almost essential for the integration of traffic light detection in automotive systems. The use of Hidden Markov Models is proposed in [12] to filter error in state estimation, increasing the detection rate up to the 50%. In [32] the authors propose an Interacting Multiple Model filter to track the position and the status of traffic lights. Position estimation accuracy increases with the number of iterations that is closely linked to the distance from the traffic light.

4   A Priori Information

Traffic lights equipped with high technology are usually found in modern and smart cities. Among its modern properties, they can be found registered in a digital map for an urban area or can be referenced by a global navigation satellite system data.

A priori knowledge of traffic light position is very useful to filter out a large number of false candidates on the images. Also, such aids to navigation system allow to activate the traffic light detector when the vehicle reaches a fixed distance from a traffic light, i.e. 150 meters in highways or even less in urban environments.

In order to create a digital prior map, some techniques are shared in [10]. In this work, promising results were obtained thanks to the numerous mapped traffic lights in the tested areas - more than 4000 traffic light position were registered. The work published in [22] also confirms the extremely significant benefits in the recognition rate due to the use of a prior map.

Additionally, in [17] the GPS position is used to compute a Region Of Interest in the image, when the distance from the traffic light is lower than 100 meters.

Finally, the experience in Public ROad Urban Driverless-Car Test[1] 2013 by VisLab group also demonstrated the reduction of false candidates and the increase of the correct detections.

5   Conclusions

Although the fully autonomous vehicles will not need the presence of traffic light in future smart cities, detection and interpretation of traffic lights meaning remains an active problem for industries and research groups. The majority of the current advance driver assistance system related to traffic light detection are based on computer vision. In this work we have reviewed the main recently advances published in this field, highlighting phases common to most approaches.

---

[1] http://vislab.it/proud

References

1. Angin, P., Bhargava, B., Helal, S.: A mobile-cloud collaborative traffic lights detector for blind navigation. In: Proceedings of the 2010 Eleventh International Conference on Mobile Data Management, MDM 2010, pp. 396–401. IEEE Computer Society, Washington, DC (2010). doi: 10.1109/MDM.2010.71
2. Cai, Z., Li, Y., Gu, M.: Real-time recognition system of traffic light in urban environment. In: 2012 IEEE Symposium on Computational Intelligence for Security and Defence Applications (CISDA), pp. 1–6, July 2012
3. Caraffi, C., Cardarelli, E., Medici, P., Porta, P., Ghisio, G., Monchiero, G.: An algorithm for italian de-restriction signs detection. In: 2008 IEEE Intelligent Vehicles Symposium, pp. 834–840, June 2008
4. de Charette, R., Nashashibi, F.: Real time visual traffic lights recognition based on spot light detection and adaptive traffic lights templates. In: 2009 IEEE Intelligent Vehicles Symposium, pp. 358–363, June 2009
5. de Charette, R., Nashashibi, F.: Traffic light recognition using image processing compared to learning processes. In: IEEE/RSJ International Conference on Intelligent Robots and Systems, IROS 2009, pp. 333–338, October 2009
6. Chung, Y., Wang, J., Chen, S.: A vision-based traffic light detection system at intersections. Journal of Taiwan Normal University: Mathematics, Science and Technology **47**(1), 67–86 (2002)
7. Diaz-Cabrera, M., Cerri, P.: Traffic light recognition during the night based on fuzzy logic clustering. In: Moreno-Díaz, R., Pichler, F., Quesada-Arencibia, A. (eds.) EUROCAST 2013, Part II. Lecture Notes in Computer Science, vol. 8112, pp. 93–100. Springer, Berlin Heidelberg (2013)
8. Diaz-Cabrera, M., Cerri, P., Medici, P.: Robust real-time traffic light detection and distance estimation using a single camera. Expert Systems with Applications **42**(8), 3911–3923 (2015)
9. Diaz-Cabrera, M., Cerri, P., Sanchez-Medina, J.J.: Suspended traffic lights detection and distance estimation using color features. In: Intelligent Transportation System Conference - ITSC 2012 IEEE, pp. 1315–1320, September 2012
10. Fairfield, N., Urmson, C.: Traffic light mapping and detection. In: 2011 IEEE International Conference on Robotics and Automation (ICRA), pp. 5421–5426, May 2011
11. Gevers, T., Smeulders, A.W.M.: Color-based object recognition. Pattern Recognition **32**(3), 453–464 (1999)
12. Gomez, A., Alencar, F., Prado, P., Osorio, F., Wolf, D.: Traffic lights detection and state estimation using hidden markov models. In: 2014 IEEE Intelligent Vehicles Symposium Proceedings, pp. 750–755, June 2014
13. Huang, Y.S., Lee, Y.S.: Detection and recognition of speed limit signs. In: 2010 International Computer Symposium (ICS), pp. 107–112, December 2010
14. Ivanchenko, V., Coughlan, J., Shen, H.: Real-time walk light detection with a mobile phone. In: Miesenberger, K., Klaus, J., Zagler, W., Karshmer, A. (eds.) ICCHP 2010, Part II. Lecture Notes in Computer Science, vol. 6180, pp. 229–234. Springer, Berlin Heidelberg (2010)
15. Jang, C., Kim, C., Kim, D., Lee, M., Sunwoo, M.: Multiple exposure images based traffic light recognition. In: 2014 IEEE Intelligent Vehicles Symposium Proceedings, pp. 1313–1318, June 2014

16. Jie, Y., Xiaomin, C., Pengfei, G., Zhonglong, X.: A new traffic light detection and recognition algorithm for electronic travel aid. In: 2013 Fourth International Conference on Intelligent Control and Information Processing (ICICIP), pp. 644–648, June 2013

17. John, V., Yoneda, K., Qi, B., Liu, Z., Mita, S.: Traffic light recognition in varying illumination using deep learning and saliency map. In: 2014 IEEE 17th International Conference on Intelligent Transportation Systems (ITSC), pp. 2286–2291, October 2014

18. Kerbyson, D., Atherton, T.: Circle detection using hough transform filters. In: Fifth International Conference on Image Processing and its Applications, pp. 370–374, July 1995

19. Kim, K.T.: Stvc: Secure traffic-light to vehicle communication. In: 2012 4th International Congress on Ultra Modern Telecommunications and Control Systems and Workshops (ICUMT), pp. 96–104. IEEE (2012)

20. Kim, H.K., Shin, Y.N., Kuk, S.G., Park, J.H., Jung, H.Y.: Night-time traffic light detection based on svm with geometric moment features. World Academy of Science, Engineering and Technology 7(4), 454–457 (2013)

21. Levinson, J., Askeland, J., Dolson, J., Thrun, S.: Traffic light mapping, localization, and state detection for autonomous vehicles. In: 2011 IEEE International Conference on Robotics and Automation (ICRA), pp. 5784–5791 (2011)

22. Lindner, F., Kressel, U., Kaelberer, S.: Robust recognition of traffic signals. In: 2004 IEEE Intelligent Vehicles Symposium, pp. 49–53, June 2004

23. Mu, G., Xinyu, Z., Deyi, L., Tianlei, Z., Lifeng, A.: Traffic light detection and recognition for autonomous vehicles. The Journal of China Universities of Posts and Telecommunications 22(1), 50–56 (2015)

24. Omachi, M., Omachi, S.: Traffic light detection with color and edge information. In: 2nd IEEE International Conference on Computer Science and Information Technology, ICCSIT 2009, pp. 284–287, August 2009

25. Omachi, M., Omachi, S.: Detection of traffic light using structural information. In: 2010 IEEE 10th International Conference on Signal Processing (ICSP), pp. 809–812, October 2010

26. Premachandra, H.C.N., Yendo, T., Tehrani, M.P., Yamazato, T., Okada, H., Fujii, T., Tanimoto, M.: High-speed-camera image processing based led traffic light detection for road-to-vehicle visible light communication. In: 2010 IEEE Intelligent Vehicles Symposium (IV), pp. 793–798. IEEE (2010)

27. Roters, J., Jiang, X., Rothaus, K.: Recognition of traffic lights in live video streams on mobile devices. IEEE Transactions on Circuits and Systems for Video Technology 21(10), 1497–1511 (2011)

28. Shaded, W., Abu-Al-Nadi, D., Mismar, M.: Road traffic sign detection in color images. In: IEEE International Conference on Electronics, Circuits and Systems, pp. 890–893 (2003)

29. Shen, Y., Ozguner, U., Redmill, K., Liu, J.: A robust video based traffic light detection algorithm for intelligent vehicles. In: 2009 IEEE Intelligent Vehicles Symposium, pp. 521–526, June 2009

30. Sooksatra, S., Kondo, T.: Red traffic light detection using fast radial symmetry transform. In: 2014 11th International Conference on Electrical Engineering/Electronics, Computer, Telecommunications and Information Technology (ECTI-CON), pp. 1–6, May 2014

31. Tae-Hyun, H., In-Hak, J., Seong-Ik, C.: Detection of traffic lights for vision-based car navigation system. In: Chang, L.-W., Lie, W.-N. (eds.) PSIVT 2006. LNCS, vol. 4319, pp. 682–691. Springer, Heidelberg (2006)

32. Trehard, G., Pollard, E., Bradai, B., Nashashibi, F.: Tracking both pose and status of a traffic light via an interacting multiple model filter. In: 2014 17th International Conference on Information Fusion (FUSION), pp. 1–7, July 2014

33. Vu, A., Ramanandan, A., Chen, A., Farrell, J., Barth, M.: Real-time computer vision/dgps-aided inertial navigation system for lane-level vehicle navigation. IEEE Transactions on Intelligent Transportation Systems **13**(2), 899–913 (2012)

34. Walad, K.P., Shetty, J.: Traffic light control system using image processing. International Journal of Innovative Research in Computer and Communication Engineering 2 (2014)

35. Yu, C., Huang, C., Lang, Y.: Traffic light detection during day and night conditions by a camera. In: 2010 IEEE 10th International Conference on Signal Processing (ICSP), pp. 821–824, October 2010

Saliency-Based Keypoint Reduction
for Augmented-Reality Applications in Smart Cities

Simone Buoncompagni[1]($\boxtimes$), Dario Maio[1], Davide Maltoni[1], and Serena Papi[2]

[1] DISI, Università di Bologna, Mura Anteo Zamboni 7 40126, Bologna, Italy
simone.buoncompagni2@unibo.it
[2] CIRI ICT, Università di Bologna, via Rasi e Spinelli 146 47521, Cesena, Italy

Abstract. In this paper we show that Saliency-based keypoint selection makes natural landmark detection and object recognition quite effective and efficient, thus enabling augmented reality techniques in a plethora of applications in smart city contexts. As a case study we address a tour of a museum where a modern smart device like a tablet or smartphone can be used to recognize paintings, retrieve their pose and graphically overlay useful information.

Keywords: Saliency-based ranking · Keypoint local descriptors · Smart city · Augmented reality

1   Introduction

The growth of mobile devices equipped with high quality displays, high resolution cameras and high processing capabilities allows new computer vision applications to be deployed. In particular in the context of smart cities, augmented reality is an enabling technology for a number of applications in tourism, arts and intelligent buildings since as defined in the European context the presence of cultural facilities is a key indicator for smart cities quality evaluation [12].

It is well-known that accurate object recognition and pose detection are key building blocks to develop effective Augmented Reality (AR) applications. Moreover, when artificial landmarks (e.g., 2D-bar codes, beacons, etc. [5] [6]) cannot be used, recognizing objects and retrieving their pose in real-time can be very challenging, especially on resource-constrained platforms such as mobile devices. In [13][14] different strategies have been proposed in order to reduce the number of keypoints (and corresponding local descriptors) that need to be matched. In [1] we recently introduced a pose detection approach founded on a Saliency-based keypoint selection and reduction that has been proved to be very effective for the problem at hand.

In this work we extend approach [1] by including an object recognition phase to be carried out before pose estimation, and we design a specific application to perform a museum tour with the aid of AR. The paper is organized as follows: in section 2 we present an overview of the Saliency-based keypoint selection method introduced in [1]; in section 3 we extend our previous approach in the context of the tour of a museum; finally, in section 4 we draw some conclusions.

© Springer International Publishing Switzerland 2015
V. Murino et al. (Eds.): ICIAP 2015 Workshops, LNCS 9281, pp. 209–217, 2015.
DOI: 10.1007/978-3-319-23222-5_26

2   Saliency-Based Keypoint Selection: An Overview

In this section we summarize the method we proposed in [1] for Saliency-based key-points selection.

Given an object, a preliminary training step is performed to define the object mod-el based on its most salient keypoint descriptors. The training set is composed by a single reference image I^{ref} of the object acquired in neutral viewpoint and lighting conditions and by a set of N generated images I^1, I^2, ..., I^N which depict the same object under different conditions. A generic transformed image $I^l = Transf_l(I^{ref})$ is obtained by applying a transformation (e.g. 2D homography, a 3D projection, a light changing function) to the reference image.

To evaluate saliency, keypoints detection on the reference image I^{ref} is firstly performed and then each keypoint is mapped on the transformed images by applying $Transf_l$ functions. Descriptors for all keypoints are computed and a global analysis is performed to rank the keypoints by saliency and to retain only the m-best ones to characterize the object model. Highly salient keypoints are excellent candidates for the matching since focusing on them not only reduces the computational load but also improves keypoint matching accuracy.

Even if our approach is independent of the keypoint detector and local description, to maximize efficiency in [1] we focused on FAST detector and BRIEF descriptors. Furthermore, we proved that working in the Opponent color space [3] (instead of the RGB space) increases the robustness with respect to light changes.

For a given object, let $x_i = (u_i, v_i) \in I^{ref}$ be a keypoint selected by the FAST detection algorithm [11] and be s_i its strength returned by the FAST algorithm itself. The set of all keypoints of the reference image is $K_d(I^{ref}) = \{(x_i, s_i): x_i \in I^{ref}, i = 1, ..., J\}$. For each $x_i \in K_d(I^{ref})$, we define with $descr: (\Re^2, \Re^S \times \Re^S) \to \Re^L$ the function that computes BRIEF descriptor [2] for a keypoint x_i according to the im-age patch $P(x_i)$ of size S×S centered on x_i. Given the nature of BRIEF, $\mathbf{b}_i = descr(x_i, P(x_i)))$ is a binary vector. Therefore, two binary vectors $\mathbf{b}_i$ and $\mathbf{b}_j$ are compared by using the Hamming distance $H(\mathbf{b}_i, \mathbf{b}_j)$ that can be computed very effi-ciently through a bitwise XOR operation followed by a bit count.

Keypoint saliency is expressed in terms of detectability, distinctiveness and repea-tability (see [1] for equations), defined as follows:

- The *distinctiveness* $D(x_i)$ of a keypoint $x_i \in K_d(I^{ref})$ is proportional to the di-versity among the x_i descriptor and the descriptors of other keypoints $x_j \in K_d(I^{ref})$, $j \neq i$ in the same image.
- The *repeatability* $R(x_i)$ of a keypoint $x_i \in K_d(I^{ref})$ is proportional to the simi-larity among its descriptor $\mathbf{b}_i$ and the descriptors of corresponding keypoints un-der a set T of given transformations   (e.g. viewpoint and lighting).
- The *detectability* $F(x_i)$ of a keypoint depends of the score values returned by the keypoint detection algorithm (i.e. in FAST, the score is the corner strength [2]) and quantifies the aptitude of a given keypoint to be detected under various view-point and lighting changes. The detectability of a keypoint $x_i \in K_d(I^{ref})$ is simp-ly an average (normalized in the range [0,1]) over the scores of all keypoints in the original image and its transformed versions.

It is worth noting that while detectability is related to keypoint stability under transformation, repeatability and distinctiveness are related to the discriminant power of descriptors. Detectability, distinctiveness and repeatability are finally combined in order to determine the *keypoint Saliency S*, as follows:

$$S(\boldsymbol{x}_i) = \omega_R R(\boldsymbol{x}_i) + \omega_D D(\boldsymbol{x}_i) + \omega_F F(\boldsymbol{x}_i) \tag{1}$$

where ω_R, ω_D and ω_F are weights assigned to repeatability, distinctiveness and detectability, respectively.

3 A Case Study: A Museum Tour with Augmented Reality

The Saliency-based approach proposed in [1] is here extended with a (pre)matching phase and applied to the painting recognition and pose estimation, which constitute useful building blocks to develop AR based museum tour. A number of AR solutions in the field of cultural heritage and mobile multimedia guides have been recently proposed [7][8][9][10]. Authors of [7] and [9] introduced an exhaustive overview of the main challenges related to conception, implementation, testing and assessment of a smart museum. In PALM-Cities Project [10] technologies such as NFC and QR Codes have been adopted to handle the interaction with the user whereas in [7] an hybrid approach based on markerless tracking plus a rotation sensor is used to allow free movements of the user mobile device.

Similarly to [7], in our application the user is expected to enjoy paintings in a markerless environment by interacting with a mobile device (e.g. tablet, smartphone or smart glasses) provided with a camera that captures videos of paintings under different conditions (i.e., moderate changes of viewpoint and lighting).

Once a painting has been recognized and its pose has been retrieved the application can properly superimpose to the live camera view useful pictorial or textual information concerning the painting itself (see Fig. 1 for an example).

An overview of the approach is presented in Fig. 2: during the training phase we use a single reference image of each painting to compute the painting model including only the most salient keypoints. Models are then stored in a database which is made available to the user's mobile device.

In this study we consider 10 famous paintings (see Fig. 3). For each painting p we downloaded the reference image I_p^{ref} from the web and printed it on paper (A3 format). Paintings were then hanged to the walls of our lab to simulate a museum room.

Fig. 1. Example of augmented information geometrically coherent with the painting pose.

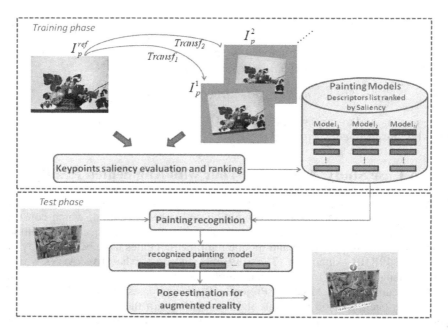

Fig. 2. Overview of the proposed application based on keypoint saliency evaluation.

Fig. 3. The 10 famous paintings we consider in our study.

For each reference image, we generated 80 artificial transformations to be used for the training phase: the variations considered are random homographic transformations within predefined parameter ranges.

Test was performed using a smart device and capturing videos of each printed painting while moving in front of the painting; for each video we selected 30 frames characterized by different lighting and pose conditions, hence our test set is composed of 300 images (see Fig. 4 for some examples).

We performed two different experiments: the former to evaluate recognition accuracy and the latter to evaluate the correctness of the estimated pose. In both these experiments our Saliency-based ranking is compared to a standard FAST score-based ranking. For each test image I^{test}, the painting recognition phase is implemented as follows:

- all keypoints are extracted (FAST) and their local descriptors (BRIEF) computed;
- for each painting model I_p^{ref}, characterized by its m-most salient keypoints $K_d^m(I_p^{ref})$:
  - we associate each keypoint in $K_d^m(I_p^{ref})$ to the keypoint in I^{test} with smallest Hamming distance (between BREIF descriptors);
  - we enforce geometrical constraints among keypoint correspondences using RANSAC algorithm [4] to filter out outliers;
  - the set of inliers returned by RANSAC is then used to compute a similarity score Φ between I^{test} and I_p^{ref} as follows:

$$\Phi(I^{test}, I_p^{ref}) = \frac{\# \, Ransac \, Inliers}{\# \, K_d^m(I_p^{ref})} \qquad (2)$$

- finally, recognition is performed according to maximum similarity.

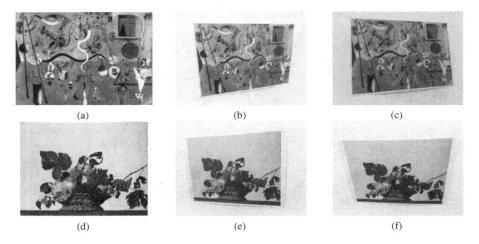

Fig. 4. Samples of the dataset used in our case study: (a) and (d) are the reference images of two different paintings, (b), (c), (e), (f) are test frames acquired live with a tablet.

Tests have been repeated for $n = 300$ and for different values of m ranging from 1% to 100% of the total number of keypoints. This allows to evaluate the effect on recognition of progressive reduction of the keypoint number.

In Table 1 we show the recognition rate obtained by considering only the most salient descriptors when our Saliency-based ranking and a standard FAST-scores ranking are applied. In general we can observe that our method is more effective than the FAST-scores based one. Moreover it turns out that by applying our Saliency evaluation a lower percentage of keypoints is sufficient to reach top performance with respect to FAST-scores ranking (only 4% of the keypoints for our approach versus 15% for FAST-scores).

Table 1. Recognition results for Saliency-based selection and Fast-scores selection.

m-most salient considered keypoint (%)	"Saliency-Based" Recognition rate (%)	"Fast-based" Recognition rate(%)
1	74.58333	53.75
2	92.5	80.41667
3	97.91667	90.83333
4	**98.75**	90
5	98.75	94.16667
10	97.91667	95.83333
15	96.66667	**97.91667**
20	97.08333	97.91667
100	88.75	88.75

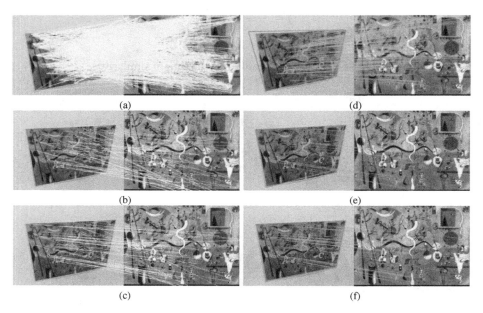

Fig. 5. Painting transformation recovery through RANSAC algorithm by taking as input: (d) all FAST keypoints; (e) 5% m-best keypoints ranked according to FAST score, (f) 5% m-best keypoints ranked according to our Saliency-based approach. Yellow segments (a), (b) and (c) denote initial keypoint pairing and orange segments (d), (e) and (f) final RANSAC inliers; the green rectangle denotes the homographic transformation inferred by RANSAC.

A second evaluation has been carried out to assess correctness and computational load of pose estimation. Since a painting can be considered as a full planar object, pose is computed by estimating a homographic transformation through the RANSAC algorithm [4] given a set of keypoint correspondences with the reference model.

Fig. 5 shows the result of pose estimation for a painting sample by considering three different cases: (a) model including all keypoints, (b) only 5% m-best keypoints selected according to FAST scores and (c) only 5% m-best keypoints selected according to our approach.

Although RANSAC is somewhat robust with respect to outliers, the advantages of using only relevant keypoints are here evident in terms of precision of the recovered viewpoint transformation. We also note how our ranking leads to consolidate a higher number of inliers and therefore a better viewpoint estimation with respect to the FAST-scores based selection.

To numerically quantify pose estimation accuracy we manually marked (as ground truth) the four painting corners both for each reference image and each test frame. A pose is then considered correct when the projected painting corners (according to the estimated homography) have a spatial distance from the corresponding ground truth lower than a prefixed threshold.

In the graph of Fig. 6a we show the percentage of "correct pose" estimation averaged over all 300 tests images.

We can easily note that, in both cases, the curves have an increasing trend up to a relatively small value m of best keypoints and then start decreasing. The optimal percentage of keypoint falls in the range [5%, 20%] in our approach, and in [15%, 30%] when selection is performed according to FAST scores.

Fig. 6b shows the average processing time for a single frame analysis as function of the keypoints percentage. For this experiment we used a Samsung ATIV Smart PC (Intel Atom Processor Z2760 1.5 Ghz) tablet device. Even if the code (written in C# for .NET) was not highly optimized, by selecting a percentage of keypoints below 5% we can provide a frame rate from 3 to 5 frame/s, ensuring, at the same time, good accuracy in terms of object recognition and pose estimation.

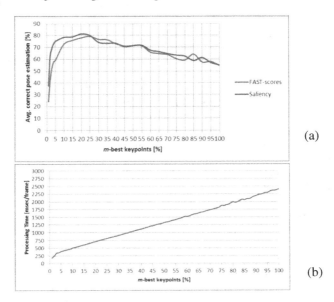

(a)

(b)

Fig. 6. (a) Average percentage of correct poses by varying the percentage of the keypoints ranked both according to Fast-scores and our Saliency-based approach; (b) Average processing time (milliseconds) required for a single frame analysis including painting recognition and pose estimation on Intel Atom Processor Z2760 1.5 Ghz.

4 Conclusions

In this paper we proved the feasibility of a markerless AR application running on mobile devices. Initial results with a limited database (10 paintings, 300 test poses) are quite promising. The main strength of the proposed Saliency-based ranking and selection relies in the significant reduction of the amount of features to be matched, thus allowing real-time implementation on resource-limited computer architectures without compromising recognition accuracy. In the future, we intend to study the efficacy and efficiency of this technique when scaling to larger datasets and with different combinations of feature detectors / local descriptors. On the one side, we expect that painting recognition accuracy and efficiency can be negatively affected when a large number of painting models are stored in the database. However, for the application considered this is not a serious problem since a single tag (e.g. NFC, e-beacon, etc.) could be placed inside each room to coarse localize the user and restrict the database search to the paintings located inside the current room.

References

1. Buoncompagni, S., Maio, D., Maltoni, D., Papi, S.: Saliency-based keypoint selection for fast object detection and matching. Pattern Recognition Letters **62**, 32–40 (2015)
2. Calonder, M., Lepetit, V., Strecha, C., Fua, P.: BRIEF: binary robust independent elementary features. In: Daniilidis, K., Maragos, P., Paragios, N. (eds.) ECCV 2010, Part IV. LNCS, vol. 6314, pp. 778–792. Springer, Heidelberg (2010)
3. Van De Sande, K.E., Gevers, T., Snoek, C.G.: Evaluating color descriptors for object and scene recognition. IEEE Transactions on Pattern Analysis and Machine Intelligence **32**(9), 1582–1596 (2010)
4. Fischler, M.A., Bolles, R.C.: Random sample consensus: a paradigm for model fitting with applications to image analysis and automated cartography. Communications of the ACM **24**(6), 381–395 (1981)
5. Parikh, D., Jancke, G.: Localization and segmentation of a 2D high capacity color barcode. In: IEEE Workshop on Applications of Computer Vision, WACV 2008, pp. 1–6, January 7–9, 2008
6. Furht, B.: Handbook of augmented reality, vol. 71. Springer, New York (2011)
7. Miyashita, T., et al.: An augmented reality museum guide. In: Proceedings of the 7th IEEE/ACM International Symposium on Mixed and Augmented Reality. IEEE Computer Society (2008)
8. Damala, A., Marchal, I., Houlier, P.: Merging augmented reality based features in mobile multimedia museum guides. In: CIPA Conference on Anticipating the Future of the Cultural Past, 2007, October 1–6, 2007
9. Damala, A., et al.: Bridging the gap between the digital and the physical: design and evaluation of a mobile augmented reality guide for the museum visit. In: Proceedings of the 3rd International Conference on Digital Interactive Media in Entertainment and Arts. ACM (2008)
10. Caridi, A., Coccoli, M., Volpi, V.: Wolfsoniana smart museum. a pilot plant installation of the PALM-cities project. In: UMAP Workshops (2013)

11. Rosten, E., Porter, R., Drummond, T.: Faster and better: A machine learning approach to corner detection. IEEE Transactions on Pattern Analysis and Machine Intelligence **32**(1), 105–119 (2010)
12. http://www.smart-cities.eu/download/smart_cities_final_report.pdf
13. Carneiro, G., Jepson, A.D.: The quantitative characterization of the distinctiveness and robustness of local image descriptors. Image and Vision Computing **27**(8), 1143–1156 (2009)
14. Hartmann, W., Havlena, M., Schindler, K.: Predicting matchability. In: Conference on Computer Vision and Pattern Recognition (2014)

A Likelihood-Based Background Model for Real Time Processing of Color Filter Array Videos

Vito Renó$^{(\boxtimes)}$, Roberto Marani, Nicola Mosca, Massimiliano Nitti,
Tiziana D'Orazio, and Ettore Stella

Institute of Intelligent Systems for Automation,
Italian National Research Council, Bari, Italy
reno@ba.issia.cnr.it

Abstract. One of the first tasks executed by a vision system made of
fixed cameras is the background (BG) subtraction and a particularly
challenging context for real time applications is the athletic one because
of illumination changes, moving objects and cluttered scenes. The aim
of this work is to extract a BG model based on statistical likelihood able
to process color filter array (CFA) images taking into account the intrinsic variance of each gray level of the sensor, named Likelihood Bayer
Background (LBB). The BG model should be not so computationally
complex while highly responsive to extract a robust foreground. Moreover, the mathematical operations used in the formulation should be
parallelizable, working on image patches, and computationally efficient,
exploiting the dynamics of a pixel within its integer range. Both simulations and experiments on real video sequences demonstrate that this
BG model approach shows great performances and robustness during the
real time processing of scenes extracted from a soccer match.

1 Introduction

Artificial vision systems (AVSs) equipped with fixed cameras usually need to
implement the BG subtraction as the first low level computational task. The
output of such process generally is the input for a large amount of software
modules that can implement, for example, object tracking or scene understanding. Today, the amount of data processed by an AVS can be dramatically huge
because state of the art cameras can achieve very high throughputs in the order
of Gb/s. Researchers and engineers are investigating on how to move low level
computational load directly on smart cameras [2] reducing the amount of information that needs to be transferred on computers for processing purposes.

Generally speaking, BG models can be classified as *Temporal difference methods* and *Background subtraction methods*: the former group obtains the foreground subtracting and thresholding two consecutive frames; the latter group
builds a dynamic model that is updated over time and subtracted to each frame
that needs to be processed. One of the most used BG subtraction method is
the Adaptive Mixture of Gaussians (MoG) proposed by Stauffer and Grimson
[13] that uses Gaussian distributions to represent the variation of pixel intensity.

© Springer International Publishing Switzerland 2015
V. Murino et al. (Eds.): ICIAP 2015 Workshops, LNCS 9281, pp. 218–225, 2015.
DOI: 10.1007/978-3-319-23222-5_27

Two examples of subsequent improvements of this algorithm are the MoGv2 [16] that adaptively updates the parameters of the model over time and its variant on Bayer pattern inputs [14]. Other BG algorithms known in literature include: the Eigenbackground [8] introduced by Oliver et al., that models the BG in a vector subspace obtained via PCA; the Codebook [7] proposed by Kim et al., that implements a quantization of the pixel values using codebooks in order to compress the model size; the GMG [5] by Godbehere et al., that estimates the entire pixel intensity distribution rather than its parameters using dynamic information and updating only the probability distributions associated with background pixels; models based on Hidden Markov Models (HMMs) [11] to represent pixel intensity variations as discrete states.

The possibility of implementing code directly on smart cameras opens new research trends applied to AVSs. In this context, a BG model able to work with CFA images can be implemented directly on embedded chips. Computationally efficient and parallelizable operations are required to find the best trade-off between complexity and reliable results in real time. The Adaptive light-weight algorithm detailed in [1] and applied to process atheltic videos is an example of relevant research interest. According to [15], this type of scenes can be used to detect salient events (i.e. offsides or goals during football matches [3,4,6]), analyse and track objects (i.e. ball and players), perform 3D reconstructions or analyse tactics. Therefore, a robust BG needs to be responsive to light changes and fast in the updates, even if it is modelled with a few bootstrapping frames.

In this paper a BG model able to deal with CFA raw images taking into account the intrinsic sensor variance of each gray value is presented. The variance raises as the gray level increases, therefore LBB exploits this information instead of the classical approaches that evaluate single pixels over time. Finally, each Bayer patch is labelled as BG by means of a likelihood-based approach. The rest of the work is organized as follows: in the second section the proposed algorithm is detailed, the third section contains experiments and results carried out on athletic videos and the last one discusses the conclusions and future works.

2 Methodology

2.1 Algorithm Description

LBB is divided in three main building blocks that are summarized in List. 1.1, namely initialization, processing and update. The first step is executed only once and initializes the BG image setting each pixel to half intensity. This all gray logic is due to the absence of any *a priori* knowledge about the scene. The processing phase is composed of: variance, likelihood, fine tuning and energy. The last one is the same presented in [10], while the other are detailed singularly in the following sub sections. The BG image is updated according to PIIB logic [10] enriched by a binary update mask M. Hence, each BG pixel value is increased or decreased by κ if the corresponding M value is set to true (in our implementation $\kappa = 1$). In addition, LBB calculates a second version of the background that does not take care of M (BG_{nu}) with the aim of avoiding ghosts on the scene, as it will be described later.

Listing 1.1. Algorithm pseudocode

```
Background Initialization
for each frame
    Variance process
    for each patch
        Likelihood process
    if(Background is learned)
        Fine tuning process
    Background Update
    Energy Process
```

2.2 Variance Process

The variance considered in the this method is not related to the observations of a single pixel over time, but is a function of the gray level and so it models the different responses of the sensor to different light intensities. Therefore, for each frame, the location of the occurrences of each generic gray value γ is first stored in a set

$$\text{Obs}(\gamma) = \{k = (u, v) | BG(u, v) = \gamma\} \tag{1}$$

Then, the variance V at the time t, associated to the γ-th gray level is iteratively updated with the following formula:

$$V_t(\gamma) = \frac{V_{t-1}(\gamma) \cdot N_{t-1}(\gamma) + \sum_k |I_t(k) - BG(k)|^2}{N_t(\gamma)} \tag{2}$$

where $k \in \text{Obs}(\gamma)$, $N(\gamma)$ is the number of times the γ-th gray level occurred over time and BG is the background. In the equations BG is substituted with the latest available frame (I_{t-1}) while the BG is being learned, namely until the energy gradient descent reaches its minimum value. Fig. 1 shows an example of convergence of this model while estimating μ and σ values of known normal distributions, that will be discussed in the next section.

2.3 Likelihood Process

This task is executed for each Bayer squared patch $P_i = (p_1, \ldots, p_4)^T$ of the image, so that P_i contains two green level values, a red one and a blue one. Considering the pixels as normal independent random variables, the likelihood of observing a background patch given a set of parameters $\theta = (\mu_1, \ldots, \mu_4, \sigma_1, \ldots, \sigma_4)$ can be calculated with the formula:

$$\mathcal{L}(\theta | P_i) = \prod_{j=1}^{4} f_{\mu_j, \sigma_j}(p_j) = \ell_i \tag{3}$$

where $\mu_j = BG(p_j)$, $\sigma_j = V_t(BG(p_j))^{\frac{1}{2}}$ and $f_{\mu_j,\sigma_j}(p_j)$ is the normal probability density function with mean μ_j and standard deviation σ_j computed in p_j. Therefore, the mean value of a pixel is its corresponding BG value, while the variance depends on its gray level, since different intensity values might have different variances. Following the same steps described in the previous section, the BG is substituted with the latest captured frame until the model is in the learning phase. Formally, a threshold $\tau_L = 0$ is used to classify each patch as background or foreground. In our implementation $\tau_L = 10^{-10}$, considering that 0 can not be achieved due to noise and floating point representation issues—experiments show that the value is small enough to guarantee a stable and reliable BG. The binary update mask of a BG patch is set to true, while it is false in case of a foreground patch. This selective update is useful to achieve robustness and to avoid updating when an object is moving on the scene.

2.4 Fine Tuning Process

The fine tuning task takes place only when the BG has been learned by the system and enriches the pipeline with two modules: a cosine similarity filter [9] and a ghost filter. The first one exploits the dot product between two vectors, specifically a foreground Bayer patch (P_f) and its corresponding background (P_b), both $\in \mathbb{N}^4$. The cosine of the angle between the two patches is filtered to blacken the foreground if it is similar to the background according to the following equation:

$$P_f = 0 \text{ if } \frac{P_f \cdot P_b}{|P_f||P_b|} > \tau_{\mathrm{S}} \tag{4}$$

where $\tau_{\mathrm{S}} \sim 1$.

The ghost filter is needed when there are no stable background frames at the beginning of a video, i.e. when the bootstrap phase contains almost stationary objects that are likely to be inserted in the background. In these cases, a movement of the object when the BG has been learned causes the presence of a ghost in the foreground. This phenomenon is removed comparing the incoming frame I_t with the background fully updated at each iteration BG_{nu} in correspondence of the ghost patch P_g. If $|I_t(P_g) - BG_{nu}(P_g)| = 0$, then the background is updated setting $BG(P_g) = BG_{nu}(P_g)$.

3 Experiments and Results

The model presented in Sect. 2 has been first tested in Matlab in order to numerically confirm its correctness. For this reason, samples from ~ 200 normal distributions with known (μ, σ) have been extracted. Fig. 1(a) shows that, starting from 128 (half intensity for 1 byte unsigned variables), each estimated mean tends to the input one in ~ 100 frames in the worst case. The distribution with input mean $\mu = 119$ (magenta) converges immediately in a couple of iterations, while for $\mu = 20$ (blue) more iterations are needed to achieve the result. This is due to the update process that consists of unary increments or decrements

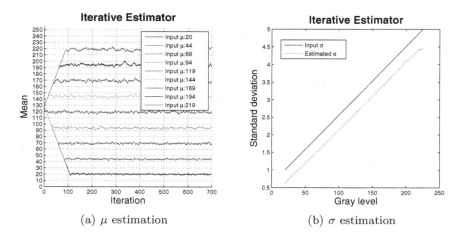

(a) μ estimation   (b) σ estimation

Fig. 1. Examples of convergence of the Iterative Estimator of Mean and Standard deviation.

at each iteration, as pointed out in Sect. 2.1. Fig. 1(b) shows the convergence of the standard deviation estimator after $\sim$ 10M iterations. In particular, the estimated σ tends to the input one subtracted by a bias due to the iterative formulation showed in (2). Moreover, LBB has been evaluated against the GMG and MoGv2 algorithms implemented in the BGS Library [12]. The test has been conducted on the same dataset presented in [10], that contains five videos that represent a football match. AR- scenes are focused on the penalty area and the size of each frame is 1600×736, while a larger area of 1920×1080 pixels is captured in the FG- ones. The five scenes contain some typical situations of a soccer match, for example: a cluttered scene with illumination changes (AR1); the shoot of a penalty kick that implies almost all players around the penalty area (AR2); the shoot of a free kick (AR3) and two actions that are filmed from a wider point of view (FG1 and FG2). In FG2 some players are warming up, so the scene is more dynamic than the one in FG1. Each BG model is evaluated after 20, 40, 60 and 80 seconds after the starting frame f_0.

Fig. 2 contains the qualitative analysis of some frames in terms of ground truth and foreground masks. Rows 1 and 3 contain a cluttered scene where a high number of players is moving in in the penalty area. Here, the MoGv2 (Fig. 2 (d)) shows a weak output due to the constant update of model parameters that is including the players in the BG, while the other approaches (Fig. 2 (c) - (e)) produce a more stable output. The frames in the second row show a scene where the advertising is changing. Here, LBB is updating the BG mask while the other algorithms already did it, due to the updating speed implemented by the unary increment described in Sect. 2.1. This corresponds to the LBB outlier in Fig. 3(a) with low precision and high recall, that gradually tends to a stable configuration when the BG mask is updated. The quantitative results have been extracted calculating the F-Measure, Precision and Recall on four different frames, representing the considered time interval. Each ground truth frame has been manually obtained starting from the raw video. Let TP be the number of true positives pixels, FP be the number of false positives pixels, TN be the number of true negatives pixels and FN be the number of false negatives pixels on the foreground mask. Accordingly, Precision P, Recall R and F-Measure F are defined as:

$$P = \frac{TP}{TP+FP}, \ R = \frac{TP}{TP+FN}, \ F = 2 \cdot \frac{P \cdot R}{P+R} \tag{5}$$

Fig. 3 summarizes the metrics calculated for each video sequence. The comparison of LBB Precision and Recall values against the best value among GMG and MoGv2 shows that the average LBB R value is 39% better than the others, while the P value is generally comparable. This result is shown in Fig. 3(a) where each point in the P-R plane is referred to a run of a specific algorithm (red for MoGv2, blue for GMG and green for LBB). According to this representation, the ground truth has coordinates $(1,1)$, therefore points in the upper right part of the figure correspond to the best results. High R values for LBB demonstrate that the approach is robust to false negative outputs. Fig. 3(b) shows the 3D bar chart representation of the F-measure. The AR sequences represent a complex situation with a high number of moving people in foreground and here the F-Measure of LBB is higher than the other methods used for the comparison. In the FG ones LBB and GMG behave in a similar way and show comparable results in terms of F-Measure. In particular, the FG1 sequence starts with an advertising change and here LBB has a low F-Measure in the first frame (FG1 - 1) because the foreground mask is noisy, but then the F-Measure increases, so the model is correctly updated in the subsequent frames. The overall average of the LBB F-Measure is 18% better than GMG and MoGv2, thus confirming that the proposed method is capable of modelling such scenarios.

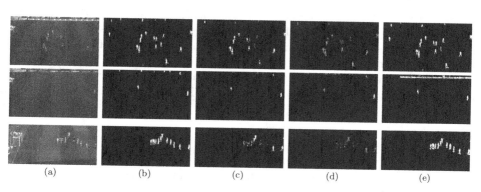

(a)   (b)   (c)   (d)   (e)

Fig. 2. Qualitative results for some frames. The columns contain, respectively, the original frame (a), the ground truth (b) and the foreground masks obtained with GMG (c), MoGv2 (d) and LBB (e).

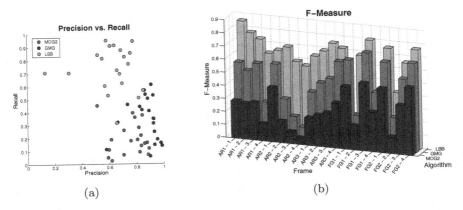

Fig. 3. Quantitative results on the dataset in terms of Precision, Recall 3(a) and F-Measure 3(b).

4   Conclusion

In this paper a likelihood-based background model for real time processing of CFA images is presented. The algorithm is designed with respect to the state of the art output format for vision cameras and implements a statistical model that takes into account the BG as the mean image while modelling the variance of each gray level processing its occurrences in the whole frames. For this reason, the variance is not calculated with respect to the observations of a single pixel over time, but is related to the intrinsic nature of the sensor. Looking at Fig. 3, LBB is able to obtain good performances while processing soccer videos. Even if the precision is lower than the other methods experimented, the recall value is significantly higher, as it is noticeable looking at the position of LBB markers in the P-R plane. These results confirm the robustness of the proposed approach in the athletic video processing context. Finally, the formulation of the algorithm enables its implementation directly on smart cameras (e.g. on FPGA or ARM cpus) and future works will regard both embedding and experimentation on other type of raw videos, for example in the field of surveillance.

References

1. Casares, M., Velipasalar, S., Pinto, A.: Light-weight salient foreground detection for embedded smart cameras. Computer Vision and Image Understanding **114**(11), 1223–1237 (2010). special issue on Embedded Vision
2. Cherian, S., Singh, C., Manikandan, M.: Implementation of real time moving object detection using background subtraction in fpga. In: International Conference on Communications and Signal Processing, ICCSP 2014, pp. 867–871 (2014)
3. D'Orazio, T., Leo, M., Spagnolo, P., Mazzeo, P., Mosca, N., Nitti, M., Distante, A.: An investigation into the feasibility of real-time soccer offside detection from

a multiple camera system. IEEE Transactions on Circuits and Systems for Video Technology **19**(12), 1804–1818 (2009)

4. D'Orazio, T., Leo, M., Spagnolo, P., Nitti, M., Mosca, N., Distante, A.: A visual system for real time detection of goal events during soccer matches. Computer Vision and Image Understanding **113**(5), 622–632 (2009). computer Vision Based Analysis in Sport Environments

5. Godbehere, A., Matsukawa, A., Goldberg, K.: Visual tracking of human visitors under variable-lighting conditions for a responsive audio art installation. In: American Control Conference, ACC 2012, pp. 4305–4312 (2012)

6. Hamid, R., Kumar, R., Hodgins, J., Essa, I.: A visualization framework for team sports captured using multiple static cameras. Computer Vision and Image Understanding **118**, 171–183 (2014)

7. Kim, K., Chalidabhongse, T.H., Harwood, D., Davis, L.: Real-time foreground-background segmentation using codebook model. Real-time Imaging **11**(3), 172–185 (2005)

8. Oliver, N., Rosario, B., Pentland, A.: A bayesian computer vision system for modeling human interactions. IEEE Transactions on Pattern Analysis and Machine Intelligence **22**(8), 831–843 (2000)

9. Qian, G., Sural, S., Gu, Y., Pramanik, S.: Similarity between euclidean and cosine angle distance for nearest neighbor queries. In: Proceedings of the 2004 ACM Symposium on Applied Computing, SAC 2004, pp. 1232–1237. ACM, New York (2004)

10. Renò, V., Marani, R., D'Orazio, T., Stella, E., Nitti, M.: An adaptive parallel background model for high-throughput video applications and smart cameras embedding. In: Proceedings of the International Conference on Distributed Smart Cameras, ICDSC 2014, pp. 30:1–30:6. ACM, New York (2014)

11. Rittscher, J., Kato, J., Joga, S., Blake, A.: A probabilistic background model for tracking. In: Vernon, D. (ed.) ECCV 2000. LNCS, vol. 1843, pp. 336–350. Springer, Heidelberg (2000)

12. Sobral, A.: BGSLibrary: An opencv c++ background subtraction library. In: IX Workshop de Visão Computacional (WVC 2013). Rio de Janeiro, Brazil, June 2013

13. Stauffer, C., Grimson, W.: Learning patterns of activity using real-time tracking. IEEE Transactions on Pattern Analysis and Machine Intelligence **22**(8), 747–757 (2000)

14. Suhr, J.K., Jung, H.G., Li, G., Kim, J.: Mixture of gaussians-based background subtraction for bayer-pattern image sequences. IEEE Transactions on Circuits and Systems for Video Technology **21**(3), 365–370 (2011)

15. Yu, X., Farin, D.: Current and emerging topics in sports video processing. In: IEEE International Conference on Multimedia and Expo, ICME 2005, pp. 526–529 (2005)

16. Zivkovic, Z.: Improved adaptive gaussian mixture model for background subtraction. In: Proceedings of the 17th International Conference on Pattern Recognition, ICPR 2004, vol. 2, pp. 28–31, August 2004

Smart Maintenance to Support Digital Life

Federico Bergenti[1(✉)], Massimo Chiappone[2], and Danilo Gotta[2]

[1] Dipartimento di Matematica e Informatica,
Università degli Studi di Parma, 43124 Parma, Italy
federico.bergenti@unipr.it
[2] Telecom Italia S.p.A., 10148 Torino, Italy
{massimo.chiappone,danilo.gotta}@telecomitalia.it

Abstract. This paper describes experiments performed to validate the possibility of delivering smart maintenance to utilities and telecommunication operators. First, the paper describes the reference architectural model of smart cities and it introduces smart maintenance and social smart maintenance. Then, the paper outlines performed experiments and relative results.

Keywords: Social smart maintenance · Business process management · Agent technology · Workflow technology

1   Introduction

One of the most important annual reports that analyze various aspects of societal changes in Italy is entitled *Digital Evolution of the Species* [1]. The concept of the report is reminiscent of how, in the last two decades, the growth of the society–in Italy and in all other western countries–has been affected by technological innovations in a way so incisive as to suggest a new *species* of human being. Such a new species lives in technological territories–both real and virtual–where people and objects are interconnected, and where information circulates so fast that it causes revolutions in lifestyles, and in the whole social context. The digital evolution of the species is short, Darwinian metaphor of how the technological revolution has brought, worldwide, a profound transformation in the habits, up to the point of speaking about the today's digital life, in contrast to a recent past when mechanical and analog devices were used to support people in all aspects of their daily life.

Connectivity as one of the enabling elements of the digital life because it is the fuel without which there can be no digital exchange. The (real) technological territories, in which such exchanges have their highest concentration, are, with no doubt, the today's cities, and the tomorrow's *smart cities*.

This paper is organized as follows: Section 2 briefly recap the reference architectural model of smart cities that this work assumes. It also introduces *smart maintenance* and *social smart maintenance*. Section 3 describes ongoing experiments in the scope of social smart maintenance which targets utilities and telecommunication operators. Section 4 briefly concludes the paper.

© Springer International Publishing Switzerland 2015
V. Murino et al. (Eds.): ICIAP 2015 Workshops, LNCS 9281, pp. 226–233, 2015.
DOI: 10.1007/978-3-319-23222-5_28

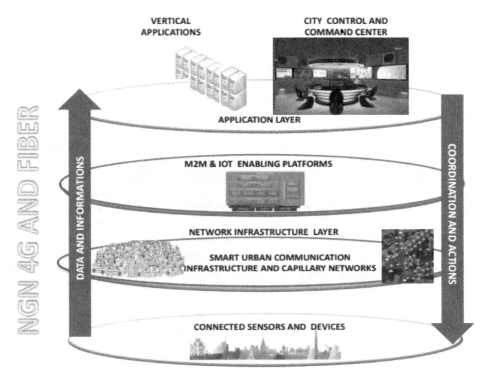

Fig. 1. Reference architectural model of a smart city

2   The Reference Architectural Model

The architectural model of upcoming smart cites, which is the reference for the work described in this paper, is shown in Fig. 1. This architectural model is simpler than other admissible models found in the literature, but it is structured just like all other models: a layered architecture ground on the possibilities that smart devices offer today, and will increasingly offer in the future.

Starting from the bottom of Fig. 1, the first layer is the layer of sensors and actuators, which are spread all around the smart city. In the smart city they become smart devices, and they become always interconnected devices. Ambient sensors, smart streetlights, surveillance cameras, media totems, traffic sensors, are just few examples of the wide range of devices that are spread around urban areas to enable *smart services* to citizens. In this simple model, also citizens' smart appliances are part of the network of sensors, and citizens themselves become sensors–*smart citizens as smart sensors*–and actuators with a high degree of autonomy. Increasingly often applications in traffic, weather, pollution, and tourism, are based on the possibility for users to provide information. Users become sensors of application-specific parameters and they also enrich basic information, with user-generated contents, that add value to the basic services. But citizens can also be somehow driven, and in this sense they become smart actuators. Gaming is a key ingredient in turning smart citizens into smart actuators, and their smart appliances are part of this picture because they allow ludic content to be delivered to citizens to engage them into games that can be used to control their collective behavior (see, e.g., [2]).

The middle layer in Fig. 1 is that of the network infrastructure and of the connectivity. In smart cities such a layer is not limited to broadband connectivity, either wired or wireless, but it also encompasses short-range connectivity–the so called *capillary networks*–which is of crucial importance for populating of smart objects the *Internet of Things (IoT)*, and for implementing innovative services in the city. Such networks are made of gateways and concentrators which gather data from sensors via low-power wireless links. This network infrastructure is shared among a large number of services, and it carries a large amount of data. Data coming from sensors and devices of the lower layer are sent in the network through gateways, which serve as connection points between the short range networks of sensors and traditional long range networks.

The third is the layer of *Machine-2-Machine (M2M)* management platforms and of cloud computing. This is the layer where storage capacity and computational capabilities reside, and where management processes are found. Such processes enable and control connections, they analyze and route data, they guarantee the security of transactions and the *Quality of Experience (QoE)*, and they also ensure to service providers the ability to interface their applications and to create new applications and services.

Finally, the last layer, enabled by management platforms, we find vertical application responsible for the management of services and objects deployed in cities. This layer contains vertical applications, like e-school, e-health, smart mobility, smart lighting, smart metering, and smart waste management. This is the layer in which *city command centers* are deployed–real or virtual–places that support service management of a smart city, and where decision makers can have an overview of the QoE that the city as a whole is providing to citizens. The city command centers gather information from underlying layers and they provide synthetic views via dedicated real-time *dashboards* offering, e.g., views of the correlation of integrated phenomena, graphical maps with views of the vitality of the city, and views dedicated to the early detection of critical levels of important parameters like pollution, noise, and environmental hazards.

Regardless of the size of the domain that various stakeholders of the smart city exert on the elements of the architectural model in Fig. 1, it is crucial to emphasize that an increasingly rich and diverse connectivity available to citizens, businesses, utilities and governments make the places where such a connectivity is more dense–the smart cities–real accelerators of digital life, thus activating a virtuous circle of benefits for all stakeholders.

Telecom Italia uses the presented architectural model for various research and experimental activities, like the ones demonstrated in the *Open Air Lab* in Turin[1]. The Open Air Lab is a new laboratory dedicated to digital life, and to the changes that ICT is driving in urban scenarios. As depicted in Fig. 2, the Open Air Lab provides a unified view of various research subjects, including smart mobility and smart parking, efficient waste management, urban surveillance, and smart metering of services.

---

[1] Open Air Lab app: *https://play.google.com/store/apps/details?id=it.telecomitalia.openairlab*

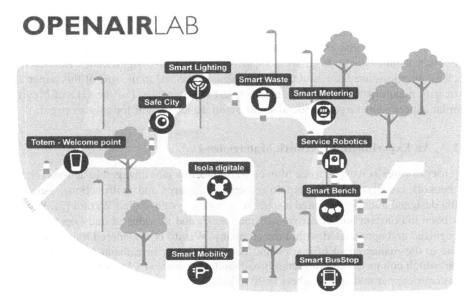

OPENAIRLAB

Fig. 2. The structure of the Open Air Lab in Turin

In the scope of a smart city, also maintenance functions and processes can exploit the availability of the infrastructures briefly summarized in Fig. 1 to improve their quality of service to service providers and to citizens. We say that smart cities provide the tools to enable *smart maintenance*, the evolution of the ordinary infrastructure maintenance by means of systematic and synergic use of smart devices (from the bottom layer), undisrupted connectivity (from the second layer), M2M and IoT (from the third layer), and applications (from the top layer). Given that smart maintenance is structured just like citizens' daily activities, it is reasonable to allow citizens entering in the maintenance processes, turning smart maintenance into *social smart mainten-ance*. Smart citizens become sensors of maintenance processes, and they contribute user-generated contents to support maintenance activities. This is the case, e.g., of citizens proactively signaling problems in the urban infrastructures, taking part of social games that award proactive participation in maintenance processes. Moreover, social smart maintenance can sometimes use smart citizens as actuators capable of performing entry-level maintenance activities, like self-configuration or self-repair of infrastructures.

3   Experiments

Maintenance is traditionally a core function of service providers and it is normally assumed that only professionals with specific skills can execute maintenance tasks with the required quality. This is main reason why smart maintenance is entering the vocabulary of service providers quite slowly. Skilled professionals do not need technological help to carry out their tasks; they do not need automatized (and rigid) help because they are the real field experts. Similarly, social smart maintenance includes average citizens in the picture, and it implicitly assumes that maintenance processes would benefit from such an inclusion. We have significant evidence that such assumptions are false, and the experiments described in the rest of this paper are primarily meant to validate the values of smart maintenance. For the sake of brevity, similar experiments targeting social smart maintenance are left for another paper.

3.1   An Experiment in Network Management

In order to support its workforce of over 10,000 technicians engaged in actions related to network configuration and repairing network failures and malfunctions, Telecom Italia designed and implemented a specific software system called Wizard [3]. Wizard has been in constant and effective use since 2007, and its value in daily operations is recognized and appreciated within the company. Wizard is considered today a cornerstone in the management of one of the most penetrating broadband networks in Europe, which counts 6.9 million retail broadband accesses and 13 million retail connections over copper and optical fibers in 2013 [4].

From the practical point of view of field technicians, Wizard guides them in a complete, integrated and exhaustive way throughout all steps of problem-solving activities. Wizard provides technicians with a direct connection with back-end systems responsible for all tasks related to network and service management. Technicians agree that Wizard is a direct responsible for significantly reducing the duration of problem-solving activities because it monitors the activities that they perform in real time, and because it can proactively trigger suitable crosschecks with relevant OSS (Operations Support Systems).

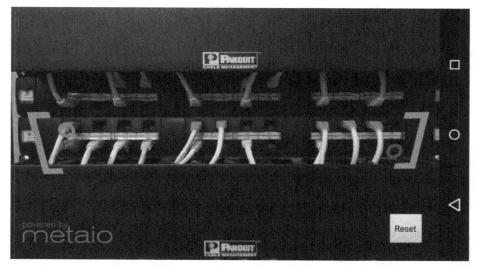

Fig. 3. A screenshot of the application used to support maintenance of network elements

From a methodological point of view, Wizard is considered a valuable tool to support network and service management because it enforces the use of a formalized notation based on workflows to represent the operative knowledge of the company. The methodological approach that Wizard promotes enables a significant reduction of durations and costs of maintenance activities because technicians are provided with a friendly and unambiguous description of the activities that they are demanded to perform in common and uncommon situations.

Today, Wizard is the primary means to support the work of field technicians, and it is in everyday use by technicians to manage an average of 5,000, and a peak of 15,000, work requests. Such work requests are nontrivial maintenance tasks that directly involve technicians–and sometimes customers–and that often allow direct resolution of access network malfunctions.

Wizard was developed on top of WADE (Workflows and Agents Development Environment) [5, 6], the BPM (Business Process Management) platform that evolves the popular agent platform JADE (Java Agent and DEvelopment framework) [7]. Both platforms are open source and they share the support mailing list and the Web site *jade.tilab.com*. JADE and WADE are considered by a large community of users and developers one of the most advanced incarnations of agent technology, and they provide Wizard with the advanced work coordination capabilities of agents (see, e.g., [8, 9]) . Technically, JADE is a software framework that facilitates the development of interoperable multi-agent systems. JADE has a long and outstanding tradition of mobile developments [10, 11] that has been recently revitalized with a specific support for Android [12]. WADE is built on top of JADE and it enriches JADE with the workflow metaphor to provide developers with a robust environment for embedding workflows into agents. WADE is a solid technology that has proven its solidity in large-scale network and service management for over 5 years [10].

The presented experiments integrate Augmented Reality (AR) in network operations (see, e.g., [13]) via Metaio SDK (*www.metaio.com/sdk*) version 5, and they were meant to simulate in a controlled environment the critical parts of so called port change workflows. Such workflows are normally activated to support maintenance of faulty ports in network equipment at customers' premises. They require the technician identifying two ports in the network equipment and performing a manual rerouting of connections. Such workflows are quite common in the daily operations of technicians and they are performed for more than 10% of the work requests managed by Wizard. Fig. 3 exemplifies the class of network equipment considered in the first experimental campaign. The equipment shown in the figure was used to validate the possibility of adopting AR to: identify the actual equipment that the technician is facing by visually searching it into a database of installed equipment; and point the technician to the two ports that would need to be rerouted by highlighting their position in the scene with appropriate markers. The gray markers in Fig. 3 inform the user that the equipment was identified, while the green and the red circles point the technician to the port to disconnect and connect, respectively.

3.2   An Experiments in Smart Metering

Telecom Italia is involved in the design of capillary networks that can be used by multiple utilities. Sensors in such networks send measured data to the services that the management platform provides. SmartView is a mobile application that helps gathering data and that support assurance actions on gas meters. SmartView can be used with full functionality by Telecom's field technicians involved in maintenance and delivery; it can be used with reduced functionality by personnel of the utility; and it can even be used with minimal functionality by citizens. In this last case, SmartView is an interesting example of social smart maintenance.

SmartView uses AR technology via the Metaio SDK to identify and track real-world objects and to augment the view of the world that it feeds to the user with contextual information. It is normally used with a tablet, but it was successfully experimented with smartphones and smartglasses. The technician involved in maintenance activities at a specific gas meter is driven to the place and uses a tablet to picture the meter. Contextual information immediately appears on the screen of the tablet to help the technician in performing the maintenance activities. Such contextual information include, as needed, commercial information about the contract and the service usage. Moreover, the technician can perform actions on the meter directly from the tablet. The technician can activate, deactivate, reset or set up the network connection of the meter. Moreover, the technician can read the power of signals upstream and downstream, as shown in Fig. 4a. Finally, Fig. 4b and Fig. 4c show that the technician can use SmartView to visualize the geolocalized assets of the capillary network, which involve antennas, repeaters, and gas meters.

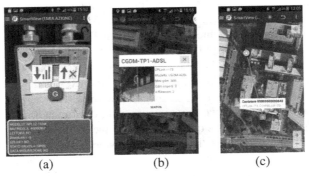

(a)   (b)   (c)

Fig. 4. View of (a) the contextual information; (b) the concentrator node; (c) the assets.

4   Conclusions

Today we live in a world where the push towards digital life come both from the top, i.e., from institutions, and from the bottom, i.e., from social habits and from the market. Cities now tend to become smart, to become territories where the connectivity becomes dense, thus favoring the digital life of citizens. In such a scenario, the research which supports the creation of innovative capillary networks is of paramount importance because it is one of the primary enablers of the desired connectivity. In the long term, such decentralized networks would cause serious maintenance issues that would require maintenance to become smart. Above smart maintenance, the decentralized nature of capillary networks would call for a decentralized approach to maintenance, and social smart maintenance would become essential to support the services offered in smart cities.

References

1. CENSIS: Undicesimo Rapporto CENSIS/UCSI sulla comunicazione, October 11, 2013
2. Bergenti F., Caire G., Gotta D.: Agent-based social gaming with AMUSE. In: Procs. 5th Int'l Conf. Ambient Systems, Networks and Technologies (ANT 2014) and 4th Int'l Conf. Sustainable Energy Information Technology (SEIT 2014) Procedia Computer Science, vol. 32, pp. 914–919 (2014)
3. Trione, L., Long, D., Gotta, D., Sacchi, G.: Wizard, WeMash, WADE: unleash the power of collective intelligence. In: Procs. Int'l Joint Conf. Autonomous Agents and Multiagent Systems, pp. 1342–1349 (2009)
4. Bergenti, F., Caire, G., Gotta, D.: Large-Scale Network and Service Management with WANTS. Industrial Agents: Emerging Applications of Software Agents in Industry. Morgan Kaufmann (2015)
5. Banzi, M., Caire, G., Gotta, D.: WADE: A software platform to develop mission critical, applications exploiting agents and workflows. In: Procs. Int'l Joint Conf. Autonomous Agents and Multi-Agent Systems, pp. 29–36 (2008)
6. Bergenti, F., Caire, G., Gotta, D.: Interactive workflows with WADE. In: Procs. IEEE Int'l Conf. Enabling Technologies: Infrastructures for Collaborative Enterprises (2012)
7. Bellifemine, F., Caire, G., Greenwood, D.: Developing multi-agent systems with JADE. Wiley Series in Agent Technology (2007)
8. Bergenti, F., Poggi, A.: Agent-based approach to manage negotiation protocols in flexible CSCW systems. In: Procs. 4th Int'l Conf. Autonomous Agents (2000)
9. Bergenti, F., Poggi, A., Somacher, M.: A collaborative platform for fixed and mobile networks. Communications of the ACM 45(11), 39–44 (2002)
10. Bergenti, F., Poggi, A.: Ubiquitous information agents. Int'l J. Cooperative Information Systems 11(34), 231–244 (2002)
11. Bergenti, F., Poggi, A., Burg, B., Caire, G.: Deploying FIPA-compliant systems on handheld devices. IEEE Internet Computing 5(4), 20–25 (2001)
12. Bergenti, F., Caire, G., Gotta, D.: Agents on the move: JADE for Android devices. In: Procs. Workshop From Objects to Agents (2014)
13. Chiappone, M., Gotta, D., Paschetta, E., Pellegrino, P., Trucco, T.: Augmented reality for TLC network operation and maintenance support. In: Procs. Int'l Working Conf. Advanced Visual Interfaces (AVI 2014), pp. 349–350. ACM Press, USA (2014)

FSSGR: Feature Selection System to Dynamic Gesture Recognition

Diego G.S. Santos, Rodrigo C. Neto, Bruno Fernandes, and Byron Bezerra$^{(\boxtimes)}$

Escola Politécnica de Pernambuco - Universidade de Pernambuco, Recife, Brazil
{dgs2,rcn,bjtf,byronleite}@ecomp.poli.br

Abstract. Dynamic gesture recognition systems based on computer vision techniques have been frequently used in some fields such as medical, games and sign language. Usually, these systems have a time execution problem caused by the elevated number of features or attributes extracted for gesture classification. This work presents a system for dynamic gesture recognition that uses Particle Swarm Optimization to reduce the feature vector while increases the classification capability. The system FSSGR, Feature Selection System to Dynamic Gesture Recognition, solved the gesture recognition problem in RPPDI dataset, achieving 99.21% of classification rate with the same vectors size of previous works on the same database, although with a better response time.

1 Introduction

Smart cities are known for be full of technological devices, many of them possessing a camera attached [1]. These devices can be used to generate several informations based on the routine of each person. Many applications have emerged from them, for example, helping the citizens based on their actions or gestures, or preventing accidents and time saving through traffic condition analysis in a street [2].

Gestures are the main way of deaf-mute people communication. The sign language is a set of gestures with a meaning that can represent the language signs of a community. But, as every language, it needs to be understood by people who surround the deaf-mute ones such as family, friends, sellers, customers and others. Systems based on computer vision can use a camera to capture the gestures performed by people and translate them using computer vision techniques so that anyone can understand.

A computer vision system generates feature vector for each image of a gesture sequence. The size of this feature vector in classification problems can compromise the execution time in fields as data mining, machine learning, pattern recognition and signal processing.

Feature selection is the process of choosing a subset of features from the original set, forming patterns in a given dataset. The subset should be plenty to describe the initial pattern, retaining a high accuracy in representing the original features.

© Springer International Publishing Switzerland 2015
V. Murino et al. (Eds.): ICIAP 2015 Workshops, LNCS 9281, pp. 234–241, 2015.
DOI: 10.1007/978-3-319-23222-5_29

Real-time computer vision systems need the ability to handle imprecise and inconsistent information in real world problems due the interaction differences by each user in the system usage. Techniques to reduce the feature vector size have been applied in real-time applications in order to reduce the processing time of them. Calinon et al. [4] use probabilistic techniques as Principal Components Analysis (PCA) to recognize and reproduce gestures.

Swarm techniques have the capacity to find a solution in a complex function, maximizing or minimizing the function, depending of the need [5]. In this original work, we start from the hypothesis that our feature vector should be reduced to maximize its quality. We select the perfect value by defining this size of our feature vector as the function to be optimized by a Swarm technique. Additionally, this work proposes a feature selection system applied in gesture recognition based on the CIPBR algorithm [6] in combination with a Binary Particle Swarm Optimization [5] (BPSO) and a selector algorithm proposed by Barros et al. [7]. Our proposed system, named Feature Selection System to Dynamic Gesture Recognition (FSSGR), aims to generate small feature vectors improving the classification rate and speeding up the system response.

2   FSSGR

We propose the FSSGR as a system to generate small feature vectors to dynamic gesture recognition aiming a better classification rate and a faster response time. The FSSGR's flow starts with the gesture images being received by CIPBR feature extractor module. In the next step, the Binary PSO selects the best size for the set of vectors using the fitness function based on Euclidian distance. The selector algorithm reduces the vectors using the size chosen by BPSO. The next subsections explain how each step of FSSGR system works.

2.1   CIPBR Feature Extractor Module

The CIPBR algorithm is an approach composed by few tasks to reduce a hand posture into two signature sets. These signatures were proposed by Keogh et al. [8]. To complete this tasks there are four modules in cascade: (1) Image binarization, (2) Radius calculation, (3) Draw maximum circumcircle, and (4) Calculate signatures.

The first module, "Image Binarization" receives the RGB hand posture image as input and reduces the number of colors to two. This binarized image serves as input to the next module as well as the original RGB image.

The "Radius Calculation" module uses the RGB image to find a wrist line and marks the wrist center point in the binarized image. A linear regression is performed on the pixels of the bracelet dressed by the user in order to find the line between forearm and hand pixels. The middle point in this line is defined as P, showed in Figure 1(b). Then, the hand posture contour is extracted from the binarized image produced by module 1. The center of mass is calculated from this hand contour using the center moments of Hu. Finally, this module calculates the distance between the center of mass and the central point of wrist line. In the Figure 1(b) is presented an output example of the "Radius Calculation" module. In this case, the cyan point is the center of mass of the contour given by C, the red point is the center point of the wrist line given by P and the line connecting these points is given by $\overline{PC}$.

Fig. 1. CIPBR module 2 output image

The third module, "Draw Maximum Circumcircle", uses the line segment $\overline{PC}$ as radius to draw a circle inside the hand contour. If this circle exceeds the hand contour boundary, a triangle is calculated using the three more distant contour points from and the biggest circle inside this triangle is used.

The last module, "Calculate Signatures", receives as input the maximum circumcircle defined in the previous step, plus points P and C. At first, the hand contour points are substantially reduced using the Andrew's monotone chain convex hull algorithm [9].

Andrew's algorithm outputs a set $\Psi = \{p_1, p_2, \ldots, p_n\}$ from Convex hull points, which is used to generate two signature sets, according to the CIPBR approach [6]. The first signature set is composed by distances $(D_{\overline{\omega Q}})$ calculated by the following way. For each point $\omega \in \Psi$, the length of the line segment $\overline{\omega C}$ is calculated based on the Euclidean distance from ω to the point C. Then, this length is decreased from the circumcircle radius, in order to obtain the $\overline{\omega Q}$ length, where the point Q is the intersection between segment $\overline{\omega C}$ and the maximum circumcicle. Therefore, the first signature set is composed by each distance $D_{\overline{\omega Q}}$, $\forall \omega \in \Psi$, calculated with the following equation (1):

$$D_{\overline{\omega Q}} = \sqrt{(\omega_x - C_x)^2 + (\omega_y - C_y)^2} - radius, \qquad (1)$$

where C is the hand posture contour's mass central point, ω_x, C_x are the x coordinates from points ω and C respectively, and ω_y, C_y are the y coordinates from points ω and C, respectively. Finally, $radius$ is the maximum circumcircle radius calculated by second module.

The second signature set consists of angles (A_w) obtained by calculating the angle between a line $\overline{wC}$ composed for each point $w \in \Psi$ of the convex hull hand shape point and the line segment $\overline{PC}$. All two signature sets are obtained in a clockwise direction always starting with point P as shown in Figure 1(b) and Figure 1(c).

Finally, to create the output feature vector, both signature sets are normalized. The first signature set is normalized dividing each distance by the radius calculated in the second module. If $D = \{d_1, d_2, \ldots, d_n\}$, the normalized vector will be $D' = \{d'_1, d'_2, \ldots, d'_n\}$:

$$d'_i = \frac{d_i}{radius} \qquad (2) \qquad\qquad a'_i = \frac{a_i}{360°} \qquad (3)$$

The set of angles is normalized by dividing each angle by $360°$, according to Equation 3. Angle and distance sets are concatenated by the following order: angles first and distances in the end of the signature vector. Therefore, the final feature vector is $F = \{ a'_1, a'_2, \ldots, a'_n, d'_1, d'_2, \ldots, d'_n \}$.

2.2   Particle Swarm Optimization

When PSO [10] is used to solve an optimization problem, a swarm of simple computational elements, called particles, is used to explore a solution space to find an optimal solution. The position from each particle represents a candidate solution in n-dimensional search space (D) defined as $X = \{x_1, x_2, x_3, \ldots, x_n\}$, where each x_n is a position in the n-th dimension. The same way, the particle velocity is represented by $V = \{v_1, v_2, v_3, \ldots, v_n\}$.

The fitness function evaluates how better each particle presents itself in each iteration. When a particle moves and its new position has a fitness value better than the previous one, this value is saved in a variable called p_{best}. To guide the swarm to the best solution, the position, where a single particle found the best solution until the current execution, is stored in a variable called g_{best}. Therefore, to update the particle velocity and position the following equations are used:

$$v_i(t + 1) = \kappa v_i(t) + c_1 r_1 [p_{i,best} - x_i(t)] + c_2 r_2 [g_{best} - x_i(t)] \qquad (4)$$

$$x_i(t + 1) = x_i(t) + v_i(t + 1) \qquad (5)$$

where $i = (1, 2, 3, \ldots, N)$ and N is the size of the swarm, c_1 which represent the private experience or "cognitive experience" and c_2 represents the "social experience" interaction usually used with value 2.05 [10]. Variables r_1 and r_2, random numbers between 0 and 1, represent how much p_{best} and g_{best} will influence the particle movement. The inertia factor κ is used to control the balance of the search algorithm between exploration and exploitation. The x_i represents particle position in $i - th$ dimension. The recursive algorithm run until the maximum number of iterations is reached.

Binary PSO. is a variation of the traditional PSO in discrete spaces. The major difference between this algorithm and canonic version is the interpretation of velocity and position. In the binary version, the particle's position and velocity are represented by $\{0\}$s and $\{1\}$s only. This change requires a reformulation in how velocity is calculated, according to the following equation:

$$If\ rand\ <\ \frac{1}{1 + e^{-v_i(t+1)}}\ then\ x_i(t+1) = 1;\ else\ x_i(t+1) = 0$$

where $rand$ is a random number between 0 and 1.

Finally, for binarization process the threshold that delimits which vector cell will represent a feature is chosen. To binarize all the feature vectors, the value which represents the general average is 1.2.

In order to choose the best size for the vectors of each gesture, a general small vector is output by BPSO. To complete this task, our system uses a fitness function based on Euclidian Distance. BPSO calculates a distance from each x_{ik} binary particle's position to the same k position in all binary vectors to the same gesture. After each iteration, all distances are added up to generate the fitness function output. Particles are improved as soon as its fitness value become smaller compared with the fitness obtained by previous iteration. The particle fitness function is:

$$fitness_i = \sum_{j=1}^{m} [\sqrt{\sum_{k=1}^{n}(x_{ik} - F_{jk})^2}] \tag{6}$$

where $[x_{i1},\ x_{i2},\ \ldots,\ x_{in}]$ is the particle $i-th$ position, and $[F_{j1},\ F_{j2},\ \ldots,\ F_{jn}]$ is the $j-th$ features in all vectors.

2.3   Selector Algorithm

BPSO chose the best feature vector size S, according the previous section. Then, the Selector Algorithm normalizes the CIPBR feature vector to fill in size S [7], producing the final vectors of our system. In this process, some rules must be respected.

First, if any vector has fewer points than S, are added 0 in the feature vector until matches the desired length S. Second, feature vectors larger than S are redefined using a selection algorithm. This algorithm consists in calculation of a window W through the division of the current vector length by S. The current vector is parsed, and each value in W position is included in the new feature vector. If the new output vector is even smaller than the desired length, the remaining positions are randomly visited and used to compose the new output vector until the desired length is achieved.

3   Experiments and Discussion

In order to evaluate our approach, a dynamic gesture recognition experiment was executed. The RPPDI Dynamic Gesture Dataset[1] [7] is used in our experiment. All gestures are composed by 14 frames, each one with 640×480 pixels captured by a smart-phone camera.

---

[1] Available at http://rppdi.ecomp.poli.br/gesture/database

The experiment consists in using the proposed system to extract small feature vectors from RPPDI gesture dataset and measure its classification effectiveness and speed. A K-Means Clustering [11] is used by HMM system [12] to find the best initial approximation and classify the feature vectors. The Baum-Welch algorithm [12] is used to train the HMM, resulting in a fast training process.

According Section 2.2, BPSO is used to find the best feature vector size S, taking into account the initial feature vectors produced by CIPBR method. The BPSO parameters adopted in this search were: 15 particles; 20 dimensions; 30 simulations; 200 iterations; $c1 = c2 = 2.05$; inertia factor of $w = 0.9 \rightarrow 0.4$; $r1 = r2 = rand[0...1]$. Based on the feature vector size chosen by BPSO, the Selector Algorithm (Section 2.3) reduces the feature vectors. These reduced vectors are classified by Hidden Markov Model system. The classification error rate is saved and the experiment is restarted and repeated 30 times. For each simulation the dataset is randomly selected, always with 2/3 of the sequences in each gesture class for training and 1/3 for test.

In Table 1 is presented the average results and standard deviations for all repetitions, for $S \in \{5, ..., 10\}$. In fact, simulations were performed with another values of S. However, the classifier has not achieved better results with feature vectors of size higher than 10. Moreover, according the Boxplot analysis, the system remains stable for feature vectors fixed in 10 elements, achieving the lowest variance among the results.

In Table 2 is presented the proposed system results in comparison with previous systems based on LCS [13] and SURF [14], as well the extensions based on the Convexity Approach: CLCS and CSURF [7]. Finally, it is presented the results achieved by Santos et al. [6] with CIPBR technique. All works used the same dataset and HMM as classifier. In column "Original V. S." is written the average size of original feature vectors, and in column "Reduced V. S." is written the average size of feature vectors after post processing these vectors. In column "Response Time" is registered the classification response time in average for one gesture.

Table 1. Classification resume by number of features.

Number of features	Classification rate	Standard deviation
5	92.34	7.32
6	92.34	5.88
7	93.88	6.81
8	90.46	8.22
9	92.71	6.11
10	99.21	0.89

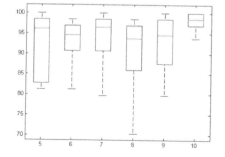

Table 2. Gesture recognition systems classification results.

Technique	Classification rate (%)	Original V. S.	Reduced V. S.	Response Time
SURF	75.0	3000	-	7.77ms
LCS	77.0	3000	-	3.07ms
CSURF	91.0	3000	15	1,19ms
CLCS	91.0	170	10	0.79ms
CIPBR	94.1	1960	10	1.78ms
FSSGR	**99.2**	1960	10	**0.70ms**

As observed in the results of Table 2, choosing the number of features selected by BPSO as input to the Selector Algorithm, improves the classification rate of the Gesture Recognition System. FSSGR solves the gesture recognition problem in RPPDI dataset with 99.21% as classification rate, while achieves the best response time. In other words, the system commits no more than 2 classification mistakes only, and several times do not commits anyone. Moreover, according the results our proposed system can reduce the feature vector to the same size achieved in previous works, although improving the classification rate and speed.

The proposed system was also run on the dataset MSRGesture3D[2], with the best settings obtained in previous experiments. In this case, our system has reached 88,98% of classification rate, surpassing the systems [15,16], both simulated under the same conditions. This indicates the proposed system does not work only in a specific dataset, but has good ability to generalize to the hand gestures recognition task.

4   Conclusion

In this paper, we proposed the FSSGR system, based on CIPBR algorithm combined with the binary PSO and a Selector Algorithm to generate a subset from a large feature vector. The reduced feature vector better represents the original one. As consequence, the proposed approach improves the classification rate whereas speeds up our hand gesture recognition system, making it suitable for several real time applications, such as the ones required in a Smart City.

In future works, more experiments will be investigated, mainly new fitness functions which allow PSO to solve feature selection issue, without any other approach to complement it, turning the process less costly. We plan as well to investigate the behavior of our system using other classifiers, such as Recurrent Neural Networks.

Acknowledgments. The authors would like to thank the support of the University of Pernambuco and the funding agencies: FACEPE, CAPES and CNPQ.

---

[2] http://research.microsoft.com/en-us/um/people/zliu/actionrecorsrc/

References

1. Yang, J., Wang, Y., Sowmya, A., Li, Z.: Vehicle detection and tracking with low-angle cameras. In: ICIP, pp. 685–688 (2010)
2. Then, Y.B., Tay, Y.H., Ho, W.T.: Estimating traffic condition using just a single image. In: ICIP, pp. 3331–3335 (2013)
3. Yang, M., Zhang, L.: Gabor feature based sparse representation for face recognition with gabor occlusion dictionary. In: Daniilidis, K., Maragos, P., Paragios, N. (eds.) ECCV 2010, Part VI. LNCS, vol. 6316, pp. 448–461. Springer, Heidelberg (2010)
4. Calinon, S., Billard, A.: Recognition and reproduction of gestures using a probabilistic framework combining pca, ica and hmm. In: Proceedings of the 22nd International Conference on Machine Learning, pp. 105–112. ACM (2005)
5. Kennedy, J., Eberhart, R.C.: A discrete binary version of the particle swarm algorithm. In: 1997 IEEE International Conference on Systems, Man, and Cybernetics, Computational Cybernetics and Simulation, vol. 5, pp. 4104–4108. IEEE (1997)
6. Fernandes, B.J.T., Santos, D.G.S., Neto, R.C., Bezerra, B.L.D.: A dynamic gesture recognition system based on cipbr algorithm. In: Computer Vision, 2014 Mexican International Conference on Artificial Intelligence. LNAI (2014)
7. Barros, P.V., Junior, N., Bisneto, J.M., Fernandes, B.J., Bezerra B.L., Fernandes, S.M.: Convexity local contour sequences for gesture recognition. In: Proceedings of the 28th Annual ACM Symposium on Applied Computing, pp. 34–39. ACM (2013)
8. Keogh, E., Wei, L., Xi, X., Lee, S.-H., Vlachos, M.: Lb_keogh supports exact indexing of shapes under rotation invariance with arbitrary representations and distance measures. In: Proceedings of the 32nd International Conference on Very large Data Bases, pp. 882–893. VLDB Endowment (2006)
9. Day, A.: Planar convex hull algorithms in theory and practice. Computer Graphics Forum **7**(3), 177–193 (1988)
10. Eberhart, R.C., Shi, Y.: Comparing inertia weights and constriction factors in particle swarm optimization. In: Proceedings of the 2000 Congress on Evolutionary Computation, vol. 1, pp. 84–88. IEEE (2000)
11. Hartigan, J.A., Wong, M.A.: Algorithm as 136: A k-means clustering algorithm. Applied statistics, pp. 100–108 (1979)
12. Normandin, Y.: Hidden markov models. Automatic Speech and Speaker Recognition: Advanced Topics **355**, 57 (2012)
13. Julka, A., Bhargava, S.: A static hand gesture recognition based on local contour sequence. International Journal of Advanced Research in Computer Science and Software Engineerin **3**(7), 918–924 (2013)
14. Bay, H., Tuytelaars, T., Van Gool, L.: SURF: Speeded up robust features. In: Leonardis, A., Bischof, H., Pinz, A. (eds.) ECCV 2006, Part I. LNCS, vol. 3951, pp. 404–417. Springer, Heidelberg (2006)
15. Wang, J., Liu, Z., Chorowski, J., Chen, Z., Wu, Y.: Robust 3D action recognition with random occupancy patterns. In: Fitzgibbon, A., Lazebnik, S., Perona, P., Sato, Y., Schmid, C. (eds.) ECCV 2012, Part II. LNCS, vol. 7573, pp. 872–885. Springer, Heidelberg (2012)
16. Klaser, A., Marszałek, M., Schmid, C.: A spatio-temporal descriptor based on 3d-gradients. In: BMVC 2008–19th British Machine Vision Conference, p. 275-1. British Machine Vision Association (2008)

Interoperability of Biometric Systems: Analysis of Geometric Characteristics of Handwritten Signatures

Giuseppe Pirlo[✉], Fabrizio Rizzi, Annalisa Vacca, and Donato Impedovo

Dipartimento di Informatica, Università degli Studi di Bari, via Orabona, 4 70125, Bari, Italy
giuseppe.pirlo@uniba.it

Abstract. Handwritten signatures are considered one of the most useful biometric traits for personal verification. In the networked society, in which a multitude of different devices can be used for signature acquisition, specific research is still needed to determine the extent to which features of an input signature depend on the characteristics of the signature apposition process.

In this paper an experimental investigation was carried out on constrained signatures, which were acquired using writing boxes having different area and shape, and the different behaviour of geometric features with respect to the writing boxes is discussed.

1   Introduction

Handwritten signature is one of the most common biometric traits for personal authentication. A signature is a rapid movement that has been defined, learned and practiced over the youth years, in literate populations, to become a very personal pattern. Therefore, it originates from a complex process that involves the human brain to process information to perform with the human writing system (based on hand, arm, etc.), using writing acquisition equipment (pen, pencil, paper, etc.). Therefore, it is not surprising that - in recent years - many efforts have been devoted to automatic signature verification, attracting researchers from different fields. More precisely, so far research efforts have been mainly devoted to determine effective features and comparison strategies for signature verification [1].

Concerning features, both functions and parameters were considered in the literature. When function-features are used, the signature is characterized by a time-function, whose values constitute the feature set. Among others, widely used functions features are position, velocity, acceleration and pressure. When parameter-features are used, a signature is characterized as a vector of parameters, each one representative of the value of a feature. Among others, widely considered parameters are total signature time duration, pen-down time ratio, number of pen-lifts, direction- and curvature-based features.

When comparison strategies are considered, both distance-based and model-based approaches have been widely investigated in the literature. Concerning distance-based verification techniques, Mahalanobis and Euclidean distances have been used for signature comparison as well as Dynamic Time Warping (DTW) and string matching

© Springer International Publishing Switzerland 2015
V. Murino et al. (Eds.): ICIAP 2015 Workshops, LNCS 9281, pp. 242–249, 2015.
DOI: 10.1007/978-3-319-23222-5_30

strategies. When model-based techniques are considered, Hidden Markov Models (HMM) have found to be well-suited for signature modelling since they are highly adaptable to personal variability and lead to results that are – in general - superior to other signature modelling techniques [2].

Notwithstanding several relevant results have been achieved so far, many aspects still remains to be investigated, in order to make signature verification feasible in a multitude of daily operations. Among the others, one of the most relevant open aspects concerns the relation between the constraints during the signature apposition process and the characteristics of the input signature. In fact, signers can use different devices (tablet, smartphone, PDA, etc.) to input their signatures and hence the verification system must be aware of the differences in the input signatures due to the acquisition conditions [3].

In this paper we perform an experimental investigation on signatures acquired under constrained conditions. More precisely, the relations between some geometric features of the input signature and size and shape of the writing area are analysed. The experimental results demonstrate that, in general, area is highly dependent on the writing area, whereas ascendants and descendants are low dependent on the writing area.

The organization of the paper is the following. Section 2 presents the experimental setup. Section 3 reports the experimental results. Section 4 addresses the conclusion of the paper and some considerations for future work.

2   Experimental Setup

The experimental setup was realized using a Wacom Intuos tablet and an Intuos Grip Pen. The Intuos Grip Pen is a cordless, battery-free and pressure-sensitive freehand writing device. Macros on the Wacom Intuos tablet ensure that the area of signature was positioned in the centre of the tablet in order to maximize comfort and sensitivity of the user. Four conditions have been considered to represent some common area and shape constraints in signature apposition:

a) Constraint 1: 4.6cm x 0.77cm rectangular box (to analyse the effect of constriction in small boxes);
b) Constraint 2: 7.0cm x 1.5cm rectangular box (space-like signatures of the identity card and bank checks);
c) Constraint 3: 14cm x 1.5cm rectangular box;
d) Constraint 4: 12cm x 7cm rectangular box (to see the biggest change of signature);

Figure 1 shows the five types of constraints that have been considered for signature apposition in this paper:

During the enrolment stage 10 signers have been involved in data acquisition. For each type of constraint, six signatures were captured from each signer. Therefore, each signer collected a total number of 6x4 = 24 genuine signatures. During testing the signer sat down and wrote comfortably to increase comfort and truthfulness.

Fig. 1a. Rectangular box (4.6cm x 0.77cm)

Fig. 1b. Rectangular box (7.0cm x 1.50cm)

Fig. 1c. Rectangular box (14.0cm x 1.50cm)

Fig. 1d. Rectangular box (12.0cm x 7.0cm)

The following figures (2a – 2l) show some examples of signatures acquisition. More precisely, they show the acquisition of signatures of three users (user 1, 2 and 3) with respect to the different types of signature constraints.

Fig. 2a. User 1 – 4.6 x 0.77

Fig. 2b. User 2 – 4.6 x 0.77

Fig. 2c. User 3 – 4.6 x 0.77

Fig. 2d. User 1 – 7 x 1.5

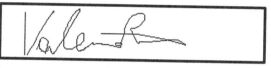

Fig. 2e. User 2 – 7 x 1.5

Fig. 2f. User 3 – 7 x 1.5

Fig. 2g. User 1 – 14 x 1.5

Fig. 2h. User 2 – 14 x 1.5

Fig. 2i. User 3 – 14 x 1.5

Fig. 2j. User 1 – 12 x 7

Fig. 2k. User 2 – 12 x 7

Fig. 2l. User 3 – 12 x 7

3   Experimental Results

A specific software system was developed in Java for the analysis of the experimental data. The signature image is the input of the system, the output is the values of some geometrical characteristics extracted from the signature:

-   F_1: Signature Area (A_s)
-   F_2: Signature Height (H_s)
-   F_3: Signature Width (W_s)
-   F_4: Ascendants of signature (H_a)
-   F_5: Descendants of signature (H_d).

More precisely, concerning F_1, F_2 and F_3, let be:

- H_s = Height of signature;
- W_s = Width of signature;
- H_i = Height of the space of signature;
- W_i = Width of the space of signature;
- $A_s = H_s * W_s$;

they are defined as follows (see Figure 3a):

- $F_1 = A_s/(H_i * Wi)$;
- $F_2 = H_s/H_i$;
- $F_3 = W_s/W_i$.

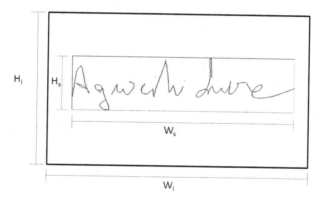

Fig. 3a. Area, height and width determination

Concerning F_4 and F_5, they are defined as follows (see Figure 3b):

- $F_4 = H_a/H_i$;
- $F_5 = H_d/H_i$.

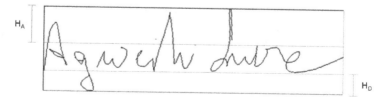

Fig. 3b. calculation of ascendants and descendants of signature

For each signer the analysis of variance (ANOVA) among pairs of groups of constrained signatures was performed [4]. ANOVA starts from the assumption that for G groups of data, it is possible to decompose the variance into two components: the variance inside the groups and the variance between groups. From these values, calculated as the sums of the standard deviations between the groups and within a single group, we can get a test variable for comparison with the value of a variable Fisher "F", taking into account the degrees of freedom, according to the significance level α to evaluate the results.

Table 2 reports, for each geometric feature, the results of dependence in relation to different pairs of constraints considered, obtained on the entire sample considered for the analysis. The values shown in the table are obtained on the basis of the results of the ANOVA for each subject (with $\alpha = 0.05$), for which the value 1 indicates dependence, while the value 0 indicates not dependence of the characteristic in relation to the pair of restrictions chosen.

Then, let be:

- N : number of users (N=10 in our tests);
- F_j : j-th features considered ($1 \leq j \leq 5$)
- C_k : k-th the couple of constraints considered, where
  - o k=1 means the couple of constraints 1 and 2
  - o k=2 means the couple of constraints 1 and 3
  - o k=3 means the couple of constraints 1 and 4
  - o k=4 means the couple of constraints 2 and 3
  - o k=5 means the couple of constraints 2 and 4
  - o k=6 means the couple of constraints 3 and 4.
- $V_{ijk} \in \{0, 1\}$: dependence/not dependence value (based on the ANOVA test) for the i-th subject, based on the j-th feature and the k-th couple of restrictions.

The value of each item in Table 2 is calculated by averaging the values V_{ijk} with respect to the number of users:

$$Xjk = \frac{1}{N} \sum_{i=1}^{N} Vijk .$$

Table 2 demonstrates that the signature area (F_1) is the characteristic most dependent on the different constraints imposed on the space of signature. Height (F_2) and width (F_3) of signature show values that oscillate, in relation to the pair of restrictions considered. Ascendants (F_4) and descendants (F_5) of signature are the characteristics that do not seem to be affected by various restrictions imposed on the area of signature.

Table 1. Dependence of the characteristics related to couples of restrictions.

Feature\Constraint	1 – 2	1 – 3	1 – 4	2 – 3	2 – 4	3 – 4
F_1	0,5	1	1	0,9	1	0,9
F_2	0,6	0,5	1	0,3	1	1
F_3	0,2	0,9	0,6	1	0,5	0,9
F_4	0,5	0,3	0,4	0,2	0,4	0
F_5	0,1	0	0,5	0,1	0,3	0,2

4   Conclusion and Future Work

An experimental investigation on the effects of the characteristics of the writing area on the geometric features of online signatures is addressed in this paper. For the purpose four different signature acquisition areas were considered (which differ in terms of area and shape) for signature acquisition and the ANOVA test was applied to verify to what extent geometric features of a signature depends on the writing area. The experimental results demonstrate that area of signature seems to be very dependent on the writing area, whereas ascendants and descendants of signature does not seem to be influenced by different constraints.

Although this study is not sufficient to derive general assumptions on the characteristics of constrained online signatures, it poses new interesting problems to the scientific community both for improving the knowledge on human behaviour in signing and for improving future systems for automatic signature verification. Among the others, an interesting aspect for assuring interoperability of signature verification systems could be the possibility to develop new (signer-dependent or signer-not dependent) techniques for normalization of constrained signatures.

References

1. Impedovo, D., Pirlo, G.: Automatic Signature Verification – State of the Art. IEEE Transactions on Systems, Man and Cybernetics - Part C: Applications and Review **38**(5), 609–635 (2008)
2. Plamondon, R., Pirlo, G., Impedovo, D.: Online signature verification. In: Doermann, D., Tombre, K. (eds.) Handbook of Document Image Processing and Recognition, pp. 917–947. Springer (2014)
3. Simsons, D., Spencer, R., Auer, S.: The Effects of Constraining Signatures. Journal of the American Society of Questioned Document Examiners **14**(1), 39–50 (2011)
4. Gelman, A.: Analysis of variance? Why it is more important than ever. The Annals of Statistics **33**, 1–53 (2005)

Computer Aided Evaluation (CAE) of Morphologic Changes in Pigmented Skin Lesions

Maria Rizzi[1(✉)], Matteo D'Aloia[2], and Gianpaolo Cice[2]

[1] Politecnico di Bari - Dipartimento di Ingegneria Elettrica e dell'Informazione, Bari, Italy
maria.rizzi@poliba.it
[2] MASVIS SRL, Conversano, Italy
{matteo.daloia,gianpaolo.cice}@masvis.com

Abstract. Mole pattern changes are important elements in detecting cancerous skin lesions, the early stage detection is a key factor to completely cure the pathology. In this paper, an automatic system for mole-tracking is indicated. The method presented is been realized as a mobile app and can be used to perform periodically a careful self-examination of their pigmented skin lesions. The implemented method receives in input two segmented images of the same pigmented skin lesion corresponding to the actual image and to the image before the last period under test. The method performs image matching and changes evaluation adopting a three stage artificial neural network and provides as output a risk indicator related to the morphology changes of the skin lesion.

Keywords: Smart health · Healthcare · Neural network · Skin lesion · Computer aided detection · Computer aided evaluation · Border detection · Edge detection · CAD · CAE

1 Introduction

Smart and healthy cities share common characteristics as they move from focusing their investment on traditional, physical infrastructures to more emphasis on digital infrastructures, including information and communication technologies. Milestones are the creation of networked and data driven cities able to keep citizens more informed, engaged and empowered. Digital infrastructures enable citizens to actively contribute to sustainable development, as well as, to self-manage their own health [1].

The objectives of smart and healthy cities are to seek improvements in safe, effective, efficient and patient-centered health and wellness services through innovations in computers, information science and engineering. Therefore, the adoption of information technologies and management systems for health care improvement is very important. For this reason, efforts mainly focus on computerization of hospitals and medical institutions [2].

Researchers look for innovative solutions and new technologies both for making the quality of patient care better and for reducing the cost of care through an early disease detection and diagnosis. Computer aided health systems allow acquisition, transmission, processing, storage, retrieval and analysis of various health and biomedical information.

© Springer International Publishing Switzerland 2015
V. Murino et al. (Eds.): ICIAP 2015 Workshops, LNCS 9281, pp. 250–257, 2015.
DOI: 10.1007/978-3-319-23222-5_31

Health service quality depends on information quality in hospital complex or in diagnostic center. Efficient hospital information system should be able to manage all patient specific data and to automated detect disease specific information for helping physicians in decision-making process within therapeutic algorithms. Moreover, in smart city achieving, databases of public hospitals and diagnostic centers should be connected together in such a way as to guarantee an effective and efficient service toward citizens. Therefore, interoperability of devices and systems is necessary. The adoption of a common standard for data facilitates interoperability of medical imaging equipment by specifying a set of media storage services, a file format and a medical directory structure.

The convergence of various information and communication technologies (i.e. smart systems, cloud computing, advanced sensing and data analysis techniques) provides potentialities for delivering automated, intelligent, and sustainable healthcare services [3].

In medical imaging, the accurate diagnosis and/or assessment of a disease depends on both image acquisition and image interpretation. Therefore, medical image interpretation process can benefit from computer technology [4, 5]. In particular, Computer Aided Detection (CADe), Computer Aided Diagnosis (CADx) and Computer Aided Evaluation (CAE) systems are becoming important tools in supporting physicians for neoplastic pathology detection and prevention [6, 7]. In particular it has been demonstrated that information content of slides of pigmented skin lesions is not modified by the digitalization process [8].

Since changes in pigmented skin lesions are important for early disease detection, dermatologists makes nevo photography to study the evolution. Lesion manual inspection and matching is subjective and tedious. For this reason, an automatic matching between lesions is useful for physicians.

In this paper, a Computer Aided system for tracking pigmented skin lesions is indicated. For the method implementation, mole macroscopic images acquired with standard cameras are used. In fact, the adoption of commercially available photographic cameras is quite common in skin lesion inspection systems, particularly for telemedicine purposes. Moreover, the implemented method can run on smartphones of the last generation which provide high resolution cameras and innovative operating systems.

In this paper, after a brief review of the most recent methods indicated in literature for the tracking of skin moles, the implemented tool is presented and its performance is evaluated. Moreover, some conclusions are drawn out.

2   Prior Researches and Adopted Approaches

As a consequence of the increase of skin tumor incidence, the interest for computer-aided skin lesion inspection and characterization has grown during the last years. In fact, the World Health Organization has evaluated a grow of about 30% over the last 10 years; worldwide each year, 132,000 subjects develop melanoma, the most common skin cancer [9].

For skin cancer early detection, mole tracking and mapping is useful.

The system indicated in [10] adopts, as input, a pair of skin back images of the same subject captured at different times. A set of anatomical landmarks are detected using a pictorial structure algorithm. Lesions that are located within the polygon defined by landmarks are identified and their anatomical spatial contexts are encoded by landmarks. Then, these lesions are matched by labelling an association graph using a tensor based algorithm. A structured support vector machine is employed for the matching.

Voronoi cells are used in [11] to measure the similarity between melanomas in successive dermatoscopy images. The melanoma registration is reduced to a bipartite graph matching problem. A minimum weight maximum cardinality matching is employed for finding the global correspondences between images.

A method for finding corresponding moles in patient skin back images at different scanning times is indicated in [12]. To calculate mole normalized spatial coordinates, a template is defined for human back and thenmolematching across images is modeled as a graph matching problem. Algebraic relations between nodes and edges in the graphs are induced in the matching cost function.

In [13], pigmented skin lesion matching problem is formulated as a relaxed labeling of an association graph. In this graph labeling problem, each node represents a mapping between a pigmented skin lesion from one image to a pigmented skin lesion in the second image. Optimal labels are obtained optimizing a high order Markov Random Field energy (MRF). A novel entropy energy term encouraging solutions with low uncertainty is proposed in the method. By interpreting the relaxed labeling as a measure of confidence, authors leverage the high confidence matching to sequentially constrain the learnt objective function defined on the association graph.

Matching probabilities of the edges of two graphs representing the spatial distribution of two pigmented skin lesion sets is evaluated in [14]. Pointwise probabilities is extracted using marginalization matrix of computed pairwise matching.

In [15] effectiveness in matching and identifying lesions in pairs of skin images of point pattern correlation, 2-point geometrical transformation, and 3-point geometrical transformation are investigated. These techniques view spots in each image as a point pattern to be matched from image to image. Experiments indicate that the 3-point transformation algorithm performs the best overall.

3   Adopted Method

In the proposed system an Artificial Neural Network (ANN) is employed for the tracking of pigmented skin lesions. In fact, ANN is robustness since it provides less operation load and has more advantageous for reducing the noise effect [16]. Moreover, ANN is more useful, because multiple inputs and outputs can be used during the stage of training [17]

ANNs are computational models based roughly on the human neural structure. They can be defined by a stimulus response transfer characteristics, called activation function, that maps input space into a specified output space [18, 19, 20].

The most commonly used network architecture consists of a number of connected nodes (neurons) which are arranged in a hierarchical sequence of different layers (input, hidden and output). Each node in a layer receives an input from all the nodes in the preceding layer, and transmits output to the nodes of the succeeding layer. The connections between nodes are weighted, putting different strengths on the information exchange between two nodes.

The nonlinear characteristic exhibited by neurons is represented by a activation function. Neuron output is computed as the weighted sum of the input signals, transformed by the activation function. Therefore, neuron output signal is given by the following relationship:

$$O = f \left(\sum_{j=1}^{n} w_j \, p_j \right) \tag{1}$$

where $(p_1, p_2, ..., p_n)$ is the neuron input vector, $(w_1, w_2, ... , w_n)$ the weight vector and $f(..)$ the activation function.

Having defined both a network architecture and a training set of input patterns, the set of weights determines the network output for each input patterns. Error between the obtained network output and the expected target output defines a potential multimodal response surface over a multidimensional hyperspace having the dimensions coincident with the number of weights.

The most used method for finding weight set is the Back Propagation (BP) procedure that is essentially a gradient method. The BP learning process operates in small iterative steps: an example case is applied to the network, and the network produces an output based on the current state of its weights. This output is compared to the target output and a mean-squared error signal is calculated. The error value is then propagated backwards through the network and small changes are made to weights in each layer. The weight changes are calculated for error signal reduction. The whole process is repeated for each of the example cases and the cycle is repeated until the overall error value drops below some pre-determined threshold. At this point the network has learned the problem "well enough": the network will never learn exactly the ideal function, but rather it will asymptotically approach an approximation of it.

The application of ANNs to nonlinear signal processing is a challenge that requires considerable engineering judgment. ANN design involves raw data pre-processing, feature extraction from the pre-processed data, selection of network model and type, network testing and evaluation. The design process is typically a complex iterative and interactive problem-specific task. The choice of both network model and type is based on precise requirements of the problem. Different ANN models and types having different features may offer special advantages for particular applications.

4   The Proposed CAE System

Images of skin lesion acquired with standard cameras represent the input of the implemented system. Macroscopic images can be segmented adopting one of the method indicated in literature, than are processed to calculate images feature. The paper aim is the accuracy in evaluating the lesion border changes with the passing of time.

In order to perform the tracking of pigmented skin lesions, an ANN has been selected as classifier for its characteristic to enhance desired responses and reduce irrelevant and unwanted responses if noisy and imprecise nonlinear data are given.

A suitable ANN classifier is designed for the mapping of skin lesions. As it is well known that any function with a finite number of discontinuities can be well approximated by a three-layer neural network with sufficient neurons in the hidden layer[21], the implemented classifier is a feed-forward ANN composed of three layers. The classifier contains 6 neurons in the input layer and 1 neuron in the output layer. In order to achieve the best performance, various ANN architectures are used which differed on the neuron number inside the hidden layer(fig.1).

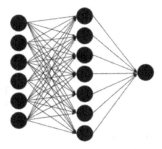

Fig. 1. The ANN architecture

Three features for image are selected for the classification process, that are: the ratio of the lesion maximum diameter to the lesion minimum diameter, the lesion compactness and eccentricity.

The maximum diameter is defined as the maximum distance between two pixels of the segmentation and the minimum diameter is the maximum distance that exists between two pixels within a segmented lesion projected on the perpendicular to the maximum diameter

Lesion compactness is defined as the ratio of the squared lesion perimeter to the lesion area and it represents the roughness of an object boundary relative to its area.

Lesion eccentricity is related to the ellipsoid hull and it is defined as: $(L_1^2 - L_2^2)^{1/2}/L_1$ where L_1 and L_2 are the major and the minor semiaxis, respectively.

Since the ANN has to map two images of the same lesion captured at different times, the vector formed by the twelve feature values (six for each image) represents an input pattern while the class to which the lesion changes belong represent the output.

A back propagation procedure is adopted for the training phase. The error is measured with the mean square error function.

During the training stage, features computed for all the images are fed into the network. Once weights and biases of neurons associated with network are initialized, the network is trained to produce expected outputs, that is 1 for appreciable changes and 0 for no appreciable changes.

In the training process, weights between neurons were adjusted iteratively so that differences between output values and target values are minimized. The training phase is terminated when 50 iterations have been performed.

5   Simulation Results

For the method implementation and validation, 200 macroscopic lesion images (100 pairs) provided from databases of various dermatology local centers are utilized. For a correct performance evaluation, the training data are not used during the testing stage. In particular 80 images (40 pairs) are adopted for the network training while 120 images (60 pairs) represent the method test bench.

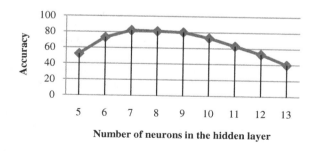

Fig. 2. One of the image pairs used as test bench

In fig.2 one of the image pair used as ANN input are shown.

The method achieves an average accuracy value in detecting lesions for which morphologic changes warrant particular attention equal about to 82%. For the accuracy evaluation, opinions of three different dermatologists are considered as a ground truth.

The best performance is obtained adopting an ANN classifier with 7 neurons in the hidden layer (fig.3).

Number of neurons in the hidden layer

Fig. 3. Method accuracy vs number of neurons in the hidden layer

6   Conclusion

The last century has produced a proliferation of innovations in health care industry aimed at enhancing life expectancy, quality of life, diagnostic and treatment options, as well as efficiency and cost effectiveness of healthcare system. Therefore, discovery of some critical pathologies in their early stage represents a healthcare benefit in fact it is useful to reduce mortality and morbidity rates, to shorten illness duration, to improve the quality of care and to limit the decay of a person functions which corresponds to increase in life expectance. In particular, the interest of biomedical scientific community for computer aided skin lesion inspection and characterization has been increased during the last years.

There is an important clinical need to follow changes in the number of moles and their appearance (size, color, texture, shape) in images from two different times.

In this paper, a computer tracking system for mapping of pigmented skin lesions adopting macroscopic images captured with standard cameras, is indicated. The method can be adopted independently from the procedure used for image lesion segmentation or image border detection. For this reason the presented tool could be implemented as the last stage of a mole tracking system which receives as inputs mole images segmented adopting any method indicated in literature.

The method simplicity and the adoption of standard camera images as inputs make the system particularly appropriate to be used in telemedicine and to run on smartphones. Therefore, the implemented system can be used as assistive devices by patients for self-manage their own health (personal health) and by primary care physicians during routine office visits.

References

1. Solanas, A., Patsakis, C., Conti, M., Ioannis, S.V., Ramos, V., Falcone, F., Postolache, O., Pérez-Martínez, P.A., Di Pietro, R., Perrea, D.N., Martínez-Ballestéc, A.: Smart Health: A Context-Aware Health Paradigm within Smart Cities. IEEE Commun. Mag. **52**, 74–81 (2014)
2. Rizzi, M., D'Aloia, M., Castagnolo, B.: Review: Health Care CAD Systems for Breast Microcalcification Cluster Detection. J. Med. Biol. Eng. **32**, 147–156 (2012)
3. Rizzi, M., Maurantonio, M., Castagnolo, B.: A Wireless Sensor Network for Security Systems Adopting the Bluetooth Technology. WSEAS Transaction on Circuits and Systems **5**, 652–657 (2006)
4. Rizzi, M., D'Aloia, M., Castagnolo, B.: High Sensitivity and Noise Immune Method to Detect Impedance Cardiography Characteristic Points Using Wavelet Transform. J. of Appl. Sci. **9**, 1412–1421 (2009)
5. Rizzi, M., D'Aloia, M., Castagnolo, B.: A New method for ICG characteristic point detection. In: 1th Int. Conf. on Bio-inspired Syst. and Signal Process., pp. 244–249. INSTICC, Portugal (2008)
6. Rizzi, M., D'Aloia, M., Castagnolo, B.: A Fully Automatic System for Detection of Breast Microcalcification Clusters. J. Med. Biol. Eng. **3**, 181–188 (2010)
7. D'Aloia, M., Rizzi, M., Di Bari, P.A.: Second Opinion System for Microcalcification Diagnosis. World Appl. Sci. J. **23**, 289–295 (2013)

8. Perednia, D.A., Gaines, J.A., Butruille, T.W.: Comparison of the Clinical Informativeness of Photographs and Digital Imaging Media with Multiple-Choice Receiver Operating Characteristic Analysis. Arch. Dermatol. **131**, 292–297 (1995)
9. Fondazione melanoma. http://www.fondazionemelanoma.org/melanoma-epi.php
10. Mirzaalian, H., Lee, T.K., Hamarneh, G.: Skin Lesion Tracking Using Structured Graphical Models. Med. Image Anal., April 2015
11. Huang, H., Bergstresser, P.: A hybrid technique for dermatological image registration. In: 7th IEEE International Conference on Bioinformatics and Bioengineering, pp. 1163–1167. IEEE Press, Boston (2007)
12. Mirzaalian, H., Hamarneh, G., Lee, T.K.: A graph-based approach to skin mole matching incorporating template-normalized coordinates. In IEEE Conference on Computer Vision and Pattern Recognition, pp. 2152–159. IEEE Press, Miami (2009)
13. Mirzaalian, H., Lee, T.K., Hamarneh, G.: Uncertainty-based feature learning for skin lesion matching using a high order MRF optimization framework. In: Ayache, N., Delingette, H., Golland, P., Mori, K. (eds.) MICCAI 2012, Part II. LNCS, vol. 7511, pp. 98–105. Springer, Heidelberg (2012)
14. Mirzaalian, H., Hamarneh, G., Lee, T.: Graph-based approach to skin mole matching incorporating template-normalized coordinates. In: IEEE Conference on Computer Vision and Pattern Recognition, pp. 2152–2159. IEEE Press, Miami (2009)
15. Perednia, D.A., White, R.G.: Automatic registration of multiple skin lesions by use of point pattern matching. Comput. Med. Imaging Graph. **16**, 205–216 (1992)
16. Egmont-Petersen, M., de Ridder, D., Handels, H.: Image Processing with Neural Networks – A Review. Pattern Recogn. **35**, 2279–2301 (2002)
17. Becerikli, Y., Demiray, H.E.: Alternative Neural Network Based Edge Detection. Neural Information Processing Letters and Reviews **10**, 193–199 (2006)
18. Rizzi, M., D'Aloia, M., Guaragnella, C., Castagnolo, B.: Health Care Improvement: Comparative Analysis of Two CAD Systems in Mammographic Screening. IEEE Trans. Syst., Man, Cybern. A, Syst., Humans **42**, 1385–1395 (2012)
19. Rizzi, M., D'Aloia, M., Castagnolo, B.: A Supervised Method for Microcalcification Cluster Diagnosis. Integr. Comput-Aid. E. **20**, 157–167 (2013)
20. Rizzi, M., D'Aloia, M.: Computer Aided System for Breast Cancer Diagnosis. Biomed. Eng-App. Bas. C. **26**, 14500331–14500338 (2014)
21. Zheng, L., He, X.: Edge detection based on modified BP algorithm of ANN. In: Pan- Sydney Area Workshop on Visual Information Processing, pp. 119–122. Australian Computer Society Press, Sydney (2003)

Analytical Method and Research of Uyghur Language Chunks Based on Digital Forensics

Yasen Aizezi[1], Anwar Jamal[1], Dilxat Mamat[1],
Ruxianguli Abdurexit[1], and Kurban Ubul[2(✉)]

[1] Xinjiang Police Institute, Urumqi, Xinjiang 830013, China
[2] School of Information Science and Engineering, Xinjiang University, Urumqi 830046, China
kurbanu@xju.edu.cn

Abstract. In the digital forensics process based on Uygur language information, stem, affix, synonym mark and other characteristics are added on the features-based English and Chinese chunks and according to relevant characteristics of Uygur language. In terms of performance evaluation indexes in this paper, accuracy rate, recall rate and F value are adopted. The test indicates that the scale of Uyghur chunks database has great effects on the model performance.

Keywords: Conditional random fields (CRF) · Uighur · Chunk analysis

1 Introduction

Chunk is a syntactic structure between word and sentence, which is also called as shallow parsing or partial parsing. It is used to identify some elements with relatively simple structure and comparatively important function and significance in a sentence. However, complete syntactic analysis tree is not served as the goal, so as to simplify complexity of the analysis and improve performance of the analysis. Abney was the first person to propose the thought of chunk analysis in 1991[1].

In recent years, people gradually attach importance to the research on Chinese chunk analysis. In 1996, Zhou Qiang made a research on chunks and basic phrases of Chinese language [5]. In 1999, Zhao Jun and Huang Changning made a research on the definition and automatic identification of basic noun phrases in Chinese language [6]. Li Sujian from the Institute of Computing Technology, Chinese Academy of Sciences proposed 12 types of Chinese chunks. Moreover, he obtained a chunk database through transformation according to the corresponding relation between these chunk types and phrase types of the Chinese tree database of the University of Pennsylvania [7]. Zhou Qiang made a large-scale research on notes of chunks in the Chinese language database [5], established a complete chunk division system, and constructed a chunk balance language database with 2,000,000 Chinese characters [8]. Zhang Yujie and others also researched the analysis on Chinese chunks [9], and [10] proposed an integral analysis model, and [11] suggested a chunk analysis method based on the division strategy.

© Springer International Publishing Switzerland 2015
V. Murino et al. (Eds.): ICIAP 2015 Workshops, LNCS 9281, pp. 258–266, 2015.
DOI: 10.1007/978-3-319-23222-5_32

As the research on the natural language processing technology of Uyghur language started late and the lexical analysis technology failed to reach an available level, the research on the syntactic analysis technology of Uyghur language is basically in a primary stage. In this paper, a research is made onto the analysis on chunks of Uyghur language. Moreover, conditional random fields are used to establish a chunk analysis algorithm.

2   Definition of Chunk and Establishment of Language Database

2.1   Definition and Division Principles of Chunk

According to the definition of Abney, chunk of Uyghur language is defined as follows in this paper:

Definition 1: chunk refers to the non-recursive, non-overlapped and non-nested phrase between word and phrase, which is more complicated than word and simpler than sentence, and which has certain syntactic functions.

A detailed interpretation of the above definition: a chunk consists of word sequence, with syntactic functions marked. Moreover, it is non-recursive and non-nested. Generally, in the chunk is a non-nested phrase. Chunk is defined in strict accordance with syntactic form; while semantics or functionality is not reflected. The purpose of chunk analysis is to identify some elements with relatively simple structure but important significance in the sentence and to erect a bridge between lexical analysis and complete syntactic analysis, so as to simplify syntactic analysis and improve the performance of syntactic analysis.

2.2   Formulation of Uyghur Language Chunk Tag Set

Prior to research on and preparation for notes, marks and specifications of the language tree database, an in-depth research is made on the establishment process of English tree database and TCT tree database. Moreover, a comparative research is made with the syntactic structure of Uyghur language. Based on the research and analysis, notes tag-set is prepared according to the following steps:

S1: preliminarily prepare a set of modern Uyghur language phrase tags collection;

S2: select from the language database 100 sentences with relatively great differences in sentence structure;

S3: automatic mark the 100 sentences, and register phenomena that existing tag-set cannot be used to mark correctly;

S4: in case that existing mark collection cannot be used to mark correctly, the mark collection should be analyzed and modified;

S5: in case that there is no any question with the tag-set, we should inspect whether the number of sentences automatic marked is 500. If the answer is no, then turn to S2; if the answer is yes, then turn to S6;

S6: end the mark phase

According to the above steps, the tag-set is repeatedly prepared and modified. Finally, 37 Uyghur language phrase structure tag-sets and 8 functional chunk tag-sets are specified. In this paper, 18 chunk mark types are defined from 37 phrase tag-sets according to relevant characteristics of chunk analysis.

2.3   Construction of Uyghur Language Chunking Corpus

At present, there are 3,000 sentences in the completed Uyghur language tree database. In this paper, chunks are selected from this database to construct the Uyghur language chunk database. Besides, in the right-side produced elements are selected for automatic calibration from the Uyghur language mark tree database and the production collection containing only non-terminal symbols and terminal symbols. Then, sentences marked by chunk in the right-side produced elements are selected. At present, there are totally 31,184 chunks in the Uyghur language chunk database established. For instance, the process of extracting chunks from the marked sentences is described as follows:

Table 1. Generative grammar classification results

Production of non-terminal symbol	mixed production	production of terminal symbol
SS->NP NP VP	UP->CP Idi	CP->bësip chüshken
VP->UP	UP->qërindashliqni UP	NP->Aq köngüllük
NP->NP NP		NP->Uning Öyidiki

The chunk shown in Table 2 is a high-frequency chunk in the Uyghur language tree database, accounting for 90.40% of all chunks.

Table 2. Ten main chunk statistics

	Mark	chunk of 2 words	chunk of 1 word	total chunks	average length
Noun chunk	CNP	7776	3924	11700	1.6646
Adjective chunk	CAP	1023	729	1752	1.5839
Verb chunk	CVP	2112	1608	3720	1.5677
Gerund chunk	CGP	2430	1251	3681	1.6601
Participle chunk	CCP	909	999	1908	1.4764
Coverb chunk	CBP	1680	822	2502	1.6715
Pronoun chunk	CPP	39	228	267	1.1461
Quantifier chunk	CQP	825	375	1200	1.6875
Numeral chunk	CMP	1116	249	1365	1.8176
Adverb chunk	CDP	66	30	96	1.6875

3   Chunk Analysis Algorithm Based on Statistical Learning Model

3.1   Description on Relevant issues of Chunk Analysis

Chunk analysis can be regarded as a machine learning process. Its task is to automatically divide blocks of sentences input and to mark the types of blocks divided under the given chunk definition and category. It can be formally described as follows:

Specify sample set $W=w_1,w_2,\ldots,w_n$ and category set $C=c_1,c_2,\ldots,c_m$, seek for a model $f:W \times C \rightarrow Boolean$ (mapping rules) from sample set W to category set C, and then judge the category of the new input sample by using the relation model obtained from this study; to be specific, set a sentence composed of word sequence $W=w_1,w_2,\ldots,w_k$, divide the sentence into several chunks, mark each word w_i with chunk mark t_i; $T=t_1,t_2,\ldots,t_n$ stands for the chunk mark sequence. Relevant results of the chunk analysis are shown as follows:

$$W=\ldots[w_i,w_{i+1},\ldots,w_{i+m}][w_{i+m+1},\ldots,w_{i+m+h}]\ldots \qquad (1)$$

$$T=\ldots[t_i,t_{i+1},\ldots,t_{i+m}][t_{i+m+1},\ldots,t_{i+m+h}]\ldots \qquad (2)$$

Mapping rules of the chunk analysis are classification laws and judgment rules automatically generated by the system according to characteristic information of each sample of machine learning. In the analysis, this mapping is one-to-one single mark classification mapping.

3.2   Research and Analysis on Chunk Analysis Methods

The issue of chunk analysis can be transformed into the issue of sequence mark. However, methods or models available for sequence mark include methods based on error transition, hidden Markov model (HMM), maximum entropy model, support vector machine (SVM), conditional random field(CRF) model, etc. In above methods or models, it is the CRF model that has optimal conditions. Therefore, CRFs are used in this paper to establish the Uyghur language chunk analysis model.

3.3   Establishment of Characteristic Space

The key of discriminant statistical model is to find out various characteristics contribute to eliminate ambiguity, to use such characteristics to combine different characteristic templates, to verify the effectiveness of such characteristic templates by means of experiment and, and to select the optimal characteristic template. On this basis, this paper establishes the characteristic space of Uyghur language chunk analysis with reference to relevant characteristics used for chunk analysis algorithms of English, Chinese and other languages based on CRFs.

In terms of the sequence of part of speech W=w1,w2,…,wk, characteristics of prefix and suffix are added into the Chinese chunk analysis model by selecting windows with the width of 5 in both English and Chinese chunk analyses, and extracting characteristics (e.g. morphology, part of speech, affix, chunk mark, etc.) of the present word wi and two words before and after this word respectively. In this paper, above characteristics are retained. Moreover, stem, affix, first-class mark of part of speech, second-class mark of part of speech, synonym mark and other elements are also added in this paper to establish the characteristic space according to characteristics of words in Uyghur language.

3.4   Establishment of Synonym Mark Database

SY (synonym) in the above characteristic space stands for synonym mark. Relevant contents of this mark are interpreted above in details. At present, there are few Uyghur language tree databases established. It is easy for inaccurate parameter estimation caused by data rarefaction by using statistical model. If words with completely the same meanings can be marked with certain marks or numbers, the issue of decreasing analysis performance resulted from the scale of language database can be remitted to a certain extent. Therefore, a Uyghur language synonym mark dictionary is established with references to existing Uyghur language synonym dictionaries. This dictionary originally has 9,902 entries, in which 1,778 are compound words. In order to guarantee the accuracy rate of synonym mark, 4,623 synonyms with strictly the same meanings are selected from the other 8,104 synonyms. Moreover, a synonym database with part-of-speech notes is established in this paper. All synonyms are classified based on meaning and part of speech. Besides, each classification is allocated with a mark. Finally, the dictionary with 971 synonym marks is established.

The CRF model is a guidance-oriented machine learning model. At first, a certain scaled mark language database should be used to evaluate relevant parameters of the model. Then, the model trained can be used for decoding, i.e. to mark unmarked language materials. The L-BFGS algorithm is used for the model training. Besides, BeamSearch algorithm is used to search for u. The width is 5. The CRF model is subject to CRFComLib training and testing.

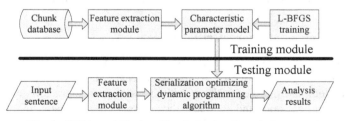

Fig. 1. CRF based Uyghur Chunk parsing System Structure

4   Test and Analysis

In this paper, 3,000 marked sentences are selected as the training and testing language database. Due to the small scale of the language database, the cross validation method is used for testing. International precision (P), recall(R) and F-measure value are adopted as performance evaluation indexes of the chunk analysis algorithm in this paper.

4.1   Feature Selection

Section of characteristic module and feature selection are key steps in judging training and application of the learning model. Features are extracted from training samples, which directly reflect various types of knowledge and cases in chunk texts. Characteristic model and feature description capability selected have direct effects on performance of the analysis system. For different language processing tasks, features selected will be different as well. Generally, there are two methods for feature selection:

- 1) According to experiences summarized from linguistic knowledge of linguists and statistical information of texts, formal characteristic templates are defined based on characters and marked in texts. Moreover, characteristic templates are used to extract characteristics from the texts, or it is called instantiation of characteristic template.
- 2) Additional information and marked are given to texts according to summary of linguistic knowledge by linguistics, such as language rules, grammatical rules, dictionaries, resource bases and other external information.
- 3) As characteristic task correlation, targeted & task-driven characteristic template and characteristic definition are always helpful for the analysis system. On the contrary, ineffective characteristics will reduce performance of the system.
- 4) According to experimental results in [93], word form, stem, affix, part of speech, synonym mark and others are used in this section to structure an atomic characteristic space. On this basis, different characteristic templates are combined for an experiment.

In order to test contribution of word form, part of speech, stem and other characteristic information, a characteristic template shown in Table 6-8 is established based on the summary in [93]. Template A is the word form template. Template B is stem information added, which can be used to observe impacts of part of speech on performance of the model. On the basis of Template B, only affix characteristic is added to Template C. In Template D, first-class part of speech mark is introduced. Both first-class and second-class part of speech marks are used in Template E. Synonym mark is introduced in Template F. In order to observe impacts of first-class and second-class marks on performance of the model, only second-class mark is used in Template G.

Table 3. Close test result

Feature Template	Precision	Recall value	F-measure
A	56.23%	57.01%	56.62%
B	58.87%	59.63%	59.25%
C	61.34%	61.97%	61.65%
D	76.02%	76.54%	76.28%
E	79.11%	78.34%	78.72%
F	81.65%	81.84%	81.74%
G	81.93%	82.30%	82.11%

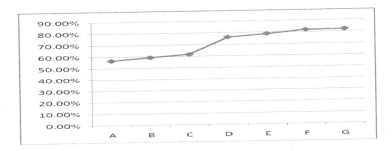

Fig. 2. Test Result Statistical Plotting

4.2   Cross Validation Test

Due to the small scale of the language database, the cross validation method is used in the test. In order to observe performances of language databases in different scales during training, the test is performed for three times:

Test A: the language database is divided into 10 subsets without cross data. Each subset has 300 sentences. The test is performed for 10 times. Finally, the average value of 10 tests is calculated.

Test B: the language database is divided into 5 subsets without cross data. Each subset has 600 sentences. The test is performed for 5 times. Finally, the average value of 5 tests is calculated.

Test C: the language database is divided into 3 subsets without cross data. Each subset has 1,000 sentences. The test is performed for 3 times. Finally, the average value of 3 tests is calculated.

Table 4. Open test result

Test	Proportion	Precision	Recall	F-measure value
A	9:1	80.23%	80.45%	80.34%
B	8:2	76.61%	77.14%	76.87%
C	2:1	66.52%	67.01%	66.76%

According to the experimental results, the scale of language database has great effects on the model. The principal reason is that the scale of language database trained with the model is not strong enough to make the model reach a saturated mode. That is, the expansion of the language database scale cannot improve the status of model performance.

5   Conclusion

In this work, 3,000 marked sentences are used as the language database for training and testing. The cross validation method is adopted in the lab. The precisions of the training and testing language databases are 9:1, 8:2, 2:1; and the recall rates are 80.34%, 76.87%, and 66.76%.

Acknowledgment. This paper is supported by the National Social Science Fund of China (No. 13CFX055), Science Research Program of the Higher Education Institute of Xinjiang (No. XJEDU2013I11, XJEDU2013I34), and Natural Science Fund of Xinjiang (No. 2015211A016).

References

1. Abney, S.P.: Parsing by Chunks. Computation and Psycholinguistics, 257–278 (1991)
2. Sang, T.K., Buchholz, S.: Introduction to the Conll-2000 shared task: chunking. In: Proceeding of CoNLL-2000, Lisbon, Portugal, pp. 127–132 (2000)
3. Kinyon, A.: A Language-independent shallow-parser compiler. In: Proceedings of 39th ACL Conference, Tourouse, France, pp. 322–329 (2001)
4. Hammerton, J., Osborne, M., Armstrong, S.: Introduction to Special Issue on Machine Learning Approaches to Shallow Parsing. Journal of Machine Learning Research (2), 551–558 (2002)
5. Qiang, Z.: Research on Automatic Division and Marking of Phrases in Chinese Language Database, pp. 1–9. Peking University (1996)
6. Jun, Z., Changning, H.: Model for Chinese BaseNP Structure Analysis. Chinese Journal of Computers **22**(2), 141–146 (1999)
7. Sujian, L., Qun, L., Zhifeng, Y.: Chunk Analysis based on Maximum Entropy Model. Chinese Journal of Computers **25**(12), 1722–1727 (2003)

8. Yuqi, Z., Qiang, Z.: Automatic Identification of Chinese Base Phrases. Journal of Chinese Information Processing **16**(6), 1–8 (2002)

9. Chen, W., Zhang, Y., Isahara, H.: An empirical study of chinese chunking. In: Proceedings of the 44th Annual Meeting of ACL, Sydney, Australia, pp. 97–104 (2006)

10. Guanglu, S.: Technical Research on Chinese Chunk Analysis based on Statistical Learning. Harbin Institute of Technology (2008)

11. Qiaoli, Z., Xin, L., Wenjing, L., Dongfeng, C.: Chunk Analysis based on Division Strategy. Journal of Chinese Information Processing **26**(5), 120–128 (2012)

CLICK TEATRO Project:
Augmented Reality and Promotion of Theater Events

Donato Barbuzzi(✉), Bachir Boussahel, Francesca De Carlo,
Angelo Galiano, Donato Impedovo, and Annalisa Longo

DYRECTA LAB s.r.l., V, Simplicio 45, 70014 Conversano, BA, Italy
donato.barbuzzi@dyrecta.com

Abstract. This work describes the activity related to the field of Augmented Reality (AR) developed in the "Integrated Multimedia Assets to promote TheaTrical" (CLICK TEATRO) living lab project.

The "Integrated Multimedia Assets to promote TheaTrical" project realizes a system addressed to the citizens in order to create a link between theater activities and commercial operators. Through the use of an App for Smartphone, the user will receive content related to the show (additional content, interviews, etc.) and service associated (restaurants, car parks, hotels, bar, etc.). This information will be generated and managed by means of Augmented Reality tools.

Finally, the involved activities will enter in a virtuous circle, in fact the user will gain discount bonus to be used for purchasing other tickets.. The app has been developed for iOS systems.

Keywords: Augmented reality · Image matching · AR code · AR marker · AR markerless · Living lab

1 Introduction

The Living Lab (LL) project modality has been introduced by Mitchell [1] [2], it represents a user-centric approach for conceiving, prototyping, validating and refining complex solutions in real life contexts. In the European Union the LL strategy has a specific network called ENoLL [3] which was founded in November 2006. The EU intends the LL as a "real-life test and experimentation environment where users and producers co-create innovations". Many LL Project have been funded [4] [5] to cover the areas of interest such as smart cities.

In Italy there are many different activities of LL [13]: a relevant role is played by the Apulia Region which, through its in house consultancy company, InnovaPuglia, has launched different calls for proposal known as "Apulian ICT Living Labs" [6]. The calls are constituted by two steps: in the first one enterprises, research centers, academies and public organizations are invited to submit needs that can be met with a LL project, successively (second steps) project proposals are presented to satisfy the previous needs.

Based on Apulian ICT Living Labs paradigm, CLICK TEATRO initiative responds to a "user need" expressed by the Teatro Pubblico Pugliese (TPP) [7], which

© Springer International Publishing Switzerland 2015
V. Murino et al. (Eds.): ICIAP 2015 Workshops, LNCS 9281, pp. 267–274, 2015.
DOI: 10.1007/978-3-319-23222-5_33

promotes the dissemination and promotion of the performing arts also working as a promoter of the fund. This activity is important to contact all stakeholders, from the spectator theater to the actor, the manager of business activities related to the tourist on the region. The aim is to investigate and test new tools of advertising.

This paper is organized as follows: Section 2 presents an overview on the Augmented Reality. CLICK TEATRO Project and its application are, respectively, in Section 3 and 4. Section 5 reports an evaluation of system's usability and Section 6 the conclusion.

2   Augmented Reality: An Overview

Technologies based on Augmented Reality (AR) enhance our perception and help us to see, hear, and feel our environments in new and enriched ways. AR supports us in fields such as education, maintenance, design and reconnaissance, to name but a few.

On the reality-virtuality continuum by Milgram and Kishino [8] [9], AR is a part of the general area of mixed reality.

The difference between augmented reality and virtual environment is that augmented reality adds virtual objects in real time to a real environment. This tool has a great emotional impact finding application in various areas also very different from each other.

An AR system [10] [11] [12] combines real and virtual objects in a real environment, registers (aligns) real and virtual objects with each other and runs interactively, in three dimensions, and in real time.

Displays, trackers, graphics computers and software remain essential in many AR experiences. In particular, the augmented reality can be used through a workstation (PC or MAC) with webcam, through the use of mobile devices equipped with camera (smartphone or tablet) or through the use of particular viewers (smart glasses). Thanks to these devices is taken up the surrounding environment, the engine "AR Engine" reworks the flow in real time by adding multimedia content to the real context. In this work smartphone-based AR tools have been applied to the aims of the projects.

3   CLICK TEATRO System

CLICK TEATRO system has been planned in order to create a link between theater activities and commercial operators. Figure 1 shows an overview of the system. Through the use of a Mobile App the user receives content related to the shows and services associated. The Augmented reality tool represents a modern way to perform a kind of "visual search". Each user can also access his/her personal wallet and be reached by targeted communication related to his/her personal interest generated by the system (TPP and/or other organizations) or self-generated by artificial intelligence algorithms.

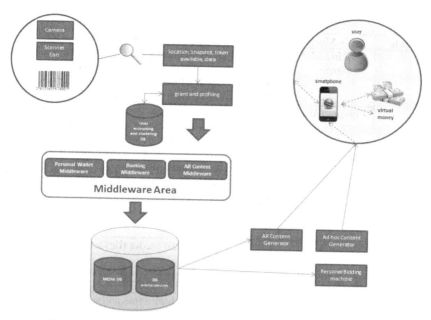

Fig. 1. Interaction macro process in CLICK TEATRO framework

The system includes several modules described (briefly) in Table 1.

4   Augmented Reality and CLICK TEATRO

Two applications of AR have been considered and developed:

- AR for poster of theatrical events;
- AR for a localized event.

In the first case (Fig. 2-a) the user will shoot, using the smartphone camera, a billboard or a poster of a theatrical event. Above the actual picture will be superimposed objects with additional content related to the show. A specific marker is reported on the poster so the related code can be recognized by the Mobile App and transmitted to the AR Content Middleware in order to get back (by the AR Content Generator) the related info. Typically these additional info also include the possibility to directly buy tickets. The communication between the App and the remote server are performed by means of web-services.

The second application (Fig. 2-b) gives the possibility, to the user, to frame the landscape: the AR engine shows events and POI (Point of Interest) in the neighbors within a certain range. In this case a markerless AR solution is adopted: the system uses the GPS capabilities of the smartphone/tablet to identify and interact with resources. The AR Content module actives the following functions:

Table 1. Description of system modules

Module	Sub-Module	Description
Middlleware Area	*Booking Mid-dleware*	This module manages the on-line ticketing system, theater events, additional information and services associated with a theatrical event. These services are close to the structure hosting the event.
	Personal Wal-let (PW)	This module manages the user portfolio. In particular, it allows the displays of accrued credit and the insertion of a new credit by scanning the EAN code reported on a receipt or manually typing the code (released by a merchant of the net).
	AR Content	This module allows the use of content available in augmented reality mode.
DB	*User account-ing*	Used for the storage and retrieval of user's profiles during the login phase.
	Media BD	This DB stores all media files associated to services and events.
	Event DB	All events are here stored.
Back Office	*Bidding Ma-chine (BM)*	Those modules represents a system for the: • User's profiling;
	Ad hoc content generator	• Identification of events of interest based on artificial intelligence techniques; • Delivery of recommended events to the target user.
	AR Content Generator	It allows the management of AR System.
Front Office	*Mobile App*	It ensures the access to all services.

a   b

Fig. 2. Application of AR for a poster of a theatrical event (a) and on POI (b).

- display of theatrical events in the nearby;
- display of associate services (restaurants, parking, hotels, bar, etc.).

Figure 3 shows data flows and modules interactions.

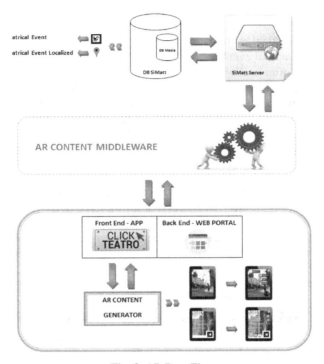

Fig. 3. AR Data Flow

Additional files and media are stored into a database. These contents are useful to enrich and complete the information in the events of the Public Theatre Pugliese in order to obtain an Augmented Reality.

The system has been prototyped for iOS smartphone and the following applications have been used:

1. METAIO for Augmented Reality software. More specifically, it has been used for EAN code recognition, POI identification and marker recognition;
2. APIs, provided by third party companies for the realization of the web services related to the modules: *Booking Middleware*, *AR content Middleware*, *Personal Wallet Middleware* and *Personal Bidding Machine*.

5   Evaluation of System's Usability

Tests have been performed according the Living Lab approach. At the moment tests are going on, however some results are already available. More specifically 20 users have been interviewed by means of a questionnaire consisted of 20 questions grouped in 9 distinct tasks:

- Task1: Find a theatrical event by Category;
- Task2: Buy a theatrical event;
- Task3: Visit the offer available on local services;
- Task4: Test of augmented reality through the use of a poster;
- Task5: Test of augmented reality through theater events located;
- Task6: Virtual wallet usage to view credit accrued and to accumulate new credits;
- Task7: Search a theatrical event among those Suggested by the system;
- Task8: Search and navigate a theatrical event;
- Task9: Usability Evaluation.

Results have been evaluated in terms of "Success Rate" evaluated for each task used to evaluate the usability of the system. Table 2 shows some of the results obtained: for each question the user answered with a value between 1 (strongly disagree) and 6 (totally agree). A failure (F) of the task is represented with the values 1-2, a partial success (P) of the task with the values 3-4 and a success (S) of the task with the values 5-6.

Table 2. Usability testing results

	Task1	Task2	Task3	Task4	Task5	Task6	Task7	Task8	Task9
User1	S	F	F	S	S	S	S	P	P
User2	S	F	F	S	S	P	S	S	P
...									
User20	S	S	F	S	S	S	S	S	P

The usability has been evaluated by considering the Success Rate. This parameter has been calculated as:

$$Success\ Rate = \frac{S + P*0,5}{S+P+F} \qquad (1)$$

So, experimental results carried out are: S=125, P=33 and F=22 . The overall success rate obtained (79%) demonstrates the ability to complete more than half of the assigned tasks.

More specifically, the students had greater difficulty in task 2 (S=4, P=5 and F=11) related to the buying a theatrical event and task 3 (S=8, P=4 and F=8) related to buying and displaying deals on local services, while greater success has been obtained in task 4 (S=20) and task 5 (S=20), respectively, related to the tests of Augmented Reality through the use of a poster and theater events located.

6   Conclusion

This paper presents the system developed for the project CLICK TEATRO. It involves two applications of Augmented Reality on Mobile environments. The first is marker-based and it is used to add info on a poster of a theatrical event (additional content, interviews, etc.) and service associated with its use (restaurants, car parks, hotels, bar, etc.). The second solution is marker-less and based on the GPS position of the device: real landscape is enriched with POI (Point of Interest) in the near by. The system has been prototyped for iOS smartphone and some tests have been performed in order to evaluate it in real environments and use cases: a success rate of the 79% was observed. Problems were identified related to the buying a theatrical event or buying and displaying deals on local services.

Acknowledgment. This work is supported by the P.O. FESR PUGLIA 2007-2013 – ASSE I – Linea di intervento 1.4 – Azione 1.4.2 – "Investiamo nel vostro futuro" – project "Sistema Integrato Multimediale Attivo per la promozione TeaTrale".

References

1. Hamalainen, T.T.: Living lab methods and tools fostering everyday life innovation. In: Proc. of 18th International Conference on Engineering, Technology and Innovation, pp. 1–8 (2012)
2. Dusko, L., Chatzimichailidou, M.M.: Review on living labs. In: Proc. Of COLLA 2011 First International Conference on Advanced Collaborative Networks, Systems and Applications, pp. 28–33 (2011)
3. European Network of Living Lab, November 2006. http://www.openlivinglabs.eu
4. Sallstrom, A., Pallot, M., Hernandez-Munoz, J.M., Santoro, R., Trousse, B., Schaffers, H.: Integrating living labs with future internet experimental platforms for co-creating services within smart cities. In: 17th International Conference on Concurrent Enterprising, pp. 1–11
5. Ishmael, J., Knowles, W., Rouncefield, M., Race, N., Stuart, M., Wright, G., Mu, M.: P2P-Based IPTV Services: Design, Deployment, and QoE Measurement. IEEE Trans. on Multimedia **14**, 1515–1527 (2012)
6. Living Labs ict Apulia innovation in progress. http://livinglabs.regione.puglia.it/
7. Mappatura dei Fabbisogni - Pubblicazione del, May 20, 2014. http://www.sistema.puglia.it/SistemaPuglia/smartpuglia2020
8. Caudell, T., Barfield, W.: Fundamentals of Wearable-Computers and Augmented Reality. CRC Press, Mahwah (2001)
9. Zhigeng, A.D., Yang, H., Zhu, J., Shi, J., Pan, Z.: Virtual reality and mixed reality for virtual learning environments. Computers & Graphics **30**(1), 20–28 (2006)
10. Azuma, R.T.: A survey of augmented reality. Presence **6**(4), 355–385 (1997)

11. Baillot, Y., Behringer, R., Feiner, S.K., Julier, S., MacIntyre, B., Azuma, R.T.: Recent advances in augmented reality. IEEE Computer Graphics and Applications **21**(6), 34–47 (2001)
12. Poelman, R., van Krevelen, D.W.F.: A Survey of Augmented Reality Technologies, Applications and Limitations. The International Journal of, Virtual Reality **9**(2), 1–20 (2010)
13. Galiano, A., Impedovo, D., Pezzuto, M.: OpenKnowledge and OpenGovernment: the experience of the Municip@zione Living Lab project. Journal of e-Leraning and Knowledge Society Je-LKS, Special Issue on, Steps Toward the Digital Agenda: Open Data to Open Knowledge **10**(2), 53–64 (2014). ISSN: 1826-6223, e-ISSN: 1971-8829

A Marker-Based Image Processing Method for Detecting Available Parking Slots from UAVs

Matteo D'Aloia[1(✉)], Maria Rizzi[2], Ruggero Russo[1],
Marianna Notarnicola[1], and Leonardo Pellicani[3]

[1] Masvis srl, Conversano, Italy
{matteo.daloia,ruggero.russo,marianna.notarnicola}@masvis.com
[2] Politecnico di Bari - Dipartimento di Ingegneria Elettrica e dell'Informazione, Bari, Italy
maria.rizzi@poliba.it
[3] Dyrecta Lab srl, Conversano, Italy
leonardo.pellicani@dyrecta.com

Abstract. Due to the considerable number of vehicles in many cities, parking problem is a long-term phenomenon and represents one of the main causes of traffic congestion. Unmanned Aerial Vehicles (UAVs) can handle automatic monitoring of traffic, pollution and other interesting services in urban areas non-invasively. UAVs are usually equipped with one or more onboard cameras and with other electronic sensors. In this context, a method for parking slot occupancy detection in parking areas is presented. For recognition of free parking spaces, pictures of urban areas captured by the onboard camera of the UAV are georeferenced and processed for marker detection. The implemented system shows good results in terms of robustness and reliability. Moreover, it paves the way for an improved management of urban spaces.

Keywords: Image processing · Shape recognition · Smart parking · UAV · Urban areas · Marker detection

1 Introduction

Unmanned Aerial Vehicles (UAVs), commonly called drones, are currently proposed for civil applications with strong involvement in smart city applications. An interesting application of UAVs is the management of parking areas and specifically the detection of parking slot occupancy.

Bad management of free parking slots can cause various problems such as traffic congestion, increase of exhaust emissions and pollution. Moreover, searching for a free parking slot can be time consuming and stressful for citizens. To solve these issues as far as possible, some cities are adopting smart parking systems. Current smart parking systems are based on installation of multiple cameras and/or multiple sensors; they imply costs related to materials, installation and periodic maintenance. Moreover, in the case of sensor networks, battery discharging could represent a problem [1].

The use of drones in monitoring parking lots in urban areas allows patrons to set-up a cost effective and scalable monitoring system based on few units that continuously monitor the whole city by contiguous areas.

© Springer International Publishing Switzerland 2015
V. Murino et al. (Eds.): ICIAP 2015 Workshops, LNCS 9281, pp. 275–281, 2015.
DOI: 10.1007/978-3-319-23222-5_34

Data retrieved from aerial images by UAVs could be employed to develop mobile applications that give live information on parking availability, zone by zone in a city. In this way, both citizens would have a better everyday city live and city governments would be able to develop better plans of dynamic parking fees based on live and more detailed parking status.

In this paper, authors suppose that all parking slots are labeled with a proper marker (a white distinctive shape printed on asphalt). Images captured by camera installed on UAV are analyzed to recognize markers independently from the camera point of view, so occupancy of parking slots of a given urban area is detected.

For marker recognition phase, shape matching technique is adopted. Tests carried out have shown high reliability in counting of parking slots. The implemented tool processes aerial images with unknown point of view. As in many cases, the reliability of detection phase depends on image quality. Generally, image quality is not a main issue in this context because drones can be equipped with high resolution imagery systems. On the other side, the developed method is scale-invariant, rotation-invariant and contemplates a certain degree of perspective distortion. Furthermore, it is relatively insensitive to changes in light conditions.

In the following sections, the procedure for parking slot detection is presented in details.

2   Parking Status Recognition

Nowadays, a lot of choices for occupation state monitoring of parking spaces are indicated.

Among current methods, techniques based on hardware integration in urban architecture are achieving a certain amount of success as a result of their reliability. The most diffuse system uses sensor networks; every sensor is able to recognize presence or absence of a vehicle on the associated spot region. Installation and maintenance costs are the main drawback of this solution. In fact, every parking slot shall be equipped with a sensor which is often put beneath the road surface. Moreover, all sensors are equipped with independent energy sources that need periodic replacements.

Evolution in the detection of vehicles in car park space is represented by live processing of images captured adopting cameras strategically located within the area to be monitored. Drawbacks of this solution are installation costs and presence of obstacle in field of view.

Unlike sensor-based systems, in this solution a single device controls more than one parking slot at a time, reducing the number of devices to be installed in a parking area. After installation a set up phase is necessary to locate Regions Of Interest (ROIs) in the frame. The adoption of fixed cameras allows to make easier and improve the procedure of parking status detection and to make it more reliable [3,4,5,6,7,8].

A new frontier to solve parking management problems in urban areas could be represented by the introduction of Unmanned Aerial Vehicles (UAVs) for operations of parking status recognition.

In the proposed solution, the adoption of a single UAV, enables the monitoring of hundreds of parking slots using an onboard computer vision (CV) system able to detect free parking spaces by recognizing custom markers on the ground. Every marker is related to a parking slot. While flying over an urban area, drone is able to recognize parking markers thus determining the state of parking spaces.

Adopting a non-static vision system, ROIs cannot be set a priori and pre-processing steps are required. To assure that the number of detected free parking spaces is uniquely related to a precise urban area, the onboard CV system shall per-form–image analysis just on non-overlapped frames. This could be obtained using standard methods of image processing in conjunction with other data from different sources for georeferencing purpose.

The development of a robust algorithm is challenging because it should detect parking markers in changeable light conditions and despite perspective distortions.

3   Parking Markers Detection

In this section, all the image processing steps adopted in the detection algorithm are described. In Fig.1, a test image is specified. The depicted condition is recommended for testing the algorithm reliability because perspective distortion of marker printed on ground grows as the view becomes less frontal. At the end of this section, results of marker recognition for the proposed test image are indicated.

Fig. 1. Test image, a custom marker is printed on ground in a parking slot

3.1   Implemented Procedure

Reference Marker Data Import. The reference marker is analyzed and its profile is extracted (Fig. 2).

The marker profile is represented by a vector containing the distances (in pixels) of each point of the marker contour from the centroid of the marker itself (Fig. 3). Extraction of marker profile is an one-off operation. In fact, the obtained value is stored in a variable after it has been evaluated.

Fig. 2. Reference marker

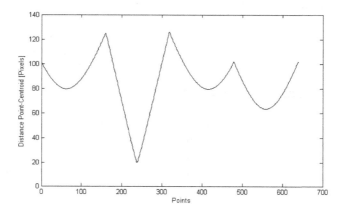

Fig. 3. Profile of the reference marker

Image Acquisition and Segmentation. The mxn image under test is captured by high resolution color camera, transformed in gray levels and imported in the workspace as a mxn matrix. Otsu's method is used to determine optimum threshold level which minimizes intra-class variance [9]. The evaluated value is used to generate a binary image. For marker detection, white blobs contained in the binary image have to be analyzed (Fig. 4).

Fig. 4. Segmented image

Edge Detection and Shape Contours. Edge detection is performed on the obtained binary image using Sobel operator (Fig. 5). Therefore, a new binary image is generated whose white pixels are contour pixels. Sobel operator has been chosen for its low computational cost [10]. As is widely known, edge recognition methods, such as those based on-Sobel operator, are very sensitive to noise [11, 12]. Since in the implemented procedure, Sobel-based edge detection is performed on binary images which are characterized by maximum contrast, the algorithm high noise sensitivity is irrelevant.

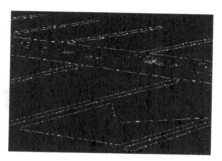

Fig. 5. Marker close-up after edge detection phase

Morphological Processing. To pick out objects to be compared with the reference marker, morphological operations are adopted

Thresholding evaluation for connected objects. The implemented procedure does not analyzed all the objects recognized as bright. In fact, based on the image height and the image resolution, the expected value of the number of contour points composing the marker is calculated. Therefore, objects having a number of contour pixels higher or lower than the expected value multiplied by a user-defined flexibility parameter, are not taken into account (Fig. 6).

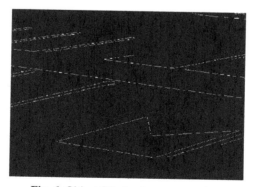

Fig. 6. Object filtering by area opening

Edge linking, Filling, and Labeling. A morphological closing operation is performed on the binary image to link any broken contour using a disk with 2 pixels radius.

The next phase realizes a morphological reconstruction; in fact every hole in any connected component is filled adopting the algorithm in [13]. In this context, holes represent every set of background points which cannot be reached by background filling starting by the image edges. The last operation performs labelling: every connected component in the binary image is labelled with a number. The same numerical value is assigned to pixels of the same object while background pixels are set to 0. The procedure adopted for object labeling is detailed in [14].

Object Warping. Because of the original reference marker is inscribed into a square, every labelled object is warped (Fig. 7). Even if this operation introduces some distortion, it makes reconstruction easier because it reduces perspective distortion and allows a more accurate comparison.

Fig. 7. Object thus isolated in the original image (left) is warped into a square (right)

Profile Extraction. Profile is extracted for each warped object adopting the same method used for reference image. For the object classification, the profile of every object is compared with the reference marker profile.

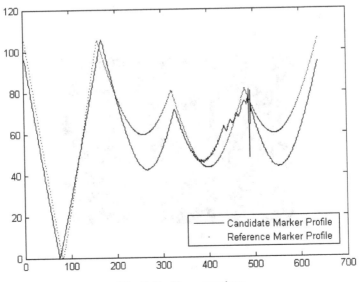

Fig. 8. Profile comparison

Profile Matching. *Offset, Scaling, Resampling, and Alignment.* To optimize the profile matching, some operations are necessary. Therefore, every object is resampled with the same number of points of the reference profile, offset between profiles is subtracted, amplitude is normalized to the maximum value of the reference profile and profiles are aligned using a dynamic time warping algorithm (Fig. 8)

Cross-correlation. Normalized cross-correlation coefficient is calculated between reference and candidate profiles. If the coefficient value is higher than a user-defined threshold, the object under test is recognized as a marker and its coordinates are stored on the original image for further uses.

The marker printed on asphalt in the test image has been successfully recognized with a cross-correlation coefficient value greater than 0.9916.

References

1. Zonouz, A.E.: Smart Parking Lot Using Quadcopter Network. https://traffic.mobilityidea contest.spigit.com/Page/ViewIdea?ideaid=400
2. Mohammed, F., Idries, A., Mohamed, N., Al-Jaroodi, J., Jawhar, I.: UAVs for smart cities: opportunities and challenges. In: International Conference on Unmanned Aircraft Systems, pp. 267–273. IEEE Press, Orlando (2014)
3. Idris, M.Y.I., Leng, Y.Y., Tamil, E.M., Noor, N.M., Razar, Z.: Car Park System: A Review of Smart Parking System and its Technology. Inform. Tech. J. **8**, 101–113 (2009)
4. Prokhorov, D.V.: Method and System for Object Recognition Based on a Trainable Dynamic System. US Patent 8705849 B2 (2014)
5. Jazayeri, A., Cai, H., Zheng, J.Y., Tuceryan, M.: Vehicle Detection and Tracking in Car Video Based on Motion Model. IEEE Trans. Intell. Transport. Syst. **12**, 583–595 (2011)
6. Klappenecker, A., Lee, H., Welch, J.L.: Finding Available Parking Spaces Made Easy. Ad Hoc Networks **12**, 243–249 (2014)
7. True, N.: Vacant Parking Space Detection in Static Images, Thesis, University of California, San Diego, La Jolla, CA (2007)
8. Michalopoulos, P.G.: Vehicle Detection Video Through Image Processing: the Autoscope System. IEEE Trans. Veh. Tech. **40**, 21–29 (1991)
9. Otsu, N.: A Threshold Selection Method for Gray-Level Histograms. IEEE Trans. Sys. Man. Cyber. **9**, 62–66 (1975)
10. Tavares, J.M.R.S., Jorge, R.M.N.: Computational Vision and Medical Image Processing: VipIMAGE 2011. CRC Press, London (2011)
11. Pham, N., Morrison, A., Schwock, J., Aviet-Ronen, S., Iakovlev, V., Tsao, M., Ho, J., Hedley, D.W.: Quantitative Image Analysis of Immunohistochemical Stains Using a CMYK Color Model. Diagn Pathol, pp. 2–8 (2007)
12. Chandrasekar, C., Shrivakshan, G.T.: A Comparison of Various Edge Detection Techniques Used in Image Processing. IJCSI International Journal of Computer Science Issues **9**, 269–276 (2012)
13. Soille, P.: Morphological Image Analysis, Principles and Applications. Springer, New York (1999)
14. Haralick, R.M., Shapiro, L.G.: Computer and Robot Vision, vol. I. Addison-Wesley, Boston (1992)

Crosswalk Recognition Through Point-Cloud Processing and Deep-Learning Suited to a Wearable Mobility Aid for the Visually Impaired

Matteo Poggi[✉], Luca Nanni, and Stefano Mattoccia

Department of Computer Science and Engineering (DISI), University of Bologna,
Viale Risorgimento, 2, 40136 Bologna, Italy
{matteo.poggi8,stefano.mattoccia}@unibo.it, luca.nanni10@studio.unibo.it

Abstract. In smart-cities, computer vision has the potential to dramatically improve the quality of life of people suffering of visual impairments. In this field, we have been working on a wearable mobility aid aimed at detecting in real-time obstacles in front of a visually impaired. Our approach relies on a custom RGBD camera, with FPGA on-board processing, worn as traditional eyeglasses and effective point-cloud processing implemented on a compact and lightweight embedded computer. This latter device also provides feedback to the user by means of an haptic interface as well as audio messages. In this paper we address crosswalk recognition that, as pointed out by several visually impaired users involved in the evaluation of our system, is a crucial requirement in the design of an effective mobility aid. Specifically, we propose a reliable methodology to detect and categorize crosswalks by leveraging on point-cloud processing and deep-learning techniques. The experimental results reported, on 10000+ frames, confirm that the proposed approach is invariant to head/camera pose and extremely effective even when dealing with large occlusions typically found in urban environments.

Keywords: Wearable · Embedded 3d vision · Deep learning · Crosswalk detection

1 Introduction and Related Work

Autonomous mobility, especially in urban environments, can be a challenging task for people suffering of visual impairments. Although some stationary obstacles can be learned day by day, many others change dynamically and thus can't be learned. For this reason, several mobility devices aimed at detecting obstacles, possibly by means of a contact-less strategy, have been proposed. Nevertheless, despite this fact, this strategy is not adopted by the white cane, the most widely adopted mobility aid by visually impaired users. Moreover, the white cane does not allow to perceive other crucial features such as pedestrian crossings.

Many vision-based systems have been proposed to deal with crosswalk recognition, or more in general urban road markings recognition, for different purposes. Most devices were proposed for vehicles, as assistive device as well as as

© Springer International Publishing Switzerland 2015
V. Murino et al. (Eds.): ICIAP 2015 Workshops, LNCS 9281, pp. 282–289, 2015.
DOI: 10.1007/978-3-319-23222-5_35

part of autonomous driving systems, such as [1] that detects crosswalks by applying several filters on 2D images and [2] that relies on a bird-view re-projection of the 2D image. Some methods exploit 3D data [3,4] while others also rely on non-vision techniques; for example, Suzuki et al. [5] use 2D image processing and radar technology. In this field, an interesting study, aimed at analyzing drivers behavior in presence of different urban road markings, has been proposed in [6].

Other approaches have been designed to aid the visually impaired. In [7], an effective methodology was proposed to detect crosswalks, estimating their extension, and traffic lights, detecting the emitted color. Some of them, such as [8] and [9], have been implemented on a smartphone. Radvanyi et al. [10] proposed a wearable device based on a neural network to detect ground plane in 2D images and then recognizing crosswalks. In [11], the 3D data obtained through a stereo vision system is processed applying the Hough transform in the 2D and 3D domain to detect crosswalks and stairs. Crosswatch system [12] allows self localization by recognizing specific street patterns. In this paper we propose an effective methodology to detect crosswalks by leveraging 3D data provided by a custom RGBD camera and a *Convolutional Neural Network* (CNN).

2   Overview of the Wearable Mobility Aid

In this section we provide a brief overview of our wearable mobility aid for obstacle detection, proposed in its early development phase in [13].

It consists of a custom RGBD sensor developed by our research group [14], based on stereo vision technology, and an embedded ARM board. Our system is purely based on vision technology and is powered by a small accumulator that enables hours of battery life. The 3D sensor provides dense and accurate depth map processing synchronized stereo images at more than 30 fps (up to 640 × 480 resolution) according to state-of-the-art 3D vision algorithms implemented into a low cost FPGA (Spartan 6 model 75 in the current setup). Specifically, we have mapped into the FPGA a complete stereo vision pipeline including a custom and modified version of the SGM algorithm [15]. The output of the RGBD sensor (reference rectified image and disparity map as shown in Figure1 a) and b)) is sent, via USB at about 20 fps, to the embedded computer, Odroid U3 [16], for obstacle detection. The early stage of the visual processing pipeline, greatly improved wrt the implementation shown in [13] consists of the following steps: disparity map to point-cloud conversion, ground plane segmentation according to a robust RANSAC [17] framework applied to the point-cloud, head pose estimation wrt the ground plane and refinement based on Kalman filtering. Once obtained the ground plane equation and the head pose we re-project, from a top-view perspective, points not laying on the ground plane and in this domain we compute, within vertical bins (of size 2 × 2 cm in the current setup), statistics concerned with heights (e.g., min and max values) and occupancy to accurately detect potential obstacles. According to suggestions provided by visually impaired users involved in the testing phase, the original field of view of the camera is restricted to the three nearby VOIs shown in Figure 1 c). Tactile and

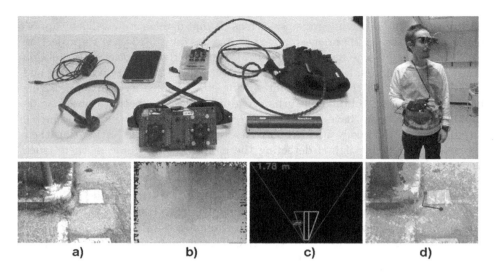

Fig. 1. On top, the adopted wearable mobility aid. It consists of a custom RGBD sensor, an Odroid U3 system, a haptic glove, a battery (enabling 3+ hours autonomy) and optional audio interfaces (purple). On bottom, overview of the obstacle detection approach deployed on it. a) Reference rectified image - b) Disparity map computed on FPGA (colder colors encode farther points) - c) Top-view re-projection with three sensed *volumes of interest* (VOI) in front of the user and, highlighted, the obstacles - d) Segmented ground plane (green) with superimposed head pose wrt the ground plane and detected obstacle regions (red).

audio feedback are provided by means of a vibro-tactile glove, bone conductive headset and smartphone. The whole hardware setup described so far and depicted in Figure 1 weights about 250 g, including the battery.

3   Proposed Crosswalk Recognition Approach

In this paper we propose a crucial enhancement to the outlined mobility aid providing reliable crosswalk recognition. This additional feature, not available with a white cane, would greatly improve the knowledge of the explored environment enabling the visually impaired to properly locate the presence and the direction of pedestrian crossings as well as to improve his/her self localization. To detect crosswalk and recognize their orientation, according to the four categories depicted at the left of Figure 2, wrt the user we rely on point-cloud processing and a CNN. In particular, two main phases are carried out:

- Head pose estimation, aimed at warping the ground plane according to the estimated head position computed from point-cloud data provided by the RGBD sensor
- Detection of pedestrian crossings and categorization of their orientation with respect to the user on the segmented and warped ground plane images

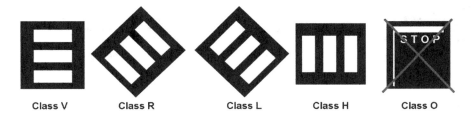

Class V   **Class R**   **Class L**   **Class H**   **Class O**

Fig. 2. Proposed ontology. The CNN is trained to detect and classify pedestrian crossings according to four possible orientation wrt the user's point of view: *vertical* (V), *horizontal* (H), *diagonal left* (L) and *diagonal right* (R). A further class, referred to as *other* (O), takes into account any other case.

3.1 Head Pose Estimation and Image Refinement

Our system, starting from the dense disparity map provided by the RGBD sensor, computes on the embedded CPU the point-cloud according to (1) mapping each point with a valid disparity value to the corresponding 3D point of coordinates (X_c, Y_c, Z_c) wrt the camera reference system by knowing the baseline of the stereo camera b, the focal length f, the optical center (u_0, v_0) and the coordinate (u, v) of the point at disparity d.

$$Z_c = \frac{bf}{d} \quad X_c = \frac{Z_c(u - u_0)}{f} \quad Y_c = \frac{Z_c(v - v_0)}{f} \tag{1}$$

From the point-cloud, a robust RANSAC framework [17] allows us to obtain a reliable estimation of the ground plane equation. This information enables to discriminate between ground plane (where crosswalk markers are painted) and any other object not laying on this surface. Then, the segmented ground plane image/point-cloud is further processed before getting analyzed by the CNN, which could wrongly estimate the direction taken by the crosswalk in presence of head/camera tilting. In particular, we found that recognition accuracy improves when the head/camera is aligned to the floor (i.e., when the normal vector of the ground plane, if drawn on the image, appears to be vertical). To follow this strategy, the angle that aligns the ground plane normal with the vertical direction is computed and used to warp the segmented image accordingly. Once obtained such normalized representation of the ground plane from point-cloud data, the warped image can be processed by the CNN to detect and classify potential pedestrian crossings.

3.2 CNN Architecture for Crosswalk Recognition

Machine learning techniques have been widely adopted in many practical applications and deep-learning is one of the most effective techniques for visual recognition. A deep neural network is a multilayer architecture with layers connected by non-linear transformations. In computer vision, CNNs are deep neural networks made of several layers, called *convolutional layers*, that extract features

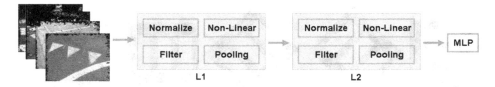

Fig. 3. Architecture of the CNN based on two convolutional layers showing their modules.

from the images by applying several normalization and filtering operations, and a final classifier, typically, a *Multi Layer Perceptron* (MLP). Compared to other machine learning techniques, such as Bag of Visual Words [18], that rely on an explicit feature extraction phase, a CNN allows for a higher level of abstraction deploying adaptive convolutional layers. LeCun et al. [19] reported how such multistage architectures yield to significant improvements compared to a single layer architecture.

In our approach the CNN takes as input the warped image of the ground plane, detects the presence of a crosswalk and, if found, its orientation. The user is made aware of the outcome of this process with an audio message. In our architecture, we adopt a 2-layers plus MLP structure, as shown in Figure 3, mapped within the Torch 7 framework [20]. Specifically, the two convolutional layers and the MLP have been designed as follows:

- Layer 1: *Filter* performs spatial convolution to extracts 256 10×10 feature maps by using 5×5 filters and fan-in equal to 1, *Non-Linear* applies hyperbolic tangent as squashing function (enhancing strong features and suppressing weak ones), *Pooling*, on 2×2 regions and 2×2 stride, obtaining 16 14×14 maps, *Normalize* performs feature normalization
- Layer 2: *Filter* performs spatial convolution to extracts 16 28×28 feature maps by using 5×5 filters and fan-in equal to 4, *Non-Linear* applies hyperbolic tangent as in Layer 1, *Pooling*, on 2×2 regions and 2×2 stride, obtaining 256 5×5 maps, *Normalize* performs feature normalization
- MLP: made by a 128 neurons level fully connected to a 5 neurons further level, adopting hyperbolic tangent for back propagation

4   Experimental Results

For the experimental validation we trained the CNN on a dataset composed of about 2500 images acquired with our wearable mobility aid in urban scenarios. For each of the 5 classes depicted in Figure 2 we have acquired about 500 training instances. After a 15 *epochs* training period the test set composed of 100 images per class has been subject of categorization returning a 100% correctness ratio. Eventually, to properly evaluate the effectiveness of the proposed approach in challenging urban environments including scenes with large and multiple occlusions, difficult illumination conditions, ruined crosswalk patterns and so on, we

Table 1. Confusion matrices computed on the validation set (10165 frames). On the left, by processing the raw segmented images, we obtain 0 false negatives (i.e., undetected crosswalks) and 741 false positives (5.97%). On the right, by processing the segmented images after head pose refinement, we obtain 0 false negatives and 995 false positives (6.63%).

1983	162	96	0	0	V, 88.48%	2198	19	24	0	0	V, **98.08%**
58	814	0	19	0	R, 91.35%	28	859	0	4	0	R, **96.40%**
45	0	874	14	0	L, 93.67%	25	0	903	5	0	L, **96.78%**
0	4	3	97	0	H, 93.27%	0	0	3	101	0	H, **97.12%**
60	58	78	411	5369	O, 89.84%	95	65	91	423	5302	O, 88.72%

acquired a validation dataset composed of 10000+ frames. In Table 1 we report *confusion matrices* summarizing the results on such dataset. A confusion matrix has N rows and N columns, with N the number of classes in the ontology, and highlights the following:

- The main diagonal contains the number of correct instances for each class
- On each row, the accuracy percentage is reported for a class, showing how many frames are miss-recognized and the class they are wrongly assigned to
- On each column, it shows how many frames, for each other class, are wrongly categorized as belonging to a different class

The table, on the left, shows results concerning recognition accuracy obtained by processing the raw ground plane segmentation image without head pose refinement. We can notice a high correctness rate for crosswalk recognition, which is between 88% and 94% for each of the four classes V, R, L, H. Moreover, it is worth noticing that wrongly categorized crosswalk frames are always assigned to a different zebra crossing pattern and never miss-categorized as class O. Therefore, the crosswalk recognition rate is 100%. On the other hand, we can also notice that we have 10.16% of the frames belonging to class O wrongly classified, resulting in a false positive percentage (i.e., images wrongly categorized as crosswalk) of 5.97% on the overall validation set.

Applying the head pose refinement, on the right in Table 1, we obtain an average recognition accuracy improvement between 3% and 5% on classes R, L and H, with a major increase close to 10% for V. Figure 4 shows 2 out 10000+ frames of the validation dataset; in particular the first row reports a scenario where the head pose refinement phase allows to detect the correct class (H). On the other hand, the number of frames of class O wrongly categorized as crosswalk slightly increases by less than 1% on the overall dataset.

In general, false positives are mainly due to particular challenging environments when framing regions containing shadows close to areas exposed to sunlight. However, it is worth observing that our current training set has a limited cardinality and an extended dataset, currently under acquisition, would certainly allow to further reduce the number of false detections. Finally, we report that on the Odroid U3 our approach computes plane detection plus head pose

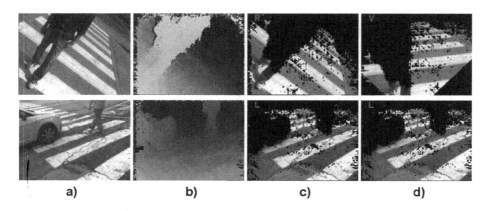

a)   b)   c)   d)

Fig. 4. Two frames from the validation set (10000+ instances). a) the reference rectified image - b) the raw disparity map computed by the RGBD sensor - c) the detected ground plane - d) refined/warped ground plane according to the normal vector. c) and d) also show the recognized orientation, corrected by pose refinement on the first frame.

refinement in about 20 ms and crosswalk recognition in 180 ms thus allowing a prompt feedback to the user.

5 Conclusions

In this paper, an effective crosswalk recognition pipeline leveraging 3D data provided by a compact RGBD sensor and deep-learning has been proposed. Despite the small cardinality of the current training set, experimental results on 10000+ images acquire in challenging urban environments, show a quite high recognition accuracy even in presence of large occlusions. Moreover, its computational efficiency makes it suitable for real-time crosswalk recognition even on the target embedded device deployed for a wearable mobility aid. A larger dataset would improve the accuracy, with no computational overhead and this approach could also be extended to detect and recognize other road markings for several purposes.

References

1. Haselhoff, A., Kummert, A.: On visual crosswalk detection for driver assistance systems. In: 2010 IEEE Intelligent Vehicles Symposium (IV), pp. 883–888, June 2010
2. Wu, T., Ranganathan, A.: A practical system for road marking detection and recognition. In: 2012 IEEE Intelligent Vehicles Symposium (IV), pp. 25–30, June 2012
3. Mancini, A., Frontoni, E., Zingaretti, P.: Automatic road object extraction from mobile mapping systems. In: 2012 IEEE/ASME International Conference on Mechatronics and Embedded Systems and Applications (MESA), pp. 281–286, July 2012

4. Hata, A., Wolf, D.: Road marking detection using lidar reflective intensity data and its application to vehicle localization. In: 2014 IEEE 17th International Conference on Intelligent Transportation Systems (ITSC), pp. 584–589, October 2014

5. Suzuki, S., Raksincharoensak, P., Shimizu, I., Nagai, M., Adomat, R.: Sensor fusion-based pedestrian collision warning system with crosswalk detection. In: 2010 IEEE Intelligent Vehicles Symposium (IV), pp. 355–360, June 2010

6. Ishizaki, R., Morimoto, M., Fujii, K.: An evaluation method of driving behavior by in-vehicle data camera. In: 2012 Fifth International Conference on Emerging Trends in Engineering and Technology (ICETET), pp. 293–297, November 2012

7. Shioyama, T., Wu, H., Nishibe, Y., Nakamura, N., Kitawaki, S.: Image analysis of crosswalk. In: proceedings of the 11th International Conference on Image Analysis and Processing, pp. 168–173, September 2001

8. Ivanchenko, V., Coughlan, J., Shen, H.: Detecting and locating crosswalks using a camera phone. In: IEEE Computer Society Conference on Computer Vision and Pattern Recognition Workshops, CVPRW 2008, pp. 1–8, June 2008

9. Ahmetovic, D., Bernareggi, C., Gerino, A., Mascetti, S.: Zebrarecognizer: efficient and precise localization of pedestrian crossings. In: 2014 22nd International Conference on Pattern Recognition (ICPR), pp. 2566–2571, August 2014

10. Radvanyi, M., Varga, B., Karacs, K.: Advanced crosswalk detection for the bionic eyeglass. In: 2010 12th International Workshop on Cellular Nanoscale Networks and Their Applications (CNNA), pp. 1–5, February 2010

11. Wang, S., Tian, Y.: Detecting stairs and pedestrian crosswalks for the blind by rgbd camera. In: 2012 IEEE International Conference on Bioinformatics and Biomedicine Workshops (BIBMW), pp. 732–739, October 2012

12. Murali, V.N., Coughlan, J.M.: Smartphone-based crosswalk detection and localization for visually impaired pedestrians. In: 2013 IEEE International Conference on Multimedia and Expo Workshops (ICMEW), pp. 1–7, July 2013

13. Mattoccia, S., Macri', P.: 3d glasses to improve autonomous mobility of people visually impaired. In: Agapito, L., Bronstein, M.M., Rother, C. (eds.) ECCV Workshop. LNCS, vol. 8927, pp. 539–554. Springer, Switzerland (2014)

14. Mattoccia, S., Marchio, I., Casadio, M.: A compact 3d camera suited for mobile and embedded vision applications. In: 2014 IEEE Conference on Computer Vision and Pattern Recognition Workshops (CVPRW), pp. 195–196, June 2014

15. Hirschmüller, H.: Stereo processing by semiglobal matching and mutual information. IEEE Trans. Pattern Anal. Mach. Intell. 30(2), 328–341 (2008)

16. Hard-Kernel: Odroid u3. http://hardkernel.com/main/main.php

17. Choi, S., Kim, T., Yu, W.: Performance evaluation of ransac family. In: BMVC (2009)

18. Csurka, G., Dance, C.R., Fan, L., Willamowski, J., Bray, C.: Visual categorization with bags of keypoints. In: Workshop on Statistical Learning in Computer Vision, ECCV, pp. 1–22 (2004)

19. Jarrett, K., Kavukcuoglu, K., Ranzato, M.A., LeCun, Y.: What is the best multi-stage architecture for object recognition? In: Proc. International Conference on Computer Vision (ICCV 2009). IEEE (2009)

20. Collobert, R., Kavukcuoglu, K., Farabet, C.: Torch7: a matlab-like environment for machine learning. In: BigLearn, NIPS Workshop (2011)

Early Diagnosis of Neurodegenerative Diseases by Handwritten Signature Analysis

Giuseppe Pirlo[1], Moises Diaz[2], Miguel Angel Ferrer[2], Donato Impedovo[3(✉)],
Fabrizio Occhionero[1], and Urbano Zurlo[1]

[1] Dipartimento di Informatica, Università Degli Studi di Bari, Bari, Italy
`giuseppe.pirlo@uniba.it`
[2] Instituto Universitario Para el Desarrollo Tecnológico y la Innovación en Comunicaciones,
Universidad de Las Palmas de Gran Canaria, Las Palmas, Spain
[3] DyrectaLab, Bari, Italy
`impedovo@gmail.com`

Abstract. Handwritten signatures are generally considered a powerful biometric traits for personal verification. Recently, handwritten signatures have been also investigated for early diagnosis of neurodegenerative diseases. This paper presents a new approach for early diagnosis of neurodegenerative diseases by the analysis of handwritten dynamic signatures. For the purpose, the sigma-lognormal model was considered and dynamic parameters are extracted for signatures. Based on these parameters, the health condition of the signer is analysed in terms of Alzheimer disease. The approach is cheap and effective, therefore it can be considered as a very promising direction for further research.

Keywords: Biometrics · Alzheimer Pre-diagnosis system · Handwritten signature · Sigma- lognormal

1 Introduction

Writing is one of the oldest representations of the intelligence of human beings. It arises mainly because of trade, accounting and administration. It represents a graphic reproduction of the spoken language, by means of a set of signs, called graphemes. Writing your own name is one of the first actions that are taught; therefore the signature is a graphic sign that is repeated countless times in everyone's life. The signature contains a huge amount of information related not only to the representation of the name and surname of the signatory, but also to his/her writing system (hand, arm, etc.) and psychophysical state. Therefore, the signature is rightly considered as a biometric trait of extraordinary importance for the verification of digital identity. Also it is the subject of many studies both by forensic experts, computer scientific and even medical doctor [1].

More recently, in view of the extraordinary information of the signer conveyed by his/her signature, it was also considered as a useful means for the pre-diagnosis of neurodegenerative diseases. Among these diseases, the Alzheimer's disease is the

V. Murino et al. (Eds.): ICIAP 2015 Workshops, LNCS 9281, pp. 290–297, 2015.
DOI: 10.1007/978-3-319-23222-5_36

most common form of degenerative dementia progressively debilitating that leads to loss of cognitive function. Alzheimer's affects, in fact, on a person's ability to carry out the simplest daily activities, going to hit the brain areas that control functions such as memory, thinking, speech and writing; the latter disorder is defined as agraphia.

Therefore, the inability to be able to communicate through writing can be seen as an early manifestation of Alzheimer's disease [2, 3].

For the analysis of a handwritten signature, in this paper the Sigma-lognormal model is used, that is based on the kinematics theory of human movements. This model allows the representation of the information of motor commands and the time it takes the neuromuscular system to produce a complex movement, such as to affix the signature [4, 5]. According to the Sigma-lognormal model, a set of well-defined parameters are extracted from the signature and used for early diagnosis of Alzheimer disease. The experimental tests demonstrate the effectiveness of the proposed approach and some directions for further research.

The organization of this paper is as follows. Section 2 describes the Sigma-lognormal model used for the representation of the signatures. In Section 3 we present the set of features and the classification algorithms that were considered for the early diagnosis. Section 4 presents the system and some experimental results. Section 5 presents the conclusion of the works and some possible directions for future research.

2   The Sigma-Lognormal Model

The kinematic theory of rapid human movement, relies on the Sigma-Lognormal model to represent the information of both the motor commands and timing properties of the neuromuscular system involved in the production of complex movements like signature [4, 5]. In recent years, several scientific contributions demonstrated the utility of such a theory in handwriting signature analysis and processing [6, 7].

The Sigma-Lognormal model considers the resulting speed of a single stroke j as having a lognormal shape Λ scaled by a command parameter (D) and time-shifted by the time occurrence of the command (t0):

$$\left| v_j(t; P_j) \right| = D_j \Lambda(t - t_{oj}; \mu_j, \sigma_j^2) = \frac{D_j}{(t - t_{oj})\sqrt{2\pi}} \exp\left\{ \frac{\left[\ln(t - t_{oj}) - \mu_j \right]^2}{-2\sigma_j^2} \right\} \tag{1}$$

where $P_j = [D_j, t_{0j}, \mu_j, \sigma_j, \Theta_{sj}, \Theta_{ej}]$ represents the sets of Sigma-Lognormal parameters:

- D_j : amplitude of the input commands;
- t_{0j} : time occurrence of the input commands, a time-shift parameter;
- μ_j: log-time delays, the time delay of the neuromuscular system expressed on a logarithmic time scale;

- σ_j: log-response times, which are the response times of the neuromuscular system expressed on a logarithmic time scale;
- Θ_{sj}: starting angle of the circular trajectories described by the lognormal model along pivot;
- Θ_{ej}: ending angle of the circular trajectories described by the lognormal model along pivot.

Additionally, from the hypothesis that every lognormal stroke represents the movement as happening along a pivot, the angular position can be computed as:

$$\phi_j(t;P_j) = \theta_{sj} + \frac{\theta_{ej} - \theta_{sj}}{D_j} \int_0^t \left|\vec{v}(\tau;P_j)\right| d\tau \tag{2}$$

In this context, a signature can be seen as the output of a generator that produces a set of individual strokes superimposed in time. The resulting complex trajectories can be modeled as a vector summation of lognormal distributions (being N_{LN} the total number of lognormal curves in which the handwritten trace is decomposed):

$$\vec{v}(t) = \sum \Lambda(t) = \sum_{j=1}^{N_{LN}} \vec{v}_j(t;P_j) \tag{3}$$

For each of the components of the signature, and then for each stroke, it can define some profiles that add information to those already expressed by the parameters of the Sigma-Lognormal.

According to the Sigma-Lognormal model, in this paper a signature S^t is characterized in the generation domain by a sequence of couples

$$S^r = (z^r_1, z^r_2, z^r_3, \dots z^r_j, \dots, z^r_m) \tag{4}$$

where each couple $z^r_j = (t_j, v_j(t_j))$ describes the j-th lognormal curve in which the signature is decomposed (in eq. (6) it is supposed that a signature is decomposed in m lognormal curves).

In this paper, the Script Studio software was used to analyze and graph the signatures through Sigma-Lognormal Model.

3   Alzheimer Pre-diagnosis System Experimental Results

In this work, a set of twelve features to distinguish between pathologic from non-pathologic dynamic signatures are defined as follows: (the label assigned to each feature is shown in brackets):

- Maximum speed of the signing divided by the time of writing (vDIVt);
- Number of log-normal in the signature (N.LogNorm);
- Number of Log-Normal divided by the time (n.logNormDIVt);

- Average and Standard Deviation of the value μ (Med_MU, DevSt_MU_);
- Average and Standard Deviation of the value σ (Med_Sigma_, DevSt_Sigma);
- Average and Standard Deviation of the value D (Med_D, DevSt_D);
- Maximum and minimum speed learned while writing (V.Max, V.Min);
- Number of peaks in the graph speed / time (Peaks);

The selected features are worked out to build a classifier through different machine learning techniques provided by R (a free development environment for statistical analysis).

More precisely, we're considered to distinguish the healthy and non healthy signatures.:

- CART algorithm;
- BAGGING CART algorithm;
- Support Vector Machines(SVM) with linear kernel.

The CART algorithm builds the decision tree in the following way: it starts from the data grouped in a single node (root node) and performs, to each step, an exhaustive search on all possible subdivisions. In each step the best subdivision is chosen, that is the subdivision producing branches as homogeneous as possible. To check if a signature belongs to a pathological case or not, just compare the values in vectors of features of each signature with the conditions present on the branches of the tree. The classification for both trees is carried starting from the root and down to the branch that meets the condition, proceed until there comes a leaf node that indicates the class of the signature.

The BAGGING CART algorithm creates more patterns of the same type obtained from different subsamples of the same group of data. Forecasts of each model are combined together to provide a better result. This approach has proved appropriate for methods with high variance. As before the classification shall be made starting from the root node and go down gradually.

Last classifier used is a SVM with linear kernel. A SVM uses a representation of the pattern examples as points in space, mapped so that the examples of the separate categories are clearly (linearly) divided. This means that the gap between categories should be as wide as possible. When additional test examples are considered, they are mapped into that same space and are classified according to the side they belong.

Finally, a user-friendly interface was developed for Alzheimer Pre-diagnosis, which exploits the handwritten signature after the Sigma-Lognormal parameters extraction. It has been so named "APs" (Alzheimer Pre-diagnosis System).

4   Experimental Results

For the experimental test of the system, a set of dynamic signatures was considered belonging to a private database.

The set consists of sixty-two signatures divided into two groups: Patologic and Healthy (Figure 1). The first group is composed of twenty-nine signatures, the second group is composed of thirty signatures.

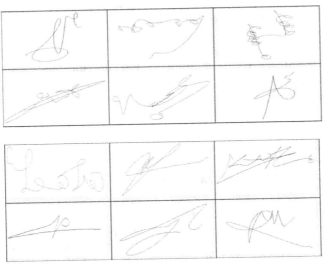

Fig. 1. The first table contains examples of pathological signatures, instead the second contains healthy.

Figure 2 and 3 show the decision trees obtained from the training data using the CART and the BAGGING CART algorithm, respectively. Figure 4 shows the result obtained using the SVM algorithm (with linear kernel), when the features Peaks vs logDIVt are considered (we chose these features since they are the best to separate the two classes).

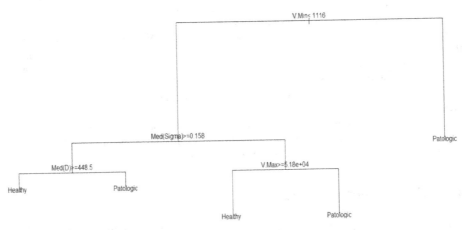

Fig. 2. Decision Tree: CART.

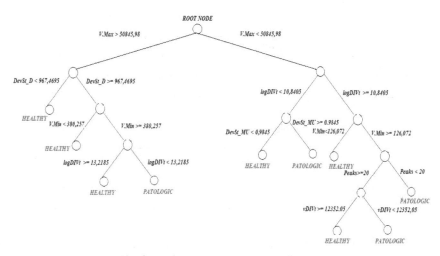

Fig. 3. Decision Tree: BAGGING CART.

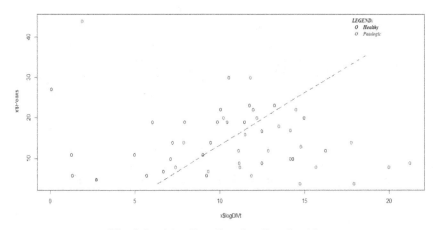

Fig. 4. Decision Tree: Bagging Cart algorithm.

Table 1-3 reports the classification results.

Table 1. Decision Tree (Cart Algorithm)

	Healthy	Patologic
Healthy	24	8
Patologic	7	22

Table 2. Decision Tree (Bagging Cart Algorithm)

	Healthy	Patologic
Healthy	31	1
Patologic	1	28

Table 3. Support Vector Machines

	Healthy	Patologic
Healthy	25	7
Patologic	10	19

Table 4 reports the False Acceptance Rate (FAR) and the False Rejection Rate (FRR) for the three classifiers.

Table 4. Experimental Results

	FAR	FRR
Decision Tree (CART)	25%	24%
Decision Tree (Bagging)	3%	3%
SVM	21%	34%

As the result demonstrates, the algorithms to generate decision trees are more efficient (in our case) than SVM. In particular, in our test, the Bagging Cart outperforms significantly both the Cart decision tree and the SVM classifier.

5   Conclusions

This paper addresses the possibility to use handwriting signatures to predict neurodegenerative diseases. For the purpose, the Sigma-Lognormal model was considered for handwritten signature analysis and specific key-features are used for the early diagnosis of Alzheimer, using a bagging cart classification tree.

Some experimental results show that this approach allows a fast pre-diagnosis, inexpensive and non-invasive. Of course, more research is still necessary to evaluate the effectiveness and robustness of the approach using other data sets, also to evaluate the extent to which this approach can be used as a screening standard routine for the early diagnosis of Alzheimer disease.

References

1. Diaz-Cabrera, M., Ferrer, M.A., Morales, A.: Modeling the Lexical Morphology of Western Handwritten Signatures. PLoS ONE **10**(4), e0123254 (2015). doi:10.1371/journal.pone.0123254
2. Vigliotti, A.: Grafologia medica: sindrome demenziale e analisi della scrittura. www.neuroscienze.net
3. Impedovo, D., Pirlo, G., Mangini, F.M., Barbuzzi, D., Rollo, A., Balestrucci, A., Impedovo, S., Sarcinella, L., et al.: Writing generation model for health care neuromuscular system investigation. In: Formenti, E., Tagliaferri, R., Wit, E. (eds.) CIBB 2013. LNCS, vol. 8452, pp. 137–148. Springer, Heidelberg (2014)
4. Djioua, M., Plamondon, R.: Studying the Variability of Handwriting Patterns using the Kinematic Theory. Human Movement Science **28**(5), 588–601 (2009)
5. O'Reilly, C., Plamondon, R.: Development of a Sigma-Lognormal Representation for On- Line Signatures. Pattern Recognition **42**, 3324–3337 (2009)
6. Galbally, J. Plamondon, R., Fierrez, J., Martinez-Diaz, M.: Quality analysis of dynamic signature based on the Sigma-Lognormal model. In: Proc. IAPR Intl. Conf. on Document Analysis and Recognition, ICDAR, pp. 633–637 (2011)
7. Diaz, M., Fischer, A., Plamondon, R., Ferrer, M.A.: Towards an automatic on-line signature verifier using only one reference per signer. In: Proc. IAPR Intl. Conf. on Document Analysis and Recognition, ICDAR, pp. 1–5 (2015)

A New Context-Aware Computing Method for Urban Safety

Hyeon-Woo Kang and Hang-Bong Kang[✉]

Department of Digital Media, Catholic University of Korea, Bucheon, Gyonggi-Do, Korea
znxlwm@gmail.com, hbkang@catholic.ac.kr

Abstract. Recently, various research efforts have been made to analyze urban environments. Particularly, predicting urban safety from by means of visual perception is very important for most people. In this paper, we propose a context-aware urban safety prediction method by measuring the contexts of urban environments through visual information. In our context-aware evaluation, we define and extract positive and negative visual associations with urban safety. Then, we add these associations to a computational model of urban safety. Our experimental results show better performance than previous approaches.

Keywords: Urban safety · Context · Visual perception · Context-aware computing

1 Introduction

Recently, considerable research efforts have been devoted to analyzing urban environments [1] - [6]. In particular, research on the connection between criminal disorder and urban environments suggests that criminal behavior can be explained in terms of neighborhood disorder; this is known as the 'broken window theory'. That is, if we ignore apparently trivial disorders in the community, that trivial disorder will spread to the entire community [7], [8]. So, it is important to explore those disorders in predicting criminal behavior from urban environment data.

In previous work [2] - [6], many researchers attempted to explore street safety, wealth, uniqueness and interesting spots based on visual perception of urban environments. Salesses et al. [2] and Naik et al. [3] proposed predicting street safety using Support Vector Regression (SVR) from global features such as Histogram of Gradients (HOG), GIST and DeCAF. Ordonez et al. [4] explored perceptual characteristics of urban environments in terms of wealth, uniqueness, and safety. They also proposed computational models to jointly predict urban perceptual characteristics. Arietta et al. [5] showed predictive relationships between visual elements and city attributes such as crime rates, theft rates and danger perception. Khosla et al. [6] proposed an approach to look beyond the immediately visible urban scene using visual elements for predicting the distance to interesting places or crime rates for those places. This method of gathering predictive perceptual characteristics from visual data is similar to the tasks needed to measure the aesthetic quality of images [9] or their memorability [10].

© Springer International Publishing Switzerland 2015
V. Murino et al. (Eds.): ICIAP 2015 Workshops, LNCS 9281, pp. 298–305, 2015.
DOI: 10.1007/978-3-319-23222-5_37

(a)   (b)

Fig. 1. (a) safe place (safety score : 6.08), (b) unsafe place (safety score : 3.03)

However, for accurate safety analysis, these approaches still need to explore appropriate semantic information in predicting their perceptual characteristics. For example, Fig. 1(a) and 1(b) from the Place Pulse 1.0 dataset [2] show a safe and an unsafe place, respectively, measured using the street-score method [3]. In this approach, Fig. 2a is same place as Fig. 1a, except that there is a car. Even though the generic car in Fig. 2a may be replaced by a police-car or a crashed car such as Fig. 2b and Fig. 2c, the safety scores in Fig. 2 are still similar to Fig. 1a. This is because the semantic information regarding cars was not reflected well in predicting street-scores. Thus, if we predict public safety for a given location, it is necessary to extract much more information from visual perception than its basic semantics. In other words, context awareness is required to analyze visual perceptions regarding urban environments.

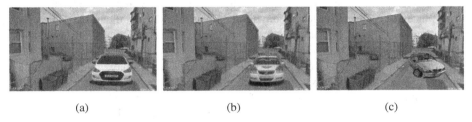

(a)   (b)   (c)

Fig. 2. (a) Normal car (safety score : 2.87), (b) Police car (safety score : 3.02), (c) Crashed car (safety score : 2.88)

In this paper, we proposed a new approach to incorporate contextual information into predicting urban safety using visual perception. We extract contextual information as a combination of spatial and temporal contexts. Then, we measure the effects of context in visual perception as an index of positives and negatives. Finally, we compute urban safety using our contextual information.

2   Context Modeling

To evaluate safety scores for given places by using urban visual perception, it is desirable to adapt a safety metric to the changing context information on the given place [11]. In this Section, we will discuss the context information gained from visual perception that may affect the safety metric.

(a) Pedestrian   (b) Police car   (c) Crashed car   (d) Night

Fig. 3. Examples of spatial and temporal context

2.1   Context Information

We define the context information of visual perception V on urban environments as the combination of spatial and temporal contexts in visual perception. It is as follows:

$$V = S + T \qquad (1)$$

The spatial context S includes various objects and their relationships. In view of urban safety, variables such as people, buildings, cars, streets, surrounding environments and activities at a given place are important elements to model spatial context S.

The temporal context T refers to the time slot and relationships within it. In view of urban safety, the time slot in a given place is strongly related to crime rates. The same place may feel safe during daylight, but unsafe during the night. Therefore, these elements should be included in the temporal context T. Fig. 3 shows some examples of spatial and temporal context.

Based on this spatial and temporal context information, we have to change the urban safety metric accordingly. From the point of view of the safety metric, some context information will increase urban safety values, but other kinds may decrease it. Thus, it is necessary to extract positive and negative contextual objects for urban safety from both spatial and temporal contexts.

2.2   Positive Contextual Objects in Urban Safety

We define positive contextual objects in urban safety as police car, policeman, a crowd of people, a clean street with numerous flowers and natural light etc. If those objects or environments exist at any given spot, they make people feel safe. Therefore, it is necessary to detect those positive contextual objects when measuring urban safety by visual perception.

To compute the positive contextual effects, we re-scored the images in which positive objects were introduced. Using these data, the positive contextual effects are computed as follows:

$$P_k = (\sum_i p_{i,k} - p_{oi,k}) / n_k \qquad (2)$$

where n_k is the number of total images including object class k, $p_{i,k}$ is the score of the modified image, and $po_{i,k}$ is the score of the original image.

2.3   Negative Contextual Objects in Urban Safety

As negative contextual objects in urban safety, we define crashed cars, streets covered with graffiti, dark night, etc. If these objects or surrounding environments feature in a given place, people feel less safe there. Thus, these negative contextual objects should also be considered in predicting urban safety.

To compute the negative contextual effects, we also re-scored the images in which positive objects are placed appropriately. The negative contextual effects are computed as follows:

$$N_k = (\sum_i no_{i,k} - n_{i,k}) / n_k \tag{3}$$

where n_k is the number of total images including object class k, $n_{i,k}$ is the score from the modified image, and $no_{i,k}$ is the score of the original image.

2.4   Contextual Effects in Urban Safety

Using the positive and negative contexts, we can compute the visual contextual effects for safety as follows:

$$V = P_{k1} - N_{k2} \tag{4}$$

where k_1 and k_2 are the object class for the positive and negative contexts, respectively.

3   Context Aware Computing for Safety Prediction

3.1   Context Extraction

Fig. 4 shows our context extraction methods. Spatial and temporal context extraction from the image is performed separately and independently. In the spatial context object detection step, we extract meaningful objects from visual perception using Felzenszwalb et al's approach [20]. This approach represents objects using mixtures of deformable part models. These models are trained using a discriminative method that requires only bounding boxes for the objects in an image. This approach uses strong low-level features based on histograms of oriented gradients (HOG) [12], [13] as image representation. HOG used to create an HOG feature pyramid. The HOG feature pyramid is composed of the HOG features of each scale of a standard image pyramid. The HOG pyramid is decomposed into deformable parts and spatial relations among the deformable parts.

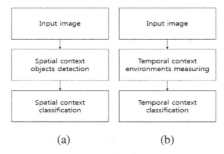

(a)   (b)

Fig. 4. Context extraction methods: (a) Spatial context extraction method. (b) Temporal context extraction method

Learning was represented as latent SVM (discriminative learning with latent variables). Latent SVM is the general class of energy-based models. This approach used part positions and hard negatives as latent variables. This approach is a detector with good performance.

For spatial context classification, the extracted objects are classified into positive, neutral and negative contexts using the Random Forest algorithm. For example, the detected cars are categorized as contributing to a positive context (e.g., police car), a neutral context (e.g., normal car), or a negative context (e.g., crashed car).

Similarly, temporal context is also computed in two stages. In the temporal context environment measurement, a given time is determined by extracting four attributes such as daytime, dawn/evening, night and dawn from visual perception. To detect attributes related with time, we extract HOG, self-similarity features (SSIM), GIST and geometric context color histograms [17]. Using these features and image attributes regarding time at a given place, we train Support Vector Regression (SVR). Following this, we determine the time of the visual perception using SVR.

In the temporal context classification, temporal context is classified into positive and negative categories. The temporal context of noon or daytime is classified as a positive context, but dawn or evening and night is classified as a negative context.

3.2   Context Aware Urban Safety Metric

Based on context information including positive and negative context, we propose a new urban safety metric. Our urban safety metric $U_{(s,t)}$ is computed as follows:

$$U_{(s,t)} = street\_score + V = street\_score + P_k - N_k$$

$$= street\_score + \left(\sum_{k1} p_{i,k1} - po_{i,k1}\right)/n_{k1} - \left(\sum_{k2} no_{j,k2} - n_{j,k2}\right)/n_{k2} \qquad (5)$$

where s and t refer to spatial and temporal context, respectively.

4 Experimental Results

To predict urban safety from visual data using context-awareness, we computed the positive and negative contexts of that place. This contextual information is reflected in the urban safety score of a given place. Fig. 5 shows an overview of our approach. Using visual perception values, we detect spatial and temporal context information that affects urban safety. Then, we classify those contexts into positive and negative context using SVM and SVR which are trained by Place Pulse DB [2]. After that, we compute the safety score for a given place by incorporating positive and negative context information. In this Section, we will discuss some experimental results for context-aware urban safety.

For detecting contexts from visual data, we constructed a DB consisting of several categories of objects such as cars, pedestrians, different time of the day, etc. In the case of cars, the car detection average precision score from PASCAL 2006 dataset is 0.64. To detect the temporal context, we extract HOG, SSIM, GIST and geometric context color histograms. Then, we learned visual attributes such as daytime, evening, night and dawn using SVR.

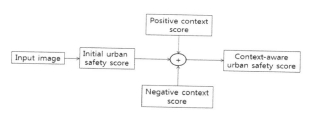

Fig. 5. An overview of our approach

Table 1 and Table 2 show weight values of each piece of contextual information relating to spatial and temporal context. To compute the weight values for spatial and temporal contextual information, we perform 3,000 crowd-sourced scoring experiments on police-car, crashed car, pedestrian and time slot. After that, we compute the weight values for police-car, crashed car and pedestrian. We also run similar experiments for time slot data. Fig. 6 shows our experimental results on the Place Pulse 1.0 dataset [2] and compares them with a previous approach. Our approach dealt with and reflected context information more accurately.

Table 1. Spatial context weights

Spatial context objects	Weights
Police-car	2.01
Crashed car	-1.76
Pedestrian	0.6

Table 2. Temporal context weights

Temporal context objects	Weights
Dawn	-1.20
Night	-2.47

5   Conclusions

In this paper, we proposed a context-aware urban safety computing method based on visual perception. We detect context information related to urban safety and extract positive and negative contexts to compute safety values accurately. By incorporating both positive and negative contexts, our urban safety computing method shows better results compared to previous approaches.

In the future, we will extend our work into a pervasive computing environment for a robust safety prediction system in which various sensor data are captured and handled. In addition, a more sophisticated high level context extraction method should be developed.

Acknowlededgements. This work was supported by the Basic Science Research Program through the National Research Foundation (NRF) funded by the Ministry of Education, Science and Technology in Korea (2010-0024641).

References

1. Lynch, K.: The image of the city, vol. 1. MIT press (1960)
2. Salesses, P., Schechtner, K., Hidalgo, C.A.: The collaborative image of the city: mapping the inequality of urban perception. PloS one **8**(7) (2013)
3. Naik, N., Philipoom, J., Raskar, R., Hidalgo, C.: Streetscore-predicting the perceived safety of one million streetscapes. In: Proceedings of the IEEE Conference on Computer Vision and Pattern Recognition Workshops, pp. 793–799 (2014)
4. Ordonez, V., Berg, T.L.: Learning high-level judgments of urban perception. In: Fleet, D., Pajdla, T., Schiele, B., Tuytelaars, T. (eds.) ECCV 2014, Part VI. LNCS, vol. 8694, pp. 494–510. Springer, Heidelberg (2014)
5. Arietta, S., Efros, A., Ramamoorthi, R., Agrawala, M.: City forensics: Using visual elements to predict non-visual city attributes. IEEE Transactions on Visualization and Computer Graphics **20**, 2624–2633 (2014)
6. Khosla, A., An, B., Lim, J.J., Torralba, A.: Looking beyond the visible scene. In: IEEE Conference on Computer Vision and Pattern Recognition (CVPR) (2014)
7. Wilson, J.Q., Kelling, G.L.: Broken windows. Atlantic monthly **249**(3), 29–38 (1982)
8. Keizer, K., Lindenberg, S., Steg, L.: The spreading of disorder. Science **322**(5908), 1681–1685 (2008)
9. Marchesotti, L., Perronnin, F., Larlus, D., Csurka, G.: Assessing the aesthetic quality of photographs using generic image descriptors. In: 2011 IEEE International Conference on Computer Vision (ICCV), pp. 1784–1791 (2011)

10. Isola, P., Xiao, J., Parikh, D., Torralba, A., Oliva, A.: What makes a photograph memorable? In: 2011 IEEE Conference on Computer Vision and Pattern Recognition(CVPR), pp. 145–152 (2014)
11. Bettini, C., Brdiczka, O., Henricksen, K., Indulska, J., Nicklas, D., Ranganathan, A., Riboni, D.: A survey of context modelling and reasoning techniques. Pervasive and Mobile Computing 6(2), 161–180 (2010)
12. Dalal, N., Triggs, B.: Histograms of oriented gradients for human detection. IEEE Computer Vision and Pattern Recognition 1, 886–893 (2005)
13. Vondrick, C., Khosla, A., Malisiewicz, T., Torralba, A.: HOGgles: visualizing object detection features. In: ICCV 2013, pp. 1–8 (2013)
14. Stefano, L.D., Mattoccia, S., Tombari, F.: An efficient algorithm for exhausrive template matching based on normalized cross correlation. In: Image Analysis and Recognition, pp. 322–327 (2004)
15. Chang, C.C., Lin, C.J.: Libsvm: a library for support vector machines. ACM Transactions on Intelligent Systems and Technology (TIST) 2(3) (2011)
16. Duda, R.O., Hart, P.E., Stork, D.G.: Pattern Classification. Wiely (2000)
17. Laffont, P.Y., Ren, Z., Tao, X., Qian, C., Hays J.: Transient Attributes for High-Level Understanding and Editing of Outdoor Scenes. ACM Transactions on Graphics – Proceedings of ACM SIGGRAPH 2014 33(4) (2014)
18. Lu, C., Lin, D., Jia, J., Tang, C.: Two-class weather classification. In: CVPR (2014)
19. Roser, M., Moosmann, F.: Classification of weather situations on single color images, intelligent vehicles symposium, pp. 798–803 (2008)
20. Felzenszwalb, P., McAllester, D., Fowlkes, C.: Discriminatively and trained, multiscale, deformable part model. In: CVPR (2008)

MADiMa 2015 - 1st International Workshop on Multimedia Assisted Dietary Management

Estimating the Nutrient Content of Commercial Foods from their Label Using Numerical Optimization

Jieun Kim$^{(\boxtimes)}$ and Mireille Boutin

Purdue University, West Lafayette, IN 47907, USA
mboutin@purdue.edu

Abstract. We propose a method for automatically estimating the amount of a given nutrient contained in a commercial food. The method applies when no part of any ingredient is removed in the preparation process. First, we automatically bound the amount of each ingredient used to prepare the food using the information provided on its label (Ingredient list and Nutrition Facts Label) along with the nutrition information for at least some of the ingredients. Using these bounds (minimum and maximum amount for each ingredient), we obtain an initial set of bounds (minimum and maximum amount) for the nutrient considered. We then utilize the Simplex algorithm to refine these bounds on the nutrient content. Our motivating application is the management of medical diets that require keeping track of certain nutrients such as phenylalanine (Phe) in the case of the inherited metabolic disease phenylketonuria (PKU). To test our method, we used it to estimate the Phe content of 25 commercial foods. In a majority of cases (17/25), the bounds obtained were within 10.4mg of each other and thus our method provided a very accurate . estimate (±5.2mg) for the Phe content of the foods.

1   Introduction

Some medical diets require keeping track of one's intake of certain nutrients. In order to do this, patients need to have access to the nutritional information for the food they consume. While many nutrients are listed on the Nutrition Facts Label of commercial foods, the information provided is not complete. Indeed, not all nutrients are listed on the label, and the content for the ones that are listed is rounded. Being able to automatically determine the amount of a nutrient contained in the food would thus be helpful for these patients.

Our motivating application is the management of inborn errors of metabolism, the most common of which is phenylketonuria (PKU). PKU is characterized by an inability to metabolize Phenylalanine (Phe) [2], which leads to an abnormal accumulation of Phe in the patient's blood. High blood Phe levels affect the patient's neurological system; they are especially detrimental to the intellectual growth of infants. Thus, one of the main goals in the clinical management of PKU is to maintain low blood Phe levels. For most patients, this is achieved by following a strict Phe-restricted diet [5] which requires measuring

© Springer International Publishing Switzerland 2015
V. Murino et al. (Eds.): ICIAP 2015 Workshops, LNCS 9281, pp. 309–316, 2015.
DOI: 10.1007/978-3-319-23222-5_38

the food consumed and multiplying the amount by a food specific Phe ratio. Unfortunately, the Phe content of commercial foods is not listed on the Nutrition Facts Label, and so patients must obtain the Phe ratios from a food list (e.g., [4,6,7]). As these databases only list a limited number of foods, alternative methods for finding the Phe content of foods would be desirable.

In this paper, we propose to estimate the content of a given nutrient such as Phe by obtaining a minimum bound and a maximum bound for the nutrient amount contained in the food. To do this, we use the food label (Nutrition Fact Label and Ingredient list), along with the USDA Food Database [7] (USDA database).

From the food label, we get the serving size x and the n ingredients used in the recipe. Let A_i denote the weight (in grams) of ingredient i, for $i = 1, \ldots, n$. Since the ingredients are listed in decreasing order of weight, we have $A_i \geq A_{i+1}$. If no part of any ingredient is removed in the preparation process, we thus have

$$x \geq A_1 \geq A_2 \geq \ldots \geq A_n > 0, \tag{1}$$
$$A_1 + A_2 + \ldots + A_n = x. \tag{2}$$

The food label gives us the rounded content y^{nut} of many nutrients. Let Δ^{nut} be the rounding error for the content of nutrient "nut". We can look for the amount y_i^{nut} of nutrient "nut" in one gram of ingredient i in the USDA database. If no part of any ingredient is removed in the preparation process, we have

$$y^{nut} - \Delta^{nut} \leq \sum_{i=1}^{n} y_i^{nut} A_i \leq y^{nut} + \Delta^{nut}. \tag{3}$$

In a preliminary version of this work [3], we proposed an iterative method for finding bounds, $A_{i_{min}}$ and $A_{i_{max}}$, for each ingredient amount A_i, which is applicable even if the nutrient data for some of the ingredients is missing. The bounds obtained this way yield a first set of bounds for the amount of the considered nutrient (e.g., Phe) contained in the food. This is Step 1 of our proposed method for nutrient content estimation, which we describe in Section 2. This step requires prior knowledge of the amount of the considered nutrient (e.g., Phe) for each ingredient. For example, when trying to estimate the Phe content of the food, then the Phe contents for all the ingredients must be known. Since many ingredients not listed in the USDA database clearly do not contain a significant amount of proteins (e.g., food coloring, natural flavor, etc.) and thus can be considered free of Phe, this is a reasonable assumption.

In Step 2 of our method, we make use of the Simplex algorithm in order to further narrow the interval of bounds for the nutrient content. This step is described in Section 3. Our method (Step 1 and Step 2) is applied to the problem of approximating the ingredient amounts and estimating the Phe content of various commercial foods in Section 4. We conclude in Section 5.

2 Step 1: Nutrient Content Estimation Using Approximate Ingredient Amounts

If we knew A_i, the amount of ingredient i, along with p_i, the number of milligrams of a given nutrient per gram of ingredient i, then $p_i A_i$ would be the nutrient contributed by ingredient i, and the total given nutrient in the food would be $\Sigma_{i=1}^n p_i A_i$. Therefore, we have the following bounds for the nutrient content (NUT),

$$\Sigma_{i=1}^n p_i A_{i_{min}} \leq NUT \leq \Sigma_{i=1}^n p_i A_{i_{max}}. \tag{4}$$

An approximate inverse recipe method to estimate a minimal and maximal bound for each ingredient $(A_{i_{min}}, A_{i_{max}})$, previously proposed in [3]. We briefly describe the method in Section 2.1. These estimates shall then be put into Equation (4) to obtain a first set of bounds for the content of the considered nutrient NUT.

2.1 Estimating Ingredient Amounts Based on an Approximate Inverse Recipe Method

To obtain an initial range estimate for each ingredient i, Procedure 1 is applied. Then, the initial bounds $A_{i_{min}} \leq A_i \leq A_{i_{max}}$ are narrowed further using Procedure 2.

Further refinement can be obtained using Procedures 3 and Procedure 4. We apply Procedure 3 to increase the minimal bound and Procedure 4 to decrease the maximal bound. Note that the minimal bound can only be refined if y_i^{nut} is known for all i. Otherwise, the bound remains as it is. This is not the case for the maximal bound.

Procedure 1. Initial bound

$A_{1_{min}} \leftarrow \frac{x}{n}, \quad A_{1_{max}} \leftarrow x$
for $i = 2$ to n **do**
  $A_{i_{min}} \leftarrow 0, \quad A_{i_{max}} \leftarrow \frac{x}{i}$
  for given nutrient with content y^{nut} **do**
    if $y_1^{nut} \neq 0$ **then**
      $A_{1_{max}} \leftarrow min(A_{1_{max}}, \frac{y^{nut} + \Delta^{nut}}{y_1^{nut} - \Delta_1^{nut}})$
    for $i = 2$ to n **do**
      if $y_i \neq 0$ **then**
        $A_{i_{max}} \leftarrow min(A_{i_{max}}, A_{i-1_{max}}, \frac{y^{nut} + \Delta^{nut}}{y_i^{nut} - \Delta_i^{nut}})$
      else
        $A_{i_{max}} \leftarrow min(A_{i_{max}}, A_{i-1_{max}})$

To estimate the A_i's, we first select a set of nutrients that are listed on the Nutrition Facts Label (e.g., carbohydrates, sodium, protein, etc.). We then apply Procedure 1 (running over all selected nutrients), followed by Procedure 2.

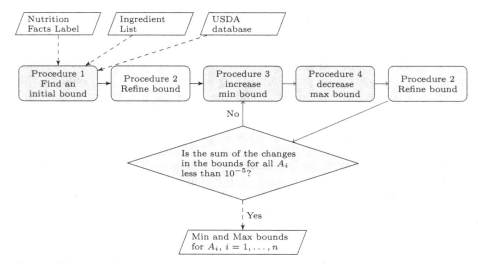

Fig. 1. Schematic Diagram of Proposed Method to Estimate the Ingredient Amounts

---

Procedure 2. Refining bound

---

for $i = 1$ to n do
$\quad A_{i_{min}} \leftarrow max(A_{i_{min}}, x - \Sigma_{j=1, j \neq i}^{n} A_{j_{max}})$
$\quad A_{i_{max}} \leftarrow min(A_{i_{max}}, x - \Sigma_{j=1, j \neq i}^{n} A_{j_{min}})$

Procedure 3. To increase the minimal bound

---

for given nutrient with content y^{nut} such that y_k^{nut} exists $\forall k$ do
$\quad$ if $y_n^{nut} \neq 0$ then
$\qquad A_{n_{min}} \leftarrow max(A_{n_{min}}, \frac{(y^{nut} - \Delta^{nut}) - \Sigma_{k=1}^{n-1}(y_k^{nut} + \Delta_k^{nut})A_{k_{max}}}{y_n^{nut} + \Delta_n^{nut}})$
$\quad$ for $i = n-1$ to 1 do
$\qquad$ if $y_i^{nut} \neq 0$ then
$\qquad\quad A_{i_{min}} \leftarrow max(A_{i_{min}}, A_{i+1_{min}}, \frac{(y^{nut} - \Delta^{nut}) - \Sigma_{k=1, k \neq i}^{n}(y_k^{nut} + \Delta_k^{nut})A_{k_{max}}}{y_i^{nut} + \Delta_i^{nut}})$

Procedure 4. To decrease the maximal bound

---

for given nutrient with content y^{nut} do
$\quad$ for $k = 1$ to n do
$\qquad$ if y_k^{nut} does not exist then
$\qquad\quad y_k^{nut} \leftarrow 0, \quad \Delta_k^{nut} \leftarrow 0$
$\quad$ if $y_1^{nut} \neq 0$ then
$\qquad A_{1_{max}} \leftarrow min(A_{1_{max}}, \frac{(y^{nut} + \Delta^{nut}) - \Sigma_{k=2}^{n}(y_k^{nut} - \Delta_k^{nut})A_{k_{min}}}{y_1^{nut} - \Delta_1^{nut}})$
$\quad$ for $i = 2$ to n do
$\qquad$ if $y_i^{nut} \neq 0$ then
$\qquad\quad A_{i_{max}} \leftarrow min(A_{i_{max}}, A_{i-1_{max}}, \frac{(y^{nut} + \Delta^{nut}) - \Sigma_{k=1, k \neq i}^{n}(y_k^{nut} - \Delta_k^{nut})A_{k_{min}}}{y_i^{nut} - \Delta_i^{nut}})$

After that, we keep repeating Procedure 3 and Procedure 4 (running over all selected nutrients), followed by Procedure 2, until our estimates change by less than 10^{-5} between consecutive repetitions. This is illustrated in Figure 1.

The accuracy of our method depends on the food considered and can vary from one ingredient to the next. However it is not necessary that all ingredient amounts be precisely estimated in order to get a good estimate on the content of the query nutrient NUT.

3   Step 2: Nutrient Content Estimate Refinement Using Simplex Algorithm

Observe that the bounds obtained using Equation (4) correspond to ingredient amounts that can violate Equation (2). More specifically, neither $\sum_{i=1}^{n} A_{i_{min}}$ nor $\sum_{i=1}^{n} A_{i_{max}}$ equal to a serving size x in general. This indicates that it should be possible to further refine the content estimate obtained in Step 1. We propose to do this using the Simplex algorithm [1] which is a well-known linear programming tool. The Simplex algorithm first finds an initial feasible solution in Phase I. Then, in Phase II, it moves along the edges of the polytope defined by the constraints while evaluating the cost until it reaches an extreme value. In the case of the nutrient content estimation problem, the cost function is the summation of the nutrient content coming from each ingredient, the nutrient content (NUT), $\sum_{i=1}^{n} p_i A_i$.

The linear constraints of the nutrient content estimation problem are defined by Definition 1. A feasible solution to this problem, a set of A_i, must be selected from the obtained minimal and maximal bounds for each ingredient and should satisfy our assumption that there is no loss of any ingredient. Therefore, the linear constraints are composed of Equation (1), Equation (2), and the obtained ranges of ingredient amounts in Section 2.1.

Definition 1. Nutrient content estimate using the Simplex algorithm

minimize, maximize $\sum_{i=1}^{n} p_i A_i$ *where*

$$\begin{cases} \sum_{i=1}^{n} A_i = x \\ x \geq A_1 \geq A_2 \geq \cdots \geq A_n > 0 \\ A_{i_{min}} \leq A_i \leq A_{i_{max}}, \quad i = 1, \ldots, n \end{cases}$$

Since all constraints are equalities, any feasible solutions satisfying the constraints are points on the edges of a (n-1)-dimensional polytope. Hence, once an initial feasible point is found from Phase I of the Simplex algorithm, in Phase II, we look through the extreme points of the polytope until the cost at any adjacent points of an extreme point does not decrease anymore. The cost at the point becomes the minimum of the nutrient content for a serving size x gram of a food. Similarly, once the cost function does not increase anymore, we set the maximum bound for the nutrient content to the value of the cost function.

4   Numerical Experiment: Application to Phenylalanine (Phe) Content Estimation

We experimented with our method to estimate the Phenylalanine (Phe) content for 25 commercial food items. The results are shown in Table 1. The table presents the minimum and maximum bounds for each food obtained by our method using six nutrients (protein, sodium, calories, carbohydrates, fat, and cholesterol). Both the results after Step 1 (column 4) and Step 2 (column 5) are given in order to see the improvement resulting from performing Step 2.

For comparison, the Phe data from two databases, USDA database [7] and a low-protein food database [6], are written in the first and second column of Table 1. When there exists no data related to the item from that database, we indicated the case with 'N/A'. As we expected, only a part of the food items considered has Phe data in the USDA database (6/25) or Phe data in the low-protein food database (14/25). Furthermore, some of the data listed in our table may be inexact as we were unable to find the specific brand of product considered and used a generic version instead. For example, the Phe content for Tomato soup specifically from Campbell company is not presented in the USDA database while the USDA database contains the Phe content of Tomato soup for any brand.

In contrast, Step 1 of our approximate method was able to provide bounds for the Phe content of all targeted food items, as shown in the fourth column of Table 1 where the estimated minimum and maximum values for the Phe content are written in parenthesis. The range between the minimum and the maximum bounds was less than 10mg for 16 food items, and less than 25mg for 19 food items. The estimated bounds for the Phe content were within no more than 3 mg from at least one of the databases for 22 items, which is 88% of the 25 foods considered. In the case of butter, rice krispies cereal and waffles, our range exclude the Phe value from both databases. This is most likely due to the violation of our assumption that no part of any ingredient is discarded during the preparation process. For example, there is considerable drying in the preparation of cereal, and liquid (whey) is discarded in the preparation of butter.

After Step 2, the interval between bounds for the Phe content narrowed significantly more in 10 cases (see the fifth column of Table 1). Step 2 narrowed the range of the estimated Phe bounds for one serving of Salsa Sauce from 24.68mg to 10.33mg. In the case of garlic mashed potatoes and sweet potato tot, the ranges of the estimated bounds for Phe content decreased to the values less than half of the ranges after Step 1. Moreover, the largest range between the minimum and maximum bounds after Step 2 became 54.76mg, less than one third of the highest range after Step 1 (165.61mg). The Simplex algorithm in Step 2 could not find an initial feasible solution for 9 items; these are denoted by 'DNE^c' in the table. This could be because an ingredient used to prepare the food did not coincide with the ingredient listed in the USDA database. Another inconsistency could have occurred because we neglected ingredients with negligible amounts for which the USDA database did not provide any data. However, even though we could not improve the bounds for the Phe content any further for these 9

Table 1. Comparison of phenylalanine content estimates obtained with our methods and two food composition databases.

Description(serving size)	USDA database[7]	low-protein food database[6]	After Step 1	After Step 2
Carr's Whole Wheat Crackers(17g)	81.6mg	75mg	(53.61mg, 85.11mg)	(53.61mg, 85.11mg)
Ketchup(17g)	4.42mg	10.2mg	(0.70mg, 7.09mg)	(1.20mg, 6.57mg)
KIT KAT Milk Chocolate(42g)	113.4mg	131.86mg	(129.56mg, 238.91mg)	(144.27mg, 191.53mg)
Campbell's Tomato soup(122g)	68.32mg[a]	66.90mg	(33.21mg, 102.91mg)	(40.69mg, 95.45mg)
Cheerios Cereal(28g)	175.84mg	165mg	(179.86mg, 180.51mg)	DNE[c]
Rice Krispies Cereal(33g)	116.82mg	107mg	(91.54mg, 94.80mg)	DNE[c]
Enchilada Sauce(60g)	N/A	6mg	(0.41mg, 35.69mg)	(0.41mg, 34.14mg)
Eggo waffle(70g)	N/A	238mg	(196.26mg, 216.35mg)	(196.26mg, 216.35mg)
Garlic chili pepper sauce(9g)	N/A	1.93mg	(1.37mg, 6.96mg)	(2.65mg, 5.27mg)
Salsa sauce(30g)	N/A	11mg	(1.53mg, 26.21mg)	(7.90mg, 18.23mg)
Garlic mashed potatoes(124g)	N/A	N/A[b]	(56.89mg, 222.50mg)	(139.51mg, 162.23mg)
Butter with Canola Oil(14g)	N/A	6mg	(11.88mg, 17.66mg)	(12.06mg, 17.66mg)
Go-Gurt(64g)	N/A	120mg	(116.38mg, 120.95mg)	DNE[c]
Jell-O Gelatin Snacks(98g)	N/A	23.76mg	(10.01mg, 30.44mg)	(10.01mg, 30.44mg)
Marshmallow Peeps(42g)	N/A	21mg	(19.17mg, 23.56mg)	DNE[c]
Ore-Ida French fries(84g)	N/A	76mg	(77.64mg, 78.77mg)	(77.64mg, 78.76mg)
Spicy Brown Mustard(5g)	N/A	8mg	(9.87mg, 10.35mg)	(10.11mg, 10.16mg)
Starburst Fruit Chews(40g)	N/A	5.42mg	(0.00mg, 4.48mg)	DNE[c]
Vinaigrette Balsamic Dressing(31g)	N/A	3mg	(0.00mg, 5.53mg)	(0.00mg, 5.53mg)
Yoplait Original Strawberry(170g)	N/A	284.67mg	(287.11mg, 291.08mg)	DNE[c]
ALTOIDS peppermint(2g)	N/A	N/A	(0.43mg, 4.22mg)	DNE[c]
Jell-O Cheesecake Pudding(26g)	N/A	N/A	(0.91mg, 0.98mg)	DNE[c]
Sweet potato Tot(85g)	N/A	N/A	(54.87mg, 113.77mg)	(71.91mg, 95.82mg)
Taco Shells(32g)	N/A	N/A	(36.69mg, 38.31mg)	(36.69mg, 38.31mg)
Vanilla bean Ice cream(87g)	N/A	N/A	(206.87mg, 211.09mg)	DNE[c]

[a] Any brand Tomato soup, condensed. Not Campbell's product.
[b] Database has a value, but with a different protein content.
[c] Simplex algorithm could not find a solution

items after Step 2, notice that the bounds after Step 1 in these cases were already very close to each other, with a difference of less than 5mg per serving size.

5   Summary and Conclusions

The Food Safety and Inspection Service of the USDA (United States Department of Agriculture) mandates food companies to label their products with an Ingredient list and a Nutrition Facts Label. This information is important, but incomplete. Indeed, some nutrients such as Phenylalanine (Phe) are not listed on the label. This is problematic for individuals with inherited metabolic disorders such as PKU who must carefully monitor their Phe intake. In an attempt to help these individuals to manage their medical diets, we proposed a method for estimating the content of a given nutrient automatically from the food label information. We assume that no part of any ingredient is removed while preparing a food. This gives two constraints: the sum of each ingredient content equals to a serving size for the food and the weighted sum of a nutrient content for one gram of each ingredient equals to the nutrient content for one serving of the food. We also use the fact that the ingredients are listed in decreasing amounts (per weight). The proposed method is applicable even if the nutrient content of some of the ingredients is not fully known.

We applied our method to the problem of Phe content estimation. Our approach finds bounds for the Phe content of a food based on the estimated ingredient amounts in Step 1. Step 2 refines the results using linear programming (Simplex algorithm). We showed our results for various commercial foods in Table 1. The intervals between the estimated bounds for the Phe content after Step 2 were within 10.4mg for 17 items and within 24mg for 21 items out of the 25 foods considered. In contrast, the intervals were within 10mg for 16 items and within 25mg for 19 items after Step 1.

While two current databases did not contain Phe data for all the food we considered, our method provided a Phe content estimate for all of them. Hence, we believe that our work provides a useful tool to help PKU patients manage their diet. Moreover, our method can be used to estimate other nutrient contents, or to increase the precision of the nutrient content listed on the Nutrition Facts Label. So it should be helpful in managing other diets as well.

References

1. Benhamadou, M.: On the simplex algorithm algorithm revised form. Advances in Engineering Software **33**(11), 769–777 (2002)
2. Huttenlocher, P.R.: The neuropathology of phenylketonuria: human and animal studies. European Journal of Pediatrics **159**(2), S102–S106 (2000)
3. Kim, J., Boutin, M.: An approximate inverse recipe method with application to automatic food analysis. In: 2014 IEEE Symposium on Computational Intelligence in Healthcare and e-health (CICARE), pp. 32–39. IEEE (2014)
4. Kim, J., Boutin, M.: A list of phenylalanine to protein ratios for common foods. ECE Technical Reports. Paper 456 (2014). http://docs.lib.purdue.edu/ecetr/456
5. National Institute of Health: Consensus development conference statement. Phenylketonuria: Screening and Management (October 16–18, 2000). http://www.nichd.nih.gov/publications/pubs/pku/sub3.cfm
6. Schuett, V.E.: Low Protein Food List for PKU, 3rd edn (2010)
7. U.S. Department of Agriculture, Agricultural Research Service: USDA national nutrient database for standard reference, release 25. Nutrient Data Laboratory Home Page (2012). http://www.ars.usda.gov/ba/bhnrc/ndl

The Use of Temporal Information
in Food Image Analysis

Yu Wang[1]([⊠]), Ye He[2], Fengqing Zhu[1], Carol Boushey[3], and Edward Delp[1]

[1] School of Electrical and Computer Engineering, Purdue University,
West Lafayette, Indiana, USA
wang1317@purdue.edu
[2] Google, Mountain View, California, USA
[3] Cancer Epidemiology Program, University of Hawaii Cancer Center,
Honolulu, Hawaii, USA

Abstract. We have developed a dietary assessment system that uses food images captured by a mobile device. Food identification is a crucial component of our system. Achieving a high classification rates is challenging due to the large number of food categories and variability in food appearance. In this paper, we propose to improve food classification by incorporating temporal information. We employ recursive Bayesian estimation to incrementally learn from a person's eating history. We show an improvement of food classification accuracy by 11% can be achieved.

1 Introduction

Mobile devices will transform the healthcare industry by increasing accessibility to quality care and wellness management. Dietary intake provides valuable insights for fitness monitoring as well as mounting intervention programs for chronic diseases. Accurate methods to assess food and nutrient intake are essential [7,15]. We have developed a dietary assessment system, known as the mobile Food Record (mFR) [1,18], to automatically estimate food type, volume, nutrients, and energy from a food image captured by a mobile device [18,19]. The mFR system consists of: a web-based user interface, a mobile application and a backend system including a computational server and an associated database system [2,18].

To achieve high classification accuracy in food images is challenging due to lighting and pose variations, background noise and occlusion. One type of food can have various serving styles (different portion sizes, distinct appearance). As a result, the use of contextual information may reduce the complexity of food image analysis. "Context" refers to any prior knowledge that is not derived from the image pixel values [4]. The use of contextual information has gained attention in psychology and computer vision with respect to its effects on visual search,

E. Delp—This work was sponsored by grant from the National Institutes of Health under grant NIEH/NIH 2R01ES012459-06. Address all correspondence to E. J. Delp: ace@ecn.purdue.edu or see www.tadaproject.org.

V. Murino et al. (Eds.): ICIAP 2015 Workshops, LNCS 9281, pp. 317–325, 2015.
DOI: 10.1007/978-3-319-23222-5_39

localization and recognition [4,14,16]. There has been work in using contextual information in food image analysis. Matsuda et al [13] proposed to use manifold ranking method to improve food classification rate using food co-occurrence statistics. Beijbom et al [5] made use of geographic location as context and focused on identifying foods in restaurants. In previous work [9] we incorporated two types of contextual knowledge, food co-occurrence patterns and an individual's food consumption frequency for a week.

In this paper, we propose to incorporate temporal information to learn a person's dietary pattern based on a recursive Bayesian model to improve food classification accuracy. The learning process is achieved by incorporating user feedback in the food classification. The user feedback consists of confirmed, modified, or added food labels based on the food image analysis.

2   Food Image Analysis

2.1   Image Acquisition and User Feedback

In our mFR system, a mobile application is used to capture a pair of before and after meal images at each eating occasion [18]. The images are sent to the server for automatic image analysis. Results are sent back to the user for confirmation and review using the mobile application [2]. In this paper, we used food images collected from one of our dietary assessment studies, where 45 participants were asked to acquire a pair of before and after meal images at each eating occasion for roughly 7 days. A total of 1453 food images were analyzed classifying 56 commonly eaten food items using the methods described in [10,11,19]. Figure 1 shows the food consumption pattern of a subset of foods from our data. Each square in Fig.1 indicates the consumption frequency of a particular food, λ_i, for a participant, S_j, where the consumption frequency is defined as followed,

$$Freq(\lambda_i^{S_j}) = \frac{N_i}{N_{\text{total}}} \ . \tag{1}$$

N_i is the number of times that S_j has consumed λ_i and N_{total} is the total number of food items that S_j has consumed. The food consumption pattern for S_j is $[Freq(\lambda_1^{S_j}), \ldots, Freq(\lambda_n^{S_j})]$, where n is the total number of food categories.

To evaluate our learning model, we manually selected participants with similar food consumption patterns to build personalized eating datasets for a month. We measure the similarity using Euclidean distance between each food consumption pattern and used *K-means* to find clusters. For example, one of the personalized eating dataset contains food images from participant 14, 17, 20 and 32, which can be treated as images from a single participant for a month. As illustrated in Fig.1, participant 14, 17, 20 and 32 all show relatively high consumption frequency of milk, salad mix and lasagna. We constructed three separate datasets, each features a different food consumption style and contains approximately 120 images. We labeled them as *Dataset 1, 2 and 3* from *User 1, 2 and 3*.

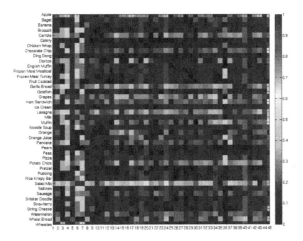

Fig. 1. A food consumption pattern. Horizontal axis represents the participants and vertical axis represents food items.

2.2 Image Segmentation and Food Identification

We used graph based segmentation using local variation [8,10]. The internal difference of a segmented region is defined to be the largest weight in the minimum spanning tree while the difference between two segmented regions is defined to be the minimum weight edge connecting the two regions [8]. The ratio of the region difference to the internal difference within at least one of the two regions determines whether two regions are segmented or not. The degree to which the difference between regions must be larger than minimum internal difference is controlled by a threshold k, where k roughly controls the size of the regions in the resulting segmentation. In our experiments, k was initially set to 150. For each segment, a set of color, texture and local region features are extracted and classified using k-Nearest Neighbor (KNN), vocabulary trees and Support Vector Machines (SVM) [12,19]. Finally we combine the decisions from all the feature channels using a majority vote rule.

3 Temporal Context

Temporal context in this paper refers to which days a person eats a particular food. An example might be that person A drinks 2% milk everyday while person B never has milk but eats Greek yogurt everyday. Such time-related eating habits can be of great help when designing a personalized training model because it allows the classifier to only select among the food classes relevant to an individual's dietary pattern [9]. According to representative cross-sectional surveys collected between 1999-2008, less than 1,000 foods capture 99% of the foods consumed in the United States for individuals between 11-65 years old and that the number of foods consumed by each person is far less [6].

3.1 Recursive Bayesian Model

In this paper, we use recursive Bayesian estimation to incrementally learn a person's dietary pattern [3,17]. We model whether a person, S_j eats a particular food, λ_i as an independent Bernoulli trial,

$$W = \begin{cases} 1, X \\ 0, 1 - X \end{cases} .$$

where $W = 1, X$ represents S_j eats λ_i with a possibility, X, and X is assumed to follow a Gaussian-like distribution with the support from 0 to 1.

We would like to estimate the probability, P_{λ_i}, that a person, S_j, will eat a particular food, λ on the next day given the past. Let $p_{\lambda_i}(x^k)$ be the probability density function (PDF) representing S_j eats λ_i on the kth day, and z^k be the observation whether S_j eats λ_i on the kth day. In our case, the observation, z^k is obtained from the user feedback in the mFR. The following equations describe the posteriori update step in the recursive Bayesian network,

$$p_{\lambda_i}(x^k|z^{1:k}) = \frac{p_{\lambda_i}(z^k|x^k)p_{\lambda_i}(x^k|z^{1:k-1})}{p_{\lambda_i}(z^k|z^{1:k-1})} = \frac{\text{likelihood} \times \text{prior}}{\text{normalization term}} . \quad (2)$$

Initially, $p_{\lambda_i}(x^1)$ is assumed to follow a Gaussian-like distribution centered at 0.5 with unit variance. The likelihood and prior PDFs are updated according to the user's feedback. If the user eats λ on the kth day, $p_{\lambda_i}(z^k|x^k)$ becomes the Gaussian-like distribution centered at 1 with unit variance, otherwise the distribution centers at 0. $p_{\lambda_i}(x^k|z^{1:k})$ is used to predict $p_{\lambda_i}(x^{k+1}|z^{1:k})$ and the PDF is computed by multiplying the likelihood and prior followed by normalization between 0 and 1. On the $k + 1^{\text{th}}$ day, the optimal estimate of P_{λ_i} is computed as $P_{\lambda_i} = \arg\max_x p_{\lambda_i}(x^k|z^{1:k})$.

For all the foods in the training dataset, we have a set of probabilities,

$$\Psi^{k+1} = \left[P^{k+1}_{\lambda_1}, \ldots, P^{k+1}_{\lambda_n}\right]^{\text{T}} .$$

where n is the total number of food categories. We further define the context-based confidence scores (CCS) to be:

$$\Phi^{k+1} = \left[\phi^{k+1}_{\lambda_1}, \ldots, \phi^{k+1}_{\lambda_n}\right]^{\text{T}} = \left[\omega P^{k+1}_{\lambda_1}, \ldots, \omega P^{k+1}_{\lambda_n}\right]^{\text{T}} . \quad (3)$$

where ω controls the trust weight we assigned to the context-based decisions (more details in Sect.3.2).

3.2 Decision Fusion

So far, we have obtained the confidence scores from both image analysis based on multiple feature channels and temporal context. From the image analysis, a set of candidate classes was assigned to each segmented region, S_q, associated with the corresponding confidence scores for each food class:

$$\Lambda^{\text{auto}}_{\text{cand}} = \left[\lambda^{\text{auto}}_1, \ldots, \lambda^{\text{auto}}_n\right]^{\text{T}} , \quad \Phi^{\text{auto}}_{\text{cand}} = \left[\phi^{\text{auto}}_1, \ldots, \phi^{\text{auto}}_n\right]^{\text{T}} .$$

where $\Lambda_{\text{cand}}^{\text{auto}}$ represents the candidate set, $\Phi_{\text{cand}}^{\text{auto}}$ indicates the corresponding confidence scores of n different food classes in the training dataset, i.e., $n = 56$ food classes in our dataset. From (3), we know the context-based decision for each food class on a certain day. To combine the above two source of decisions, we used a strategy of maximum confidence score. The final score is determined as:

$$\Phi_{\text{cand}}^{\text{final}} = \left[\phi_1^{\text{auto}}, \ldots, \phi_n^{\text{auto}}\right]^{\text{T}} + \left[\omega P_{\lambda_1} \ldots \omega P_{\lambda_n}\right]^{\text{T}} . \tag{4}$$

ω, also in (3), is set to be $1/h$ of the maximum automatic analysis based confidence score: $\omega = \frac{1}{h} \max(\Phi_{\text{cand}}^{\text{auto}})$. In our experiments, we observed best results when h was set to 4-5.

4   Experimental Results

Three separate datasets (i.e. *Dataset 1, 2 and 3* described above) with a total of 358 food images were used with and without temporal context. Fifty-six unique food items were contained in the datasets. Each dataset features different food composition and consumption style. For example, milk, lasagna, mixed salad and garlic bread are the most frequently-consumed foods in *Dataset 1* while *Dataset 2* does not have any frequently-consumed foods except milk. *Dataset 3* represents a significant dietary pattern change within a month. The first three weeks in *Dataset 3* have similar food consumption style as *Dataset 1*. However, we selected data from participant 7 in Fig.1 for the last week, which has noticeably different eating pattern.

Figure 2 shows how the recursive Bayesian network updates the prediction probabilities for three example food items in *Dataset 1*. On Day 1, every food has the same prediction of 0.5. In the end, the predictions of milk, orange and pretzel converge to 0.99, 0.34 and 0.12 respectively. Milk was consumed almost every day in *Dataset 1*, so the blue curve in Fig.2 gradually increases to show improved confidence. Note the prediction for pretzel decreases and the red curve for orange oscillates around 0.3 because pretzel or orange were consumed less frequently.

Note we used the food label with the highest confidence score from classifier, and define the classification accuracy as, $\Theta = \frac{TP}{TP+FP+TN}$, where TP denotes True Positives (correctly detected food segments), FP denotes False Positives (incorrectly detected food segments or misidentified foods) and TN denotes True Negatives (food not detected).

As we show below the classification accuracy from the highest confidence score is in the range of 50-65%. In the typical operation of our mFR system we report the top 4 food labels and have a classification accuracy of 80-85% [11]. In this paper we want to emphasize how the contextual information improves the classifier performance.

Figure 3 demonstrates the food classification accuracy improvement. The blue lines in Fig.3(a), 3(b) and 3(c) indicate the average daily food classification accuracy with temporal context, Θ_{context}, while the red lines indicate the one

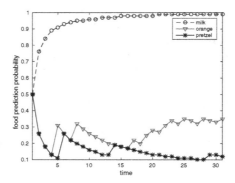

Fig. 2. Food occurrence prediction of three food items (Blue: Milk; Red: Orange; Black: Pretzel).

without, Θ_{auto}. The accuracy improvement is illustrated in Fig.3(b) is determined by $\frac{\Theta_{\text{context}} - \Theta_{\text{auto}}}{\Theta_{\text{auto}}}$. As shown in Fig.3(d), the accuracy improvement drops from Day 10 to Day 20 as the baseline (classification accuracy without context) increases from 47% to 57%. This implies that the proposed method is more effective when the automatic image analysis does not work well. If we set a threshold for the baseline, the average accuracy improvement when the baseline is above 0.55 is just 6.92% compared to 32.97% when the baseline is below 0.55. The 80% accuracy rate achieved with temporal context on Day 25 demonstrates the effectiveness of the proposed method when the automatic image analysis result is poor. In *Dataset 2* , the classification accuracy without context is always above 0.55 (see the red line in Fig.3(b)). The deep valley shown in Fig.3(e) implies the learning process in the first week. Nevertheless, Fig.3(d) and Fig.3(e) both illustrate an ascent trend of accuracy improvement.

We selected the images of the last 7 days to have a noticeably different food consumption pattern compared to the first 23 days in *Dataset 3*. We would like to verify the behavior of our training model under circumstance where a person may change their eating style. As expected, the blue line and the red line intersect in Fig.3(c) on Day 24. We witnessed a huge drop in Fig.3(f) followed by the re-learning state. The accuracy improvement is negative on Day 24, because the context-based prediction puts more confidence on the specific food, which *Dataset 3* no longer contains after changing one's eating habit, for example, milk is not consumed on Day 24. Due to the dietary change in *Dataset 3*, the increasing trend of classification accuracy is not as conspicuous as Fig.3(d) and Fig.3(e). Table 1 summarizes two statistics for the datasets, average daily classification accuracy (in %) and average daily accuracy improvement (in %). Due to our dataset selection, the classification accuracy using automatic image analysis alone in *Dataset 2* is significantly higher than other datasets. Thus, the accuracy improvement for *Dataset 2* is expected to be lower (3.85%). The fact that *Dataset 2* has less frequently-consumed foods also contributed to the lower

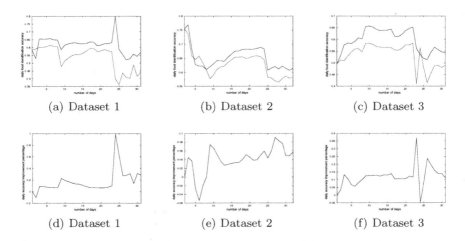

(a) Dataset 1   (b) Dataset 2   (c) Dataset 3

(d) Dataset 1   (e) Dataset 2   (f) Dataset 3

Fig. 3. Learning curves for one month. Daily classification rates with(blue) and without(red) temporal context are illustrated in (a),(b) and (c). Corresponding accuracy improvements are shown in (d),(e) and (f).

accuracy improvement. When a person has a more consistent eating pattern, such as *User 1*'s dataset, the classification accuracy gain using temporal contextual information is significantly higher (18.45%). On average, the proposed method of utilizing temporal context shows approximately $11\%(\approx \frac{18.45+3.85+12.39}{3}\%)$ improvement (see Table 1).

Table 1. Food classification performance statistics

statistics	user ID	with context	without context
average daily	user1	61.88	53.23
classification	user2	65.25	62.90
accuracy(%)	user3	59.69	53.28
average daily	user1	18.45	
accuracy	user2	3.85	
improvement(%)	user3	12.39	

5 Conclusions

In this paper we investigated the use of temporal context to improve food classification accuracy. We used a recursive Bayesian network to achieve active learning. Experimental results showed the classification accuracy was improved by 11% on average. In the future, we plan to extend our learning model by combining various ranges of eating history and separating eating occasions based on the time of day.

References

1. The TADA project. http://tadaproject.org
2. Ahmad, Z., Khanna, N., Kerr, D., Boushey, C., Delp, E.: A mobile phone user interface for image-based dietary assessment. In: Proceedings of the IS&T/SPIE Conference on Mobile Devices and Multimedia 9030, 903007-1-9, San Francisco, CA (February 2014)
3. Arulampalam, S., Maskell, S., Gordon, N., Clapp, T.: A tutorial on particle filters for online nonlinear/non-gaussian bayesian tracking. IEEE Transactions on Signal Processing 50(2), 174–188 (2002)
4. Bar, M.: Visual objects in context. Nature Reviews Neuroscience 5(8), 617–629 (2004)
5. Beijbom, O., Joshi, N., Morris, D., Saponas, S., Khullar, S.: Menu-match: Restaurant-specific food logging from images. In: Winter Conference on Applications of Computer Vision, pp. 844–851, Waikoloa, HI (January 2015)
6. Eicher-Miller, H., Boushey, C.: The most frequently reported foods and beverages differ by age among participants of nhanes 1999–2008. The Journal of the Federation of American Societies for Experimental Biology 26, 256–261 (2012)
7. Fagot-Campagna, A., Saaddine, J., Flegal, K., Beckles, G.: Diabetes, impaired fasting glucose, and elevated hba1c in us adolescents: the third national health and nutrition examination survey. Diabetes Care 24(5), 834–837 (2001)
8. Felzenszwalb, P., Huttenlocher, D.: Image segmentation using local variation. In: Proceedings of IEEE International Conference on Computer Vision and Pattern Recognition, pp. 98–104, Santa Barbara, CA (June 1998)
9. He, Y., Xu, C., Khanna, N., Boushey, C., Delp, E.: Context based food image analysis. In: Proceedings of IEEE International Conference on Image Processing, pp. 2748–2752, Melbourne, Australia (September 2013)
10. He, Y., Xu, C., Khanna, N., Boushey, C., Delp, E.: Food image analysis: segmentation, identification and weight estimation. In: Proceeding of the IEEE International Conference on Multimedia and Expo, pp. 1–6, San Jose, CA (July 2013)
11. He, Y., Xu, C., Khanna, N., Boushey, C., Delp, E.: Analysis of food images: Features and classification. In: Proceedings of the IEEE International Conference on Image Processing, pp. 2744–2748, Paris, France (October 2014)
12. Manjunath, B., Ohm, J.R., Vasudevan, V., Yamada, A.: Color and texture descriptors. IEEE Transactions on Circuits and Systems for Video Technology 11(6), 703–715 (2001)
13. Matsuda, Y., Yanai, K.: Multiple-food recognition considering co-occurrence employing manifold ranking. In: Proceedings of the IEEE International Conference on Pattern Recognition, pp. 2017–2020, Tsukuba, Japan (November 2012)
14. McFee, B., Galleguillos, C., Lanckriet, G.: Contextual object localization with multiple kernel nearest-neighbor. IEEE Transactions on Image Processing 20(2), 570–585 (2011)
15. Ogden, C., Carroll, M., Curtin, L., Lamb, M., Flegal, K.: Prevalence of high body mass index in us children and adolescents, 2007–2008. Jama 303(3), 242–249 (2010)
16. Rabinovich, A., Vedaldi, A., Galleguillos, C., Wiewiora, E., Belongie, S.: Objects in context. In: Proceedings of IEEE International Conference on Computer vision, pp. 1–8, Rio de Janeiro, Brazil (October 2007)

17. Sarkka, S.: Bayesian Filtering and Smoothing. Cambridge University Press, Cambridge (2013)
18. Zhu, F., Bosch, M., Woo, I., Kim, S., Boushey, C., Ebert, D., Delp, E.: The use of mobile devices in aiding dietary assessment and evaluation. IEEE Journal of Selected Topics in Signal Processing **4**(4), 756–766 (2010)
19. Zhu, F., Bosch, M., Khanna, N., Boushey, C., Delp, E.: Multiple hypotheses image segmentation and classification with application to dietary assessment. IEEE Journal of Biomedical and Health Informatics **19**(1), 377–388 (2015)

Tastes and Textures Estimation of Foods Based on the Analysis of Its Ingredients List and Image

Hiroki Matsunaga[1], Keisuke Doman[1,2], Takatsugu Hirayama[1], Ichiro Ide[1(✉)], Daisuke Deguchi[1,3], and Hiroshi Murase[1]

[1] Graduate School of Information Science, Nagoya University, Furo-cho, Chikusa-ku, Nagoya 464-8601, Japan
matsunagah@murase.m.is.nagoya-u.ac.jp,
kdoman@sist.chukyo-u.ac.jp,{hirayama,ide,murase}@is.nagoya-u.ac.jp,
ddeguchi@nagoya-u.jp
[2] School of Engineering, Chukyo University, 101 Tokodachi, Kaizu-cho, Toyota 470-0393, Japan
[3] Information Strategy Office, Nagoya University, Furo-cho, Chikusa-ku, Nagoya 464-8601, Japan

Abstract. Recently, the number of cooking recipes on the Web is increasing. However, it is difficult to search them by tastes or textures although they are actually important considering the nature of the contents. Therefore, we propose a method for estimating the tastes and the textures of a cooking recipe by analyzing them. Concretely, the proposed method refers to an ingredients feature from the "ingredients list" and image features from the "food image" in a cooking recipe. We confirmed the effectiveness of the proposed method through an experiment.

1 Introduction

Recently, the number of cooking recipes on the Web is increasing. An example of a cooking recipe posted on the Web is shown in Fig. 1. Currently, users would usually search from a large number of cooking recipes for those that suit their requirements by means of keywords matching with the recipe title or the list of ingredients. However, it is difficult to search cooking recipes by tastes or textures although they are actually important considering the nature of the contents. Labeling each recipe with its tastes and textures could be a solution, but we cannot expect all users who post cooking recipes on the Web to do so.

As related work, a tastes sensor has been developed by Tahara and Toko [8]. It imitates the biological effects on the surface of the human tongues, and measures the tastes of food in the aspect of the five basic tastes; *sweet*, *sour*, *salty*, *bitter*, and *umami*. However, normal users that post cooking recipes on the Web cannot make use of this sensor casually, since it is very expensive. In addition, it cannot measure textures.

H. Matsunaga—Currently at IVIS, Inc.

V. Murino et al. (Eds.): ICIAP 2015 Workshops, LNCS 9281, pp. 326–333, 2015.
DOI: 10.1007/978-3-319-23222-5_40

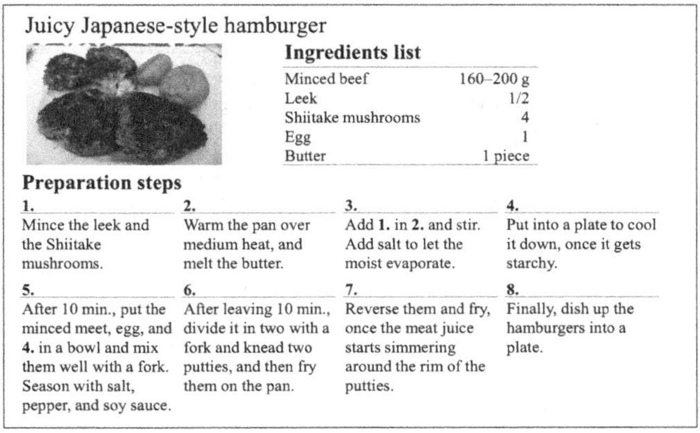

Juicy Japanese-style hamburger			

	Ingredients list	
	Minced beef	160–200 g
	Leek	1/2
	Shiitake mushrooms	4
	Egg	1
	Butter	1 piece

Preparation steps

1.	**2.**	**3.**	**4.**
Mince the leek and the Shiitake mushrooms.	Warm the pan over medium heat, and melt the butter.	Add **1.** in **2.** and stir. Add salt to let the moist evaporate.	Put into a plate to cool it down, once it gets starchy.
5.	**6.**	**7.**	**8.**
After 10 min., put the minced meet, egg, and **4.** in a bowl and mix them well with a fork. Season with salt, pepper, and soy sauce.	After leaving 10 min., divide it in two with a fork and knead two putties, and then fry them on the pan.	Reverse them and fry, once the meat juice starts simmering around the rim of the putties.	Finally, dish up the hamburgers into a plate.

Fig. 1. Example of a cooking recipe posted on the Web[1] by one of the authors.

Thus, we are aiming at estimating the tastes and the textures of a food by analyzing cooking recipes. Concretely, the proposed method refers to an ingredients feature from the "ingredients list" and image features from the "food image" in a cooking recipe.

In the following sections, we first introduce the proposed method on tastes estimation in Sect. 2, and then report its results in Sect. 3.1. In addition, we also report the result of applying the same scheme to textures estimation in Sect. 3.2. Finally, we conclude the paper in Sect. 4.

2   Tastes Estimation Method

As shown in Fig. 1, a typical cooking recipe posted on the Web is composed of a "title", a "food image", an "ingredients list", and "preparation steps". The proposed method estimates the tastes of a food in two steps referring to the "ingredients list" and the "food image"; the training step and the estimation step, as shown in Fig. 2 and described below. Note that here, we assume that the structure of a cooking recipe could be automatically analyzed, and the "food image" and the "ingredients list" are available for immediate processing.

2.1   Training Step

Classifiers are constructed for each taste class. Each classifier is a one-versus-rest classifier that judges whether the food has the specific taste or not.

The process flow of the training step is shown in Fig. 2(a). First, an ingredients feature is extracted from the "ingredients list". Next, image features are extracted from the "food image". Classifiers for each taste class are constructed using these two features extracted from a large-number of cooking recipes with taste labels.

---

[1] Translated from http://cookpad.com/recipe/1452708/.

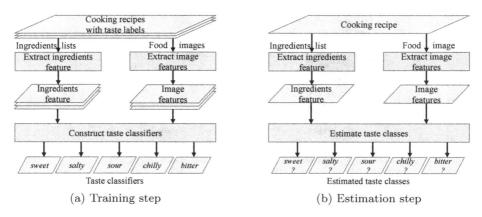

Fig. 2. Process flow of the proposed method.

Ingredients Feature. First, an ingredients dictionary is built by accumulating all ingredients that appear in a cooking recipe dataset. Next, an ingredients feature vector is formed for each cooking recipe, as a binary vector with the value 1 for ingredients that appear in the recipe, and 0 for all the others.

Image Features. First, in order to extract image features precisely, regions that include plates and tables are cropped. Here, GrabCut [7] was employed following the practice in the food recognition system proposed by Kawano et al. [5]. In our case, GrabCut is given the entire input image as the initial region. Next, as image features, Hue-Saturation histogram, Hue-Saturation correlogram [4], BoF representation [1] of SIFT features [6], and HOG [2] are extracted.

Taste Classifiers. An SVM [9] classifier for each taste class is constructed, that learns the features extracted from the cooking recipes with manually labeled taste labels.

2.2   Estimation Step

As in the training step, an ingredients feature and image features are extracted from an input cooking recipe, and then each of the trained SVM classifiers estimates if it has the corresponding taste or not.

3   Experiments

We evaluated the effectiveness of the proposed method through tastes estimation experiments in Sect. 3.1. In addition, for reference, we also report preliminary results on the application of the same scheme to textures in Sect. 3.2.

Table 1. Number of cooking recipes labeled with taste classes by subjects.

Taste class	*sweet*	*sour*	*chilly*	*salty*	*bitter*
Number of cooking recipes	1,254	366	241	537	213

Table 2. Number of cooking recipes labeled with taste classes by referring to user comments.

Taste class	*sweet*	*sour*	*chilly*	*salty*	*bitter*
Number of cooking recipes	4,849	1,093	907	495	362

3.1 Tastes Estimation Experiments

Construction of Datasets. We first constructed a dataset of cooking recipes labeled by human subjects through a subjective experiment. First, 2,700 cooking recipes were randomly selected from 440,000 cooking recipes in the "Rakuten recipe dataset"[2]. Then, 45 Japanese male and female subjects were asked to label them with taste classes. Here, each subject was presented the "title", the "food image", and the "ingredients list" of 60 cooking recipes, and was asked to choose up to two out of five taste classes; *sweet, sour, chilly, salty,* and *bitter.* The subjects were also allowed to choose "unknown" if they could not decide, in which case, the corresponding cooking recipe was excluded from the dataset. As a result, we obtained 1,827 cooking recipes labeled with taste classes. The number of the cooking recipes labeled with each taste class in this dataset is shown in Table 1.

However, since manual labeling requires sufficient amount of man-power, it is difficult to create a larger dataset. Thus, we also constructed a second dataset by referring to expressions related to each taste class from user comments posted to each cooking recipe. This allows us to create a larger dataset automatically, although it may degrade the reliability of the labels.

First, morphological analysis was applied to the comments. Next, each word was matched with a dictionary of taste-related expressions for each taste class, which we prepared manually beforehand. If a match was found, the corresponding taste class was labeled, and if not, the cooking recipe was excluded from the dataset. Note that multiple labeling was allowed. As a result, we obtained 7,706 cooking recipes with taste labels as the second dataset. The number of cooking recipes labeled with each taste class in this dataset is shown in Table 2.

Experimental Method. We conducted experiments to evaluate the effectiveness of the proposed method using each of the two datasets. When constructing a classifier for a taste class, cooking recipes labeled with the corresponding taste

---

[2] Rakuten Inc., "Rakuten datasets," http://www.nii.ac.jp/cscenter/idr/rakuten/rakuten.html

label were used as positive samples, while all the others were used as negative samples. Since there was a large difference between the numbers of positive and negative samples in the datasets, each class was weighted according to the inverse of the sample size in the SVM training step. We compared the proposed method with two comparative methods; one that used only the ingredients feature, and one that used only image features. Each method was evaluated through eight-fold cross validation. Precision, recall, and F-measure were used as the evaluation criteria.

Results. The experimental results from the first dataset labeled by the subjects are shown in Table 3. From the results, we confirmed the effectiveness of the proposed method for all the taste classes.

The experimental results from the second dataset labeled by referring to user comments are likewise shown in Table 4. Since the results were similar and sometimes better than those obtained from the first dataset, we considered that the larger size of the dataset contributed more than the degradation of the labels.

Discussion. For the *salty* class labeled by subjects, the highest F-measure was obtained when only the ingredients feature was used. A representative ingredient that causes a food to become *salty* will be "salt". Actually, many cooking recipes labeled as *salty* contained "salt". This would be a reason that the ingredients feature was effective to estimate the *salty* class, while it lead to lower accuracy when using only the image feature, since "salt" is usually not visually perceivable. Thus, selecting different features for each class, could improve the accuracy.

3.2   Application to Textures Estimation

In order to evaluate if the proposed scheme could also be applied to textures estimation, we performed a similar experiment as that in Sect. 3.1 for textures. According to a research by Hayakawa et al. [3], there are 445 texture expressions in the Japanese language. Here, we targeted the following five texture expressions that were most frequently used in the comments; *shaki-shaki*, *fuwa-fuwa*, *toro-toro*, *saku-saku*, and *hoku-hoku*.

Construction of a Dataset. To label the cooking recipes with the five texture classes, we applied the same procedure as that for the second dataset created in Sect. 3.1 that was labeled by referring to user comments. As a result, we obtained 5,219 cooking recipes with texture labels. The number of cooking recipes labeled with each texture class is shown in Table 5.

Experimental Method. We conducted an experiment to evaluate the applicability of the proposed scheme to textures estimation using the dataset, in the same manner as in Sect. 3.1.

Table 3. Estimation results from taste classes labeled by subjects.

(a) *sweet* class

Method	Precision	Recall	F-measure
Proposed method	0.813	0.838	**0.825**
Ingredients feature	**0.818**	0.828	0.822
Image features	0.701	**0.928**	0.798

(b) *sour* class

Precision	Recall	F-measure
0.405	0.390	**0.397**
0.393	0.336	0.362
0.209	**0.672**	0.319

(c) *chilly* class

Method	Precision	Recall	F-measure
Proposed method	**0.393**	0.220	**0.282**
Ingredients feature	0.325	**0.227**	0.256
Image features	0.227	0.104	0.142

(d) *salty* class

Precision	Recall	F-measure
0.538	**0.545**	0.542
0.561	0.533	**0.547**
0.337	0.384	0.359

(e) *bitter* class

Method	Precision	Recall	F-measure
Proposed method	**0.409**	0.399	**0.404**
Ingredients feature	0.342	**0.418**	0.376
Image features	0.246	0.192	0.216

Table 4. Estimation results from taste classes labeled by referring to user comments.

(a) *sweet* class

Method	Precision	Recall	F-measure
Proposed method	**0.755**	**0.844**	**0.797**
Ingredients feature	0.743	0.837	0.787
Image features	0.706	0.703	0.705

(b) *sour* class

Precision	Recall	F-measure
0.408	0.410	**0.409**
0.552	0.282	0.373
0.167	**0.485**	0.243

(c) *chilly* class

Method	Precision	Recall	F-measure
Proposed method	0.511	0.260	0.345
Ingredients feature	**0.576**	0.294	**0.388**
Image features	0.196	**0.615**	0.298

(d) *salty* class

Precision	Recall	F-measure
0.398	0.225	**0.287**
0.348	0.091	0.144
0.089	**0.503**	0.152

(e) *bitter* class

Method	Precision	Recall	F-measure
Proposed method	0.680	0.350	**0.462**
Ingredients feature	**0.777**	0.329	**0.462**
Image features	0.086	**0.439**	0.144

Table 5. Number of the cooking recipes labeled with texture classes by referring to user comments.

Texture class	shaki- shaki	fuwa- fuwa	toro- toro	saku- saku	hoku- hoku
Number of cooking recipes	1,445	1,353	843	828	750

Table 6. Estimation accuracy for texture classes labeled by referring to user comments.

(a) *shaki-shaki* class

Method	Precision	Recall	F-measure
Proposed method	0.767	0.689	0.726
Ingredients feature	**0.778**	**0.691**	**0.732**
Image features	0.487	0.544	0.514

(b) *fuwa-fuwa* class

Precision	Recall	F-measure
0.708	0.593	**0.645**
0.702	0.593	0.643
0.317	**0.678**	0.432

(c) *toro-toro* class

Method	Precision	Recall	F-measure
Proposed method	0.282	0.507	0.363
Ingredients feature	**0.289**	0.547	**0.378**
Image features	0.207	**0.603**	0.310

(d) *saku-saku* class

Precision	Recall	F-measure
0.642	0.465	**0.539**
0.639	0.448	0.526
0.245	**0.587**	0.346

(e) *hoku-hoku* class

Method	Precision	Recall	F-measure
Proposed method	0.771	0.598	0.650
Ingredients feature	**0.773**	0.601	**0.660**
Image features	0.224	**0.649**	0.333

Results. The experimental results are shown in Table 6. Compared with the experimental results of the tastes estimation in Sect. 3.1, the F-measures were in the same level, so we confirmed that the proposed method could also be applied to textures estimation.

Discussion. For some texture classes, the highest F-measure was obtained when only the ingredients feature was used. We found that in many cases, cooking recipes that were selected as positive samples in each texture class were those on a specific dish. For example, most cooking recipes on a "salad" were labeled with the *shaki-shaki* class. Some dishes often share the same ingredients and follow similar preparation steps, but they could have various visual appearances, so indeed image features may not necessarily be effective in such cases.

In this experiment, we selected only five out of the 445 texture expressions, so in order to truly confirm the effectiveness of the proposed scheme for textures estimation, we need to extend the number of texture classes. However, it may be difficult to do so due to the insufficient numbers of positive samples available.

4   Conclusion

We proposed an estimation method of tastes and textures from cooking recipes. The proposed method analyzed the text feature extracted from the "ingredients list" and the image features extracted from the "food image" in a cooking recipe.

Experimental results showed the effectiveness of the proposed method for all taste classes. The proposed scheme also showed its extensibility to textures estimation. Future work includes introducing additional information, such as the "preparation steps" and the quantity of ingredients.

Acknowledgments. Part of this work was supported by Grant-in-Aid for Scientific Research (24240028). We thank Rakuten Inc. for providing their recipe contents.

References

1. Csurka, G., Bray, C., Dance, C., Fan, L.: Visual categorization with bags of keypoints. In: Proc. ECCV 2004 Workshop on Statistical Learning in Computer Vision, pp. 59–74 (May 2004)
2. Dalal, N., Triggs, W.: Histograms of oriented gradients for human detection. In: Proc. 2005 IEEE Computer Society Conf. on Computer Vision and Pattern Recognition, pp. 886–893 (June 2005)
3. Hayakawa, F., Kazami, Y., Nishinari, K., Ioku, K., Akuzawa, S., Yamano, Y., Baba, Y., Kohyama, K.: Classification of Japanese texture terms. J. of Texture Studies **44**(2), 140–159 (2013)
4. Huang, J., Kumar, S.R., Mitra, M., Jing, W., Zabih, Z.: Image indexing using color correlogram. In: Proc. 1997 IEEE Computer Society Conf. on Computer Vision and Pattern Recognition, pp. 762–768 (June 1997)
5. Kawano, Y., Yanai, K.: Foodcam: A real-time food recognition system on a smartphone. Multimedia Tools and Applications, 1–27 (April 2014)
6. Lowe, D.: Object recognition from local scale-invariant features. In: Proc. 1999 IEEE Int. Conf. on Computer Vision, pp. 1150–1157 (September 1999)
7. Rother, C., Kolmogorov, V., Blake, A.: Grabcut: Interactive foreground extraction using iterated graphcuts. ACM Trans. on Graphics **23**(3), 309–314 (2004)
8. Tahara, Y., Toko, K.: Electronic tongues –A review. IEEE Sensors J. **13**(8), 3001–3011 (2013)
9. Vapnik, V.: The nature of statistical learning theory. Springer, New York (1998)

Food Recognition and Leftover Estimation for Daily Diet Monitoring

Gianluigi Ciocca, Paolo Napoletano[(⊠)], and Raimondo Schettini

DISCo (Dipartimento di Informatica, Sistemistica e Comunicazione),
Università degli Studi di Milano-Bicocca, Viale Sarca 336, 20126 Milano, Italy
{ciocca,napoletano,schettini}@disco.unimib.it

Abstract. Here we propose a system for automatic dietary monitoring of canteen customers based on robust computer vision techniques. The proposed system recognizes foods and estimates food leftovers. Results achieved on 1000 customers of a real canteen are promising.

Keywords: Food recognition · Leftover estimation · Diet monitoring

1 Introduction

Automatic food recognition is an important task to support the user in his daily dietary monitoring. Nowadays, technology can support the users in keep tracks of their food consumption in a more user friendly way allowing for a more comprehensive daily dietary monitoring. Recent findings showed that computer vision techniques can help to automatically recognize food [17] and estimate its quantity [25].

The works that tackle the problem of food recognition are based on different classification strategies. For example, [14] uses a k-NN classifier on local and global features; in [11] a vocabulary is constructed on textons and the images are classified using SVM; the same classifier is used in [22] where local binary pattern and relationship between SIFT interest points are used to code the local and spatial information. SVM, Artificial Neural Networks and Random Forest classification methods are evaluated in [2] on 5000 food images organized into 11 classes described in terms of different bag-of-features. Recently, deep learning algorithms are receiving great attention due to their efficiency in dealing with, and solving complex problems. Convolutional neural network (CNN) belongs to this kind of algorithms and have been successfully used in [15] and [16] on large food image datasets. Most of food recognition works, exploits only the information derived from the picture itself. A different approach is described in [4] where the context of where the picture was taken is also exploited.

Food quantity estimation is very important in the context of a dietary monitoring since on it depends the assessment of the food intakes. One of the first work that presents a system that recognizes each food item on the plate and then estimates its quantity is [25]. The problem is tackled using binary classifiers for

© Springer International Publishing Switzerland 2015
V. Murino et al. (Eds.): ICIAP 2015 Workshops, LNCS 9281, pp. 334–341, 2015.
DOI: 10.1007/978-3-319-23222-5_41

recognition, and 3D reconstruction to measure the food volumes. A calibrated camera and a calibration card are used in [26] for food recognition and portion estimation. Also the TADA dietary assessment system [21] uses a token (checkboard in this case) for food quantity estimation. Instead of using an auxiliary token, the size of the thumb is used in [23], [24], and [27]. 3D information is often exploited. For example, 3D template matching is used in [6] and [13] while 3D shape reconstruction is used in the already cited [25] and in [13]. In the latter, 3D shape reconstruction is used for food with regular shape, while area-based weight estimation is used for food without regular shape.

Food recognition and quantity estimation algorithms are used in more general, often mobile, systems for dietary monitoring purposes [2]. Examples of such systems are FoodLog [19], DietCam [20], Menu-Match [3], and FoodCam [18]. FoodLog is an online system that relies on the users to take images of their eating occasions using a camera and then send the images to a system to be processed. DietCam is a mobile application that is able to recognize foods and automatically calculate calorie content of the meal on a server. Other mobile applications are the ones presented in [28], and [1]. FoodCam is expressly designed to perform real-time food recognition on the device using efficient image representation and fast classification. Very few works consider the problem of leftover estimation. Often the problem is treated as a special case of the problem of food recognition and quantity estimation [23,28].

2 Proposed System

In this paper, we propose a system for automatic dietary monitoring of canteen customers that is based on robust computer vision techniques for automatic food recognition and leftover estimation in a canteen scenario. Although the canteen scenario includes some apparent simplifications, such as controlled image acquisition conditions, known weekly menu etc., the problem of food recognition and leftover estimation is still a challenging problem due to the enormous variations in the tray and plate composition. The visual appearance of the same dish may greatly change depending on how it is placed on the plate. Our system is able to identify and recognize the food category and estimate the amount of food in each plate. Moreover, it is designed to evaluate the leftovers as well as allowing an estimation of the truly consumed foods. Food consuption is associated to the user identity through the use of visual marker on their mobile phone. This information can be stored in more general profiling system to keep track of the user's food consumption over several days with a minimum inconvenience.

Figure 1 illustrates the user interaction and data processing involved in our system. Specifically there are seven steps:

1. The user starts its mobile application showing his personal identification number coded into a visual marker. The mobile phone is placed on the tray and the user choses the dishes placing them on the tray.

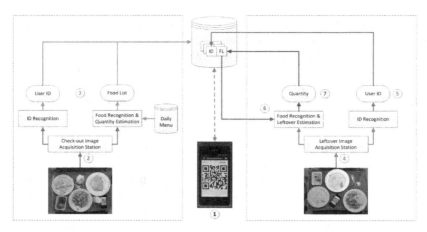

Fig. 1. The seven steps of our food recognition and leftover estimation system for automatic dietary monitoring of canteen customers. All the processing is carried out as a server application. The user ID is embedded into a visual marker displayed on his mobile phone.

2. Once the tray reaches the check-out acquisition station, an image of the tray is taken using a camera placed above the tray. The image is sent to the server application.
3. The image is processed. The user ID is decoded from the visual marker and the food recognition phase starts. The food recognition module detects each plate and the food placed in it is recognized according to the daily menu. The obtained food list is stored on a database into the user's dietary profile.
4. After the meal, an image of the tray containing eaten foods is taken at the leftover acquisition station and sent to the server for processing.
5. First the user ID is decoded and then used to retrieve the previous stored food list from the database.
6. The food list is used as input to the leftover estimation module that first performs food recognition. With respect to the Step 3, different processing and parameters of the food recognition are used in this step.
7. The information about the leftovers, and thus about the eaten foods, is finally logged back in the database.

As it can be seen from Figure 1, the link between the food recognition phase and the leftover estimation phase is done via the QR code representing the user ID. Its detection and recognition are performed immediately after the image acquisition through the ZBar[1] library.

2.1   Food Recognition

The overall processing pipeline is shown in Figure 2, and works as follows. To speed up the processing while maintaining enough information, the input images

---
[1] http://zbar.sourceforge.net/

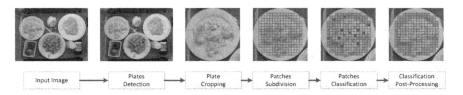

| Input Image | → | Plates Detection | → | Plate Cropping | → | Patches Subdivision | → | Patches Classification | → | Classification Post-Processing |

Fig. 2. Patch-based food recognition processing pipeline.

are sub-sampled to 1024×768 pixels. Since we are interested only on the food placed on the plates, plate detection is performed using the Hough transform for circles, with suitable parameters. To cope with the problem of having multiple foods on the same plate, we designed a patch-based food recognition algorithm. Each plate is cropped and subdivided into patches and each patch is classified into one of the candidate foods. The size of the patches influences the classification accuracy. Small patches increase the number of misclassification between patches of different classes, while large patches make the classification too noisy since non relevant information could be included in every single patch. After having experimented with different patch sizes, we found a tradeoff and we set the size to 40×40 pixels. From each patch, a visual descriptor is extracted and submitted to a pre-trained k-NN classifier in order to receive a classification label. The labels of the the patches are then post-processed to remove spurious labels in order to have more homogeneous groups of labels that correspond to the food regions.

We have experimented with several descriptors listed in Table 1 from different classes of approaches, such as color based, statistical, spatial-frequency or spectral, structural and hybrid [5,7,9,10]. Detailed results are reported in Section 3. It must be noted that the sample space of the classifier is constructed such that its scope is limited to samples taken from foods belonging to the daily menu list. Among the samples we have also included patches of non-food items such as plates, tablecloth, cutlery, etc. The list of recognized foods is assembled in a food list that is stored into the user's profile. Along with the food identities, the food quantities are also assessed and stored to be used for leftover estimation. These quantities, that represent reference baselines, are determined by counting the number of patches of each food.

2.2   Leftover Estimation

Within the canteen scenario, the personnel is bounded to follow the regulations provided by nutritionists in the form of nutritional tables, and to serve a specific amount of food (that depends on its calories and nutrients). This somewhat simplifies the problem of the estimation of the food quantity. In this scenario, it is more important to precisely identify what kind of foods have been chosen by the users in a given day, how much of these foods have been eaten, and to compare them with the user's dietary recommendations.

Table 1. Visual descriptors tested in our system

Name	Description	Length
CEDD	Color and Edge Directivity Descriptor	144
Gabor	Gabor features. Mean and st.dev. of RGB DFT at $(\theta, f) = (4,4)$	96
OG	Opponent Gabor. Gabor on iter-intra channel combinations	264
LBP	Non-uniform, invariant Local Binary Pattern with (r,n)=(1,8)	54
LCC	Local Color Contrast	499
CM	Two sets of five normalized Chromaticity Moments	10
CWT	Complex Wavelet features. RGB mean and st.dev. at three scales	18

The processing pipeline starts with the user identification that is done as in the previous section. After that, the list of the daily food taken by the user is retrieved from the server database and is used to match plates before and after meal. Such a food list is also used to limit the search space of the leftover estimation. The estimation of the leftover quantity is performed by counting the food patches of each food. For a given customer (i) and a given food class (c), we define the ratio (r_{ic}^{est}). This is the ratio between the number of patches found by the leftover estimation module and the number of patches previously found by the recognition module. This is an estimation of the amount of eaten food c by the customer i:

$$r_{ic}^{est} = \frac{\#Patches\ leftover}{\#Patches\ before}.$$

Once we have identified this ratio, the corresponding amount of calories is deduced by the precompiled nutritional tables.

3   Experiments

We experimented our system in a real scenario. We monitored and recorded the meal of 1000 customers of a real canteen that corresponded to 2000 tray images (1000 before and 1000 after the meal). Each customer selected 3 dishes from the daily menu that included 15 different dishes. The images have been acquired through an automatic photographic system that includes a raspberry motherboard, an embedded camera and a motion sensor. The system automatically detects when the tray has to be acquired. All the 2000 images have been manually annotated in order to provide the ground-truth for both recognition and leftover estimation. The annotations have been created using the IAT - image annotation tool [8], that permitted to draw a polygon around the food. For a customer i, the assesment of the leftover quantity of a food c is obtained as the ratio between the areas of annotated polygons before and after the meal (r_{ic}^{gt}).

We have selected 300 customers (600 tray images) to train the system and 700 for testing. The training set has been selected such that all the 15 dishes were equally represented. The training step has been performed with a k-NN algorithm with $k = 7$. The food distribution of the 700 test customers is reported in Table 2. As can be seen, the food classes are not uniformly distributed

To cope with the class imbalance problem of the test set we jointly used two assessment metrics for food recognition: the *Standard Accuracy (SA)* and the

Table 2. Food recognition rate of all the visual descriptors considered. Best performance are reported in bold.

Classes	w_c(%)	visual descriptors						
		CEDD	OG	Gabor	LBP	LLC	CM	CWT
bistecca	(3.8%)	100.00	100.00	100.00	27.50	97.50	91.25	80.00
carote	(7.6%)	100.00	100.00	100.00	100.00	100.00	98.75	100.00
cavolfiore	(8.6%)	100.00	100.00	98.89	97.22	98.33	97.22	100.00
fagiolini	(7.6%)	100.00	100.00	100.00	99.38	100.00	100.00	98.33
frittata	(7.6%)	100.00	100.00	100.00	99.38	100.00	100.00	96.25
fusilli ragu	(8.6%)	100.00	100.00	100.00	81.25	93.75	83.12	100.00
insalata mista	(2.4%)	100.00	100.00	100.00	85.56	100.00	97.22	100.00
lenticchie	(7.1%)	98.67	92.00	42.00	58.00	100.00	90.00	32.00
minestra	(6.7%)	100.00	99.33	96.67	68.00	94.67	28.67	57.33
pasta cime rapa	(8.6%)	100.00	100.00	97.86	99.29	97.86	93.57	100.00
pasta sugo	(2.4%)	100.00	100.00	100.00	100.00	100.00	100.00	100.00
piselli	(7.1%)	99.33	100.00	100.00	28.00	76.00	100.00	98.00
pollo ferri	(7.6%)	96.86	97.48	98.67	94.67	100.00	88.00	98.00
scaloppina	(8.6%)	98.90	99.45	67.30	62.26	76.10	93.71	69.18
tortino	(5.7%)	91.67	90.83	79.17	22.50	79.17	83.33	80.00
SA		**99.05**	99.00	94.33	74.14	95.05	89.57	90.38
MAA		**99.03**	98.61	92.00	69.16	94.11	89.51	87.20

Macro Average Accuracy (MAA) [12]. Denoting NP_c the number of positives, i.e., the number of times the class c occurs in the dataset; TP_c the number of *true positives* for class c, i.e., the number of times that the system recognizes the dish c; C the number of classes, for each class, the metrics can be defined as follows:

$$SA = \frac{\sum_{c=1}^{C} TP_c}{\sum_{c=1}^{C} NP_c}; \quad MAA = \frac{1}{C} \sum_{c=1}^{C} A_c = \frac{1}{C} \sum_{c=1}^{C} \frac{TP_c}{NP_c}.$$

Regarding the food recognition task, the system showed a very high performance based on both assessment metrics, see Table 2. The *CEDD* descriptor achieved the highest accuracy while the LBP and CWT achieved the lowest accuracy. Concerning the evaluation of the leftover estimation module, we measured the overall relative error (*Error*) as:

$$Error = \sum_{c=1}^{C} w_c \sum_{i=1}^{I} |r_{ic}^{gt} - r_{ic}^{est}|,$$

where w_c is the class weight and I is the number of test customers. The class weight is defined as the number of elements of the class divided by the total number of elements. The system is capable of estimating the relative quantity of eaten food with an average error of about 15 percentage points, with the best and worst cases being 7 and 34 percentage points respectively.

4   Conclusions

The proposed food recognition and leftover estimation system can serve multiple purposes: first, at the check-out station, the food recognition allows to keep track the eaten food and the user's dietary habits; second, using the list of recognized foods, an automatic billing procedure can be activated speeding up the check-out; third, by evaluation the leftovers, we can better estimate the food intakes in terms of calories ingested. Results achieved on a real canteen scenario are promising with an average accuracy in recognition of about 99%, and and average error in food estimation of 15 percentage points.

Acknowledgments. This work is part of the research Project titled Feedin' Italy. The project is co-funded by European Union, The italian government, and Regione Lombardia under CE regulations 1083/2006 and 1828/2006.

References

1. Ahmad, Z., Khanna, N., Kerr, D.A., Boushey, C.J., Delp, E.J.: A mobile phone user interface for image-based dietary assessment. In: IS&T/SPIE Electronic Imaging, p. 903007. International Society for Optics and Photonics (2014)
2. Anthimopoulos, M.M., Gianola, L., Scarnato, L., Diem, P., Mougiakakou, S.G.: A food recognition system for diabetic patients based on an optimized bag-of-features model. IEEE Journal of Biomedical and Health Informatics **18**(4), 1261–1271 (2014)
3. Beijbom, O., Joshi, N., Morris, D., Saponas, S., Khullar, S.: Menu-match: restaurant-specific food logging from images. In: 2015 IEEE Winter Conference on Applications of Computer Vision (WACV), pp. 844–851. IEEE (2015)
4. Bettadapura, V., Thomaz, E., Parnami, A., Abowd, G., Essa, I.: Leveraging context to support automated food recognition in restaurants. In: 2015 IEEE Winter Conference on Applications of Computer Vision (WACV), pp. 580–587 (2015)
5. Bianconi, F., Harvey, R., Southam, P., Fernández, A.: Theoretical and experimental comparison of different approaches for color texture classification. Journal of Electronic Imaging **20**(4) (2011)
6. Chae, J., Woo, I., Kim, S., Maciejewski, R., Zhu, F., Delp, E.J., Boushey, C.J., Ebert, D.S.: Volume estimation using food specific shape templates in mobile image-based dietary assessment. In: IS&T/SPIE Electronic Imaging, p. 78730. International Society for Optics and Photonics (2011)
7. Chatzichristofis, S.A., Boutalis, Y.S.: CEDD: color and edge directivity descriptor: a compact descriptor for image indexing and retrieval. In: Gasteratos, A., Vincze, M., Tsotsos, J.K. (eds.) ICVS 2008. LNCS, vol. 5008, pp. 312–322. Springer, Heidelberg (2008)
8. Ciocca, G., Napoletano, P., Schettini, R.: Iat-image annotation tool: Manual. arXiv preprint arXiv:1502.05212 (2015)
9. Cusano, C., Napoletano, P., Schettini, R.: Intensity and color descriptors for texture classification. In: IS&T/SPIE Electronic Imaging, p. 866113. International Society for Optics and Photonics (2013)
10. Cusano, C., Napoletano, P., Schettini, R.: Combining local binary patterns and local color contrast for texture classification under varying illumination. JOSA A **31**(7), 1453–1461 (2014)
11. Farinella, G., Moltisanti, M., Battiato, S.: Classifying food images represented as bag of textons. In: 2014 IEEE International Conference on Image Processing (ICIP), pp. 5212–5216 (2014)
12. He, H., Ma, Y.: Imbalanced Learning: Foundations, Algorithms, and Applications. John Wiley & Sons (2013)

13. He, Y., Xu, C., Khanna, N., Boushey, C., Delp, E.: Food image analysis: segmentation, identification and weight estimation. In: 2013 IEEE International Conference on Multimedia and Expo (ICME), pp. 1–6 (2013)
14. He, Y., Xu, C., Khanna, N., Boushey, C., Delp, E.: Analysis of food images: features and classification. In: 2014 IEEE International Conference on Image Processing (ICIP), pp. 2744–2748 (2014)
15. Kagaya, H., Aizawa, K., Ogawa, M.: Food detection and recognition using convolutional neural network. In: Proceedings of the ACM International Conference on Multimedia, MM 2014, pp. 1085–1088 (2014)
16. Kawano, Y., Yanai, K.: Food image recognition with deep convolutional features. In: Proceedings of the 2014 ACM International Joint Conference on Pervasive and Ubiquitous Computing, UbiComp 2014 Adjunct, pp. 589–593 (2014)
17. Kawano, Y., Yanai, K.: Foodcam-256: a large-scale real-time mobile food recognitionsystem employing high-dimensional features and compression of classifier weights. In: Proceedings of the ACM International Conference on Multimedia, MM 2014, pp. 761–762 (2014)
18. Kawano, Y., Yanai, K.: Foodcam: A real-time food recognition system on a smartphone. Multimedia Tools and Applications, 1–25 (2014)
19. Kitamura, K., Yamasaki, T., Aizawa, K.: Foodlog: capture, analysis and retrieval of personal food images via web. In: Proceedings of the ACM Multimedia 2009 Workshop on Multimedia for Cooking and Eating Activities, pp. 23–30 (2009)
20. Kong, F., Tan, J.: Dietcam: Automatic dietary assessment with mobile camera phones. Pervasive and Mobile Computing 8(1), 147–163 (2012)
21. Mariappan, A., Bosch, M., Zhu, F., Boushey, C.J., Kerr, D.A., Ebert, D.S., Delp, E.J.: Personal dietary assessment using mobile devices, vol. 7246, pp. 72460Z-1–72460Z-12 (2009)
22. Nguyen, D.T., Zong, Z., Ogunbona, P.O., Probst, Y., Li, W.: Food image classification using local appearance and global structural information. Neurocomputing 140, 242–251 (2014)
23. Pouladzadeh, P., Shirmohammadi, S., Al-Maghrabi, R.: Measuring calorie and nutrition from food image. IEEE Transactions on Instrumentation and Measurement 63(8), 1947–1956 (2014)
24. Pouladzadeh, P., Villalobos, G., Almaghrabi, R., Shirmohammadi, S.: A novel svm based food recognition method for calorie measurement applications. In: 2012 IEEE International Conference on Multimedia and Expo Workshops (ICMEW), pp. 495–498 (2012)
25. Puri, M., Zhu, Z., Yu, Q., Divakaran, A., Sawhney, H.: Recognition and volume estimation of food intake using a mobile device. In: 2009 Workshop on Applications of Computer Vision (WACV), pp. 1–8 (2009)
26. Sun, M., Liu, Q., Schmidt, K., Yang, J., Yao, N., Fernstrom, J., Fernstrom, M., DeLany, J.P., Sclabassi, R.: Determination of food portion size by image processing. In: 30th Annual International Conference of the IEEE Engineering in Medicine and Biology Society, EMBS 2008, pp. 871–874 (2008)
27. Villalobos, G., Almaghrabi, R., Pouladzadeh, P., Shirmohammadi, S.: An image processing approach for calorie intake measurement. In: 2012 IEEE International Symposium on Medical Measurements and Applications Proceedings, pp. 1–5 (2012)
28. Zhu, F., Bosch, M., Woo, I., Kim, S., Boushey, C., Ebert, D., Delp, E.: The use of mobile devices in aiding dietary assessment and evaluation. IEEE Journal of Selected Topics in Signal Processing 4(4), 756–766 (2010)

Mobile Computing and Artificial Intelligence for Diet Management

Alessandro Mazzei[1(✉)], Luca Anselma[1], Franco De Michieli[2],
Andrea Bolioli[3], Matteo Casu[3], Jelle Gerbrandy[4], and Ivan Lunardi[5]

[1] Dip. Informatica, Università di Torino, Torino, Italy
{alessandro.mazzei,luca.anselma}@unito.it
[2] Dip. Scienze Mediche, Università di Torino, Torino, Italy
franco.demichieli@unito.it
[3] CELI s.r.l., Torino, Italy
{abolioli,mcasu}@celi.com
[4] Gerbrandy s.r.l., Torino, Italy
jelle@gerbrandy.com
[5] Synesthesia s.r.l., Torino, Italy
lunardi@synestesia.com

Abstract. This paper proposes a software architecture for automatic diet management and recipes analysis. We devise a *virtual dietitian* that is able: (1) to recover the nutritional information directly from a specific recipe, (2) to reason over recipes and diets with *flexibility*, i.e. by allowing some forms of diet disobedience, and (3) to persuade the user to minimize these acts of disobedience.

1 Introduction

The increasing pervasiveness of technology is drawing some new scenarios on man-machine interaction. We are surrounded by computers and this revolutionary state of affairs can be exploited in order to enlarge the power of our senses [9]. Cloud computing technologies allow to consider mobile devices as a number of sophisticated sensors that enhance the human senses and, sometimes, change them in new surprising forms. The term "Quantified Self" has recently been adopted to indicate technologies that allow for a ubiquitous monitoring of human activities. Moreover, in recent years there has been a growing interest in using multimedia applications on mobile devices as *persuasive* technologies. For instance "UbiFit Garden" is a mobile application developed to encourage people to maintain a good level of physical activity in daily life. The users can see their weekly progress in the background of their smartphones [4].

The daily diet is one of the most important factors influencing diseases, in particular obesity. As highlighted by the World Health Organization, this factor is primarily due to the recent changes in the lifestyle [16]. The necessity to encourage world's population toward a healthy diet has been sponsored by the FAO [13] and each nation has tried to specialize these guidelines by adopting strategies related to its *food history*; for instance, for USA refer to

© Springer International Publishing Switzerland 2015
V. Murino et al. (Eds.): ICIAP 2015 Workshops, LNCS 9281, pp. 342–349, 2015.
DOI: 10.1007/978-3-319-23222-5_42

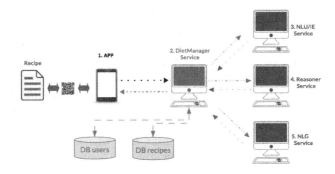

Fig. 1. The architecture of the diet management system.

http://www.choosemyplate.gov/ and for UK http://www.nutrition.org.uk. The Italian Society for Human Nutrition has recently produced a prototypical study with recommendations for the use of specialized operators [1]. A less specialized Italian text, with recommendations easier to read, has been released in 2003 (http://nut.entecra.it/648/linee_guida.html). This complex scenario suggests the possibility to integrate the directives on nutrition in the daily diet of people by using multimedia facilities of mobile devices. A smartphone can be considered as an innovative super-sense that creates new kinds of interaction with the food. For example, we can imagine to print the QR code of a specific dish on a restaurant menu to allow to retrieve "on the cloud" that specific recipe. The information about the dish could be analyzed by an artificial dietitian in order to assess the compatibility of the course with a diet.

We want to design a *virtual dietitian*, i.e. an artificial intelligence (henceforth AI) software that is able to reason over recipes and diet with *flexibility*. In our opinion, a major strength of our design is the possibility for the user to not follow the recommendation produced by the system. So, the AI should make the system *tolerant* to some forms of diet disobedience, but it should also be *persuasive* to minimize these acts of disobedience. In this paper we describe a cloud-based software architecture developed in the project MADiMAN (Multimedia Application for DIet MANagement – http://di.unito.it/madiman) that uses Natural Language Processing (NLP) and Automatic Reasoning techniques for diet management. The paper is organized as follows. In Section 2 we describe the general architecture of the system. In Section 3 we describe three AI software modules designed for analyzing the recipes, for reasoning over the diet and for generating a message to motivate the user toward the right choice. Finally, Section 4 concludes the paper.

2   A Cloud Architecture for Diet Management

In our scenario the interaction between man and food is mediated by an intelligent recommendation system that, on the basis of various variables, encourages or discourages the user to eat a dish that she intends to eat. The main factors that the system needs to account for are: (1) the diet that the user intends to follow, (2) the food that has been eaten in the last days, and (3) the nutritional values of the ingredients of the dish and its specific recipe.

The system is composed of five modules/web services (see Figure 1): a smartphone application (APP), a central module that manages the information flow (DietMAnager), a Natural Language Understanding / Information Extraction (NLU/IE) module, a reasoning module (Reasoner), a natural language generator module (NLGenerator). Upon a registration where the user provides her anthropometric data, the information flow follows this pattern:

1. The user, by using the APP, recovers the QR-code of a specific recipe, or finds the recipe using full-text search.
2. The APP, using the DietManager service, retrieves the user diet together with the list of the food that the user has eaten in the last days. Moreover, the DietManager retrieves the specific recipe of the specific dish.
3. The NLU/IE module computes the salient nutrition information about the specific course.
4. The Reasoner, using the user diet and the list of the food that has been eaten in the last days, produces the final recommendation about the dish for the user.
5. The NLGenerator uses the recommendation given by the Reasoner, produces an explanation for the user in plain natural language and/or in a multimedial format, e.g. by using icons.
6. The DietManager sends the result produced by the NLGenerator to the APP: the user will see this final result on her smartphone. If the user decides to eat the dish, the APP will send this information to the DietManager that will update the list of food eaten.

The DietManager plays the role of a hub for the stateless communications with the web services. So, all web services expose REST (REpresentational State Transfer) interfaces following the best practices for creating simple scalable web services.In the next Section we discuss the main issues of the three web services.

3   AI for Diet Management

The AI allows us to add flexibility to the web services. In Section 3.1 we describe the module for automatic analysis of recipes, in Section 3.2 we describe the reasoning system based on STP (Simple Temporal Problems), and in Section 3.3 we describe a persuasive NLG module.

3.1   NLP for Recipe Analysis

Many smartphone applications use food databases to store the nutritional content of a recipe, but such databases provide only a generic version of the recipes. So, these applications do not allow for a precise computation of the nutritional values of a specific recipe. It is common knowledge that a recipe may vary from cook to cook, both in the quantity of the ingredients and in the methods of preparation. The automatic analysis of recipes is performed to accurately calculate the nutritional values of a specific recipe.

The NLU/IE module is based on an NLP pipeline with the following components: tokenizer, normalizer, sentence splitter, Part-of-Speech tagger, lemmatizer, Named Entities extractor, chunker. The pipeline implements the Apache UIMA (Apache Unstructured Information Management Architecture), and the architecture components are implemented as UIMA annotators [7]. Each component analyzes the text and produces a sort of annotation that will be used by the next component. The UIMA facilitates a rapid component integration, testing and evaluation. The goal of the NLU/IE module is the extraction of a set of pairs *ingredient*-quantity for each recipe. Moreover, the analyzer needs to recover some special information for the diet, such as the presence of particular cooking techniques (e.g. frying). The extraction of such information is rule-based, and occurs at end of the pipeline execution. Thus, the NLU/IE spots expressions of quantities in the text of the recipes, obtaining nutrients for the current recipe.

Although machine learning has been successfully used for similar tasks ([10]) we chose a rule-based approach for different reasons, namely a robust experience with rule-based systems by the team, and the fact of having at disposal a rich gazetteer for ingredients. Besides, a rule-based approach permitted to quickly set up the first experiments with results easily verifiable by hand, so that a linguist developer could analyze the major issues that emerged in order to report them.

The extraction can be performed by using a rule engine with condition-action rules acting on the analyzed text. For our experiments we used Drools (http://www.drools.org), a state-of-the-art Business Rules Engine developed by the JBoss Community. We integrated Drools engine into our implementation of the Apache UIMA framework. Besides being efficient, Drools is well maintained, comes under a Apache 2.0 License and is well integrated with common Java developers' tools such as Eclipse.

An example of pattern captured by the system has the form:

```
<number> ("g"|"gr"|"gram") "of" <ingredient>
```

(a number followed by an expression for grams, followed by an ingredient) and sets a new "Quantity" annotation on the document, positioned where the pattern was spotted.

We mention here two challenging issues we have encountered: 1. in order to normalize all quantities in grams, we have to know the specific weight for each liquid mentioned in text (water, wine, and so on); 2. some quantities occur often under vague; expressions ("a glass of water", "a handful of almonds", etc.); this problem can be softened assuming standard quantities for the various expressions (e.g. a glass of water is of approximately 250 milliliters and weighs approximately 250 grams) – furthermore, in some cultures (e.g. anglo-saxon) such relations between expressions and volumes are quite standardized.

3.2 Reasoning over Recipes and Diet

Since our approach to automatic reasoning for diet management is based on the STP framework [5], first we introduce STP, then we describe how we exploit STP to reason on a diet and how we interpret the results from STP.

An STP [5] is composed by a conjunction of STP constraints of the form $c \leq x - y \leq d$, where x and y are temporal points and c and d are numbers (their domain can be either discrete or real). An STP constraint can be interpreted as "the temporal distance between the time points x and y is between a lower bound c and an upper bound d". It is also possible to impose strict inequalities and $-\infty$ and $+\infty$ can be used to denote the fact that there is no lower or upper bound, respectively. STP can be represented as a graph whose nodes correspond to the temporal points of the STP and whose arcs are labeled with the temporal distance between the points. The problem of determining the consistency of an STP can be solved efficiently by an all-pairs shortest paths algorithm such as Floyd-Warshall's one, which also obtains the minimal network, that is the minimum and maximum distance between each pair of points.

Dietary recommendations are often expressed as Dietary Reference Values (henceforth DRVs) for (macro)nutrients that are recommended to be assumed for significant amounts of time. In particular, from the basal metabolic rate and physical activity level it is possible to estimate the total energy requirement and then obtain the DRVs for an individual. For example, if we assume that a patient has a total energy requirement of 2450 kcal/day, the DRVs in [1] provide that the appropriate amount of the macronutrients is of 260 kcal/day of proteins, 735 kcal/day of lipids and 1455 kcal/day of carbohydrates. In this section we focus on the total energy requirement; the macronutrients can be dealt with separately in the same way. The basic idea is to represent DRVs as STPs. More precisely, we use an STP constraint to represent both the DRVs and the actual values of the ingested food. For example, a recommendation to eat at lunch between 500 kcal and 600 kcal is represented by the STP constraint $500 \leq lunch_E - lunch_S \leq 600$, where $lunch_E$ and $lunch_S$ represent the end and the start of the lunch, respectively. To allow a user to make small deviations with regard to the "ideal" diet, we impose less strict constraints over the shortest periods (i.e., days or meals) and stricter constraints over the longest periods (i.e., months, weeks). For example the recommended energy requirement results in a constraint such as $2450 \cdot 7 \leq week_E - week_S \leq 2450 \cdot 7$ over a week and as $2450 - 10\% \leq Sunday_E - Sunday_S \leq 2450 + 10\%$ for a single day (e.g., Sunday). For single meals we further relax the constraints.

In order to effectively support the user, the system must also take into account what she actually eats. Therefore, a new, provisional, STP is generated where – in addition to the constraints derived from the DRVs – also the new STP constraints deriving from the meals that the user has actually consumed are added. The new constraints possibly restrict the values that the constraints in the original STP allow. The constraint propagation determines whether the new constraints are consistent and provides the new minimal network with the new implied relations. For example, let us suppose that the user on Sunday, Monday and

Tuesday had an actual intake of 2690 kcal for each day. This corresponds to adding to the STP the new constraints $2690 \leq Sunday_E - Sunday_S \leq 2690$, ..., $2690 \leq Tuesday_E - Tuesday_S \leq 2690$. Then, propagating the constraints of the new STP, we discover that (i) the intake is compatible with the diet (in fact the STP is consistent) and (ii) on each remaining day of the week the user has to assume between 2205 kcal and 2465 kcal.

We wish to provide the user with user-friendly information not limited to a visualization of the minimal network. The minimal network allows us to classify the macronutrients of the dish that the user intends to eat in the following cases: I.1) *permanently inconsistent,* I.2) *occasionally inconsistent,* C.1) *consistent and not balanced,* C.2) *consistent and well-balanced* and C.3) *consistent and perfectly balanced.* In the cases I.1 and i.2 the dish is inconsistent. In case I.1) the value of a macronutrient is inconsistent with the DRVs as represented in the user's diet. The dish cannot be accepted even independently of the other food she may possibly eat. In case I.2) the dish, taken in isolation, does not violate the DRVs, but, considering the past meals she has already eaten, it would preclude to be consistent with the diet. In cases C.1), C.2) and C.3) the value of the macronutrient is consistent with the diet, but a consistent but not balanced choice of a dish could have consequences on the rest of the user's diet because the user will have to "recover" from it. We assume that the mean value in the relative STP constraint is the "ideal" value according to the DRVs and we consider two parametric user-adjustable thresholds relative to the mean: according to the deviation with respect to the mean we classify the macronutrient as not balanced (case C.1), well balanced (case C.2) or perfectly balanced (case C.3). In particular, in the cases C.1) and C.2) we distinguish between lack or excess of a specific macronutrient for a dish: if it is lacking (in excess) with regard to the ideal value, we tag the dish with the keyword *IPO* (*IPER*). This information is exploited in the generation of the messages.

3.3   Motivating with NLG

In order to motivate an user to follow a good choice for eating, we reformulate the result of the reasoning into a textual form. This text will be combined with a suggestion in order to create a final output text. We designed a template-based system that, starting from the numerical results of the reasoning, returns a text message by following a number of textual patterns. That is, for each case in the reasoner output, we produce a textual template that will be filled with the specific content of the reasoning. These templates have been designed by basically considering three models of persuasion: (i) CAPTology, (ii) the Cialdini's Six Principles of Influence, (iii) the persuasive use of the emoticons [3,6,8].

In CAPTology (Computers As Persuasive Technologies), the principal idea is that the computer is perceived in three coexisting forms, Tool-Media-SocialActor. As a tool, the computer can enhance the capabilities of a user: our system calculates the nutritional contents of a dish, and so it enhances the ability to correctly judge the compatibility of the dish with a diet. As a media the

Table 1. The persuasive message templates.

C	D	Message Template	Translation
I.1	IPO	Questo piatto non va affatto bene, contiene davvero pochissime proteine!	This dish is not good at all, it's too poor in proteins!
I.2	IPO	Ora non puoi mangiare questo piatto perché è poco proteico. Ma se domenica mangi un bel piatto di fagioli allora lunedì potrai mangiarlo.	You cannot have this dish now because it doesn't provide enough proteins, but if you eat a nice dish of beans on Sunday, you can have it on Monday.
C.1	IPO	Va bene mangiare le patatine ma nei prossimi giorni dovrai mangiare più proteine.	It's OK to eat chips but in the next days you'll have to eat more proteins.
C.2	IPO	Questo piatto va bene, è solo un po' scarso di proteine. Nei prossimi giorni anche fagioli però! :)	This dish is OK, but it's a bit poor in proteins. In the next days you'll need beans too! :)
C.3	-	Ottima scelta! Questo piatto è perfetto per la tua dieta :)	Great choice! This dish is perfect for your diet :)

computer "provides experience": in our system, the human memory is enhanced by the reasoner, which indirectly reminds the user what she ate in the last days. As a social actor the computer creates an empathic relationship with the user reminding her the "social rules". Specifically, we designed the templates to guide the user towards the choice of a balanced meal, convincing her, by using a *friendly* recommendations, to follow the diet that herself decided. The six principles of Cialdini are: (1) Reciprocity: "people feel obligated to return a favor", (2) Scarcity: "people will value scarce products", (3) Authority: "people value the opinion of experts", (4) Consistency: "people do as they said they would", (5) Consensus: "people do as other people do", (6) Liking: "we say yes to people we like". In particular, our templates follow two of these principles, i.e. authority and consistency. Finally, in some messages we decided to use emoticons, since they can increase the communicative strength of a message by creating a tone of friendship, in particular for positive messages [6].

We use five templates to communicate the five cases in the reasoner output: in Table 1 we report the cases obtained by the reasoner output interpretation (column **C**), the direction of the deviation (column **D**), the Italian templates, and their rough English translation. For space reason, we do not describe the algorithm used in the generation module to combine the three distinct outputs of the reasoner on the three distinct macronutrients (i.e. proteins, lipids and carbohydrates). In short, the messages corresponding to each macronutrient need to be *aggregated* into a single message. A number of constraints related to coordination and relative clauses needed to be accounted for [14].

4   Conclusions

In this paper we proposed a software architecture for diet management: we discussed the main issues related to the modules used to analyze a recipe, to reason over the diet and to generate a message for the user.

There is a number of academic studies related to our project, e.g. [2,11,12,15], and there is also a great number of smartphone applications related to nutrition on the Italian and international markets, e.g. *DailyBurn, Lose It!, MyNetDiary,*

WeightWatchers. However, our dietary system presents three elements of novelty:
(1) the recovery of nutritional information directly from the recipes by using
NLU/IE techniques, (2) the use of automatic reasoning as a tool for verifying
the compatibility of a specific recipe with a specific diet, and (3) the use of NLG
techniques to produce the answer.

In the next future we intend to test our system by using a simulation. We
plan to use a real database of recipes and a number of realistic diets into the
context of a hospital.

References

1. LARN - Livelli di Assunzione di Riferimento di Nutrienti ed energia per la popo-
   lazione italiana - IV Revisione. SICS (2014)
2. Balintfy, J.L.: Menu planning by computer. Commun. ACM **7**(4), 255–259 (1964)
3. Cialdini, R.B.: Influence: science and practice. Pearson Education, Boston (2009)
4. Consolvo, S., et al.: Activity sensing in the wild: a field trial of ubifit garden. In:
   Proceedings of the SIGCHI Conference on Human Factors in Computing Systems,
   CHI 2008, pp. 1797–1806. ACM, New York (2008)
5. Dechter, R., Meiri, I., Pearl, J.: Temporal constraint networks. Artif. Intell.
   49(1–3), 61–95 (1991)
6. Derks, D., Bos, A.E.R., von Grumbkow, J.: Emoticons in computer-mediated
   communication: Social motives and social context. Cyberpsy., Behavior, and Soc.
   Networking **11**(1), 99–101 (2008)
7. Ferrucci, D., Lally, A.: UIMA: An architectural approach to unstructured information processing in the corporate research environment. Nat. Lang. Eng. **10**(3–4),
   327–348 (2004). http://dx.doi.org/10.1017/S1351324904003523
8. Fogg, B.: Persuasive Technology. Using computers to change what we think and
   do. Morgan Kaufmann Publishers / Elsevier, San Francisco (2002)
9. Furht, B. (ed.): Handbook of Augmented Reality. Springer (2011)
10. Greene, E.: Extracting structured data from recipes using conditional random fields
    (2015). http://open.blogs.nytimes.com/2015/04/09/extracting-structured-data-
    from-recipes-using-conditional-random-fields
11. Iizuka, K., Okawada, T., Matsuyama, K., Kurihashi, S., Iizuka, Y.: Food menu
    selection support system: considering constraint conditions for safe dietary life. In:
    Proceedings of the ACM Multimedia 2012 Workshop on Multimedia for Cooking
    and Eating Activities, CEA 2012, pp. 53–58. ACM, New York (2012)
12. Mankoff, J., Hsieh, G., Hung, H.C., Nitao, E.: Using low-cost sensing to support
    nutritional awareness. In: Borriello, G., Holmquist, L.E. (eds.) UbiComp 2002.
    LNCS, vol. 2498, pp. 371–376. Springer, Heidelberg (2002)
13. Nishida, C., Uauy, R., Kumanyika, S., Shetty, P.: The joint WHO/FAO expert
    consultation on diet, nutrition and the prevention of chronic diseases: process,
    product and policy implications. Public Health Nutrition **7**, 245–250 (2004)
14. Reiter, E., Dale, R.: Building Natural Language Generation Systems. Cambridge
    University Press, New York (2000)
15. Siek, K., Connelly, K., Rogers, Y., Rohwer, P., Lambert, D., Welch, J.: When
    do we eat? an evaluation of food items input into an electronic food monitoring
    application. In: Pervasive Health Conference and Workshops, pp. 1–10 (2006)
16. World Health Organization: Global strategy on diet, physical activity and health
    (WHA57.17). In: 75th World Health Assembly (2004)

Highly Accurate Food/Non-Food Image Classification Based on a Deep Convolutional Neural Network

Hokuto Kagaya[1(✉)] and Kiyoharu Aizawa[1,2]

[1] Graduate School of Interdisciplinary Information Studies,
The University of Tokyo, Tokyo, Japan
{kagaya,aizawa}@hal.t.u-tokyo.ac.jp
[2] Department of Information and Communication Engineering,
The University of Tokyo, Tokyo, Japan

Abstract. "Food" is an emerging topic of interest for multimedia and computer vision community. In this paper, we investigate food/non-food classification of images. We show that CNN, which is the state of the art technique for general object classification, can perform accurately for this problem. For the experiments, we used three different datasets of images: (1) images we collected from Instagram, (2) Food-101 and Caltech-256 dataset (3) dataset we used in [4]. We investigated the combinations of training and testing using the all three of them. As a result, we achieved high accuracy 96, 95 and 99% in the three datasets respectively.

Keywords: Food/Non-Food classification · Convolutional neural network · Deep learning

1 Introduction

"Food" is an emerging topic of interest for multimedia and computer vision community. It is a very important issue for healthcare. We have been developing a novel food recording tool, "FoodLog" [1, 2], which helps users easily record their everyday meals by the assistance of image retrieval.

However, analysis of food images is in general very challenging. For example, recognition of a food item in an image is still difficult because intra-class variance is high and inter-class variance is low. Moreover, the number of food classes is not well determined yet.

In this paper, we investigate a problem of food/non-food classification. Given an image, we want to find if the image contains food or not. It is a binary classification of images. One of the applications of such classification is a pre-processing for food image recognition.

In recent years, the number of photographs uploaded to social networking services (SNS) has been explosively increasing. Photo/video sharing services such as Instagram, Flickr and Pinterest are very popular. When users upload a photo to them, they add keywords or hash tags explaining the image content. However, in reality, the hash tags they use are not very reliable. Fig. 1 shows a search result by "#food" of Instagram. Although "food" is specified in the search, there are more non-food images in

© Springer International Publishing Switzerland 2015
V. Murino et al. (Eds.): ICIAP 2015 Workshops, LNCS 9281, pp. 350–357, 2015.
DOI: 10.1007/978-3-319-23222-5_43

the results. In order to show food images, we need to automatically filter the results by the binary food/non-food classification.

In our study, we arranged three datasets for the experiments: Instagram, Food-101[5] and the one we used in [4]. We adopted convolutional neural network (CNN) [3] as feature extractor and classifier, which is the state-of-the-art technique.

Fig. 1. Top two pages of search results by query "*#food*" in Instagram.

2   Related Work

This study is an extension of our previous study on food image recognition. In our previous paper [4], we have addressed the effectiveness of CNN for food image recognition and detection (classification). We had also presented food/non-food classification by SVM with hand-crafted features for personal food logging applications [1].

Analysis of food images has attracted much attention of multimedia and computer vision communities. Bossard et al., [5] built a publicly available food image dataset, Food-101, and they examined the efficiency of their method to mine discriminative parts using Random Forests. We utilize this dataset in the experiment. Li et al. [6] presented food recognition using a small dataset: their study was a part of their Technology Assisted Dietary Assessment project. From the point of view of the datasets, Pittsburgh Fast-food Image Dataset [7] is one of the earliest datasets. It consists of American fast-food images. Kawano et al., [8] introduced a UEC Food-256 Dataset, which is a dataset constructed by crowdsourcing. These food recognition related works did not handle food/non-food classification.

As mentioned earlier, food/non-food classification will be beneficial to searching food images in current photo sharing SNS, as well as to pre-processing of food recognition.

3   CNN-Based Approach to Food/Non-Food Classification

The CNN offers a state-of-the-art technique for general image recognition. It is a multilayer neural network, whose neurons take small patches of the previous layer as input. It is robust against small shifts and rotations. A CNN mainly comprises convolution layers and pooling layers.

The biggest advantage of CNN is to be able to learn high-level efficient features from data. We expect that CNN will extract important features of "food" images. We utilize the Network in Network model [9] as CNN architecture, because it is fast for training, performs better than the AlexNet [14] and it is memory efficient. We call our model "CNN-NIN" for the rest of the paper. It has four convolution layers with two mlpconv layers (see the detail in [9]). Additionally, to Copy mid-level image representations in CNN is very efficient for computation time and accuracy [13]. Therefore, we employ the model pre-trained by ImageNet that is publicly avail-able, and after copying the model parameters, we fine-tune them for our datasets. We revise the dimension of outputs from 1000 to 2 for food/non-food classification.

We also train CNN from scratch and compare the results with the fine-tuned model. In our research, we use caffe [10] as the CNN library, which is a standard GPU implementation in C++ and python.

4   Datasets

We introduce three dataset in this section. The datasets we collected from Instagram and Food-101/Caltech-256 are described later. The dataset used in [4] is made of 1,234 food images and 1,980 non-food images collected from social media. We utilize it for a comparative study in Section 5.3.

Fig. 2. 16 samples from Instagram Food/Non-Food Dataset. Left one is positive, right one is negative.

Fig. 3. 16 samples of images from Food-101/Caltech-256. Left one is positive, right one is negative.

Fig. 4. 16 examples of images from the dataset used in [4]. Left one is positive, right one is negative.

4.1   Instagram-#Food Dataset (IFD)

We built an Instagram Food/Non-Food Dataset (IFD, in short). We collected them from the search results of "#food" in Instagram and manually annotated images with food or non-food labels. Our annotation criteria are as follows: 1) The main content of image should be food. 2) Food in the image should be real, not illustration. The first criterion is relatively subjective. If the image captures some objects with food in the background, we excluded them from the dataset. In the dataset, we finally have 4,230 food images and 5,428 non-food images. We will open the dataset to the public[1].

4.2   Food-101/Caltech-256 Dataset (FCD)

We also built another dataset using widely available datasets. We used Food-101 [5] as food images and Caltech-256 as non-food image (This dataset is called FCD, in short). Food-101 images were originally downloaded from foodspotting.com, which is a sharing site that allows users to upload images with additional information. Among 1,000 images of each class, we chose 250 images so that the variance of a color feature (64-dim color histogram) within the class becomes high. Color feature is one of the most important features for food image recognition [4, 12]. As a result, we chose 25,250 positive food images in total.

Caltech-256[11] is a standard dataset for general image recognition and categorization. We use it for negative samples after excluding the images related to food. The categories of Caltech-256 excluded from dataset are shown in Table 1. Finally, we chose 28,322 non-food images.

Table 1. The categories excluded from Caltech-256.

Excluded categories
crab, mussels, octopus, grape, mushroom, tomato, watermelon, beer-mug, cereal-box, coffee-mug, soda-can, wine-bottle, teapot, cake, ice-cream-cone, fried-egg, hamburger, hot-dog, spaghetti, sushi, drinking-straw, frying-pan

5   Experiment

In this section, we show the experimental results on three datasets: IFD, FCD and our previous dataset. In Section 5.1, 5.2 and 5.3, we present the results of evaluation within the same dataset. In 5.3, we compare our results with previous results of conventional methods. We show the results of the evaluation across the datasets in Section 5.4. Finally, the result of comparative study between the from-scratch model and the fine-tune model is shown in Section 5.5.

Table 2. Experimental results of IFD and FCD with different train/test ratios.

Train/test Ratio		0.5	0.6	0.7	0.8	0.9
Accura-	IFD	94.5	94.7	94.5	94.8	95.1
cy (%)	FCD	96.2	96.3	96.2	96.4	96.1

5.1   Instagram Food/Non-Food Dataset   (IFD)

Firstly, we examined accuracy of training/testing ratio, which is the ratio of the number of training samples and that of testing. We randomly selected images from IFD, and then evaluated the accuracy.

---

[1] https://www.hal.t.u-tokyo.ac.jp/~kagaya/ifd.html

The top row of Table 2 shows the results by different training/testing ratios, which is the averaged value over five trials. As can be seen, all values are about 96% for all ratios. The differences in the training/testing ratios are few, hence we fixed the ratio at 0.8 for the rest of the paper. Fig. 5 shows confusion matrix of the trials with train/test ratio 0.8; from the results, differences of the accuracies among classes (food or non-food) were not observed. Table 3 shows some examples of classified images. The results that were not classified as food included food products and small food regions. Some results which were not classified as non-food included flowers (similar to food) or objects of colors similar to foods.

Table 3. Classification examples of IFD. Incorrect results may be influenced by its background, products, small food regions.

	Ground truth : food	Ground truth : non-food
Correct		
Incor-rect		

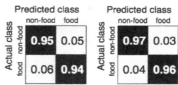

Fig. 5. (left) confusion matrix in the experiments of IFD (average over 5 trials with train/test ratio 0.8). (right) confusion matrix in the experiments of FCD (average over 5 trials with train/test ratio 0.8).

5.2   Food-101/Caltech-256 Dataset (FCD)

We conducted the evaluation using Food-101/Caltech-256 Dataset in the same manner as Section 5.1. The accuracies are shown in the bottom row of Table 2, and a confusion matrix of one particular trial is shown in Fig. 5 (right), both of which show a similar trend to the results of IFD. Example images are shown in Table 4.

5.3   Dataset Used in [4]

In this section, we show a comparative study of the proposed method against our two previous methods, which are the baseline method based on SVM of handcrafted features in our FoodLog system and Alex-Net CNN.

Table 5 shows the results of the comparisons. The values are averaged over ten trials[2] of different combinations of training and testing images using the dataset of [4].

---

[2]   The manner of evaluation for the existing method in [4] differs a little. See the detail in [4].

As shown in Table 5, the proposed CNN-NIN produced the best accurate performance among the three methods.

Table 4. Classification examples of FCD.

	round truth : food	round truth : non-food
Correct		
Incor-rect		

Table 5. Comparison with the previous methods.

Method	Accuracy
Baseline ([1, 4])	89.7 ± 0.73%
CNN [4]	93.8 ± 1.39%
CNN-NIN (this paper)	**99.1 ± 0.81%**

5.4   Cross Dataset Evaluation

The three datasets may have statistical differences in food/non-food images. To examine the effects of the difference of datasets, we evaluated accuracies of the proposed system using different datasets for training and testing. We conducted two evaluations as follows:

(A)   Training: FCD   and   Testing: IFD
(B)   Training: IFD   and Testing: FCD

Table 6 shows accuracies, and Fig. 6 shows the confusion matrices of (A) and (B). The accuracy of food images classification was degraded in (A), and that of non-food images was degraded in (B). It is considered that IFD and FCD datasets have slight differences. The dataset should be larger for the classification to be robust.

Table 6. Result for (A) and (B).

Experiment	Accuracy
(A)	91.5%
(B)	90.6%

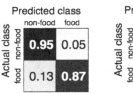

Fig. 6. (left) Confusion matrix of (A).
(right) Confusion matrix of (B).

Table 7. Examples incorrectly classified by the model in (A) but correctly classified by the model of IFD

Ground truth : food	Ground truth : non-food

We compared the model of (A) with one of the model of IFD (section 5.1), using the best accuracy in five trials. In other words, we compared the model trained by the same dataset as when testing with the model trained by the different one. The images for testing are those not used in the training of this model in Section 5.1. Table 7 shows some examples. As seen in Table 7, Instagram images in which colors were modified were not correctly classified.

5.5 Fine-Tune Model vs. from-Scratch for Cross Dataset Evaluation

To examine the effects of differences of CNN trainings, we conducted evaluations for comparison between a fine-tune model and a from-scratch model using the datasets of (A). Fine-tune models were made as follows: We used a pre-trained model trained using ImageNet images [15]. Following the method in [13], the transferred parameters were copied from the pre-trained model and the last one or two layers were adapted. In addition, we used the pre-trained model as the initial weights and re-trained, too. We also evaluated CNN made from scratch.

Table 8 shows the result of the experiments. Fine-tune models were better than the from-scratch regarding accuracy and computational time required for training. The size of the datasets would be much larger the from-scratch could be better. Among the three fine tune ones, re-training version was the best.

Table 8. Results of comparison between from-scratch and fine-tuning

Method	Transferred Parameters	New adaption Layers	Accuracy
Fine-tune	Re-train	Last one	**91.5%**
Fine-tune	Fixed	Last one	89.6%
Fine-tune	Fixed	Last two	91.1%
From-scratch	-	-	86.4%

6   Conclusion

In this paper, we have examined the effectiveness of a CNN-based approach for food/non-food classification with three datasets. The datasets were collected from publicly available images and social media. The model for this task can be applied to pre-processing of food item recognition or filter the search result of queries related to food, meals or dishes. In the future, food/non-food classification could be applied to more complex processing of food images.

References

1. Kitamura, K., Yamasaki, T., Aizawa, K.: Food log by analyzing food images. In: Proceedings of the 16th ACM International Conference on Multimedia, pp. 999–1000. ACM, October, 2008
2. Aizawa, K., Ogawa, M.: FoodLog: Multimedia Tool for Healthcare Applications. IEEE MultiMedia **22**(2), 4–9 (2015)
3. LeCun, Y., Boser, B., Denker, J.S., Henderson, D., Howard, R.E., Hubbard, W., Jackel, L.D.: Backpropagation applied to handwritten zip code recognition. Neural computation **1**(4), 541–551 (1989)
4. Kagaya, H., Aizawa, K., Ogawa, M.: Food detection and recognition using convolutional neural network. In: Proceedings of the ACM International Conference on Multimedia, pp. 1085–1088. ACM, November 2014
5. Bossard, L., Guillaumin, M., Van Gool, L.: Food-101 – mining discriminative components with random forests. In: Fleet, D., Pajdla, T., Schiele, B., Tuytelaars, T. (eds.) ECCV 2014, Part VI. LNCS, vol. 8694, pp. 446–461. Springer, Heidelberg (2014)
6. He, Y., Xu, C., Khanna, N., Boushey, C.J., Delp, E.J.: Analysis of food images: features and classification. In: 2014 IEEE International Conference on Image Processing (ICIP), pp. 2744–2748. IEEE, October 2014
7. Chen, M., Dhingra, K., Wu, W., Yang, L., Sukthankar, R., Yang, J.: PFID: pittsburgh fast-food image dataset. In: 2009 16th IEEE International Conference on Image Processing (ICIP), pp. 289–292. IEEE, November 2009
8. Kawano, Y., Yanai, K.: FoodCam-256: a large-scale real-time mobile food recognitionsystem employing high-dimensional features and compression of classifier weights. In: Proceedings of the ACM International Conference on Multimedia, pp. 761–762. ACM, November 2014
9. Lin, M., Chen, Q., Yan, S.: Network in network. In: Proceedings of International Conference on Learning Representations (2014)
10. Jia, Y., Shelhamer, E., Donahue, J., Karayev, S., Long, J., Girshick, R., Darrell, T.: Caffe: convolutional architecture for fast feature embedding. In: Proceedings of the ACM International Conference on Multimedia, pp. 675–678. ACM, November 2014
11. Griffin, G., Holub, A., Perona, P.: Caltech-256 object category dataset (2007)
12. Bosch, M., Zhu, F., Khanna, N., Boushey, C.J., Delp, E.J.: Combining global and local features for food identification in dietary assessment. In: IEEE Transactions on Image Processing: A Publication of the IEEE Signal Processing Society, 2011, pp. 1789–1792 (2011). doi:10.1109/ICIP.2011.6115809
13. Oquab, M., Bottou, L., Laptev, I., Sivic, J.: Learning and transferring mid-level image representations using convolutional neural networks. In: 2014 IEEE Conference on Computer Vision and Pattern Recognition (CVPR), pp. 1717–1724. IEEE, June 2014
14. Krizhevsky, A., Sutskever, I., Hinton, G.E.: ImageNet Classification with Deep Convolutional Neural Networks, NIPS 2012: Neural Information Processing Systems, Lake Tahoe, Nevada
15. Deng, J., Dong, W., Socher, R., Li, L.-J., Li, K., Fei-Fei, L.: ImageNet: a large-scale hierarchical image database. In: IEEE Computer Vision and Pattern Recognition (CVPR) (2009)

A Printer Indexing System for Color Calibration with Applications in Dietary Assessment

Shaobo Fang[1], Chang Liu[1], Fengqing Zhu[1],
Carol Boushey[2], and Edward Delp[1]($\boxtimes$)

[1] School of Electrical and Computer Engineering, Purdue University,
West Lafayette, IN, USA
ace@ecn.purdue.edu
http://www.tadaproject.org
[2] Cancer Epidemiology Program, University of Hawaii Cancer Center,
Honolulu, HI, USA

Abstract. In image based dietary assessment, color is a very important feature in food identification. One issue with using color in image analysis in the calibration of the color imaging capture system. In this paper we propose an indexing system for color camera calibration using printed color checkerboards also known as fiducial markers (FMs). To use the FM for color calibration one must know which printer was used to print the FM so that the correct color calibration matrix can be used for calibration. We have designed a printer indexing scheme that allows one to determine which printer was used to print the FM based on a unique arrangement of color squares and binarized marks (used for error control) printed on the FM. Using normalized cross correlation and pattern detection, the index corresponding to the printer for a particular FM can be determined. Our experimental results show this scheme is robust against most types of lighting conditions.

1 Introduction

In this paper we describe a printer indexing system for color image calibration used in a mobile telephone dietary assessment system, the Technology Assisted Dietary Assessment (TADA) system, that we have been developing for the past seven years [1,3,15]. The TADA system, and the associated mobile Food Record (mFR), allows users to acquire food images using a mobile telephone [1]. Image processing and analysis methods are then used to determine the food type and nutrient value of the food [1,14,15]. The current system uses color as an important feature for identifying food types, therefore it is crucial to maintain the consistency of color for accurate food classification [14]. A color calibration process based on reference information is required prior to food classification to eliminate the influences of varying lighting conditions and mitigate variations in camera sensor response. To provide reference information, we have designed a color

---

E. Delp—This work was sponsored by grant from the National Institutes of Health under grant NIEH/NIH 2R01ES012459-06.

V. Murino et al. (Eds.): ICIAP 2015 Workshops, LNCS 9281, pp. 358–365, 2015.
DOI: 10.1007/978-3-319-23222-5_44

checkerboard pattern or a fiducial marker (FM) as illustrated in Figure 1(a). This color checkerboard consists of M colors where $M = 11$ including background "white" for our current version of the FM. The fiducial marker is included in the scene by the user to serve as a reference for the estimation of scale and pose of the objects in the scene and to provide reference information for color calibration [12]. Our research group has generated and distributed all the FMs used in our previous studies by printing the FMs on the same printer (a Canon i9900). As the number of users in our studies increases, we need to develop a method for the users to generate the FM themselves.

(a) Canon i9900   (b) Canon PIXMA   (c) HP   LaserJet
                        Pro-100   M551

Fig. 1. Food images from our TADA system with the fiducial marker (FM) present.

The issue of reproducing colors is a fundamentally difficult problem [10]. We have tested printing the FMs using various printers and significant color mismatch can be observed based on both the perception of a human observer (see Figure 3) and our estimates of the sRGB values [7]. Therefore we must design a system that allows us to know which printer was used to print the FM so that we can properly color calibrate the images. Our goal is to design the FM so that we can determine the printer by extracting the printer index from an image of the FM. Note that by "printer index" we mean a number that we can use to associate to a particular printer used to print the FM. We assume for this paper that we know the color calibration matrix for the printer. We are in the process of planning a large study whereby the number of simultaneous users of the mFR will be in the 100s. For this study we are designing a process where a user will be sent an FM as a digital file (e.g. a pdf file) with the indexing described in this paper that assigns that FM to the particular user. They will be asked to print the FM and send the printed FM back to us for extraction of the color calibration matrix. This process is beyond the scope of this paper. In this paper we are describing the FM indexing scheme and it relative robustness. One approach for printer indexing is to add a QR code containing the printer index in addition to the FM. However, this would require an additional step for the user to scan the QR code, thus increasing user burden [3]. Another approach we have used in the past for printer identification is based on texture features [5]. Unfortunately a texture-based printer identification technique will have issues with insufficient texture details in the FMs we use. We are interested in developing a method that will embed the index information in the fiducial marker without interfering with the color calibration and image analysis processes.

Fig. 2. Magnified FM in Figure 1(c).

Fig. 3. FM color differences using two printers.

2   Color Correction and Printer Indexing

2.1   Color Correction

Color is one of the key variables in imaging [7,10]. It is difficult to maintain color consistency due to illumination of the scene and camera settings such as auto exposure and auto white balance. Existing approaches attempt to increase the robustness of color descriptors based on features such as the RGB histogram, color moments and C-SIFT [6,9]. Our approach for color correction is a linear RGB mapping based on the von-Kries model [4]. Before we can calibrate the colors in an image acquired with our mFR one needs to calibrate the printer and determine its calibration matrix. This is done for a specific printer by printing the FM assigned to that printer and using a spectral radiometer to determine the sRGB estimates under CIE standard illuminant D65 [8]. A $M \times 3$ color reference matrix, where M is the number of checkerboard colors, is constructed and denoted as C_{ref}. C_{ref} is constructed by assigning color sRGB estimates to the rows of C_{ref} based on the appearances of colors using a raster scan order, with the background color "white" last. The location associated with "red" square on the fiducial marker as indicated in Figure 3 will always be used as the starting point for raster scan order.

For color calibration, both the presence of the FM and the pixel coordinates of vertices for each color square in the FM need to be detected in the image we want to color correct. In our system, the detection is done on a gray scale version of the image [11]. Once the pixel coordinates of the vertices of the color squares are obtained, the sRGB values for each of the M colors in FMs are then estimated by examining the pixels in each color square. A color matrix for the image to be color corrected, denoted as C_{test}, is then constructed similarly to C_{ref}. Note that C_{test} is constructed using the lighting conditions in the scene and not the CIE standard illuminant D65. Color calibration is conducted using C_{ref} based on linear least squares [12]. The color correction matrix $D \in \mathbb{R}^{3 \times 3}$ is:

$$\hat{D} = \underset{D \in \mathbb{R}^{3 \times 3}}{\arg\min} \sum_{j=1}^{M} ||(\boldsymbol{C}_{ref_j})^t - D(\boldsymbol{C}_{test_j})^t||^2 \tag{1}$$

where $\hat{D}$ is the estimated color correction matrix, and $\boldsymbol{C}_{ref_j}, \boldsymbol{C}_{test_j} \in \mathbb{R}^{1 \times 3}$ are the jth color, $j \in \{1, \cdots, M\}$. The image can be color corrected pixel by pixel as:

$$C_{corrected}^t = \hat{D} C_{original}^t \tag{2}$$

where $C_{original} \in \mathbb{R}^{1 \times 3}$ is the original uncorrected sRGB values at any pixel location and $C_{corrected} \in \mathbb{R}^{1 \times 3}$ is the color corrected result.

2.2 Printer Indexing System

We are interested in constructing an indexing system that allows us to identify from an image containing an FM which printer is used to print the FM. We designed the indexing system by associating each printer with a unique FM with different color squares arrangement. Rearranging the color squares on the checkerboard with no constraint yields a theoretical maximum of N_{max} permutations (or printers) where $N_{max} = 10! = 3,628,000$ and it is sufficient to address our needs. Denote i as the index for the ith FM (or the ith printer) and its corresponding color reference matrix is $C_{ref}^{(i)} \in \mathbb{R}^{M \times 3}$.

C_{test} is the color matrix estimated from an image to be color corrected, we shall refer to this image as the test image. Denote the lighting condition as I, the conditional probability that the FM with assigned index i is in the test image is defined as:

$$p(C_{test}|C_{ref}^{(i)}, I) \tag{3}$$

We want to estimate the index $\hat{i}$ based on (3) such that:

$$\hat{i} = \arg\max_{i \in \{1,\dots,N\}} \{p(C_{test}|C_{ref}^{(i)}, I)\} \tag{4}$$

We will find $\hat{i}$ using normalized cross correlation (NCC).

Normalized cross correlation is a method for template or image matching [2,13]. Our experimental results indicate that NCC can minimize the impact of the external lighting condition when estimating the printer index. The printer index is estimated using the NCC score between C_{test} and $C_{ref}^{(i)}$ where the NCC score, $f(C_{test}, C_{ref}^{(i)})$, is defined as:

$$f(C_{test}, C_{ref}^{(i)}) = \frac{1}{3 \cdot M - 1} \frac{\sum_{k=1}^{3 \cdot M} \{(C_{test}(k) - \mu_{C_{test}})(C_{ref}^{(i)}(k) - \mu_{C_{ref}^{(i)}})\}}{\sigma_{C_{test}} \sigma_{C_{ref}^{(i)}}} \tag{5}$$

where C_{test} and $C_{ref}^{(i)}$ are vectorized as C_{test}, $C_{ref}^{(i)} \in \mathbb{R}^{1 \times 3 \cdot M}$, $M = 11$, μ and σ^2 are mean and sample standard deviation, respectively. Based on the above definition, we have the estimated index as:

$$\hat{i} = \arg\max_{i \in \{1,\dots,N\}} \{f(C_{test}, C_{ref}^{(i)})\} \tag{6}$$

After we obtain the estimate $\hat{i}$, we use the reference information associated with this specific FM for color calibration as described in Section 2.1.

2.3   Error Control Using Binarized Marks

From our experiments, we observed that similar FM colors (such as red, orange and brown) may be very difficult to differentiate under certain lighting conditions (e.g. a dim restaurant) or due to poor printing quality. For these similar colors that are likely to cause incorrect index decisions using NCC, we define "similar colors" sets. For example, red, orange and brown can form a "similar colors" set. If similar colors can not be differentiated, the assumption that each FM has a unique arrangement of color squares can no longer hold true. To address this issue, we propose the use of a "binarized mark" that we can add to the FM to serve as an error control method in addition to NCC. Binarized marks are combinations of small black squares placed at the center of one or more white squares as illustrated in Figure 2.

A numeric value can be generated from the binarized mark based on the detection of the black square. Following raster scan order begins at the second white square in the FM, each subsequent white square represents a "bit" in the binary sequence starting from the least significant bit. A bit is assigned a "1" when a black square is present and "0" otherwise. The corresponding numeric value in decimal can be obtained by converting the binary sequence. For the FM shown in Figure 2, the binary sequence is "000000011" and accordingly the numeric value in decimal is "3". Since the length of the binary sequence is 9, only $2^9 = 512$ binarized marks can be generated. However, the theoretical maximum number of printers we can index is $N_{max} = 3,628,800$. Since we "assign" a binarized mark to every FM, we will quickly run out of binarized marks without having identical binarized marks assigned to each FM. Since we cannot assign a unique binarized mark to each FM, we need to define a criteria for assigning binarized marks to the FMs.

We define a threshold T to activate the error control. For a given printer index $\hat{i}$ obtained from (6), if there is no other $i \in \{1, \cdots, N\}$ and $i \neq \hat{i}$ such that the NCC score defined in (5) satisfies the following:

$$f(C_{test}, C_{ref}^{(\hat{i})}) - f(C_{test}, C_{ref}^{(i)}) < T \tag{7}$$

we can safely assume that using the NCC score is sufficient for indexing the printer, hence no binarized marks are needed in this case. We set $T = 0.01$ based on our experimental results. Otherwise, error control method is activated and printer index can be corrected based on the detection of the binarized mark. As a result, we only need to assign a unique binarized mark to each FM that meets the criteria of (7). Based on our experimental results, we have observed that the number of FMs with "similar colors" swapped generally do not exceed the maximum number of binarized marks that can be generated, which is 512. For example, in the case where similar FM colors such as red, orange and brown are swapped, we only need $3! = 6$ binarized marks to guarantee the correct printer indexing.

3   Experimental Results

The initial evaluation of our printer indexing system is based on FMs we printed using several printers. Our test images contain various foods images with different FMs taken under several lighting conditions. There is no other information in the test images that can indicate which FM is used in a specific test image. After extracting the color information from the FMs and the binarized marks, we estimated the index i using the methods described in Section 2.2. The indexing is estimated primarily using the NCC score. Binarzied marks will be used only when error control is activated as described in (7). The ground truth is obtained by a human observer examining the arrangement of color squares. The accuracy of indexing decisions can then be obtained by comparing to the ground truth.

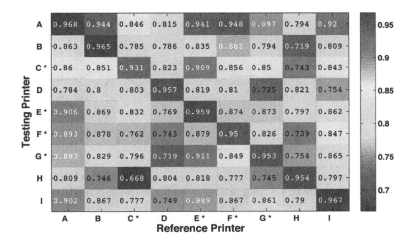

Fig. 4. Accuracy of estimated printer index based on average NCC scores from 9 printers, with each printer associated with a unique FM as listed below: (A) Canon i9900 (original FM), (B) Canon PIXMA Pro-100 (red and brown swapped), (C*) HP LaserJet M551 (green and dark green swapped), (D) Canon PIXMA Pro-10 (green and yellow swapped), (E*) HP Color LaserJet 4700 (red and magenta swapped), (F*) Ricoh Aficio MP C6501 (yellow and orange swapped), (G*) TOSHIBA e-STUDIO 3530c (blue and cyan swapped), (H) Epson WF3540 (green, yellow and dark green swapped), (I) HP D110a (red and orange swapped)

We are interested in testing the NCC-based method for a variety of FMs. To conduct such a test we generated 9 FMs, where 1 had no color swapped (original FM with the following colors in raster scan order: red, green, blue, black, brown, cyan, magenta, yellow, dark green and orange), 7 had two colors swapped compared to the original one (red and brown, green and dark green, green and yellow, red and magenta, yellow and orange, blue and cyan, red and orange), and 1 had three colors swapped compared to the original one (green, yellow and dark green). Figure 1(b) and (c) show examples of images with FMs that have color swapped and binarized marks.

We have obtained 579 test images with different lighting conditions using 9 models of laser and inkjet printers. These lighting conditions include incandescent and fluorescent lightings with various luminance, sunlight, shadows and more complex lighting conditions in the restaurants. The index decisions can be made accurately as reflected by the average NCC scores illustrated in Figure 4. The average NCC scores for each FM are obtained from test images containing the same FM. Note that printers with "*" in Figure 4 are laser printers.

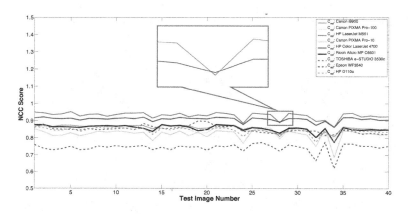

Fig. 5. A test set of 40 images from 9 printers. The two lines inside the red rectangular area show an example where a wrong printer indexing decision is made based on NCC scores alone.

We also test the accuracy of printer indexing based on NCC scores for each test image from a subset of the 579 test images used above. This subset of test images contains 40 images with the same FM printed from a HP LaserJet M551 printer. For this particular example, color squares green and dark green are swapped compared to the original FM (no color swapped). A wrong indexing decision is made based on NCC scores alone as shown in the zoomed in red rectangular area of Figure 5. The printer is indexed to HP Color LaserJet 4700 instead of HP LaserJet M551 without activating error control for one of the test images. The test image that generates the wrong indexing decision is shown in Figure 1(c), with a zoomed in image of the fiducial marker shown in Figure 2. However, the criteria for activating the error control method as defined in (7) is satisfied for this test image. Therefore, by detecting the binarized marks, the correct indexing decision can be made.

4   Conclusion

In this paper we have described a printer indexing system for use in color image correction. We have shown that the printer index can be accurately estimated.

We are currently investigating how to use this approach in user studies that may have hundreds of printers by constructing a database of color calibration information.

References

1. The TADA project. http://tadaproject.org
2. Briechle, K., Hanebeck, U.: Template matching using fast normalized cross correlation. In: Proceedings of the SPIE Optical Pattern Recognition XII, Orlando, FL, vol. 4387, pp. 95–102, April 2001
3. Daugherty, B., Schap, T., Ettienne-Gittens, R., Zhu, F., Bosch, M., Delp, E., Ebert, D., Kerr, D., Boushey, C.: Novel technologies for assessing dietary intake: Evaluating the usability of a mobile telephone food record among adults and adolescents. Journal of Medical Internet Research **14**(2), e58 (2012)
4. von Kries, J.: Chromatic adaptation. Festschrift der Albrecht-Ludwigs-Universit, pp. 145–158 (1902)
5. Mikkilineni, A., Chiang, P., Ali, G., Chiu, G., Allebach, J., Delp, E.: Printer identification based on graylevel co-occurrence features for security and forensic applications. In: Proceedings of the SPIE Security, Steganography, and Watermarking of Multimedia Contents VII, San Jose, CA, vol. 5681, pp. 430–440, January 2005
6. Mindru, F., Tuytelaars, T., Van Gool, L., Moons, T.: Moment invariants for recognition under changing viewpoint and illumination. Computer Vision and Image Understanding **94**(1–3), 3–27 (2004)
7. Sharma, G.: Digital Color Imaging Handbook. CRC Press, Boca Raton (2002)
8. Stokes, M., Anderson, M., Chandrasekar, S., Motta, R.: A standard default color space for the internet-srgb. Microsoft and Hewlett-Packard Joint Report (1996)
9. van de Sande, K., Gevers, T., Snoek, C.: Evaluating color descriptors for object and scene recognition. IEEE Transactions on Pattern Analysis and Machine Intelligence **32**(9), 1582–1596 (2010)
10. Wandell, B.: Foundations of Vision. Sinauer Associates Inc., Sunderland (1995)
11. Xu, C., Khanna, N., Boushey, C.J., Delp, E.J.: Low complexity image quality measures for dietary assessment using mobile devices. In: Proceedings of the IEEE International Symposium on Multimedia, Dana Point, CA, pp. 351–356, December 2011
12. Xu, C., Zhu, F., Khanna, N., Boushey, C., Delp, E.: Image enhancement and quality measures for dietary assessment using mobile devices. In: Proceedings of the IS&T/SPIE Conference on Computational Imaging X, San Francisco, CA, vol. 8296, pp. 82960Q–82960Q-10, January 2012
13. Zhao, F., Huang, Q., Gao, W.: Image matching by normalized cross-correlation. In: Proceedings of the IEEE International Conference on Acoustics, Speech, and Signal Processing, Toulouse, France, vol. 2, pp. 729–732, May 2006
14. Zhu, F., Bosch, M., Khanna, N., Boushey, C., Delp, E.: Multiple hypotheses image segmentation and classification with application to dietary assessment. IEEE Journal of Biomedical and Health Informatics **19**(1), 377–388 (2015)
15. Zhu, F., Bosch, M., Woo, I., Kim, S., Boushey, C., Ebert, D., Delp, E.: The use of mobile devices in aiding dietary assessment and evaluation. IEEE Journal of Selected Topics in Signal Processing **4**(4), 756–766 (2010)

Food Object Recognition Using a Mobile Device: State of the Art

Simon Knez and Luka Šajn[(✉)]

Faculty of Computer and Information Science, University of Ljubljana,
Ljubljana, Slovenia
vbknez@hotmail.com, luka.sajn@fri.uni-lj.si

Abstract. In this paper nine mobile food recognition systems are described based on their system architecture and their core properties (the core properties and experimental results are shown on the last page). While the mobile hardware increased its power through the years (2009 - 2013) and the food detection algorithms got optimized, still there was no uniform approach to the question of food detection. Also, some system used additional information for better detection, like voice data, OCR and bounding boxes. Three systems included a volume estimation feature. First five systems were implemented on a client-server architecture, while the last three took advantage of the available hardware in later years and proposed a client only based architecture.

1 Introduction

Because of the raise of diet related diseases, a lot of easy to use applications were made for the purpose of dieting guidance. At first, dieting guidance was mediated by manual monitoring of eating activity (keeping records of foods and beverages consumed), followed by storing them on a web site application with instant analysis (web sites like Calorie King, CRON-O-Meter, Selfnutritiondata, etc.). All this applications allow the user to get information about the nutrients of the selected food, but they need to know which food and how much of it has been eaten. For the purpose of easier tracking of food activity, a merge of object detection and previous diet monitoring systems was bound to happen. The first food object detection algorithm, that was implemented for practical use on a mobile device, was described in the paper of Joutou in the year 2009 [1]. New approaches to lower the amount of knowledge and hardware needed for the users analysis of eating followed. The outline of the paper is as follows: section 2 describes the methods of analysis of the applications, section 3 reviews these applications. In section 4 the paper concludes.

2 Methods

2.1 Comparisons of Applications

In this paper nine mobile food recognition applications are described. Each application is described by its core features and its system architecture. At the end

© Springer International Publishing Switzerland 2015
V. Murino et al. (Eds.): ICIAP 2015 Workshops, LNCS 9281, pp. 366–374, 2015.
DOI: 10.1007/978-3-319-23222-5_45

of the paper, a table of all used algorithms for food recognition are listed and grouped into 5 stages of object recognition.

2.2 The Applications

Nine applications were described in this paper, aging from the year 2009 to the year 2013: Joutou and Yanai, 2009 [1], Puri et al., 2009 [2],Hoashi, Joutou and Yanai, 2010 [3], Kong and Tan, 2012 [4], Rahman et al., 2012 [5], Kawano and Yanai, 2013 [6], Kawano and Yanai, 2013 [7], Anthimopoulos et al., 2013 [8] and Pouladzadeh, Shirmohammadi and Arici, 2013 [9].

3   Review of Applications

All of the reviewed applications in this paper use the mobile phone to record eating activity via images. To automatically detect what food objects were eaten a food object recognition algorithm is needed. Object recognition algorithms are mostly comprised of the following steps or stages: image acquisition, image processing, image segmentation, image feature extraction and image classification. Image acquisition deals with different techniques of data capturing (some applications use one image, some use multiple images, some use OCR or voice data), while the processing stage deals with different pixel normalization techniques for the reduction of the noise present. These two stages are needed for better image segmentation, where ROIs - regions of interest are extracted. Regions of interest (usually background, foreground subtraction) allow to shorten the processing time of the later stage of feature extraction, since the area of analysis is smaller and object specific. The next stage is to extract different features from the segmented images. Many different image features techniques can be used. This features are later used for the classification. After the classification is done, the algorithm outputs the class to which the inputed set of features belongs to. After the output, it is in the hands of the front-end developer to display the results in a desired shape or form (caloric analysis, recommendation for further eating activities, recipes suggestions...). Because of the difference of availability of technology and the object detection algorithms, mobile food detection applications differ through the years in most of the stages. While some aspects of a particular stage co-exist, newer and better one replaced the old ones or are added to the mix.

3.1   Joutou and Yanai, 2009

According to the authors, this is the first food detection system, which demonstrated practical implications on a mobile phone. The main future of the implemented food detection algorithm is the multiple-kernel-learning (MKL) classification. In simple terms, the MKL algorithm classifies object based on the features and their corresponding weights. This means that the importance of a particular image feature changes dynamically, depending on the food category.

This goes very well in hand with food objects, especially when we move from simple fruit or vegetable detection, to detection of complex meals. In the following year (2010) this system was extended, to recognize 85 different food categories [3]. The goal of the authors was to retain the success rate of classification of the previous system. For this, eight additional HoG (histogram of oriented gradients) features were added.

3.2   Puri et al., 2009

In the paper of Puri et al. [2], the authors described and proposed a food item and volume estimation system. In the paper the authors recognize that dietary assessment of food is a very difficult procedure even for nutritional experts. The difficulty lies especially in dishes where some nutrients are occluded. Therefore an algorithm based system of food and volume detection needs as much information as possible. A method based on a Food Intake Visual and Voice Recognizer (FIVR) system was proposed. The system is then implemented using a mobile device and so uses image as well as voice data for food recognition and volume estimation[1]. The system is created to recognize multiple items on a plate. All the algorithms for image segmentation and classification are executed on a server. The mobile phone is used only for recording of voice and image data.

The System Architecture. The main feature of the application is that it enables to recognize foods and estimate its volume. The system architecture is as follows: the user initially takes three pictures of a meal (the scene setup can be seen in Fig. 1[2]. Than the users accompanies this pictures with a speech data, to create food labels for the items on the plate. These data is then sent to the server[3]. The food is identified based on the speech data. For each identified food object, 3D reconstruction follows to estimate its volume. After the volume estimation, data of foods and their corresponding volumes are stored on the server and sent to the user via a text message. The message includes nutritional facts of each item.

3.3   Kong and Tan, 2012

In the paper of Kong and Tan [4] the DietCam mobile phone application was introduced. Similar to the system of Puri et al. [2] this system is used for food detection as well as volume estimation. The main difference in the case of the DietCam is, that it executes both functions only on the basis of images. Additionally, the mobile application uses the accelerometer, for calculating the angle of the device, which comes in handy for multiple view approach of picture recording. Besides regular food images, optical character recognition technique (OCR) is used for reading the food labels.

---

[1] For volume estimation 3D reconstruction method is used
[2] The image was derived from the paper [2]
[3] The system runs on an Intel Xeon workstation with a 3GHz CPU and 4GB of RAM.

The System Architecture. The system architecture can be described as follows: first the users captures 3 pictures of different item poses or a video around the food item. Then the information is sent in a XML format to the server, where all the processes of image processing, feature extraction, classification and a 3D reconstruction for food item volume estimation are executed. First the image manager extracts the important features, which are used for the classification. The classification is first executed using a local database, where instances of users' images are stored. If none of the stored instances can be used for classification of the recorded food item, than the global database of all food images is used. This two step process allows for a quicker and more effective classification of food objects. After the classification, the volume of the food items is estimated via 3D reconstruction. The system has also the possibility to extract the residues of the meal, which is later used for total calories consumed. After this stages, the calories and foods consumed are send to the mobile phone and stored into the database.

3.4   Rahman et al., 2012

In the paper of Rahman, Pickering and Kerr [5] a new texture feature was proposed, which would increase the food recognition accuracy on a mobile platform. The proposed texture feature would be based on Gabor filter banks, which would produce scale and rotation invariant global texture features. The main difference with other dietary consulting applications is that it uses multiple scale and orientation images for food items. This allows for a better food item detection in different poses. For the implementation of this new texture feature, the Technology Assisted Dietary Assessment (TADA) was used. The system executes food detection as well as volume estimation.

The System Architecture. The TADA system architecture is based on a interaction between a mobile device for image acquisition and server for image processing, segmentation, feature extraction, classification as well as volume estimation. The user starts with taking a photo of a food item, which is accompanied with a color calibration marker 1^4. Besides the photo, the user also sends some additional data, like the date, time and geolocation. This information is then sent to the server where food identification and volume estimation is executed (based on the underlying processes). The results of food identification and volume estimation is later sent to the user, for a approval and possible adjustments. After the confirmation, the eating activity is stored on the server, based on the nutritional database (which is also located on the server). Finally, the results of nutrient calculations are sent to a researcher for further analysis, which would in future work incorporate user feedback for food group analysis and dietary recommendations.

---

[4] The image was derived from the paper [5]

Fig. 1. The right image displays an instances of a scene used in [5], the left image displays the effects of color normalization in [2]

3.5   Kawano and Yanai, 2013

Kawano and Yanai have proposed a lightweight system for food object recognition, where all of the processing is executed on the mobile phone device[6]. This is the first application to do so. The purpose of executing all of the stages of food detection locally on the mobile phone was, to eliminate the un-desired delay and costs between the client and the server, as a result of data transmission. For additionally speed up, the user can draw bounding boxes around the food items, which allows for a quick image segmentation. Because food detection is executing in real-time fashion, the user can adjust the camera angles if the food detection algorithm doesn't detect the correct food item. This is done via an additional feature, which proposes the camera angle, where more information about the food should be visible. The system does not automatically estimate the volume of the items, but it allows the user to indicate the volume with a slider on the screen. In the same year (2010) the system was optimized by reducing the time for food detection inside the bounding boxes [7]. This has been successfully achieved using Fisher vectors [10] and different image features [5]. The optimized version had better processing time of food recognition (down from 0.26 seconds to 0.065 seconds) and slighty better success rate while doubling the number of categories (from 50 to 100). In 2015 these two systems were implemented on a android platform for public use [11].

The System Architecture. The system architecture in this application is as follows. First the user points with his camera to the desired food item. Because food detection is executed in real time, the application is collecting frames continuously. Next, the user draws bounding boxes around the food items, which allows for a quick segmentation. After the user created ROIs, food detection is executed in each of them. The results of the food detection algorithm is a list of top 5 candidates and the direction of the region of food items. The direction

---

[5] To see the difference in the features used in both systems, see the Fig. 1

is displayed as an arrow on the screen, besides the food item in Fig. 2[6]. After the returned candidate list the user has two choices. If the correct food item is on the list, than the user can adjust the estimated volume of the food and select the food item (by touching the list element). If the top 5 candidate list does not include the correct food item, the user moves the mobile phone in the proposed direction indicated by the arrow. By doing so, the food detection algorithm is again executed. This adjustment continues until the desired food item is detected. After the selection of the desired food item, the food item and the nutritional information are displayed on the screen. Also, the user can save the meal records to a server. He can later access this information on the Web.

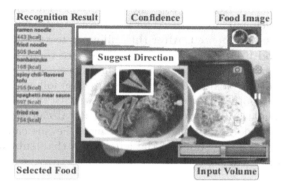

Fig. 2. The implementation of the system on a mobile device. Bounding boxes are user made, the arrows present the direction of the food items, and the sidebar includes top 5 candidates with their nutritional properties (kilo calories). Below the food items, there is a volume estimation slider.

3.6   Anthimopoulos et al., 2013

In [8] a system for carbohydrate counting was proposed and was aimed especially for helping patients with type 1 diabetes. The classification of the images is based on six different categories: meat, breaded food, rice, pasta, potatoes and vegetables and is therefore not food specific. The goal is to separate and identify regions of the before mentioned food groups on a plate. The special property of this system is complexity of the food segmentation which is accomplished with different algorithms. [7]

The System Architecture. The system architecture starts with a photo taken by the mobile phone camera. Later the recorded image gets segmented and recognized as on of the six food categories. Based on the segmentation and the classified food category, the system can return the estimated carbohydrate value and the corresponding insulin dose, based on the patients data.

---

[6] The image was derived from the paper [6]
[7] The algorithms used are listed in Tab. 1.

3.7   Pouladzadeh, Shirmohammadi and Arici, 2013

In the paper of Pouladzadeh [9] a system of automatic food measurement was proposed. Besides the food detection, the aim of the system is to estimate the eaten calories, by using before and after pictures of the meal (similar to the system proposed by Kong in his DietCam, described in section 3.3). The system is client based i.e. all of the the stages of food detection are executed on the mobile device.

The System Architecture. The system architecture is as follows: the user records two images of the food - one from the top and another from the side. When taking the picture from the top, the user needs to accompany the image with its' thumb, which will later be used for volume estimation. One of the images is than processed and segmented. After this, different features are extracted for each segmented food item. The extracted features are then used for a correct classification. The application sends the user the information about the classification for the approval[8]. Next, the food area estimation follows. Area estimation is produced by using both pictures of the food item, with the help of the thumb. With the area estimation and nutritional labels, total caloric consumption is calculated. If the user does not finish the whole meal, he/she can later record an image of the leftovers. The volume of the leftovers is than subtracted from the volume of the initial meal.

4   Conclusions and Discussion

Nine different mobile phone applications for tracking the eating activity were described in this paper. Through their review, we took a look at different approaches dealing with different system architectures. The main problem in correctly detecting food items is the vast inter-class variability of food items. Since food items are hand made, they differ in shape, texture and size, even if they present the same food instance. While these aspects can be solved with different algorithms which use local and global feature extraction (HoG, SIFT, SURF, deformable parts model etc.) another problem in food detection is occlusion, especially for food items in a complex meal. While detecting a whole food is mostly solved[9] (system described in section 3.7 demonstrated a 92% classification rate for 30 basic food items), the issue with complex food items, which includes chopping, mixing and covering food items with other food items is much more challenging. As mentioned in [9], even a human dietitian would not be able to recognize constituents of such meals by only looking at the plate. Solving this problem with images only will be therefore a hard if not impossible challenge. By using additional sensors for taste, the problem of occlusions might be solved or at least help to produce even better classification results.The last issue in food

---

[8] If the user does not approve, he/she can correct the information, that were sent as the result of classification
[9] Whole foods being un-processed foods

Table 1. Comparison of main features of the system and their experimental results described in their papers. The first row presents the literature index, the architecture row display if the system is implemented solely on a mobile platform or with a help of a server, the next 5 rows show the basic properties of the food recognition stages. The last two rows display the results of the experiment in each paper. First the number of categories is listed and next the success rate the system achieved.

Paper	System Architecture	Acquisition	Processing	Food detection algorithms Segmentation	Features	Class.	Experiment Cat.	Success
[1]	Client-Server	1 picture	None	Manual clipping	BoF, Color, Gabor	SVM + MKL	50	61.34%
[2]	Client-Server	3 pictures, Voice, Checker box	None	None	Color, MR, Adaboost, Volume	SVM + χ^2	150	+90%
[3]	Client-Server	1 picture	None	Manual clipping	Bof, Color, Gabor, HoG	SVM + MKL	85	62.5%
[4]	Client-Server	3 pictures, checker board, credit card, OCR, user input	redundancy elimination - SIFT	fg-bg subtraction., template subtraction	SIFT, volume	local-global DB, K-means clustering	Not listed	92%
[5]	Client-Server	1 picture, checker board, user confirmation	Spatial and color calibration	fg-bg subtraction	Invariant Gabor	Not desc.	209	95%
[6]	Client	1 Picture, bounding box, food item selection	None	Bounding box	Bag-of-SURFS, RGB color, reliable direction	linear SVM	50	81.55%
[7]	Client	1 Picture, bounding box, food item selection	None	Bounding box	HoG, RGB color	linear SVM + Fisher vector	100	79.2%
[9]	Client	2 Pictures, users thumb	Cropping, padding	K-means clustering for color, texture segmentation	Color, texture, shape	SVM + RBF kernel	30	92.21%
[8]	Client	1 Picture, plate	CIELAB, pyramid mean-shift filtering, region growing	Region merging, bg-subtraction	Color, texture	Hierarchical k-means clustering	6	87%

detection that is described in this paper is volume estimation. Some systems like [2,4,5,9] implemented the feature of automatic volume estimation, which is costly. But relatively good estimations are generated in all of those systems. This allows to calculate a much more accurate calorie consumption. Comparison of all the described systems, their properties and the results of their experiment[10] are shown in the Tab. 1.

References

1. Joutou, T., Yanai, K.: A food image recognition system with multiple kernel learning. In: 2009 16th IEEE International Conference on Image Processing (ICIP), pp. 285–288. IEEE (2009)
2. Puri, M., Zhu, Z., Yu, Q., Divakaran, A., Sawhney, H.: Recognition and volume estimation of food intake using a mobile device. In: 2009 Workshop on Applications of Computer Vision (WACV), pp. 1–8. IEEE (2009)
3. Hoashi, H., Joutou, T., Yanai, K.: Image recognition of 85 food categories by feature fusion. In: 2010 IEEE International Symposium on Multimedia (ISM), pp. 296–301. IEEE (2010)
4. Kong, F., Tan, J.: Dietcam: Automatic dietary assessment with mobile camera phones. Pervasive and Mobile Computing 8(1), 147–163 (2012)
5. Rahmana, M.H., Pickering, M.R., Kerr, D., Boushey, C.J., Delp, E.J.: A new texture feature for improved food recognition accuracy in a mobile phone based dietary assessment system. In: 2012 IEEE International Conference on Multimedia and Expo Workshops (ICMEW), pp. 418–423. IEEE (2012)
6. Kawano, Y., Yanai, K.: Real-time mobile food recognition system. In: 2013 IEEE Conference on Computer Vision and Pattern Recognition Workshops (CVPRW), pp. 1–7. IEEE (2013)
7. Kawano, Y., Yanai, K.: Rapid mobile object recognition using fisher vector. In: 2013 2nd IAPR Asian Conference on Pattern Recognition (ACPR), pp. 476–480. IEEE (2013)
8. Anthimopoulos, M., Dehais, J., Diem, P., Mougiakakou, S.: Segmentation and recognition of multi-food meal images for carbohydrate counting. In: 2013 IEEE 13th International Conference on Bioinformatics and Bioengineering (BIBE), pp. 1–4. IEEE (2013)
9. Pouladzadeh, P., Shirmohammadi, S., Arici, T.: Intelligent svm based food intake measurement system. In: 2013 IEEE International Conference on Computational Intelligence and Virtual Environments for Measurement Systems and Applications (CIVEMSA), pp. 87–92. IEEE (2013)
10. Perronnin, F., Sánchez, J., Mensink, T.: Improving the fisher kernel for large-scale image classification. In: Daniilidis, K., Maragos, P., Paragios, N. (eds.) ECCV 2010, Part IV. LNCS, vol. 6314, pp. 143–156. Springer, Heidelberg (2010)
11. Kawano, Y., Yanai, K.: Foodcam: A real-time food recognition system on a smartphone. Multimedia Tools and Applications, 1–25 (2015)

---

[10] For a description of the experimental design, see the corresponding papers.

On the Exploitation of One Class Classification to Distinguish Food Vs Non-Food Images

Giovanni Maria Farinella[⊠], Dario Allegra,
Filippo Stanco, and Sebastiano Battiato

Image Processing Laboratory, Department of Mathematics and Computer Science,
University of Catania, Catania, Italy
{gfarinella,allegra,fstanco,battiato}@dmi.unict.it

Abstract. In the last years automatic food image understanding has become an important research challenge for the society. This is because of the serious impact that food intake has in human life. Food recognition engines, can help the monitoring of the patient diet and his food intake habits. Nevertheless, distinguish among different classes of food is not the first question for assisted dietary monitoring systems. Prior to ask what class of food is depicted in an image, a computer vision system should be able to distinguish between food vs non-food images. In this work we consider one-class classification method to distinguish food vs non-food images. The UNICT-FD889 dataset is used for training purpose, whereas other two datasets of food and non-food images has been downloaded from Flickr to test the method. Taking into account previous works, we used Bag-of-Words representation considering different feature spaces to build the codebook. To give possibility to the community to work on the considered problem, the datasets used in our experiments are made publicly available.

Keywords: Food understanding · One class classification · Bag of words

1 Introduction and Motivation

Food has always influenced human lives and cultural development. It has a key role for health and market economy. The current technologies to acquire visual data (e.g., smartphones and wearable cameras) allow new possible applications in food domain. As example, a food intake monitoring can be useful when people have to be assisted during their daily meals. The collected data can help to understand the habits (or eating disorders) of a patient to prevent diseases like obesity or diabetes. An intake monitoring system could replace the traditionally dietary assessment based on self-reporting, which is often inaccurate [1–8]. In the last years wearable system for diet monitoring has taken a role for the monitoring of food intake [9]. Considering wearable glasses cameras, the first capability to address for an automatic diet monitoring system is the recognition of the frames of the acquired videos related to food. A food vs non-food classifier can be use to create automatic food-log to discover the intake behaviour of a person. Food

© Springer International Publishing Switzerland 2015
V. Murino et al. (Eds.): ICIAP 2015 Workshops, LNCS 9281, pp. 375–383, 2015.
DOI: 10.1007/978-3-319-23222-5_46

image understanding is important also for marketing purpose. A restaurant could provide a mobile software which processes a photo of food plate and reports several information such as cuisine type, the used ingredients, a list of other similar dishes or a video on how to cook that plate. Mobile apps can be exploited to recommend a restaurant serving food similar to the one of a selected picture by making retrieval with respect the food images of a menu [10,11].

Several works have been published on food image classification in the last years. Jiménez et al. [12] proposed one of the first food classification pipeline. They proposed to detect spherical fruits in natural environment and to exploit data acquired with a 3D laser scanner for recognition purpose. Multiple Kernel Learning SVM (MKL-SVM) is investigated by Joutou et al. [13]. In [7] the authors proposed a food recognition system based on the Bag of Words model which uses color features (e.g., histrograms, color moments) and dense SIFT on color space (DSIFT). Ravì et al. [14] developed a real-time mobile system for hierarchical food classification, exploiting Fischer Vector representation and a set of linear classifiers. Matsuda et al. [15,16] introduced a new dataset (UEC FOOD 100) with food images belonging to 100 classes. Other datasets are introduced in [11,17]. Specifically, [17] introduced PFID dataset composed by 1098 fast-food images belonging to 61 different classes. In [11] the UNICT-FD889 dataset has been introduced. This dataset contains 3583 instances with over 800 food plates acquired with mobile devices in real meal scenario.

All the works mentioned above perform recognition among different food classes and assume that the analyzed image contains food. However, to build food monitoring systems able to perform a food-log (e.g., with the use of wearable cameras) the discrimination between food vs non-food images is the first issue to address.

In this paper we focus our attention on food vs non-food images classification. This problem has been taken into account in [18,19]. In [18] Kitamura et al. presented a food-logging web system which consider food vs non-food problem to analyse the food intake balance and visualise a food log. Circle detection and color information are exploited as feature to identify the presence of dishes in images. However in real scenario not all the images of food include the plate. Moreover the shape of the plates can be different from a plate to another. Kagaya et al. [19] used deep learning for food detection and recognition. As in [18], to perform a proper training of the method proposed in [19] both food images and non-food ones have to be employed. This means that to train a food vs non-food classifier, the variability of the non-food classes have to be captured in dataset used for training purpose. Despite could be simple to collect images of food (e.g., by considering the current available food datasets or by crawling images from website dedicated to food[1]), the collection of a proper representative dataset of non-food images can be a challenging task. Differently than previous works, in this paper we investigate one-class classification (OCC)[20] to recognize when an image is belonging to the food class. Multi-class classification methods, such as the ones proposed in the aforementioned works, aim to classify an unknown

---

[1] https://www.flickr.com/groups/foodphotography/

image into one of several predefined categories (two classes in case of food vs non-food classification). One-class classification approaches allow to obtain a model of a single class, so the images that do not fit the model are labeled as an "anomaly" with respect to that class. In this paper, the Bag of Words model is employed to represent images. Three different descriptors are compared: Texton, SIFT and PRICoLBP. One-class classification is performed by using one-class Support Vector Machine (OSVM). To learn about the food class we have used the UNICT-FD889 dataset, since it presents variability and because the images are collected in real meal scenario with a mobile phone. We also used two more datasets for testing purpose which can be employed as benchmark to compare food vs non-food classification algorithms.

The reminder of the paper is organized as follows. In Section 2 the proposed approach for food vs non-food recognition is described. Section 3 reports the experimental results. Finally, Section 4 concludes the paper providing hints for future works.

2   Proposed Method

We consider the one-class classification paradigm (OCC) for food vs non-food classification problem [20,21]. One-class classification algorithms learns about the class to be identified assuming that representative training data of all the other possible classes are not available or very difficult to obtain. We consider this paradigm for food vs non-food classification since in a training phase could be simple to have example of what a food image looks like, but it is very difficult to define all the images related to the non-food class. If one considers the problem of detecting food frames in videos acquired with wearable glasses, the non-food class is composed by all the possible scene that a human can observe in his life. This motivated us to perform a benchmark experiment where the unique class to be used for learning purpose is the food one. As training data to represent the food space we have used the UNICT-FD889 dataset introduced in [11]. It contains 3583 food images related to 889 different plates acquired with an iPhone in real scenarios during meals. Some examples of the images belonging to the UNICT-FD889 are shown at the first three rows of Fig. 1. To test the discriminative capability of the approach, two more datasets of food and non-food images, respectively composed by 4805 and 8005 images, have been considered. The images of the two dataset used for testing have been downloaded from Flickr (see Fig. 1) by considering only images acquired with an iPhone at their original resolution. We employed three different image descriptors as baseline for our experiments: Bag of SIFT [22,23], PRICoLBP [24] and Bag of Textons [11,25].

For Bag of SIFT we have considered a dense sampling on a grid with spacing of 8 pixels. For each grid point a 16×16 patch is extracted and SIFT descriptor is computed consider the color domain as in [7]. The codebook to be used for a Bag of SIFT representation has been obtained through K-Means clustering with $K = 2200$. To obtain the gray and color PRICoLBP representations [24] we used the original code provided by the authors at URL http://qixianbiao.github.io. With the original parameters PRICoLBP representation is a 1180-dimensional vector for gray whereas 3540-dimensional vector for RGB images. To compute the Bag of Textons representation [11,25] we considered both the MR8 and the Schmid bank of filters. We considered Textons in both gray and LAB color domains. Also in this case we used a vocabulary of 2200 Textons to represent images.

3   Experimental Settings and Results

We have performed two experiments to assess the performances of the SVM One Class Classification with the considered descriptors. In all the experiments we employed the LibSVM library [26] with a Sigmoid kernel with $\gamma = 10^{-5}$ and an OSVM tolerance $\nu = 0.35$.

In the first experiment we have considered the UNICT-FD889 dataset for training the OSVM classifier. Tests have been repeated three times and the results are obtained by averaging on the three runs. For the training phase the UNICT-FD889 dataset has been divided in three parts. For each run two parts of the dataset (2855 food images) have been used for training the classifier. The remaining 728 food images have been used for testing purpose. To test the performances on the non-food class in each run we have used the 8005 images downloaded from Flickr. The results obtained in this first experiment are shown in Fig 2(a). Food classification rate is similar for all representations, while non-food classification rate is strongly dependent from the descriptor, and varies between

Fig. 1. Top: UNICT-FD889 image examples. Middle: examples of non-food images downloaded from Flickr. Bottom: examples of food images downloaded from Flickr.

26.21% and 94.44%. As in [11], Textons outperform PRICoLBP (PLBP). More-over, the Schmid bank of filters (LABSch) seems to outperform MR8 filters. The best performances are obtained when the Bag of SIFT representation (BoS) is employed. Color domain helps all the descriptors except PRICoLBP. Since SIFT and Textons capture different image's aspects (i.e., SIFT summarises spatial histograms of gradients, whereas Textons encode textures) we have tested a simple concatenation of Bag of SIFT and Bag of Textons. This test shows an improvement in the discrimination capability (94.44% for non-food and 65.43% for food). The achieved results encourage the usage of multiple descriptors to have a low false positive rate (i.e., very few images of non-food class misclassified as food). Some example of misclassified images are shown in Fig 3. As last test we have concatenated Bag of Schmid Textons, Bag of SIFT and PRICoLBP (all obtained considering color domain). The results confirm that PRICoLBP do not add useful information for food vs non-food classification (Fig. 2(a)).

In the second experiment we used the whole UNICT-FD889 dataset to perform training (3583 images). For testing purpose we have used the same dataset of non-food images employed for the first experiment (8005 images) and one more food dataset (4805 images) obtained from Flickr by downloading (and visually reviewing) images with the tag "food". This experiment is more challenging than the first one since the food images used in the training and the once used in the testing phases look very different. Despite the Flickr images with "food" tag are related to images containing food, these can contain also other objects not belonging to the food class (e.g., sometime the percentage of the pixels related to food are much less than the once of the background and other objects). There is also a huge variability in the scale of the food plates, as well as photometric variability, and there are examples of dishes which never appear into the training dataset. In this experiment we considered only Textons and SIFT descriptors on color domain since they obtained the best performances in the first experiments. The results obtained in this second experiment are shown in Fig 2(b). Also in this case seems that combination of the descriptors can help for the task under consideration. We report some examples of misclassified images in Fig. 4.

We would highlight once more that in our experiments images of non-food class have not been used for training the classifier. Considering the results of the two experiments, it is clear that by learning from the food class only it is possible to achieve low false positive rate for food vs non-food classification already with simple image representations. This means that in a possible wearable systems for food monitoring which have to automatically collect food images there will be few outlier to be manually removed by nutrition experts. Note that the trade-off between good true positive rate and low false positive rate can be tuned by the parameters used in one class classification. On the other hand, the classification accuracy of the food class is still to low to be considered useful to monitor the food intake and the behaviour of a person. By considering the two experiments the main observation with respect to this last aspect is that, when the food class to be recognized is represented in the training, the food classification performance is higher (i.e., when images of food used for testing are visually similar

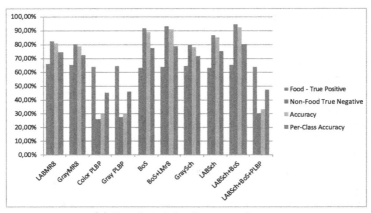

(a) Results of the first experiment.

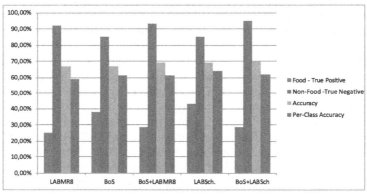

(b) Results of the second experiment.

Fig. 2. Food vs Non-Food classification results.

to the once in the training, despite high geometric and photometric variabilities). Also, the combination of different features can contribute to have a better discrimination. Our conjecture for food vs non-food classification is that by considering a big representative food image dataset, where the food dishes appear in a appropriate scale (i.e., the food plate is the main or the only object, as usually occurs when a user snap a food during meals), and by considering appropriate image representation, the food vs non-food classification become a feasible task.

One more consideration made from the outcome of the experiments is related to the description level to consider the task about of food vs non food classification. Sometime in literature this problem has been called food detection [19]. We believe that food detection and food vs non-food classification are two different tasks. As demonstrated by the second experiment, when images contain food but also background and other objects, the food vs non-food classification become

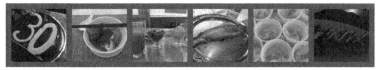

(a) Images of food classified as non-food.

(b) Images of non-food classified as food.

Fig. 3. Some misclassification examples for (a) food class and (b) non-food class related to the first experiment.

(a) Images of food classified as non-food.

(b) Images of non-food classified as food.

Fig. 4. Some misclassification examples for (a) food class and (b) non-food class related to the second experiment.

more difficult. This is mainly because the whole image is considered during food vs non-food classification. On the other hand, a food detector have to be able to localize where the food appears rather than classify the whole image (i.e., draw a bounding box in the part of the image in which the food appear discarding the other parts).

The benchmark datasets used in our experiments (as well as the training and testing information needed to properly compare other approaches on the problem considered in this paper) are available at the following link: http://iplab.dmi.unict.it/madima2015/

4   Conclusion

Food understanding is an interesting challenge for the computer vision research community and it is demanded to build food intake monitoring systems.

Although different progress have been done in recent years regarding multiclass food classification, food vs non-food classification is still the first problem to solve. We believe that this task is different from food detection where the main aim is to localize the region of the image containing pixels of food. In this work we focus our attention on the application of One Class Classification method to distinguish food images vs other classes. The motivation beyond the exploration of this method comes from the consideration that the non-food class is very difficult to be represented in a dataset if one consider a system that have to work for example on wearable glasses. The preliminary experiments presented in this paper gave us some hints for further research directions, such as for example the need to better define the food vs non-food problem considering the context where the system have to be employed. We guess that augmenting the food dataset, the one class classification approach can achieve better results. Further studies should also consider more complex approaches to extract features (e.g., in an unsupervised way with Deep Learning based approaches [19,27]), and to combine and represent the images (e.g., using also spatial information) for the considered one class classification task.

References

1. Kong, F., Tan, J.: Dietcam: Automatic dietary assessment with mobile camera phones. Pervasive and Mobile Computing **8**(1), 147–163 (2012)
2. Kim, S., Schap, T., Bosch, M., Maciejewski, R., Delp, E.J., Ebert, D.S., Boushey, C.J.: Development of a mobile user interface for image-based dietary assessment. In: International Conference on Mobile and Ubiquitous Multimedia, pp. 13:1–13:7 (2010)
3. Feasibility testing of an automated image-capture method to aid dietary recall
4. Xu, C., He, Y., Khannan, N., Parra, A., Boushey, C., Delp, E.: Image-based food volume estimation. In: International Workshop on Multimedia for Cooking and Eating Activities, pp. 75–80 (2013)
5. Zhu, F., Bosch, M., Woo, I., Kim, S., Boushey, C.J., Ebert, D.S., Delp, E.J.: The use of mobile devices in aiding dietary assessment and evaluation. Journal of Selected Topics Signal Processing **4**(4), 756–766 (2010)
6. O'Loughlin, G., Cullen, S.J., McGoldrick, A., O'Connor, S., Blain, R., O'Malley, S., Warrington, G.D.: Using a wearable camera to increase the accuracy of dietary analysis. American Journal of Preventive Medicine **44**(3), 297–301 (2013)
7. Anthimopoulos, M.M., Gianola, L., Scarnato, L., Diem, P., Mougiakakou, S.G.: A food recognition system for diabetic patients based on an optimized bag-of-features model. IEEE Journal of Biomedical and Health Informatics **18**(4), 1261–1271 (2014)
8. Puri, M., Zhiwei, Z., Qian, Y., Divakaran, A., Sawhney, H.: Recognition and volume estimation of food intake using a mobile device. In: Workshop on Applications of Computer Vision, pp. 1–8 (2009)
9. Fontana, J.M., Sazonon, E.: Detection and characterization of food intake by wearable sensors. In: Wearable Sensors, pp. 591–616 (2014)
10. Beijbom, O., Joshi, N., Morris, D., Saponas, S., Khullar, S.: Menu-match: restaurant-specific food logging from images. In: IEEE Winter Conference on Applications of Computer Vision, pp. 844–851 (2015)

11. Farinella, G.M., Allegra, D., Stanco, F.: A benchmark dataset to study the representation of food images. In: Agapito, L., Bronstein, M.M., Rother, C. (eds.) ECCV 2014 Workshops. LNCS, vol. 8927, pp. 584–599. Springer, Heidelberg (2015)
12. Jiménez, A.R., Jain, A.K., Ruz, R.C., Rovira, J.L.P.: Automatic fruit recognition: a survey and new results using range/attenuation images. Pattern Recognition 32(10), 1719–1736 (1999)
13. Joutou, T., Yanai, K.: A food image recognition system with multiple kernel learning. In IEEE International Conference in Image Processing, pp. 285–288 (2009)
14. Ravì, D., Lo, B., Yang, G.F: Real-time food intake classification and energy expenditure estimation on a mobile device. In: Body Sensor Networks Conference (2015)
15. Matsuda, Y., Hoashi, H., Yanai, K.: Recognition of multiple-food images by detecting candidate regions. In: IEEE International Conference on Multimedia and Expo, pp. 25–30 (2012)
16. Matsuda, Y., Yanai, K.: Multiple-food recognition considering co-occurrence employing manifold ranking. In: International Conference on Pattern Recognition, pp. 2017–2020 (2012)
17. Chen, M., Dhingra, K., Wu, W., Yang, L., Sukthankar, R., Yang, J.: Pfid: Pittsburgh fast-food image dataset. In: IEEE International Conference on Image Processing (2009)
18. Kitamura, K., Yamasaki, T., Aizawa, K.: Foodlog: capture, analysis and retrieval of personal food images via web. In: Proceedings of the Workshop on Multimedia for Cooking and Eating Activities, pp. 23–30 (2009)
19. Kagaya, H., Aizawa, K., Ogawa, M.: Food detection and recognition using convolutional neural network. In: Proceedings of the ACM International Conference on Multimedia, pp. 1085–1088 (2014)
20. Khan, S.S., Madden, M.G.: A survey of recent trends in one class classification. In: Coyle, L., Freyne, J. (eds.) AICS 2009. LNCS, vol. 6206, pp. 188–197. Springer, Heidelberg (2010)
21. Schölkopf, B., Platt, J.C., Shawe-Taylor, J.C., Smola, A.J., Williamson, R.C.: Estimating the support of a high-dimensional distribution. Neural Computation 13(7), 1443–1471 (2001)
22. Lowe, D.G.: Object recognition from local scale-invariant features. IEEE International Conference on Computer Vision 2, 1150–1157 (1999)
23. Lowe, D.G.: Distinctive image features from scale-invariant keypoints. International Journal of Computer Vision 60(2), 91–110 (2004)
24. Qi, X., Xiao, R., Guo, J., Zhang, L.: Pairwise rotation invariant co-occurrence local binary pattern. In: Fitzgibbon, A., Lazebnik, S., Perona, P., Sato, Y., Schmid, C. (eds.) ECCV 2012, Part VI. LNCS, vol. 7577, pp. 158–171. Springer, Heidelberg (2012)
25. Farinella,G.M., Moltisanti, M., Battiato, S.: Classifying food images represented as bag of textons. In: IEEE International Conference on Image Processing, pp. 5212–5216 (2014)
26. Chang, C.-C., Lin, C.-J.: LIBSVM: a library for support vector machines (2001)
27. LeCun, Y., Bengio, Y., Hinton, G.: Deep learning. Nature 512 (2015)

Food Recognition Using Consensus Vocabularies

Giovanni Maria Farinella, Marco Moltisanti$^{(\boxtimes)}$, and Sebastiano Battiato

Image Processing LAB, Department of Mathematics and Computer Science,
Universitá degli Studi di Catania, Catania, Italy
{gfarinella,moltisanti,battiato}@dmi.unict.it

Abstract. Food recognition is an interesting and challenging problem
with applications in medical, social and anthropological research areas.
The high variability of food images makes the recognition task difficult
for current state-of-the-art methods. It has been proved that the exploitation of multiple features to capture complementary aspects of the image
contents is useful to improve the discrimination of different food items.
In this paper we exploit an image representation based on the consensus among visual vocabularies built on different feature spaces. Starting
from a set of visual codebooks, a consensus clustering technique is used
to build a consensus vocabulary used to represent food pictures with
a Bag-of-Visual-Words paradigm. This new representation is employed
together with a SVM for recognition purpose.

1 Introduction and Motivation

People love food. This fact, coupled with the great diffusion of low cost imaging devices (e.g., wearable cameras, smartphones), makes the food one of the
most photographed objects. The analysis of food images can drive to a wider
comprehension of the relationship between people and their meals. For instance,
automatic food recognition can be useful to build diet monitoring systems to
combat obesity, by providing to the experts (e.g., nutritionists) objective measures to assess patients' food intake. Also, food recognition is a challenging and
exciting task for computer vision researchers due its both high intra-class and
low inter-class variabilities of visual content [16].

Several works have been published in last years addressing the problem of
food classification [2–4,7,8,14–18]. Jimenez *et al.* [3] proposed an automatic
recognition method able to detect spherical fruits (e.g., oranges) in natural environment. To this purposes they used range images, obtained via a 3D laser
scanner. Joutou *et al.* [4] used a Multiple Kernel Learning SVM (MKL-SVM)
to exploit different kinds of features. They combined Bag-of-SIFT with color
histograms and Gabor filters to discriminate between images of a dataset considering by 50 different food categories. Matsuda *et al.* [7,8] introduced a new
dataset with food belonging to 100 classes. In [7] they employed Bag-of-SIFT on
Spatial Pyramid, Histograms of Gradient, color histogram and Gabor filters to
train a MKL-SVM after a detection of candidate regions based on Deformable
Part Models. The trained models were used to classify multiple instances of

© Springer International Publishing Switzerland 2015
V. Murino et al. (Eds.): ICIAP 2015 Workshops, LNCS 9281, pp. 384–392, 2015.
DOI: 10.1007/978-3-319-23222-5_47

Fig. 1. Three different instances of the same food in the PFID dataset [2].

Fig. 2. Six different point of view of one instance of food in the PFID dataset [2].

food. In [8] they extended their previous work including a ranking algorithm to be used for image retrieval purpose.

Most of the aforementioned approaches propose, along with a classification engine, a new dataset. However, it is difficult to find papers where different techniques are compared on the same dataset [16]. This makes not easy to fully understand which are the peculiarities of the different techniques and which is the best method for food recognition so far. We consider the Pittsburgh Fast-food Image Dataset (PFID) [2]. This dataset is composed by 1098 food images belonging to 61 different categories. Each class contains 3 different instances of the food (i.e., same food class but acquired in different days and in different restaurants - see Fig. 1), and 6 images of different viewpoints for each instance (see Fig. 2). The main contribution of [2] is the dataset itself. As baseline tests, the authors provide the food recognition results by employing Color Histograms and Bag-of-SIFT and a linear SVM classifier. This dataset, as well as the experimental protocol and the results, can be used to properly compare different algorithms.

Considering the aforementioned PFID dataset, Yang et al. [14] outperformed the baseline results of [2] using statistics of pairwise local feature in order to encode spatial relationship between different ingredients. As first step, a Semantic Textons Forest (STF) [11] is used to assign a soft label to represent the distribution over ingredients (beef, chicken, pork, bread, vegetable, tomato and tomato sauce, cheese and butter, egg/other). Then the food images are represented with the OM features, which are computed taking into account orientation (O) and midpoint (M) of the segment that connects two previously labelled pixels. These features are hence used with a SVM for classification (using a χ^2 kernel). A successive work considering the PFID dataset for testing purposes [15] pointed out that a classic Bag of Textons approach for texture discrimination outperforms the methods presented in [2] and [14]. The aforementioned approaches proposed in [14] have been considered in the experimental phase of this work for comparison purposes.

It is worth noting that some of the aforementioned food recognition techniques use combination of different features [4,7,8,14]. By exploiting multiple features it is possible to capture different aspects of food appearance (e.g., color,

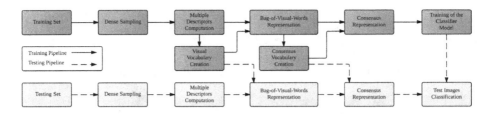

Fig. 3. Proposed image representation pipeline based on Consensus Vocabularies.

shape, texture, spatial relationships) and hence improve the recognition accuracy. On the other hand, image representations based on the alignment of multiple visual vocabularies (Bag-of-Visual-Phrases) built on different feature spaces have been used to address other Computer Vision problems (e.g., near duplicate image retrieval [1, 19]).

In this paper we propose a new way to encode different and complementary aspects of local regions, which we call *Consensus Vocabularies*. Starting from vocabularies built on classic SIFT [6] and SPIN [5] features, we use consensus clustering [12] to build a the final vocabulary to be used for the image representation. The proposed representation is coupled with a Support Vector Machine classifier for food recognition. Our method is compared with respect to other state-of-the-art approaches on the PFID dataset [2, 14, 15]. At the best of our knowledge, although consensus clustering is a well known topic in Pattern Recognition, it has not been previously exploited to build visual vocabularies for image representation and recognition purposes.

The remainder of this paper is structured as follows: Section 2 presents the proposed approach to build the image representation. In Section 3 the experimental settings and the results are described. Finally, Section 4 concludes the paper with hints for further works.

2   Consensus Vocabularies

In this work, we propose to augment the classic Bag-of-Features approach by exploiting a representation based on consensus vocabularies obtained from different visual codebooks computed on different and complementary descriptors. In our representation pipeline, we start by generating different partitions of SIFT [17] and SPIN [5] feature spaces employing a K-means clustering (as in the classic visual vocabularies in the Bag-of-Feature method). The generated partitions are then used to feed the consensus clustering algorithm. In this work we employ the technique proposed in [12]. As output, the consensus clustering gives a vocabulary which is then used to represent each image belonging to both training and testing sets. We use SIFT and SPIN features because they are able to capture different local information. SIFT is useful to capture local gradients [6], whereas SPIN are more powerful in encoding textures [20]. By employing the different descriptors and different runs of the clustering algorithms (i.e., input partitions for the consensus clustering), we can tune the diversity of the partitions to build the final vocabulary. Of course, different consensus clustering strategies can be used for the proposed method [10, 12]. We chosen the algorithm proposed in [12] since it is based on categorical clustering (i.e., can be applied straightforward on pre-built visual vocabularies) and because it does not need to solve the clusters correspondence problem to build the final consensus partition. The consensus partition is obtained as the solution of a maximum likelihood problem using an Expectation-Maximization approach. Figure 3 shows the general pipeline of both training and testing pipelines.

Let $\mathbf{I} = \{I_1, \ldots, I_T\}$ be the training set. Through a dense sampling of each image I_i, we obtain a set of interest points $\mathbf{X}^{(i)} = \{x_1^{(i)}, \ldots, x_{N_i}^{(i)}\}$ on which each feature descriptor is computed. Let $\mathbf{F} = \{F_1, \ldots, F_M\}$ be a set of descriptors. For each descriptor $F_m \in \mathbf{F}$ we compute the set of features $\mathbf{Y}_m^{(i)} = \left\{y_{1,m}^{(i)} = F_m\left(x_1^{(i)}\right), \ldots, y_{N_i,m}^{(i)} = F_m\left(x_{N_i}^{(i)}\right)\right\}$ related to the image $I_i \in \mathbf{I}$. Hence, $\mathbf{Y}_m = \{\mathbf{Y}_m^{(1)} \ldots \mathbf{Y}_m^{(T)}\}$ is the set of all feature descriptors of type m computed over the image set $\mathbf{I}$. Let $\mathbf{C} = \{C_1, \ldots, C_P\}$ be the set of the considered clustering algorithms and let $\mathbf{\Theta}^{(p)} = \{\theta_1^{(p)}, \ldots, \theta_{Q_p}^{(p)}\}$ be the set of the parameters considered for the clustering algorithm $C_p \in \mathbf{C}$ (i.e., the parameters corresponding to different runs of a specific algorithm). Each set $\mathbf{Y}_m$ is clustered taking into account a specific clustering algorithm $C_p \in \mathbf{C}$ and considering the set of parameters $\mathbf{\Theta}^{(p)}$. This gives as output a set of visual vocabularies for each feature of type m. Let $\mathbf{V} = \{V_1 \ldots V_H\}$ be the set of all vocabularies obtained with the aforementioned procedure. Each set $\mathbf{Y}_m$ is therefore represented with the *ids* related to the visual words belonging to the obtained vocabularies of type m. In this way each interest point $x_n^{(i)} \in I_{(i)}$ is projected into the vocabulary spaces:

$$
\begin{array}{c|ccc}
Input & V_1 & \cdots & V_H \\
\hline
x_1^{(1)} & V_1\left(x_1^{(1)}\right) & \cdots & V_H\left(x_1^{(1)}\right) \\
\vdots & \vdots & \ddots & \vdots \\
x_{N_1}^{(1)} & V_1\left(x_{N_1}^{(1)}\right) & \cdots & V_H\left(x_{N_1}^{(1)}\right) \\
\vdots & \vdots & \ddots & \vdots \\
x_1^{(T)} & V_1\left(x_1^{(T)}\right) & \cdots & V_H\left(x_1^{(T)}\right) \\
\vdots & \vdots & \ddots & \vdots \\
x_{N_T}^{(T)} & V_1\left(x_{N_T}^{(T)}\right) & \cdots & V_H\left(x_{N_T}^{(T)}\right)
\end{array}
\tag{1}
$$

At this point we employ the consensus clustering [12] to build a vocabulary. We define $\mathbf{v}_n^{(i)} = \left(V_1\left(x_n^{(i)}\right), \ldots, V_H\left(x_n^{(i)}\right)\right)$ as the vector that contains all the *ids* labels for the interesting point x_n^i. Considering the set of all vectors $\mathbf{v}_n^{(i)}$, the consensus clustering algorithm is used to find a consensus partition V_c called the *Consensus Vocabulary*.

The original formulation of the consensus clustering assigns each vector $\mathbf{v}_n^{(i)}$ to the most likely cluster of the consensus partition in a hard way. Taking into account possible visual words ambiguities [9,13], we use a soft assignment. Specifically, we employ the probability vector $\mathbf{z}_n^{(i)}$ given by the consensus algorithm to establish the membership degree of each vector $\mathbf{v}_n^{(i)}$ to the different consensus clusters. Every image I_i is hence represented as the normalized sum of all the $\mathbf{z}_n^{(i)}$:

$$\mathbf{S}_{I_i} = \frac{1}{N_i} \sum_{n=1}^{N_i} \mathbf{z}_n^{(i)} \tag{2}$$

To represent test images $\overline{I}_i$, we first project their interesting points in the set of vocabulary $\mathbf{V}$, and then the consensus vocabulary is used to compute the final signature in the same way as for the training images (Eq. 2).

To perform the classification, a multiclass SVM with a pre-computed kernel and cosine distance is used. Given two signature vectors $\mathbf{S}_{I_i}, \mathbf{S}_{I_j}$, the cosine distance $d_{\cos}$ is calculated as follows:

$$d_{\cos}\left(\mathbf{S}_{I_i}, \mathbf{S}_{I_j}\right) = 1 - \frac{\mathbf{S}_{I_i} \mathbf{S}_{I_j}'}{\sqrt{\left(\mathbf{S}_{I_i} \mathbf{S}_{I_i}'\right)\left(\mathbf{S}_{I_j} \mathbf{S}_{I_j}'\right)}}. \tag{3}$$

The kernel is defined as:

$$k_{\cos}\left(\mathbf{S}_{I_i}, \mathbf{S}_{I_j}\right) = e^{-d_{\cos}\left(\mathbf{S}_{I_i}, \mathbf{S}_{I_j}\right)}. \tag{4}$$

3   Experimental Results

To assess the proposed approach we have used the PFID dataset [2] described in Section 1. Our method has been compared against the two baseline methods reported in [2] as well as with respect to the different methods proposed in [14]. As in [14], we followed the experimental protocol of [2] by performing a 3-fold cross-validation for our experiments. We used 12 images from two instances of each class for training and the 6 remaining images of the third instance for testing.

A dense sampling procedure to extract the descriptors has been considered by using a spatial grid with steps of 8 pixels in both horizontal and vertical directions. The descriptors are computed on patches of 24×24 pixels centered on each point of the spatial grid. The visual vocabularies to be used as input for the consensus clustering have been obtained considering three different runs of the K-means clustering for each descriptor. We have used $K = 200$ on each run with a random initialization. So, each point into the spacial grid of the dense sampling has been projected into the 6-dimensional feature space of the computed visual vocabularies (3 on the SIFT features and 3 on the SPIN features). For the final consensus vocabulary, we chose a size of 300 consensus words. This means that the final food image is represented with a very small vector.

Table 1. Per-Class accuracy of the different methods on the 7 Major Classes of the PFID dataset. In each row, the two highest values are underlined, while the maximum is reported in **bold**.

Class	Per-Class Accuracy % (# of images)					
	Color [2]	BoW SIFT [2]	GIR-STF [11,14]	OM [14]	BoW Textons [15]	Proposed
Sandwich	69.0 (157.3)	75.0 (171)	79.0 (180.1)	86.0 (196.1)	87.6 (199.7)	**89.0 (203)**
Salad & Sides	16.0 (5.8)	45.0 (16.2)	79.0 (28.4)	**93.0 (33.5)**	84.3 (30.3)	69.4 (25)
Bagel	13.0 (3.1)	15.0 (3.6)	33.0 (7.9)	40.0 (9.6)	**70.8 (17)**	62.5 (15)
Donut	0.0 (0)	18.0 (4.3)	14.0 (3.4)	17.0 (4.1)	**43.1 (10.3)**	29.2 (7)
Chicken	49.0 (11.8)	36.0 (8.6)	73.0 (17.5)	82.0 (19.7)	66.7 (16)	**91.7 (22)**
Taco	39.0 (4.7)	24.0 (2.9)	40.0 (4.8)	65.0 (7.8)	**69.4 (8.3)**	50.0 (6)
Bread & Pastry	8.0 (1.4)	3.0 (0.5)	47.0 (8.5)	**67.0 (12.1)**	53.7 (9.7)	66.7 (12)
Average	27.7 (26.3)	30.9 (29.6)	52.1 (35.8)	64.3 (40.4)	**67.9 (41.6)**	65.5 (41.4)

After representing images as described in Section 2, we trained the SVM classifier, using the training images and pre-computed kernel with cosine distance. The trained classifier has been then employed on the test images. The classification accuracy achieved employing consensus vocabularies on the 61 classes is reported in Figure 4a, along with the accuracies of the compared state-of-the-art approaches. The low accuracy in discriminating among the 61 different classes is mainly due to foods items of the PFID dataset have very similar appearances (and similar ingredients) despite they belong to different classes [15].

It is important to note that our method, differently than [14], does not need any manual labeling of the different ingredients composing the food items to be employed to produce the representation. Although the labeling of the different food ingredients is possible for a small set of plates, the up-scaling to a huge number of categories (composed by many ingredients) became not feasible, making the approach described in [14] difficult to be applied.

As in [14], we have also performed tests re-organizing the 61 PFID food categories into seven major groups (e.g. sandwiches, salads and sides, chicken, breads and pastries, donuts, bagels, tacos). Results obtained by the different approaches are reported in Fig. 4b. In Table 1 the per-class accuracies of the results of the different methods on the seven major classes of the PFID dataset are reported. Since the number of images belonging to the different classes is not balanced, for a better understanding of the results, the number of images is reported together with the per-class accuracy. Also in this case, our approach obtains better performances with respect to the best performing one proposed in [14].

We want also to underline that, despite the approach in [15] has better results in terms of accuracy, the proposed method is valuable under a theoretical perspective. In fact, it shows that the results obtained using a combination of different features are almost as good as standard techniques, but it captures different aspects of the image, such as local gradient and textures. Note that the representation proposed in [15] can be exploited together with SIFT and SPIN to build a novel Consensus vocabulary which takes into account the power of Textons in

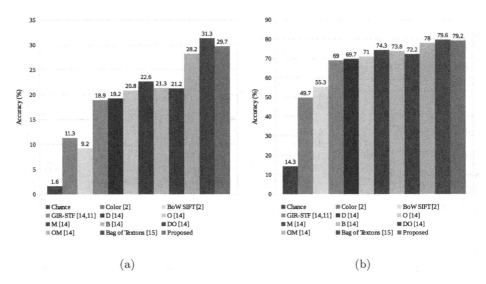

(a)   (b)

Fig. 4. Classification accuracy on the 61 categories (4a) and on the 7 major classes (4b) of the PFID dataset [2].

representing patterns. Moreover, the final vocabulary size used in this approach is much lower than the one used in [15].

4   Conclusions and Future Works

This paper introduces an augmented version of the Bag of Words approach useful to combine different feature descriptors. We propose to build a consensus vocabulary starting from different visual codebooks. The images are represented as a Bag of Consensus Words taking into account different aspects of local regions. The proposed image representation has been assessed by considering the problem of food recognition, obtaining results which closely match the state of the art. Future works could be devoted to the exploitation of consensus vocabularies on different computer vision applications, and by considering other type of features (as well as the spatial relationship among them) to build the final consensus codebook. Also, an in-depth analysis of the performances at varying of the involved parameters and considering bigger datasets (e.g., the UNICTFD-889 [16]) should be performed. Moreover the impact of the size of the consensus vocabulary both in terms of recognition rate and computational time should be investigated.

References

1. Battiato, S., Farinella, G.M., Puglisi, G., Ravì, D.: Aligning codebooks for near duplicate image detection. Multimedia Tools and Applications, 1–24 (2013)
2. Chen, M., Dhingra, K., Wu, W., Yang, L., Sukthankar, R., Yang, J.: Pfid: Pittsburgh fast-food image dataset. IEEE International Conference on Image Processing, 289–292 (2009)
3. Jiménez, A.R., Jain, A.K., Ceres, R., Pons, J.: Automatic fruit recognition: a survey and new results using range/attenuation images. Pattern recognition 32(10), 1719–1736 (1999)
4. Joutou, T., Yanai, K.: A food image recognition system with multiple kernel learning. IEEE International Conference on Image Processing, 285–288 (2009)
5. Lazebnik, S., Schmid, C., Ponce, J.: A sparse texture representation using local affine regions. IEEE Transactions on Pattern Analysis and Machine Intelligence 27(8), 1265–1278 (2005)
6. Lowe, D.G.: Distinctive image features from scale-invariant keypoints. International Journal of Computer Vision 60(2), 91–110 (2004)
7. Matsuda, Y., Hoashi, H., Yanai, K.: Recognition of multiple-food images by detecting candidate regions. IEEE International Conference on Multimedia and Expo, 25–30 (2012)
8. Matsuda, Y., Yanai, K.: Multiple-food recognition considering co-occurrence employing manifold ranking. In: International Conference on Pattern Recognition, pp. 2017–2020 (2012)
9. Perronnin, F.: Universal and adapted vocabularies for generic visual categorization. IEEE Transactions on Pattern Analysis and Machine Intelligence 30(7), 1243–1256 (2008)
10. Saffari, A., Bischof, H.: Clustering in a boosting framework, pp. 75–82. Computer Vision Winter Workshop (2007)
11. Shotton, J., Johnson, M., Cipolla, R.: Semantic texton forests for image categorization and segmentation. IEEE Conference on Computer Vision and Pattern Recognition, 1–8 (2008)
12. Topchy, A., Jain, A.K., Punch, W.: Clustering ensembles: Models of consensus and weak partitions. IEEE Transactions on Pattern Analysis and Machine Intelligence 27(12), 1866–1881 (2005)
13. van Gemert, J.C., Veenman, C.J., Smeulders, A.W., Geusebroek, J.-M.: Visual word ambiguity. IEEE Transactions on Pattern Analysis and Machine Intelligence 32(7), 1271–1283 (2010)
14. Yang, S., Chen, M., Pomerleau, D., Sukthankar, R.: Food recognition using statistics of pairwise local features. IEEE Conference on Computer Vision and Pattern Recognition, 2249–2256 (2010)
15. Farinella, G.M., Moltisanti, M., Battiato, S.: Classifying Food Images Represented as Bag of Textons. IEEE International Conference on Image Processing, 5212–5216 (2014)
16. Farinella, G.M., Allegra, D., Stanco, F.: A benchmark dataset to study the representation of food images. In: Agapito, L., Bronstein, M.M., Rother, C. (eds.) ECCV 2014 Workshops. LNCS, vol. 8927, pp. 584–599. Springer, Heidelberg (2015)
17. Anthimopoulos, M.M., Gianola, L., Scarnato, L., Diem, P., Mougiakakou, S.G.: A Food Recognition System for Diabetic Patients Based on an Optimized Bag-of-Features Model. IEEE Journal of Biomedical and Health Informatics 18(4), 1261–1271 (2014)

18. Bossard, L., Guillaumin, M., Van Gool, L.: Food-101 – mining discriminative components with random forests. In: Fleet, D., Pajdla, T., Schiele, B., Tuytelaars, T. (eds.) ECCV 2014, Part VI. LNCS, vol. 8694, pp. 446–461. Springer, Heidelberg (2014)
19. Hu, Y., Cheng, X., Chia, L.-T., Xie, X., Rajan, D., Tan, A.-H.: Coherent Phrase Model for Efficient Image Near-Duplicate Retrieval. IEEE Transactions on Multimedia **11**(8), 1434–1445 (2009)
20. Varma, M., Zisserman, A.: A Statistical Approach to Texture Classication from Single Images. International Journal of Computer Vision **62**(1-2), 61–81 (2005)

Using Small Checkerboards as Size Reference: A Model-Based Approach

Hamid Hassannejad$^{(\boxtimes)}$, Guido Matrella,
Monica Mordonini, and Stefano Cagnoni

Dipartimento di Ingegneria Dell'Informazione, Università degli Studi di Parma,
Parma, Italy
{hamid.hassannejad,guido.matrella,
monica.mordonini,stefano.cagnoni}@unipr.it

Abstract. Monitoring diet is crucial for preventing or dealing with many chronic diseases. Therefore, plenty of different methods have been developed to serve this purpose. Among these, automatic diet monitoring based on mobile devices are of particular interest. An automatic system is supposed to be able to detect type and amount of food intake. This work suggests using a small checkerboard in food images as size reference as an aid for estimating food amount. Although checkerboard is a simple pattern, most of the off-the-shelf algorithms do not perform well in detecting small checkerboards. This paper extends a previous work presenting a new stochastic model-based algorithm to detect small checkerboards. The algorithm first locates the checkerboard in the food image and then applies a customized corner detection algorithm to the located region. Experimental results show notably better performance in comparison to basic methods and to the previous version of the method.

Keywords: Corner detection · Small checkerboard · Model-based method

1 Introduction

According to World Health Organization, in 2014 the global prevalence of diabetes was estimated to be 9% among adults aged 18+ years while at least 2.8 million people die each year as a result of being overweight or obese [1]. There are many other health problems which are directly related to diet. These facts have fostered the emergence of many services which help people monitor their diet. Moreover, there have been many efforts to make the monitoring easier and more precise by automating it.

Food volume estimation is the most direct approach to automate the computation of calories or nutrients of food intake. Volume estimation from images can be obtained through different procedures, but only up to a scale. Therefore, in many studies, an object of known size is used as reference for volume estimation. In [2], for instance, the user puts his/her finger besides the dish. In [4], a specific

© Springer International Publishing Switzerland 2015
V. Murino et al. (Eds.): ICIAP 2015 Workshops, LNCS 9281, pp. 393–400, 2015.
DOI: 10.1007/978-3-319-23222-5_48

pattern of known size printed on a card is used as reference. Many studies have followed the same idea using a checkerboard as reference [6][9].

The simplicity of the checkerboard pattern and the existence of effective algorithms to detect it are some of the reasons for choosing it over other options. Nevertheless, off-the-shelf checkerboard detection algorithms are usually designed to be means for camera calibration or pose-detection processes. They are usually tuned for specific situations like: flat checkerboards, a big checkerboard, that is often the only object in the image, etc. Thus, for applications which do not satisfy these requirements, different algorithms, or modified versions of available ones, are needed. Checkerboards which are used as size references usually consist of few squares and occupy a relatively small portion of the image. This situation makes it difficult for 'standard' checkerboard detectors. Figure 1 shows three examples in which OpenCV and Matlab checkerboard detection algorithms fail. The OpenCV algorithm is available through the *findChessboardCorners()* function, and the Matlab algorithm is available through the *detectCheckerboardPoints* function (hereafter, they will be referred to, respectively, as *basic method 1* and *basic method 2*).

In [3] we have introduced a method to locate small checkerboard in an image. We used a small checkerboard, printed on a PVC card, as size reference. The method can be used as a pre-processing step before applying off-the-shelf checkerboard detection algorithms. This paper is an extension of that approach. The locating algorithm is improved and a new method to detect checkerboard corners is presented. The method, first, locates the checkerboard in the image using a model-based approach. Later, the detected region is processed by a customized corner detection algorithm to obtain exact coordination of the checkerboard corners. It is shown that this idea outperforms the basic algorithms.

Fig. 1. First row: typical images used for calibration. Second row: Examples of images in which checkerboard is used as size reference for food volume estimation, on which both OpenCV and Matlab functions for detecting checkerboards fail, while, they are correctly located by model-based algorithm (green areas)

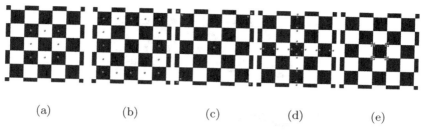

(a)   (b)   (c)   (d)   (e)

Fig. 2. Key points are evaluated in five steps to compute the similarity degree between the projected model and the image.

Moreover, the stochastic nature of the proposed method gives it an important advantage. In the case of food intake monitoring, missing the checkerboard in an image would cost the user the trouble of providing another image of the food, and even so there would not be any guarantee that, under the same condition, the algorithm would work with the new image. While, the stochastic nature of the proposed method makes it possible to run a new attempt on the same image, when the first run fails.

2 Method

The method consists of two main steps: locating the checkerboard in the image and then detecting the checkerboard corners in the located area.

2.1 Locating the Checkerboard

To locate the checkerboard, we use the same approach as [8]. The procedure we adopted estimates the pose of an object based on a 3D model and can be utilized with any projection system and any general object model. In this method, a hypothesis of checkerboard location can be evaluated by rigidly transforming a model of the checkerboard and then projecting it onto the image according to a perspective transform. The likelihood of the hypothesis is evaluated using a similarity measure between the projected model and the actual content of the image region onto which the pattern is projected.

This procedure allows one to turn checkerboard detection into an optimization problem, in which the parameters to be optimized are the coefficients of the rigid transformation and of the projection. Using such a similarity measure as fitness function, a meta-heuristic is then used to generate hypotheses, until similarity reaches a predefined threshold, which means that the checkerboard has been located.

One of the advantages over other model-based approaches is that this approach does not need any preliminary preprocessing of the image or any projection of a full 3D model [5].

In this work, the Differential Evolution (DE) is employed for optimization. DE is a relatively simple evolutionary optimization algorithm. It iteratively tries

Fig. 3. Camera coordinate system (green) and world coordinate system (blue). The input vector of the fitness functions presents the transformation (translation and rotation) which matches the camera coordinate system to the world coordinate system.

to improve a candidate solution to one optimization problem with respect to a given measure of quality [7].

The fitness function calculates the degree of similarity between the re-projected model and the image. In this work the input argument of the fitness function is a vector of six parameters which represents the pose of the object with respect to the camera. The first three parameters represent translation in the 3D coordinate system and the other three represent rotation around the coordinate system axes. These parameters describe the transformation which matches the camera coordinate system (blue) in figure 3 to the world coordination system (green).

To do so, 73 key points are used to describe the checkerboard model. The similarity degree is calculated in 5 steps. In each step a subset of key points is checked and a similarity term is added to the fitness. The solution passes to the next step if at least a certain degree of similarity has been reached, otherwise it rejects the hypothesis returning a bad fitness value. Figure 2 shows the key points checked in every step of the fitness function. A perfect match will be given a score of 54, however any score higher than 48 can be considered an acceptable match in this work. In comparison to the previous work [3], we applied some improvements in evaluating of the selected points and we also improved the tunning of the thresholds to reach more consistent results on divers images.

2.2 Corners Detection

Since the approximate location of the checkerboard is detected during the first phase, it is possible to design a customized algorithm to detect the checkerboard corners on the cropped image. Algorithm 1 describes the process flow of the corner detection method. The method is developed based on the fact that the checkerboard is in the center of the cropped image and covers most of the image.

The process starts with calculating gray scale image and then single precision image of the RGB input. Then, second derivative of the single precision image is

---

Algorithm 1. Corner detection algorithm

---

function FINDCHECKERBOARDCORNERS

$\quad Image \leftarrow GetCroppedRGBImage()$
$\quad Image \leftarrow RGB2SinglePrecision(Image)$
$\qquad\qquad\qquad\qquad\qquad\qquad$ ▷ Calculate second derivatives at zero and 45 degrees
$\quad D0 \leftarrow CalcSecondDerivative(Image, 0)$
$\quad D45 \leftarrow CalcSecondDerivative(Image, 45)$
$\qquad\qquad\qquad\qquad\qquad\qquad\qquad\qquad\qquad$ ▷ Find the pixels with higer values
$\quad Corners0 \leftarrow FindCorners(D0)$
$\quad Corners45 \leftarrow FindCorners(D45)$
$\qquad\qquad\qquad\qquad\qquad\qquad\qquad$ ▷ Find 3 closest corners to the image center
$\quad CentralCorners0 \leftarrow Find3CentralCorners(Corners0)$
$\quad CentralCorners45 \leftarrow Find3CentralCorners(Corners45)$
$\qquad\qquad\qquad$ ▷ Expand the candidate checkerboards based on the central corners
$\quad Candidates0 \leftarrow ExpandCentralCorners(CentralCorners0)$
$\quad Candidates45 \leftarrow ExpandCentralCorners(CentralCorners45)$
$\qquad\qquad\qquad\qquad\qquad\qquad\qquad\qquad\qquad$ ▷ Choose the best candidate
$\quad BestCandidate \leftarrow ScoreCandidates(Candidates0, Candidates45)$
$\quad$ **return** $BestCandidate$

end function

---

calculated in two direction: zero degree and 45 degrees. This allows the algorithm to detect the corners of the checkerboards with various poses.

In both of the derivative images, the pixels with higher values are identified as corners. This set contain checkerboard corners as well as other generic corners inside the cropped image. Then, the fact that the checkerboard is located in the center of the image is applied: three corners which are the closests to the image center are belong to the central square of the checkerboard (one can not be sure about the fourth one, due to approximation in locating of the checkerboard). Afterwards, the other corners of the checkerboard will be detected by gradually growing it from the central square.

However, There will be 3 candidates in each derivative image. Figure 4 demonstrates 3 different options of checkerboard expansion based of the three selected corners. Obviously there is only one correct choice. Since, there are two derivative images, that is 6 candidates in total. To find the true checkerboard, each candidate will be scored based on the compliance with the known checkerboard structure (in this case a 5×5 one). The candidate with the higher score would be selected as the true checkerboard.

3   Experimental Results

The algorithm has been tested over four sets of images, for a total of 458 images in each of which a 5×5 checkerboard, printed on a plastic card. The images of each set have been taken by a different mobile device and in different environments.

In one case (Samsung Galaxy S3), since the high resolution default images led to worse results using basic corner detection algorithms, a scaled version of the images was tested as well. The fourth set therefore contains the images in the third set scaled by a factor of 0.5.

In this work an implementation of DE with binomial crossover was used to locate the checkerboard. DE was iterated up to 1000 times for every image. Moreover, if the algorithm failed to locate the checkerboard in first attempt, it was repeated from scratch with a new population. For every image, DE is allowed to run up to four times.

Table 1 demonstrates the results of the algorithm in locating checkerboards. In more than 98% of the cases the checkerboard was correctly located. In 89% of the cases it was found within the first try of DE; on the average, DE has been repeated 1.24 times for each image.

Table 1. Results of the DE-based checkerboard locating algorithm.

	Images No.	Success	First try Success	DE tries
Motorola MotoG	179	176	143	1.34
Samsung Galaxy Note 1	19	19	11	1.3
Samsung Galaxy S3	130	129	123	1.2
Samsung Galaxy S3 scaled (0.5)	130	127	125	1.13
Total	458	451	402	1.24

Table 2 shows the result of the corner detection algorithms. Five different methods have been evaluated. Besides the basic methods and the proposed method, the results of combining of the locating method and basic methods have been reported. In the latter case, before applying the basic methods on the original image, the region selected by the locating algorithm was fed to the algorithm. If it failed, the original image was used.

As shown in table 2, there was an obvious improvement in both speed and performance of the basic algorithms when they used the pre-processed images (cropped checkerboard found by DE). Locating the checkerboard reduced the total processing time (including pre-processing) of the basic methods respectively by 23% and 71%, whereas the number of correctly detected checkerboards

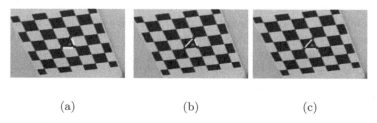

(a)   (b)   (c)

Fig. 4. Center of image (red) and 3 closest corners on a located checkerboard. Only one combination (a) is correct which its expansion reproduces the checkerboard.

Table 2. Results of the checkerboard corner detection algorithms.

		Motorola MotoG	Samsung Galaxy Note 1	Samsung Galaxy S3	Samsung Galaxy S3 scaled (0.5)	Total
Total number of images		179	19	130	130	458
Basic method 1	Detection	118	12	24	94	248
	Time (ms)	3368393	179775	16276198	909017	20733383
Basic method 1 with located checkerboard	Detection	133	14	51	100	298
	Time (ms)	2618700	133823	12512673	710783	15975979
Basic method 2	Detection	159	12	88	121	380
	Time (ms)	1267700	42853	626590	195250	2132393
Basic method 2 with located checkerboard	Detection	171	18	102	128	419
	Time (ms)	269817	21682	222827	104179	618505
Proposed method	Detection	173	19	128	127	447
	Time (ms)	200976	21324	114170	88669	425139

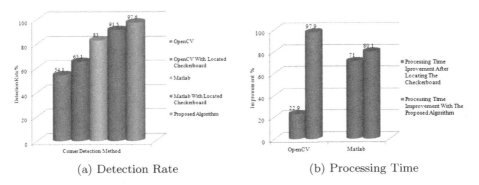

(a) Detection Rate   (b) Processing Time

Fig. 5. Results summary: (a) Improvement of the detection rate after applying the locating approach or using the proposed algorithm. (b) Processing time improvement in compare to the basic methods.

increased by 20% and 10%. Yet, the best results come with the proposed algorithm both regarding detection rate and processing time. Figure 5 shows a summary of the results.

Moreover, one can notice that the proposed method is much less sensitive to the image resolution, whereas basic methods are dramatically affected by high resolution images, which are common in new smart-phones. It is an advantage of simple models selected to be evaluated in locating phase and corner detection phase.

4   Conclusions and Future Works

A small checkerboard, can be a proper reference for many applications. Therefore, this algorithm could be a valuable asset in automatic size-estimation applications and, in particular, for food amount estimation.

The proposed algorithm offers very satisfying performance in detecting of small checkerboard corners. It includes an improved version of a previous ly developed pre-processing algorithm used to locating the checkerboard and a new customized corner detection algorithm. We could show that, adding the locating phase as pre-processing step, improves existing checkerboard detection algorithms as regards both processing time and successful detection rate of small checkerboards. Moreover, the customized corner detection algorithm outperforms basic methods even after improving them by pre-processing phase.

A symmetric checkerboard as the one used in this work may cause inconsistent pose detections. The procedure we described is applicable to any pattern, so an asymmetric checkerboard could be used in applications in which the accuracy of DE-based object location is more critical. Finally, taking into consideration the intrinsic parallel nature of DE, parallelizing the algorithm on GPU using platforms like CUDA or OpenCL could be considered to further improving processing time.

Acknowledgments. This work is funded by the Helicopter Project (an EU granted Ambient Assisted Living Joint Project). We want to thank in particular, the project partner METEDA S.R.L.

References

1. Diabetes (2015). http://www.who.int/mediacentre/factsheets/fs312/en/
2. Almaghrabi, R., Villalobos, G., Pouladzadeh, P., Shirmohammadi, S.: A novel method for measuring nutrition intake based on food image. In: 2012 IEEE International Instrumentation and Measurement Technology Conference (I2MTC), pp. 366–370, May 2012
3. Hassannejad, H., Matrella, G., Mordonini, M., Cagnoni, S.: A stochastic approach to detect small checkerboards . accepted in AI*IA 2015 (2015)
4. Martin, C.K., Kaya, S., Gunturk, B.K.: Quantification of food intake using food image analysis. In: Annual International Conference of the IEEE Engineering in Medicine and Biology Society, EMBC 2009, pp. 6869–6872. IEEE (2009)
5. Mussi, L., Cagnoni, S., Daolio, F.: Gpu-based road sign detection using particle swarm optimization. In: Ninth International Conference on Intelligent Systems Design and Applications, ISDA 2009, pp. 152–157. IEEE (2009)
6. Rahman, M.H., Li, Q., Pickering, M., Frater, M., Kerr, D., Bouchey, C., Delp, E.: Food volume estimation in a mobile phone based dietary assessment system. In: 2012 Eighth International Conference on Signal Image Technology and Internet Based Systems (SITIS), pp. 988–995. IEEE (2012)
7. Storn, R., Price, K.: Differential evolution-a simple and efficient adaptive scheme for global optimization over continuous spaces, vol. 3. ICSI Berkeley (1995)
8. Ugolotti, R., Nashed, Y.S.G., Cagnoni, S.: Real-time GPU based road sign detection and classification. In: Coello, C.A.C., Cutello, V., Deb, K., Forrest, S., Nicosia, G., Pavone, M. (eds.) PPSN 2012, Part I. LNCS, vol. 7491, pp. 153–162. Springer, Heidelberg (2012)
9. Zhu, F., Bosch, M., Woo, I., Kim, S., Boushey, C.J., Ebert, D.S., Delp, E.J.: The use of mobile devices in aiding dietary assessment and evaluation. IEEE Journal of Selected Topics in Signal Processing 4(4), 756–766 (2010)

Fractal Nature of Chewing Sounds

Vasileios Papapanagiotou[1]([✉]), Christos Diou[1], Zhou Lingchuan[2],
Janet van den Boer[3], Monica Mars[3], and Anastasios Delopoulos[1]

[1] Aristotle University of Thessaloniki, Thessaloniki, Greece
{vassilis,diou}@mug.ee.auth.gr
http://mug.ee.auth.gr
[2] CSEM SA, Landquart, Switzerland
lingchuan.zhou@csem.ch
[3] Wagenigen University, Wagenigen, Netherlands
monica.mars@wur.nl, adelo@eng.auth.gr

Abstract. In the battle against Obesity as well as Eating Disorders, non-intrusive dietary monitoring has been investigated by many researchers. For this purpose, one of the most promising modalities is the acoustic signal captured by a common microphone placed inside the outer ear canal. Various chewing detection algorithms for this type of signals exist in the literature. In this work, we perform a systematic analysis of the fractal nature of chewing sounds, and find that the Fractal Dimension is substantially different between chewing and talking. This holds even for severely down-sampled versions of the recordings. We derive chewing detectors based on the the fractal dimension of the recorded signals that can clearly discriminate chewing from non-chewing sounds. We experimentally evaluate snacking detection based on the proposed chewing detector, and we compare our approach against well known counterparts. Experimental results on a large dataset of 10 subjects and total recordings duration of more than 8 hours demonstrate the high effectiveness of our method. Furthermore, there exists indication that discrimination between different properties (such as crispness) is possible.

1 Introduction

Monitoring and managing dietary behaviour has received extensive focus during the last few years, since both Obesity (OB) and Eating Disorders (ED), such as Anorexia Nervosa (AN) and Bulimia Nervosa (BN), currently affect a very large portion of the population[1][2]. Recent advancements in the field of mobile computing have enabled the use of wearable sensors for monitoring the human behaviour in various aspects of everyday life. Vast development and enhancement of the capabilities of mobile phones, as well as networking, combined with various wearable sensors (e.g. smart watches) have practically transformed them into personal monitoring devices, that can be used to exploit data otherwise

---

[1] www.who.int/gho/ncd/risk_factors/overweight/en/
[2] www.anad.org/get-information/about-eating-disorders/eating-disorders-statistics/

© Springer International Publishing Switzerland 2015
V. Murino et al. (Eds.): ICIAP 2015 Workshops, LNCS 9281, pp. 401–408, 2015.
DOI: 10.1007/978-3-319-23222-5_49

unavailable even to clinician experts. This data can be used to detect risks (for example for the development of OB or ED, such as the case of the SPLENDID project[3]) and even help reduce those risks.

Regarding the monitoring of dietary activities and behaviour, one of the most commonly proposed sensors in bibliography is the microphone, either open-air or bone conduction. The microphone is usually placed in an unobtrusive location, such as housed in a set of ear phones, and continuously records audio throughout the day, or during long periods of a day. The streamed audio is analysed, usually in real-time, and chewing activity is detected. Most proposed algorithms for the processing of such signals employ well known methods from the field of digital signal processing, such as computation of various statistical features of buffered audio segments, and usually combine them with statistical machine learning methods. Other approaches try to model the distinct structure of chewing sounds, employing heuristically defined rules.

O. Amft was one of the first to systematically analyse chewing sounds, and develop an off-line algorithm to detect chews on continuous streaming audio data. In [2], various positions of a condenser microphone recording at 44.1 kHz are studied, to determine the optimal for automatic chewing detection. Placing the microphone at the inner ear, directed towards the ear drum was found to yield the best results, as in this position chewing sounds are recorded louder than speech sounds. Thus, recognition of chewing sounds is based on the amplitude of the recorded signal. The useful frequency content is determined from 0 to 10 kHz (requiring 20 kHz sampling rate). Furthermore, a speech recognition system is used to reject talking and further increase the precision of chewing detection. In a later work, a complex pipeline is proposed in [1] that (a) estimates various multi-resolution statistical features of audio segments, (b) performs feature selection, and (c) uses a feature similarity measure to detect chews. The detection system is able to discriminate between three food types of distinct texture qualities (crispiness and wetness). However, the computational burden is significantly high, increasing the required resources for a real-time implementation.

In [8], seven chewing detection algorithms are evaluated on a common dataset. The dataset includes recordings of 51 subjects, consuming 6 different food types, using a microphone recording at 11,025 Hz. One algorithm requires the use of a second microphone, placed behind the ear, and uses the difference of the signals' power between the two microphones to detect chews. Another algorithm associates chewing sounds with a particular shape of the signal energy (a local maximum followed by an interval of lower energy). Another one is based on the principle that the power spectrum of chewing sounds is centred around specific frequencies, and thus can be used to distinguish chewing from other sounds. Other algorithms detect chewing regions by identifying the dominant frequency at which chews occur, which is commonly around 1 and 3 Hz. Authors report accuracy from 50% to 60% and precision from 75% to 91% on average. However, it is important to note that the recording of the dataset was performed in

---

[3] splendid-program.eu/

laboratory conditions and the participants were instructed not to talk or make any other disturbing sound, which makes the recognition task significantly easier.

In this work, we explore the Fractal Dimension (FD) of chewing sounds, as recorded by such an open air microphone placed inside the outer ear canal, in comparison to the FD of other sounds recorded by this sensor, such as talking, coughing, ambient noise and silence. Section 2 presents the analysis and the method for computing the FD, whereas in Section 3 further analysis is performed to design a detection algorithm. In Section 4 various experiments are presented, including the application of the detection algorithm on a large dataset for the purpose of detecting snacking events. Results are compared to other state-of-the-art algorithms. Finally, Section 5 concludes this work.

2   Fractal Dimension of Chewing Sounds

Mandelbrot [4] defines the FD of a graph of a real valued function as its Hausdorff Dimension (HD). In the work of Maragos et al. [6], an algorithm for estimating the FD of such real valued functions is presented, based on a morphological covering of the function using the erosion and dilation operators [3].

Given a real valued function $x(t), 0 \leq t \leq T$, its graph can be defined formally as $F = \{(t, x(t)) \in \mathbf{R}^2 : t \in [0, T]\}$. The FD can then be defined as follows. Given a morphological element B and a scaling factor ϵ, the FD is estimated as

$$D = 2 - \lim_{\epsilon \to 0} \frac{\log (A_B(\epsilon))}{\log (\epsilon)} \tag{1}$$

where $A_B(\epsilon)$ is the area resulting from dilating the graph by ϵB. In the case where B is a compact, single-connected, symmetric planar set, the two-dimensional processing of the signal can be avoided [5,7]. If we define the structuring function $G_\epsilon(t) = \sup \{y \in \mathbf{R} : (t, y) \in \epsilon B\}$, then the area $A_B(\epsilon)$ can be approximated by

$$A_B(\epsilon) \approx \int_0^T ([x \oplus G_\epsilon](t) - [x \ominus G_\epsilon](t)) \, dt \tag{2}$$

where $[x \oplus G_\epsilon](t)$ and $[x \ominus G_\epsilon](t)$ are the dilation and erosion of $x(t)$ by $G_\epsilon(t)$.

In the case of discrete signals, and for discrete structure elements, we can approximate $A_B(\epsilon)$ as

$$A_B(\epsilon) \approx \sum_{n=0}^{N-1} \left[x_k^d(n) - x_k^e(n)\right], \epsilon = \epsilon_0 k, k = 0, 1, 2, \ldots, M \tag{3}$$

where the discrete version of dilation $x_k^d(n)$ and erosion $x_k^e(n)$ at level k are computed recursively as

$$x_0^d(n) = x(n) \tag{4}$$

$$x_0^e(n) = x(n) \tag{5}$$

$$x_k^d(n) = [x_{k-1}^d \oplus v](n) \tag{6}$$

$$x_k^e(n) = [x_{k-1}^e \ominus v](n) \tag{7}$$

In practice, we choose a flat structure element v of length $L = \lceil f_s T \rceil$ where $T = 3$ msec, and thus

$$x_k^d(n) = \max\{x_{k-1}^d(n+i) : i = -\lfloor \tfrac{L}{2} \rfloor, \ldots, 0, \ldots, \lceil \tfrac{L}{2} \rceil - 1\} \qquad (8)$$

For the erosion, the max operator is replaced with min.

According to [5], the FD D can be estimated by linear fitting on $\log(A_B(\epsilon)) = (2-D)\log(\epsilon)$, for discrete scales of $\epsilon = k\epsilon_0$, $k = 1, 2, \ldots, M$. Instead, we estimate D as the mean of local gradients

$$D = \frac{1}{M} \sum_{\epsilon=1}^{M} \frac{\log(A_B((k+1)\epsilon_0)) - \log(A_B(k\epsilon_0))}{\log(k+1) - \log(k)} \qquad (9)$$

In order to examine the fractal properties of chewing sounds, in particular compared to other sounds commonly recorded by such a microphone as the one used in this work (e.g. talking, coughing, etc), we extract recordings of individual chews of six food types of various properties (such as crispness), as well as segments of approximately same duration of coughing, talking, and silence (and some ambient noise). The number of audio segments for each category are presented in Table 1. The recordings that contain these segments belong to a much larger dataset which is presented in Section 4, and used in the final experiment of snacking detection.

Table 1. The extracted audio segments of chewing and non-chewing segments.

Food Type	No.	Type	No.
Apple	156	Cough	15
Banana	63	Pause	1032
Bread	84	Talking	147
Candy bar	96		
Chewing gum	126		
Potato chips	149		
Total	674	Total	1194

Fig. 1 shows the data points for 20 chews of "apple" and audio segments of "talking", for $k = 1, 2, \ldots, 40$. We use both the audio segments, and their time-derivatives. The fact that these curves are approximately linear is a strong indication that these chew segments are highly fractal in nature. Note that for some audio segments, the curves' gradients tend to decrease for larger values of k. This is not accurate however, but rather a computational artifact, since for such values of k the length of the equivalent structuring element is comparable to the length of the audio segment, causing this inaccurate result.

Furthermore, only a few data points are required to estimate the FD. In the following, we have selected $M = 6$. Selecting such a low value for M, combined with the computationally lighter method for computing the dilation and erosion banks (by iterative application of the same structuring element), allows the implementation of a fast and computationally inexpensive detection algorithm. Finally, it also avoids the problem of the computational artifacts caused by excessively large structuring elements, as noted above.

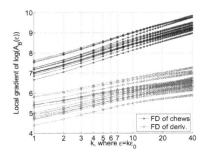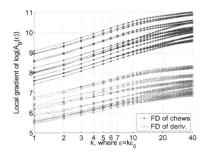

Fig. 1. Local gradient for $\log(A_B(\epsilon))$ versus $k = 1, 2, \ldots, 40$ (in log-scale), for 20 chew segments (blue) and their derivatives (red) of "apple" (left), and 15 segments of "coughing" (right).

3 Designing a Detection Algorithm

In order to examine the fractal nature of the chewing sounds, we compute the FD of the extracted audio segments and their derivatives, at various sampling rates, lower than the original. This is achieved by resampling the original recordings. Fig. 2 (*left*) shows the results for "apple" and "talking". The mean ($\pm$ standard deviation) curves of the FD of the signals are presented, sampling at frequencies $0.5, 1, 2, 4, 8, 16$ and 32 kHz, as well as for the original frequency of 44.1 kHz, in a log-scale plot. The statistics are not affected by the down-sampling, even for as low as 2 kHz, which corresponds to a narrow frequency content of only 1 kHz. Very similar results are obtained for all six food types. This observation reduces the detector requirements for the sampling frequency at just 2 kHz, significantly reducing the computational effort required to process the audio signals.

Using the down-sampled (at 2 kHz) segments, a three-dimension feature vector is computed for each, using the FD of the segment D_x, the FD of the derivative of the segment D_s, and the segment energy E. The features for all the extracted segments are shown in Fig. 2 (*right*). The six food types have been grouped into two clusters for visual clarity, whereas the non-chewing categories are presented separately. As it can be seen, the union of the two chewing clusters is almost linearly separable from "silence", based solely on the energy feature, which is expected. Furthermore, it as also separable (again almost linearly) from "talking" and "coughing".

These results are particularly encouraging. First, the fact that these five classes form separable clusters is strong evidence of the fractal nature of chewing sounds, and enables the detection of chewing sounds based on their fractal dimension. At second, they are also promising in discriminating between different food type properties. For example, the first cluster (as presented in Fig. 2 (*right*)) includes chews of "banana" and "potato chips". "Banana" is not crispy, which results in a relatively lower FD. "Potato chips" are crispy at first, but quickly transform into a wet bolus after the very few first chews. On the other

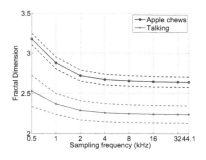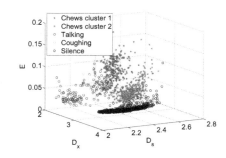

Fig. 2. *Left:* Mean (± standard deviation) of FD of apple chews, and talking segments, across various sampling frequencies (log-scale), showing (a) the linear separability of the two classes, and (b) that down-sampling up to 2 kHz does not significantly alter the actual value of FD. *Right:* Feature vectors for the entire dataset, at 2 kHz. Chews cluster 1 includes "banana" and "potato chips", cluster 2 the remaining 4 food types.

hand, the food types of the second cluster are consistently crispy throughout an entire bite (e.g. "chewing gum").

Finally, in order to enable processing of streamed audio data, we experiment with various lengths of sliding windows along each audio segment, in order to determine the minimum length that captures its fractal properties. We have found that a window length of 300 msec is sufficient to detect parts of chews, and thus enable robust chewing detection.

4   Experiments

A dataset was recorded at the Wageningen University, Netherlands, in the framework of EU funded program SPLENDID. It contains recordings of 10 individuals wearing a prototype sensor consisting of an FG-23329 microphone housed in an ear bud, and connected using audio cable to recording apparatus. Various activities were performed by each subject in randomised sequences, and include pauses, talking, listening to another person speaking, coughing, and consuming a variety of different foods and liquids, such as apples, lettuce, potato chips, toffee, water, milk, etc. The recording for each subject lasted approximately 30 minutes. It is important to notice that during the recordings there was no request for absolute silence. In contrast, some chewing activities were performed under non-silent conditions. For example, the subject was asked to consume a specific type of food while listening to the supervisor talking. The extracted chews of Table 1 belong to the recordings of two subjects of the dataset.

In order to validate our findings, we perform a classification experiment. We form a classification problem with three classes: "chew", "talk/cough" and "silence". The classification method is a two step process. First, the energy of the segment is compared to a threshold; this essentially removes all segments of "silence". Second, an optimal straight line on the $D_x \times D_s$ plane discriminates between "chew" and non-chew. Table 2 presents the results, however we show each food type and non-chewing activity separately, to gain a better understanding of the misclassification cases. Out of the 6 different food types, only 7 potato chip chews have been misclassified as talking or coughing, which indicates a clear discrimination between chewing and talking/coughing. On the other hand, only 9 chews have been misclassified as silence; most probably due to the lower energy of those segments. Classification accuracy in the 3-class problem is 95.4%, whereas for the binary "chew" vs. non-chew problem is 96.5% (using all of the extracted segments).

In order to examine the efficiency of the proposed algorithm in real time conditions, we apply our algorithm on the large dataset presented in this Section, so as to detect individual chews. This is achieved by thresholding the energy against an adaptively computed mean energy, and using the optimal separating line from the previous experiment on the $D_x \times D_s$ feature space. A median filter is then applied as a post processing step. Finally, chews are created from subsequent windows that are classified as chewing. We then apply an aggregation method to obtain chewing bouts (each chewing bout contains multiple chews) and evaluate this result, as a binary classification problem, based on duration of predicted intervals. To compare our algorithm with other known algorithms of the literature, we also apply some algorithms of [8] so as to detect individual chews, and use the same aggregation method to obtain the corresponding chewing regions. The aggregation algorithm assigns chews to the same bout if they are no more than 5 seconds apart. This relatively relaxed condition allows the chewing detection to "miss" a chew (or two) without fragmenting the bout. This yields consecutive intervals of chewing and non-chewing activity. We present the prediction precision and recall of each algorithm in Table 3. The proposed algorithm maintains a balance between high precision and recall, compared to other algorithms such as Ch. Band Power, that achieves higher precision (by 1%) at the cost of much lower recall.

Table 2. Confusion matrix for the classification experiment with linear kernel and three classes: "chew", "talk/cough" and "silence". Energy threshold is 0.0202, and the separating line in the $D_x \times D_s$ plane is $y = -2.62x + 8.73$.

Class	Chew	T/C	Sil.
Apple	156	0	0
Banana	62	0	3
Bread	83	0	1
Candy bar	95	0	1
Chewing gum	120	0	6
Cough	2	13	0
Pause	27	0	1005
Potato chips	142	7	0
Talking	21	106	20

Furthermore, we subsequently aggregate chewing bouts to snacks, by assigning to the same snack all bouts that are no more than 45 seconds apart. This interval seems realistic in real time application. However, in the dataset, subjects performed activities based on a schedule, and recordings of different snacking events are sometimes recorded much closer than 45 seconds. In these cases, we explicitly split the chewing bouts properly into different snacks. We then use a one-to-one method to assign predicted snacks to ground truth snacks. Table 3 presents the precision and accuracy at the snack classification level.

5 Conclusions

Table 3. Precision and recall for chew bouts and slnacks

Algorithm	Chew bout Prec	Rec	Snack Prec Rec
Max. Sound En.	0.85	0.75	0.77 0.90
Max. Spec. B. En.	0.89	0.76	0.81 0.89
L. P. Filtering	0.86	0.78	0.79 0.94
Ch. Band Power	0.92	0.61	0.92 0.87
Fractal Dim.	0.91	0.87	0.86 0.98

In this work, we explored the FD of chewing sounds, as a means to automatic monitoring of dietary activity, using a wearable microphone sensor. We have performed a systematic analysis of the fractal nature of chewing sounds, which indicates that chewing sounds are highly fractal. Thus, the FD can be used to discriminate chewing from non-chewing sounds, such as talking, coughing, or silence. This property persists even after significant down-sampling of the audio into very narrow spectral bandwidth. Furthermore, promising evidence was found that FD can be used to discriminate between different food properties, such as crispness. Based on these findings, we then proposed a chewing detection algorithm, and tested it on a large, realistic dataset. Results show an improvement in both precision and recall compared to other literature algorithms.

Acknowledgments. The work leading to these results has received funding from the European Community's ICT Programme under Grant Agreement No. 610746, 01/10/2013 - 30/09/2016.

References

1. Amft, O., Kusserow, M., Troster, G.: Bite weight prediction from acoustic recognition of chewing. IEEE Transactions on Biomedical Engineering **56**(6), 1663–1672 (2009)
2. Amft, O., Stäger, M., Lukowicz, P., Tröster, G.: Analysis of chewing sounds for dietary monitoring. In: Beigl, M., Intille, S.S., Rekimoto, J., Tokuda, H. (eds.) UbiComp 2005. LNCS, vol. 3660, pp. 56–72. Springer, Heidelberg (2005)
3. Gonzalez, R.C., Woods, R.E.: Digital image processing (2002)
4. Mandelbrot, B.B.: The fractal geometry of nature/revised and enlarged ed., 495p., 1. WH Freeman and Co., New York (1983)
5. Maragos, P.: Fractal signal analysis using mathematical morphology. Advances in electronics and electron physics **88**, 199–246 (1994)
6. Maragos, P., Potamianos, A.: Fractal dimensions of speech sounds: Computation and application to automatic speech recognition. The Journal of the Acoustical Society of America **105**(3), 1925–1932 (1999)
7. Maragos, P., Sun, F.-K.: Measuring the fractal dimension of signals: morphological covers and iterative optimization. IEEE Transactions on signal Processing **41**(1), 108–121 (1993)
8. Päßler, S., Fischer, W.-J.: Evaluation of algorithms for chew event detection. In: Proceedings of the 7th International Conference on Body Area Networks, ICST (Institute for Computer Sciences, Social-Informatics and Telecommunications Engineering), pp. 20–26 (2012)

Objective and Subjective Meal Registration via a Smartphone Application

Ioannis Moulos[1](✉), Christos Maramis[1], Ioannis Ioakimidis[2], Janet van den Boer[3], Jenny Nolstam[4], Monica Mars[3], Cecilia Bergh[4], and Nicos Maglaveras[1]

[1] Lab of Medical Informatics, Aristotle University of Thessaloniki, Thessaloniki, Greece
{joemoul,chmaramis,nicmag}@med.auth.gr
[2] Division for Applied Neuroendocrinology, Karolinska Intitutet, Stockholm, Sweden
ioannis.ioakimidis@ki.se
[3] Division of Human Nutrition, Wageningen University, Wageningen, The Netherlands
{janet.vandenboer,monica.mars}@wur.nl
[4] Mando Group AB, Stockholm, Sweden
jenny@jennynolstam.se, Cecilia.Bergh@mando.se

Abstract. SPLENDID is a research programme that develops a novel preventive intervention for young people at risk for obesity and eating disorders. The SPLENDID app, a novel smartphone application that mediates the monitoring and modification of the participants' eating and activity behaviors, resides in the intervention's core. The app receives and manages eating and physical activity related signals from three communicating sensors as well as subjective user input. In this paper, we present two discrete meal registration mechanisms – subjective and objective – that have been implemented and incorporated in the SPLENDID app, along with the relevant user feedback. In objective meal registration, the app records meal information with the help of a portable food weight scale, while an electronic meal report is employed for the subjective registration. Certain components of the proposed registration mechanisms and the relevant feedback have been evaluated with respect to usability on forty young adolescents, yielding promising results.

Keywords: Sensory meal recording · Subjective meal reporting · Smartphone application · Obesity · Eating disorders

1   Introduction

Obesity and eating disorders (ED), such as boulimia nervosa, have emerged as major concern for public health, affecting – among other age categories – young adults and adolescents at a worrisome increasing pace. As a result, several treatment interventions (surgical, pharmacological, and lifestyle) have been proposed and, in most cases, rejected as ineffective. Contemporary approaches attempt to *prevent* obesity and eating disorders with the help of modern technology, such as sensors and mobile phones. In this scope, the ongoing EU-funded research programme SPLENDID develops an ICT system for delivering a novel lifestyle intervention for the prevention of obesity

© Springer International Publishing Switzerland 2015
V. Murino et al. (Eds.): ICIAP 2015 Workshops, LNCS 9281, pp. 409–416, 2015.
DOI: 10.1007/978-3-319-23222-5_50

and ED on young populations [1]. The SPLENDID system is going to monitor the eating and physical activity behavior of its users (adolescents and young adults) by integrating objective recordings from 3 wearable sensors and – subjective – user input. Its goal is to evaluate a list of eating and physical activity indicators defined by the SPLENDID intervention in order to assess the risk of a user for obesity or ED. For those at risk, the SPLENDID system – using the same sensors – will attempt to permanently modify their hazardous eating and physical activity habits with the help of personalized behavioral goals and performance feedback mechanisms.

In the heart of the SPLENDID system, one can find the SPLENDID app [2], a modern smartphone application that is responsible for (1) collecting the recordings from the communicating sensors, (2) providing a bidirectional interface to the end-users for collecting subjective input and presenting the feedback of the system, and (3) communicating with the Decision Support System of SPLENDID, which calculates the behavioral indicators and evaluates the obesity and ED risk for the end-user. The various components of the SPLENDID system are outlined in Fig. 1.

The objective of this work is to present the novel meal ICT-enabled approach of SPLENDID for meal registration via the SPLENDID app. This offers an alternative to standard objective meal registration methods (e.g., meal image acquisition). Two novel mechanisms have been developed for registering meals into the SPLENDID app: Objective meal recording with the help of the Mandometer, i.e., a food weight scale with Bluetooth communication capabilities, and subjective self-reporting of meals via an electronic questionnaire. The mechanism that provides user feedback concerning the registered meals is also in scope of this work. The design and implementation (by means of the resulting screens of the app) of all three developed mechanisms are presented along with their partial evaluation with respect to usability in two experiments.

2   Related Work

Several smartphone applications for dietary management employ multimedia for meal registration. Most of them make use of wearable sensors (e.g., smartphone cameras, barcode scanners, RFID readers and IR sensors) to objectively capture characteristics of the user meals. However, monitoring and feedback features can be found to apps such as SapoFitness [3], an application that keeps a daily record of one's food intake and daily exercise, motivating the user to use the system. MANUP [4] is a mobile application that targets health literacy improvement, promoting physical activity and eating.

Relevant applications target weight management are mentioned; SmartLossSM [5] a smartphone-based weight loss intervention using additional wireless sensors such as scale and activity monitor. My Meal Mate [6] is a smartphone application, designed to support weight loss. The app helps the users to record food and drink intake, allowing them to take photos of foods while applying goal-setting information to automatically generate a specific daily energy target for them.

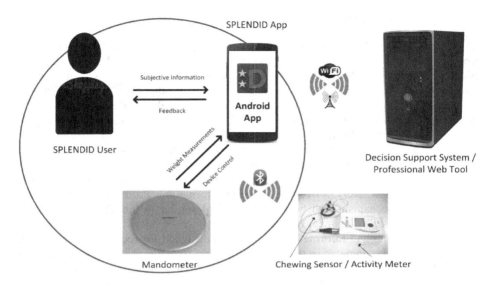

Fig. 1. Overview of the SPLENDID System indicating the main components and actors along with their interactions and means of communication. The part of the system that is of interest for the present paper has been included in a red circle.

3   Methods

The ability to monitor the eating activity of the end-users, i.e., meal occurrences and characteristics, is critical for the SPLENDID intervention, since this is the primary input for the behavioral indicators extraction and risk assessment algorithms of the system. Therefore, functionalities for registering the meals of the end-users into the SPLENDID system in as much detail as possible had to be designed. Evidently, the preferred means of registration requires the recording of the meal with one of the available sensors (objective information). However, in a real-world system like SPLENDID, a backup solution for subjectively reporting a past meal is also needed to ensure that at least some information about the non-recorded meals is registered into the system. At the same time, the provision of feedback to the end-users concerning (1) their eating and physical activity, and (2) the proximity to the set behavioral goals is of major importance for the SPLENDID intervention, as this feedback can help their recollection and motivate the modification of their eating and physical activity behavior. Specifically for meal registration, the most straightforward user feedback concerns an aggregated presentation of past registered meals.

The functionalities presented in the remainder of this section have been integrated into the SPLENDID app, which has been developed as an Android application. The flows of screens that carry out the aforementioned functionalities are displayed on Fig. 2 as actual screen captures from an Android Smartphone.

3.1   Objective Meal Registration

The primary sensor that is employed for meal recording is the Mandometer, a portable weight scale that periodically takes food weight measurements and sends them via Bluetooth to the SPLENDID app, which stores the resulting food weight time-series into its database. The SPLENDID app is able to drive the Mandometer (establish connection send start/stop recording signals, etc.). The meal recording functionality is delivered through a useable user interface (UI) that requests also the input of subjective meal information by the user. The Chewing Sensor, a currently developed ear plugged device incorporating an open air microphone and a photophethysmography (PPG) sensor, is SPLENDID's alternative for meal recording. When available, the Chewing Sensor will be able to generate and send to the SPLENDID app audio and visual signals respectively conveying chewing information. From the UI standpoint, this recording mechanism will be almost identical similar to the already developed functionality for recording meal with Mandometer.

A modern, clean and informative UI has been designed for recording a meal with the help of the Mandometer in the SPLENDID app (see Fig. 2): After selecting the meal registration option in the main screen of the app, the users specify the recording device and fill in the type of the meal (breakfast, lunch, dinner and snack). Then, they follow the illustrative instructions on how to put the food on the plate and initiate the recording process by pressing the "Start" button. The Mandometer starts sending via Bluetooth food weight measurements at 1Hz frequency, until the users press the "Finish" button to complete the recording. While the meal is in progress, a dialogue asking the users for their satiety level pops up every 2 minutes; the users specify their satiety with the help of vertical slider.

The recorded data combined with the subjective input of the users (e.g., satiety) comprise the primary input for the advanced computational algorithms of SPLENDID that extract the behavioral indicators and subsequently assess the risk of the users for obesity or ED.

3.2   Subjective Meal Registration

The – subjective – self-reporting mechanism enhances the overall meal registration functionalities of the SPLENDID app by complementing the sensor-based recording approach. This is considered as an alternative to objective recording for the cases where the latter is not possible. In this context, the main information about a meal is subjectively completed by the user.

This functionality reuses some of the meal recording screens and also introduces some resembling screens (see Fig. 2): After initiating the meal registration process in the main screen of the app, the users select the self-report option. Then, they specify the type/kind and estimated quantity of food and drink that they consumed, along with the time the meal took place. The reporting process concludes by asking the users to rate their satiety level at the specific time of meal reporting.

This feature manages to fill in the gaps at times when the sensor recording is unavailable by collecting some basic information about the meal in a subjective fashion. As above, this information is also fed to indicator extraction and risk assessment algorithms of the SPLENDID system.

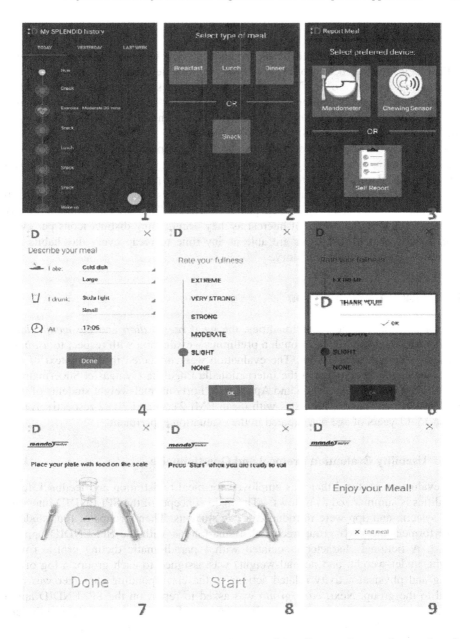

Fig. 2. Screens developed for the discussed functionalities. To complete meal reporting, the user navigates through screens 1, 2, 3, 4, 5, 6 and back to 1, while for meal recording, the screen flow is 1, 2, 3, 5 (recurs every 2 min), 7, 8, 9 and back to 1. Feedback is provided via screen 1.

3.3   User Feedback

The provision of up-to-date feedback through the app has been considered to be a critical factor for the success of the entire intervention, helping users' recollection and encouraging them to go on. The meal related feedback mechanism presented here serves mainly user recollection. The provided feedback concerns both user provided and sensor acquired information and it is delivered in an ambient manner via a modern, visual modality, i.e., the SPLENDID timeline.

The SPLENDID timeline (see Screen 1 in Fig. 2) is part of the main screen of the app. The timeline is an easily understandable visual log of the past events of interest for the SPLENDID intervention. Piece of information presented in the timeline include the occurrence and the type of the meals the users had during the day, as well as, the duration and intensity of their physical activity. The timeline is automatically updated to display the events of interest as they occur, using distinct icons per event type. In this context, the users are able at any time to recap every day habits and monitor their eating/activity history.

4   Usability Evaluation

Among the implemented functionalities, the *meal registration* and the *meal-related feedback* have already gone through a preliminary evaluation with respect to *usability* but also *aesthetics and design*. The evaluation was conducted in the context of two pilot studies that took place at the Internationalla Engelska Gymnasiet Södermalm in Stockholm (Sweden) on March and April 2015. Forty normal-weight students of both genders (19 males and 21 females with mean BMI 21.59 and 20.92 respectively) between 15-17 years of age participated in the evaluation experiment.

4.1   Usability Evaluation Protocol and Questionnaire

The evaluation protocol that was employed for meal registration and feedback functionalities is summarized as follows: The main concepts of the SPLENDID intervention, system, and app were introduced to the students. Then, groups of four students were formed and each group received a smartphone with the SPLENDID app installed. A fictional character associated with a paradigmatic dieting profile (overweight, under-weight, and normal-weight) was assigned to each group; a log of the eating and physical activity related actions of the corresponding character was provided to the group. Next, *each group* was asked to report on the SPLENDID app a specific meal of their character according the provided log and then observe the updated timeline. After that, *each student* was asked to fill in a questionnaire.

The objective of the developed questionnaire is to evaluate the usability of the demonstrated functionalities of the SPLENDID app as well as their *ease of completion* with the help of an enhanced version of the widely used System Usability Scale (SUS) [7]. An enhanced version of SUS was designed including 13 statements, i.e., the original 10 statements of SUS followed by three statements proposed by the authors (see Table 1). Same as in the original SUS, generally positive statements are alternating with generally negative ones and the users have to specify their extent of agreement/disagreement with each statement using a Likert scale of 5 categories (spanning from "Strongly agree" to "Strongly disagree").

4.2   Analysis of Usability Evaluation Results

The SUS scoring function was employed for the original SUS, resulting in scores in the range [0,100]. The same rationale was applied to the enhanced SUS which was then normalized in the aforementioned range to allow direct comparison with the original SUS. The summarized scores that were achieved are presented in Table 2.

Table 1. Proposed statements extending the System Usability Scale (SUS)

Order	Statement
11	I had to do more things than needed while using the app
12	It was easy to enter information in the app
13	The app had too many screens for what it does

Table 2. Mean and standard deviation (STD) of achieved scores for original and enhanced SUS

		Males	Females	All
SUS	Mean	73.62	68.21	70.78
	STD	8.77	14.14	12.06
Enhanced SUS	Mean	74.58	69.42	72.29
	STD	9.20	11.94	11.31

According to the scientific literature on usability testing, a SUS score above 68 is considered to be above average [8]. Table 2 makes clear that SPLENDID app passes this threshold (for both genders when considered separately and the ensemble of the participants). Moreover, the mean scores become even higher when the *ease of task completion* qualities are taken into account (enhanced SUS).

5   Conclusions

In this paper, we have presented the design, implementation and partial usability evaluation of the mechanisms that have been developed for meal registration and relevant user feedback in the SPLENDID app. The developed functionalities of the app allow its end-users to record each meal as a time series of food weight measurements acquired by a wirelessly connected weight scale and also either complement or replace – when there is no other way – this objective information with self-reported subjective information about the consumed food and beverage. The meal registration is accompanied with a functionality of aggregated feedback on past meals, to help users' recollection.

The next step of this work would be the exploitation of the second available sensor for meal recording, i.e., the Chewing Sensor that generates audio and optical time-series – air acoustic signal and photophethysmogram, respectively. Another feature that is planned to be included in the meal registration process is the acquisition of a digital photograph of the meal by means of the smartphone camera to be used for the visual annotation of the meal in the SPLENDID system. Once the development of the app is over, the main evaluation goal is to conduct well-sized pilot studies for assessing the efficiency of the app – and the proposed mechanisms – in monitoring and, subsequently, facilitating the modification of the eating habits of the users.

Acknowledgement. The work leading to these results has received funding from the European Community's ICT Programme under Grant Agreement No. 610746, 1/10/13 – 30/9/16.

References

1. Maramis, C., Diou, C., Ioakeimidis, I., Lekka, I., Dudnik, G., Mars, M., et al.: Preventing obesity and eating disorders through behavioural modifications: the SPLENDID vision. In: 2014 EAI 4th International Conference on Wireless Mobile Communication and Health-care (Mobihealth), pp. 7-10. IEEE, November 2014
2. Moulos, I., Maramis, C., Mourouzis, A., Maglaveras, N.: Designing the user interfaces of a behavior modification intervention for obesity & eating disorders prevention. Studies in Health Technology and Informatics **210**, 647–651 (2014)
3. Silva, B.M., Lopes, I.M., Rodrigues, J.J., Ray, P.: SapoFitness: a mobile health application for dietary evaluation. In: 2011 13th IEEE International Conference on e-Health Network-ing Applications and Services (Healthcom), pp. 375-380. IEEE, June 2011
4. Duncan, M., Vandelanotte, C., Kolt, G.S., Rosenkranz, R.R., Caperchione, C.M., George, E.S., et al.: Effectiveness of a web-and mobile phone-based intervention to promote physical activity and healthy eating in middle-aged males: randomized controlled trial of the ManUp study. Journal of Medical Internet Research **16**(6) (2014)
5. Martin, C.K., Miller, A.C., Thomas, D.M., Champagne, C.M., Han, H., Church, T.: Effica-cy of SmartLossSM, a smartphone-based weight loss intervention: Results from a rando-mized controlled trial. Obesity **23**(5), 935–942 (2015)
6. Carter, M.C., Burley, V.J., Nykjaer, C., Cade, J.E.: 'My Meal Mate' (MMM): validation of the diet measures captured on a smartphone application to facilitate weight loss. British Journal of Nutrition **109**(03), 539–546 (2013)
7. Brooke, J.: SUS-A quick and dirty usability scale. Usability Evaluation in Industry **189**(194), 4–7 (1996)
8. Bangor, A., Kortum, P., Miller, J.: Determining what individual SUS scores mean: Adding an adjective rating scale. Journal of Usability Studies **4**(3), 114–123 (2009)

Towards an Engaging Mobile Food Record for Teenagers

Maurizio Caon[1(✉)], Stefano Carrino[1], Federica Prinelli[2], Valentina Ciociola[2], Fulvio Adorni[2], Claudio Lafortuna[2], Sarah Tabozzi[2], José Serrano[3], Laura Condon[4], Omar Abou Khaled[1], and Elena Mugellini[1]

[1] University of Applied Sciences and Arts Western Switzerland, Fribourg, Switzerland
{maurizio.caon,stefano.carrino,omar.aboukhaled,
elena.mugellini}@hes-so.ch
[2] Consiglio Nazionale delle Ricerche, Milan, Italy
{federica.prinelli,valentina.ciociola,fulvio.adorni,claudio.lafo
rtuna,sarah.tabozzi}@cnr.it
[3] Universitat de Lleida, Lleida, Spain
jceserrano@mex.udl.cat
[4] University of Nottingham, Nottingham, UK
laura.condon@nottingham.ac.uk

Abstract. In the frame of the PEGASO European project, we aim at promoting healthier lifestyles among teenagers focusing on the alimentary education and physical activity. This paper presents a novel concept of mobile food record developed following a multidisciplinary approach to innovate both the monitoring and the user experience. This mobile food record does not count calories but is focused on tracking dietary patterns and support the adoption of target behaviours. Moreover, the introduction of game mechanics developed through participatory design techniques aims at sustaining engagement in the long term.

1 Introduction

The evaluation of dietary intake provides useful information for intervention programs aimed to prevent chronic diseases such as obesity [1]. For the assessment of food intake, three conventional tools are widely used for both adults and adolescents: the food frequency questionnaire (FFQ), food record (or diary), and 24-hour dietary recall. Each one with strengths and weaknesses [2].

Several issues have to be taken into account for monitoring dietary intake and especially designing a tool, which is able to evaluate the dietary habits of adolescents, and considering that youths have particular food choices and meal habits compared with children and adults. They differ in irregular eating patterns, frequent snacking and frequent skipping of meals, particularly breakfast [3]. Furthermore, the measurement of energy and nutrient intakes in adolescents is particularly challenging because they are more limited in their abilities to estimate portion sizes accurately in comparison with adults [4].

With the advent of new technologies, such as mobile phones, tablets, and other devices, the possibilities for rapid dietary data logging and real-time dietary analysis are

© Springer International Publishing Switzerland 2015
V. Murino et al. (Eds.): ICIAP 2015 Workshops, LNCS 9281, pp. 417–424, 2015.
DOI: 10.1007/978-3-319-23222-5_51

growing. Recent results reported that individuals, especially adolescents, prefer the use of a technology-based approach, rather than the traditional paper food record [5] suggesting that for this particular target population, dietary methods incorporating new mobile technology might increase the user adherence.

Due to the complexity of diet and the interaction among dietary components, instead of traditional methods of examining single foods or nutrients, holistic approaches able to capture the variation in overall food intake have been suggested. Dietary pattern is a set of habits regarding consumption of food and beverages and is characterised on the basis of usual consumption of foods and food groups and more closely describe real world conditions [6]. Furthermore, it has been reported that the relationship between diet and obesity, should focus not only on energy and macronutrient intake, but also on dietary patterns [7].

A number of specific food items and dietary behaviours have been associated with weight gain and chronic diseases in youth, including inadequate fruit and vegetable intake [8], breakfast skipping [9], frequent consumption of fast-food (energy-dense take-away meals) [10], increased sugar-sweetened beverages intake [11]. Snacking between meals (with high-calorie foods) has been associated with increased incidence of overweight and obesity increased [12]. Taken together, these data suggest specific areas of focus around which a nutrition education and a healthy diet promotion program may be structured.

Another important factor for the success of a food record is the user experience design. Indeed, teenagers have specific interests and understanding how it is possible to convey their attention in order to sustain their engagement over time is crucial. Moreover, other factors such as fashion and peer pressure play a critical role not only in the positive acceptance of the tool but also in the dietary habits [13].

In this paper, we present the multidisciplinary approach thought to design a food record application for smartphones that could be desirable for teenagers. In next section, we will present the context of the PEGASO project and the overview of its technological system. Successively, we will explain how we changed perspective on the food tracking in order to simplify the interaction and, at the same time, to go beyond the mere calorie counting function in order to focus on the change of target behavioural patterns that are associated with unhealthy lifestyles. Then, we will present the user experience design that aims at sustaining teenagers' engagement over time, and enhancing usability and acceptance. Finally, we will conclude this paper describing the work that we will conduct in the next months for the validation of the prototype developed using this approach.

2   The PEGASO System

Obesity is becoming epidemic and the World Health Organization estimated it to be the first leading risk related to nutrition for global deaths outranking famine [14]. Considering that besides genetic factors, the scarce health literacy level plays a crucial role in the spreading of this disease and that, as reported by the World Health Organization, over 60% of children who are overweight before puberty will be overweight in early adulthood, it becomes obvious that the best moment to intervene in order to promote healthy lifestyles is during adolescence. For all these reasons, the EU-funded PEGASO project aims at developing a whole services ecosystem that should be able to motivate teenagers to learn and to apply a healthy life-style effortlessly in order to prevent diseases related to nutrition in adulthood, especially obesity [15]. In this ecosystem, a special role is played by the ICT system, which has been designed to use the smartphone as main interface for the interaction with the users. The smartphone has been chosen as main communication device because the current generation of teenagers already perceive it as a companion and this relationship is predicted to become stronger in the future [16]. In PEGASO, the smartphone provides a set of applications that enable users to access multiple services and games that aim to promote healthy lifestyles, in particular to motivate teenagers in performing physical activity and to adopt healthy dietary habits. In this ecosystem of interrelated applications and services, the food record application plays an important role in order to allow users to monitor and self-manage their alimentary patterns.

All these applications send the information to the cloud, where there is a semantic repository developed by experts in physiology, nutrition, and psychology that allows modelling the user's characteristics: this is called the Virtual Individual Model (VIM) [17]. The VIM allows structuring the information about the single individual about her characterisation of body structure, physiological status, physical activity behaviours, dietary patterns and psychosocial determinants. This information will be used to provide tailored interventions to the user applying the strategy that is estimate to have the biggest impact to change user's behaviour.

3 From Calories to Target Behaviours

Many food record applications for smartphones have been developed in the last years and they can be found in the most popular application stores, such as Apple Store and Google Play. All these applications provide the possibility to record information about eaten food and to count the relative amount of calories consumed. In the PEGASO project we developed a new kind of food record application for smartphone, which is able to monitor the dietary behaviours of adolescents and also to provide an immediate educational feedback based on dietary data inserted by the users.

This food record app has been designed to be used at different levels, depending on user compliance and usability, from the simplest level to the most complex and complete. Before filling in data, at the first log in, a demo will provide some information related with definition of specific dietary concepts and food categories user will find in different levels, in order to help her understand the purpose and the functionality of the food record app.

PEGASO nutritional theory, underlying the selection of parameters composing the VIM and the definition of target behaviours to be monitored and possibly changed, is consistent with the Food-Based Dietary Guidelines principles [18], commissioned to EFSA by EC, which derive from the Nutrient-based recommendations, explicitly referring to chemistry and human physiology of digestion.

The multidimensional analysis of alimentary behaviour built for the project is based on the nutritional principles agreed by the main international agencies and health organisations [19] and on evidences supporting the association of unhealthy patterns of food assumptions [20]. It is able to encompass the energy content of foods, and also aspects of quality of foods and composition/frequency of meals, based on the relation with metabolic/physiological processes.

The list of dietary behaviours identified is: fruit consumption, vegetable consumption, sugar-sweetened drinks consumption, breakfast skipping, snacking habits, and fast-food intake.

This food record app consists of a detailed list of all foods (items) grouped into categories (groups) consumed by the user and recorded at the time the foods are eaten. Ideally, to record the intake following each meal or snack is better than waiting until the end of the day and trying to recall food items and amounts. This will prove to be more accurate and representative of the actual intake. Because a single day or few days of intake is unlikely to be representative of usual individual intake, the collection of multiple days of intake (preferable 3 week days plus week end) will be request in order to guarantee data completeness and reliability of the collected information.

The basis for placing a food item into 12 food groups was the similarity of nutrients, the typology and frequency of consumption together with the necessity to be well identifiable and recognisable by youths [21]. At each log in, the user will have to choose the type of meal (breakfast, lunch, dinner or morning/afternoon snack) after that she can add the different food groups in which her food/foods is/are included. This food record application is structured in three different levels, and each level provides to system different kinds of data and information. In order to capture the complexity of human diets in a single value, taking into account the interactions between nutrients, food preparation methods and eating patterns, the Diet Quality Indexes for adolescents (DQI-A) was used in order to give an immediate feedback to the user by means of pyramid and charts [22]. The major components of this DQI-A are dietary diversity, dietary quality, dietary equilibrium and meal patterns [23]. The diet diversity expresses the degree of variation of food intake in the diet; the diet equilibrium is calculated as the adequacy of intake of each food group based on known food group intake recommendations; the diet quality is expressed as whether the user makes the optimal food quality choices within a food groups.

4   User Experience Design

In order to develop an effective mobile food record application, it is necessary to implement a design that can sustain users' engagement over time. In order to understand what teenagers think about technology and health, and to empathically explore what are their desires and needs, we conducted several focus groups in three countries: Italy, Spain and UK. During these focus groups, we found out some crucial elements for the development of desirable food records: the use of the smartphone is perceived as a motivating means to acquire information about healthy lifestyles; the display of information should not be tiring, hence the use of multimedia, especially images, was suggested; the food record should be interesting and for this reason they suggested it could implement games in it (other researchers drew the same conclusion as in [24]). It is obvious that the user experience design is a crucial factor for the successful acceptance of the food record by the adolescents. Understanding that the gamification of the interface could be a winning choice [25], we conducted a workshop with 15 teenagers to generate ideas for the implementation of an engaging gamified food record application for smartphones. During this participatory design session, we explored different possible solutions for the information entry and feedback taking into account both non-automatised approaches: tracking individual food items via a database and tracking food categories [26]. Moreover, we explored some game mechanisms that could be perceived as motivating and fun. Hence, we developed a prototype of a mobile food record based on the results coming from the focus groups and the workshop, and we integrated the strategy proposed by the experts in nutrition in order to allow for the monitoring of dietary patterns.

The prototype has been designed to evolve with the user: during the first period of use, the user interface allows the user only to select which food categories she ate during her last meal, Fig. 1 a), and the feedback just displays the diversity index, as depicted in Fig. 1 b). After some time and regular use, the user can access a more advanced interface, which allows specifying how many servings for each food category she ate during her last meal, Fig. 2 a); also the feedback becomes more complex: the user can monitor diversity index and the equilibrium index, with also a graphical representation of the eaten food amount with reference to the recommended daily quantity Fig. 2 b). It is also possible to monitor the dietary behaviour during the last week and during the last month. This evolving interface allows providing a sense of progression, which is a very motivating mechanism in videogames. The visualisation of the alimentary information has been chosen by the teenagers during the workshop (depicted in Fig. 1 and Fig.2): the food categories have been represented with pictures and the sole action required to entry the information is a simple tap; the feedback has been found particularly appealing because it was playful, and probably also the affective affordance of the smiley can enhance the engagement with the user. In addition, for every meal entry they can take a picture of the food and upload it.

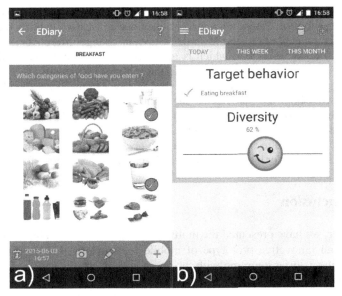

Fig. 1. The user interface in the beginner mode: a) shows the entry interface based on 12 food categories; b) shows the feedback about the diet diversity index and about the target behaviours.

Fig. 2. The user interface in the expert mode: a) shows the entry interface based on 12 food categories with the possibility to specify the number of servings; b) shows the feedback about the diet equilibrium index (the radar chart shows the amount of each food category input and the circles the suggested daily quantity), obviously this interface comprehends also the diet diversity and the target behaviour feedback.

This food record shows also the adherence to the target dietary behaviour that the user chose to monitor. Providing a target behaviour consists of making the teenager to set a goal, which is the first step towards behaviour change. Moreover, it provides that possibility to focus on a goal, which is motivating, and the constant feedback allows her to improve her behaviour and provides the sense of progression.

Another game mechanism integrated in this prototype comes from the ideas generated during the workshop: the participants suggested that it could be motivating to receive games or other goods as a reward. Therefore, in this prototype, the regular use of the food record and the successful adherence to the target behaviour make the user to earn points; these points, associated to the user account, can be spent as a virtual currency in order to access special services or buy virtual items within the PEGASO ecosystem.

5   Conclusion

In this paper, we have presented the multidisciplinary approach adopted for the development of an innovative prototype of mobile food record. The presented approach substitutes the calories counting with the Diet Quality Indexes and enables the user to select a target behaviour supporting its change towards a healthy lifestyle. Moreover, we presented the results of the participatory design conducted with teenagers showing the integration of game mechanisms in the design of the prototype to make the user experience more engaging. In addition, we reported the choices made for the interface design in order to enhance the usability for both food entry and for the feedback display.

Currently, we are organising a test with teenagers in UK, Italy and Spain to assess the usability of the current prototype, to understand their opinion about the interaction design and to understand if this is the right direction to follow. The feedback from these formative test sessions will be used to improve and finalise the current prototype for the final pilot studies that will be conducted next year.

Acknowledgements. The PEGASO project is co-funded by the European Commission under the 7th Framework Programme. The authors of the paper wish to thank all the project partners for their contribution to the work.

References

1. Ogden, C.L., Carroll, M.D., Curtin, L.R., Lamb, M.M., Flegal, K.M.: Prevalence of high body mass index in US children and adolescents, 2007-2008. Jama **303**(3), 242–249 (2010)
2. Thompson, F.E., Subar, A.F.: Dietary assessment methodology. Nutrition in the Prevention and Treatment of Disease **2**, 3–39 (2008)
3. Moreno, L.A., Kersting, M., De Henauw, S., Gonzalez-Gross, M., Sichert-Hellert, W., Matthys, C., Mesana, M.I., Ross, N.: How to measure dietary intake and food habits in adolescence: the European perspective. International Journal of Obesity **29**, S66–S77 (2005)
4. Livingstone, M.B.E., Robson, P.J., Wallace, J.M.W.: Issues in dietary intake assessment of children and adolescents. British Journal of Nutrition **92**(S2), S213–S222 (2004)
5. Boushey, C.J., Kerr, D.A., Wright, J., Lutes, K.D., Ebert, D.S., Delp, E.J.: Use of technology in children's dietary assessment. European Journal of Clinical Nutrition **63**, S50–S57 (2009)
6. Hu, F.B.: Dietary pattern analysis: a new direction in nutritional epidemiology. Current Opinion in Lipidology **13**(1), 3–9 (2002)
7. Nicklas, T.A., Baranowski, T., Cullen, K.W., Berenson, G.: Eating patterns, dietary quality and obesity. Journal of the American College of Nutrition **20**(6), 599–608 (2001)
8. Boeing, H., Bechthold, A., Bub, A., Ellinger, S., Haller, D., Kroke, A., Leschik-Bonnet, E., Müller, M.J., Oberritter, H., Schulze, M., Stehle, P., Watzl, B.: Critical review: vegetables and fruit in the prevention of chronic diseases. European Journal of Nutrition **51**(6), 637–663 (2012)
9. Szajewska, H., Ruszczyński, M.: Systematic review demonstrating that breakfast consumption influences body weight outcomes in children and adolescents in Europe. Critical Reviews in Food Science and Nutrition **50**(2), 113–119 (2010)
10. Braithwaite, I., Stewart, A.W., Hancox, R.J., Beasley, R., Murphy, R., Mitchell, E.A., et al.: Fast-food consumption and body mass index in children and adolescents: an international cross-sectional study. BMJ Open **4**(12), e005813 (2014)
11. Larson, N., Neumark-Sztainer, D., Laska, M.N., Story, M.: Young adults and eating away from home: associations with dietary intake patterns and weight status differ by choice of restaurant. Journal of the American Dietetic Association **111**(11), 1696–1703 (2011)

12. Piernas, C., Popkin, B.M.: Snacking increased among US adults between 1977 and 2006. The Journal of Nutrition **140**(2), 325–332 (2010)
13. Salvy, S.J., De La Haye, K., Bowker, J.C., Hermans, R.C.: Influence of peers and friends on children's and adolescents' eating and activity behaviors. Physiology & Behavior **106**(3), 369–378 (2012)
14. World Health Organization: Obesity: preventing and managing the global epidemic. Report of a WHO consultation. WHO technical report series no. 894, WHO, Geneva (2000)
15. Carrino, S., Caon, M., Abou Khaled, O., Andreoni, G., Mugellini, E.: PEGASO: towards a life companion. In: Duffy, V.G. (ed.) DHM 2014. LNCS, vol. 8529, pp. 325–331. Springer, Heidelberg (2014)
16. Siewiorek, D.: Generation smartphone. Spectrum, IEEE **49**(9), 54–58 (2012)
17. Caon, M., Carrino, S., Lafortuna, C. L., Serrano, J.C., Coulson, N.S., Sacco, M., Khaled, O.A., Mugellini, E.: Tailoring motivational mechanisms to engage teenagers in healthy life-style: a concept. In: AHFE Conference on Advances in Human Aspects of Healthcare (2014)
18. EFSA Panel on Dietetic Products, Nutrition, and Allergies (NDA). Scientific Opinion on establishing Food-Based Dietary Guidelines. EFSA Journal **8**, 1460 (2010)
19. WHO European Region: Food Based Dietary Guidelines in the European Region. EUR/03/5045414 (2003)
20. Deshmukh-Taskar, P.R., Nicklas, T.A., O'Neil, C.E., Keast, D.R., Radcliffe, J.D., Cho, S.: The relationship of breakfast skipping and type of breakfast consumption with nutrient intake and weight status in children and adolescents: the National Health and Nutrition Examination Survey 1999-2006. J. Am. Diet. Assoc. **110**, 869–878 (2010)
21. Vyncke, K., Cruz Fernandez, E., Fajó-Pascual, M., Cuenca-García, M., De Keyzer, W., Gonzalez-Gross, M., Moreno, L.A., Beghin, L., Breidenassel, C., Kersting, M., Albers, U., Diethelm, K., Mouratidou, T., Grammatikaki, E., De Vriendt, T., Marcos, A., Bammann, K., Börnhorst, C., Leclercq, C., Manios, Y., Dallongeville, J., Vereecken, C., Maes, L., Gwozdz, W., Van Winckel, M., Gottrand, F., Sjöström, M., Díaz, L.E., Geelen, A., Hallström, L., Widhalm, K., Kafatos, A., Molnar, D., De Henauw, S., Huybrechts, I.: Validation of the Diet Quality Index for Adolescents by comparison with biomarkers, nutrient and food intakes: the HELENA study. British Journal of Nutrition **109**(11), 2067–2078 (2013)
22. Huybrechts, I., Vereecken, C., De Bacquer, D., et al.: Reproducibility and validity of a diet quality index for children assessed using a FFQ. British Journal of Nutrition **104**, 135–144 (2010)
23. Vereecken, C., De, H.S., Maes, L., Moreno, L., Manios, Y., Phillipp, K., Plada, M., De Bourdeaudhuij, I., HELENA Study Group: Reliability and validity of a healthy diet determinants questionnaire for adolescents. Public Health Nutr. **12**, 1830–1838 (2009)
24. Boushey, C.J., Harray, A.J., Kerr, D.A., Schap, T.E., Paterson, S., Aflague, T., Bosch Ruiz, M., Ahmad, Z., Delp, E.J.: How Willing Are Adolescents to Record Their Dietary Intake? The Mobile Food Record. JMIR mHealth and uHealth **3**(2), e47 (2015)
25. Lister, C., West, J.H., Cannon, B., Sax, T., Brodegard, D.: Just a Fad? Gamification in Health and Fitness Apps. JMIR Serious Games **2**(2), e9 (2014)
26. Consolvo, S., Klasnja, P., McDonald, D.W., Landay, J.A.: Designing for Healthy Lifestyles: Design Considerations for Mobile Technologies to Encourage Consumer Health and Wellness. Human-Computer Interaction **6**(3–4), 167–315 (2012)

MANGO - Mobile Augmented Reality with Functional Eating Guidance and Food Awareness

Georg Waltner[1](✉), Michael Schwarz[2], Stefan Ladstätter[2], Anna Weber[2],
Patrick Luley[2], Horst Bischof[1], Meinrad Lindschinger[3], Irene Schmid[3],
and Lucas Paletta[2]

[1] Graz University of Technology, Graz, Austria
{waltner,bischof}@icg.tugraz.at
[2] JOANNEUM RESEARCH Forschungsgesellschaft MbH, Graz, Austria
{michael.schwarz,stefan.ladstaetter,anna.weber,
patrick.luley,lucas.paletta}@joanneum.at
[3] Institute for Nutritional and Metabolic Diseases, Schwarzl Outpatient Clinic,
Lassnitzhöhe, Austria
office@lindschinger.at

Abstract. The prevention of cardiovascular diseases becomes more and more important, as malnutrition accompanies today's fast moving society. While most people know the importance of adequate nutrition, information on advantageous food is often not at hand, such as in daily activities. Decision making on individual dietary management is closely linked to the food shopping decision. Since food shopping often requires fast decision making, due to stressful and crowded situations, the user needs a meaningful assistance, with clear and rapidly available associations from food items to dietary recommendations. This paper presents first results of the Austrian project (MANGO) which develops mobile assistance for instant, situated information access via Augmented Reality (AR) functionality to support the user during everyday grocery shopping. Within a modern diet - the functional eating concept - the user is advised which fruits and vegetables to buy according to his individual profile. This specific oxidative stress profile is created through a short in-app survey. Using a built-in image recognition system, the application automatically classifies video captured food using machine learning and computer vision methodology, such as Random Forests classification and multiple color feature spaces. The user can decide to display additional nutrition information along with alternative proposals. We demonstrate, that the application is able to recognize food classes in real-time, under real world shopping conditions, and associates dietary recommendations using situated AR assistance.

Keywords: Mobile application · Video based food recognition · Augmented reality · Nutrition recommender · Functional eating concept

1 Introduction

There is a scientific consensus that modern eating habits - including excessive use of salt, fat and sugar - are one of the key factors resulting in cardiovascular

© Springer International Publishing Switzerland 2015
V. Murino et al. (Eds.): ICIAP 2015 Workshops, LNCS 9281, pp. 425–432, 2015.
DOI: 10.1007/978-3-319-23222-5_52

Fig. 1. Innovative interface functionality of the mobile application: The user applies the app similar to a "functional eating lens", moving the smart-phone in video camera modus over food appearances (left) and receives responses about the degree of recommendation from a functional eating perspective (green bars) on the recognized food items, with alternatives fitting to his nutrition plan. She can access more details and health recommendations associated with the selected food item.

diseases (CVD) [1]. According to the WHO [2], more than half of all deaths across the European Region are caused by CVD. National and European institutions expend much effort into long term prevention and information strategies, including distribution of booklets and other literature. While the literature on nutrition is steadily growing and information is readily available on the Internet, it is not practicable to carry books around or search online for specific nutrition facts when going grocery shopping. In the New Media Age, almost every person is equipped with devices such as mobile phones or tablets. Surprisingly, only very few applications are available that were developed with scientific background and can be easily utilized from persons without prior knowledge. We present early results with the aim to provide the nutrition aware user a mobile augmented reality technology that enables situated dietary information assistance and through this simplifies food choices with global aim to improves the user's overall health and well-being. We resort to the functional eating diet, devised by an experienced physician and based on investigation of a large dataset (16k entries). With focus on oxidative stress it defines pillars that stand for different stress types and are connected to nutrition recommendations; following these recommendations enables a person to alleviate stress and reduce the risk of CVD. By integrating a real-time image recognition system into the app, we facilitate the information retrieval which provides added benefit to the user (Fig. 1). This system is evaluated on a novel grocery dataset (containing fruit and vegetable classes) which had to be created from scratch, as existing food datasets concentrate on restaurant dishes only.

2   Related Work

A variety of dietary apps are commercially available, which rely on manual input of food and food volume (e.g. taking pictures or using food databases). These apps no longer focus on solely counting calorie intake, but provide tailored diet plans (e.g. Diet Point Weight Loss) or detailed nutritional information (e.g. LoseIt). Popular fitness apps like Endomondo and Runkeeper (MyFitness-Pal) integrate data from wireless scales or activity trackers (Fitbit, Withings,...). Community support ensures a steady growth of food databases (e.g. MyFitness-Pal database with over 5 million foods), providing motivation by competing with other users or receiving feedback. Some apps assist with food logging or a integrated barcode scanner; e.g. ShopWell is a shopping assistant rating scanned groceries according to a personalized profile (health conditions, food allergies, athletic training) and provides health recommendations.

For image-based food recognition a large amount of research prototypes exist (e.g. [3]), however, hardly any commercial applications are available. A promising work was introduced by [4], capable of identifying food and portion size for calorie count estimation. The application also incorporates contextual features (restaurant locations, user profiles) for refinement and result augmentation. Besides mobile food recognition approaches, more sophisticated methods mostly focus on distinguishing dishes or ingredients. [5] classify images in food and non-food categories under user interaction utilization. Multiple Kernel Learning (MKL) is examined by [6], [7] use pairwise features and [8] explore the use of a bag-of-texton framework. [9] use depth information to classify and quantify Chinese food categories. A candidate region detection process is used by [10], they classify food with a Support Vector Machine (SVM). [11] learn a Bag-of-Features (BoF) model on HSV-SIFT and color moment features to estimate carbohydrate content for diabetic patients. [12] present a combination of Random Forests (RF) and SVM to mine typical image components which are discriminative for 101 food categories collected from the web. Deep convolutional features and a SVM classifier are used by [13]. In the context of fruit and vegetable recognition, [14] present a system for facilitating the supermarket checkout process. [15] use a feed-forward neural network for fruit recognition. An overview of commercial vision systems can be found in [16], [17] and [18]. Similar to our method, [19] present a mobile cooking recipe recommendation system employing object recognition for food ingredients. Their approach is based on a BoF (SURF and color histograms) using a linear SVM classifier. In contrast to our method, most afore-mentioned approaches are intractable to handle on mobile devices due to the complexity of the recognition systems. Also the images are often manually selected or acquired in a controlled laboratory environment, while our data is collected in supermarkets from individuals without background on computer vision. Additionally, we employ recognition in a temporal context, as our inputs are videos and not images. While incorporating a barcode reader and/or Optical Character Recognition (OCR) could improve recognition, we want to create a general system independent of store specific barcodes, price tags or food packages. We focus mainly on unpackaged, loose grocery items.

3   Functional Eating Dietary Concept

Functional eating is a modern diet, developed based on medical expertise particularly concerning demand oriented nutrition. On a dataset including over 16000 entries, [20, 21] show that the measurement of oxidative stress is one of the main factors which can be alleviated by a an optimal food combination. Combining food in a certain way further results in health benefits and improved performance, accompanied by a better taste experience. Often only few fruit types are able to cover the demand for individual vitamins and minerals, therefore a correct food combination is directly connected to the general well-being and health of people, as well as an increased mental and physical performance. Age- and gender-related diversities and differing stress profiles (with respect to work, family or sport) lead to person-specific nutrition profiles. As proposed by [22], functional eating addresses oxidative stress reduction by presenting seven pillars for different nutrition requirements, they are depicted in Fig. 2. These pillars are incorporated into a mobile application that provides feedback on the user's food choices during grocery shopping. The user gets recommendations triggered by his individual profile and is presented detailed nutrition information about food items.

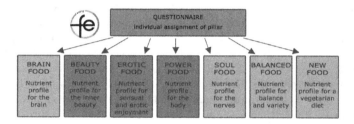

Fig. 2. Functional eating offers seven pillars corresponding to specific nutrition guidelines. After questionnaire completion, a person is assigned to one of the tailored diet pillars.

4   Mobile Augmented Reality and Information System

The MANGO project aims at the development of a mobile application with situated nutrition assistance for dietary management on the basis of an augmented reality based recommender component. The food information and recommender assistant provides an intuitive interface with video based food recognition. The nutritional advice in the frame of functional eating is tailored to fit the user's profile which has been assessed by a dietary questionnaire in advance. After scanning a food item, the food recognition result is shown on the mobile display, together with alternatives for nutrition, associated with a ranking bar indicating how well the food matches the dietary user profile. By clicking on a result, detailed information is shown, including macronutrients with corresponding health claims as well as further food recommendations matching the user's profile (Fig. 1). Complementing the image-based food recognition, the app allows to browse or search through a rich food database specially created for the application in the global context of functional eating. Users might also read an introduction about the

(a)   (b)   (c)   (d)   (e)   (f)

Fig. 3. (a) On the welcome screen, the user chooses between camera mode, a food database and functional eating information. (b) Food database with information about ingredients and health claims. (c,d) Information screens about functional eating and the beauty food pillar. (e,f) The user fills in a questionnaire to determine his nutrition profile and is assigned to the most suitable pillar.

underlying functional eating nutrition concept. See Fig. 3 for app details and Fig. 1 for a usage example.

4.1 Food Recognition Methodology

For video (image) classification we use a Random Forest, a classifier that gained popularity after introduction in [23]. RF have multiple advantages over other classifiers like Support Vector Machines or Neural Networks (NN). They are capable of handling large training datasets, are inherently suited for multiclass problems, avoid overfitting due to random feature selection and are comparably fast to train and evaluate. A random forest is an ensemble of decision trees, which are trained separately by random feature selection and choosing the optimal node splits from this feature pool. Arriving samples at every forest leaf are stored as class probability histograms; during testing the results of all trees are averaged and the class with the maximum average probability is selected as classification result. We use the discriminative color descriptor [24] and a combination of color histograms, namely RGB, HSV and LAB and concatenate the features to a single vector. We have also explored different shape and texture descriptors like SURF [25], SIFT [26], HOG [27], PHOG [28], wavelet moments or Gabor wavelets. Since the accuracy did not improve significantly and the cost in terms of computing time was too high for real time performance on mobile devices, we removed them from the framework. The features are calculated on image patches in a sliding window fashion. After patch classification, rather than taking the cumulative maximum of the predicted patch classes, we fuse the results by calculating the mean and median over all patch histograms and take the averaged maximum of both as classification result. This gives robustness to outliers and minors their impact on the final result.

5 Experimental Results

For evaluation we recorded 1719 videos from different supermarkets and generated a dataset containing 23 classes (e.g. tomatoes) with 98 subclasses (e.g. tomatoes on the vine, mixed tomatoes, beef tomatoes, Kumato tomatoes). The videos were recorded with five different standard android smartphones (Full HD). We evaluate our experiments on the entire dataset, as well as on a smaller sub-dataset of 12 classes for the mobile application prototype. These classes were chosen from seasonal available food groups at that time, to allow for an in-market user study. From the videos we extracted 150 images per class, samples can be seen in Fig. 4. We perform experiments on a desktop PC to evaluate our

Fig. 4. Datasets: Sample images for each of the 35 food classes and the 12 classes used in the prototype application. From top left to bottom right: cherries, apricots, strawberries, blackberries, blueberries, chanterelles, champignons, tomatoes on the vine, green salad, pears, broccoli, cauliflower, cabbage, grapes, bananas, herbs, horseradish, plums, damsons, raspberries, red currants, black currants, white currants, brown mushrooms, red apples, green apples, mixed tomatoes, beef tomatoes, Kumato tomatoes, iceberg salad, Lollo rosso salad, yellow peppers, red peppers, green peppers, mixed peppers.

approach with a greater amount of classes using the entire dataset. By dividing some of the 23 classes according to intra-class differences (e.g. green/red apples), we obtain 35 classes, which are evaluated by the RF with a 50%/50% split, using previously discussed features. The mobile classifier (app) is trained and evaluated with a 80%/20% split on the sub-dataset of 12 classes. In addition to the top vote, we also calculate bullseye scores for top 2 and top 3 votes for the classifier, as in the app's food scanning mode three proposals are displayed to the user. We achieve a classification rate of 80.30% for predicting the correct food category with the maximum confidence vote, and subsequently a rate of 92.28% for the top 2 and 97.20% for the top 3 class classifications. Our first prototype runs at 5fps. Table 1 shows a comparison of our two approaches. On one hand, the mobile prototype results evaluated on the 12 class sub-dataset (MANGO-12) on the other hand the evaluation on the entire dataset (MANGO-35). Our method could not be evaluated on the most similar mobile approach of [19], as their dataset is not publicly available.

Table 1. Evaluation on the MANGO-12 and MANGO-35 datasets on a mobile phone and a desktop PC respectively. Top 1 to top 3 bullseye scores are displayed.

Dataset	Classes	Acquisition	Classifier	Top 1	Top 2	Top 3
MANGO-12	12	mobile phone	mobile phone	80.30%	92.28%	97.20%
MANGO-35	35	mobile phone	desktop PC	67.25%	85.97%	91.97%

6   Conclusion

We have presented an innovative mobile assistant solution, that supports the user in his grocery shopping and situated dietary management decisions . Within the app we incorporated the functional eating diet as scientific basis and included an early, promising prototype of an automated video based food recognition component. Future developments will include more food classes and enhanced adaptive classifiers, which are a main subject of ongoing research. As there exist only few public food datasets (such as [10,12,29]) and these contain dishes in contrast to grocery items, we plan to publish our fruit and vegetable dataset in the future along with fine and coarse category labels.

Acknowledgments. This work was supported by the Austrian Research Promotion Agency (FFG) under the project Mobile Augmented Reality for Nutrition Guidance and Food Awareness (836488).

References

1. Waxman, A., Norum, K.R.: Why a global strategy on diet, physical activity and health? The growing burden of non-communicable diseases. Public Health Nutrition **7**, 381–383 (2004)
2. World Health Organization: European Action Plan for Food and Nutrition Policy, pp. 2007–2012 (2008)
3. Oliveira, L., Costa, V., Neves, G., Oliveira, T., Jorge, E., Lizarraga, M.: A mobile, lightweight, poll-based food identification system. Pattern Recognition **47**(5), 1941–1952 (2014)
4. Zhang, W., Yu, Q., Siddiquie, B., Divakaran, A., Sawhney, H.: "Snap-n-Eat" Food Recognition and Nutrition Estimation on a Smartphone. DST (2015)
5. Maruyama, Y., de Silva, G.C., Yamasaki, T., Aizawa, K.: Personalization of food image analysis. In: VSMM, pp. 75–78 (2010)
6. Hoashi, H., Joutou, T., Yanai, K.: Image recognition of 85 food categories by feature fusion. In: ISM, pp. 296–301 (2010)
7. Yang, S., Chen, M., Pomerleau, D., Sukthankar, R.: Food recognition using statistics of pairwise local features. In: CVPR, pp. 2249–2256 (2010)
8. Farinella, G.M., Moltisanti, M., Battiato, S.: Classifying food images represented as bag of textons. In: ICIP, pp. 5212–5216 (2014)
9. Chen, M.Y., Yang, Y.H., Ho, C.J., Wang, S.H., Liu, S.M., Chang, E., Yeh, C.H., Ouhyoung, M.: Automatic Chinese Food Identification and Quantity Estimation. In: SIGGRAPH, pp. 29:1–29:4 (2012)

10. Matsuda, Y., Hoashi, H., Yanai, K.: Recognition of multiple-food images by detecting candidate regions. In: ICME, pp. 25–30 (2012)
11. Anthimopoulos, M.M., Gianola, L., Scarnato, L., Diem, P., Mougiakakou, S.G.: A Food Recognition System for Diabetic Patients Based on an Optimized Bag-of-Features Model. JBHI **18**(4), 1261–1271 (2014)
12. Bossard, L., Guillaumin, M., Van Gool, L.: Food-101 – mining discriminative components with random forests. In: Fleet, D., Pajdla, T., Schiele, B., Tuytelaars, T. (eds.) ECCV 2014, Part VI. LNCS, vol. 8694, pp. 446–461. Springer, Heidelberg (2014)
13. Kawano, Y., Yanai, K.: Food image recognition with deep convolutional features. In: UbiComp Adjunct, pp. 589–593 (2014)
14. Bolle, R.M., Connell, J.H., Haas, N., Mohan, R., Taubin, G.: Veggievision: a produce recognition system. In: WACV, pp. 244–251 (1996)
15. Zhang, Y., Wang, S., Ji, G., Phillips, P.: Fruit classification using computer vision and feedforward neural network. Journal of Food Engineering **143**, 167–177 (2014)
16. Jiménez, A.R., Jain, A.K., Ceres, R., Pons, J.L.: Automatic fruit recognition: a survey and new results using Range/Attenuation images. Pattern Recognition **32**(10), 1719–1736 (1999)
17. Zhang, B., Huang, W., Li, J., Zhao, C., Fan, S., Wu, J., Liu, C.: Principles, developments and applications of computer vision for external quality inspection of fruits and vegetables: A review. Food Research International **62**, 326–343 (2014)
18. Costa, C., Antonucci, F., Pallottino, F., Aguzzi, J., Sun, D.W., Menesatti, P.: Shape Analysis of Agricultural Products: A Review of Recent Research Advances and Potential Application to Computer Vision. FABT **4**(5), 673–692 (2011)
19. Maruyama, T., Kawano, Y., Yanai, K.: Real-time mobile recipe recommendation system using food ingredient recognition. In: IMMPD Workshop, pp. 27–34 (2012)
20. Lindschinger, M., Nadlinger, K., Adelwöhrer, N., Holweg, K., Wögerbauer, M., Birkmayer, J., Smolle, K.H., Wonisch, W.: Oxidative stress: potential of distinct peroxide determination systems. CCLM **42**(8), 907–914 (2004)
21. Wonisch, W., Falk, A., Sundl, I., Winklhofer-Roob, B., Lindschinger, M.: Oxidative stress increases continuously with bmi and age with unfavourable profiles in males. Aging Male **15**(3), 159–165 (2012)
22. Karalus, B., Lindschinger, M.: Eat yourself beautiful, smart and sexy with functional eating (in German). Riva Verlag, Munich (2008)
23. Breiman, L.: Random Forests. Machine Learning **45**(1), 5–32 (2001)
24. Khan, R., van de Weijer, J., Khan, F.S., Muselet, D., Ducottet, C., Barat, C.: Discriminative color descriptors. In: CVPR, pp. 2866–2873 (2013)
25. Bay, H., Tuytelaars, T., Van Gool, L.: SURF: speeded up robust features. In: Leonardis, A., Bischof, H., Pinz, A. (eds.) ECCV 2006, Part I. LNCS, vol. 3951, pp. 404–417. Springer, Heidelberg (2006)
26. Lowe, D.G.: Distinctive Image Features from Scale-Invariant Keypoints. IJCV **60**(2), 91–110 (2004)
27. Dalal, N., Triggs, B.: Histograms of Oriented Gradients for Human Detection. In: CVPR, vol. 1, pp. 886–893 (2005)
28. Bosch, A., Zisserman, A., Munoz, X.: Representing shape with a spatial pyramid kernel. In: CIVR, New York, NY, USA, pp. 401–408 (2007)
29. Chen, M., Dhingra, K., Wu, W., Yang, L., Sukthankar, R.: PFID: pittsburgh fast-food image dataset. In: ICIP, pp. 289–292 (2009)

Dish Detection and Segmentation for Dietary Assessment on Smartphones

Joachim Dehais[1,2]([✉]), Marios Anthimopoulos[1,3], and Stavroula Mougiakakou[1,4]

[1] ARTORG Center for Biomedical Engineering Research, University of Bern,
Bern, Switzerland
{joachim.dehais,marios.anthimopoulos,
stavroula.mougiakakou}@artorg.unibe.ch
[2] Graduate School of Cellular and Biomedical Sciences, University of Bern, Bern, Switzerland
[3] Department of Emergency Medicine, Bern University Hospital, Bern, Switzerland
[4] Department of Endocrinology, Diabetes and Clinical Nutrition,
Bern University Hospital, Bern, Switzerland

Abstract. Diet-related chronic diseases severely affect personal and global health. However, managing or treating these diseases currently requires long training and high personal involvement to succeed. Computer vision systems could assist with the assessment of diet by detecting and recognizing different foods and their portions in images. We propose novel methods for detecting a dish in an image and segmenting its contents with and without user interaction. All methods were evaluated on a database of over 1600 manually annotated images. The dish detection scored an average of 99% accuracy with a .2s/image run time, while the automatic and semi-automatic dish segmentation methods reached average accuracies of 88% and 91% respectively, with an average run time of .5s/image, outperforming competing solutions.

Keywords: Diet assessment · Diabetes · Obesity · Image segmentation · Computer vision · Smartphone

1 Introduction

The epidemic spread of diet-related chronic diseases such as obesity and diabetes has severely affected public health on a global scale over the last decades. Diet management is key to prevent and treat such diseases; yet, traditional methods often fail because patients lack the motivation and skills to assess their food intake. This situation demands novel tools and services to provide automatic, personalized, and accurate diet assessment, which are now feasible thanks to powerful smartphones and the recent advances of computer vision. Recently, a plethora of solutions has been proposed for the automatic recognition of food images and the assessment of their nutritional content. Some methods classify food images directly into one meal type and then retrieve the nutritional content from databases. These methods address meals with specific composition and size (e.g. fast food restaurants) but are insufficient for meals with arbitrary content and portions. For such cases, another category of systems exists,

© Springer International Publishing Switzerland 2015
V. Murino et al. (Eds.): ICIAP 2015 Workshops, LNCS 9281, pp. 433–440, 2015.
DOI: 10.1007/978-3-319-23222-5_53

which first detect and segment food items, then classify them separately, and finally estimate food portions from their 3D shape. Here, we focus on the first two stages of such a system.

To deal with the automatic food detection/segmentation problem, the existing solutions make assumptions on the number, color, and shape of dishes in the image, as well as the possible number of food items in each dish and the visual properties of the background. Shroff et al. [1] assume disconnected food items and a background of uniform light color, making a simple adaptive thresholding method usable. He et al. [2] experimented with active contours [3], normalized cuts [4] and local variation [5], and concluded that the latter is the most suitable choice. In their experiments, multiple dishes were considered, and the background was defined as the region with the most frequent color. In [6], Zhu et al. used feedback from recognition to choose the number of segments in normalized cuts. Matsuda et al. [7] also considered multiple candidate food regions by using: (i) the whole image, (ii) a deformable part model [8], (iii) a circle detector based on Hough transform [9] and (iv) the JSEG segmentation method [10]. Then, all of the candidate regions are classified and a predefined number of them are kept according to their classification confidence, without providing their locations in the image. Bettadapura et al. [11] use the hierarchical image segmentation of [12] together with unspecified location heuristics and assumptions for segmentation. Puri et al. [13] consider a single circular dish, detected with a fixed time RANSAC circle detection method [14], and classify dense image patches to generate a segmentation map. Classification makes this approach inherently limited by the performance of the food patch recognizer. Anthimopoulos et al. [15] make similar assumptions and use a RANSAC-based ellipse detector for the dish, followed by mean-shift filtering in the CIELab color space for the segmentation of the contained food.

Semi-automatic methods have also been proposed to improve the accuracy of food detection and segmentation. Kawano et al. [16] assume multiple dishes containing single foods and ask the user to draw a box around each dish, then adjust the boxes using grab-cut [17] and recognize the content. Morikawa et al. [18] proposed a system where the user taps on each food item, providing seeds which then grow on square patches using RGB histogram similarity and empirically found thresholds. Oliveira et al. [19] also proposed a region-growing method in which the regions grow using spatial variation and average color similarity. Different color spaces are used along with experimentally found thresholds. From the multiple results the one with the best classification confidence is kept.

In this study we assume that the taken food image contains a single elliptical dish with possibly multiple food items and propose:

- A fast and robust dish detection method using multi-layered RANSAC
- A fast automatic method for food segmentation using non-parametric region growing/merging and CIELab color similarity
- A semi-automatic version of the segmentation that enhances the results with minimum user input

2   Proposed Methods

The proposed system first detects the dish based on its elliptic projection, then segments it and localizes the different food items. We propose two segmentation methods based on a region growing paradigm: one automatic, and one semi-automatic.

2.1   Dish Detection

The dish is detected through the combination of edge detection, grouping, and robust model fitting (Fig.1). For edge detection we use the Canny filter [20] on images downscaled to a height of 240px with their intensity histogram equalized (Fig. 1(b)). The edge components are further filtered by eliminating junctions between edge curves, sharp corners, and small segments (Fig. 1(c)). The classical robust estimator RANSAC [21] is modified to an equivalent of groupSAC [22], where groups of edge curves are randomly sampled and tested on the complete edge set. The size of the sampled groups starts from one curve and increases up to five as long as increasing the size results in finding an ellipse with more support. Whenever the algorithm finds an ellipse with more support, iterative local optimization (LO) [23] takes the inliers to the new best ellipse, and randomly samples them to generate new ellipses, potentially with larger support. (Fig. 1(d)).

| (a) | (b) | (c) | (d) |

Fig. 1. Dish detection: (a) original image, (b) Canny edges, (c) filtered edge segments, (d) detected dish border

2.2   Segmentation

For the segmentation of the dish we adopt the Seeded Region Growing (SRG) method [24]: a fast nonparametric partitioning method for image segmentation. SRG iteratively expands seed regions until the image is fully covered. At each iteration, only the neighboring pixels of the seed regions are considered for expansion, and the one pixel with the lowest distance from its region is absorbed in it. Its neighbors are then added to the border list, to be considered in future iterations. Once all pixels have been added to a region, the process stops, and the image is segmented. As distance between a pixel and a region, we modify the CIE94 distance [25] on the CIELab color space, putting emphasis on the color component, hence reducing the effect of intensity changes often caused by shadows:

$$\text{dist}(L,a,b,L^{'},a^{'},b^{'})=\sqrt{|\Delta L_N|+\Delta C_N{}^2+\Delta H_N{}^2}, \text{ with} \qquad (1)$$

$$\Delta L_N=(L\text{-}L^{'}), \qquad (2)$$

$$\Delta C_N=(\sqrt{a^2+b^2}\text{-}\sqrt{a^{'2}+b^{'2}})/(1+0.045\sqrt{a^2+b^2}), \qquad (3)$$

$$\Delta H_N=\sqrt{(a\text{-}a^{'})^2+(b\text{-}b^{'})^2\text{-}\Delta C_N{}^2}/(1+0.015\sqrt{a^2+b^2}) \qquad (4)$$

Eq.1 is an asymmetric distance; to make it symmetric we apply it twice, with either the pixel or the region color as the origin, and the maximum of the two is used. The color of a region is defined as the median L and the average a and b values over all the region pixels. Pixels outside the dish are not considered while a small band of pixels on the inside of the dish border is automatically labeled as the dish seed in both the automatic and the semi-automatic version.

Automatic Segmentation. For the automatic segmentation, a fixed number of seeds are generated on a regular grid (Fig. 2(a)), and SRG grows these into small, consistent regions (Fig. 2(b)). The regions are then merged together iteratively using the Statistical Region Merging paradigm (SRM) [26] with a modified merging cost (Fig. 2(c)). SRM, like SRG, is a nonparametric aggregation process: in each iteration, the two regions with the smallest merging cost are merged, until a stopping criterion is met. The merging cost we use is the ratio of color distance (eq. 1) divided by square root of the edge length between two regions. The merging process continues until all regions are larger than a certain ratio of the dish area and all inter-region color distances are larger than a fixed threshold.

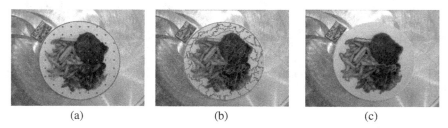

(a)   (b)   (c)

Fig. 2. Automatic segmentation: (a) grid seeds (b) grown regions (c) merged regions after removing the dish region

Semi-automatic Segmentation. In the semi-automatic version of the method the seed regions are given by the user. A dedicated smartphone interface displays the image and allows the user to draw paths over each food item by touching the screen. Fig. 3(a) shows an example input, where colored curves represents user-given seeds. The SRG algorithm grows these seeds as previously described, directly producing the final segmentation (Fig. 3(b)). Knowing the number and the approximate locations of the food items through the user seeds allows this method to outperform the automatic one, especially in difficult cases. The semi-automatic method is thus designed to be used whenever the automatic segmentation fails.

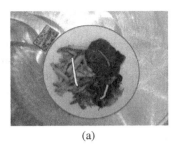
(a)

(b)

Fig. 3. Semi-automatic segmentation: (a) user seeds (b) grown regions after removing the dish region

3   Experimental Results

3.1   Data and Experimental Setup

All proposed methods are evaluated on a dataset of 1620 meal images, with each image containing one fully visible dish. The meals were provided by the restaurants of the Bern university hospital, Inselspital, and photographed by us to obtain typical and complex cases. The dataset thus presents a large variety of food types, viewing angles, backgrounds and lighting conditions. Segmentation maps were manually created and provide the exact area of the dish and the different food items, where each food item is made of a single connected component. To test the semi-automatic segmentation, we used for seeds the pixels of each segment with a distance to the border in the top 3% (~.1% of the total region area).

Both the dish detection and segmentation are evaluated using region-based metrics similar to the Huang and Dom Index (HDI) [27]. Let $S = \{S_i\}_{i=1}^{m}$ and $T = \{T_i\}_{i=1}^{n}$ be two segmentations, where S_i (resp. T_i) is region i from segmentation S (resp. T) and m, n are the number of segments in S and T. We define two normalized directional indices based on worst and average segmentation performance:

$$\text{NI}_{min}(T{=}{>}S){=}\text{Min}_i\left(\frac{\text{Max}_j(|S_i \cap T_j|)}{|S_i|}\right) \qquad (5)$$

$$\text{NI}_{sum}(T{=}{>}S){=}\frac{\Sigma_i \text{Max}_j(|S_i \cap T_j|)}{\Sigma_i |S_i|} \qquad (6)$$

For each index, the indices for the two directions are combined in the harmonic mean to give the final two indices for the evaluation:

$$F_x{=}\frac{2{*}\text{NI}_x(T{=}{>}S){*}\text{NI}_x(S{=}{>}T)}{\text{NI}_x(T{=}{>}S){+}\text{NI}_x(S{=}{>}T)}, \; x = \text{min or sum} \qquad (7)$$

The background segment is excluded from the computation of the measures to make the results independent from the size of the dish. Average processing times are also provided; the experiments were conducted on an Intel i7-3770 CPU.

3.2   Results

Dish Detection. Because there is just one dish per image, indices (5) and (6) are equal when evaluating the dish detection. The average F score achieved by the proposed method is 99.1%, showing its robustness to different lighting and shooting conditions. The average processing time per image is 0.19 seconds, small enough to be used directly on mobile phones.

Table 1. Performance comparison for different color spaces and distances

Automatic	Average F_{min} (%)	Average F_{sum} (%)
RGB - Euclidian	45.7	61.1
CIE94 [25]	69.6	80.2
Proposed	80	88.2
Semi-Automatic	Average F_{min} (%)	Average F_{sum} (%)
RGB - Euclidian	57.9	72.3
CIE94[25]	66	78.2
Proposed distance	82.9	90.8

Segmentation. We first evaluate the influence of the color distance and the merging cost used for region growing and merging. As can be seen in Table 1, the proposed distance outperformed the RGB Euclidian distance by 20-30% and the CIE94 perceptual distance by nearly 10% for both automatic and semi-automatic methods and both evaluation metrics. Furthermore, Table 2 shows a considerable improvement for the automatic segmentation by including the length of the shared edge between segments in the merging cost.

Table 2. Comparison of merging cost

Merging Cost	Average F_{min} (%)	Average F_{sum} (%)
Color distance	74.7	85.8
Color distance/$\sqrt{edge}$	80	88.2

Table 3 compares the proposed food segmentation with methods from the related literature; for all methods, the true location of the dish was used to remove the background and dish segments. Flood fill corresponds to a version of region growing with a threshold on the maximal distance between a pixel and a region, similar to [18], but using the proposed distance and the dish seed (eq.1). For automatic segmentation the proposed system was closely followed by [15] in terms of accuracy, although the latter was more than four times slower. Local variation was less accurate and even slower, followed by ultrametric contours. For the semi-automatic case, the proposed method was about 1% better than flood fill, a non-negligible improvement considering the high accuracies of both methods.

Table 3. Comparison of segmentation methods

Automatic	Average F_{min} (%)	Average F_{sum} (%)	Time (s/image)
Proposed	80	88.2	0.45
Mean-shift [15]	78.2	87.5	2.1
Local Variation [5]	66.7	82.6	2.8
Ultrametric contours [12]	54.1	69.2	19
Semi-Automatic	Average F_{min} (%)	Average F_{sum} (%)	Time (s/image)
Proposed	82.9	90.8	0.49
Flood fill	81.2	89.9	0.52

4   Conclusion

We have presented methods to automatically and semi-automatically detect and segment food in images. The methods make limited assumptions: a single dish is present in the image, with circular or elliptic shape, and an arbitrary number of food items. First, the dish is detected and the different food items are segmented automatically, or with user interaction if needed. The average performance was 99% for the dish detection, 88% for the automatic segmentation and 91% for the semi-automatic, outperforming existing methods. The methods have been implemented in a client-server model, used remotely from a smartphone. Future work includes the extension of the methods to images with multiple dishes, the combination with 3D shape of the scene to improve the segmentation, and the porting of the methods to smartphones.

Acknowledgement. This work was funded in part by the Bern University Hospital "Inselspital" and the European Union Seventh Framework Programme (FP7-PEOPLE-2011-IAPP) under grant agreement n° 286408 [www.gocarb.eu].

References

1. Shroff, G, Smailagic, A., Siewiorek, D.P.: Wearable context-aware food recognition for calorie monitoring. In: 12th IEEE ISWC, pp. 119–120 (2008)
2. He, Y., Khanna, N., Boushey, C.J., Delp, E.J.: Image segmentation for image-based dietary assessment: a comparative study. In: IEEE ISSCS 2013
3. Kass, M., Witkin, A., Terzopoulos, D.: Snakes: Active contour models. Int. J. Comput. Vis. **1**, 321–331 (1998)
4. Shi, J., Malik, J.: Normalized cuts and image segmentation. IEEE Tran. Pattern Anal. Mach. Intell. **22**(8), 888–905 (2000)
5. Felzenszwalb, P.F., Huttenlocher, D.P.: Image segmentation using local variation. In: IEEE Conference on Computer Vision and Pattern Recognition, pp. 98–104 (1998)

6. Zhu, F., Bosch, M., Khanna, N., Boushey, C.J., Delp, E.J.: Multiple Hypotheses Image Segmentation and Classification With Application to Dietary Assessment. IEEE J. Biomed. Health Inform. **19**(1), 377–388 (2015)
7. Matsuda, Y., Hoashi, H., Yanai, K.: Recognition of multiple-food images by detecting candidate regions. In: IEEE ICME, 2012, pp. 25–30 (2012)
8. Felzenszwalb, P.F., Girshick, R.B., McAllester, D., Ramanan, D.: Object detection with discriminatively trained part-based models. IEEE Trans. Pattern Anal. Mach. Intell. **32**(9), 1627–1645 (2010)
9. Duda, R.O., Hart, P.E.: Use of the Hough Transformation to Detect Lines and Curves in Pictures. Comm. ACM **15**, 11–15 (1972)
10. Deng, Y., Manjunath, B.S.: Unsupervised segmentation of color-texture regions in images and video. IEEE Trans. Pattern Anal. Mach. Intell. **23**(8), 800–810
11. Bettadapura, V., Thomaz, E., Parnami, A., Abowd, G.D., Essa, I.A.: Leveraging Context to Support Automated Food Recognition in Restaurants. In: WACV 2015, pp. 580–587
12. Arbelaez, P., Maire, M., Fowlkes, C., Malik, J.: Contour detection and hierarchical image segmentation. IEEE Trans. Pattern Anal. Mach. Intell. **33**(5), 898–916 (2011)
13. Puri, M., Zhu, Z., Yu, Q., Divakaran, A., Sawhney, H.: Recognition and volume estimation of food intake using a mobile device. In: IEEE WACV, pp. 1–8 (2009)
14. Cai, W., Yu, Q., Wang, H., Zheng, J.: A fast contour-based approach to circle and ellipse detection. In: 5th IEEE WCICA (2004)
15. Anthimopoulos, M., Dehais, J., Diem, P., Mougiakakou, S.: Segmentation and recognition of multi-food meal images for carbohydrate counting. In: IEEE BIBE (2013)
16. Kawano, Y., Yanai, K.: FoodCam: A real-time food recognition system on a smartphone. Multimedia Tools and Applications, pp. 1–25 (2014)
17. Rother, C., Kolmogorov, V., Blake, A.: GrabCut: Interactive foreground extraction using iterated graph cuts. ACM Trans. Graph. **23**, 309–314 (2004)
18. Morikawa, C., Sugiyama, H., Aizawa, K.: Food region segmentation in meal images using touch points. In: ACM Workshop on Multimedia for Cooking And Eating Activities (2012)
19. Oliveira, L., Costa, V., Neves, G., Oliveira, T., Jorge, E., Lizarraga, M.: A mobile, lightweight, poll-based food identification system. Pattern Recognition **47**, 1941–1952 (2014)
20. Canny, J.: A Computational Approach to Edge Detetion. IEEE Trans. Pattern Analysis and Machine Intelligence **8**(6), 679–698 (1986)
21. Fischler, M.A., Bolles, R.C.: Random Sample Consensus: A Paradigm for Model Fitting with Applications to Image Analysis and Automated Cartography. Comm. of the ACM **24**(6), 381–395 (1981)
22. Ni, K., Jin, H., Dellaert, F.: Groupsac: efficient consensus in the presence of groupings. In: IEEE 12th International Conference on Computer Vision, pp. 2193–2200 (2009)
23. Chum, O., Matas, J., Kittler, J.: Locally optimized RANSAC. In: Michaelis, B., Krell, G. (eds.) DAGM 2003. LNCS, vol. 2781, pp. 236–243. Springer, Heidelberg (2003)
24. Adams, R., Bischof, L.: Seeded region growing. IEEE Transactions on Pattern Analysis and Machine Intelligence **16**(6), 641–647 (1994)
25. McDonald, R., Smith, K.J.: CIE94a new color difference formula. Journal of the Society of Dyers and Colourists **111**(12), 376–379 (1995)
26. Nock, R., Nielsen, F.: Statistical region merging. IEEE Trans. Pattern Analysis and Machine Intelligence **26**(11), 1452–1458 (2004)
27. Huang, Q., Dom, B.: Quantitative methods of evaluating image segmentation. International Conference on Image Processing **3**, 53–56 (1995)

FooDD: Food Detection Dataset for Calorie Measurement Using Food Images

Parisa Pouladzadeh[1(✉)], Abdulsalam Yassine[1], and Shervin Shirmohammadi[1,2]

[1] Distributed and Collaborative Virtual Environments Research Laboratory,
University of Ottawa, Ottawa, Canada
{ppouladzadeh,ayassine,shervin}@discover.uottawa.ca
[2] Colleges of Engineering and Natural Sciences, Istanbul Şehir University, Istanbul, Turkey

Abstract. Food detection, classification, and analysis have been the topic of in-depth studies for a variety of applications related to eating habits and dietary assessment. For the specific topic of calorie measurement of food portions with single and mixed food items, the research community needs a dataset of images for testing and training. In this paper we introduce FooDD: a Food Detection Dataset of 3000 images that offer variety of food photos taken from different cameras with different illuminations. We also provide examples of food detection using graph cut segmentation and deep learning algorithms.

Keywords: Food image dataset · Calorie measurement · Food detection

1 Introduction

Food images, taken by people using their smartphones, are used in many proposed systems for food recognition, detection, and classification. Detection of food ingredients from their image is a key process in calorie measurement systems used for treatment of chronical illness such as diabetes, blood pressure, obesity, etc. However, for the specific topic of calorie measurement of food portions with single and mixed food items, the research community is lacking a public and free dataset of images for testing and training, making comparison across different food recognition methods more challenging. For this purpose, in this paper we introduce a dataset of 3000 images, offering a variety of food poses taken from different cameras with different illuminations. Acquisition of an accurate dataset will, at the end, support the realization of effective treatment programs for patients. In our previous work [1][2][3], we proposed a system using Vision-Based Measurement (VBM) [6] to improve the accuracy of food intake reporting. Our system runs on smartphones and allows the user to take a picture of the food and measure the calorie intake automatically. This paper presents the food image dataset. Furthermore, we provide examples of food detection using graph cut segmentation [4] and deep learning algorithms [5]. Our dataset can aid further research on different types of food recognition and learning algorithms. The rest of the paper is organized as follows: In section 2 we evaluate existing food datasets and explain the novelty and contribution of our dataset. In section 3, we briefly explain our food

© Springer International Publishing Switzerland 2015
V. Murino et al. (Eds.): ICIAP 2015 Workshops, LNCS 9281, pp. 441–448, 2015.
DOI: 10.1007/978-3-319-23222-5_54

recognition system, while in section 4 we present the dataset collection methodology. Section 5 describes our proposed system. Finally, in section 6, we conclude the paper.

2 Related Work

In [12], the authors have collected 101 different fast food images such as burgers, pizza, salads, etc. But the collection has only fast food images. The dataset in [13] introduces 101 food categories, with 101,000 images, which are mostly mixed food. They sampled 750 training images automatically. Additionally, 250 test images were collected for each class, and were manually cleaned. However, the training images were not cleaned, and thus contain some amount of noise. In [14], the proposed framework consists of images from the Web with the category of names. The noise is filtered out using a "foodness" classifier and an adaptive SVM. Also in [15], the authors investigate features and their combinations for food image analysis and a classification approach based on k-nearest neighbors and vocabulary trees. The system is evaluated on a food image dataset consisting of 1453 images in 42 food categories acquired by 45 participants in natural eating conditions. In [16], the authors collected the dataset from different restaurant food images which contains 61 different categories of food items. Also in [17] and [18], the authors collected a dataset of different food images with different smart phones. In our dataset, we collected around 3000 different images with different categorization as we are going to discuss in next sections. We considered both single and mixed food portions. By so doing, our system is trained to achieve higher accuracy in mixed and non-mixed food. Also, by having the user's finger in the image, we can easily calculate the size of each food in order to have better calorie estimation. Compared to other food datasets, our dataset has a number of advantages and is in fact the only dataset that provides all of the following features:

1- We include both single and mixed food portions. By so doing, the food recognition system trained with our dataset can achieve higher accuracy in mixed and non-mixed food.
2- We use multiple brands of cameras to capture the image of the same food item, providing an opportunity for the food recognition system to become more robust with changes in camera brands.
3- We provide multiple lighting conditions, again for the same food item, allowing more research in developing systems that are more resilient to lighting changes.
4- We provide multiple shooting angles for the same food item, allowing the development of more accurate food recognition methods.
5- We provide a calibration reference (user's thumb) in our images, allowing more accurate measurement of the size of food ingredients, leading to higher accuracy in calories measurement.

In our dataset we have collected around 3000 different images with different categorization as we are going to discuss in next sections.

3   Food Recognition

In this section, we briefly explain how our food recognition system works. For a complete description with details about specific image processing and machine learning techniques, design choices, experiments, and the required accuracy, we refer the readers to [1] [2], and [3]. To measure food calorie, we use a mobile device with camera that supports wireless connection, such as any of today's smartphones. The system will enable the mobile device to take pictures of the food for analysis and immediate response to the user. The overall system design is shown in Figure 1.

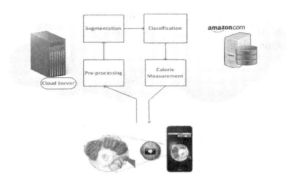

Fig. 1. Overall System Design

First, in order to have accurate results for our segmentation, a simple transformation must be performed on the image to change the image size into standard format. To do so, the size of each image will be compared with standard size categorizes. If the image size is not compatible with any size category, some cropping or padding techniques will be applied to the image. We have defined one size category, i.e. 970 × 720 for simplicity. Larger images will be adjusted to this size, before performing any image processing technique. In next step, at the segmentation step, each image is analyzed to extract various segments of the food portion. We paid significant attention to the segmentation mechanism design to ensure that images are processed appropriately. Particularly, we have used color segmentation, k-mean clustering, and texture segmentation tools. Furthermore, in our classification and food recognition analysis, we have nominated Cloud SVM and deep neural network method to increase the accuracy of the recognition system. Finally we have measure the calorie of the food.

4   Dataset Collection

For the collection of the food images in our dataset, we divided the food images into two different collections; single food portions and mixed food portions. We took into consideration important factors that affect the accuracy of our results. Specifically, we used a variety of the following components: Camera, Lighting, Shooting Angle, White Plate, Thumb, Single and Mixed Food. Each component will be described in details in the following subsections.

4.1   Camera

The camera itself will have an effect on the results in terms of its lens, hardware, and software. As such, we used three different cameras for our experiments, consisting of Canon SD1400 (14.1-megapixel resolution, 2.7-inch Pure Color System LCD, 28mm wide-angle lens; 4x optical zoom and Optical Image Stabilizer) iPhone 4(5 megapixel resolution, LED flash, VGA-quality photos and video at up to 30 frames per second with the front camera), and Samsung S4 cameras (13 megapixel resolution, 41, auto-focus, LED flash, Dual shot).

4.2   Lighting

Lighting and illumination is one of the important parameters which affect the system outcome because illumination directly affects the image segmentation algorithm, which in turn affects the rest of the algorithms. To take this into account, we put the same plate in three different locations with different illuminations (sunlight) and we took pictures.

4.3   Shooting Angle

Another effective parameter is the angle of photography; we have chosen three different angles which are approximately 30, 90, and 150 degrees from the plate of food for all pictures. This means that for each plate in 3 different lighting locations we have also taken 3 pictures from different angles.

4.4   White Plate

For all images we have considered a white plate to ignore the background of the images. By using white plate, food segmentation and food recognition will be easier to perform.

4.5   Thumb

The thumb of the user and its placement on the plate are also shown in Figure 2. There is a one-time calibration process for the thumb, which is used as a size reference to measure the real-life size of food portions in the picture [1]. An example of food picture capturing and thumb isolation and measurement are shown in Figure 1. Compared to the calibration methods of similar systems, using the thumb is more flexible, controllable, and reliable. For users with thumb disability or amputated thumbs, another finger or a coin can be used instead, the latter still more ubiquitous than special plates or cards used in other systems.

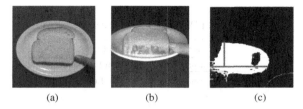

(a)   (b)   (c)

Fig. 2. (a, b) Test images with thumb (c) Calculation of the thumb dimensions [1]

4.6   Single and Mixed Food

We have divided our food into two different groups: single food and fruits such as apple, orange, and bread, and mixed food which includes different food portions in a plate of food such as salad, pizza, and kebab with rice.

4.7   Food Item Types

The dataset contains images taken with different cameras, illuminations, and angles. Having a wide variety of food and fruits gives a better and more reliable dataset in order to increase the accuracy of calorie food measurement systems. The name and number of single food images which are included in the dataset are shown in Figure 3. In the dataset, the images are divided into 6 categories considering the capturing device, background, and lighting condition. For example, images in category 1 are captured with a Samsung camera, within a light environment with a white background, and from different shooting angles.

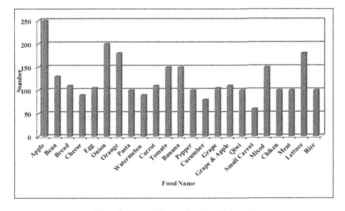

Fig. 3. Food Items in the Dataset

The categories in the dataset are shown in Table I. Each category contains more than 100 images, including various food items from Figure 3. Figure 4 shows sample images takes by the user. Note that the thumb is used as a calibration means to determine the size of the food items in the image [1].

Table 1. I Different Food Categories

Category	Camera	Lighting
1	Samsung-S4	Light Environment
2	Samsung-S4	Dark Environment
3	IOS-4	Light Environment
4	IOS-4	Dark Environment
5	CanonSD1400	Light Environment
6	CanonSD1400	Dark Environment

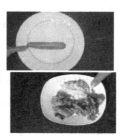

Fig. 4. Sample food images taken by the user

5   Experimental Results

This section presents the experimental results of our system using the food images dataset. In this work, we have combined Graph cut segmentation and deep neural network. The dataset is used in the learning process of these two methods, which allow us to improve the accuracy of our food classification and recognition significant compared to our previous work [1][3]. By recognizing the food portions and also by having the size and shape of the food portions from graph cut algorithm, we can calculate the calorie of the whole food portions.

In this experiment, our dataset comprises of 30 different categories of food and fruits. These food and fruit images are divided into training and testing sets, where around 50% of the images from each group are used to train the system and the remaining images serve as the testing set.

The results are shown in Figure 5. We can see that graph cut segmentation outperforms normal segmentation but is outperformed by Deep Neural Network algorithm which has 100% accuracy in our dataset. In addition, our system recognized food portions very accurately in about 3 seconds, on average.

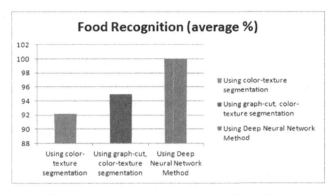

Fig. 5. Food Recognition Accuracy for Single Food

6   Dataset Availability and Format

The dataset is available for free as long as it is used for research purposes. Instructions on how to obtain it are posted at our website[1].

7   Conclusion

Food detection and classification is a problem gaining much importance in health-related applications. Since algorithms to accomplish this task are currently being developed and refined, diverse and complementary datasets for evaluation are not only helpful but also necessary to aid research. In this paper, we provided a dataset comprising 3000 food images. In this dataset, we placed careful attention in generating the food images characteristics pertained to camera type, shooting angle, and illumination variations. A strong feature of our dataset is the good distribution of single and mixed food images. Thus, it can be used to facilitate testing and benchmarking of various food detection algorithms. We provided experimental results using color-texture segmentation, graph cut segmentation, and deep neural network algorithms on this dataset, and invite researchers to devise suitable benchmarks and share with the research community.

References

1. Pouladzadeh, P., Shirmohammadi, S., Almaghrabi, R.: Measuring Calorie and Nutrition from Food Image. IEEE Transactions on Instrumentation & Measurement **63**(8), 1947–1956 (2014)
2. Pouladzadeh, P., Shirmohammadi, S., Bakirov, A., Bulut, A., Yassine, A.: Cloud-Based SVM for Food Categorization. Multimedia Tools and Applications, p. 18. Springer, June 3, 2014. doi: 10.1007/s11042-014-2116-x

3. Pouladzadeh, P., Shirmohammadi, Yassine, A.: Using graph cut segmentation for food calorie measurement. In: IEEE International Symposium on Medical Measurements and Applications, pp. 1–6, June 2014

4. Yuri, Y.B., Lea, G.F.: Graph Cuts and Efficient N-D Image Segmentation. International Journal of Computer Vision **70**(2), 109–131 (2006)

5. Krizhevsky, A., Sutskever, I., and Hinton, G.: ImageNet classification with deep convolutional neural networks. Advances in Neural Information Processing Systems (NIPS) (2012)

6. Shirmohammadi, S., Ferrero, A.: Camera as the Instrument: The Rising Trend of Vision Based Measurement. IEEE Instrumentation and Measurement Magazine **17**(3), 41–47 (2014)

7. Sun, M., et al.: Determination of food portion size by image processing. Engineering in Medicine and Biology Society, 871–874, August 2008

8. Schölkopf, B., Smola, A., Williamson, R., Bartlett, P.L.: New support vector algorithms. Neural Computation **12**(5), 1207–1245 (2000)

9. Burke, L.E., et al.: Self-monitoring dietary intake: current andfuture practices. Journal of renal nutrition the official journal of the Council on Renal Nutrition of the National Kidney Foundation **15**(3), 281–290 (2005)

10. Beasley, J.: The pros and cons of using pdas for dietary self-monitoring. J. Am. Diet Assoc. **107**(5), 739 (2007)

11. Gao, C., Kong, F., Tan, J.: Healthaware: tackling obesity with health aware smart phone systems. In: IEEE International Conference on Robotics and Biometics, pp. 1549–1554 (2009)

12. Chen, M., Dhingra, K., Wu, W., Yang, L., Sukthankar, R., Yang, J.: PFID: pittsburgh fast-food image dataset. In: International Conference on Image Processing, pp. 289–292 (2009)

13. Bossard, L., Guillaumin, M., Van Gool, L.: Food-101 – mining discriminative components with random forests. In: Fleet, D., Pajdla, T., Schiele, B., Tuytelaars, T. (eds.) ECCV 2014, Part VI. LNCS, vol. 8694, pp. 446–461. Springer, Heidelberg (2014)

14. Kawano, Y., Yanai, K.: Automatic expansion of a food image dataset leveraging existing categories with domain adaptation. In: Agapito, L., Bronstein, M.M., Rother, C. (eds.) ECCV 2014 Workshops. LNCS, vol. 8927, pp. 3–17. Springer, Heidelberg (2015)

15. He, Y., Xu, C., Khanna, N, Boushey, C.J., Delp, E.J.: Analysis of food images: features and classification. In: IEEE International Conference on Image Processing (ICIP), pp. 2744–2748 (2014)

16. Kong, F., Tan, J.: DietCam: regular shape food recognition with a camera phone. In: International Conference on Body Sensor Networks (BSN), pp. 127–132 (2011)

17. Farinella, G.M., Allegra, D., Stanco, F.: A benchmark dataset to study the representation of food images. In: Agapito, L., Bronstein, M.M., Rother, C. (eds.) ECCV 2014 Workshops. LNCS, vol. 8927, pp. 584–599. Springer, Heidelberg (2015)

18. Kawano, Y., Yanai, K.: FoodCam: A real-time food recognition system on a smartphone. Multimedia Tools and Applications. Springer, April 12, 2014

CNN-Based Food Image Segmentation Without Pixel-Wise Annotation

Wataru Shimoda and Keiji Yanai[✉]

Department of Informatics, The University of Electro-Communications,
1-5-1 Chofugaoka, Chofu-shi, Tokyo 182-8585, Japan
{shimoda-k,yana}@mm.inf.uec.ac.jp

Abstract. We propose a CNN-based food image segmentation which requires no pixel-wise annotation. The proposed method consists of food region proposals by selective search and bounding box clustering, back propagation based saliency map estimation with the CNN model fine-tuned with the UEC-FOOD100 dataset, GrabCut guided by the estimated saliency maps and region integration by non-maximum suppression. In the experiments, the proposed method outperformed RCNN regarding food region detection as well as the PASCAL VOC detection task.

Keywords: Food segmentation · Convolutional neural network · Deep learning · UEC-FOOD

1 Introduction

Food image recognition is one of the promising applications of visual object recognition, since it will help estimate food calories and analyze people's eating habits for health-care. Therefore, many works have been published so far [1–3,9, 12,14,20]. However, most of the works assumed that one food image contained only one food item. They cannot handle an image which contains two or more food items such as a hamburger-and-french-fries image. To list up all food items in a given food photo and estimate calories of them, segmentation of foods is needed. Some works attempted food region segmentation [8,10,14,15].

Matsuda et al. [14] proposed to used multiple methods to detect food regions such as Felzenszwalb's deformable part model (DPM) [5], a circle detector and the JSEG region segmentation method [4]. He et al. [8] employed Local Variation [6] to segment food regions for estimating total calories of foods in a given food photo. In some works for mobile food recognition [10,15], they asked users to point rough locations of each food item in a food photo, and perform Grab-Cut [16] to extract food item segments.

Meanwhile, recently the effectiveness of Deep Convolutional Neural Network (DCNN) have been proved for large-scale object recognition at ImageNet Large-Scale Visual Recognition Challenge (ILSVRC) 2012. Krizhevsky et al. [13] won

© Springer International Publishing Switzerland 2015
V. Murino et al. (Eds.): ICIAP 2015 Workshops, LNCS 9281, pp. 449–457, 2015.
DOI: 10.1007/978-3-319-23222-5_55

ILSVRC2012 with a large margin to all the other teams who employed a conventional hand-crafted feature approach. In the DCNN approach, an input data of DCNN is a resized image, and the output is a class-label probability. That is, DCNN includes all the object recognition steps such as local feature extraction, feature coding, and learning. In general, the advantage of DCNN is that it can estimate optimal feature representations for datasets adaptively, the characteristics of which the conventional hand-crafted feature approach do not have. In the conventional approach, we extract local features such as SIFT and SURF first, and then code them into bag-of-feature or Fisher Vector representations. Regarding food image recognition, the classification accuracy on the UEC-FOOD100 dataset [14] was improved from 59.6% [12] to 72.26% [11] by replacing Fisher Vector and liner SVM with DCNN.

By taking advantage of excellent ability of DCNN to represent objects, DCNN-based region detection and segmentation methods are proposed. RCNN [7] is the representative one of object detection, while Simonyan et al. [17] proposed a DCNN-based weakly-supervised segmentation method employing back-propagation-based saliency maps and GrabCut [16]. Both of them needs no pixel-wise annotation. The former method needs bounding box annotation, while the latter method needs even no bounding box annotation.

In this paper, we propose a new region segmentation method which combines the ideas of RCNN [7] and Simonyan et al. [17]. In RCNN, firstly, region proposals were generated by selective search [19], then extracted DCNN activation features from all the proposal, applied SVM to evaluate proposals and integrated them by non-maximum suppression to produce object bounding boxes. They fine-tuned DCNN pre-trained with ImageNet 1000 categories using the PASCAL VOC dataset having 20 categories.

Meanwhile, Simonyan et al. [17] proposed a method to generate object saliency maps by back propagation (BP) over a pre-trained DCNN, and showed it enabled semantic object segmentation by applying GrabCut [16] using saliency maps as seeds.

In this paper, we firstly obtain region proposals by selective search [19], secondly estimate saliency maps with BP-based methods over the pre-trained DCNN for each of the region proposals after aggregation of overlapped proposals, thirdly apply GrabCut using the obtained saliency maps as seeds of GrabCut, and finally apply non-maximum suppression to obtain final region results.

In the experiments, we examined food region segmentation with UEC-FOOD100 [14] and compared the proposed method and RCNN [7] regarding food detection performance in the bounding box level. In addition, we used PASCAL VOC 2007 as well. Our method outperformed RCNN by both of the dataset.

Although DCNN [9,11] has been applied to food image classification problem so far, no work tackled food image segmentation problems with DCNN-based methods. As long as we know, this is the first work to apply a DCNN-based segmentation method to food image segmentation task.

2 Proposed Method

The proposed method on DCNN-based region detection consists of the following steps as shown in Fig. 1:

(1) Apply selective search and obtain 2000 bounding box proposals at most.
(2) Group them and select bounding boxes.
(3) Perform back propagation over the pre-trained DCNN regarding all the selected bounding boxes.
(4) Obtain saliency maps by averaging BP outputs within each group.
(5) Extract segments based on the saliency maps with GrabCut.
(6) Apply non-maximum suppression (NMS) to obtain final region results.

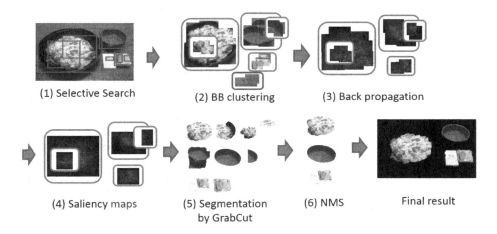

Fig. 1. The processing flow of the propose method.

2.1 Selective Search

In the work by Simonyan et al. [17], they applied their method to a whole image. This brings acceptable results for images containing only one prominent object, while it it difficult to handle images containing many objects. Especially, in case that a target image includes multiple same-class objects, Simonyan et al.'s method sometimes extracts multiple objects as one large object region and fails to extract individual object regions, since they employed GrabCut which is a generic region segmentation method.

Then, first, we apply selective search [19] to obtain food region candidates where we perform estimation of saliency maps and region segmentation, which is inspired by RCNN [7]. We obtain 2000 region proposals represented by bounding boxes at most from the selective search implementation. [1]

---

[1] Downloaded from http://koen.me/research/selectivesearch/

2.2   Bounding Box Grouping

2000 bounding boxes (BB) are too many to perform estimation of BP-based saliency maps and GrabCut within each of them. Therefore, we perform bounding box clustering to reduce the number of bounding boxes. We group the bounding boxes based on the ratio of intersection over union (IOU) into 20 BB groups at most, and we removed the groups the number of the members of which is less than 15 BBs. The rest BB groups are regarded as food region candidates. Note that BB groups sometimes contain other BB groups inside them, as shown in Fig. 1(2), because we cluster BBs according to the ratio of intersection over union (IOU).

2.3   Saliency Maps by Back Propagation over Trained DCNN

According to Simonyan et al. [17], we estimate food saliency maps which represents rough position of target objects employing back propagation (BP) over the trained DCNN. In general, BP is used for training of DCNNs, which propagates errors between estimated values and ground truth values in an output layer from an output layer to an input layer in the backward direction. In case of training, the weights of DCNNs are modified so that total errors are reduced. Reducing errors is equivalent to increasing the output scores of given classes. If propagating errors to an input image, we can obtain a map indicating which pixels need to be changed to increase the scores of given classes. Such pixels are expected to correspond to the object location in the images. This is the explanation why BP can be used for object region estimation. The advantage of this method is that it does not need neither pixel-wise annotation or bounding box annotation as training data. The only thing needed is a trained DCNN with labeled images.

We estimate saliency maps of each of the selected bounding boxes (Fig. 1 (3)) and unify saliency maps within each BB group. In the experiments, we fine-tuned AlexNet [13] with the UEC-FOOD100 dataset [14] and used it to estimate food categories and saliency maps.

To perform BP, both forward pass and backward pass computation are needed. Forward pass computation is equivalent to classification by DCNN. We provide a region cropped within each selected BB to DCNN in the forwarding direction, and obtain soft-max scores of all the categories. Then, we select the top five categories, and provide the vector where only the elements corresponding to the top five categories are 1 and the rest elements are 0 into the backward pass. Note that the size of an input image is fixed to 227×227 in case of using AlexNet. We resize (shrink or enlarge) cropped regions to fit to the fixed size.

To estimate object saliency maps, two other methods than the BP-based method proposed by Simonyan et al. [17] exists. One is deconvolution (deconv) proposed by Zeiler et al. [21], the other is guided back propagation (guided BP) proposed by Springerberg et al. [18]. Basic ideas of the three method are the same. Only the ways to back propagation through ReLUs (rectified linear units) are different. Refer the further detail to [18]. Originally, guided BP and deconv were proposed as visualizing methods of inside of a CNN which was regarded as a black box for analysis and understanding of it. Guided BP can emphasis edges of objects, which is good for visualizing trained filters inside a DCNN. Fig. 2 shows saliency maps, and GrabCut results obtained by the three methods.

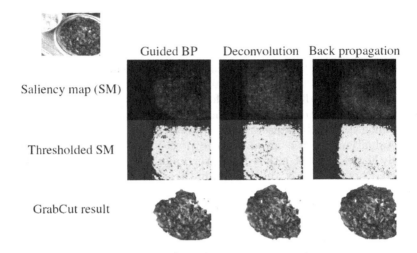

Fig. 2. Saliency maps, thresholded saliency maps and GrabCut results generated by three kinds of BP-variant methods: Guided BP, Deconvolution, Back Propagation.

After obtaining saliency maps of BBs, we average them within each BB group and obtain saliency maps of BB groups as shown in Fig. 1(4). The pixels with higher values are expected to correspond to objects.

2.4   Segmentation by GrabCut

In this step, we apply GrabCut [16] to each BB group region to extract whole object regions, because BP can estimate only most discriminative parts of objects. To use GrabCut, both foreground and background color models are needed. In the similar way as Simonyan et al. [17], the foreground model are estimated from the pixels with the top 3% saliency, while the background model are estimeted from the lower 40% saliency. The red regions and the blue regions represent the foreground and the background regions in the thresholded images shown in Fig. 2. Because we apply GrabCut to each BB group independently, we obtain several regions for one objects as shown in Fig.1 (5).

To integrate overlapped regions, we apply non-maximum supression (NMS), and we obtain non-overlapped regions as shown in Fig. 1 (6). Finally, we estimate rectangular regions bounding obtained segmented regions, and provide them to the trained CNN to obtained labels for each of the segmented regions. In addition, in the experiments, we use the extracted bounding boxes for evaluation.

3   Experiments

In the experiments, we used the UEC-FOOD100 dataset [14] and the PASCAL VOC 2007 detection dataset, both of which have bounding box information as well as class labels.

3.1   Food Detection Evaluation

The UEC-FOOD100 dataset [14] contains one hundred kinds of food photos. The total number of the food photos is 12740 including 1174 multiple-food photos. In the experiment, we used 1174 multiple-food photos including 3045 food items for testing, while we used the rest 11566 photos for fine-tuning a DCNN pre-trained with the ImageNet 1000 dataset.

For evaluation, we use mean average precision. We count it as a correct result only if the ratio of intersection over union (IOU) exceeds 50% between the detected bounding box and the ground truth bounding box. Note that we evaluated results regarding not segmentation but only bounding boxes, since UEC-FOOD has no pixel-wise annotation.

(1) original   (2) R-CNN results   (3) ours results   (4) ground truth

Fig. 3. The results of food region segmentation for UEC-FOOD100. (1) original food photo, (2) detected BB, (3) estimated food segments, (4) ground truth BB. ([] represents food ID: [01] rice, [05] pork cutlet, [17] humberger, [24] beef noodle, [36] miso soup, [39] oden, [93] kinpira-style salad, [94] rice ball, [98] french fries.)

Table 1. Mean average precision over all the 100 categories, 53 categories (more than 10 items of which are included in the test data), and 11 categories (more than 50 items of which are included in the test data).

UEC-FOOD100 mAP	100class (all)	53class (#item ≥ 10)	11class (#item ≥ 50)
guided back propagation (GBP)	**50.7**	52.5	51.4
deconvolution (deconv)	48.0	54.1	**55.4**
back propagation (BP)	49.9	**55.3**	**55.4**

Table 2. The results by RCNN and the proposed methods.

UEC-FOOD100 mAP	100class (all)	53class (#item ≥ 10)	11class (#item ≥ 50)
R-CNN	26.0	21.8	25.7
proposed method	**49.9**	55.3	**55.4**

Table 3. The results for the PASCAL VOC 2007 detection dataset.

	aero	bike	bird	boat	btl	bus	car	cat	chair	cow	dtable	dog	horse	mbike	person	plant	sheep	sofa	train	tv	mAP
R-CNN	64.2	69.7	50.0	41.9	32.0	62.6	71.0	60.7	32.7	58.5	46.5	56.1	60.6	66.8	54.2	31.5	52.8	48.9	57.9	64.7	**54.2**
proposed	81.5	70.2	65.2	39.7	37.8	63.9	83.2	67.8	27.0	65.3	39.5	63.6	63.2	73.2	61.2	37.3	63.5	39.8	70.0	60.8	**58.7**

Fig.3 shows some examples of the detected BB and food regions. The red letters with yellow backgrounds represent food IDs and corresponding output scores from the DCNN. Most of the food items were correctly detected. In the top row, "[93] kinpira-style salad" was correctly detected, although it was not annotated in the ground truth data. In the bottom row, "[24] beef noodle" was detected as only half of the ground truth region due to failure of GrabCut.

Next, we compared three kinds of BP-variant methods which are used for estimating saliency maps. Tab.1 shows mean average precisions by three methods regarding estimated bounding boxes. Although the results by BP were better than the results by the other methods, the difference was not so large.

We compared our results with the results by RCNN. For RCNN as well as the proposed method, we used the same DCNN fine-tuned with the single food images of UEC-FOOD 100. Tab.2 shows the results. Unexpectedly, the mean AP by RCNN was much lower than the proposed method. Fig.4 shows some example results. Compared to the bounding boxes estimated by the proposed methods, RCNN detected too small bounding boxes which cannot be counted as correct bounding boxes.

3.2   Evaluation on Pascal VOC 2007 Detection Task

For more fair comparison with RCNN [7], we also applied our method to Pascal VOC 2007 detection dataset. We used the pre-trained model on PASCAL VOC 2007 included in the RCNN package [2]. In the same way as UEC-FOOD, we compare both performance in mean average precision. The results are shown in Fig.3. Our method outperformed RCNN by 4.5 points.

---

[2] Downloaded from https://github.com/rbgirshick/rcnn

(1) original   (2) R-CNN results   (3) ours results   (4) ground truth

Fig. 4. Examples of the detection results by R-CNN and the proposed method.

4   Conclusions

In this paper, we proposed a DCNN-based food image segmentation which requires no pixel-wise annotation. The proposed method consists of food region proposals by selective search and bounding box clustering, back propagation based saliency map estimation with the DCNN fine-tuned with the UEC-FOOD100 dataset, GrabCut guided by the estimated saliency maps and region integration by non-maximum supression. In the experiments, the proposed method outperformed RCNN regarding food region detection as well as the PAS-CAL VOC detection task.

For future work, we plan to implement the proposed method on mobile devices as a real-time food region recognition system for estimating more accurate food calorie intake.

References

1. Bosch, M., Zhu, F., Khanna, N., Boushey, C.J., Delp, E.J.: Combining global and local features for food identification in dietary assessment. In: Proc. of IEEE International Conference on Image Processing (2011)
2. Bossard, L., Guillaumin, M., Van Gool, L.: Food-101 – mining discriminative components with random forests. In: Fleet, D., Pajdla, T., Schiele, B., Tuytelaars, T. (eds.) ECCV 2014, Part VI. LNCS, vol. 8694, pp. 446–461. Springer, Heidelberg (2014)
3. Chen, M., Yang, Y., Ho, C., Wang, S., Liu, S., Chang, E., Yeh, C., Ouhyoung, M.: Automatic chinese food identification and quantity estimation. In: SIGGRAPH Asia (2012)
4. Deng, Y., Manjunath, B.S.: Unsupervised segmentation of color-texture regions in images and video. IEEE Transactions on Pattern Analysis and Machine Intelligence **23**(8), 800–810 (2001)

5. Felzenszwalb, P.F., Girshick, R.B., McAllester, D., Ramanan, D.: Object detection with discriminatively trained part based models. IEEE Transactions on Pattern Analysis and Machine Intelligence 32(9), 1627–1645 (2010)
6. Felzenszwalb, P.F., Huttenlocher, D.P.: Image segmentation using local variation. In: Proc. of IEEE Computer Vision and Pattern Recognition, pp. 98–104 (1998)
7. Girshick, R., Donahue, J., Darrell, T., Malik, J.: Rich feature hierarchies for accurate object detection and semantic segmentation. In: Proc. of IEEE Computer Vision and Pattern Recognition, pp. 580–587 (2014)
8. He, Y., Xu, C., Khanna, N., Boushey, C.J., Delp, E.J.: Food image analysis: segmentation, identification and weight estimation. In: Proc. of IEEE International Conference on Multimedia and Expo., pp. 1–6 (2013)
9. Kagaya, H., Aizawa, K., Ogawa, M.: Food detection and recognition using convolutional neural network. In: Proc. of ACM International Conference Multimedia, pp. 1085–1088 (2014)
10. Kawano, Y., Yanai, K.: Real-time mobile food recognition system. In: Proc. of IEEE CVPR International Workshop on Mobile Vision (IWMV) (2013)
11. Kawano, Y., Yanai, K.: Food image recognition with deep convolutional features. In: Proc. of ACM UbiComp Workshop on Workshop on Smart Technology for Cooking and Eating Activities (CEA) (2014)
12. Kawano, Y., Yanai, K.: Foodcam: A real-time food recognition system on a smartphone. Multimedia Tools and Applications, 1–25 (2014)
13. Krizhevsky, A., Sutskever, I., Hinton, G.E.: Imagenet classification with deep convolutional neural networks. In: Advances in Neural Information Processing Systems (2012)
14. Matsuda, Y., Hoashi, H., Yanai, K.: Recognition of multiple-food images by detecting candidate regions. In: Proc. of IEEE International Conference on Multimedia and Expo., pp. 1554–1564 (2012)
15. Morikawa, C., Sugiyama, H., Aizawa, K.: Food region segmentation in meal images using touch points. In: Proc. of ACM MM WS on Multimedia for Cooking and Eating Activities (CEA), pp. 7–12 (2012)
16. Rother, C., Kolmogorov, V., Blake, A.: Grabcut: Interactive foreground extraction using iterated graph cuts. ACM Transactions on Graphics (TOG) 23(3), 309–314 (2004)
17. Simonyan, K., Vedaldi, A., Zisserman, A.: Deep inside convolutional networks: visualising image classification models and saliency maps. In: Proc. of International Conference on Learning Represenation Workshop Track (2014). http://arxiv.org/abs/1312.6034
18. Springenberg, J.T., Dosovitskiy, A., Brox, T., Riedmiller, M.: Striving for simplicity: the all convolutional net. In: Proc. of International Conference on Learning Represenation Workshop Track (2015). http://arxiv.org/abs/1412.6806
19. Uijlings, J.R.R., van de Sande, K.E.A., Gevers, T., Smeulders, A.W.M.: Selective search for object recognition. International Journal of Computer Vision 104(2), 154–171 (2013)
20. Yang, S., Chen, M., Pomerleau, D., Sukthankar, R.: Food recognition using statistics of pairwise local features. In: Proc. of IEEE Computer Vision and Pattern Recognition (2010)
21. Zeiler, M.D., Fergus, R.: Visualizing and understanding convolutional networks. In: Fleet, D., Pajdla, T., Schiele, B., Tuytelaars, T. (eds.) ECCV 2014, Part I. LNCS, vol. 8689, pp. 818–833. Springer, Heidelberg (2014)

Food Recognition for Dietary Assessment Using Deep Convolutional Neural Networks

Stergios Christodoulidis[1,2(✉)], Marios Anthimopoulos[1,3],
and Stavroula Mougiakakou[1,4]

[1] ARTORG Center for Biomedical Engineering Research,
University of Bern, Bern, Switzerland
{stergios.christodoulidis,marios.anthimopoulos,
stavroula.mougiakakou}@artorg.unibe.ch
[2] Graduate School of Cellular and Biomedical Sciences,
University of Bern, Bern, Switzerland
[3] Department of Emergency Medicine, Bern University Hospital, Bern, Switzerland
[4] Department of Endocrinology, Diabetes and Clinical Nutrition,
Bern University Hospital, Bern, Switzerland

Abstract. Diet management is a key factor for the prevention and treatment of diet-related chronic diseases. Computer vision systems aim to provide automated food intake assessment using meal images. We propose a method for the recognition of already segmented food items in meal images. The method uses a 6-layer deep convolutional neural network to classify food image patches. For each food item, overlapping patches are extracted and classified and the class with the majority of votes is assigned to it. Experiments on a manually annotated dataset with 573 food items justified the choice of the involved components and proved the effectiveness of the proposed system yielding an overall accuracy of 84.9%.

Keywords: Food recognition · Convolutional neural networks · Dietary management · Machine learning

1 Introduction

Diet-related chronic diseases like obesity and diabetes have become a major health concern over the last decades. Diet management is a key factor for the prevention and treatment of such diseases, however traditional methods often fail due to the inability of patients to assess accurately their food intake. This situation raises an urgent need for novel tools that will provide automatic, personalized and accurate diet assessment. Recently, the widespread use of smartphones with enhanced capabilities together with the advances in computer vision, enabled the development of novel systems for dietary management on mobile phones. Such a system takes as input one or more images of a meal and either classifies them as a whole or segments the food items and recognizes them separately. Portion estimation is also provided by some systems based on the 3D reconstruction of food. Finally, the meal's nutritional content is estimated using

© Springer International Publishing Switzerland 2015
V. Murino et al. (Eds.): ICIAP 2015 Workshops, LNCS 9281, pp. 458–465, 2015.
DOI: 10.1007/978-3-319-23222-5_56

nutritional databases and returned to the user. Here, we focus on food recognition which constitutes the common denominator in this new generation of systems. To this end, various approaches have been proposed derived from the particularly active fields of image classification and object recognition. The problem is usually divided into two tasks: description and classification.

Some systems employed handcrafted global descriptors, capturing mainly color and texture information: quantized color histograms [1, 2], first-order color statistics [3, 4, 5], Gabor filtering [6], [7] and local binary patterns (LBP) [2] have been used among others. In order to achieve a description adapted to the problem, visual codebooks have been utilized, created by clustering local descriptors. The most popular choices for local descriptors are: the classic SIFT [1] and its color variants [9], [10] as well as the histogram of oriented gradients (HoG) [11, 12, 13]. Other kinds of local descriptors include filter banks like the maximum response filters [8], [14] or even raw values of neighboring pixels [15]. Visual codebooks are often created within bag of features (BoF) approaches where image patches are described and assigned to the closest visual word from the codebook, while the resulting histogram constitutes the global descriptor [1], [9], [10], [16]. When filter banks are used for the local description the term texton analysis is used instead [8], [14], [15]. Other approaches attempted to reduce the quantization error introduced by the hard assignment of each patch to a single visual word. Sparse coding was used in [6] which represents patches as sparse linear combinations of visual words. On the other hand, the locality-constrained linear coding (LLC) used in [3], [12] enforces locality instead of sparsity producing smaller coefficients for distant visual words. Finally, the Fisher vector (FV) approach used in [11], [13], [17] fits a Gaussian mixture model (GMM) to the local feature space instead of clustering, and then characterize a patch by its deviation from the GMM distribution. For the classification, the support vector machines (SVM) have been the most popular choice. Gaussian kernels were used in many systems [2], [5] whereas for histogram based features the chi-squared kernel is reported to be the best choice [8], [15]. For highly dimensional features spaces even linear kernels often perform satisfactorily [13]. Finally, multiple kernel learning has also been used for the fusion of different types of features [7], [10].

Recently, an approach based on deep convolutional neural networks (CNN) [18] gained attention by winning the ImageNet Large-Scale Visual Recognition Challenge and outperforming by far the competition. The eight-layer network of [18] was used in [11] for the classification of Japanese food images in 100 classes. However, due to the huge size of the network and the limited amount of images (14,461), the results were not adequate so a FV representation on HoG and RGB values was also employed to provide complementary description. In [20], a four-layer CNN was used for food recognition. A dataset with 170,000 images belonging to 10 classes was created and images were downscaled to 80×80 and then randomly cropped to 64×64 before fed to the CNN.

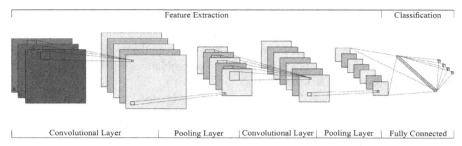

Fig. 1. Typical architecture of a convolutional neural network

In this study, we propose a system for the recognition of already segmented food items in meal images using a deep CNN, trained on fixed-size local patches. Our approach exploits the outstanding descriptive ability of a CNN, while the patch-wise model allows the generation of sufficient training samples, provides additional spatial flexibility for the recognition and ignores background pixels.

2   Methods

Before describing the architecture and the different components of the proposed system, we provide a brief introduction to the deep CNNs.

2.1   Convolutional Neural Networks

CNNs are multi-layered artificial neural networks which incorporate both unsupervised feature extraction and classification. A CNN consists of a series of convolutional and pooling layers that perform feature extraction followed by one or more fully connected layers for the classification. Convolutional layers are characterized by sparse connectivity and weight sharing. The inputs of a unit in a convolutional layer come from just a small rectangular subset of units of the previous layer. In addition, the nodes of a convolutional layer are grouped in feature maps sharing the same weights. The inputs of each feature map are tiled in such a way that correspond to overlapping regions of the previous layer making the aforementioned procedure equivalent to convolution while the shared weights within each map correspond to the kernels . The output of convolution passes through an activation function that produces nonlinearities in an element-wise fashion. A pooling layer follows which subsamples the previous layer by aggregating small rectangular subsets of values. Max or mean pooling is applied replacing the input values with the maximum or the mean value, respectively. A number of fully connected layers follow with the last one having a number of units equal to the number of classes. This part of the network performs the supervised classification and takes as input the values of the last pooling layer which constitute the feature set. For training the CNN a gradient descent method is applied using back propagation. A schematic representation of a CNN with two pairs of convolutional-pooling layers and two fully connected layers is depicted in Fig. 1.

2.2   System Description

The proposed system recognizes already segmented food items using an ensemble learning model. For the classification of a food item, a set of overlapping square patches is extracted from the corresponding area on the image and each of them is classified by a CNN into one of the considered food classes. The class with the majority of votes coming from the local classifications is finally assigned to the food item. Our approach is comprised by three main stages: preprocessing, network training and food recognition. An overview of the system is depicted in Fig. 2.

Preprocessing. This stage aims at preparing the data for the CNN training procedure. First, non-overlapping patches of size 32×32 are extracted from the inside of each food item in the dataset. In order to increase the amount of training data and prevent over-fitting we artificially augment the training patch dataset by using label-preserving transformations such as flip and rotation as well as the combinations of the two. In total, 16 transformations are used. Then, we calculate the mean over the training image patches and subtract it from all the patches of the dataset so the CNN takes as input mean centered RGB pixel values.

Network Training. Using the created patch dataset we train a deep CNN with a six layer architecture. The network has four convolutional layers with 5×5 kernels; the first three layers have 32 kernels while the last has 64, producing equal number of feature maps. All the activation functions are set to the rectified linear unit (ReLU) since it has been reported to minimize the classification error of the network faster than other activation functions such as *tanh* [18]. Each convolutional layer is followed by a

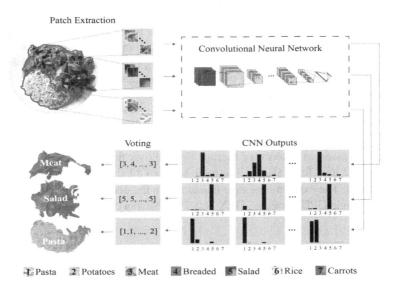

Fig. 2. The proposed system overview.

pooling layer with 3×3 pooling regions and stride equal to two; the first one outputs the maximum value out of each pooling region while the following three use the average. The last two layers of the network are fully connected with 128 and 7 units, respectively. On these layers, random dropout of units was used to prevent overfitting [21]. The output of each hidden neuron was set to zero with a probability p forcing the network to learn more robust features for the description of the input regardless of the inactive neurons. Here, the dropout probability p is set to 0.5. The softmax function is used so as to normalize the outputs of the last layer so each output is between zero and one and they all sum up to one. This way, the output values represent a categorical probability distribution so a cross-entropy loss function is used to calculate the error used by gradient descent training. Finally, as far as the weight learning is concerned, a schema with a decay of the learning rate along with a momentum coefficient was used. The base learning rate is set to 0.001 with an exponential decay policy and the momentum is set to 0.9.

Food Recognition. For the recognition of the food items a voting scheme is used. For each food item to be classified, images patches are extracted preprocessed and fed to the CNN. The most frequent class occurring from the classification of the patches is then assigned to the food item.

3   Experimental Setup and Results

3.1   Experimental Setup

For training and testing the proposed system we used a dataset of 246 images of different meals served in the restaurants of Bern University hospital, "Inselspital". The images contain in total 573 food items, belonging to seven broad food classes, namely pasta, potatoes, meat, breaded food, rice, green salad and carrots. For each image an annotation map has been manually created containing the area and the class label of the existing food items. The evaluation procedure for the classification of both patches and food items is based on a 5-fold cross-validation scheme which is applied on a food item level in order to avoid biased results. For each fold, we used the ground truth maps to extract a number of 32×32 patches leading to a set of nearly 160,000 training patches per fold which proved to be sufficient for training the CNN. The performance in the experiments is assessed in terms of average F-score over the different classes in a patch (pF_{avg}) or food item level (F_{avg}). The total accuracy of the food item classification is also considered. The experiments were conducted in the deep learning framework Caffe [22] using a single GPU (GeForce GTX 760, 2GB Memory, 1152 Cores).

3.2   Results

The configuration of the CNN was initially based on the cifar-10 solution[1]. However, in order to find the most suitable configuration for the proposed system, a number of

---

[1] https://code.google.com/p/cuda-convnet/wiki/Methodology

experiments were conducted on the involved components and their parameters. Table 1 presents the results for the different configurations that were tested. The optimal number of convolutional-pooling layers was four. The use of the dropout technique for the penultimate layer further improved the results. However, the use of a local response normalization (LRN) after the activation functions did not present a clear improvement.

Table 1. Results for the different architectures that were investigated. For all the convolutional layers 5x5 kernels was used and for all the pooling layers 3x3 pooling regions. Notation: cp – convolutional-pooling layers, fc – fully connected layers, pF_{avg}- the f-score on a patch level.

CNN architecture	$pF_{avg}(\%)$
32cp – 32cp – 128fc – 7fc	66.5
32cp – 32cp – 64cp – 128fc – 7fc	68.7
32cp – 32cp – 32cp – 64cp – 128fc – 7fc	69.5
32cp – 32cp – 32cp – 64cp – 64cp – 128fc – 7fc	67.1
32cp – 32cp – 32cp – 64cp – 128fc – 7fc + LRN	70.4
32cp – 32cp – 32cp – 64cp – 128fc – 7fc + Dropout	**71.79**
32cp – 32cp – 32cp – 64cp – 128fc – 7fc + LRN + Dropout	71.28

Table 2. Results of the proposed method for different voting schemes and variants compared to a method from the literature

Classification Method	Accuracy	F_{avg}	Time (sec/item)
Patch-wise CNN + Weighted voting + step=16	84.6	82.8	0.28
Patch-wise CNN + Max voting + step=32	83.5	81.4	0.11
Patch-wise CNN + Max voting + step=16	**84.9**	**82.7**	**0.28**
Patch-wise CNN + Max voting + step=8	84.7	82.5	0.92
Learned histogram + Multi-scale LBP + SVM	82.2	79.7	0.1

Fig. 3 presents the 32 convolutional kernels from the first layer of the proposed network. It can be observed that the kernels capture mainly color information which is the primal feature for the discrimination among foods. After configuring the CNN architecture for the classification of patches, we conducted an investigation regarding the best use of this fixed-scale classifier for the recognition of food items. Two are the main involved elements; the voting scheme and the density of the classification. For the voting, we tested two techniques: (i) voting only for the best candidate class (Max

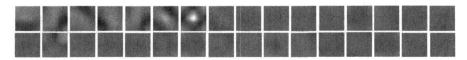

Fig. 3. The kernels from the first layer of the proposed CNN

voting) and (ii) voting for all the classes using the CNN output, after the softmax normalization, as weights (weighted voting). For the density of the classified patches on each food item we used several step values resulting in different overlaps. Table 2 shows the corresponding results. As it can be seen, the max voting scheme presented slightly better performance while a maximum overlap of 50% (step = 16) among the extracted patches was proved to be optimal. Table 2 also provides a comparison with a method from the state of the art in the same dataset. The method is based on [2] and uses adapted color histograms and multi-scale LBP features fed to an SVM with a Gaussian kernel. The proposed recognition system scored nearly 3% more in both metrics showing the potential of CNN in the food recognition problem. The average processing time per image for the selected configuration was 0.28 seconds which is more than most conventional methods but still acceptable

4   Conclusions

We proposed a method for the recognition of already segmented food items using a CNN. The classification is applied in a patch-wise manner and a voting technique was used to determine the class of each food item. The patch-wise model together with the data augmentation trick allowed us to extract a sufficient amount of samples to train a 6-layer CNN. The experimental results proved the effectiveness of the system that achieved an overall accuracy of 84.9%. The presented results are preliminary; future work should include a more thorough investigation on the optimal architecture as well as the training parameters of the network. Moreover, the use of alternative classifiers combined with the CNN features could further enhance the performance.

Acknowledgments. This work was funded in part by the Bern University Hospital "Inselspital", the European Union Seventh Framework Programme (FP7-PEOPLE-2011-IAPsP) under grant agreement n° 286408 [www.gocarb.eu] and the Swiss National Science Foundation n° 156511 [p3.snf.ch/project-156511].

References

1. Chen, M., Dhingra, K., Wu, W., Yang, L., Sukthankar, R.,Yang, J.: PFID: Pittsburgh fast-food image dataset. In: 16th IEEE International Conference on Image Processing (2009)
2. Anthimopoulos, M., Dehais, J., Diem, P., Mougiakakou, S.: Segmentation and recognition of multi-food meal images for carbohydrate counting. In: IEEE BIBE (2013)
3. Aizawa, K., Maruyama, Y., He, L., Morikawa, C.: Food Balance Estimation by Using Personal Dietary Tendencies in a Multimedia Food Log. IEEE Transactions on Multimedia **15**(8), 2176–2185 (2013)
4. Fengqing, Z., Bosch, M., Khanna, N., Boushey, C.J., Delp, E.J.: Multiple Hypotheses Image Segmentation and Classification With Application to Dietary Assessment. IEEE Journal of Biomedical and Health Informatics **19**(1), 377–388 (2015)

5. Oliveira, L., Costa, V., Neves, G., Oliveira, T., Jorge, E., Lizarraga, M.: A mobile, lightweight, poll-based food identification system. Pattern Recognition **47**, 1941–1952 (2014)
6. Chen, M.Y., Yang, Y.H., Ho, C.J., Wang, S.H., Liu, S.M., Chang, E., Yeh, C.H., Ouhyoung, M.: Automatic chinese food identification and quantity estimation. In: SIGGRAPH Asia 2012 (2012)
7. Matsuda, Y., Hoashi, H., Yanai, K.: Recognition of multiple-food images by detecting candidate regions. In: IEEE International Conference on Multimedia and Expo (2012)
8. Puri, M., Zhu, Z., Yu, Q., Divakaran, A., Sawhney, H.: Recognition and volume estimation of food intake using a mobile device. In: IEEE WACV, pp. 1–8 (2009)
9. Anthimopoulos, M.M., Gianola, L., Scarnato, L., Diem, P., Mougiakakou, S.G.: A Food Recognition System for Diabetic Patients Based on an Optimized Bag-of-Features Model. IEEE Journal of Biomedical and Health Informatics **18**(4), 1261–1271 (2014)
10. Bettadapura, V., Thomaz, E., Parnami, A., Abowd, G.D., Essa, I.A.: Leveraging context to support automated food recognition in restaurants. In: WACV 2015, pp. 580–587 (2015)
11. Kawano, Y., Yanai, K.: Food image recognition with deep convolutional features. In: ACM UbiComp Workshop on Cooking and Eating Activities (CEA) (2014)
12. Beijbom, O., Joshi, N., Morris, D., Saponas, S., Khullar, S.: Menu-match: restaurant-specific food logging from images. In: 2015 IEEE Winter Conference on Applications of Computer Vision, pp. 844–851 (2015)
13. Kawano, Y., Yanai, K.: FoodCam: A real-time food recognition system on a smartphone. Multimedia Tools and Applications (2014)
14. Farinella, G.M., Moltisanti, M., Battiato, S.: Classifying food images represented as bag of textons. In: IEEE International Conference on Image Processing (ICIP), pp. 5212–5216 (2014)
15. Yang, S., Chen, M., Pomerleau, D., Sukthankar, R.: Food recognition using statistics of pairwise local features. In: CVPR 2010 (2010)
16. Nguyen, D.T., Zong, Z., Ogunbona, P., Probst, Y.C., Li, W.: Food image classification using local appearance and global structural information. Neurocomputing **140**, 242–251 (2014)
17. Bossard, L., Guillaumin, M., Van Gool, L.: Food-101 – Mining discriminative components with random forests. In: Fleet, D., Pajdla, T., Schiele, B., Tuytelaars, T. (eds.) ECCV 2014, Part VI. LNCS, vol. 8694, pp. 446–461. Springer, Heidelberg (2014)
18. Krizhevsky, A., Sutskever, I., Hinton, G.: ImageNet classification with deep convolutional neural networks. In: NIPS 2012 (2012)
19. Russakovsky, O., Deng, J., Su, H., Krause, J., Satheesh, S., Ma, S., Huang, Z., Karpathy, A., Khosla, A., Bernstein, M., Berg, A.C., Fei-Fei, L.: ImageNet Large Scale Visual Recognition Challenge (2014)
20. Kagaya, H., Aizawa, K., Ogawa, K.: Food Detection and Recognition Using Convolutional Neural Network. ACM Multimedia, 1085–1088 (2014)
21. Hinton, G., Srivastava, N., Krizhevsky, A., Sutskever, I., Salakhutdinov, R.: Improving neural networks by preventing co-adaptation of feature detectors. http://arxiv.org/abs/1207.0580
22. Yangqing, J.: Caffe: An open source convolutional architecture for fast feature embedding (2013). http://caffe.berkeleyvision.org

SBMI 2015 - Scene Background Modeling and Initialization

Towards Benchmarking Scene Background Initialization

Lucia Maddalena[1](✉) and Alfredo Petrosino[2]

[1] Institute for High-Performance Computing and Networking,
National Research Council, Naples, Italy
lucia.maddalena@cnr.it
[2] Department of Science and Technology, University of Naples Parthenope,
Naples, Italy
alfredo.petrosino@uniparthenope.it

Abstract. Given a set of images of a scene taken at different times, the availability of an initial background model that describes the scene without foreground objects is the prerequisite for a wide range of applications, ranging from video surveillance to computational photography. Even though several methods have been proposed for scene background initialization, the lack of a common groundtruthed dataset and of a common set of metrics makes it difficult to compare their performance. To move first steps towards an easy and fair comparison of these methods, we assembled a dataset of sequences frequently adopted for background initialization, selected or created ground truths for quantitative evaluation through a selected suite of metrics, and compared results obtained by some existing methods, making all the material publicly available.

Keywords: Background initialization · Video analysis · Video surveillance

1 Introduction

The scene background modeling process is characterized by three main tasks: 1) *model representation*, that describes the kind of model used to represent the background; 2) *model initialization*, that regards the initialization of this model; and 3) *model update*, that concerns the mechanism used for adapting the model to background changes along the sequence. These tasks have been addressed by several methods, as acknowledged by several surveys (e.g., [2,4]). However, most of these methods focus on the representation and the update issues, whereas limited attention is given to the model initialization. The problem of scene background initialization is of interest for a very vast audience, due to its wide range of application areas. Indeed, the availability of an initial background model that describes the scene without foreground objects is the prerequisite, or at least can be of help, for many applications, including video surveillance, video segmentation, video compression, video inpainting, privacy protection for videos, and computational photography (see [6]).

© Springer International Publishing Switzerland 2015
V. Murino et al. (Eds.): ICIAP 2015 Workshops, LNCS 9281, pp. 469–476, 2015.
DOI: 10.1007/978-3-319-23222-5_57

We state the general problem of *background initialization*, also known as bootstrapping, background estimation, background reconstruction, initial background extraction, or background generation, as follows: *Given a set of images of a scene taken at different times, in which the background is occluded by any number of foreground objects, the aim is to determine a model describing the scene background with no foreground objects.*

Depending on the application, the set of images can consist of a subset of initial sequence frames adopted for background training (e.g., for video surveillance), a set of non-time sequence photographs (e.g., for computational photography), or the entire available sequence. In the following, this set of images will be generally referred to as the *bootstrap sequence*.

In order to move first steps towards an easy and fair comparison of existing and future background initialization methods, we assembled the SBI dataset, a set of sequences frequently adopted for background initialization, including ground truths for quantitative evaluation through a selected suite of metrics (made publicly available through http://sbmi2015.na.icar.cnr.it), and compared results obtained by some existing methods.

2   Sequences

The SBI dataset includes seven bootstrap sequences extracted by original publicly available sequences that are frequently used in the literature to evaluate background initialization algorithms. COST 211 (sequence *Hall&Monitor* can be found at http://www.ics.forth.gr/cvrl/demos/NEMESIS/hall_monitor. mpg), ATON (dataset available at http://cvrr.ucsd.edu/aton/shadow/index. html), and PBI (dataset available at http://www.diegm.uniud.it/fusiello/demo/ bkg/). In Table 1 we report, for each sequence, the name, the dataset it belongs

Table 1. Information on sequences adopted for evaluation

Name	Dataset	Original frames	Used frames	Original Resolution	Final Resolution
Hall&Monitor	COST 211	0-299	4-299	352x240	352x240
HighwayI	ATON	0-439	0-439	320x240	320x240
HighwayII	ATON	0-499	0-499	320x240	320x240
CaVignal	PBI	0-257	0-257	200x136	200x136
Foliage	PBI	0-399	6-399	200x148	200x144
People&Foliage	PBI	0-349	0-340	320x240	320x240
Snellen	PBI	0-333	0-320	146x150	144x144

to, the number of available frames, the subset of the frames adopted for testing, the original and the final resolution. The subsets have been selected in order to avoid the inclusion into the testing sequences of *empty* frames (frames not including foreground objects), while the final resolution has been chosen in order to avoid problems in the computation of boundary patches for block-based methods. The ground truths (GT) have been manually obtained by either choosing one of the sequence frames free of foreground objects (not included into the subsets of used frames) or by stitching together empty background regions from different sequence frames.

3   Metrics

The metrics adopted to evaluate the accuracy of the estimated background models have been chosen among those used in the literature for background estimation. They are described in Table 2, where GT (Ground Truth) is the image containing the *true* background, CB (Computed Background) is the estimated background image computed with one of the background initialization methods, L is the maximum number of grey levels, N is the number of image pixels, and MSE is the Mean Squared Error between GT and CB images. While the last metric is defined only for color images, all the other metrics are expressly defined for gray-scale images. In the case of color images, they are generally applied to either the gray-scale converted image or the luminance component Y of a color space such as YCbCr. The latter approach has been chosen for measurements reported in §4.

Table 2. Metrics adopted for evaluation

Name	Description	Range
AGE	Average Gray-level Error: Average of the gray-level absolute difference between GT and CB images.	$[0, L\text{-}1]$
EPs	Total number of Error Pixels: An *error pixel* is a pixel of CB whose value differs from the value of the corresponding pixel in GT by more than some threshold τ (in the experiments τ=20).	$[0, N]$
pEPs	Percentage of Error Pixels: EPs/N.	$[0, 1]$
CEPs	Total number of Clustered Error Pixels: A *clustered error pixel* is any error pixel whose 4-connected neighbors are also error pixels.	$[0, N]$
pCEPs	Percentage of Clustered Error Pixels: CEPs/N.	$[0, 1]$
PSNR	Peak-Signal-to-Noise-Ratio: $PSNR = 10 \cdot \log_{10}\left((L-1)^2/MSE\right)$.	
MS-SSIM	MultiScale Structural Similarity Index: Defined in [10].	$[0, 1]$
CQM	Color image Quality Measure: Defined in [11].	

4   Experimental Results and Comparisons

In this study, we compared the results on the SBI dataset of six background initialization methods, whose classifications according to [6] are summarized in Table 3. In the reported experiments, the temporal **Median** for the color bootstrap sequences is computed for each pixel as the one that minimizes

Table 3. Classifications of the compared methods

	pixel-level	region-level	hybrid	recursive	non-recursive	blind	selective
Temporal Statistics:							
Median [7]	X				X	X	
SC-SOBS [5]			X	X			X
Subintervals of Stable Intensity:							
WS2006 [9]	X				X		X
CA2008 [3]	X				X		X
Model Completion:							
RSL2011 [8]		X		X			X
Optimal Labeling:							
Photomontage [1]		X		X			X

the sum of L_∞ distances of the pixel from all the other pixels. The **SC-SOBS** [5] background estimate is obtained as the result of the initial training of the software SC-SOBS (publicly available in the download section of the CVPRLab at http://cvprlab.uniparthenope.it) using for all the sequences the same default parameter values. Once the neural background model is computed, the background estimate is extracted for each pixel by choosing the modeling weight vector that is closest to the ground truth. **WS2006** has been implemented based on [9], and parameter values have been chosen among those suggested by the authors and providing the best overall results. Results for **RSL2011** [8] have been obtained through the related software publicly available at http://arma.sourceforge.net/background_est/. Results for **Photomontage** [1] have been obtained through the related software publicly available at http://grail.cs.washington.edu/projects/photomontage/ choosing the maximum likelihood image objective as data term for achieving visual smoothness. Finally, results for **CA2008** [3] have been kindly provided by the authors.

Fig. 1 shows the background images obtained by the compared methods on the SBI dataset, while Table 4 reports accuracy results according to the metrics described in §3 (in boldface the best results for each metric and each sequence).

For sequence *Hall&Monitor*, we observe few differences in initializing the background in image regions where foreground objects are more persistent during the sequence. A man walking straight down the corridor occupies the same image region for more than 65% of the sequence frames, while the briefcase is left on the small table for the last 60%. WS2006, RSL2011, Photomontage, and CA2008 well handle the walking man, but only CA2008 does not include the abandoned briefcase into the background. This qualitative analysis is confirmed by accuracy results in terms of pEPs and pCEPs values reported in Table 4. Moreover, AGE values are quite low for all the compared methods, due to the reduced size of foreground objects as compared to the image size. However, the worst AGE values are achieved by RSL2011 and Photomontage, despite their quite good qualitative results. Finally, all the compared methods achieve

Fig. 1. Background initialization results on the SBI dataset obtained by: a) GT, b) Median, c) SC-SOBS, d) WS2006, e) RSL2011, f) Photomontage, g) CA2008

similar values of PSNR, MS-SSIM, and CQM, as overall, apart from reduced sized defects related to foreground objects, they all succeed in providing a sufficiently faithful representation of the empty background.

For both *HighwayI* and *HighwayII* sequences, all the compared methods succeed in providing an accurate estimated background. This is due to the fact that, even though the highway is always fairly crowded by passing cars, the background is revealed for at least 50% of the entire bootstrap sequence length and no cars remain stationary during the sequence. The above qualitative considerations are only partially confirmed by performance results reported in Table 4. Indeed, different AGE and pEPs values are achieved by qualitatively similar estimated backgrounds, while similar low pCEPs values and high MS-SSIM, PSNR, and CQM values are achieved by all the compared methods.

Sequence *CaVignal* represents a major burden for most of the compared methods. Indeed, the only man appearing in the sequence stands still on the left of the scene for the first 60% of sequence frames; then starts walking and rests on the right of the scene for the last 10% of sequence frames. The persistent clutter at the beginning of the scene leads most of the compared methods to include the man on the left into the estimated background, while the persistent clutter at the end of the scene leads only WS2006 to partially include the man on the right into

Table 4. Accuracy results of the compared methods on the SBI dataset

	Method	AGE	EPs	pEPs	CEPs	pCEPs	MS-SSIM	PSNR	CQM
Hall&Monitor	Median	2.7105	839	0.9931%	451	0.5339%	0.9640	30.4656	42.6705
	SC-SOBS	**2.4493**	828	0.9801%	272	0.3220%	0.9653	30.4384	**43.1867**
	WS2006	2.6644	470	0.5563%	26	0.0308%	0.9821	30.9313	40.0949
	RSL2011	3.2687	703	0.8321%	398	0.4711%	0.9584	28.4428	37.9971
	Photomontage	2.7986	**305**	**0.3610%**	69	0.0817%	0.9819	**33.3715**	41.7323
	CA2008	2.4737	337	0.3989%	**0**	**0.0000%**	**0.9878**	32.2503	41.2399
Highway1	Median	1.4275	120	0.1563%	11	0.0143%	0.9924	40.1432	62.5723
	SC-SOBS	**1.2286**	**3**	**0.0039%**	**0**	**0.0000%**	**0.9949**	**42.6868**	**65.5755**
	WS2006	2.5185	526	0.6849%	19	0.0247%	0.9816	35.6885	56.9113
	RSL2011	2.8139	267	0.3477%	33	0.0430%	0.9830	36.0290	51.9835
	Photomontage	2.1745	313	0.4076%	37	0.0482%	0.9830	37.1250	59.0270
	CA2008	2.9477	895	1.1654%	65	0.0846%	0.9752	33.9800	56.1319
Highway2	Median	1.7278	245	0.3190%	1	0.0013%	0.9961	34.6639	42.3162
	SC-SOBS	**0.6536**	**7**	**0.0091%**	**0**	**0.0000%**	**0.9982**	**44.6312**	**54.3785**
	WS2006	2.4906	375	0.4883%	10	0.0130%	0.9927	33.9515	40.5088
	RSL2011	5.6807	956	1.2448%	316	0.4115%	0.9766	28.6703	35.0821
	Photomontage	2.4306	452	0.5885%	4	0.0052%	0.9909	34.3975	41.7656
	CA2008	2.4340	486	0.6328%	43	0.0560%	0.9919	33.5545	39.4813
CaVignal	Median	10.3082	2846	10.4632%	2205	8.1066%	0.7984	18.1355	33.1438
	SC-SOBS	4.0941	869	3.1949%	436	1.6029%	0.8779	21.8507	42.2652
	WS2006	2.5403	408	1.5000%	129	0.4743%	0.9289	27.1089	37.0609
	RSL2011	**1.6132**	**4**	**0.0147%**	**0**	**0.0000%**	**0.9967**	**41.3795**	**52.5856**
	Photomontage	11.2665	3052	11.2206%	2408	8.8529%	0.7919	17.6257	32.0570
	CA2008	9.2569	17	0.0625%	**0**	**0.0000%**	0.9932	27.5197	39.7879
Foliage	Median	27.0135	13626	47.3125%	8772	30.4583%	0.6444	16.7842	28.7321
	SC-SOBS	3.8215	160	0.5556%	0	0.0000%	0.9900	31.7713	39.1387
	WS2006	6.8649	821	2.8507%	2	0.0069%	0.9754	27.2438	34.9776
	RSL2011	2.2773	43	0.1493%	11	0.0382%	0.9951	36.7450	43.1208
	Photomontage	**1.8592**	**0**	**0.0000%**	**0**	**0.0000%**	**0.9974**	**39.1779**	**45.6052**
	CA2008	18.3613	3327	11.5521%	1258	4.3681%	0.9092	18.7767	29.9137
People&Foliage	Median	24.4211	24760	32.2396%	19446	25.3203%	0.6114	15.1870	27.4979
	SC-SOBS	15.1031	10770	14.0234%	3849	5.0117%	0.7561	16.6189	35.3667
	WS2006	5.4243	2743	3.5716%	71	0.0924%	0.9269	22.6952	31.3847
	RSL2011	2.0980	612	0.7969%	434	0.5651%	0.9905	32.5550	37.0598
	Photomontage	**1.4103**	**3**	**0.0039%**	**0**	**0.0000%**	**0.9973**	**41.0866**	**47.1517**
	CA2008	19.7347	9401	12.2409%	4755	6.1914%	0.8220	17.1567	25.9970
Snellen	Median	42.3981	12898	62.2010%	11814	56.9734%	0.6932	13.6573	36.0691
	SC-SOBS	16.8898	7746	37.3553%	5055	24.3779%	0.9303	21.2571	44.7498
	WS2006	23.0010	4804	23.1674%	2544	12.2685%	0.7481	15.6158	24.9930
	RSL2011	**1.8095**	**133**	**0.6414%**	**99**	**0.4774%**	**0.9979**	**38.0295**	**50.2600**
	Photomontage	29.9797	6946	33.4973%	6318	30.4688%	0.5926	14.1466	26.9210
	CA2008	40.5218	9173	44.2371%	6359	30.6665%	0.6886	12.9428	24.0239

the background. RSL2011 and CA2008 perfectly handle the persistent clutter, even though only RSL2011 accordingly achieves the best accuracy results for all the metrics.

For sequence *Foliage*, even though moving leaves occupy most of the background area for most of the time, many of the compared methods achieve a quite good representation of the scene background. Indeed, only Median produces a greenish halo due to the foreground leaves over almost the entire scene area, and accordingly achieves the worst accuracy results for all the metrics.

In sequence *People&Foliage*, the artificially added leaves and men occupy almost all the scene area in almost all the sequence frames. Only Photomontage and RSL2011 appear to well handle the wide clutter, also achieving the best accuracy results for all the metrics.

In sequence *Snellen*, the foreground leaves occupy almost all the scene area in almost all the sequence frames. This leads most of the methods to include the contribution of leaves into the final background model. The best qualitative result can be attributed to RSL2011, as confirmed by the quantitative analysis in terms of all the adopted metrics.

Overall, we can observe that most of the best performing background initialization methods are region-based or hybrid, confirming the importance of taking into account spatio-temporal inter-pixel relations. Also selectivity in choosing the best candidate pixels, shared by all the best performing methods, appears to be important for achieving accurate results. Instead, all the common methodological schemes shared by the compared methods can lead to accurate results, showing no preferred scheme, and the same can be said concerning recursivity.

5 Concluding Remarks and Future Perspectives

We proposed a benchmarking study for scene background initialization, moving the first steps towards a fair and easy comparison of existing and future methods, on a common dataset of groundtruthed sequences, with a common set of metrics, and based on reproducible results. The assembled SBI dataset, the ground truths, and a tool to compute the suite of metrics were made publicly available.

Based on the benchmarking study, first considerations have been drawn. Concerning main issues in background initialization, low speed (or steadiness), rather than great size, of foreground objects included into the bootstrap sequence is a major burden for most of the methods. All the common methodologies shared by the compared methods can lead to accurate results, showing no preferred scheme, and the same can be said concerning recursivity. Anyway, the best results are generally achieved by methods that are region-based or hybrid, and selective; thus, these are the methods to be preferred. Concerning the evaluation of background initialization methods, among the eight selected metrics frequently adopted in the literature, pEPs and MS-SSIM confirm to be strongly indicative of the performance of background initialization methods.

Further insight will be certainly achieved by extending the dataset to include more sequences, also from other video categories (e.g., night videos and hardly crowded scenes), the notion of ground truth, in order to better handle the case of multimodal backgrounds, and the evaluation metrics, also evaluating their robustness in handling different scene conditions and their combination to provide global evaluation scores.

Acknowledgments. This research was supported by Project PON01_01430 PT2LOG under the Research and Competitiveness PON, funded by the European Union (EU) via structural funds, with the responsibility of the Italian Ministry of Education, University, and Research (MIUR).

References

1. Agarwala, A., Dontcheva, M., Agrawala, M., Drucker, S., Colburn, A., Curless, B., Salesin, D., Cohen, M.: Interactive digital photomontage. ACM Trans. Graph. **23**(3), 294–302 (2004)
2. Bouwmans, T.: Traditional and recent approaches in background modeling for foreground detection: An overview. Computer Science Review **1112**, 31–66 (2014)
3. Chen, C.C., Aggarwal, J.: An adaptive background model initialization algorithm with objects moving at different depths. In: 15th IEEE International Conference on Image Processing, 2008. ICIP 2008, pp. 2664–2667 (2008)
4. Elhabian, S., El Sayed, K., Ahmed, S.: Moving object detection in spatial domain using background removal techniques: State-of-art. Recent Patents on Computer Science **1**(1), 32–54 (2008)
5. Maddalena, L., Petrosino, A.: The SOBS algorithm: what are the limits? In: Proc. CVPR Workshops, pp. 21–26, June 2012
6. Maddalena, L., Petrosino, A.: Background model initialization for static cameras. In: Bouwmans, T., Porikli, F., Hferlin, B., Vacavant, A. (eds.) Background Modeling and Foreground Detection for Video Surveillance, pp. 3-1-3-16. Chapman & Hall/CRC (2014)
7. Maddalena, L., Petrosino, A.: The 3dSOBS+ algorithm for moving object detection. Comput. Vis. Image Underst. **122**, 65–73 (2014)
8. Reddy, V., Sanderson, C., Lovell, B.C.: A low-complexity algorithm for static background estimation from cluttered image sequences in surveillance contexts. EURASIP J. Image Video Process. **2011**, 1:1–1:14 (2011)
9. Wang, H., Suter, D.: A novel robust statistical method for background initialization and visual surveillance. In: Narayanan, P.J., Nayar, S.K., Shum, H.-Y. (eds.) ACCV 2006. LNCS, vol. 3851, pp. 328–337. Springer, Heidelberg (2006)
10. Wang, Z., Simoncelli, E., Bovik, A.: Multiscale structural similarity for image quality assessment. In: Conference Record of the Thirty-Seventh Asilomar Conference on Signals, Systems and Computers, 2004, vol. 2, pp. 1398–1402 (2003)
11. Yalman, Y., Erturk, I.: A new color image quality measure based on YUV transformation and PSNR for human vision system. Turkish J. of Electrical Eng. & Comput. Sci. **21**, 603–612 (2013)

Simple Median-Based Method for Stationary Background Generation Using Background Subtraction Algorithms

Benjamin Laugraud$^{(\boxtimes)}$, Sébastien Piérard, Marc Braham,
and Marc Van Droogenbroeck

INTELSIG Laboratory, University of Liège, Liège, Belgium
{blaugraud,sebastien.pierard,m.braham,m.vandroogenbroeck}@ulg.ac.be

Abstract. The estimation of the background image from a video sequence is necessary in some applications. Computing the median for each pixel over time is effective, but it fails when the background is visible for less than half of the time. In this paper, we propose a new method leveraging the segmentation performed by a background subtraction algorithm, which reduces the set of color candidates, for each pixel, before the median is applied. Our method is simple and fully generic as any background subtraction algorithm can be used. While recent background subtraction algorithms are excellent in detecting moving objects, our experiments show that the frame difference algorithm is a technique that compare advantageously to more advanced ones. Finally, we present the background images obtained on the SBI dataset, which appear to be almost perfect. The source code of our method can be downloaded at http://www.ulg.ac.be/telecom/research/sbg.

1 Introduction

Estimating the static background image from a video sequence has many interesting applications. Traditionally, the *foreground* (FG) is defined as objects or people moving in the front of the scene that form the *background* (BG). Note that a temporarily stopped FG object must be dissociated from the BG (*e.g.* a pedestrian waiting for a green light). An example of application is the rendering of non-occluded pictures of monuments, or landscapes, which are difficult to observe in crowded places. Another example is the initialization of the *background subtraction* (BGS) algorithms [3] that aim at classifying, into a *segmentation map*, for each frame of a video sequence, pixels as belonging to the FG or the BG. BGS algorithms often assume that the few first frames are motionless, which leads to inappropriate segmentation maps for the beginning of the sequences if the assumption does not hold. In order to accelerate the initialization process, they could benefit from a better estimation of the initial BG image.

The SBMI challenge [8] aims at developing methods to estimate the BG image of a scene given a video sequence taken from a static viewpoint, but with potential jitter. To evaluate such methods, the SBI dataset [8], composed

© Springer International Publishing Switzerland 2015
V. Murino et al. (Eds.): ICIAP 2015 Workshops, LNCS 9281, pp. 477–484, 2015.
DOI: 10.1007/978-3-319-23222-5_58

of 7 sequences, is provided. Their characteristics prevent the use of simple approaches such as taking the median color per pixel using all the frames (we refer to this method as the MED method hereafter), as the BG may be visible in less than 50% of the frames for some pixels [7]. Also, for some sequences, there is no image void of occluding objects, although the BG color is visible for each pixel for at least a few frames. Heuristics used in inpainting techniques [10] might be useless in this context. The BG is assumed to be unimodal, this means that we do not have to consider effects due to dynamic textures or illumination changes in the BG, and that there is only one possible BG at each instant. Moreover, as all the sequences are quite short (they are between 257 and 499 frames long), one background image should suffice to represent the static background.

In this paper, we present a simple method to estimate the BG image. Instead of estimating the BG image to initialize BGS algorithms as discussed above, we rely on BGS algorithms to generate a reference image for the BG. One could think that it is sufficient to simply extract this image from the BG modeled by such an algorithm. However, this approach has major drawbacks. Among others, despite that some BGS algorithms build an internal BG image reference, they often have a more complex *model* (*e.g.* for the Mixture of Gaussians [13]) or even store samples (*e.g.* ViBe [2]). Thus, extracting a BG image from the model of a given BGS algorithm might be complicated due to the internal mechanisms involved in the model maintenance. Rather than trying to extract a reference image directly, our idea consists in detecting motion according to the segmentation maps produced by any BGS algorithm, and integrate this process into a generic framework. Note that the optimal BGS algorithm for video-surveillance might not be best for our purpose. For example, classifying shadowed areas in the FG would help us, but this is rarely the targeted behavior of BGS algorithms.

The paper is organized as follows. Section 2 describes the method proposed in this paper, and presents the related work. Our experiments and results are provided and discussed in Section 3. Section 4 concludes this paper.

2   Proposed Method

According to Maddalena *et al.* [7], the stationary BG generation problem can be solved with the MED method when the BG is visible for half of the time. Unfortunately, for most sequences of the SBI dataset or also often in practice, this is not the case. Nevertheless, this simple idea combined to a BGS algorithm to select relevant frames, for each pixel, proves effective and produces excellent results. In our method, the median is computed on a per-pixel subset of frames (of fixed size S), selected by considering the probability p_+^* of FG elements in the neighborhood of the considered pixel, instead of the pixel only. For example, colors might be darkened in shadowed areas but still be undetected by some BGS algorithms. As casted shadows are spatially close to the associated objects, the spatial estimation of p_+^* helps discarding them. More specifically, to estimate this probability, we divide the image plane in $N \times N$ non-overlapping patches, and compute the proportion of pixels classified in the FG class, by the BGS algorithm, for the patch containing the considered pixel. Note that we discard the first frame processed by the BGS algorithm as the BGS model is undefined and this frame cannot be segmented.

In practice, all BGS algorithms require an initialization period during which their outputs are unreliable. The number of frames needed for the initialization is algorithm dependent, and can be larger than the number of available frames in the sequences of the SBI dataset. Therefore, we suggest to process the sequences several times. Let γ denote the total number of passes, which is chosen to be odd. The odd passes process the frames forwards, while the even ones process them backwards. Note that the idea of processing frames in a non chronological order to detect motion was first introduced in [14]. The internal model of the BGS algorithm is always updated, even during the last pass.

For each pixel, our method selects the S frames with the lowest probability p_+^* of FG computed for the corresponding patch. The S frames are issued from the ones processed during the γ passes, as we observed the trend that discarding the $\gamma - 1$ first passes deteriorates our results. In the case where S is too small to select all the frames with equal probabilities, we arbitrarily select the last ones encountered during the processing. Then, the BG color is estimated by taking the median of the colors in the S selected frames, the median being computed for the red, green, and blue components independently.

2.1 Related Work

Following the terminology of Maddalena *et al.* in [7], our method is:

- *Hybrid.* We combine the *pixel-level* analysis of a background subtraction algorithm with a *region-level* selection process to extract patches with the highest background probabilities.
- *Non-recursive.* Our method stores colors observed in the previous frames in a buffer, and directly derives the estimated background image by means of a temporal median filter.
- *Selective.* The median is computed in each pixel on a selection of samples with high background probability.

To the best of our knowledge, the closest method of the literature has been proposed by Amri *et al.* [1]. Its main idea lies in the application of a median filter on a set of frames, selected according to a criterion based on motion analysis. However, this method presents significant differences with our one.

Among others, due to the different targeted application (constructing a wide panoramic image from a video sequence taken with a moving camera), the work of Amri *et al.* is much more complicated. Moreover, the authors propose an iterative method processing frames until a stopping criterion is achieved. And last but not least, instead of being detected by temporal analysis, the motion is detected with a comparison between each processed frame and the last esti-mated BG image. Note that such a comparison is made by using a hysteresis thresholding technique while a raw BGS algorithm is used in our method.

3   Experiments and Results

Our proposed method has 4 parameters: the used BGS algorithm, the buffer size S, the amount of patches $N \times N$, and the number of passes γ. In our experiments, we have tested all combinations of 10 BGS algorithms, $S \in \{5, 11, 21, 51, 101, 201\}$, $N \in \{1, 3, 5, 10, 25, 50\}$, and $\gamma \in \{1, 3, 5, \ldots, 19\}$. The chosen BGS algorithms are listed in Section 3.1. The metrics used to assess the estimated BG images are detailed in Section 3.2, and results are presented and discussed in Section 3.3.

3.1   Background Subtraction Algorithms

All BGS algorithms proceed at the pixel level. The most intuitive one, the frame difference (F. Diff.), is based on a simple motion detection method which applies a threshold to the distance of colors between consecutive frames.

As noise is not spatially and temporally uniform, other algorithms have been proposed to estimate the statistical distribution of background colors over time. Wren *et al.* [15] supposed a Gaussian noise, and modeled the background with a Gaussian distribution whose mean and variance are adapted constantly (Pfinder). Stauffer *et al.* extended this idea to handle dynamic backgrounds using a mixture of Gaussians [13] (MoG G.). Zivkovic improved this by adapting the number of needed Gaussians over time [16] (MoG Z.). The Sigma-Delta algorithm (S-D) is another variant of Pfinder, proposed by Manzanera *et al.* [9], estimating the median (instead of the mean) based on a $\Sigma - \Delta$ estimator.

As an alternative, El Gammal *et al.* [4] proposed, in their KDE algorithm (KDE), to build the distribution by applying Parzen windows on a set of past samples. ViBe (ViBe), proposed by Barnich *et al.* [2], uses a pure sample-based

Fig. 1. The 7 video sequences of the SBI dataset (50th frame on the 1st row), the result obtained by the MED method (2nd row), our best result (F. Diff., $S = 21$, $N \times N = 3 \times 3$, $\gamma = 11$) (3rd row), and the corresponding ground-truth (last row).

approach and random policies to sample, in a conservative way, the observed background values. Some variants have been developed by, among others, Hofmann *et al.* [5] with PBAS (PBAS) by adding adaptive decision thresholds and update rates, and by St-Charles *et al.* [12] with SuBSENSE (SuBS.) by associating these adaptive parameters with the sampling of LBSP strings.

Finally, an approach based on self organization through artificial neural networks has been proposed by Maddalena *et al.* with the SOBS algorithm, whose idea is inspired from biologically problem-solving methods [6]. It should be noted that the implementations of the 10 used BGS algorithms are provided by the BGSLibrary [11] or by the authors.

3.2   The Metrics Used to Assess the Estimated Background Images

For each set of parameters, we have computed the eight metrics suggested by Maddalena *et al.* [8]. As two metrics are normalized versions of two others, we decided to keep only six of them: the *Average Gray-level Error (AGE)*, the *Percentage of Error Pixels (pEPs)* (a difference of values larger than 20 is considered

Table 1. Comparison of the BGS algorithms. The best set of parameters, as well as the averaged metrics are given for each algorithm. We selected the best sets of parameters according to the the averaged pEPs (arbitrary choice of metric).

BGS method	Best parameters			Averaged metrics					
	S	$N \times N$	γ	AGE	pEPs	pCEPs	PSNR	MS-SSIM	CQM
F. Diff.	21	3×3	11	**8.211**	**0.026**	**0.015**	**29.803**	**0.986**	**41.481**
Pfinder	11	1×1	1	16.361	0.160	0.123	26.227	0.886	37.915
MoG G.	51	3×3	17	11.569	0.063	0.047	28.975	0.934	39.757
MoG Z.	5	50×50	19	13.106	0.109	0.072	25.145	0.876	37.620
S-D	11	3×3	1	16.029	0.141	0.111	26.619	0.881	38.324
KDE	101	1×1	15	11.400	0.079	0.058	27.610	0.935	39.577
ViBe	21	1×1	11	15.555	0.124	0.103	27.003	0.890	37.107
PBAS	11	1×1	9	10.406	0.057	0.039	27.030	0.947	38.550
SOBS	11	1×1	7	15.990	0.159	0.121	25.229	0.878	37.022
SuBS.	5	3×3	19	10.939	0.070	0.048	26.936	0.947	39.205

Table 2. According to the pEPs metric, the optimal BGS algorithm and set of parameters depend on the considered video sequence.

Sequence	Best parameters				Metrics					
	BGS method	S	$N \times N$	γ	AGE	pEPs	pCEPs	PSNR	MS-SSIM	CQM
CaVignal	F. Diff.	51	3×3	1	9.231	0.000	0.000	27.539	0.993	39.737
Foliage	F. Diff.	201	5×5	19	12.018	0.015	0.000	26.019	0.992	34.113
HallAndMonitor	SOBS	101	5×5	1	2.000	0.000	0.000	39.118	0.994	47.195
HighwayI	MoG Z.	101	1×1	1	1.693	0.001	0.000	39.201	0.990	58.794
HighwayII	MoG Z.	101	10×10	1	1.786	0.000	0.000	39.729	0.996	48.417
PeopleAndFoliage	KDE	11	1×1	5	11.202	0.005	0.002	26.367	0.993	34.374
Snellen	F. Diff.	11	1×1	5	14.858	0.056	0.047	22.426	0.982	40.001

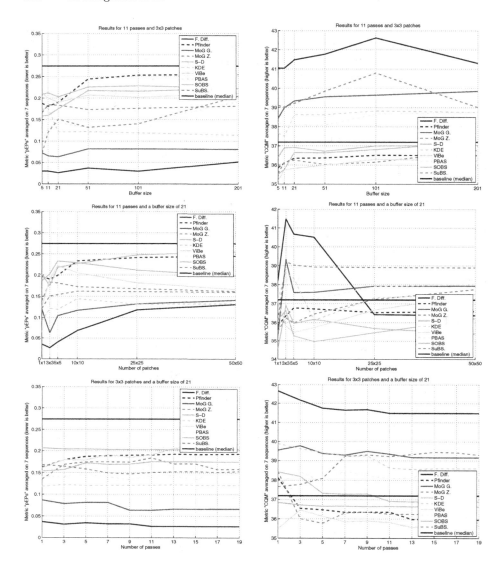

Fig. 2. According to the pEPs metric averaged over the 7 sequences, the best results are obtained with F. Diff., $S = 21$, $N \times N = 3 \times 3$, and $\gamma = 11$. This figure shows that this is at least a local optimum as it is not possible to improve this metric by varying the parameters (left column). Moreover, we observed that our conclusion about the best set of parameters is very close to those one would obtain by considering other metrics (see the metric CQM in the right column). Note that the CQM metric tends to prefer an increased buffer size and a reduced number of passes. The performance of the MED method is shown as a point of comparison (baseline).

as an error), the *Percentage of Clustered Error Pixels (pCEPs)* (any error pixel whose 4-connected neighbors are also error pixels), the *Peak-Signal-to-Noise-Ratio (PSNR)*, the *Multi-Scale Structural Similarity Index (MS-SSIM)* that estimates the perceived visual distortion, and the *Color image Quality Measure (CQM)*. The AGE, pEPs, and pCEPs are to be minimized, while the PSNR, MS-SSIM, and CQM are to be maximized. For any set of parameters, metric values were averaged over the 7 video sequences of the SBI dataset.

3.3 Results

Table 1 compares the metrics for the 10 tested BGS algorithms. On average, the frame difference algorithm performs best with respect to all metrics. The best values for the other parameters are $S = 21$, $N = 3$, and $\gamma = 11$. Despite the metrics indicate our results are imperfect, Figure 1 shows that the differences between our background images and the ground-truths are barely noticeable, to the contrary of images obtained with the MED method. However, we note in Table 2 that the best BGS algorithm depends on the sequence. Figure 2 shows the performance sensitivity with respect to parameters S, N, and γ, when they vary around the optimal values given above, and compares the performance with the MED method. Despite the small size of the SBI dataset, we observed that the different metrics agree to a large extend on the ranking of the BGS algorithms for our purpose (there is a high agreement for the top 5 methods, and the frame difference is always ranked first), even if small discrepancies exist (*e.g.* the ranking of the MED method for the pEPs and CQM metrics).

The processing time of our method tuned with its best parameters can be easily estimated in terms of pixel throughput (the number of pixels processed per second). According to our experiments, the mean pixel throughput of a naive implementation, excluding the temporal median filter, is approximately equal to 479×10^6 pixel/s for an Intel Core i7-4790K processor. Note that the most naive implementation of a temporal median filter has an asymptotic time complexity of $O(S \log S)$, and represents an additional processing load of approximately 120×10^8 pixel/s using the same processor.

4   Conclusion

In this paper, we present a simple, yet efficient, method for estimating the BG image corresponding to any video sequence taken from a fixed viewpoint. Note that the source code of our method can be downloaded at http://www.ulg.ac. be/telecom/research/sbg. The main contribution consists to embed any BGS algorithm into a generic process. For each pixel separately, this process analyses the BGS segmentation maps locally to select a subset of the frames encountered during a given number of passes. At the end of the selection process, the median is applied on the selected frames. Surprisingly, the frame difference outperforms more advanced BGS algorithms in this particular context. Results are also convincing as we obtain nearly perfect background images on the SBI dataset.

References

1. Amri, S., Barhoumi, W., Zagrouba, E.: Unsupervised background reconstruction based on iterative median blending and spatial segmentation. In: IEEE Int. Conf. Imag. Syst. and Techniques (IST), pp. 411–416. Thessaloniki, Greece, July 2010. http://dx.doi.org/10.1109/IST.2010.5548468

2. Barnich, O., Van Droogenbroeck, M.: ViBe: A universal background subtraction algorithm for video sequences. IEEE Trans. Image Process. **20**(6), 1709–1724 (2011). http://dx.doi.org/10.1109/TIP.2010.2101613

3. Bouwmans, T.: Traditional and recent approaches in background modeling for foreground detection: An overview. Computer Science Review **11–12**, 31–66 (2014). http://dx.doi.org/10.1016/j.cosrev.2014.04.001

4. Elgammal, A., Harwood, D., Davis, L.: Non-parametric model for background subtraction. In: Vernon, D. (ed.) ECCV 2000. LNCS, vol. 1843, pp. 751–767. Springer, Heidelberg (2000)

5. Hofmann, M., Tiefenbacher, P., Rigoll, G.: Background segmentation with feedback: The pixel-based adaptive segmenter. In: IEEE Int. Conf. Comput. Vision and Pattern Recognition Workshop (CVPRW). Providence, Rhode Island, USA, June 2012

6. Maddalena, L., Petrosino, A.: A self-organizing approach to background subtraction for visual surveillance applications. IEEE Trans. Image Process. **17**(7), 1168–1177 (2008)

7. Maddalena, L., Petrosino, A.: Background model initialization for static cameras. In: Background Modeling and Foreground Detection for Video Surveillance, chap. 3. Chapman and Hall/CRC (2014)

8. Maddalena, L., Petrosino, A.: Towards benchmarking scene background initialization. CoRR abs/1506.04051 (2015). http://arxiv.org/abs/1506.04051

9. Manzanera, A., Richefeu, J.: A robust and computationally efficient motion detection algorithm based on sigma-delta background estimation. In: Indian Conference on Computer Vision, Graphics and Image Processing, pp. 46–51. Kolkata, India, December 2004

10. Patwardhan, K., Sapiro, G., Bertalmio, M.: Video inpainting of occluding and occluded objects. IEEE Int. Conf. Image Process. (ICIP) **2**, 69–72 (2005)

11. Sobral, A.: BGSLibrary: An OpenCV C++ background subtraction library. In: Workshop de Visao Computacional (WVC). Rio de Janeiro, Brazil, June 2013

12. St-Charles, P.L., Bilodeau, G.A., Bergevin, R.: SuBSENSE: A universal change detection method with local adaptive sensitivity. IEEE Trans. Image Process. **24**(1), 359–373 (2015). http://dx.doi.org/10.1109/TIP.2014.2378053

13. Stauffer, C., Grimson, E.: Adaptive background mixture models for real-time tracking. In: IEEE Int. Conf. Comput. Vision and Pattern Recognition (CVPR), vol. 2, pp. 246–252. Ft. Collins, USA, June 1999

14. Van Droogenbroeck, M., Barnich, O.: Visual background extractor. World Intellectual Property Organization, WO 2009/007198, 36 pages, January 2009

15. Wren, C., Azarbayejani, A., Darrell, T., Pentland, A.: Pfinder: Real-time tracking of the human body. IEEE Trans. Pattern Anal. Mach. Intell. **19**(7), 780–785 (1997)

16. Zivkovic, Z.: Improved adaptive gausian mixture model for background subtraction. In: IEEE Int. Conf. Pattern Recognition (ICPR), vol. 2, pp. 28–31. Cambridge, UK, August 2004

Multi-modal Background Model Initialization

Domenico D. Bloisi[1]([✉]), Alfonso Grillo[2], Andrea Pennisi[1],
Luca Iocchi[1], and Claudio Passaretti[2]

[1] Sapienza University of Rome, via Ariosto, 25, 00185 Rome, Italy
{bloisi,pennisi,iocchi}@dis.uniroma1.it
[2] WT Italia, Rome, Italy
{alfonsogrillo,claudiopassaretti}@wtitalia.com

Abstract. Background subtraction is a widely used technique for detecting moving objects in image sequences. Very often background subtraction approaches assume the availability of one or more clear frames (i.e., without foreground objects) at the beginning of the image sequence in input. This strong assumption is not always correct, especially when dealing with dynamic background. In this paper, we present the results of an on-line and real-time background initialization method, called IMBS, which generates a reliable initial background model even if no clear frames are available. The accuracy of the proposed approach is calculated on a set of seven publicly available benchmark sequences. Experimental results demonstrate that IMBS generates accurate background models with respect to eight different quality metrics.

1 Introduction

Background subtraction (BS) is a popular and widely used technique that represents a fundamental building block for multiple Computer Vision applications, ranging from automatic monitoring of public spaces to augmented reality.

This work is motivated by the development of the Audio-Video Analytics Software (AVAS), joint work between WT Italia company and Sapienza University of Rome, which is designed to be a highly modular and flexible software framework for audio-video analytics. AVAS also aims at including state-of-the-art cutting-edge software components, which are properly integrated within the framework and to provide clear performance metrics and evaluation in challenging scenarios, as the one provided by scientific challenges and competitions.

A notable amount of work in BS has been done and many techniques have been developed for tackling the different aspects of the problem (see, for example, the surveys in [5,6]). In addition to the large literature, some open-source software libraries have been released, so that also non-experts can exploit BS techniques for developing Computer Vision systems. However, a number of open issues in BS still need to be addressed, in particular how to deal with sudden and gradual illumination changes (e.g., due to clouds), shadows, camera jitter (e.g., due to wind), background movement (e.g., waves on the water surface, swaying trees), and permanent and temporary changes in the background geometry (e.g., moving furniture in a room, parked cars).

© Springer International Publishing Switzerland 2015
V. Murino et al. (Eds.): ICIAP 2015 Workshops, LNCS 9281, pp. 485–492, 2015.
DOI: 10.1007/978-3-319-23222-5_59

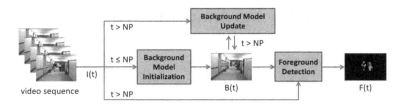

Fig. 1. Background subtraction process. *I(t)* is the current frame at time *t*, *B(t)* the background model, and *F(t)* the foreground mask. *P* is the sampling period and *N* is the total number of frames.

The BS process is carried out by comparing the current input frame with the model of the scene background and considering as foreground points the pixels that differ from the model. Thus, the problem is to generate a background model that is as reliable as possible. More formally, the BS process can be divided into three phases [4]: *background initialization*, *foreground detection*, and *model update*. Phase (1) is carried out only once, exploiting *N* frames at the beginning of the video sequence in input. Phases (2) and (3) are executed repeatedly as time progresses (see Fig. 1).

In contrast to the widely studied background model representation and model maintenance routines, limited attention has been given to the problem of initializing the background model [4]. In particular, often BS methods assume the availability of one or more *clean* frames at the beginning of the sequence, i.e., frames without foreground objects [11]. This is a strong assumption that is not always correct, because of continuous clutter presence. Generally, the model is initialized using the first frame or a background model over a set of training frames, which contains or do not contain foreground objects.

In this paper, we focus on the background initialization phase and describe the results of an on-line and real-time method, called Independent Multimodal Background Subtraction (IMBS) [1], when dealing with sequences where no clean frames are available. The software module evaluated in this paper is an extended version of IMBS with multi-thread optimization. For the evaluation, the test sequences provided by the Scene Background Modeling and Initialization (SBMI)[1] data set are used. Quantitative experimental results demonstrate that IMBS generates accurate background models for all the seven image sequences in SBMI with respect to eight different quality metrics, as well as very fast computation performance (over real-time).

The remainder of the paper is organized as follows. Related work, with particular emphasis on clustering-based BS methods and on existing software libraries, is discussed in the next Section 2 and the proposed method is summarized in Section 3. The results of the quantitative evaluation of IMBS and two other methods on the SBMI data set are reported in Section 4. Summary and conclusions are given in Section 5.

---

[1] http://sbmi2015.na.icar.cnr.it

2   Related Work

Background subtraction (BS) has been extensively studied and a rich literature with different approaches for generating accurate foreground masks exists.
Some recent surveys have been realized by Hassanpour *et al.* [8], Cristani *et
al.* [6], and Bouwmans [3]. From the large literature on BS algorithms, we have
decided to discuss some methods adopting clustering-based solutions, since our
algorithm is based on the same idea. This section describes also a set of implemented BS approaches for which open-source code and/or development libraries
are available. We believe that the possibility of having the code for the algorithms, together with challenging benchmarks, is a fundamental requirement for
achieving more and more reliable BS modules.

   BS Clustering Approaches. Fan *et al.* in [7] perform a k-means clustering
and single Gaussian model to reconstruct the background through a sequence of
scene images with foreground objects. Then, based on the statistical characteristics of the background pixel regions, the algorithm detects the moving objects.
In addition, an adaptive algorithm for foreground detection is used in combination with morphological operators and a region-labeling mechanism. Li *et al.* in
[10] propose a method for background modeling and moving objects detection
based on clustering theory. An histogram containing the pixel value over time is
used to extract the moving objects, with each peak in the histogram considered
as a cluster. Kumar and Sureshkumar in [9] propose a modification of the k-
means algorithm for computing background subtraction in real-time processing.
In their experimental results, the algorithm shows that selecting centroids can
lead to a better background subtraction and it results efficient and robust for
dynamic environment with new objects in it.

   Differently to the above-cited clustering methods, *time* is a key factor in
IMBS. Indeed, the background model is built by considering N frame samples
that are collected on the basis of a time period P. The details about IMBS are
given in Section 3.

   Open Source BS algorithms. The possibility of having the source code
of the BS methods described in the literature represents a key point towards
the goals of generating more and more accurate foreground masks and widely
applying this technology. OpenCV[2] library version 3 provides the source code
for two BS methods:

1. MOG2: An improved adaptive Gaussian mixture model [13];
2. KNN: K-nearest neighbors background subtraction described in [14].

Bgslibrary[3] is an OpenCV based C++ BS library containing the source code
for both native methods from OpenCV and several approaches published in
literature. The author also provides a JAVA graphical user interface (GUI) that
can be used for comparing different methods.

---

[2] http://opencv.org
[3] https://github.com/andrewssobral/bgslibrary

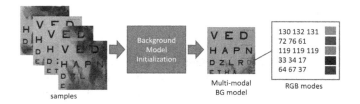

Fig. 2. IMBS stores multiple background values for each pixel.

3   IMBS Background Model Initialization

In this section, we briefly summarize the IMBS (Independent Multimodal Background Subtraction) background subtraction method experimented in this paper. Additional details can be found in [1], while the source code of IMBS is publicly available[4]. Although the method has been specifically realized for the maritime domain [2], which is characterized by non-regular and high frequency noise, IMBS can be successfully applied to many benchmark sequences, as demonstrated in Section 4.

The main idea behind IMBS is the discretization of the color distribution for each pixel, by using an on-line clustering algorithm. More specifically, for each pixel $p(i,j)$ the analysis of a set of N sample image frames is used to determine the background mode $\mathfrak{B}(i,j)$ for that pixel. $\mathfrak{B}(i,j)$ is a set of pairs $\langle c, f(c) \rangle$, where c is a value in the chosen color space (e.g., a triple in RGB or HSV space) and $f(c)$ is the number of occurrences of the value c in the sample set (see Fig. 2). After processing all the samples, only those color values that have enough occurrences are maintained in the background model. In this way, the background model contains, for each pixel, a discrete and compact multi-modal representation of its color probability distribution over time.

IMBS does not require fitting the data in some predefined distributions (e.g., Gaussian). This is the main difference with respect to a Mixture of Gaussians approach [12,13], where fitting Gaussian distributions is required and typically the number of Gaussians is limited and determined *a priori*.

Once the background model $\mathfrak{B}$ is computed, the foreground mask is determined by using a quick thresholding method: A pixel $p(i,j)$ is considered as a foreground point if the current color value is not within the distribution represented in the model, i.e., its distance from all the color values in $\mathfrak{B}(i,j)$ is above a given threshold A. IMBS requires a time $R = NP$ for creating the first background model. Then a new model, independent from the previous one, is built continuously, according to the same refresh time R.

For coping with the model update problem, IMBS adopts a conditional update policy: Given a scene sample S_k and the current foreground binary mask F, if $F(i,j) = 1$ and $S_k(i,j)$ is associated to a background mode in the background model under development, then it is labeled as a "foreground mode".

---

[4] http://www.dis.uniroma1.it/~bloisi/software/imbs.html

When computing the foreground, if $p(i, j)$ is associated with a foreground mode, then p is classified as a potential foreground point. Such a solution allows for identifying regions of the scene representing not moving foreground objects (i.e., temporarily static foreground objects).

4   Experimental Results

In order to experimentally evaluate the performance of our method, seven different image sequences, provided in the SBMI data set, have been used. The SBMI sequences have been extracted from multiple publicly available sequences that are frequently used in the literature to evaluate background initialization algorithms. In addition to our method, we used for comparison the results generated by two other BS methods, i.e., KNN and MOG2, whose implementation is available in OpenCV 3. For computing the results, we maintained the default parameters for KNN and MOG2 and we used the following parameters for IMBS: $P = 500ms$, $N = 20$, $D = 2$, and $A = 5$.

Accuracy Evaluation. The proposed method has been evaluated both qualitatively and quantitatively, by using the SBMI scripts for computing the results. Qualitative evaluation is illustrated in Fig. 3, where the first column contains a sample frame for each sequence; the second column contains ground truth images, included in the SBMI data set, that have been manually obtained by either choosing one of the sequence frames free of foreground objects (not included into the subsets of used frames) or by stitching together empty background regions from different sequence frames. The background model images computed with the KNN, MOG2, and IMBS methods are shown in the last three columns, respectively. For KNN and MOG2, we created the model images with the *getBackgroundImage* function, while for IMBS we created the model image by selecting, for each pixel p, the mode with the minimum distance d from the ground truth:

$$d = \arg \min_{k} |r_k - r_{GT}| + |g_k - g_{GT}| + |b_k - b_{GT}|$$

where (r_k, g_k, b_k) is one of the modes in $\mathfrak{B}$ for the pixel p and (r_{GT}, g_{GT}, b_{GT}) is the corresponding ground truth value.

Table 1 shows quantitative results obtained on the seven sequences with respect to the quality metrics suggested in SBMI (bold font is used to denote best performance in each metric). The quantitative results demonstrate that, when the nature of the scene is static (as in the first four sequences), then the three methods obtain comparable results. However, when the nature of the scene becomes highly dynamic (as in the last three sequences), then IMBS outperforms the other two methods. In particular, for the last two sequences it can be noted that IMBS obtains better results on all the considered metrics. This is due to the specific capacity of IMBS to model scenes with dynamic background, since IMBS does not consider a predefined distribution of the pixel values in the background. The last row in Table 1 shows that, when computing the average results on the

sample frame	ground truth	KNN	MOG2	IMBS

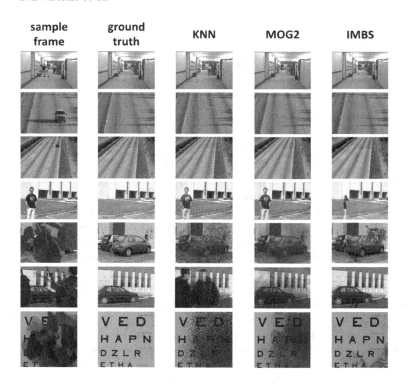

Fig. 3. Qualitative results on the Scene Background Initialization (SBI) data set.

complete SBMI data set, IMBS performs better than KNN and MOG2 with respect to all the eight considered metrics.

Computational Performance. The complete pipeline shown in Fig. 1 has been implemented to take advantage of parallel execution by using the OpenMP[5] libraries. Indeed, IMBS can process in parallel the operations for creating the background model, since an independent color distribution is generated for each pixel. In the same way, it is also possible to obtain a fast computation of the foreground mask by exploiting the parallel execution.

In order to ensure real-time performance, we measured the computational speed of IMBS by using an Intel(R) Core(TM) i7-3610QM CPU @ 2.30GHz, 8 GB RAM on 9 high-resolution video sequences of an urban scenario from the AVAS system. The results for three different high-resolution computer display standards are reported in Table 2. A computational speed of more than 30 frame per seconds can be achieved with Full High-Definition (Full HD) images. In addition, we measured also the performance on 352×240 images, obtaining a very high processing speed, i.e., more than 450 frames per second.

---

[5] http://openmp.org

Table 1. Results on the Scene Background Modeling and Initialization (SBMI) data set.

Sequence	Method	AGE	EPs	pEPs	CEPs	pCEPS	MS-SSIM	PSNR	CQM
Hall	KNN	3.9413	1019	0.0121	174	0.0021	0.9519	28.2208	37.4907
&	MOG2	2.4506	917	0.0109	378	0.0045	0.9833	34.3943	45.9714
Monitor	IMBS	**1.5762**	**80**	**0.0009**	**0**	**0.0000**	**0.9953**	**38.8691**	**48.3614**
	KNN	6.1277	4728	0.0616	24	0.0003	0.8506	25.1521	34.8174
HighwayI	MOG2	2.6031	174	0.0023	15	0.0002	0.9753	35.8635	**58.2889**
	IMBS	**1.9224**	**49**	**0.0006**	**7**	**0.0001**	**0.9889**	**39.5607**	54.8991
	KNN	3.2112	649	0.0085	4	0.0001	0.9851	32.0981	39.6454
HighwayII	MOG2	**2.0893**	305	0.0040	**0**	**0.0000**	**0.9946**	**36.1190**	**45.2643**
	IMBS	3.2424	**52**	**0.0007**	**0**	**0.0000**	0.9894	35.1272	38.3185
	KNN	15.9267	2212	0.0813	345	0.0127	0.8241	18.2332	30.9930
CaVignal	MOG2	16.9327	3031	0.1114	2277	0.0837	0.8136	18.5891	34.5104
	IMBS	**3.7573**	**839**	**0.0308**	532	0.0196	**0.9039**	**24.2900**	**38.9337**
	KNN	34.5615	11410	0.3962	1109	0.0385	0.6281	14.1761	25.6845
Foliage	MOG2	32.3624	19252	0.6685	15914	0.5526	**0.8038**	16.5991	31.5282
	IMBS	**19.4927**	**4305**	**0.1495**	1093	**0.0380**	0.8035	**18.1790**	**31.9055**
People	KNN	48.4920	36231	0.4718	22782	0.2966	0.4238	10.9196	19.8121
&	MOG2	33.8442	54590	0.7108	47110	0.6134	0.8584	16.2252	27.4728
Foliage	IMBS	**13.6299**	**8074**	**0.1051**	**1211**	**0.0158**	**0.9748**	**23.9064**	**31.8531**
	KNN	61.9389	14166	0.6832	8975	0.4328	0.4493	10.6164	22.5804
Snellen	MOG2	58.8159	15790	0.7615	14182	0.6839	0.5336	11.4143	27.0312
	IMBS	**17.5073**	**3785**	**0.1825**	**2828**	**0.1364**	**0.9521**	**21.0135**	**41.6055**
	KNN	24.8856	10059	0.2449	4773	0.1146	0.7304	19.9309	30.1462
Average	MOG2	21.2997	13437	0.3242	11411	0.2769	0.8518	24,2254	38.5810
	IMBS	**8.7326**	**2455**	**0.0671**	**810**	**0.0299**	**0.9439**	**28.7065**	**40.8395**

Table 2. IMBS computational load for different computer display standards. A comparison between mono and multi-thread solutions has been reported.

Video	Frame	FPS	
Standard	size	mono	multi
Video CD	352×240	30.75	455.23
HD	1360×768	10.44	125.07
HD+	1600×900	7.62	65.46
Full HD	1920×1080	5.73	30.22

It is worth nothing that, the possibility of working with Full HD data allows for using high-level image processing routines after the foreground extraction, such as face recognition and plate identification. Moreover, with the computational speed achieved by IMBS it is possible to process simultaneously up to four HD video streams in real-time on a single PC.

5   Summary and Conclusions

In this paper, we presented the results of a fast clustering-based background subtraction method, called IMBS [1], when dealing with the problem of background initialization. The key aspect of IMBS is the capacity of generating an accurate background model even if no clear frames (i.e., without foreground objects) are present in the image sequence in input. Experimental results on the challenging sequences of the SBMI data set demonstrate that IMBS can generate highly accurate initial background models. The results obtained by IMBS have been compared with two state-of-the-art BS methods implemented in OpenCV 3, i.e., KNN and MOG2, obtaining better results in average with respect to eight different quality metrics.

References

1. Bloisi, D., Iocchi, L.: Independent multimodal background subtraction. In: Proc. of the Third Int. Conf. on Computational Modeling of Objects Presented in Images: Fundamentals, Methods and Applications, pp. 39–44 (2012)
2. Bloisi, D.D., Iocchi, L.: ARGOS - a video surveillance system for boat trafic monitoring in venice. International Journal of Pattern Recognition and Artificial Intelligence **23**(7), 1477–1502 (2009)
3. Bouwmans, T.: Recent advanced statistical background modeling for foreground detection: A systematic survey. Recent Patents on Computer Science **4**(3), 147–176 (2011)
4. Bouwmans, T.: Traditional and recent approaches in background modeling for foreground detection: An overview. Computer Science Review **1112**, 31–66 (2014)
5. Bouwmans, T., El Baf, F., Vachon, B.: Statistical background modeling for foreground detection: A survey. In: Handbook of Pattern Recognition and Computer Vision, pp. 181–199. World scientific Publishing (2010)
6. Cristani, M., Farenzena, M., Bloisi, D., Murino, V.: Background subtraction for automated multisensor surveillance: A comprehensive review. EURASIP J. Adv. Sig. Proc. **2010**, 1–24 (2010)
7. Fan, T., Li, L., Tian, Q.: A novel adaptive motion detection based on k-means clustering. In: IEEE Int. Conf. on Computer Science and Information Technology (ICCSIT), vol. 3, pp. 136–140 (2010)
8. Hassanpour, H., Sedighi, M., Manashty, A.: Video frames background modeling: Reviewing the techniques. Journal of Signal and Information Processing **2**(2), 72–78 (2011)
9. Kumar, A., Sureshkumar, C.: Background subtraction based on threshold detection using modified k-means algorithm. In: Int. Conf. on Pattern Recognition, Informatics and Medical Engineering (PRIME), pp. 378–382 (2013)
10. Li, Q., He, D., Wang, B.: Effective moving objects detection basedon clustering background model for video surveillance. In: Congresson Image and Signal Processing (CISP), vol. 3, pp. 656–660 (2008)
11. Maddalena, L., Petrosino, A.: Background model initialization for static cameras. In: Handbook on Background Modeling and Foreground Detection for Video Surveillance, pp. 3-1-3.16. Chapman and Hall/CRC (2014)
12. Stauffer, C., Grimson, W.: Adaptive background mixture models for real-time tracking. Int. Conf. on Computer Vision **2**, 246–252 (1999)
13. GZivkovic, Z.: Improved adaptive gaussian mixture model forbackground subtraction. In: Int. Conf. on Pattern Recognition,vol. 2, pp. 28–31 (2004)
14. Zivkovic, Z., van der Heijden, F.: Efficient adaptive density estimation per image pixel for the task of background subtraction. Pattern Recognition Letters **27**(7), 773–780 (2006)

Background Modeling by Weightless Neural Networks

Massimo De Gregorio[1] and Maurizio Giordano[2] (✉)

[1] Istituto di Scienze Applicate e Sistemi Intelligenti – CNR,
Via Campi Flegrei 34, 80078 Pozzuoli, Naples, Italy
[2] Istituto di Calcolo e Reti ad Alte Prestazioni – CNR,
Via P. Castellino 111, 80131 Naples, Italy
{massimo.degregorio,maurizio.giordano}@cnr.it

Abstract. Background initialization is the task of computing a background model by processing a set of preliminary frames in a video scene. The initial background estimation serves as bootstrap model for video segmentation of foreground objects, although the background estimation could be refined and updated in steady state operation of video processing systems. In this paper we approach the background modeling problem with a weightless neural network called WiSARD^{rp}. The proposed approach is straightforward, since the computation is pixel–based and it exploits a dedicated neural network to model the pixel background by using the same training rule.

1 Introduction

Background modeling and estimation in video sequences is a challenging problem in computer vision since it is a required task in several research and commercial applications domains, such as video surveillance, segmentation, understanding, and compression, just to mention a few. Background estimation is the task of distinguishing foreground objects from background areas in video frames. Evaluation and comparison surveys of existing techniques can be found in literature [4,12,13].

Background modeling approaches can be classified into the following main categories: pixel–based [12], region–based [15] and object–based [8]. The first one mainly based on individually pixel changes. The second one based on the analysis of the single pixel with its neighborhood. The latter based on splitting the image into regions that are likely to belong to the same object. Another classification has been proposed by Bouwmans in his survey [4].

Self–organizing neural networks [10], general regression neural networks [5], self–organizing maps [14,16], and adaptive resonance theory neural networks [9] are examples of neural network based approaches to background modeling. Even if the background modeling problem has been approached with different neural architectures, the totality of them is based on a weighted neuron model. In this paper we approach the background modeling task with a weightless neural network (WNN) called WiSARD [1]. The approach is straightforward, since

© Springer International Publishing Switzerland 2015
V. Murino et al. (Eds.): ICIAP 2015 Workshops, LNCS 9281, pp. 493–501, 2015.
DOI: 10.1007/978-3-319-23222-5_60

the WNN system takes into account single pixel information to accomplish the background modeling, although, at the same time, it features highly adaptive and noise–tolerance behavior, due to a never–ending and single–policy learning phase of the adopted WNN model and its capability to absorb small variations of the model at runtime.

We apply the WNN–based background modeling method to address an important although specific topic of background estimation: how to compute an initial background model based on a set of preliminary frames of a video scene. The initial background model is a prerequisite for high quality moving object detection, either if foreground areas are computed at runtime as difference between the estimated background model and the current frame, or if it is used as bootstrapping model for successive updates at steady state system operation when foreground object detection is carried out.

With this target in mind, we did experiments and measured the performance of our method on the SBI dataset [11]. It is worth noticing that the viability and performance of WNNs in background detection has already been proved in [6], although by addressing a slightly but related topic, like change and moving object detection problem [7].

The paper is so organized: in Section 2 the adopted WNN model is introduced; in Section 3 the WNN–based method for background modeling is presented; Section 4 reports and discusses the experimental results of the method applied to videos of the SBI dataset; finally, Section 5 summarizes some concluding remarks.

2   The WiSARD^{rp} Weightless Neural Model

Weightless neural networks are based on networks of Random Access Memory (RAM) nodes [2]. The WNNs have a basis for their biological plausibility because of the straightforward analogy between the address decoding in RAMs and the integration of excitatory and inhibitory signaling performed by the neuron dendritic tree. WiSARD systems are a particular type of WNN. While the use of n–tuple RAM nodes in pattern recognition problems is old, dating about 60

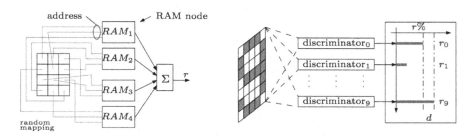

Fig. 1. A WiSARD discriminator (left) and a WiSARD multi–discriminator classifier (right)

years, with the availability of integrated circuit memories in the late 70s, the WiSARD (**W**ilkes, **S**tonham and **A**leksander **R**ecognition **D**evice) was the first artificial neural network machine to be patented and produced commercially [1].

The WiSARD model of computation is described in Figure 1. In this neural model a *discriminator* consists of a set of RAM–neurons, which store the information of occurrence of binary patterns of fixed size during the learning phase. Any sequence of bits fitting the s–sized pattern, the so–called *retina*, can be used to train a discriminator consisting of m RAMs with n–bit addressing, that is each RAM formed by 2^n memory cells, such that $s = m \times n$. In the example of Figure 1, the binary pattern (the retina) is a 3×4 image with pixels whose color can be 1 (for black) and 0 (for white); each RAM has a 3–bit addressing mechanism for cells, thus the number of required RAMs to cover the retina is $12/3 = 4$. Nevertheless, since any kind of information can be coded in binary patterns, by means of *ad hoc* data transformations a WiSARD discriminator can be enabled to learn then recognize data in both symbolic and numeric domains.

Since each RAM cell is uniquely addressed by an n–tuple of bits, the s–sized input pattern (the retina) can be partitioned into a set of n–tuples of bits, where bits forming each n–tuple have no correlation since they are pseudo–randomly extracted from the retina and associated to one RAM. For example, in Figure 1, the RAM_1, is uniquely associated to a triplet (3–tuple) of pixels. Thus, in the general case, the random mapping statically extract for the binary input pattern (stored in the retina) a number m of n–tuples of bits, and each n–tuple represents a binary address with n digits. This address is used to stimulate a RAM–neuron (by accessing one of its cells) either in writing mode (learning phase) or reading mode (classification phase).

A WiSARD *discriminator*, composed by m RAM–neurons, is trained with representative data of a specific class/category. In order to use the neuron network as a discriminator, one has to set to 0 the content of all cells of RAMs (initialization), and choose a training set formed by binary patterns of $m \times n$ bits. For each training pattern, a 1 is stored in the memory cells addressed by this input pattern. Once the training of patterns is completed, RAM contents will be set to a certain number of 0s and 1s. The information stored in RAM nodes during the training phase is used to deal with previously unseen patterns. When one of these is given as input, RAM memory contents addressed by the input pattern are read and summed by the summing device Σ which computes the number m^* of RAMs that output 1. Therefore $r = m^*/m$, which is called the *discriminator response*, provides the percentage of RAMs that outputs 1. It is easy to see that $r = 1$ if the input pattern belongs to the training set, $r = 0$ if none of its constituent n–tuples occurred in the training set. The closer is r to 1 the more "similar" is the input pattern to those patterns in the training set. The summing device enables this network of RAM nodes to exhibit – just like other ANN models based on synaptic weights – generalization and noise tolerance [3].

In this work we adopted a modified version of the WiSARD, that we call WiSARD^{rp}, which is depicted in Figure 2(a) and whose main modifications are the followings:

1. **Training phase** – RAM contents corresponding to n–tuples of binary inputs on the retina instead of being set to 1 are incremented by a positive number ρ (*reward*) at each access, up to a maximum value called *uppermark*, namely β. Thus, during training, RAM contents can store sub patterns frequencies up to a given saturation value β. At each memory cell access, while its content is increased by ρ, all other cells are decreased by ψ (*punishment*), thus lowering the frequencies of not occurring sub patterns. Punishments are applied to cells although they can never change their contents to negative values.

2. **Classification phase** – While in WiSARD, upon a read stimulus, a RAM always outputs its contents, that can be 0 or 1, in WiSARD^{rp} the output is 1 if the accessed RAM cell value is greater than a threshold, namely ω (*bleaching*), otherwise it is 0. With this modification we put a firing condition to RAMs, thus making them to contribute to the classification response only when the stored frequency of the sub patter under test overcomes a certain threshold ω.

It is easy to prove that WiSARD^{rp} with $\rho = 1$, $\psi = 0$, $\beta = +\infty$, and $\omega = 0$, behaves exactly as the original WiSARD system in the training and classification phases. On the other side, different settings of ρ, ψ, β and ω parameters implies very different behaviors of the training and classification phases. In other words, the *reward & punishment* strategy (rp) allows to size the time a sub pattern is completely unlearned once it does not occur any longer, as well as to size the time the more frequent sub patterns remain in the learned knowledge of the network. By changing these two latency times it is possible to tune WiSARD^{rp} capabilities both in classification and class model construction over a changeable and long–term training phase.

3   The BGWiS Approach to Background Modeling

The proposed method for background modeling in video sequences is called BGWiS and it exploits the WiSARD^{rp} neural network model in its core logic. The pseudocode of BGWiS is sketched in Algorithm 1 and it is based on the following assumptions:

1. **Color encoding** – The pixel color (in any color space among RGB, HSV, and Lab) is represented by three non–negative numbers, namely *color channels*, in the range 0–255. In order to use the WiSARD^{rp} as the core of our background modeling system a binarisation of pixel colors is required. As illustrated in Figure 2(a), the three channels are scaled and discretized in the range $0, 1, \ldots, nt - 1$, thus representing a color with a binary pattern of size $3 \times nt$. This black and white image is fed as input to the WiSARD^{rp} system for training and classification.

Algorithm 1. BGWiS method pseudocode

```
1  foreach frame in video sequence do
2      transform frame in the chosen color space;
3      foreach pixel in frame do
4          get response on input color from pixel discriminator (with firing threshold ω) ;
5          classify pixel as bg (if response > σ), otherwise as fg;
6          use color to train pixel discriminator (reward & punishment rule {ρ, ψ, β}) ;
7          use pixel discriminator contents to update background model;
```

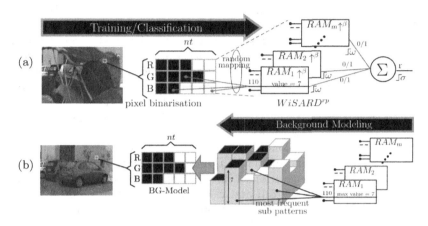

Fig. 2. Training phase (a) and background modeling phase (b) of BGWiS

2. **Background model** – In WiSARD^{rp} a pattern class is represented by the snapshot of RAM contents during time. As already mentioned, each RAM records the number of occurrences of sub patterns inside the binary input. In other words, a RAM content can be seen as the histogram of occurrences of all binary sub patterns occurred during training. In our case study, we assume that the background model of a pixel is formed by combining the most frequent sub patterns contained in RAMs. As illustrated in Figure 2(b), the background model of a pixel is computed by considering in each RAM the sub pattern addressing the cell with the greatest value.

3. **Processing loop** – In video processing learning and classification are overlapped and execute continuously. In the algorithm 1 the role of WiSARD^{rp} is twofold:

   (a) **Foreground detection** – On the basis of the learned knowledge of pixel color history which is stored in RAM cells and managed by means of the reward & punishment mechanism, the system is able to provide a classification response for the current pixel, that is a measure of its similarity to the color knowledge acquired by the WiSARD^{rp} by means of a continuous training. This response is then compared to the threshold σ to state whether the pixel in the current frame is detected as belonging either to the background or to the foreground. Afterwards, the WiSARD^{rp} is trained on the current pixel color regardless of the classification result (see line 4–6 of Algorithm 1).

(b) **Background modeling** – The learned knowledge of pixel color history contained in the discriminator neurons is used (see line 7 of Algorithm 1) to update the pixel background model, according to the logic already described (see point 2.). BGWiS system outputs a colored image representing the computed background model during the timeline.

The change–detection method proposed in the previous work [6] is based on WiSARD while the current method exploits WiSARD^{rp}. In particular, the change–detection method has no punishment ($\psi = 0$) and a fixed reward ($\rho = 1$) with both no firing threshold ($\omega = 0$) and saturation constraint ($\beta = \infty$). Another difference is the logic of the background modeling algorithm. The CDnet dataset target was foreground object detection rather than background modeling which is the target of SBI dataset. In fact, in the former challenge a set of video frames was allowed to be used only for training, while the remaining video frames were used for classification (foreground detection). In the change–detection method only pixel colors detected as background are used to further update (enrich) the background model for those pixels (i.e. in Algorithm 1 lines 6–7 are executed under the condition of line 5), unless a history buffer storing more recent foreground pixels is full and it is time to use it to reinitialize the background model. This policy, which was adopted to deal with moving/stopping objects in the scene, jointly with the aforementioned (and static) setting for ρ, ψ, β and ω, was experimentally proved to be a high performance (in the average) method in the CDnet competition. SBI videos are very different with respect to the percentage of background occlusion occurring both in space (frame area) and time (video duration). For this reason, BGWiS was designed to be flexible and reconfigurable in the parameters driving background modeling, as well as no comparison between the change–detection method of [6] and BGWiS could be carried out within the scope of SBI experiments.

4   BGWiS Experiment Settings and Results

We did experiments of BGWiS running on the SBI dataset of videos. Table 1 reports the system performance by evaluating eight metrics which, as defined on the SBI dataset website, compare for each sequence the ground truth background

Table 1. BGWiS results on SBI dataset

Sequence	AGE	EPs	pEPs	CEPs	pCEPS	MSSSIM	PSNR	CQM	ρ	ψ	β	n
HallAndMonitor	2.5177	442	0.0052	161	0.0019	0.9773	31.7928	42.2277	1	1	65	4
HighwayI	1.6885	106	0.0014	8	0.0001	0.9916	39.3795	59.4393	2	1	∞	16
HighwayII	2.2060	357	0.0046	1	0.0000	0.9948	33.2780	39.8760	2	1	∞	16
CaVignal	9.1964	25	0.0009	0	0.0000	0.9933	27.5468	39.7962	1	1	95	8
Foliage	14.7191	3060	0.1062	145	0.0050	0.9465	22.5656	33.7781	2	1	20	16
PeopleAndFoliage	32.2664	25240	0.3286	20514	0.2671	0.6849	13.9668	23.9475	1	3	∞	16
Snellen	38.4451	11324	0.5461	9928	0.4788	0.7700	14.5757	38.5964	1	3	∞	16

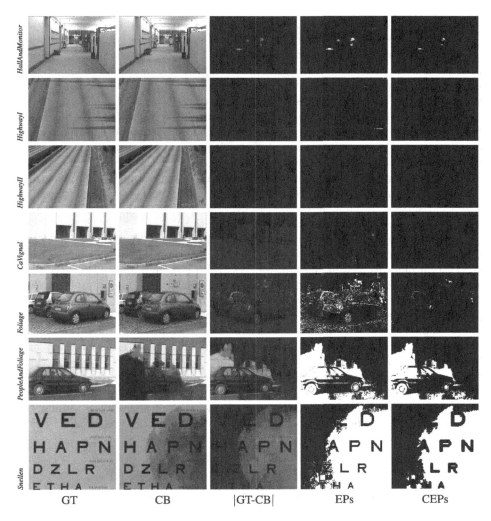

GT   CB |GT-CB| EPs   CEPs

Fig. 3. BGWiS output on SBI dataset: GT = Ground Truth; CB = Computed Background; |GT-CB| = absolute difference of GT and CB, EPs = number of CB pixels different from GT over a given threshold; CEPs = number of EPs in CB with all 4–connected neighbors pixels in EPs

image (GT) with the computed background image (CB) produced by our system at the end of the video.

In all measures we chose to transform input frames into Lab color space as a preprocessing step. As reported in Table 1, we used different parameter settings for videos, although in most cases we used 16–bit addressing for RAMs. The higher is the bit address the more precise is the color selection for the background model in bustling video scenes. In *HighwayI*, *HighwayII* and *Foliage* videos the pixel color patterns are used to access–then–reward neuron cells twice ($\rho = 2$, $\psi = 1$). Indeed, this setting allows the system to forget patterns more slowly and it is useful in those videos with object moving (or changing in shape) in a regular manner. In other cases, like *PeopleAndFoliage* and *Snellen*, the pixel color patterns are used to access–then–reward neuron cells a third than the punishment required for unseen color patterns ($\rho = 1$, $\psi = 3$).

It should be noted that in some video the saturation level of RAMs has been fixed in order to limit that foreground patterns could outnumber (in frequency) the background patterns by shortening the foreground patterns decay time. In the remaining videos the saturation level was disabled ($\beta = \infty$). It should be noted that the neuron threshold σ and bleaching ω only apply to classification phase without interfering with the background modeling computation. That is why their settings are not in Table 1. In order to generated the best CB, nt was set to 256 in all experiments (no loss of information).

Snapshots of BGWiS outputs are shown in Figure 3. By relating the performance measures of Table 1 to the snapshots of Figure 3, we can notice how the system behaves well in the first four videos. The remaining videos (*Foliage*, *PeopleAndFoliage* and *Snellen*) are challenging: in both *Foliage* and *Snellen* a waving plant frequently (more than 50% of timeline) occludes almost completely the target background; in the *PeopleAndFoliage* case a waving plant plus stationary–then–moving persons occlude more than half of the target background for almost the whole timeline. Although these three cases of study are hard to get a clean and effective background model, it is worth noticing that our system at least shows quite good results in the *Foliage* video (both in terms of the eight metrics and by evaluating at sight the difference from the ground truth). In the *Snellen* video, the computed background snapshot is similar to the ground truth, although the AGE, EPs and CEPs metrics are poor.

5   Conclusions

In this work we presented a background modeling approach for videos based on a weightless neural system, namely WiSARD^{rp}, with the aim of exploiting its features of being highly adaptive and noise–tolerance at runtime. Indeed, the adopted neural model is able to operate in a never–ending and single–policy learning phase with a *reward & punishment* mechanism, which allows it to absorb small variations of the learned model in the steady state of operation. The approach is quite simple, and by tuning a set of parameters that rule the reward & punishment mechanism of neural training, we have proved how it is possible to build on it a background modeling system showing very good performance in common case studies (like camera views of highways and traffic crossings), as well as good or promising results in more challenging video sequences (like static views with heavy and waving occlusions in space and time).

References

1. Aleksander, I., Thomas, W.V., Bowden, P.A.: WiSARD a radical step forward in image recognition. Sensor Review **4**, 120–124 (1984)
2. Aleksander, I., De Gregorio, M., França, F.M.G., Lima, P.M.V., Morton, H.: A brief introduction to weightless neural systems. In: ESANN 2009, pp. 299–305 (2009)
3. Aleksander, I., Morton, H.: An introduction to neural computing. Chapman & Hall (1990)
4. Bouwmans, T.: Recent advanced statistical background modeling for foreground detection: A systematic survey. Recent Patents on Computer Science **4**(3), 147–176 (2011)
5. Culibrk, D., et al.: A neural network approach to bayesian background modeling for video object segmentation. In: Proc. of VISAPP 2006, pp. 474–479 (2006)
6. De Gregorio, M., Giordano, M.: Change detection with weightless neural networks. In: Proc. of 2014 IEEE CVPRW, pp. 409–413 (2014)
7. Goyette, N., et al.: Changedetection.net: a new change detection benchmark dataset. In: Proc. of 2014 IEEE CVPRW, pp. 1–8 (2012)
8. Hall, D., et al.: Comparison of target detection algorithms using adaptive background models. In: Proc. 2nd Joint IEEE Int. Workshop VS-PETS, 2005, pp. 113–120 (2005)
9. Luque, R.M., Domínguez, E., Palomo, E.J., Muñoz, J.: An art-type network approach for video object detection. In: ESANN 2010, pp. 423–428 (2010)
10. Maddalena, L., Petrosino, A.: A self-organizing approach to background subtraction for visual surveillance applications. IEEE Trans. on Image Processing **17**(7), 1168–1177 (2008)
11. Maddalena, L., Petrosino, A.: Towards benchmarking scene background initialization (2015). http://arxiv.org/abs/1506.04051 (posted June 12, 2015)
12. Panahi, S., Sheikhi, S., Hadadan, S., Gheissari, N.: Evaluation of background subtraction methods. In: Proc. of DICTA 2008, pp. 357–364 (2008)
13. Piccardi, M.: Background subtraction techniques: a review. In: IEEE International Conference on Systems, Man and Cybernetics (October 2004)
14. Ramirez-Quintana, J., Chacon-Murguia, M.: Self-organizing retinotopic maps applied to background modeling for dynamic object segmentation in video sequences. In: Proc. of IJCNN 2013, pp. 1–8, August 2013
15. Shuai, Y.M., Xu, X., Sun, H., Xu, G.: Change detection based on region likelihood ratio in multitemporal sar images. In: 2006 8th Int. Conf. on Signal Processing, vol. 2 (2006)
16. Zhao, Z., Zhang, X., Fang, Y.: Stacked multilayer self-organizing map for background modeling. IEEE Transactions on Image Processing **24**(9), 2841–2850 (2015)

BMTDL for Scene Modeling on the SBI Dataset

Nicoletta Noceti(✉), Alessandra Staglianò, Alessandro Verri,
and Francesca Odone

DIBRIS, Università Degli Studi di Genova, Genova, Italy
{nicoletta.noceti,alessandra.stagliano,
alessandro.verri,francesca.odone}@unige.it

Abstract. In this paper we evaluate our method for Background Modeling Through Dictionary Learning (BMTDL) and sparse coding on the recently proposed Scene Background Initialization (SBI) dataset. The BMTDL, originally proposed in [1] for the specific purpose of detecting the foreground of a scene, leverages on the availability of long time observations, where we can treat foreground objects as noise. The SBI dataset refers to more general scene modeling problems – as for video segmentation, compression or editing – where video sequences may be generally short, and often include foreground objects occupying a large portion on the image for the majority of the sequence. The experimental analysis we report is very promising and show how the BMTDL may be also appropriate for these different and challenging conditions.

1 Introduction

In the last decades, a large body of the literature has addressed the problem of modeling and maintaining a background of the scene with the purpose of detecting variations at run time. This is a typical requirement of video-surveillance applications. An account of the related literature is out of the scope of this paper, we refer in particular to multi-variate background models, able to deal with complex outdoor scenarios. Recently, dictionary learning has been considered as an effective and elegant way to incorporate scene variations in multi-variate background models. Indeed, a video sequence is often obtained from a fixed camera looking at a slowly changing background. In this setting we can consider the atoms as denoised versions, or prototypes, of the inputs [8,9]. Over time, a richer dictionary is expected to arise in order to be able to capture greater (and permanent) changes in the background. Sparsity, which has been reported to favor discriminative power in subsequent classification tasks [10–12], here ensures a model of the background consisting of a linear combination of a few prototypes. The prototypes actually used in the model provide information can be usefully employed to reason on the time evolution of the image.

Dictionary learning approaches may be applied to different input data. A pixel-based modeling of the background, as in standard background modeling methods [2,3], does not appear to be informative enough for learning a dictionary. Thus most methods learn a dictionary of the entire image [4–7,20] even if, doing so, the peculiarities of the application domain, where changes

© Springer International Publishing Switzerland 2015
V. Murino et al. (Eds.): ICIAP 2015 Workshops, LNCS 9281, pp. 502–509, 2015.
DOI: 10.1007/978-3-319-23222-5_61

are often local and with a limited spatial extent, are not exploited. Also, different portions of the image may require models of different complexity, or more frequent updates. Our BMTDL method (Background Modeling Through Dictionary Learning) which we proposed in [1] for the specific application to change detection, adopts a space-variant patch-based model which allows us to choose an appropriate scale for the model (related to the patch size) and, in principle, to exploit prior information by selecting an appropriate size for a given position on the frame.

The concept behind BMTDL is the fact that in video-surveillance long time observations are usually available, and thus the background can slowly improve while the foreground can be soon treated as noise. This idea allowed us to address very complex illumination and scene changes, in particular periodic ones. In this work we test the applicability of BMTDL, more in general, to background modeling from a video sequence, with potential application to video segmentation, compression, and editing. Unlike video-surveillance systems, in this setting we have shorter observations, possibly including foreground objects which are stable for a majority of frames. We stressed the use of our method on the recent Scene Background Initialization (SBI) dataset [21] to test its appropriateness under general circumstances. The results we obtain are promising and appropriate of most scenarios: slowly changing foreground objects are easily dealt with, highly dynamic foreground is cleaned away. Figure 1 shows examples of the most likely background images.

Fig. 1. Examples of the (normalized) background models we obtained on the SBI dataset.

In the remainder of the paper we first briefly review the structure of our method (Sec. 2), to discuss then in detail the analysis we performed on the SBI dataset (Sec. 3). We conclude the paper with a final discussion (Sec. 4).

2   A Review of the BMTDL Algorithm

In this section we review the BMTDL algorithm, starting with a brief introduction of the mathematical core of the method, and then summarizing the main algorithmic steps. We refer the interested reader to [1] for a deeper discussion.

2.1 ℓ_1−Dictionary Learning

The goal of *sparse dictionary learning* (DL) is to build data representations by decomposing each datum into a linear combination of a few components selected from a dictionary of basic elements, called *atoms*. More technically, given a datum $\mathbf{x} \in \mathbb{R}^n$, we can assume the existence of a dictionary of K atoms $\{\mathbf{d}_1, \ldots, \mathbf{d}_K\}$ such that $\mathbf{x} \approx \mathbf{Du}$ for some sparse K-vector $\mathbf{u}$ and where $\mathbf{d}_j$ is the $j-th$ column of the $n \times K$-matrix D.

Often times, the dictionary is fixed and derived analytically, but to achieve adaptivity its atoms should be learnt directly from the input data. Actually, both dictionary atoms and data representations can be learnt from data. *Sparse coding*, also known as ℓ_1-Dictionary Learning [12], relies on solving the following functional:

$$\min_{\mathbf{D},\mathbf{u}} \|\mathbf{x} - \mathbf{Du}\|_2^2 + \lambda \|\mathbf{u}\|_1 \quad subject\ to\ \ \|\mathbf{d}_j\|_2 \le 1, \tag{1}$$

where the regularizer induces sparsity in the components of the $\mathbf{u}$ vector [14].

Algorithm 1. BMTDL algorithm described with pseudo-code

```
 1: procedure BMTDL({pᵗ_xy}ᴺₜ₌₀)              ▷ State := NORMAL
 2:     Bootstrap({pᵗ_xy}ᵏₜ₌₀)                   ▷ Init. the dictionary
 3:     for t ← k + 1, N do
 4:         err ← recError()
 5:         if (err ≤ τ_err) then
 6:             if (CLEAN_COND) then            ▷ State:=CLEAN
 7:                 dictPruning()
 8:             end if                          ▷ State:=NORMAL
 9:         else                                ▷ State:=ANOMALY
10:             if (TimeAnomCounter > τ_temp) then   ▷ State:=UPDATE
11:                 dictLearning()
12:             end if                          ▷ State:=NORMAL
13:         end if
14:     end for
15: end procedure
```

Although the joint minimization problem in $(\mathbf{D}, \mathbf{u})$ is non-convex and non-differentiable, it is convex in each variable and it can be solved by iteratively minimizing first with respect to $\mathbf{u}$ (*sparse coding step*) and then to $\mathbf{D}$ (*dictionary update step*), assorting to a procedure known as *block-coordinate descent* [12].

In this work the data are image patches of a fixed size acquired by a still camera over time. In what follows, each patch will be named $\mathbf{p}_{xy}^t$, meaning that the area we are considering is centered at the position xy of the time instant t. A patch evolving in time will participate to form and update a specific dictionary $\mathbf{D}_{xy}$. Therefore, our data are a sequence of $\mathbf{x}_i$ examples, $i = 1, \ldots$ – each one being the patch unfolded in a n-dimensional vector – where the observation at time t could possibly update the previous solution. In the machine learning terminology this would correspond to an *online learning* procedure [13].

2.2   The Background Modeling Procedure

We now summarize the algorithmic pipeline of the BMTDL method. For the sake of simplicity, we focus on processing a single image patch.

Algorithm 1 provides a sketch of the procedure. At each time instant, a patch can be in one among four possible states: states NORMAL and ANOMALY, that may be *persistent* for some time, and *transient* states UPDATE and CLEAN.

On a bootstrap phase, the dictionary $\mathbf{D}_{xy}$ is initialized with the first k patches normalized in order to constrain the atoms to have unitary norm. After initialization, the patch is in the NORMAL state.

Now a dictionary instance is available, the online procedure may start. Given a new patch instance $\mathbf{p}_{xy}^t$, the procedure attempts the decomposition with respect to the current dictionary $\mathbf{D}_{xy}$. To the purpose, we first estimate the feature vector $\mathbf{u}$ as $\mathbf{p}_{xy}^t \approx \mathbf{D}_{xy}\mathbf{u}$ by minimizing Eq. 1 with respect to $\mathbf{u}$ only. The, we compute the reconstruction error as $||\mathbf{p}_{xy}^t - \mathbf{D}_{xy}\mathbf{u}||_2/||\mathbf{p}_{xy}^t||_2$. If the reconstruction error is lower than a threshold τ_{err} – meaning that the reconstruction has been successful – the patch remains in a NORMAL status, otherwise there is a transition to the ANOMALY state. Each time an atom is employed in the reconstruction of the patch a usage counter is increased, to control later the dictionary size. When the patch is in the NORMAL state, at regular time intervals it assumes the transient stage CLEAN to undergo a pruning of its dictionary. The method checks the usage counters associated with the atoms and discards the ones which have seldom been used (they may be e.g. atoms corresponding to foreground moving object, erroneously enrolled in the model).

When a patch is in state ANOMALY, it undergoes the decomposition as well. As far as it succeeds, the patch goes back to the NORMAL state, otherwise a temporal counter that indicates the persistence of the anomaly state in the patch is increased. When the counter is large enough ($\geq \tau_{temp}$) it is likely to indicate a permanent background change: the state of the patch becomes UPDATE and the dictionary is enriched to accommodate new stable information as follows. Using the last τ_{temp} frames as training data, we learn a new dictionary $\mathbf{D}_{xy}^{update}$ of a fixed size K_{update} by minimizing Eq. 1, and add the new estimated atoms to the main dictionary $\mathbf{D}_{xy} = \mathbf{D}_{xy} \cup \mathbf{D}_{xy}^{update}$. Then the system returns in the state NORMAL and begins to process new patches with the updated dictionary.

In summary, we obtain a background model with a memory, able to model recurring background events that are detected as foreground only for the first occurence. We can control the capability of the method of adaptation to time changes, as well as its ability in detecting time-variant dynamic events, by appropriately tuning the τ_{temp} parameter. Similar considerations, together with computational issues, should guide the choice of K_{update}.

3   Experimental Results

In this section we discuss the experimental analysis we performed on the recently published Scene Background Initialization (SBI) dataset [21]. We refer the reader to [1] for a deeper evaluation of BMTDL on other benchmarks and for comparisons with other approaches. The dataset is a collection of image sequences of different complexity extracted from publicly available datasets. Together with the dataset, a set of Matlab scripts has been provided, allowing a common protocol of evaluation based on comparing the true background model GT (an image) with the estimated background model CB.

Notice that the latter is not directly available in our framework, since BMTDL provides us with a multi-variate patch model which incorporates different possible background states (corresponding to stable configurations). Therefore, to allow the evaluation, we composed an image CB by selecting the atoms which are closest to the GT image.

Table 1. Quality indexes of our background model with PS=10 and τ_{temp}=50

Sequence	AGE	EPs	pEPs	CEPs	pCEPS	MSSSIM	PSNR	Atoms
Hall&Monitor	10.15	480	0.0057	0	0.	0.99	27.59	2.13
HighwayI	20.65	36414	0.4741	12254	0.1596	0.87	21.23	5.48
HighwayII	17.04	6872	0.0895	243	0.0032	0.98	23.30	3.56
CaVignal	13.50	942	0.0362	160	0.0062	0.94	24.95	2.21
Foliage	3.84	141	0.0050	11	0.0004	0.99	34.34	5.94
People&Foliage	4.46	2276	0.0296	212	0.0028	0.94	30.46	8.94
Snellen	12.25	3307	0.1687	1050	0.0536	0.86	22.86	5.37
Avg.	11.698	7204.571	0.116	1990.000	0.032	0.937	26.391	
± std.dev	±6.177	±13083.813	±0.168	±4540.045	±0.059	±0.054	±4.687	

Once we formed our best CB, we evaluated it by means of the scripts provided with the dataset. These scripts compute a set of metrics:

- **AGE:** average of the gray-level absolute difference between GT and CB images (the lower the better).
- **EPs:** number of pixels in CB whose value differs from the value of the corresponding pixel in GT by more than a threshold th, fixed to 20 as suggested (the lower the better).
- **pEPs:** percentage of EPs with respect to the total number of pixels in the image (the lower the better).
- **CEPs:** number of pixels whose 4-connected neighbors are also error pixels (the lower the better).
- **pCEPs:** percentage of CEPs with respect to the total number of pixels in the image (the lower the better).
- **PSNR:** amounts to $10 log_{10} \frac{(L-1)^2}{MSE}$ where L is the maximum number of grey levels and MSE is the Mean Squared Error between GT and CB images. It assumes values in decibels (the higher the better).
- **(MS-SSIM)** [19]: estimate of the perceived visual distortion (the higher the better).

There is a last quality index in the evaluation that we did not consider, being referred to color images.

Table 1 reports the output of the Matlab scripts for a fixed configuration of our method corresponding to a square patch 10×10 pixels and τ_{temp} to 50 frames. The table also reports the dictionary size K, averaged over the image, (last column) which is an indication of the scene complexity. It can be noticed how the reported performances are very good on average. Observe how the average grey levels (AGE), which influence all the other metrics, are well below the threshold th. An exception is the sequence *HighwayI*, where shadows and highly dynamic foreground objects cause occasionally larger differences.

For a further analysis, we compare the effects of changing the size of the patch side (10, 20, 130 or 40 pixels) and the value of τ_{temp} (25, 50 or 100 frames).

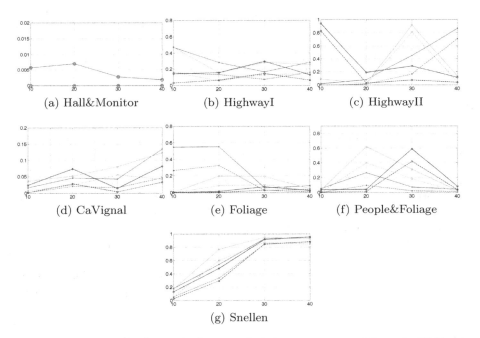

Fig. 2. Performances of the method in terms of the percentages pEPs and pCEPs (on the y-axis) as the patch side increases (on the x-axis) and for different choices of τ_{temp} (Solid line: pEPs; dotted line: pCEPs. red xs: $\tau_{temp} = 25$; green squares: $\tau_{temp} = 50$; blue circles: $\tau_{temp} = 100$.)

The results of the comparison are reported in Fig. 2, for pEPs and pCEPs indexes. Here some observations are in order. First, we can easily observe how the performances on the first, and easiest, sequence *Hall&Monitor*, is independent on the specific values of the parameters. Conversely, for the last sequence *Snellen*, an appropriate choice of the parameters is crucial (better using small patches, regardless of the update frequency).

The first of the *Highway* sequences can be more appropriately handled with a slow rate of update coupled with small image patches. This is caused by the relevant velocity and size of the foreground objects (cars), that might be enrolled in the model when updating more frequently. Different properties characterize the second *Highway* sequence (spatially smaller moving objects), for which a higher update rate is convenient with small patches, while it is beneficial to update less when image patches have higher size.

In the case of *CaVignal*, where a subject stands still for more than the half of the frames before moving, a less frequent update, in general, does not allow the enrollment of the correct background atoms.

Finally, *Foliage* and *People&Foliage* sequences differ in the background dynamic, which is still in the first and moving in the second. For *Foliage* a small image patch is not an appropriate choice. The case of *People&Foliage* is somehow peculiar in that all the plots show a similar behavior, with the presence of peaks. This testifies the need for an appropriate synchronization of the model parameters.

We may conclude with a general consideration on the performances of our method on the SBI dataset, observing that the use of small side patches is often the best option to improve the quality of the obtained CB image.

4   Discussion

In this paper we discussed the applicability of our method for background modeling, BMTDL, to the Scene Background Initialization dataset. BMTDL is based on the use of dictionary learning and sparse coding to build dictionaries at a patch level to gather background information evolving over time. Our method was first proposed as a solution for foreground segmentation in video-surveillance, where the availability of long time observations favors the refinement of background models (dictionaries).

The SBI dataset provided for our method a challenging scenario, considering more general video analysis problems where modeling the scene background is an issue, and often characterized by a lower amount of video frames. The presence of foreground objects covering large portions of the image plane for significant temporal extents further increases the level of complexity.

We discussed how to use our method to obtain an explicit background image, which was not directly available in our approach (background models are dictionaries, collection of atoms). Then, we evaluated the obtained images with the scripts provided with the SBI dataset in order to quantify the goodness of our estimated images. We obtained very promising results, showing the capability of our method to appropriately model the scene background under general circumstances and, possibly, with an appropriate tuning of the parameters.

References

1. Stagliano, A., Noceti, N., Verri, A., Odone, F.: Online Space-Variant Background Modeling With Sparse Coding. IEEE Trans. on Image Processing **24**(8), 2415–2428 (2015)

2. Stauffer, C., Grimson, W.: Adaptive background mixture models for real-time tracking. In: CVPR, vol. 2 (1999)
3. Kim, K., Chalidabhongse, T., Harwood, D., Davis, L.: Real-time foreground-background segmentation using codebook model. Real-time imaging 11(3), 172–185 (2005)
4. Dikmen, M., Tsai, F., Huang, T.: Base selection in estimating sparse foreground in video. In: ICIP, pp. 3217–3220 (2009)
5. Dikmen, M., Huang, T.: Robust estimation of foreground in surveillance videos by sparse error estimation. In: ICPR, pp. 1–4 (2008)
6. Sivalingam, R., D'Souza, A., Bazakos, M., Miezianko, R., Morellas, V., Papanikolopoulos, N.: Dictionary learning for robust background modeling. In: ICRA, pp. 4234–4239 (2011)
7. Zhao, C., Wang, X., Kuen Cham, W.: Background Subtraction via Robust Dictionary Learning. Journ. on Image and Video Proc. (2011)
8. Aharon, M., Elad, M., Bruckstein, A.: K-SVD: An algorithm for designing overcomplete dictionaries for sparse representation. IEEE Trans. on Signal Processing 54(11), 4311–4322 (2006)
9. Stagliano, A., Chiusano, G., Basso, C., Santoro, M.: Learning adaptive and sparse representations of medical images. In: Menze, B., Langs, G., Tu, Z., Criminisi, A. (eds.) MICCAI 2010. LNCS, vol. 6533, pp. 130–140. Springer, Heidelberg (2011)
10. Ranzato, M., Huang, F., Boureau, Y., LeCun, Y.: Unsupervised learning of invariant feature hierarchies with applications to object recognition. In: CVPR (2007)
11. Basso, C., Santoro, M., Verri, A., Villa, S.: PADDLE: proximal algorithm for dual dictionaries learning. In: Honkela, T. (ed.) ICANN 2011, Part I. LNCS, vol. 6791, pp. 379–386. Springer, Heidelberg (2011)
12. Lee, H., Battle, A., Raina, R., Ng, A.: Effcient sparse coding algorithms. In: NIPS, pp. 801–808 (2006)
13. Lu, C., Shi, J., Jia, J.: Online robust dictionary learning. In: CVPR, pp. 415–422 (2013)
14. Tibshirani, R.: Regression shrinkage and selection via the lasso. J. of the Royal Statistical Society, Series B, 267–288 (1996)
15. Toyama, K., Krumm, J., Brumitt, B., Meyers, B.: Wallflower: Principles and practice of background maintenance. In: ICCV, vol. 1 (1999)
16. Barnich, O., Droogenbroeck, M.V.: Vibe: A universal background subtraction algorithm for video sequences. Trans. on IP 20(6) (2011)
17. Bouwmans, T.: Recent advanced statistical background modeling for foreground detection: A systematic survey. Recent Patents on Computer Science 4(3), 147–176 (2011)
18. Brutzer, S., Hoferlin, B., Heidemann, G.: Evaluation of background subtraction techniques for video surveillance. In: CVPR, pp. 1937–1944 (2011)
19. Alman, Y., Erturk, I.: A new color image quality measure based on YUV transformation and PSNR for human vision system. Turkish Jour. of Electrical Engineering & Computer Sciences 21(2), 603 (2013)
20. David, C., Gui, V.: Sparse coding and gaussian modeling of coefficients average for background subtraction. In: ISPA, pp. 230–235 (2013)
21. Maddalena, L., Petrosino, A.: Towards Benchmarking Scene Background Initialization. arXiv:1506.04051 (2015)

Comparison of Matrix Completion Algorithms for Background Initialization in Videos

Andrews Sobral[1,2]([✉]), Thierry Bouwmans[2], and El-hadi Zahzah[1]

[1] Lab. L3I, Université de La Rochelle, 17000 La Rochelle, France
[2] Lab. MIA, Université de La Rochelle, 17000 La Rochelle, France
andrews.sobral@univ-lr.fr

Abstract. Background model initialization is commonly the first step of the background subtraction process. In practice, several challenges appear and perturb this process such as dynamic background, bootstrapping, illumination changes, noise image, etc. In this context, this work aims to investigate the background model initialization as a matrix completion problem. Thus, we consider the image sequence (or video) as a partially observed matrix. First, a simple joint motion-detection and frame-selection operation is done. The redundant frames are eliminated, and the moving regions are represented by zeros in our observation matrix. The second stage involves evaluating nine popular matrix completion algorithms with the Scene Background Initialization (SBI) data set, and analyze them with respect to the background model challenges. The experimental results show the good performance of LRGeomCG [17] method over its direct competitors.

Keywords: Matrix completion · Background modeling · Background initialization

1 Introduction

Background subtraction (BS) is an important step in many computer vision systems to detect moving objects. This basic operation consists of separating the moving objects called "foreground" from the static information called "background" [2,16]. The BS is commonly used in video surveillance applications to detect persons, vehicles, animals, etc., before operating more complex processes for intrusion detection, tracking, people counting, etc. Typically the BS process includes the following steps: a) background model initialization, b) background model maintenance and c) foreground detection. With a focus on the step (a), the BS initialization consists in creating a background model. In a simple way, this can be done by setting manually a static image that represents the background. The main reason is that it is often assumed that initialization can be achieved by exploiting some clean frames at the beginning of the sequence. Naturally, this assumption is rarely encountered in real-life scenarios, because of continuous clutter presence. In addition, this procedure presents several limitations,

© Springer International Publishing Switzerland 2015
V. Murino et al. (Eds.): ICIAP 2015 Workshops, LNCS 9281, pp. 510–518, 2015.
DOI: 10.1007/978-3-319-23222-5_62

because it needs a fixed camera with constant illumination, and the background needs to be static (commonly in indoor environments), and having no moving object in the first frames. In practice, several challenges appear and perturb this process such as noise acquisition, bootstrapping, dynamic factors, etc [11].

The main challenge is to obtain a first background model when more than half of the video frames contain foreground objects. Some authors suggest the initialization of the background model by the arithmetic mean [9] (or weighted mean) of the pixels between successive images. Practically, some algorithms are: (1) batch ones using N training frames (consecutive or not), (2) incremental with known N or (3) progressive ones with unknown N as the process generates partial backgrounds and continues until a complete background image is obtained. Furthermore, initialization algorithms depend on the number of modes and the complexity of their background models. However, BS initialization has also been achieved by many other methodologies [2,11]. We can cite for example the computation of eigen values and eigen vectors [15], and the recent research on subspace estimation by sparse representation and rank minimization [3]. The background model is recovered by the low-rank subspace that can gradually change over time, while the moving foreground objects constitute the correlated sparse outliers.

In this paper, the initialization of the background model is addressed as a matrix completion problem. The matrix completion aims at recovering a low rank matrix from partial observations of its entries. The image sequence (or video) is represented as a partially observed real-valued matrix. Figure 1 shows the proposed framework. First, a simple joint motion-detection and frame-selection operation is done. The redundant frames are eliminated, and the moving regions are represented with zeros in our observation matrix. This operation is described in the Section 2. The second stage involves evaluating nine popular matrix completion algorithms with the Scene Background Initialization (SBI) data set [12] (see Section 3). This enables to analyze them with respect to the background model challenges. Finally, in Sections 4 and 5, the experimental results are shown as well as conclusions.

Throughout the paper, we use the following notations. Scalars are denoted by lowercase letters, e.g., x; vectors are denoted by lowercase boldface letters, e.g., $\boldsymbol{x}$; matrices by uppercase boldface, e.g., $\mathbf{X}$. In this paper, only real-valued data are considered.

2   Joint Motion Detection and Frame Selection

In order to reduce the number of redundant frames, a simple joint motion detection and frame selection operation is applied. First, the color images are converted into its gray-scale representation. So, let a sequence of N gray-scale images (frames) $\mathbf{I}_0 \ldots \mathbf{I}_N$ captured from a static camera, that is, $\mathbf{I} \in \mathbb{R}^{m \times n}$ where m and n denote the frame resolution (rows by columns). The difference between two consecutive frames (motion detection step) is calculated by:

$$\mathbf{D}_t = \sqrt{(\mathbf{I}_t - \mathbf{I}_{t-1})^2} \,|\, t = 1, \ldots, N \,, \tag{1}$$

Fig. 1. Block diagram of the proposed approach. Given an input image, a joint motion detection and frame selection operation is applied. Next, a matrix completion algorithm tries to recover the background model from the partially observed matrix. In this paper, the processes described here are conducted in a batch manner.

where $\mathbf{D}_t \in \mathbb{R}^{m \times n}$ denotes the matrix of pixel-wise L_2-norm differences from frame $t - 1$ to frame t. Next, the sum of all elements of $\mathbf{D}_t$, for $t = 1, \ldots, N$, is stored in a vector $\boldsymbol{d} \in \mathbb{R}^N$ whose t-th element is given by:

$$d_t = \sum_{i=1}^{m} \sum_{j=1}^{n} \mathbf{D}_t(i, j), \tag{2}$$

where $\mathbf{D}_t(i, j)$ is the matrix element located in the row $i \in [1, \ldots, m]$ and column $j \in [1, \ldots, n]$. Then, the vector $\boldsymbol{d}$ is normalized between 0 and 1 by:

$$\hat{\mathbf{d}} = \frac{d_t - d_{min}}{d_{max} - d_{min}} \mid_{t=1,\ldots,N}, \tag{3}$$

where d_{min} and d_{max} denote the minimum value and the maximum value of the vector $\boldsymbol{d}$. The frame selection step is done by calculating the derivative of $\hat{\mathbf{d}}$ by:

$$\boldsymbol{d}' = \frac{d}{dt}\hat{\mathbf{d}}, \tag{4}$$

Next, the vector $\boldsymbol{d}'$ is also normalized by Equation 3 and represented by $\hat{\mathbf{d}}'$. Finally, the index of the more relevant frames are given by thresholding $\hat{\mathbf{d}}'$:

$$\boldsymbol{y} = \begin{cases} 1 & \text{if } |\hat{\mathbf{d}}' - \hat{\mu}'| > \tau \\ 0 & \text{otherwise} \end{cases}, \tag{5}$$

where $\hat{\mu}'$ denotes the mean value of the vector $\hat{\mathbf{d}}'$, and $\tau \in [0, \ldots, 1]$ controls the threshold operator. In this paper, $R \leq N$ represent the set of all frames where $\boldsymbol{y} = 1$, and the parameter τ was chosen experimentally for each scene: $\tau = 0.025$ for HallAndMonitor, $\tau = 0.05$ for HighwayII, $\tau = 0.10$ for HighwayI, and $\tau = 0.15$ to all other scenes. Figure 3 illustrates our frame selection operation, in this example, with $\tau = 0.025$, only 92 relevant frames are selected from a total of 296 frames ($68, 92\%$ of reduction). In the next section, the matrix completion process is described.

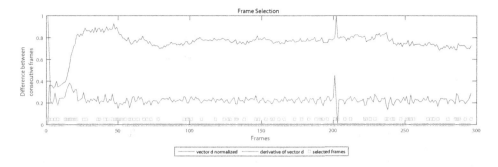

Fig. 2. Illustration of frame selection operation. The normalized vector (in blue) shows the difference between two consecutive frames. The derivative vector draw how much the normalized vector changes (in red), and then it is thresholded and the frames are selected (in orange).

3   Matrix Completion

As explained previously, the matrix completion aims to recover a low rank matrix from partial observations of its entries. Considering the general form of low rank matrix completion, the optimization problem is to find a matrix $\mathbf{L} \in \mathbb{R}^{n1 \times n2}$ with minimum rank that best approximates the matrix $\mathbf{A} \in \mathbb{R}^{n1 \times n2}$. Candès and Recht [6] show that this problem can be formulated as:

$$
\begin{aligned}
&\text{minimize} \quad rank(\mathbf{A}), \\
&\text{subject to} \quad P_\Omega(\mathbf{A}) = P_\Omega(\mathbf{L}),
\end{aligned}
\tag{6}
$$

where $rank(\mathbf{A})$ is equal to the rank of the matrix $\mathbf{A}$, and P_Ω denotes the sampling operator restricted to the elements of Ω (set of observed entries), i.e., $P_\Omega(\mathbf{A})$ has the same values as $\mathbf{A}$ for the entries in Ω and zero values for the entries outside Ω. Later, Candès and Recht [6] propose to replace the $rank(.)$ function with the nuclear norm $||\mathbf{A}||_* = \sum_{i=1}^{r} \sigma_i$ where $\sigma_1, \sigma_2, ..., \sigma_r$ are the singular values of $\mathbf{A}$ and r is the rank of $\mathbf{A}$. The nuclear norm make the problem tractable and Candès and Recht [6] have proved theoretically that the solution can be exactly recovered with a high probability. In addition, Cai et. al [4] propose an algorithm based on soft singular value thresholding (SVT) to solve this convex relaxation problem. However, in real world application the observed entries may be noisy. In order to make the Equation 6 robust to noise, Candès and Plan [5] propose a stable matrix completion approach. The equality constraint is replaced by $||P_\Omega(\mathbf{A} - \mathbf{L})||_F \leq \epsilon$, where $||.||_F$ denotes the Frobenious norm and ϵ is an upper bound on the noise level. Recently, several matrix completion algorithms have been proposed to deal with this challenge, and a complete review can be found in [21].

In this paper, we address the background model initialization as a matrix completion problem. Once frame selection process is done, the moving regions

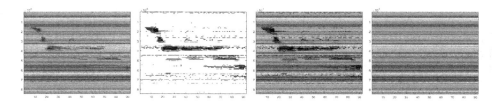

Fig. 3. Illustration of the matrix completion process. From the left to the right: a) the selected frames in vectorized form (our observation matrix), b) the moving regions are represented by non-observed entries (black pixels), c) the moving regions filled with zeros (modified version of the observation matrix), and d) the recovered matrix after the matrix completion process.

of the R selected frames are determined by:

$$\mathbf{M}_k(i,j) = \begin{cases} 1 & \text{if } 0.5(\mathbf{D}_k(i,j))^2 > \beta \\ 0 & \text{otherwise} \end{cases} \tag{7}$$

where $k \in R$, and β is the thresholding parameter (in this paper, $\beta = 1e^{-3}$ for all experiments). Next, the moving regions of each selected frame are filled with zeros by $\mathbf{I}_k \circ \overline{\mathbf{M}_k}$, where $\overline{\mathbf{M}_k}$ denotes the complement of $\mathbf{M}_k$, and $\circ$ denotes the element-wise multiplication of two matrices. For color images, each channel is processed individually, then they are vectorized into a partially observed real-valued matrix $\mathbf{A} = [vec(I_1) \dots vec(I_k)]$, where $\mathbf{A} \in \mathbb{R}^{n1 \times n2}$, $n1 = (m \times n)$, and $n2 = k$. Figure 3 illustrates our matrix completion process. It can be seen that the partially observed matrix can be recovered successfully even with the presence of many missing entries. So, let $\mathbf{L}$ the recovered matrix from the matrix completion process, the background model is estimated by calculating the average value of each row, resulting in a vector $l \in \mathbb{R}^{n1 \times 1}$, and then reshaped into a matrix $\mathbf{B} \in \mathbb{R}^{m \times n}$.

4   Experimental Results

In order to evaluate the proposed approach, nine matrix completion algorithms have been selected, and they are listed in Table 1. The algorithms were grouped in two categories, as well as its main techniques (following the same definition of Zhou et al. [21]).

In this paper, the Scene Background Initialization (SBI) data set was chosen for the background initialization task. The data set contains seven image sequences and corresponding ground truth backgrounds. It provides also MATLAB scripts for evaluating background initialization results in terms of eight metrics[1]. Figure 4 show the visual results for the top three best matrix completion algorithms, and Table 2 reports the quantitative results of each algorithm

---

[1] Please, refer to http://sbmi2015.na.icar.cnr.it/ for a complete description of each metric.

Table 1. List of low-rank matrix completion algorithms evaluated in this paper.

Category	Method	Main techniques	Reference
Rank Minimization	IALM	Augmented Lagrangian	[10, Linetal.(2010)]
	RMAMR	Augmented Lagrangian	[20, Yeetal.(2015)]
Matrix Factorization	SVP	Hard thresholding	[13, Mekaetal.(2009)]
	OptSpace	Grassmannian	[8, Keshavanetal.(2010)]
	LMaFit	Alternating	[19, Wenetal.(2012)]
	ScGrassMC	Grassmannian	[14, NgoandSaad(2012)]
	LRGeomCG	Riemannian	[17, Vandereycken(2013)]
	GROUSE	Online algorithm	[1, Balzanoetal.(2013)]
	OR1MP	Matching pursuit	[18, Wangetal.(2015)]

Fig. 4. Visual comparison for the background model initialization. From top to bottom: 1) example of input frame, 2) background model ground truth, and background model results for the top 3 best ranked MC algorithms: 3) LRGeomCG, 4) LMaFit, and 5) RMAMR.

over the data set[2]. The algorithms are ranked as follow: 1) for each algorithm we calculate its rank position for each metric, we call it as *metric rank* (i.e.

---

[2] Full experimental evaluation and related source code can be found in the main website: https://sites.google.com/site/mc4bmi/

Table 2. Quantitative results over SBI data set, and the global rank for each matrix completion method. The bold metric values show the best score for each metric. For each scene, the results are ordered by the rank column.

HallAndMonitor

Method	AGE↑	EP↑	pEP↑	CEP↑	pCEP↑	MSSSIM↑	PSNR↑	CQM↑	Scene Rank↑
LRGeomCG	2.0850	190	0.0022	0	0.0000	**0.9938**	**37.9811**	**46.5235**	1
RMAMR	2.0499	190	0.0022	0	0.0000	0.9938	37.9755	46.3222	2
LMaFit	2.0563	194	0.0023	0	0.0000	0.9938	37.8497	46.1503	3
ScGrassMC	2.0663	193	0.0023	0	0.0000	0.9937	37.9046	46.2638	4
GROUSE	2.2201	191	0.0023	0	0.0000	0.9923	37.5319	45.8704	5
ORLMP	2.3025	374	0.0044	0	0.0000	0.9926	34.6021	44.8283	6
IALM	3.6143	2336	0.0277	1190	0.0141	0.9627	30.5907	40.9249	7
SVP	4.1486	3230	0.0382	1574	0.0186	0.9474	28.2921	41.4396	8
OptSpace	6.7051	5860	0.0704	2694	0.0319	0.9299	26.1834	37.6430	9

Highway1

Method	AGE↑	EP↑	pEP↑	CEP↑	pCEP↑	MSSSIM↑	PSNR↑	CQM↑	Scene Rank↑
LRGeomCG	2.7715	192	0.0025	16	0.0002	0.9760	**35.8950**	56.6108	1
RMAMR	2.7601	193	0.0025	16	0.0002	0.9769	35.8899	**58.5283**	2
LMaFit	2.7761	195	0.0026	16	0.0002	0.9769	35.8638	58.6193	3
GROUSE	3.3206	1088	0.0142	593	0.0077	0.9714	33.4638	58.5694	4
ORLMP	6.1324	621	0.0081	138	0.0018	0.9614	30.3643	56.2661	5
IALM	5.9587	1202	0.0157	691	0.0090	0.9637	32.4145	57.9051	6
SVP	6.4223	1836	0.0239	837	0.0109	0.9507	29.5142	57.9214	7
OptSpace	14.7067	19754	0.2572	2530	0.0329	0.9095	27.0631	53.1073	8
OptSpace	14.7067	19754	0.2572	13930	0.1814	0.7957	23.8624	43.8143	9

Highway1

Method	AGE↑	EP↑	pEP↑	CEP↑	pCEP↑	MSSSIM↑	PSNR↑	CQM↑	Scene Rank↑
LRGeomCG	2.6840	268	0.0035	4	0.0001	0.9919	**35.7070**	46.1997	1
RMAMR	2.7603	271	0.0035	5	0.0001	0.9919	35.6695	**46.2002**	2
LMaFit	2.6919	275	0.0036	7	0.0001	0.9919	35.5752	46.0673	3
ScGrassMC	2.9622	360	0.0047	2	0.0000	0.9898	34.6783	46.1585	4
IALM	4.9361	306	0.0040	2	0.0000	0.9830	31.5964	46.1296	5
ORLMP	3.2010	843	0.0110	102	0.0013	0.9888	32.2682	42.0740	6
SVP	4.7779	945	0.0123	34	0.0004	0.9590	31.6017	41.8817	7
GROUSE	4.3665	1751	0.0228	700	0.0091	0.9756	31.5642	45.6062	8
OptSpace	8.6231	4722	0.0615	1307	0.0170	0.9279	25.6722	36.7406	9

CaVignal

Method	AGE↑	EP↑	pEP↑	CEP↑	pCEP↑	MSSSIM↑	PSNR↑	CQM↑	Scene Rank↑
LMaFit	11.9504	3788	0.1393	2700	0.0993	0.9027	**24.5417**	39.8279	1
LRGeomCG	11.9506	3789	0.1393	2700	0.0993	0.9096	24.3415	39.5379	2
RMAMR	12.0081	3817	0.1403	2715	0.0998	0.9027	24.3147	39.8083	3
GROUSE	12.8187	3654	0.1892	2205	0.0811	0.9846	23.4862	38.8759	4
ScGrassMC	12.3375	4084	0.1501	2942	0.1082	0.9911	23.9011	39.8237	5
IALM	12.2618	4764	0.1751	3531	0.1298	0.8779	23.7957	**40.6135**	6
SVP	12.3567	4455	0.1638	3596	0.1234	0.8855	23.7716	39.7716	7
SVP	13.2230	5628	0.2069	3982	0.1464	0.8855	23.3352	38.8300	8
OptSpace	14.1744	6176	0.2271	4214	0.1549	0.8927	23.0940	39.8862	9

Foliage

Method	AGE↑	EP↑	pEP↑	CEP↑	pCEP↑	MSSSIM↑	PSNR↑	CQM↑	Scene Rank↑
GROUSE	26.4086	17640	0.6194	13271	0.4608	0.8957	18.4042	**33.4059**	1
LRGeomCG	26.4008	18074	0.6276	13459	0.4673	**0.8970**	**18.4522**	33.2733	2
LMaFit	26.4088	18070	0.6274	13442	0.4667	0.8970	18.4490	33.2663	3
RMAMR	26.5144	18148	0.6301	13548	0.4704	0.8965	18.4160	33.2392	4
ScGrassMC	29.2600	19189	0.6660	13585	0.5342	0.6845	17.4636	33.2173	5
ORLMP	31.3878	19004	0.6580	15257	0.5298	0.6321	16.7364	33.0468	6
OptSpace	33.1405	19155	0.6651	15234	0.5290	0.6566	16.2368	31.4830	7
IALM	31.6036	19451	0.6754	14986	0.5203	0.7473	16.6016	31.0114	8
SVP	35.3522	19469	0.6760	16003	0.5557	0.7556	16.5496	33.1273	9

PeopleAndFoliage

Method	AGE↑	EP↑	pEP↑	CEP↑	pCEP↑	MSSSIM↑	PSNR↑	CQM↑	Scene Rank↑
LRGeomCG	38.7497	64150	0.8353	59210	0.7710	**0.8505**	**15.1638**	27.6167	1
OptSpace	41.8200	60020	0.7815	53183	0.6925	0.7535	14.1746	25.9930	2
IALM	42.9444	63161	0.8224	58560	0.7625	0.7951	14.1751	**27.8900**	3
GROUSE	40.3918	63856	0.8315	57097	0.7435	0.8130	14.6485	26.6857	4
ORLMP	42.5560	62335	0.8117	56809	0.7397	0.7961	14.0424	26.7915	5
ScGrassMC	39.6945	64076	0.8343	58991	0.7681	0.8472	14.9449	27.6499	6
LMaFit	38.7738	64155	0.8354	59220	0.7711	0.8501	15.1507	27.6143	7
RMAMR	38.8234	64169	0.8356	59275	0.7716	0.8502	15.1484	27.5987	8
SVP	45.0733	63916	0.8322	58603	0.7657	0.7644	13.6320	27.0416	9

Snellen

Method	AGE↑	EP↑	pEP↑	CEP↑	pCEP↑	MSSSIM↑	PSNR↑	CQM↑	Scene Rank↑
ScGrassMC	43.8219	17638	0.6602	16070	0.7750	0.8469	14.3702	**37.6651**	1
LRGeomCG	41.6853	18621	0.6980	17379	0.6381	0.8607	14.8166	37.4253	2
OptSpace	49.2605	16619	0.6016	15292	0.7375	0.7419	12.8053	29.4492	3
LMaFit	41.6688	18623	0.6981	17387	0.6365	**0.8609**	**14.8209**	37.4234	4
GROUSE	43.0691	18629	0.8984	17408	0.8393	0.8462	14.8421	37.5570	5
IALM	46.0976	16433	0.6989	17084	0.8239	0.8330	14.0292	37.1551	6
SVP	47.7772	16463	0.6992	17692	0.7504	0.7504	13.1692	36.2566	7
SVP	54.6990	17649	0.6511	16169	0.7607	0.7607	12.5506	35.6896	8
RMAMR	42.0476	18625	0.6982	17395	0.8369	0.8600	14.7872	37.3821	9

Global rank over all scenes

Method	Global rank↑
LRGeomCG	1
LMaFit	2
RMAMR	3
ScGrassMC	4
GROUSE	5
IALM	6
ORLMP	7
OptSpace	8
SVP	9

RMAMR have the first position for the AGE metric in the HallAndMonitor scene), next, 2) we sum the rank position value of each algorithm over the eight metrics, and finally, 3) we calculate the rank position over the sum, and we call it as *scene rank*. For the Global Rank, first we sum the scene rank for each MC algorithm, then we calculate its rank position over the sum. As we can see, the experimental results show the good performance of LRGeomCG [17] method over its direct competitors. Furthermore, in most cases the matrix completion algorithms outperform the traditional approaches such as Mean [9], Median [7] and MoG [22] as can be seen in the full experimental evaluation available at https://sites.google.com/site/mc4bmi/.

5 Conclusion

In this paper, we have evaluated nine recent matrix completion algorithms for the background initialization problem. Given a sequence of images, the key idea is to eliminate the redundant frames, and consider its moving regions as non-observed values. This approach results in a matrix completion problem, and the background model can be recovered even with the presence of missing entries. The experimental results on the SBI data set shows the comparative evaluation of these recent methods, and highlights the good performance of LRGeomCG [17] method over its direct competitors. Finally, MC shows a nice potential for background modeling initialization in video surveillance. Future research may concern to evaluate incremental and real-time approaches of matrix completion in streaming videos.

References

1. Balzano, L., Wright, S.J.: On GROUSE and incremental SVD. In: CAMSAP 2013, pp. 1–4 (2013). http://dx.doi.org/10.1109/CAMSAP.2013.6713992
2. Bouwmans, T.: Traditional and recent approaches in background modeling for foreground detection: An overview. Computer Science Review (2014)
3. Bouwmans, T., Zahzah, E.: Robust PCA via principal component pursuit: a review for a comparative evaluation in video surveillance. In: Special Isssue on Background Models Challenge, Computer Vision and Image Understanding. vol. 122, pp. 22–34, May 2014
4. Cai, J.F., Candès, E.J., Shen, Z.: A singular value thresholding algorithm for matrix completion. SIAM J. on Optimization **20**(4), 1956–1982 (2010)
5. Candès, E.J., Plan, Y.: Matrix completion with noise. CoRR abs/0903.3131 (2009)
6. Candès, E.J., Recht, B.: Exact matrix completion via convex optimization. CoRR abs/0805.4471 (2008). http://arxiv.org/abs/0805.4471
7. Cucchiara, R., Grana, C., Piccardi, M., Prati, A.: Detecting objects, shadows and ghosts in video streams by exploiting color and motion information. In: ICIAP 2001, pp. 360–365, September 2001
8. Keshavan, R.H., Montanari, A., Oh, S.: Matrix completion from noisy entries. The Journal of Machine Learning Research **99**, 2057–2078 (2010)
9. Lai, A.H.S., Yung, N.H.C.: A fast and accurate scoreboard algorithm for estimating stationary backgrounds in an image sequence. In: IEEE SCS 1998, pp. 241–244 (1998)

10. Lin, Z., Chen, M., Ma, Y.: The Augmented Lagrange Multiplier Method for Exact Recovery of Corrupted Low-Rank Matrices. Mathematical Programming (2010)
11. Maddalena, L., Petrosino, A.: Background model initialization for static cameras. In: Background Modeling and Foreground Detection for Video Surveillance. CRC Press, Taylor and Francis Group (2014)
12. Maddalena, L., Petrosino, A.: Towards benchmarking scene background initialization. CoRR abs/1506.04051 (2015). http://arxiv.org/abs/1506.04051
13. Meka, R., Jain, P., Dhillon, I.S.: Guaranteed rank minimization via singular value projection. CoRR abs/0909.5457 (2009)
14. Ngo, T., Saad, Y.: Scaled gradients on grassmann manifolds for matrix completion. Advances in Neural Information Processing Systems 25, 1412–1420 (2012)
15. Oliver, N.M., Rosario, B., Pentland, A.P.: A bayesian computer vision system for modeling human interactions. IEEE PAMI 22(8), 831–843 (2000)
16. Sobral, A., Vacavant, A.: A comprehensive review of background subtraction algorithms evaluated with synthetic and real videos. CVIU 122, 4–21 (2014). http://www.sciencedirect.com/science/article/pii/S1077314213002361
17. Vandereycken, B.: Low-rank matrix completion by Riemannian optimization. SIAM Journal on Optimization 23(2), 1214–1236 (2013)
18. Wang, Z., Lai, M., Lu, Z., Fan, W., Davulcu, H., Ye, J.: Orthogonal rank-one matrix pursuit for low rank matrix completion. SIAM J. Scientific Computing 37(1) (2015). http://dx.doi.org/10.1137/130934271
19. Wen, Z., Yin, W., Zhang, Y.: Solving a low-rank factorization model for matrix completion by a nonlinear successive over-relaxation algorithm. Mathematical Programming Computation 4(4), 333–361 (2012). http://dx.doi.org/10.1007/s12532-012-0044-1
20. Ye, X., Yang, J., Sun, X., Li, K., Hou, C., Wang, Y.: Foreground-background separation from video clips via motion-assisted matrix restoration. IEEE T-CSVT PP(99), 1 (2015)
21. Zhou, X., Yang, C., Zhao, H., Yu, W.: Low-rank modeling and its applications in image analysis. ACM Computing Surveys (CSUR) 47(2), 36 (2014)
22. Zivkovic, Z.: Improved adaptive gaussian mixture model for background subtraction. In: ICPR 2004, vol. 2, pp. 28–31, Auguet 2004

Real-Time Implementation of Background Modelling Algorithms in FPGA Devices

Tomasz Kryjak$^{(\boxtimes)}$ and Marek Gorgon

AGH University of Science and Technology,
Al. Mickiewicza 30, 30-059 Krakow, Poland
{tomasz.kryjak,mago}@agh.edu.pl

Abstract. The article discusses the possibilities of hardware implementation of foreground object segmentation and background modelling algorithms in FPGA. The potential benefits, as well as challenges and problems associated with porting algorithms from general-purpose processors (CPU) to reconfigurable logic (FPGA) are presented. Also several hardware implementation of well known method are reviewed: GMM, Codebook, Clustering, ViBE and PBAS.The last algorithm was also evaluated on the SBI dataset.

Keywords: Real-time image processing · Embedded systems · Smart cameras · Background modelling · Foreground object segmentation

1 Introduction

Foreground object segmentation and background modelling is one of the fundamental steps in a number of automatic video stream analysis system. This involves human detection, tracking and action recognition, abandoned or stolen object detection (advanced video surveillance systems) and vehicle traffic monitoring (video based ITS). The method is conceptually very simple. Objects are detected by comparing the current frame and the background representation (background model). Sometimes, the algorithms are supported by moving object detection e.g. using optical flow.

However, due to several factors: camera jitter, variable lighting conditions (slow or rapid changes), objects to background similarity, movement of background object (e.g. flowing water), stopped objects (pedestrian waiting for green traffic light) and objects which started to move (a car left a parking lot) the issue is not easy. A very good and extensive review of most common approach can be found in the work by Thierry Bouwmans [4].

Unfortunately, usually the methods which allow to obtain object mask of better quality are also computationally complex. Furthermore, segmentation is only one of the first stages of a vision system. In recent years, the dynamic development of so-called smart cameras can be observed. In this solution, the image processing, analysis and recognition is performed immediately after acquisition. This allows for the computation decentralization and avoid image quality deterioration due to compression. Such solutions are offered by leading manufacturers of video surveillance cameras Bosch, Ganz, Pelco.

© Springer International Publishing Switzerland 2015
V. Murino et al. (Eds.): ICIAP 2015 Workshops, LNCS 9281, pp. 519–526, 2015.
DOI: 10.1007/978-3-319-23222-5_63

1.1 FPGA Devices

When designing a smart camera, parameters like energy efficiency (GOPS/W, GFLOPS/W), as well as computation parallelisation and acceleration are very important. In systems that require image processing in real time and high quality foreground obejct masks the GPP implementation may not meet expectations due to insufficient performance computing. Therefore, FPGA (Field Programmable Gate Arrays) are a very interesting computing platform for these kind of applications. FPGA are build of many simple logic elements (flip-flops, LUTs and multiplexers). They also include internal memory resources, DSP modules and advanced I/O capabilities (with support for different standards). What's more, the devices can be reconfigured (by downloading a bitstream file) many times, even after installation in the target system. The FPGAs are used in all kinds of vision systems (introduction in the book by Bailey [2]), wire and wireless telecommunication networks, as well as automotive, defence and space industries.

FPGAs, unlike other platforms on which parallel implementation of algorithms is possible e.g. multi-core CPUs, DSPs or GPUs, provide an almost full flexibility when designing the system architecture. Moreover, the filed reprogrammability allows to preform algorithms update (firmware updates). This is not possible in ASIC (Application Specific Integrated Circuit) or ASSP (Application Specific Standard Product) based solutions. It is also worth to mention, that in recent years heterogeneous SoC (System on Chip) devices have been proposed. For example, the Zynq from Xilinx combines reconfigurable resources and an efficient dual-core ARM processor. This allows for easy hardware-software co-design.

1.2 FPGA Logic Design Methodology

The first stage always involves the analysis of the computational task, as well as an attempt to propose a parallelisation. In the fine-grain FPGA logic all types of parallelism according to Flynn's classification (SISD, SIMD, MISD, MIMD) can by realised. In the second step, the so-called software model is implemented. This is an software application, which performs calculations in the same way as the hardware (i.e. bit accurate model). At this point it is worth to discuss some limitations of FPGAs. First of all, fixed-point arithmetic is preferred[1]. Secondly, the typical operating frequency reaches 200-300 MHz. This is enough for VGA/PAL and HD processing, where the so-called pixel clock is respectively 25-27 and 150 MHz, but almost only when data is processed in pipeline. A serious challenge are algorithms, which require image content dependent data access (e.g. region growing segmentation) or storage of large amount of data (need for external RAM access).

For logic design the so-called hardware description languages (HDL) are used. The two most common are Verilog and VHDL. They provide full control of the

---

[1] In recently presented FPGAs from Altera hardware support for single precision floating arithmetic is provided.

created system. Other solutions involve high level synthesis (HLS) tools, which allows C/C++ to HDL code conversion and extensions to packages like Matlab (HDL Coder, System Generator) or LabView.

The designed system is tested in two stages. First simulations are performed. The aim is to achieve full compliance with the described earlier software model. Secondly, the system is evaluated in hardware i.e. on an FPGA development board with video stream input/output.

At this stage, several additional issues not directly related to the algorithm implementation, but important for the functionality of the entire video system should be considered. Firstly, it is necessary to communicate with the video stream source. For prototyping a good solution is HDMI, which is very intuitive and easy to use.

Second, despite the significant increase of FPGA memory resource, their size is too small to store a full image frame in STD resolution. Therefore, larger chunks of data i.e. background model or previous frame should be saved in external memory (usually DDR). These have large capacities, but the maximum data transfer rate is limited.

The third element is the broadly understood results visualisation and transfer. In the simplest case, they are displayed on an LCD screen. However, it possible to send them in the form of meta-data with a compressed video stream.

2   Background Modelling Implemented in FPGA

With the development od FPGAs, they became an interesting platform for vision systems implementation. The firsts designs were very simple image processors like: histogram computation, convolutional or median filters or colourspace conversions. Nowadays, it is possible to carry out complex operation like object classification (HOG+SVM, Haar + AdaBoost) or tracking.

The first works related to background modelling date back to year 2005. In the article by Appiah et al. [1] an FPGA implementation of a Gaussian Mixture Models (GMM) based method was descried. For each pixel, K background variants were stored, each composed of a mean and a weight. In Gorgon et al. [7] an approach based on average brightness calculation and periodic re-scaling mechanism was proposed. Real-time processing for a 768×576 pixels @ 25 fps video stream was reported.

Most publications on this subject appeared in the last four years. Definitely worth mention are:

- Hardware implementation of the GMM algorithm in Genovese and Napoli [6] – real-time image processing of 1280×720 pixels @ 20 fps video stream.
- FPGA implementation of Horprasert method in Gomez et al. [15] – real-time image processing of 1024×1024 @ 32.8 fps video stream.
- FPGA implementation of Codebook method in Gomez et al. [16] – real-time image processing of 768×576 @ 60 fps video stream.

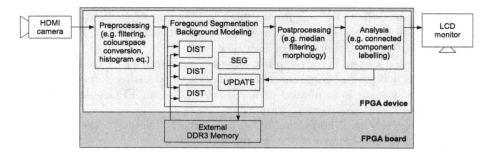

Fig. 1. Scheme of an FPGA-based system for background modelling and foreground segmentation.

2.1   The General Scheme

FPGA implementation of background modelling methods involves several issues. Firstly, most of the method that perform well in the rankings accepted by the community (e.g. *changedetection.net*) are multivariate i.e. the background model for a given pixel has more than one value. Examples are: GMM, Clustering, Codebook, ViBE, PBAS, as well as recent proposals like FTSG (Flux Tensor with Split Gaussian models). Such solutions are quite straightforward to parallelise, as shown in Fig. 1 – modules DIST.

Secondly, as the fixed point arithmetic is preferred in FPGA, the research should involve representation impact analysis (i.g. a comparison with the floating point version). Thirdly, modern FPGAs do not have enough internal memory resources to store a complex background model. For a 'typical" algorithm, for each pixel from the video stream, the corresponding model should be provided and after update saved back in RAM. On the VC707 platform from Xilinx (used by the Authors of this paper) for a video stream 720× 576 @ 50 fps the maximal transfer rate is 2048 bits per pixel clock period (at 27 MHz). For such algorithms as GMM this is satisfactory, but for example in case of ViBE or PBAS it forces some limitations.

2.2   Implemented Algorithms

We designed hardware modules of three foreground object segmentation algorithms: Clustering [10], ViBE [9], [11] and PBAS [13], [12].

Clustering. The Clustering algorithm was described in Butler et al. [5] and is a simplification of GMM. The background model for a single pixel consists of K variants, each formed by a mean and weight. The lack of the standard deviation or covariance results in a compact representation and simpler calculations.

The main objective of the research described in Kryjak et al. [10] was to show that in a modern FPGA it is possible to implement a complex background modelling algorithm and obtain real-time processing for a 1920 × 1080 @ 60 fps video stream [2]. Several improvements and modification were proposed to the algorithm, among others the use of CIE Lab colourspace and the use of edges in the background model. Furthermore, during segmentation difference in brightness, colour and texture (Normalised Gradient Difference) was used. The module was evaluated on the Wallflower dataset. The results were comparable to the state of the art (in year 2012). The vision system was implemented on the Xilinx ML605 FPGA board with Virtex 6 device. The model for a single pixel had 141 bits (3 variants, in each CIE Lab pixel (32 bits), edge information (9 bits) and weight (6 bits)) and the bandwidth to external RAM was 33459 Mb/s (HD resolution).

ViBE. The ViBE (Visual Background Extractor) algorithm was proposed in 2009 by O. Barnich and M. Van Droogenbroeck [3]. It is a hybrid method based on sample buffer (non recursive) and recursive approach. The background model consists of $N = 20$ pixel samples (greyscale or colour). The foreground - background classification is based on calculating the distance (e.g. Euclidean) between the current pixel and all samples. If at least $\#_{min}$ are smaller than a given threshold, than the pixel is considered as background.

The other features of the algorithm are:

- background model initialization based on a single frame – the N samples buffer is filled with values randomly selected from a 3×3 context,
- conservative update policy (updated are only pixels regarded as background),
- random factors in the update process (the update id performed with some probability, the sample to modify is selected randomly),
- neighbourhood update procedure, in order to eliminate "ghost" classification errors.

Hardware implementation of the ViBE algorithm on the ML 605 platform is described in Kryjak et al. [9]. The general scheme is similar to that presented in Fig. 1. Real-time processing of 640×480 @ 60 fps video stream was obtained. The model for a single pixel had 460 bits (20×23bits) and the bandwidth to external RAM was 13645 Mb/s.

An extended version of this module was described in Kryjak et al. [11]. There, the algorithm was adapted to a moving camera scenario. Camera displacement between two consecutive frames estimation was implemented. It was based on 3×3, SAD, block matching approach. The displacement was not computed for each pixel (i.e. dense optical flow), but only for certain points selected in 32×32 blocks using Harris corner detection. Then, the final displacement was defined as the median values from particular blocks. The system was implemented on the VC707 board with Virtex 7 FPGA from Xilinx. Real-time image processing was obtained for a 720×576 @ 50 fps video stream. It is worth noting, the solution is characterized by only 4 W power dissipation.

---

[2] When the module was designed, i.e. in 2012, no other hardware implementation able to process HD video stream was reported.

PBAS. The PBAS (Pixel-Based Adaptive Segmenter) described in Hofmann et al. [8] is based on ViBE. Two additional parameters were added: R (variable similarity threshold) and T (variable update rate). Both are updated using properties of the model for a given location. This improves the segmentation performance, but increases the memory requirements (additional for each pixel location R, T and some auxiliary data has to be stored).

FPGA implementation of the PBAS algorithm was described in Kryjak et al. [13]. Because of limited transfer rate to external RAM, the number of samples had to be reduced from 35 proposed by the authors of the algorithm to 19. This resulted in slight deterioration of segmentation performance (evaluation on the *changedetection.net* dataset). Finally, real-time image processing for a 720×576 @ 50 fps video stream was obtained. It is also worth to emphasize, that the model for a single pixel had the size of 1008 bits ($3 \times (19 \times 16 \text{bits} + 2 \times 16 \text{bits})$) – 19 samples containing 8-bit colour component and 8-bit minimum distance value, parameters R and T (16 bits), all these for three components). Therefore, the bandwidth to external RAM was 39867 Mb/s. The measured power dissipation was less than 7 W.

In Kryjak et al. [12] the PBAS algorithm was supported with feedback from object analysis module. It was designed to improve segmentation results is scenarios, where it is necessary to distinguish between real objects, which have stopped (e.g. abandoned luggage) and so-called "ghosts". During experiments the *Intermittent Object Motion* dataset from *changedetection.net* was used. Two features were utilized: motion (determined by consecutive frames differencing) and edges (computed for the foreground, background and object mask). The first was used to determine whether the object is not moving. The second, to distinguish between stooped objects (mask edges are similar to current frame edges) and ghost (mask edges are similar to background model edges). It is worth noting, that this rather simple approach requires connected component labelling i.e. transition from individual pixel analysis to objects (connected pixel group) analysis. In a software implementation this step is quite straightforward, however in a pipeline vision systems it is quite challenging. The system was implemented on the VC707 platform with Virtex 7 FPGA. Real-time image processing for a 720×576 @ 50 fps video stream was obtained.

2.3   Evaluation on the SBI Dataset

The SBI (Scene Background Initialization) dataset [14] was prepared for the Scene Background Modeling and Initialization Workshop. In consists of seven video sequences and 7 reference backgrounds. In addition 8 metrics are proposed to assess the initialization process. Detailed information is available on the http://sbmi2015.na.icar.cnr.it website.

After initial analysis of the sequences, from the 3 methods: Clustering, ViBE and PBAS, the last was chosen for evaluation mainly due to the implemented feedback from the object analysis module. However, it should be noted that PBAS is not a "typical" background initialisation method. The initial model is obtained using the first frame from the sequence, which for the rather short

Table 1. Result of the PBAS FPGA implementaion on the SBI dataset

Sequence	AGE	EPs	pEPs	CEPs	pCEPS	MSSSIM	PSNR	CQM
HallAndMonitor	4.5412	1962	0.0232	11	0.0001	0.9874	24.9338	31.5584
HighwayI	10.3774	10596	0.1380	7614	0.0991	0.7204	20.7564	28.1407
HighwayII	4.7919	2976	0.0388	440	0.0057	0.9490	24.6061	30.7008
CaVignal	15.1816	1682	0.0618	19	0.0007	0.9301	18.6021	27.6635
Foliage	21.3365	7063	0.2452	2676	0.0929	0.8328	17.6953	25.8441
PeopleAndFoliage	19.1997	15779	0.2055	4990	0.0650	0.8848	19.0184	26.1430
Snellen	62.3326	16310	0.7866	14306	0.6899	0.3721	10.8639	22.5839

test sequences has major impact on the experiment. Moreover, no explicit representation of the background model is provided. It consists of randomly located samples. Thus, to create a model in the form of an "image" for example the median value from the buffer should be selected. Furthermore, the calculations are independent for RGB components, which result in small errors in the background image. The obtained results are summarized in the Tab. 1.

For two sequences *CaVignal* and *HallAndMonitor* the obtained results are quite correct. The used edge analysis approach allowed to eliminate ghosts. For *HighwayII* the results are partially correct. In regions, where the movement is not very intensive, the ghosts were eliminated. However, some errors due to the median based background image "extraction" occur.

For other sequences, due to constantly moving objects (foliage or cars) it is impossible to eliminate the ghosts with the implemented approach. This issue should be further investigated.

3 Summary

In this paper examples of FPGA based hardware implementations of foreground segmentation and background modelling algorithms were presented. The general concept and design approach, as well as three modules: Clustering, ViBE and PBAS were discussed. The last was also evaluated on the SBI dataset. Using FPGA devices it is possible to obtain real-time image processing for VGA/PAL or even HD video stream resolution. The proposed modules could be used in low-power smart cameras.

Acknowledgments. The work presented in this paper was supported by AGH University of Science and Technology projects number 15.11.120.476 (first author) and 11.11.120.612 (second author).

References

1. Appiah, K., Hunter, A.: A single-chip FPGA implementation of real-time adaptive background model. In: Proceedings of the IEEE International Conference on Field-Programmable Technology, pp. 95–102 (2005)
2. Bailey, D.G.: Design for embedded image processing on FPGAs, John Wiley & Sons (2011)

3. Barnich, O., Van Droogenbroeck, M.: ViBE: A Universal Background Subtraction Algorithm for Video Sequences. IEEE Transactions on Image Processing **20**(6), 1709–1724 (2011)
4. Bouwmans, T.: Traditional and recent approaches in background modeling for foreground detection: An overview. Computer Science Review **1112**, 31–66 (2014)
5. Butler, D., Sridharan, S., Bove Jr, V.M.: Real-time adaptive background segmentation. In: Proceedings of the IEEE International Conference on Acoustics, Speech, and Signal Processing (ICASSP), pp. 349–352 (2003)
6. Genovese, M., Napoli, E.: FPGA-based architecture for real time segmentation and denoising of HD video. Journal of Real-Time Image Processing **8**(4), 389–401 (2013)
7. Gorgon, M., Pawlik, P., Jablonski, M., Przybylo, J.: FPGA-based road traffic videodetector. In: 10th Euromicro Conference on Digital System Design Architectures, Methods and Tools, pp. 412–419 (2007)
8. Hofmann, M., Tiefenbacher, P., Rigoll, G.: Background segmentation with feedback: the pixel-based adaptive segmenter. In: IEEE Computer Society Conference on Computer Vision and Pattern Recognition Workshops (CVPRW), pp. 38–43 (2012)
9. Kryjak, T., Gorgon, M.: Real-time implementation of the ViBe foreground object segmentation algorithm. In: Federated Conference on Computer Science and Information Systems (FedCSIS), pp 591–596 (2013)
10. Kryjak, T., Komorkiewicz, M., Gorgon, M.: Real-time background generation and foreground object segmentation for high defnition colour video stream in FPGA device. Journal of Real-Time Image Processing **9**(1), 61–77 (2014)
11. Kryjak, T., Gorgon, M.: Real-time implementation of foreground object detection from a moving camera using ViBE algorithm. Computer Science and Information Systems **11**(4), 1617–1637 (2014)
12. Kryjak, T., Komorkiewicz, M., Gorgon, M.: Real-time foreground object detection combining the PBAS background modelling algorithm and feedback from scene analysis module. International Journal of Electronics and Telecommunications **60**(1), 61–72 (2014)
13. Kryjak, T., Komorkiewicz, M., Gorgon, M.: Hardware implementation of the PBAS foreground detection method in FPGA. In: Proceedings of the 20th International ConferenceMixed Design of Integrated Circuits and Systems (MIXDES), pp. 479–484 (2013)
14. Maddalena, L., Petrosino, A.: Towards Benchmarking Scene Background Initialization. arXiv:1506.04051 (publicly avaliable at http://arxiv.org/abs/1506.04051) (2015)
15. Rodriguez-Gomez, R., Fernandez-Sanchez, E.J., Diaz, J., Ros, E.: FPGA Implementation for Real-Time Background Subtraction Based on Horprasert Model. Sensors **12**(1), 585–611 (2012)
16. Rodriguez-Gomez, R., Fernandez-Sanchez, E.J., Diaz, J., Ros, E.: Codebook hardware implementation on FPGA for background subtraction. Journal of Real-Time Image Processing **10**(1), 43–57 (2015)

A Perfect Estimation of a Background Image Does Not Lead to a Perfect Background Subtraction: Analysis of the Upper Bound on the Performance

Sébastien Piérard$^{(\boxtimes)}$ and Marc Van Droogenbroeck

INTELSIG Laboratory, Department of Electrical Engineering
and Computer Science, University of Liège, Liège, Belgium
{Sebastien.Pierard,M.VanDroogenbroeck}@ulg.ac.be

Abstract. The quest for the "best" background subtraction technique is ongoing. Despite that a considerable effort has been undertaken to develop flexible and efficient methods, some elementary questions are still unanswered. One of them is the existence of an intrinsic upper bound to the performance. In fact, data are affected by noise, and therefore it is illusory to believe that it is possible to achieve a perfect segmentation. This paper aims at exploring some intrinsic limitations of the principle of background subtraction. The purpose consists in studying the impact of several limiting factors separately. One of our conclusions is that even if an algorithm would be able to calculate a perfect background image, it is not sufficient to achieve a perfect segmentation with background subtraction, due to other intrinsic limitations.

1 Introduction

The background subtraction (BGS) is a well studied problem [2,10] for which, despite the impressive amount of methods proposed in the literature so far, no satisfactory technique has been found yet (for all cases) [6,7]. This paper discusses the limits of pixel-based BGS methods. They aim at classifying, for each frame of a video sequence, pixels in the foreground (FG) or background (BG) classes by performing a motion analysis. It is an online unsupervised one-class classification problem, as the goal is to learn the distribution of the background colors on-the-fly, in an unsupervised way (no sample with known label FG/BG being provided *a priori*), and to classify new colors based on the representation (named the *model*) of this sole BG class. Note that even if other types of features are sometimes considered (*e.g. local binary patterns* in [9], *local binary similarity patterns* in [13], or gradients [8]), we limit the scope of this paper to colors.

Each classification problem has an intrinsic performance limit; this holds also for background subtraction. Indeed, a perfect classifier can only be theoretically obtained when the distributions of the samples (the colors in the case studied in this paper) of the two classes have disjoint supports. For all other cases, the class overlapping introduces an upper limit to the performance. In the context

© Springer International Publishing Switzerland 2015
V. Murino et al. (Eds.): ICIAP 2015 Workshops, LNCS 9281, pp. 527–534, 2015.
DOI: 10.1007/978-3-319-23222-5_64

of BGS, a class overlapping originates from similar colors in the foreground and background. This can result, for example, from the noise in the images (this noise coming from the sensor or from the compression of the video stream), varying lighting conditions, shadows, or camouflage. We are interested in working out whether, aside from the theoretical limit, there is some room left for improving the performance of BGS techniques, or if the limit has already been reached. In the case of BGS, the performance limit also originates from the way the decisions are taken (the per-pixel decisions have to be fast in order to work in real time, and memory constraints prevent from storing a lot of information per pixel). This should also be considered when we discuss the performance limit.

The outline of this paper is as follows. Section 2 presents how the decisions are traditionally taken in BGS algorithms. Dividing the processing pipeline into the initialization and updating parts on the one hand, and the segmentation part on the other hand, allows us to present results independent of any choice for a particular BGS algorithm. As the initialization and updating parts essentially aim at estimating the background image (more information about this topic can be found in the SBMI workshop [11]), we derive a performance bound that depends on the amount of noise affecting this image (that is the model). Our approach to compute this bound is presented in Section 3. Bounds computed for a few common decision rules (the segmentation processes) are presented and discussed in Section 4. In addition, we show how these bounds vary with respect to the main characteristics of the video sequences (amount of noise, quantity and magnitude of shadows, proportion of foreground). Finally, the conclusion is given in Section 5. Our results establish that being able to compute a perfect background image does not really help to raise the performance limit, due to the other intrinsic bottlenecks of the BGS problem (even if this is important for other applications such as video inpainting or computational photography).

2   The Traditional Processing Pipeline of BGS Algorithms

The Segmentation Process. Even if online learning, unsupervised learning, and one-class classification are studied by the machine learning community, most of the BGS algorithms do not leverage machine learning techniques. The trend is to directly threshold the distances between colors stored in the model, as in a nearest neighbors analysis, or to test if the observed color follows the distribution encoded in the model. The difference originates from the constraints of the BGS: the per-pixel classifiers have to run in real time with low memory, and to adapt themselves with only a few observed samples of the (supposed) BG class.

The Variety of Models. In the simple case of the frame difference algorithm, the model is the color observed at the same location in the previous frame. To the contrary, conservative approaches try to build a model describing only the background. Strictly speaking, the model encodes the distribution of colors *predicted as being* in the background, instead of encoding the distribution of colors *being* in the background. This nuance should not be overlooked as it is intrinsic to any unsupervised one-class classification approach. A large family of BGS methods use probabilistic models of the background, often parametric ones. For example Wren *et al.* [15] supposed a Gaussian distribution, and adapt only the mean and variance of this distribution on a pixel basis. Other well-known methods of this family include the mixture of a fixed amount of Gaussians proposed by Stauffer and Grimson [14], and the mixture of Gaussians with an adaptive amount of components introduced by Zivkovic [16]. As an alternative to these probabilistic models, sample-based ones have been developed. They represent the background distribution with a set of samples drawn from this distribution. This is the case for the KDE [4] and ViBe [1] algorithms. In this study, we assume that the model is an estimated background image (this is the topic of the SBMI workshop [11]).

Motivation for Discussing the Limits of Pixel-based BGS Methods. Aside from the particular technical details of BGS algorithms, three elements of background subtraction should be considered:

1. [**Initialization**] The initialization aims at learning a good model from as few frames as possible from the video. Typically, when foreground objects are present in the first frames, the model needs time to erase the foreground objects, leading the appearance of so-called ghosts.
2. [**Updating**] The model has to be maintained to deal with temporal changes in the scene. Note that periodic or quasi-periodic modifications with high frequency are often considered as giving rise to a distribution of background colors that is a mixture, instead of a varying distribution.
3. [**Segmentation**] The result of the classification process is a segmentation map, with identified foreground or background pixels. Spatial coherence can be enhanced by post-processing the segmentation masks, or by propagating the neighboring distributions into the pixel's model as done by ViBe. Both techniques can also be combined. Note that post-processing techniques are known to always increase the performance [3,12]. In this paper, we study the performance of the BGS without any post-processing.

While authors propose sophisticated methods to increase the performance, it is interesting to understand if there are limitations, and where they originate from. To our knowledge, this question has not been explicitly studied in the literature. In order to discuss this theoretical question, we focus on the simple, but often encountered case, of a fixed background. It follows that the initialization and updating problems then become the problem of estimating the background image, which is the main focus of the SBMI workshop [11]. In this paper, we assume that the background image can be estimated, and we discuss the existence of theoretical upper bounds on the performance for pixel-based BGS algorithms.

3   Methodology

For some video sequences, foreground and background colors are so different that obtaining a perfect segmentation is trivial once the background is perfectly known. Considering such a video leads to a highly optimistic upper bound on the performance. To the contrary, in case of the *camouflage* effect, the foreground and background colors are so close that is impossible to distinguish between the two classes and that the BGS algorithms have a performance limited to that of a random classifier. Such a video leads to a very pessimistic upper bound. The upper bound of the performance is therefore video specific. The difficult question consists to determine the expected upper bound for a video sequence with unknown characteristics.

It is hard to determine the upper bound directly from state-of-the-art datasets for evaluating BGS algorithms, such as *changedetection.net* [6,7]. The reason is that they contain only a few dozens of video sequences. Due to the large variations in the characteristics of the video sequences, the small size of these datasets prevents from estimating a statistically significant averaged upper bound by averaging the performances measured experimentally on each sequence. Moreover, considering the pixels contained in a few video sequences as the test set is suboptimal as there is a natural spatial and temporal coherence in videos, leading to poor diversity and most probably to a biased estimation of the upper bound.

For studying the performance of BGS techniques taking their decisions on the pixel values, it is not necessary to have a video sequence. The reason is twofold.

1. In the absence of post-processing, the pixel-based nature ensures that the neighboring pixels do not have to be considered in order to study the behavior of the BGS for a pixel. Moreover, because we assume the background image can be computed, there is no need to consider the past of the video to study the behavior of the BGS: the model does not change over time as it represents the real background, regardless of the current frame.
2. The evaluation of the segmentation map occurs on a pixel base in most benchmarks such as *changedetection.net* [2,10], which indicates that the spatial coherence is not the primary concern. In fact, none of the 7 metrics computed on that website depends on the temporal or spatial order of pixels.

We argue that, in consequence, the expected upper bound can be obtained by choosing the test samples randomly in the space of pixels (which is of low dimension) instead of selecting them in the space of video sequences (which has an intractable dimension). Accordingly, we decide to simulate synthetic distributions at the pixel level, and to measure the upper bound experimentally. Note that our methodology could also be used to calculate upper bounds for region-based BGS methods, but in that case a statistical model of the spatial coherence would be necessary. In the absence of any prior information about the observed colors, we assume an uniform distribution of colors in the RGB space, both for the foreground and the background. All colors components are assumed to be real numbers between 0 and 1, but final RGB values are quantized over 8 bits in the input images as well as for the background image stored in the model. The noise statistic is supposed to be Gaussian, as assumed in several BGS techniques [14–16]. More precisely, we draw noise values randomly, independently for

(a) original image   (b) noise with $\sigma = 0.06$ (c) value decreased by 0.3

Fig. 1. Illustration of the magnitude of simulated imperfections.

each channel, from a centered normal distribution truncated in such a way that the noisy color is still in the range of possible colors (*i.e.* all components between 0 and 1). Noise can affect the observed images as well as the background image (that is the model). A standard deviation of 0.06 is considered as realistic (see Figure 1). The noise level in the model can be lower than the one in the input images if the BGS method uses internally a temporal noise filtering technique. We also simulate the shadows affecting the background part of the input images due to the foreground elements in the scene. In our experiments, the shadows are not present in the model, but only in the observed image. Shadows decrease the value channel; we consider a decrease of 0.3 as being typical (see Figure 1).

We wrote a software for computing ROC curves [5] with a Monte-Carlo approach, given (1) the amount of noise corrupting the input image, (2) the quality of the background image estimation that is stored in the model (that is the quantity of noise affecting it), (3) the average proportion of shadowed pixels, and (4) the corresponding decrease of value. We also compare four segmentation rules, that correspond to different ways to build the value to be thresholded:

- **[V1]** $|C_{input} - C_{model}|$ with $C \in \{R, G, B\}$ for grayscale images;
- **[V2]** $\sum_{C \in \{R,G,B\}} |C_{input} - C_{model}|$,
- **[V3]** $\max_{C \in \{R,G,B\}} |C_{input} - C_{model}|$,
- **[V4]** and $\sum_{C \in \{R,G,B\}} (C_{input} - C_{model})^2$ for color images.

These ROC curves are our upper bounds on the performance limit of BGS algorithms performing per-pixel segmentation based only on the color information.

4   Results and Discussion

The simulated ROC curves of a few upper bounds are given in Figure 2. The first observation is that ROC curves for V2, V3, and V4 are always very close, and always improve with respect to the segmentation rule V1 (based on grayscale values only). Working with one channel images is therefore suboptimal, and the performance does not depend much on the decision rule itself. The second observation, by comparing the ROC plots of the first and second rows, is that the performance is not very different when the model contains the perfect background image or a noisy version of it. *Being able to estimate a very precise background*

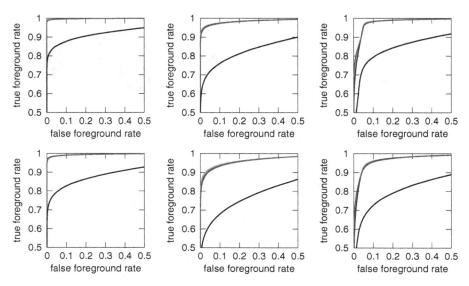

Fig. 2. Some upper bounds obtained for the performance of BGS methods, in the ROC space. In the left column, the input images have a low noise level ($\sigma = 0.04$) and no shadows. In the middle column, they have a high noise level ($\sigma = 0.08$), and no shadows. In the right column, they have a mid noise level ($\sigma = 0.06$) and 5% of their pixels in shadowed areas (decrease of value: 0.3). The model comprises a perfect background image in the upper row, and a noisy estimate of it in the lower row (the same amount of noise is added to the model and to the input images). The segmentation rules are: ■ V1, ■ V2, ■ V3, ■ V4.

image does not help much for the BGS, due to other intrinsic limitations of the BGS problem (at least under the working assumptions of this paper).

In order to show how the performance evolves with the amount of noise affecting the estimate of the background image, we need to express the performance with a numerical value instead of a curve. Once the decision threshold is set, the performance is given by a single point in the ROC space. We argue that a good way of choosing the decision threshold is to force the classifier to be unbiased. In that case, the BGS method predicts the right proportion of foreground. Unbiased classifiers are, in the ROC space, on the line passing through the points $(\mathrm{TNR}, \mathrm{TPR}) = (1, 1)$ and $(1 - p^+, p^+)$, where TNR denotes the true negative rate, TPR the true positive rate, and p^+ the prior of the positive class. The average p^+ is 4.56 % in the dataset of [6]. The performance resulting from the threshold selection is the intersection between the ROC curve and this line. Many metrics could be used to measure it. We report the balanced accuracy $\frac{\mathrm{TNR} + \mathrm{TPR}}{2}$. As there is a mapping between this value and the other metrics (see Figure 3), reporting how the balanced accuracy of the unbiased classifier varies with the amount of noise affecting the estimated background image suffices. Figure 4 shows that a very large standard deviation of noise ($\simeq 0.1$) should be reached before observing a significant decrease of performance.

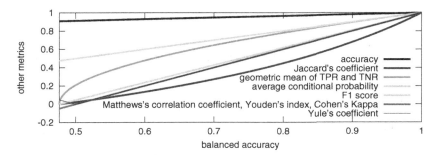

Fig. 3. Relationships between various metrics and the balanced accuracy that exist in the case of unbiased classifiers and $p^+ = 4.56\,\%$.

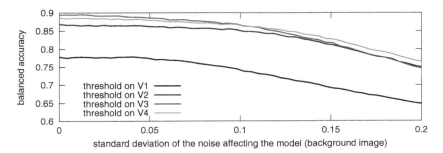

Fig. 4. The balanced accuracy of unbiased BGS methods, with respect to the amount of noise affecting the estimated background image. These results correspond to video sequences such that the noise has a standard deviation of $\sigma = 0.06$, and 5% of pixels are in shadowed areas with a value decreased by 0.3.

5   Conclusion

The SBMI workshop [11] focuses on the estimation of a background image given a video sequence taken from a static viewpoint; the background is assumed to be unimodal. In this context, we have proposed an original methodology to simulate the expected upper bound on the performance of pixel-based BGS algorithms, when their model reduces to the estimated background image. In our simulations, the provided bounds depend on the amount of noise corrupting the video sequence, the quality of the background image estimation, and the proportion of shadowed pixels. One important conclusion is that the quality of the estimate of the background image helps for the BGS, but only marginally, because of other intrinsic limitations. This questions the need for a perfect estimation of the background in general. Note that the presented methodology could also be tuned to derive bounds for a given video sequence, or a family of them (*e.g.* BGS for video surveillance of roads), by adapting the distribution of colors.

References

1. Barnich, O., Van Droogenbroeck, M.: ViBe: A universal background subtraction algorithm for video sequences. IEEE Trans. Image Process. **20**(6), 1709–1724 (2011)
2. Bouwmans, T.: Traditional and recent approaches in background modeling for foreground detection: An overview. Computer Science Review **11–12**, 31–66 (2014)
3. Brutzer, S., Höferlin, B., Heidemann, G.: Evaluation of background subtraction techniques for video surveillance. In: IEEE Int. Conf. Comput. Vision and Pattern Recognition (CVPR), Providence, Rhode Island, USA, pp. 1937–1944, June 2011
4. Elgammal, A., Harwood, D., Davis, L.: Non-parametric model for background subtraction. In: Vernon, D. (ed.) ECCV 2000. LNCS, vol. 1843, pp. 751–767. Springer, Heidelberg (2000)
5. Fawcett, T.: An introduction to ROC analysis. Pattern Recognition Letters **27**(8), 861–874 (2006)
6. Goyette, N., Jodoin, P.-M., Porikli, F., Konrad, J., Ishwar, P.: Changedetection.net: a new change detection benchmark dataset. In: IEEE Int. Conf. Comput. Vision and Pattern Recognition Workshop (CVPRW), Providence, Rhode Island, USA, June 2012
7. Goyette, N., Jodoin, P.-M., Porikli, F., Konrad, J., Ishwar, P.: A novel video dataset for change detection benchmarking. IEEE Trans. Image Process. **23**(11), 4663–4679 (2014)
8. Gruenwedel, S., Van Hese, P., Philips, W.: An edge-based approach for robust foreground detection. In: Blanc-Talon, J., Kleihorst, R., Philips, W., Popescu, D., Scheunders, P. (eds.) ACIVS 2011. LNCS, vol. 6915, pp. 554–565. Springer, Heidelberg (2011)
9. Heikkilä, M., Pietikäinen, M.: A texture-based method for modeling the background and detecting moving objects. IEEE Trans. Pattern Anal. Mach. Intell. **28**(4), 657–662 (2006)
10. Jodoin, P.-M., Piérard, S., Wang, Y., Van Droogenbroeck, M.: Overview and benchmarking of motion detection methods. In: Bouwmans, T., Porikli, F., Hoferlin, B., Vacavant, A. (eds.) Background Modeling and Foreground Detection for Video Surveillance, chapter 24. Chapman and Hall/CRC, July 2014
11. Maddalena, L., Bouwmans, T.: Scene background modeling and initialization (SBMI) workshop, September 2015. http://sbmi2015.na.icar.cnr.it
12. Parks, D., Fels, S.: Evaluation of background subtraction algorithms with post-processing. In: IEEE Int. Conf. Advanced Video and Signal Based Surveillance, Santa Fe, New Mexico, USA, pp. 192–199, September 2008
13. St-Charles, P.-L., Bilodeau, G.-A., Bergevin, R.: SuBSENSE: A universal change detection method with local adaptive sensitivity. IEEE Trans. Image Process. **24**(1), 359–373 (2015)
14. Stauffer, C., Grimson, E.: Adaptive background mixture models for real-time tracking. In: IEEE Int. Conf. Comput. Vision and Pattern Recognition (CVPR), Ft. Collins, USA, vol. 2, pp. 246–252, June 1999
15. Wren, C., Azarbayejani, A., Darrell, T., Pentland, A.: Pfinder: Real-time tracking of the human body. IEEE Trans. Pattern Anal. Mach. Intell. **19**(7), 780–785 (1997)
16. Zivkovic, Z.: Improved adaptive gausian mixture model for background subtraction. In: IEEE Int. Conf. Pattern Recognition (ICPR), , Cambridge, UK, vol. 2, pp. 28–31, August 2004

Nonlinear Background Filter to Improve Pedestrian Detection

Yi Wang[1]([✉]), Sébastien Piérard[2], Song-Zhi Su[3], and Pierre-Marc Jodoin[1]

[1] Department of Computer Science, University of Sherbrooke, Sherbrooke, Canada
{yi.wang,Pierre-Marc.Jodoin}@usherbrooke.ca
[2] INTELSIG Laboratory, Montefiore Institute, University of Liège, Liège, Belgium
Sebastien.Pierard@ulg.ac.be
[3] School of Information Science and Technology, Xiamen University, Xiamen, China
ssz@xmu.edu.cn

Abstract. In this paper, we propose a simple nonlinear filter which improves the detection of pedestrians walking in a video. We do so by first cumulating temporal gradient of moving objects into a motion history image (MHI). Then we apply to each frame of the video a motion-guided nonlinear filter whose goal is to smudge out background details while leaving untouched foreground moving objects. The resulting blurry-background image is then fed to a pedestrian detector. Experiments reveal that for a given miss rate, our motion-guided nonlinear filter can decrease the number of false positives per image (FPPI) by a factor of up to 26. Our method is simple, computationally light, and can be applied on a variety of videos to improve the performances of almost any kind of pedestrian detectors.

Keywords: Motion detection · Pedestrian detection · Motion history image · Nonlinear filtering

1 Introduction

Despite the plethora of papers published on the topic of pedestrian detection, detecting human shapes in 2D images is still an open problem. Pedestrian detection comes with fundamental difficulties that even state-of-the-art methods cannot handle properly. By their very nature, pedestrians may have different poses, they may be pictured from arbitrary angles and be occluded by objects or other pedestrians. Another issue that is fundamentally hard to cope with is background objects with a humanoid shape such as an armchair, a lamp post, or a coat rack. Since these objects have roughly the same features than human bodies, they are often wrongly classified as pedestrians [16].

In general, what differentiate pedestrian detection methods are the features they use and/or the classification rule which they implement [10]. The most widely used features are those using histograms of oriented gradients (HOG) [4]. Other commonly-implemented features are local binary patterns (LBP) [3] and

© Springer International Publishing Switzerland 2015
V. Murino et al. (Eds.): ICIAP 2015 Workshops, LNCS 9281, pp. 535–543, 2015.
DOI: 10.1007/978-3-319-23222-5_65

Haar wavelets [15]. When video is available, some methods extract spatio-temporal features such as binary motion labels from background subtraction [9] and motion tracks [13] to describe the motion of pedestrians. Other methods use richer features extracted from specialized hardware like stereo [2] or infrared cameras [8]. Recently, detectors based on deep learning [11] have been proposed. Instead of using man-made features, deep learning methods learn optimal pedestrian features automatically. As for the classifiers, the most widely implemented ones are support vector machines (SVM) and Adaboost [6]. Deformable Parts Model (DPM) [7] has also reported good results.

In this paper, we propose a new way to improve the performances of different pedestrian detectors without changing their design *per se*. Our method is based on two fundamental observations : 1) false positives produced by most pedestrian detectors are located over background objects whose visual features are close to that of a human and 2) by their very nature, pedestrians in surveillance videos are 2D moving blobs. The intuition behind our method is to use the temporal information of the video sequences as a leverage to filter out background objects while leaving untouched moving blobs (and thus pedestrians). By doing so, we get to deteriorate background visual features and thus help pedestrian detectors reduce their false detection rate.

We show that blurring adaptively the video sequences before applying existing pedestrian detection methods improves the results. The amount of blur can vary spatially and temporally, and is a function of the activity. More precisely, the filtered image is such that the graylevel in a pixel results from filtering the input image with a Gaussian filter whose standard deviation is correlated with the probability of motion in that pixel. Since the standard deviation vary spatially, our filter is nonlinear. The probability is estimated based on a Motion History Image (MHI) [5] that we compute by cumulating motion features. Experiments show that the number of false detections in the filtered images is drastically lower than on the original images without impacting much the miss rate.

Our paper comes with three main contributions. First, since our nonlinear filter is independent from the detector, it can be used by almost any pedestrian detection method. Second, our filtering method is robust to MHI inaccuracies which occur when illumination suddenly changes or when a background object moves. And third, since our filter is not optimized for detecting human shapes only, it can be used to detect other kinds of moving objects such as cars or boats.

2 Methodology

As shown in Fig. 1, our method implements a series of operations, which start with a background image that we compute by a moving average. We then compute an MHI which in turn is used by the nonlinear filter. Pedestrians are detected in the filtered image whose background has been smudged out.

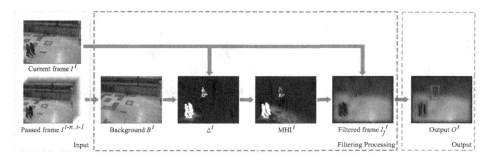

Fig. 1. Pipeline of our method. First, the background image B^t is computed with the past video frames. Then, we cumulate temporal gradients into an MHI. The MHI is then used by the filter to adjust its standard deviation to the amount of activity. Pedestrians are then detected on the filtered image.

2.1 Motion History Image

The first step of our technique is to estimate the background image B^t at each time t. It is updated at every frame with an exponential filter to account for changes in the dynamics of the video:

$$B^{t+1} = \beta I^t + (1 - \beta)B^t, \tag{1}$$

where I^t the input frame, and $\beta \in [0, 1]$ is a forgetting factor.

Based on the estimated background image, we highlight moving objects. We do so by computing a temporal gradient Δ^t

$$\Delta^t = \left| B^t - I^t \right|, \tag{2}$$

where $|\cdot|$ stands for the Euclidean norm in the RGB space. It is a naive estimation of motion at time t.

The Motion History Image MHI^t is obtained by cumulating Δ^t. Our implementation of MHI^t differs from that of Davis *et al.* [5] as we cumulate temporal gradients instead of binary motion maps:

$$\text{MHI}^t = \max(\Delta^t, \alpha\Delta^t + (1 - \alpha)\text{MHI}^{t-1}), \tag{3}$$

where $\alpha \in [0, 1]$ is the updating ratio for MHI. The max operator ensures that the MHI always contains the latest and largest temporal gradient. Without it, Eq.(3) would be a simple exponential moving average unable to grasp short burst of activity caused by fast moving objects.

Computing MHI with Eq.(3) has two main advantages over Davis *et al.*'s method. First, the use of an α ratio allows to adjust the speed at which the MHI is renewed. Second, Eq.(3) requires no detection threshold (we cumulate gradients but not binary motion maps) which is one less parameter to adjust.

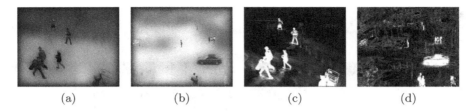

(a)	(b)	(c)	(d)

Fig. 2. Example of two filtered images (a, b) and their associate MHI (c, d).

Using MHI instead of a motion detection method to characterize activity has 3 main advantages. First, as opposed to motion detection methods, the MHI summarizes motion information of several frames. In other words, MHI pixel values aggregate the recent motion history that occurred at that location. Thus, MHI comes with a spectrum of values (not just binary values) which allows us to smoothly adjust the filter's standard deviation. Second, aggregating motion information of previous frames adds robustness to the system when a pedestrian stops moving for a short while. Third, MHI helps compensating for camouflage problems. This happens when sections of a moving object have a low temporal gradient. By cumulating gradients in time, we empirically noticed that sections of the moving object with a larger gradient often compensate for another one with a low gradient.

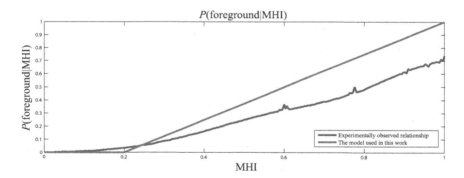

Fig. 3. The blue plot shows the empirical relationship $P(\text{foreground}|\text{MHI})$ obtained after processing all 54 videos from the changedetection.net dataset. As can be seen, the posterior probability and MHI values are almost linearly correlated. The red curve shows the model used in this work.

2.2 Motion-guided Filtering

As mentioned previously, background objects with humanoid shapes often lead to false detections. To decrease the false positive rate, we propose a nonlinear motion-guided filter whose goal is to blur out background details. In order to do so, we need to characterize the probability of a region to be associated to a moving blob, *i.e.* $P(\text{foreground}^t|\text{MHI}^t)$. This formulation is based on the working assumption that MHI^t is a discrete variable.

In order to define the probabilistic model between foreground pixels and MHI^t values, we conducted an experiment on the changedetection.net 2014 dataset, the largest video dataset with pixel-accurate groundtruth. We took all 54 videos, computed an MHI for each frame and empirically computed $P(\text{foreground}|\text{MHI})$ by counting foreground and background pixels for each MHI value. This experiment resulted into the graphic of Fig. 3. As can be seen, pixels with MHI values smaller than 0.2 hardly correlate to any motion while those with values above 0.2 have a linear relationship with the probability of the foreground. Considering the noise of the data and motion detection errors, $P(\text{foreground}|\text{MHI})$ can never reach 1 in practice. However, for our foreground model we set $P(\text{foreground}|\text{MHI}) \in [0,1]$:

$$P(\text{foreground}|\text{MHI}) = \max(0,\ 1.25(\text{MHI} - 0.2)), \tag{4}$$

In order for our filter to adapt to the content of the video (*i.e.* to filter out background areas while leaving untouched moving blobs), we use a Gaussian filter $\mathcal{G}(0, \sigma)$ whose standard deviation is a function of the posterior probability estimated at position (x, y). More specifically:

$$I_f^t = I^t * \mathcal{G}(0, \sigma^t), \tag{5}$$

$$\sigma_{x,y}^t = \sigma_{max} \times (1 - P_{x,y}(\text{foreground}|\text{MHI})), \tag{6}$$

where σ_{max} is set as $\frac{1}{5}$ of the height of the image and $P_{x,y}$ is the posterior probability at position (x, y). The reason that σ_{max} is a function of the image size is to account for high-resolution images whose background details are much larger pixel-wise. We also observed that a Gaussian filter with a standard deviation of σ_{max} eliminates background details in such a decisive manner that detecting pedestrians in those areas is very unlikely.

It should be stressed that the proposed filter aims at improving pedestrian detectors with a low risk of deteriorating their results. In particular, it is a well known fact that background subtraction techniques are highly sensitive to changes in the lighting conditions, to hard shadows, camera jitter and background motion [14]. Under these conditions, the temporal gradient Δ^t contains false positives which lead to an overestimation of activity within the MHI. That being said, more activity within the MHI leads to less filtering and thus performances close to the ones obtained by the detector alone.

|(a) small pedestrians|(b) top-down|(c) baseline|

Fig. 4. Examples of video sequences from the three categories.

3 Experiments and Results

3.1 Setup

We evaluated our method on 13 videos with pedestrians from 3 datasets, namely Caviar [1], changedetection.net [14] and the CUHK Square dataset [12]. The 13 videos were separated into 3 categories:

1. the **small pedestrians** category contains pedestrians with an height of at most 50 pixels;
2. the **top-down** category shows pedestrians filmed by a camera looking downward. Pedestrians in those videos all suffer from perspective distortion;
3. the **baseline** category contains videos showing easily detectable pedestrians.

For evaluation, we extract a subset of N (uniformly spaced) frames per video, where N is the number of frames in the shortest video of the category. All the frames selected in a category are considered as a unique set. This selection allows one to avoid biasing the results in favor of longer videos (their lengths vary from 400 to 7200 frames). Snapshots from the 3 categories are shown in Fig. 4.

We tested our method with 3 widely-implemented pedestrian detectors, namely **HOG+SVM** from Dalal and Triggs [4], the **C4** contour-based method by Wu *et al.* [16], and **DPM** by Felzenszwalb *et al.* [7]. For every video, the background image B^1 was initialized with a temporal median filter over the first 200 frames. The MHI update ratio α and the background update ratio β were set to 0.8 and 0.016 after some empirical validation.

3.2 Results

Fig. 5 shows pedestrian detection results with and without our motion-guided nonlinear filter. As one can see, in every case the number of false detections is much smaller in the filtered images than in the original images. Since the number of true detections is the same, the use of a filtered image significantly improves accuracy.

We also evaluated the performance by drawing miss rate *vs* FPPI curves, as shown in Fig. 6. Again here, the motion-guided nonlinear filter drastically

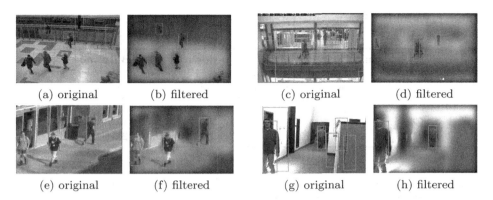

(a) original   (b) filtered   (c) original   (d) filtered

(e) original   (f) filtered   (g) original   (h) filtered

Fig. 5. Results obtained on original (*i.e.* without our technique) and filtered (*i.e.* with it) images with the detectors HOG+SVM (1st row), C4(2nd row left) and DPM (2nd row right).

reduces the FPPI for all 3 detectors. The reader shall notice that results from our filtering method have a miss rate 1.1 to 1.9 times larger (the end of the dotted lines are slightly higher than the full lines) which is nonetheless negligible compared with the FPPI reduction which is between 2.4 and 16.5 times smaller. It is thus clear that our nonlinear filter can be used to improve the performance of existing pedestrian detectors on different kinds of videos.

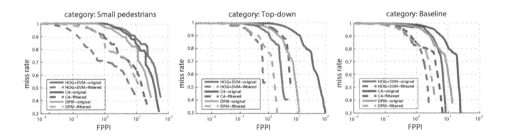

Fig. 6. Miss rate - FPPI curves for all 3 categories. Curves with different colors correspond to different detectors. Solid curves are for the original results without our pre-processing filtering, whereas the dashed ones are for the results with our filtering.

In Table 1 and Table 2, we further illustrated the quantitative analysis of our results. In Table 1, we selected the last point of each curve in Fig. 6 and compared the miss rate and FPPI value before and after applying nonlinear filtering on each detector with the same set of parameters. As can be seen, the FPPI decreases on average by a factor of 5.8 for each detector while the miss rate increases on average by a factor of only 1.3.

Table 1. Factor by which the miss rate increases and the FPPI decreases after applying our nonlinear filter.

Detector	Small pedestrians		Top-down		Baseline	
	miss rate increase	FPPI decrease	miss rate increase	FPPI decrease	miss rate increase	FPPI decrease
HOG+SVM	1.1	6.5	1.3	6.4	1.4	3.5
C4	1.2	2.4	1.9	16.5	1.1	3.6
DPM	1.3	2.5	1.5	6.8	1.2	3.8

Table 2. The FPPI value for a fixed miss rate of 0.7.

Detector		Small pedestrians	Top-down	Baseline
HOG+SVM	Original	**10.4**	2.6	5.9
	Filtered	**0.4**	0.6	1.6
C4	Original	6.6	35.3	18.5
	Filtered	2.0	5.2	3.8
DPM	Original	**4.0**	7.1	8.3
	Filtered	**1.9**	1.3	2.3

Table 2 compares the FPPI with and without our nonlinear motion-guided filter for a fix miss rate of 0.7. The table shows that our method reduces the FPPI values by a factor between 2.1 and 26 (see the bold values in the table).

Experiments were conducted on a 2.8GHz Intel Core2 Quad computer with a Matlab implementation. On average, it takes approximately 0.03 secs to update the background, compute the MHI and filter an image. This time does not depend on the number of pedestrians. Considering that it takes 0.06 sec to detect a pedestrian with HOG+SVM, 0.1 sec with C4 and 1.8 sec with DPM, our pre-processing (filtering) method does not bring a major processing overhead.

4   Conclusion

In this paper, we proposed a novel nonlinear filtering method which can be combined with almost any existing pedestrian detector. The method extracts motion features and cumulates it into an MHI. The MHI is then used to determine the standard deviation of a Gaussian filter which is used to nonlinearly filter video frames. Our method is easy to implement, fast and robust on different kinds of challenging circumstances. A drawback of this method is that if a pedestrian is a stationary from the first images, it would be integrated into background. We test our system with 3 widely used detectors on 3 categories of videos. The experiment results show that our nonlinear filter significantly decreases the false positive rate while keeping almost unchanged the miss rate.

References

1. http://homepages.inf.ed.ac.uk/rbf/caviar/
2. Benenson, R., Mathias, M., Timofte, R., Van Gool, L.: Pedestrian detection at 100 frames per second. In: IEEE-C-CVPR, pp. 2903–2910 (2012)
3. Chen, G., Ding, Y., Xiao, J., Han, T.X.: Detection evolution with multi-order contextual co-occurrence. In: IEEE-C-CVPR, pp. 1798–1805 (2013)
4. Dalal, N., Triggs, B., Schmid, C.: Human detection using oriented histograms of flow and appearance. In: Leonardis, A., Bischof, H., Pinz, A. (eds.) ECCV 2006. LNCS, vol. 3952, pp. 428–441. Springer, Heidelberg (2006)
5. Davis, J.W.: Hierarchical motion history images for recognizing human motion. In: IEEE-W-Det. and Rec. of Eve. in Vid., pp. 39–46 (2001)
6. Dollar, P., Wojek, C., Schiele, B., Perona, P.: Pedestrian detection: An evaluation of the state of the art. IEEE-T-PAMI **34**(4), 743–761 (2012)
7. Felzenszwalb, P.F., Girshick, R.B., McAllester, D., Ramanan, D.: Object detection with discriminatively trained part based models. IEEE-T-PAMI (2010)
8. Fernández-Caballero, A., Castillo, J., Serrano-Cuerda, J., Maldonado-Bascón, S.: Real-time human segmentation in infrared videos. Exp. Sys. with App. **38**(3), 2577–2584 (2011)
9. Lin, Z., Davis, L.S.: Shape-based human detection and segmentation via hierarchical part-template matching. IEEE-T-PAMI **32**(4), 604–618 (2010)
10. Ouyang, W., Wang, X.: Single-pedestrian detection aided by multi-pedestrian detection. In: IEEE-C-CVPR, pp. 3198–3205 (2013)
11. Sermanet, P., Kavukcuoglu, K., Chintala, S., LeCun, Y.: Pedestrian detection with unsupervised multi-stage feature learning. In: IEEE-C-CVPR (2013)
12. Wang, M., Li, W., Wang, X.: Transferring a generic pedestrian detector towards specific scenes. In: IEEE-C-CVPR, pp. 3274–3281 (2012)
13. Wang, X., Wang, M., Li, W.: Scene-specific pedestrian detection for static video surveillance. IEEE-T-PAMI **36**(2), 361–374 (2014)
14. Wang, Y., Jodoin, P.M., Porikli, F., Konrad, J., Benezeth, Y., Ishwar, P.: Cdnet 2014: an expanded change detection benchmark dataset. In: IEEE-W-CVPRW, pp. 393–400 (2014)
15. Wojek, C., Schiele, B.: A performance evaluation of single and multi-feature people detection. In: Pat. Rec., pp. 82–91 (2008)
16. Wu, J., Rehg, J.M.: Centrist: A visual descriptor for scene categorization. IEEE-T-PAMI **33**(8), 1489–1501 (2011)

QoEM 2015 - Workshop on Image and Video Processing for Quality of Multimedia Experience

Full-Reference SSIM Metric for Video Quality Assessment with Saliency-Based Features

Eduardo Romani[1(✉)], Wyllian Bezerra da Silva[2], Keiko Verônica Ono Fonseca[1],
Dubravko Culibrk[3], and Alexandre de Almeida Prado Pohl[1]

[1] Graduate Program on Electrical and Computer Engineering (CPGEI), Federal Technological
University–Paraná (UTFPR), Curitiba, Brazil
romaniseduardo@gmail.com, {keiko,pohl}@utfpr.edu.br
[2] Federal University of Santa Catarina – Santa Catarina (UFSC), Florianópolis, Brazil
willianbs@gmail.com
[3] Department of Industrial Engineering - Faculty of Technical Sciences,
University of Novi Sad, Novi Sad, Serbia
dubravko.culibrk@gmail.com

Abstract. This paper uses models of visual attention in order to estimate the human visual perception and thus improve metrics of Video Quality Assessment. This work reports on the use of the saliency based model in a full-reference structural similarity metric for creating new metrics that take into account regions that greatly attract the human attention. Correlation results with the differential mean opinion score values from the LIVE Video Quality Database are presented and discussed.

Keywords: Video quality assessment · Salient model · Human visual system

1 Introduction

Today there is a growing quantity of available multimedia content, particularly videos, creating a need for their quality evaluation and measurement. Video Quality Assessment (VQA) techniques concern the development of metrics that attempt to estimate the video quality as perceived by the Human Visual System (HVS). They are meant to assess the degradations related to lossy compression, losses in transmission and/or reception processes or even due to problems related to the original video content, for example. In order to determine the efficiency of a metric at predicting the human perception of video quality, a correlation between objective and subjective of video sequences is needed, which is achieved by calculating the correlation between objective and subjective scores (Mean Opinion Score - MOS [1] or Differential Mean Opinion Score - DMOS [1]).

VQA metrics can be classified as Full-Reference (FR), Reduce-Reference (RR) or No-Reference (NR), depending if the whole, reduced or no information about the original video is available to estimate the level of degradation. Many studies have already been developed based on encoding artifacts for all types of metrics. For instance, video

© Springer International Publishing Switzerland 2015
V. Murino et al. (Eds.): ICIAP 2015 Workshops, LNCS 9281, pp. 547–554, 2015.
DOI: 10.1007/978-3-319-23222-5_66

degradation can be assessed by relating the information about encoding characteristics, such as blocking and blurring features [2]. Several FR metrics have been developed, going from the most simple ones, such as the Peak Signal-to-Noise Ratio (PSNR), obtained by the ratio between the maximum power of a signal and its noise, to techniques that involve the structural similarity with motion associated weighting, such as the Speed-Weighted Structural SIMilarity Index (SW-SSIM) [3] and to more complex ones, such as the Motion-based Video Integrity Evaluation (MOVIE) [4], based in the spatio-temporal domains using the Gabor filter. Among RR metrics, there is the Spatial-Temporal Reduce Reference Entropic Differences (STRRED) [5], calculated by the entropic differences. And concerning NR metrics, the No-Reference Video Quality Assessment based on the Extreme Learning Machine algorithm (NRVQA-ELM) [6, p.8] uses the spatio-temporal features with a Neural Network in the prediction method.

A good prediction method should emulate the perceived quality of the HVS. Therefore, in addition to the analysis of encoding effects, VQA techniques have been recently developed, which includes the temporal analysis and the human attention models. For instance, it is known that the visual system focus the attention on objects of interest [7]. This is an evolutionary ability that permits the human being to rapidly localize salient

objects in a scene, such as a possible prey or predators.

In this way, salient models are being included in VQA techniques, as they are able to highlight video regions with discrepancies, which greatly attracts the human attention since movements, differences in texture and artifacts are better perceived by the HVS in visual focus regions than in regions of peripheral vision. Models of visual attention are widely used in computer vision [7], in eye tracking [8], and recently they have also been used in VQAs [9], [10].

This work presents results on the use of the saliency based model to improve the quality assessment. As a starting point, the FR metric proposed by Wang [11] is used, which is based on the characteristics between the frame structure of the original video and the degraded video. The metric is then modified by introducing the saliency-based model in the processing, resulting in metrics that contain the salient and the not-salient characteristics. Results show that there is an improvement in prediction compared to the original metric when salient features are used. In the experiments the LIVE Video Quality Database [12] is employed, which follows the recommendations of the Video Quality Experts Group (VQEG) [1] for subjective assessments and is widely used in the VQA testing. For comparison purposes the Pearson Linear Correlation Coefficient (PLCC) [13] and Spearman's Rank-Order Correlation Coefficient (SROCC) [13] are considered.

This work is divided, as follows: section 2 contains a basic description of the saliency model and section 3 describes the modified FR metric SSIM using the same model. Next, section 4 presents the experimental results and the analysis, followed by the conclusion in section 5.

2   The Salient Model

The salient model used in this paper has been developed by Culibrk [9], and is based on the bottom-up processing [14] for modeling visual attention, in which the presented stimulus process establishes a region of saliencies, i.e., a region with outliers in a given context. In this type of processing a disparate region is detected through its outliers in relation to its adjacent region, as, for instance, a red sign 'Stop' in a landscape with trees, and in a scene in which an object moves in one direction and at a different speed from the rest of the content, such as a moving car in a highway.

The algorithm employs the principles of multi-scale processing in the background, where two background frames are obtained by Infinite Impulse Response (IIR) filters for each frame. The principles of cross-scale motion consistency, temporal coherence and outlier detection are also used. The multiscale processing is similar to that proposed by Itti [7], in which a Gaussian pyramid is formed with scales and backgrounds frames. The method uses the maps of crominance, intensity and orientation to extract the conspicuity maps of the frame, then, a linear combination of these maps create a saliency map of the spatial information for one frame. A novelty filter in the form of Mexican hat function is applied to the two background and the current frame to extract the motion information, hereupon one single image obtained by the temporal filtering is formed. Finally, an outlier detector is used to detect the salient regions, defining regions that differ significantly from the context of the video sequence. This approach makes it possible to consider cross-scale consistency and the spatial coherence.

Through this method a binary map of saliencies is extracted for each frame. The processed frame of the video sequence is showed in Figure 1(a). Figure 1(b) shows the map of saliencies extracted of the same frame. A filter is proposed in this paper to create blocks with size of 8x8 pixels. These blocks can then be characterized as salients or not. They are used to eliminate small regions of saliency (sizes less then 8 pixels salients per block) and to create macro salient regions. The filter focus on regions mostly affected by the HVS attention, aiming at reducing small noise and optimizing the salient algorithm used to improve FR and NR metrics predictions. Figure 1(c) presents how the filter works: white regions are the superposition of the salient map from Figure 1(b) and the filtered salient map of Figure 1(d), the gray regions are areas formed by just one of that two maps, and the black areas have no salient regions in both maps. In the zoom area showed by the red square it is possible to see the amount of pixels in one block and, by the definition of the filter, blocks with less than 8 pixels salients per block do not integrate a salient block. The result of this process can be seen in Figure 1(d).

Looking to the final result in Figure 1(d) it is easy to see some examples of salient (white) regions determined by the crominance discrepancy in the two wheels of the tractor, the orientation differences in the boundaries of the object (tractor) and intensity enhancement in the ceiling of the tractor. There are also some salient regions caused by the motion information, which can not be perceived, like the spatial features, because it is generated by the temporal filter that requires more than just one frame. The salient map described in this section is used to characterize the new metrics approach in section 3.

a)   b)

c)   d)

Fig. 1. Salient model Extraction. a) Processed frame. b) Salient map after using [9] model. c) Filter 8x8 for the extraction of macro regions of saliencies. d) Filtered salient map.

Fig. 2. SSIM map extracted from the processed frame of Figure 1(a).

3   Salient-Based SSIM

Considering that the HVS is adapted for extracting structural information from a scene, the FR SSIM metric [11] analyses the structural similarity between the processed and the reference video. The SSIM uses the fact that the luminance of a frame is composed by illumination and reflection of objects, but the structure is not affected by the illumination, so it can be isolated from the structure of the frame.

Assuming the signal x as the reference frame and signal y as the degraded frame, Wang [11, p. 605] proposed a method comparing three components: luminance, contrast and structure, given by

$$SSIM(x, y) = [l(x, y)]^\alpha . [c(x, y)]^\beta . [s(x, y)]^\gamma, \tag{1}$$

where α, β and γ are parameters used to adjust the importance of each component. In this paper, α, β and γ received value '1' like suggested by Bovik [2] to simplify the equation. With (1) it is possible to plot the SSIM map presented in Figure 2 for the degraded frame of Figure 1(a).

A visual inspection in the structural similarity map represented in Figure 2 reveals the structural differences between two consecutives frames of the video sequence, outlining the object boundaries, in this case, the tractor.

In (2) the overall frame quality is presented.

$$MSSIM(X, Y) = \frac{1}{M} \sum_{j=1}^{M} SSIM(x_j, y_j), \tag{2}$$

To create versions of salient and not-salient SSIM it is necessary to calculate separately the corresponding regions of interest. In this paper the salient map extracted from the degraded frame is used. Considering MS_j as the binary Map of Saliencies exemplified in Figure 1(d) and counting the total of numbers "1" in the binary frame the total number of salient regions in the frame can be obtained, as follows

$$M_s = \sum_{j=1}^{M} MS_j, \tag{3}$$

Then, (4) and (5) calculate the overall SSIM value of the salient regions and of the not-salient regions of the frame, respectively.

$$MSSIM\_S = \frac{1}{M_s} \sum_{j=1}^{M} SSIM(x_j, y_j), \qquad if\ MS_j = 1, \tag{4}$$

$$MSSIM\_NS = \frac{1}{M-M_s} \sum_{j=1}^{M} SSIM(x_j, y_j), \qquad if\ MS_j = 0. \tag{5}$$

Finally, to obtain the metric score of the video sequence, the average of the MSSIM of all frames is calculated.

$$SSIM\_std = \frac{1}{N_f} \sum_{i=1}^{N_f} MSSIM_i, \tag{6}$$

$$SSIM\_S = \frac{1}{N_f} \sum_{i=1}^{N_f} MSSIM\_S_i, \tag{7}$$

$$SSIM\_NS = \frac{1}{N_f} \sum_{i=1}^{N_f} MSSIM\_NS_i, \tag{8}$$

where N_f is the total number of frames of the video sequence, SSIM_std (6) is the standard metric as proposed by Wang [11], and SSIM_S (7) and SSIM_NS (8) are the proposed salient and not-salient SSIM modified metrics, respectively.

The analysis of the results of these three metrics is correlated to the DMOS values of video sequences using the PLCC and SROCC coefficients. The data is presented in Table I.

4   Experimental Results

The correlation of DMOS for videos in the LIVE Database with the saliency-based metrics is analyzed using PLCC (accuracy) and SROCC (monotonicity). Table I shows the results of the standard SSIM_std [11] metric and the proposed SSIM_S (7) and SSIM_NS (8) for all frames of the videos of LIVE database, subdividing in categories according to different types of videos. Numbers in bold emphasizes the best outcomes.

The SSIM_S metric presents an improvement of SROCC in all categories listed in the table, when compared to the results of the SSIM_std. The most significant SROCC results were obtained with the SSIM_S metric for Wireless and IP videos with an increase of 21.5% and 12.8%, respectively. Looking at the SROCC values, when all videos are analyzed together (last row of Table I), an improvement of 11.05% using the proposed salient method is observed, i.e., the relationship between the SSIM_S and the DMOS by a monotonic function presents a better correlation than the one using the original SSIM_std method.

For the PLCC, a significant improvement in the Wireless (24,5%), IP (9,3%) and "all" (11,2%) video categories is observed. However, in the case of H.264 and MPEG videos the best values were presented with the SSIM_NS method, but in these cases the difference lies within 1% and does not affect the general result in a significant way.

Table 1. PLCC (accuracy) and SROCC (monotonicity) between DMOS of LIVE database [12] and the metrics SSIM [11], SSIM Salient and SSIM Not-Salient.

Video Type	SSIM_std [11]		SSIM_S (7)		SSIM_NS (8)	
	PLCC	SROCC	PLCC	SROCC	PLCC	SROCC
Wireless	0,5283	0,5221	**0,6577**	**0,6345**	0,4371	0,4163
IP	0,6137	0,4812	**0,6709**	**0,5430**	0,5812	0,4888
H.264	0,6900	0,6503	0,6831	**0,6598**	**0,7024**	0,6398
MPEG	0,5767	0,5581	0,5813	**0,5699**	**0,5826**	0,5527
ALL	0,5440	0,5248	**0,6048**	**0,5828**	0,4979	0,4714

The overall analysis points to the fact that the metric SSIM_S presents the best results for both PLCC and SROCC. We can also note that the main variations occur in the lowest correlation values of the original metric SSIM_std, given by the Wireless, IP and ALL video categories. The most significant improvement occurs when one does not know the specific video category and the SSIM_S metric is applied to the the set of "All" videos.

Observing the results of the SSIM_NS, the PLCC values of H.264 and MPEG videos are higher than the other metrics correlations, but don`t have a significant improvement. In general, the metric shows very low results, which reinforces the fact that the salient regions have more influence in the human visual system than the not-salient regions.

The strength of the metric arises from the fact that the salient model highlight the regions of the video with the higher discrepancies in orientation, crominance, intensity and motion, leading to a better correlation to the HVS evaluation.

5   Conclusion

The impact of saliencies in VQA metrics has been explored in this paper. Saliency-based features are employed in the standard FR SSIM [11] metric, resulting in two alternative metrics: SSIM_S based in the characteristics of the region of frames with the salient information and SSIM_NS with the complementary not-salient information. The comparison with the original metric is performed with the LIVE Video Quality Database.

The results obtained with the FR SSIM_S show consistent improvements compared to the original metric, as it can be noticed from values shown in Tables I. The use of the saliency-based model increases the correlation with the human perception, therefore enhancing the benefits of using saliencies in VQAs. This study also shows that the technique can be used in future approaches, such as the ones that employ NR metrics, which have been developed in past researches of the group, such as the NRVQA-ELM [6] and NRVQA-LM [15] techniques.

References

1. Methodology for the Subjective Assessment of the Quality of Television Pictures, ITU-R BT.500 Std. (2002)
2. Wang, Z., Sheikh, H.R., Bovik, A.C.: No-reference perceptual quality assessment of JPEG compressed images. In: Proc. IEEE Int. Conf. Image Process., pp. 477–480 (2002)
3. Wang, Z., Li, Q.: Video quality assessment using a statistical model of human visual speed perception. J. Opt. Soc. Amer. A 24(12), B61–B69 (2007)
4. Seshadrinathan, K., Bovik, A.C.: Motion-based perceptual quality assessment of video. IEEE Trans. Image Process. 19(2), 335–350 (2010)
5. Soundararajan, R., Bovik, A.C.: Video quality assessment by reduced reference spatio-temporal entropic differencing. IEEE Transactions on Circuits and Systems for Video Technology 3(4), 684–694 (2013)
6. Silva, W.B.: Métodos sem referência baseados em características espaço-temporais para avaliação objetiva de qualidade de vídeo digital. Ph.D. dissertation, Federal Technological University - Paraná, March 2013
7. Itti, L., Koch, C.: Computational modelling of visual attention. Nature Reviews Neuroscience 2(3), 194–203 (2001)
8. Liang, Z., Fu, H., Chi, Z., Feng, D.: Refining a region based attention model using eye tracking data. In: Proc. IEEE Int. Conf. Image Process., pp. 1105–1008, September 2010

9. Culibrk, D., Mirkovic, M., Zlokolica, V., Pokric, M., Crnojevic, V., Kukolj, D.: Salient motion features for video quality assessment. IEEE Transactions on Image Processing **20**(4), 948–958 (2011)

10. Wang, Y., Jiang, T., Ma, S., Gao, W.: Novel sapatio-temporal structural information based video quality metric. IEEE Transactions on Circuits and Systems for Video Technology **22**(7), 989–998 (2012)

11. Wang, Z., Bovik, A.C., Sheikh, H.R., Simoncelli, E.P.: Image quality assessment: From error visibility to structural similarity. IEEE Transactions on Image Processing **13**(4), 600–612 (2004)

12. Seshadrinathan, K., Soundararajan, R., Bovik, A.C., Cormack, L.K.: Study of subjective and objective quality assessment of video. IEEE Transactions on Image Processing **19**(16), 1427–1441 (2010)

13. O'Rourke, N., Hatcher, L., Stepanski, E.J.: A Step-by-Step Approach to Using SAS for Univariate & Multivariate Statistics, 2nd edn. Wiley-Interscience New York, NY (2008)

14. Connor, C., Egeth, H., Yantis, S.: Visual attention: Bottom-up versus top-down. Current Biology **14**(19), R850–R852 (2004)

15. Silva, W.B., Pohl, A.A.P.: No-reference video quality assessment method based on levenberg-marquardt minimization. In: XXX Simpósio Brasileiro de Telecomunicações (SBrT 2012), September 2012

Video Quality Assessment for Mobile Devices on Mobile Devices

Milan Mirkovic$^{(\boxtimes)}$, Dubravko Culibrk, Srdjan Sladojevic, and Andras Anderla

Faculty of Technical Sciences, University of Novi Sad, Novi Sad, Serbia
mirkovic.milan@gmail.com

Abstract. Pervasiveness of mobile devices and ubiquitous broadband Internet access have laid foundations for video content to be consumed increasingly on smart phones or tablets. As over 85% of the global consumer traffic by 2016 is estimated to be generated by streaming video content, video quality as perceived by end-users of such devices is becoming an important issue. Most of the studies concerned with Video Quality Assessment (VQA) for mobile devices have been carried out in a carefully controlled environment, thus potentially failing to take into account variables or effects present in real-world conditions. In this paper, we compare the results of traditional approach to VQA for mobile devices to those obtained in real-world conditions by using a physical mobile device, for the same video test-set. Results indicate that a difference in perceived video quality between the two settings exists, thus laying foundations for further research to explain the reasons behind it.

Keywords: Video quality assessment · Subjective · Mobile devices

1 Introduction

Recent years have witnessed a tremendous increase in usage of mobile devices to access the Internet and its services. Fierce competition on the end-user electronics market has caused smart phones to become accessible to everyone, and similar situation in the telecommunications department has made broadband Internet access cheap and ubiquitous. As a consequence, vast majority of population in developed countries now owns a cell phone [1], while one quarter of the smart phone owners also possess a tablet [2]. These devices are becoming more potent and versatile by the day and the result of this evolution is not only a change in people's habits when day-to-day tasks are in question, but a shift in the way some traditional services are perceived (such as TV, mail or telephony). This shift is especially noticeable when video content is concerned, as more and more of it gets consumed "on the move" [3]. In fact, some estimates have it that 86% of the global consumer traffic by 2016 will be generated by streaming video content [4]. Such high percentage inevitably raises the issue of quality of the delivered content, as perceived by the end-users.

© Springer International Publishing Switzerland 2015
V. Murino et al. (Eds.): ICIAP 2015 Workshops, LNCS 9281, pp. 555–562, 2015.
DOI: 10.1007/978-3-319-23222-5_67

Successful design and validation of different quality assessment approaches first requires the ground truth data, which in the domain of Video Quality Assessment (VQA) takes the form of degraded sequences and the Mean Opinion Scores (MOS) gathered mostly in laboratory tests on human observers. The sequences are degraded through multimedia coding and decoding processes and the effects of transmission are simulated by eliminating a certain proportion of packets from the encoded data, before passing the data to the decoder [5]. Important constraint when VQA for mobile devices is concerned however, is that close-to-ideal laboratory conditions can rarely be encountered in the real world.

In this paper, we consider network-induced video impairments and their effect on video quality as perceived by the consumers when observed in controlled laboratory conditions on a desktop monitor, versus when observed on a physical mobile device (i.e. a tablet) in a real-world scenario. Our main research hypothesis is that there are differences in the way the same video material is perceived (quality-wise) depending on the screen/device and setting (environment, context) of its presentation. As artefacts introduced to streaming videos are to a large degree dependant on network conditions and people are familiar with them appearing when watching content on mobile devices, we chose to focus on these to derive a set of videos for our experiments.

The rest of the paper is organized as follows: Section 2 provides an overview of the related work in the field, Section 3 describes the proposed approach in more detail, Section 4 presents the results of experiments conducted and Section 5 concludes the paper with a brief discussion and pointers for future research.

2 Background and Related Work

A recent survey by Winkler provides a fairly exhaustive list of publicly available video quality databases [5]. Winkler lists a total of 11 different databases, covering MPEG-2, Dirac wavelet, and H.264 codecs and simulated packet losses for wireless and wired IP transmission. When focusing on mobile devices, the only concession made in published databases is the reduction of the spatial resolution of sequences, due to the expected smaller screen sizes. The subjective quality assessment experiments are, however, carried out in the laboratory environment and conditions recommended for general multimedia were laid out at the time when majority of it was consumed over classic television and computer screens.

Most of the research in the field of VQA for mobile devices is aimed towards the evaluation of effect of different codecs, bitrates and content on perceived video quality. Winkler et. al. compare two coding standards used for mobile applications (MPEG-4 and Motion JPEG2000) by simulating the transmission errors of a WCDMA channel using representative bit error patterns provided by ITU-T [6]. They analyse the subjective scores obtained from assessors and use them to compare codec performance as well as the effects of transmission errors on visual quality, in a controlled environment using desktop computers for assessment. In subsequent work, they use similar experimental setting to explore the interactions between audio and video on perceived audiovisual quality, and confirm that both the product and linear combination of the two components are an effective model of the audiovisual quality [7]. Similarly to Winkler, Jumisko-Pyykko et. al. compare the performance of different codecs and audio/video bitrates but use physical mobile devices (smart phones) for obtaining subjective quality scores, and conclude that presenting different content clearly requires different audio-video bitrate ratios at relatively low bitrates levels [8]. In addition, work of Jumisko et. al. [9] as well as that of Mirkovic et. al. [10] shows that the personal interest in content presented to the assessors might be an important factor for video quality evaluation, and they recommend measuring the evaluator's interest in content in subjective assessment studies. Although in the work of Jumisko et. al. actual mobile devices have been used to obtain MOS, the experiments were executed in a controlled environment.

At the same time, there is an ongoing debate spanning different research areas on whether and how do results obtained in a controlled environment (i.e. in a laboratory) correlate with those observed in field experiments. Opinions – and indeed results – vary across domains, but a consensus on the matter has still not be reached. While it is generally accepted that laboratory studies are good at telling whether or not some manipulation of an independent variable causes changes in the dependent variable, many scholars assume that these results do not generalize to the "real world" [11]. Even though some studies have shown otherwise [12][13], they acknowledge that the failure to find high correspondence between lab and field studies in a given domain or with a specific phenomenon should not be seen as a failure of the researchers in either setting, but should be seen as an indicator that further conceptual analysis and additional empirical tests are needed to discover the source of the discrepancy.

As we are aware of no mobile-device-targeted VQA study that attempts analyse the effect of network impairments as they occur in real-world scenarios and compare them to quality results obtained through traditional approach in a controlled environment, we aim to establish a connection (or show the lack of) in this research.

3   Methodology

To create the test set, we adopted the following approach: a video was streamed by the server and delivered to an Android mobile phone, which logged the packets received as well as the times they were received at, starting from the first packet received. An application that relies on the FFMpeg library [14] was developed for the Android platform and used to this extent. At the same time, we have developed a client (PC) application that is able to receive a video stream and uses a log file generated on the mobile device as input, to impair the stream it is receiving.

The client application drops packets not present in the log file, and decodes video frames using the rest. To ensure successful decoding, first 10 packets containing coding parameters are not dropped. Timestamps from the log file are used to withhold the received packets until the reception time-stamp time has passed as measured from the first packet received. The result is a set of decoded frames. The decoded frames are generated using default error concealment of the FFMpeg. Those frames missing completely are created by copying them from the last decoded frame, to create the video of the original frame rate.

Using this approach, we created a test set consisting of 50 impaired videos and 10 reference videos, that we used to obtain MOS from human assessors. To do this, we employ a standard methodology (as recommended in [15]), but first divide assessors into two groups: (i) "laboratory" – where the experiment is conducted in a controlled environment as proposed by the ITU-T and (ii) "field" – where the experiment is conducted in real-world conditions.

We also ask assessors to provide us with more details about their opinion on the perceived quality of the test-set as a whole. With the "laboratory" group we do this via a post-experiment questionnaire where the participants are asked to evaluate the effect of 4 distinct factors (namely "freeze", "jerkiness", "blockiness/distortion" and "large grey areas") on a grading scale, and leave them with the option to provide additional qualitative comments. With the "field" group we conduct brief post-experiment interview where we ask assessors for their opinion.

3.1   Test Set

To create the test set, we used reference videos available within the LIVE Video Quality Database. Videos used were: Pedestrian Area, River Bed, Rush Hour, Tractor, Station, Sunflower, Blue Sky, Shield, Park Run and Mobile & Calendar.

The spatial resolution of all videos was 768x432 pixels, but they were first resized to a resolution of 384x216, as this is a resolution more appropriate for mobile device applications. In addition, all videos were converted to 25 fps frame rate. Finally, they were compressed using x264vfw, which is the the VfW (Video for Windows) version of a well known x264 encoder and ffh264 decoder (from FFmpeg/Libav project) [14]. Since the sequences are short, the logs in various scenarios were acquired by concatenating all ten videos and streaming this content in a single session. The merged video is 493s long, and has 12,325 frames. The video is split into 29,615 RTP packets for streaming. In this aspect, we evaluated three common scenarios: (i) static device over GSM, where the stream was received by a static mobile device, (ii) driving scenario, where the stream was received over GSM, while driving on the highway at the average speed of around 65 mph, and (iii) WiFi scenario, where content was streamed over WiFi network to a static mobile device.

The ratio of received packets and decoded frames was as follows: (i) static GSM scenario – 9,210 packets received and 4,377 frames decoded, (ii) highway GSM scenario – 1,908 packets received and 657 frames decoded, and (iii) WiFi scenario – 11,837 packets received and 5,239 frames decoded. For each scenario a log file was created, for the whole duration of streaming. As our logs were much longer than the average length of the test sequence, we first chose interesting transmission segments based on the running average of the number of packets received over an interval twice the maximum sequence length (20 second) interval. Based on this, our three multimedia use scenarios yielded 5 network

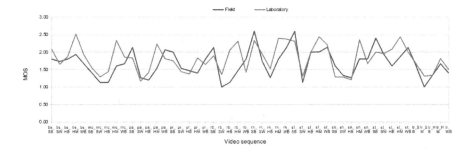

Fig. 1. Comparison of MOS obtained for each of the videos

impairment scenarios: static GSM best segment (SB), static GSM worst (SW), highway GSM best (HB), highway GSM average (HM) and WiFi best (WB) segment. The performance in the worst segments of highway scenario yielded too few packets to create viable impaired test sequences, so we opted for average segments, while the performance in the WiFi scenario was selected to represent ideal streaming conditions, so we opted for the best segment.

Once the segments were chosen, we reproduced those reception scenarios using our impairment application, which was run on the same machine as the server, in order to avoid any additional packet loss. The decoded frames were saved to disk as bitmaps, along with the decoding times from the log. To create impaired videos, a Matlab script was created to concatenate the frames and fill in the missing frames by copying the last decoded frame. Thus, the freeze effects were created when no frames were available from the decoder. For each original sequence, we created 5 impaired videos. E.g. for video named bs, we created bs1, bs2, bs3, bs4 and bs5 which represent network impairments scenarios logged in scenarios SB, SW, HB, HM and WB.

4   Experiment and Results

Subjective assessment was conducted for the 50 videos created. DSIS Variant I method was used [15], where the assessor is first presented with an unimpaired, reference sequence, and then with the same sequence impaired. He/she is then asked to vote on the second sequence, keeping in mind the first. Voting is done on a 1 to 5 scale, 1 being the lowest score where perceived impairments are very annoying and 5 being the highest, where impairments cannot be perceived. Sequences with different levels of impairments are randomly presented to assessors to avoid ordering effects.

The final MOS value for a sequence is the average score over all assessors for that sequence. Average MOS for a Scenario is calculated as the average of all MOS assigned to videos impaired using the same Scenario settings.

For the "laboratory" group, the environment where the tests were conducted was set up in a dedicated computer laboratory as proposed in [16] [17]. Sequences were presented to assessors on a 18.5" LG Flatron monitor (E1941), which was operated at its native resolution of 1366x768 pixels. For the "field" group, the tests were conducted on a Asus Transformer Pad TF300T tablet device (10.1" touch-screen operated at a native resolution of 1280x800 pixels) in an office, and a custom-developed software was used for voting. Assessors in this group were allowed to freely position the tablet device in terms of viewing distance and angle, in order to make themselves comfortable and to reduce the potential glare. In addition, each of them was allowed to choose the position they found the most comfortable for performing the assessment (sitting at the table, in the easy chair or being laid-back in the lazy-bag), to account for the fact that different people have different habits when it comes to watching videos on mobile devices.

The actual test in case of each group consisted of one session of about 25 minutes, including training. Before the test, written instructions were given to subjects, and a test session was run that consisted of videos demonstrating the extremes of expected video quality ranges. It was also specifically pointed out that the assessment should be focused on the quality and not the content of the video. In the "laboratory" group, 48 subjects – 41 male and 7 female participated in the test, their age ranging from 18 to 54. In the "field" group, 15 subjects – 11 male and 4 female participated, their age ranging from 24 to 64. Even though there is a considerable difference in the size of groups, number of assessors in the "field" group conforms with the recommendations for the minimum number of participants given in [15]. None of the assessors in either group were familiar with video processing, nor had previously participated in similar tests. All of the subjects reported normal or corrected vision prior to testing.

Obtained MOS results for each video separately and over all scenarios are presented in Figure 1 and Table 1 respectively. Due to the severe impairments introduced to original videos that were easily identifiable by simple overview of the resulting test-set, we have expected MOS to gravitate towards the low end of the scale. To identify differences between different scenarios, we performed Analysis of Variance (ANOVA) for scores obtained within each group. When "laboratory" group is concerned, ANOVA showed that for all but one video (video labelled "st") statistically significant differences exist between scenarios ($p<0.05$), meaning that assessors found a difference in quality of videos belonging to different Scenarios. Post-hoc analysis was run (Tukey's test) to identify where exactly these differences laid, and it revealed that for majority of videos this difference is due to scenario HM, mean of which significantly differs from mean of at least one other scenario (and often differs from 3 or all 4 of scenarios).

For the "field" group, assessors found differences in video quality (which are statistically significant) between different scenarios for only 4 out of 10 videos ($p<0.05$ for those labeled "pa", "rb", "rh" and "sf"). Post-hoc analysis showed that these differences were largely due to scenario SB, which scored higher than at least one other scenario (usually scenario SW).

Analysis of additional questionnaire and interview materials revealed that the two groups identified the same impairment ("video freeze") as the most influential on their opinions. What is interesting though, is that in the case of "laboratory" group this impairment contributes positively to the score given (i.e.

Table 1. MOS and % of decoded frames for different scenarios

Scenario	Average % of decoded frames	MOS "Laboratory"	MOS "Field"
SB	61.20	1.87	2.03
SW	17.30	1.47	1.38
HB	15.60	1.63	1.42
HM	6.60	2.27	1.71
WB	60.40	1.84	1.86

to a degree, the more prominent the effect, the higher score is given), while in the case of "field" group it affects the score in the opposite manner (more "freezing" will annoy the assessors and cause video to receive lower score).

5 Conclusions and Future Work

Results suggest that people tend to be more tolerant to impairments when observing videos on mobile devices in a relaxed environment than when watching the same sequences in controlled, laboratory conditions. Part of explanation for this might lay in the fact that people behave differently (e.g. they are more concentrated on the task or pay attention to details more closely) when they are asked to do something in a laboratory as opposed when being asked to do the same thing in a more informal setting. This has to do with human psychology and the wish to perform well, but also might be a good cue for researchers in the domain of VQA to relax their criteria a little when it comes to real-world applications, or to find means to exploit these phenomenons to devise more efficient ways for video streaming. Also, another important contributor to the results obtained might be the tacit expectation when it comes to observing videos on mobile devices; people might simply have a lower criteria for the quality they expect to observe because of effects they are used to experiencing when consuming videos on phones or tablets – such as "jerkiness" (which occurs commonly due to video buffering) or "freezing" (loss of connection).

We presented results of an initial study that was not designed to take into account or control all the variables that might bear some weight on final conclusion whether people really have a different perception of video quality when observed in different settings and on different devices. We discovered that some discrepancy exists between the MOS obtained through traditional methods and those acquired "in the field", so future research aimed at discovering what are the reasons for this disagreement is needed. In particular, we intend to design experiments which should take into account both psychological (i.e. behaviour related) and technological (i.e. intrinsic to devices) factors that might influence the VQA process in order to improve the current methods for obtaining subjective quality scores.

Acknowledgments. This research was supported by the FP7 Marie-Curie project QoSTREAM (Grant Agreement 295220).

References

1. Lenhart, A., Purcell, K., Smith, A., Zickuhr, K.: Social media & mobile internet use among teens and young adults. Technical report, Pew Internet & American Life Project, Washington, DC (2010)
2. ComScore: Today's U.S. Tablet Owner Revealed (2012)
3. O'Hara, K., Mitchell, A., Vorbau, A.: Consuming video on mobile devices. In: Proceedings of the SIGCHI Conference on Human Factors in Computing Systems, pp. 857–866. ACM (2007)
4. CISCO: Cisco Visual Networking Index : Forecast and Methodology, 2011–2016. Technical report, CISCO (2012)
5. Winkler, S.: Analysis of Public Image and Video Databases for Quality Assessment. IEEE Journal of Selected Topics in Signal Processing **6**, 616–625 (2012)
6. Winkler, S., Dufaux, F.: Video quality evaluation for mobile applications. In: Proceedings of SPIE Conference on Visual Communications and Image Processing, Lugano, Switzerland, pp. 593–603 (2003)
7. Winkler, S., Faller, C.: Audiovisual quality evaluation of low-bitrate video. In: SPIE/IS&T Human Vision and Electronic Imaging, pp. 139–148. Citeseer (2005)
8. Jumisko-Pyykko, S., Hakkinen, J.: Evaluation of subjective video quality of mobile devices. In: Proceedings of the 13th Annual ACM International Conference on Multimedia - MULTIMEDIA 2005, pp. 535–538 (2005)
9. Jumisko, S., Ilvonen, V.: Vaananen-vainio mattila, K.: Effect of TV content in subjective assessment of video quality on mobile devices. In: Proceedings of SPIE, vol. 5684, pp. 243–254 (2005)
10. Mirkovic, M., Vrgovic, P., Culibrk, D., Stefanovic, D., Anderla, A.: Evaluating the role of content in subjective video quality assessment. The Scientific World Journal **2014** (2014)
11. Campbell, D.: Factors relevant to the validity of experiments in social settings. Psychological Bulletin **54**, 297 (1957)
12. Anderson, C., Lindsay, J., Bushman, B.: Research in the psychological laboratory truth or triviality? Current Directions in Psychological Science **8**, 3–9 (1999)
13. Wolfe, J., Roberts, C.: A further study of the external validity of business games: five-year peer group indicators. Simulation & Gaming **24**, 21–33 (1993)
14. Bellard, F., Niedermayer, M.: FFMpeg (2007)
15. ITU-T: Subjective video quality assessment methods for multimedia applications (1999)
16. Winkler, S., Campos, R.: Video quality evaluation for internet streaming applications. In: Proceedings of SPIE Human Vision and Electronic Imaging, pp. 104–115 (2003)
17. ITUT: Methodology for the subjective assessment of the quality of television pictures (2002)

An Efficient SIMD Implementation of the H.265 Decoder for Mobile Architecture

Massimo Bariani[1], Paolo Lambruschini[1(✉)], Marco Raggio[1], and Luca Pezzoni[2]

[1] DITEN, University of Genoa, Genoa, Italy
{bariani,lambruschini,raggio}@dibe.unige.it
[2] AST, STMicroelectronics, Milan, Italy
luca.pezzoni@st.com

Abstract. This paper focuses on an efficient optimization of the H.265 video decoder on suitable architectures for mobile devices. The solutions developed to support the H.265 features, and the achieved performances are shown. The most demanding modules have been optimized with Single Instruction Multiple Data (SIMD) instructions and we keep in special account the memory handling, with the minimization of the memory transfer. The effectiveness of the proposed solutions has been demonstrated on ARM architecture. In particular, we have selected the dual-core Cortex A9 processor with NEON SIMD extension.

Keywords: H.265 · SIMD optimization · ARM NEON · Video compression · Mobile application

1 Introduction

Video compression algorithms play a fundamental role in enjoying the multimedia contents, allowing high video quality thanks to the remarkable enhancement of video resolutions. This is especially true in mobile environment where wired networks are not present and the wireless bandwidth can be reduced. Several compression standards have been developed in the past years: VC-1 also known with the name SMPTE 421M[1], MPEG-2/H.262 [2], and H.264/AVC [3][4].

The nowadays trend sees a constant improvement of screen resolutions and display capabilities of mobile devices. The last smartphones and tablets can address video in Ultra High Definition (UHD) format [5], with a resolution of 3840 × 2160 (8.3 megapixel). In the future, mobile devices will handle even higher resolutions, may be the Full Ultra High Definition (FUHD) format, with a resolution of 7680×4320 (33.2 megapixel).

The internet traffic has grown significantly in recent years, especially boosted by video content. Moreover, in next future it will rise approximately 85 percent of global consumer traffic [6]. Video will make up about 72% of the data consumed by mobile devices by 2019[7].

In this scenario, the continuous improvement of video resolutions leads to very high bandwidth occupation and this can be a serious issue especially on mobile network.

© Springer International Publishing Switzerland 2015
V. Murino et al. (Eds.): ICIAP 2015 Workshops, LNCS 9281, pp. 563–570, 2015.
DOI: 10.1007/978-3-319-23222-5_68

Therefore, the performance enhancement of compression algorithms plays an important role, reducing the amount of data transmitted to enjoy multimedia contents.

To face the challenge of transfer very high resolution video contents, in recent years, a new video compression standard was developed: High Efficiency Video Coding (HEVC/H.265) [8] [9]. HEVC/H.265 aim is to increase the compression efficiency by 50% if compared to the H.264/AVC, while maintaining the same level of visual quality.

In Fig. 1, the HEVC decoder block diagram is illustrated. The main difference with H.264 previous standard is the picture partitioning that is not fixed to 16x16 pixels blocks, but is flexible.

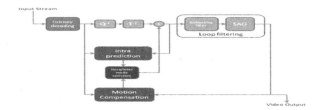

Fig. 1. HEVC decoder block diagram

Analogous to the concept of H.264 macroblock, HEVC defines the Coding Tree Unit (CTU) having maximum dimension 64x64 pixels [8][9]. The CTU is subdivided in square areas named Coding Unit (CU), with a quadtree scheme, which are the base blocks for the intra and inter coding. Their size can vary from 64x64 to 8x8 pixels.

The basic unit used in the prediction process is the Prediction Unit (PU). Each CU (NxN dimension) can contain: 1 PU (NxN), 2 PUs (NxN/2 or N/2xN), or 4 PUs (N/2xN/2), and their dimension can range from 64x64 to 4x4 pixels. The Discrete Cosine Transform (DCT) is utilized in the HEVC standard for coding the residual. Transform and quantization are applied to the Transform Unit (TU). Each CU can be spitted in several TUs having size ranging from 32x32 to 4x4 pixels.

The intra prediction keeps the same structure of the H.264 algorithm, but the number of intra modes increases from 9 to 35.

Moreover, one additional module is involved in the loop filtering process: the Sample Adaptive Offset (SAO). The basic concept of SAO filter is to classify reconstructed pixels in different categories using intensity or edge properties. An offset is added to the pixels in each category to reduce distortion. SAO is applied after the deblocking filter, as shown in Fig. 1. Further details of HEVC algorithm can be found in literature [8] or in the ITU-T formal publication [9].

In this paper, we will focus on an optimized software implementation of the HEVC/H.265 decoder, exploiting data-level parallelism. In the description of the proposed approach, special regards is dedicated to the new H.265 features, highlighting the issues in exploiting data-level parallelism and proposing our solutions. Starting from our previous work on HEVC [15] [16], we have decided to further optimize the decoder in order to increase the achieved performance. New strategy to exploit the ARM architecture will be shown on this paper.

2   SIMD Implementation

Starting from results on performance achieved with test performed in our previous work [15] [16], we have decided to focus the optimization on the most computation demand modules of H.265.

The analysis of the H.265 decoder profiles shows that even after our past optimization [15] [16] the most onerous module is the Motion Compensation (MC), similarly to what happened before. Besides MC, inverse transform and deblocking filter are still considerably time-consuming.

Our approach in previous software development was to use the Single-Instruction-Multiple-Data (SIMD) instructions to exploit the data level parallelism during the execution. We have decided to push more deeply this SIMD optimization with a better memory handling. One of the major limits of the NEON intrinsic [14] is the impossibility to specify the alignment in the operations of load/store. We have developed specific assembler optimization to bypass this limit. The architecture utilized to validate the effectiveness of the presented work is ARM Cortex A9 with NEON extension [14].

In order to take advantage of SIMD instructions, usually software developers have to strongly modify the original source code. Main changes regard the data manipulation: SIMD instructions often require having data ordered in specific ways to fully exploit their parallelism. The amount of control-flow code is another factor that can substantially impact the performance of a SIMD implementation. In order to effectively increment the performance, the code should be linear with a well-defined flow of operations. All these changes are necessary for a generic SIMD implementation, regardless of the particular instruction-set.

In the following, the details about the optimization of H.265 modules are provided.

2.1   Deblocking Filter

Blocking artifacts are well known, since they are one of the most visible distortions due to block based video compression algorithm. For this reason, H.265 filters data before the visualization. The filtering module shown in the decoder scheme of Fig. 1 is performed in loop (loop filtering). This means that the filtered data are used inside the process loop for the motion compensation of the next frames. In order to improve the video quality, H.265 exploits a H.264-like deblocking filter, followed by the newly added SAO filter.

The deblocking filter [8] [9] processes the edges among all the possible block partitions (CUs, PUs, TUs), except for 4x4 block that are not filtered. Each edge can be processed using either a strong or a weak filter.

The first step of the optimization was to exploit SIMD instruction for minimizing the number of memory accesses. In the ANSI-C implementation several instructions for loading and storing pixels were executed. Code reorganization has been performed in order to efficiently group load/store operations at the beginning/end of each vertical and horizontal phase. Each SIMD instruction loads from memory four elements in the horizontal phase and eight elements in the vertical phase. The memory access have been optimized exploiting prefetch from cache and aligned load/store from memory. Aligned load are not always possible, but when are possible the performance increase can be significant. An example of code developed for prefetch is shown in Fig. 2.

```
#define __pldw(x) asm volatile ( " pld [%[addr]]\n" :: [addr] "r" (x));
#define __pld_2i(x, o) asm volatile ( " pld [%[addr], %[offset]]\n" :: [addr] "r" (x), [offset] "I" (o));

#define __pld_2r(x, o) asm volatile ( " pld [%[addr], %[offset]]\n" :: [addr] "r" (x), [offset] "r" (o));
```

Fig. 2. Source code for prefetch

An example of code developed for aligned load/store is shown in Fig. 3.

```
#define _vld1u8_alig(y,x,a) asm("vld1.8 %h[out], [%[addr], :%c[alig]]\n" : [out]"=w"(y) : [addr]"r"(x), [alig]"I"(a))

#define _vst1u8_alig(x,y,a) asm ("vst1.8 %h[in], [%[addr], :%c[alig]]\n" : : [addr]"r"(x), [in]"w"(y), [alig]"I"(a))
```

Fig. 3. Source code for aligned load

We have decided to write assembler code for prefetch and aligned load/store because NEON extension does not handle this feature. Even load/store with increment are exploited, in order to perform load/store and pointer updating with one instruction. All optimization with aligned load/store are possible only when data are aligned in memory. We have aligned the frame at 64 byte, but not all the operation in the decoder access to aligned data. Sometimes pixels involved in the process are unaligned. In the deblocking filter aligned load/store can be well exploited in the horizontal phase, while in the vertical the gain is negligible.

2.2   SAO Filter

The Sample Adaptive Offset (SAO) process [8] [9] is applied to the reconstruction signal after the deblocking filter. It utilizes a set of offset values given in the slice header. SAO divides a picture into CTU-aligned regions to obtain local statistical information. The aim of SAO is to reduce the distortion by adding an offset to pixels of each category in these regions [15] [16].

There are four patterns selecting the type of processing for each region (see Fig. 4). The selected pattern is sent in the bit-stream.

For every SAO type four categories can be selected, the category selection must be also computed at the decoder side. Categories are calculated comparing the value of the current pixel (denoted as "C" in Fig. 4) with the value of the two neighbouring pixels. Each category selects an offset value to be added to the original pixel.

Fig. 4. 3-pixel patterns for the pixel classification in EO

One of the main issues of SAO implementation is that the category must always be computed referring to the original pixels, but the pixels are modified by the process itself. For this reason usual implementations works on two buffers, making a copy of input data before starting the process. In our implementation, we directly work on the decoded frame buffer in order to avoid copies, but we always keep in memory one or two CTU lines depending on the EO type. For example, in the vertical edge filter (90° pattern), we always load a line ahead the current line, we keep both current and next line in two temporal buffers while filtering the current line and writing the results to the decoded frame buffer. After the whole line has been completed, we switch next and current buffers and load a new line. For supporting this mechanism for all the edge offset types, we have to additionally store one frame line and one CTU column in order to manage the CTU border filtering.

Even though the operations slightly differ between the four EO types, the SIMD implementation structure is similar. The main difference is the way data is loaded into vector registers. We always load CTU-aligned vectors and misalign them to obtain the needed input pixels. For example, in the horizontal edge filter, after we load the current line, we shift the vector register one element to obtain the vector of pixels on the right.

In the SAO module we have exploited prefetch and aligned load/store like previously shown for deblocking filter. For the SAO module, to exploit aligned load/store we transfer more data than what strictly necessary.

2.3   Motion Compensation

The motion compensation (MC) is the most expensive task in H.265 decoder. It has the purpose to create the temporal predictor that will be added to the decoded prediction error for creating the reconstructed block. The temporal predictor is created from the previously decoded images called reference frame.

The MC could be unidirectional when it uses only a predictor coming from one reference frames, or could be bidirectional. In this last case, it takes two different predictors coming from two different reference frames, and it merges them for creating the final predictor (see Fig. 5).

The MC could be applied to each PU, so in the worst case we could have up to two different predictors for each 4x4 smallest PU.

For creating the temporal predictors, the MC also needs to make a pixel interpolation because the movement between the actual images and the reference frames could be fractionally.

In H.265 the luma interpolation has a ¼ of pixel precision and it uses a separable horizontal and vertical FIR filter at 8 taps.

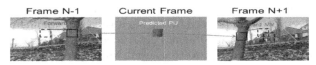

Fig. 5. Uni/Bidirectional MC.

For the Chroma Interpolation the precision is up to 1/8 pixels and it uses a separable 4 taps FIR filter.

We did a deep function specialization in order to separate luma from chroma motion compensation, monodirectional from bidirectional prediction, and no interpolation, only horizontal interpolation, only vertical interpolation or diagonal one. This process results in having 24 different functions specialized for each case.

Another modification that we have done is to work always with 8x8 PUs, also when we have a 4x4 PU. In this way we could always use all the 128-bit NEON registers in an efficient way. In this way prefetch and aligned load/store can be well exploited and time for memory transfer is minimized.

3   Results

In order to evaluate the achieved performance after the optimization process, several tests have been performed on a set of test sequences, addressing 720p resolution and different coding features. Some of the results are shown in the following tables. The utilized architecture is the ARM Cortex A9 @1.2GHz.

The following tables show results for different quantization values (QP) and different configurations: low-delay using B slices (LB), low-delay using P slices (LP), and random-access (RA). The decoder performance is measured in frames per second.

Table 1. Decoder Performance on Standard Sequences

Sequences	Number of frames	QP	Optimized decoder [fps]			JCT-VC decoder [fps]			Speed-up		
			LB	LP	RA	LB	LP	RA	LB	LP	RA
FourPeople	600	22	30.06	35.31	27.49	4.71	4.94	4.41	6.38	7.15	6.23
		27	38.43	49.01	31.96	5.86	6.16	5.05	6.56	7.96	6.33
		32	44.34	57.44	35.49	6.63	6.87	5.39	6.69	8.36	6.58
		37	50.09	65.06	38.10	7.34	7.45	5.70	6.82	8.73	6.68
Johnny	600	22	29.80	36.33	28.96	4.69	5.01	4.37	6.35	7.25	6.63
		27	39.10	52.14	36.65	5.82	6.41	5.12	6.72	8.13	7.16
		32	45.13	60.21	39.26	6.54	7.07	5.45	6.90	8.52	7.20
		37	49.86	66.86	42.25	7.28	7.55	5.74	6.85	8.86	7.36
KristenAndSara	600	22	27.17	32.88	26.12	4.16	4.58	4.00	6.53	7.18	6.53
		27	34.52	43.69	31.75	5.02	5.56	4.57	6.88	7.86	6.95
		32	40.46	51.96	35.47	5.69	6.20	4.94	7.11	8.38	7.18
		37	45.70	58.36	38.64	6.39	6.74	5.29	7.15	8.66	7.30
SlideEditing	300	22	48.21	64.23	39.93	8.38	8.31	5.98	5.75	7.73	6.68
		27	51.61	67.43	40.56	8.48	8.40	6.01	6.09	8.03	6.75
		32	52.56	71.62	38.77	8.54	8.45	5.96	6.15	8.48	6.50
		37	55.08	73.67	39.35	8.71	8.61	6.05	6.32	8.56	6.50
SlideShow	500	22	37.02	45.42	31.25	5.90	5.96	4.90	6.27	7.62	6.38
		27	40.83	50.40	33.38	6.19	6.22	5.08	6.60	8.10	6.57
		32	46.22	56.51	34.96	6.48	6.53	5.25	7.13	8.65	6.66
		37	49.12	60.55	37.02	6.80	6.83	5.36	7.22	8.86	6.91

In Table 1, the decoding performance for a set of standard sequences is shown. The execution time is strongly influenced by the input stream configuration, but the optimized code is able to streams at 30 frames per seconds (fps). The random-access configuration shows the lower results, whereas using low-delay with only P slices lead to better performance.

In the same table, we compare our results to the performance obtained with the reference decoder of the Joint Collaborative Team on Video Coding (JCT-VC), in order to put the here presented work in perspective. In particular, we refer to the H.265 decoder from the official software repository [18]. In the last three columns of the tables, we show the speed-up of our optimized decoder vs. the JCT-VC decoder. As can be noticed, the achieved performances are increased respect to our previous work.

4   Conclusions and Future Work

Video compression algorithms are computationally heavy and each new video standard introduces novelties that increase the rate of compression, but also increase the complexity of the algorithms [19]. The major issue is to conciliate the real-time requirement with the execution time achievable with the architectures available in mobile environment with a computational power usually limited.

The work presented in this paper illustrates our solutions, implemented and evaluated on a widely spread processor in mobile panorama, the ARM Cortex-A9. The experimental results show that the resulting H.265 decoder is able to achieve real-time performance for 720p video sequences.

Ongoing work is addressing multi-core implementation based on previous research on VC1 decoder [20][21]. The main issue in exploiting multi-core in video decoders is the data dependency. Usually, little portions of code can be concurrently executed without having to wait for data outgoing from other modules. Moreover, most of the available parallelism resides at block level, but this fine-grain parallelism has the drawback of data communication between cores. A promising solution seems to be the subdivision of the processing into two stages: the first module for parsing and entropy decoding, and the second for the rest of the decoding process. Referring to Fig. 1, the first core will execute the entropy decoding on frame N+1, while the second core will decode the frame N. In this way, it is possible subdivide the computational weight in two cores limiting the amount of data communication.

References

1. VC-1 Compressed Video Bitstream Format and Decoding Process. SMPTE 421M-2006, SMPTE Standard (2006)
2. International Telecommunication Union: ITU-T Recommendation H.262 (11/94): generic coding of moving pictures and associated audio information – part 2: video (1994)
3. Advanced Video Coding, ITU-T Rec. H.264 and ISO/IEC 14496-10:2009, March 2010
4. Wiegand, T., Sullivan, G.J., Bjøntegaard, G., Luthra, A.: Overview of the H.264/AVC video coding standard. IEEE Trans. Circuits Syst. Video Tech. 13(7), 560–576 (2003)
5. Nakasu, E.: Super Hi-Vision on the Horizon: A Future TV System That Conveys an Enhanced Sense of Reality and Presence. IEEE Consumer Electronics Magazine 1(2), 36–42 (2012)
6. Cisco Corporation: Cisco Visual Networking Index: Forecast and Methodology, 2013-2018, June 2014. http://www.cisco.com/c/en/us/solutions/collateral/service-provider/ip-ngn-ip-next-generation-network/white_paper_c11-481360.html

7. Cisco Corporation: Cisco Visual Networking Index: Global Mobile Data Traffic Forecast Update, 2014–2019, February 2015. http://www.cisco.com/c/en/us/solutions/collateral/service-provider/visual-networking-index-vni/white_paper_c11-520862.html

8. Sullivan, G.J., Ohm, J.R., Han, W.J., Wiegand, T.: Overview of the High Efficiency Video Coding (HEVC) Standard. Circuits and Systems for Video Technology. IEEE Trans. on Circuits and Systems for Video Technology **22**(2), 1649–1668 (2012)

9. H.265: High efficiency video coding, ITU-T Rec.H.265 and ISO/IEC 23008-2 MPEG-H Part 2, November 2013

10. Guo, Z., Zhou, D., Goto, S.: An optimized MC interpolation architecture for HEVC. In: IEEE International Conference on Acoustics, Speech and Signal Processing (ICASSP), March 2012

11. High efficiency video coding, Recommendation ITU-T H.265 / ISO/IEC 23008-2:2013, April 2013

12. Bossen, F., Bross, B., Suhring, K., Flynn, D.: HEVC Complexity and Implementation Analysis. IEEE Trans. On Circuits and Systems for Video Technology, December 2012

13. Alvarez-Mesa, M., Chi, C.C., Juurlink, B., George, V., Schierl, T.: Parallel video decoding in the emerging HEVC standard. In: IEEE International Conference on Acoustics, Speech and Signal Processing (ICASSP), March 2012

14. ARM White Paper: The ARM Cortex-A9 Processors, September 2009

15. Bariani, M., Lambruschini, P., Raggio, M.: An optimized SIMD implementation of the HEVC/H.265 video decoder. In: Wireless Telecommunications Symposium (WTS) (2014). doi:10.1109/WTS.2014.6835018

16. Bariani, M., Lambruschini, P., Raggio, M.: An optimized software implementation of the HEVC/H.265 video decoder. In: 2014 IEEE 11th Consumer Communications and Networking Conference (CCNC). doi:10.1109/CCNC.2014.7056307

17. Bariani, M., Lambruschini, P., Raggio, M.: An Efficient Multi-Core SIMD Implementation for H.264/AVC Encoder. VLSI Design **2012**, 14 (2012). Article ID 413747, doi:10.1155/2012/413747

18. https://hevc.hhi.fraunhofer.de/svn/svn_HEVCSoftware/

19. Ohm, J.R., Sullivan, G.J., Schwarz, H., Tan, T.K., Wiegand, T.: Comparison of the Coding Efficiency of Video Coding Standards—Including High Efficiency Video Coding (HEVC). IEEE Trans. on Circuits and Systems for Video Technology **22**(12), 1669–1684 (2012)

20. Bariani, M., Lambruschini, P., Raggio, M.: VC-1 decoder on STMicroelectronics P2012 architecture. In: Proc. of 8th Annual Intl. Workshop 'STreaming Day', Univ. of Udine, Udine, IT, September 2010. http://stday2010.uniud.it/stday2010/stday_2010.html

21. Paulin, P.: Programming challenges & solutions for multi-processor SoCs: an industrial perspective. In: 2011 48th ACM/EDAC/IEEE Design Automation Conference (DAC)

Kinematics Analysis Multimedia System for Rehabilitation

Minxiang Ye[1](✉), Cheng Yang[1], Vladimir Stankovic[1], Lina Stankovic[1], and Andrew Kerr[2]

[1] Department of Electronic and Electrical Engineering,
University of Strathclyde, Glasgow, UK
[2] Biomedical Engineering Department,
University of Strathclyde, Glasgow, UK
minxiang.ye.2013@uni.strath.ac.uk

Abstract. Driven by recent advances in information and communications technology, tele-rehabilitation services based on multimedia processing are emerging. Gait analysis is common for many rehabilitation programs, being, for example, periodically performed in the post-stroke recovery assessment. Since current optical diagnostic and patient assessment tools tend to be expensive and not portable, this paper proposes a novel marker-based tracking system using a single depth camera which provides a cost-effective solution that enables tele-rehabilitation services from home and local clinics. The proposed system can simultaneously generate motion patterns even within a complex background using the proposed geometric model-based algorithm and autonomously provide gait analysis results using a customised user-friendly application that facilitates seamless navigation through the captured scene and multi-view video data processing, designed using feedback from practitioners to maximise user experience. The locally processed rehabilitation data can be accessed by cross-platform mobile devices using cloud-based services enabling emerging tele-rehabilitation practices.

Keywords: Multimedia signal processing · Gait analysis · Optical marker · Multimedia content analysis

1 Introduction

The recent emergence of tele-rehabilitation services that aim to provide clinical rehabilitation diagnostics to patients in the comfort of their own home, calls for a radical shift in rehabilitation technology: from bulky, expensive equipment ideal for large rehabilitation facilities, to portable and affordable technology that can be operated in the home setting. The advances in information and communications technology have been making this shift possible through novel, cheap, and compact communications and media processing tools, with a large development space in terms of user-friendliness and accuracy of diagnostics. Furthermore, post-stroke rehabilitation with pleasant user experience would significantly benefit from tele-rehabilitation.

© Springer International Publishing Switzerland 2015
V. Murino et al. (Eds.): ICIAP 2015 Workshops, LNCS 9281, pp. 571–579, 2015.
DOI: 10.1007/978-3-319-23222-5_69

During typical clinical rehabilitation programs, the walking patterns of stroke patients are periodically assessed [1], which can be performed by using optical motion capture systems such as VICON [2]. These systems provide accurate walking patterns by tracking markers attached to relevant joints using multiple cameras, at the cost of high expense, operational expertise and large laboratory space.

To provide the service to patients who do not have access to these facilities, simple marker-based or markerless tracking systems using multiple or single RGB camera have been proposed. However, these systems have limitations, such as operational expertise and time-consuming processing [3], and requirement for specific colour of the underlying cloths, such as the single RGB camera systems of [4], [5], [1] and multiple RGB camera systems, such as [6]. An attractive alternative is to use Microsoft (MS) Kinect sensor [7] with its own SDK capable of tracking 25 skeleton joints. However, it is demonstrated in [8], [9], [10] that Kinect's skeleton results are too noisy and not suitable for clinical applications.

In this paper, we develop a novel application using a single depth camera (MS Kinect), combining the benefits of the 3D reconstruction ability of Kinect and high accuracy from VICON-like optical marker-based tracking. The proposed multimedia system provides a convenient solution for tracking multiple retro-reflective markers simultaneously, solving a geometric model-based identification problem even within a complex background. Our proposed geometric model detector automatically locates all labelled markers and constructs the corresponding digital models. We use a blob detector to detect all markers, introduce a novel algorithm to estimate the depth value in the center region of each marker to restore its 3D trajectory, which is in turn used to calculate the required 3D joint angles. In experiments, we adopt the cubic Bezier curve interpolation [11] for gap filling, calculate the joint angles, visualize movement patterns, analyze gait cycle and measure step and stride length, swing and stance phases.

Our designed multimedia application provides visualization for all raw and processed data autonomously and potentially provides an interactive multimedia communication service with mobile terminal devices via cloud servers. Result validation with VICON clearly shows the ability to reconstruct sagittal view gait cycles accurately.

2   Proposed System

The proposed multimedia system enables 3D kinematics reconstruction with high accuracy and robustness, using attached joint marker trajectories estimation to perform automatic computation and kinematics data visualization such as segment angle, movement patterns, gait cycle, step and stride length, swing and stance phases, etc [12]. The system consists of three parts: (1) Preprocessing - cleaning invalid data and building subject reference model before processing. (2) Tracking - detecting and labeling each marker. (3) Kinematics Analysis and visualization - computing and presenting kinematics data. The overall platform visually presents all processed data enabling user interaction using a high level graphic user interface (GUI) framework and is capable of interacting with cloud servers or other remote terminal devices as an inquiry service for tele-rehabilitation.

2.1 Preparation

Data acquisition is done by capturing infrared (IR) and depth image sequences using MS Kinect v2 [7]. We adopt a depth-map projection method from [13] to map space coordinates of tracked markers to the camera space. To keep the region of interest on the IR map and remove background, we model offline the scene by a virtual trapezoidal cylindrical model shown in Fig.1 due to blob noise from reflective materials that introduce redundant high intensity pixels into IR images and blank holes into depth images.

In Fig. 1, we define the central point x for subject modeling whose distance L to the Kinect sensor can be estimated by extracting the floor square corners (p1, p2, p3, p4 in Fig.1). The start and end points of a straight walking line and a valid scene region (solid line shown in Fig.1) can be estimated by a field of view angles $\beta_w = 70°$ and $\beta_h = 60°$ and a predefined reliable depth range [14]. In this way, our multimedia application will present the actual start and end points within the RGB stream using mapping functions from MS Kinect v2 SDK [7], which simplifies walking line calibration.

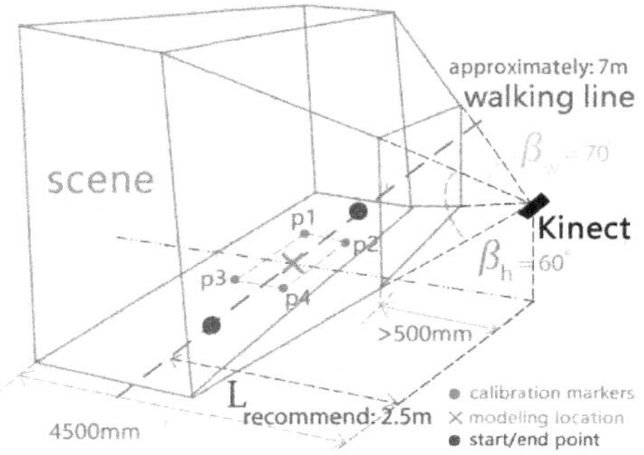

Fig. 1. Virtual Scene.

Next, we split the defined sagittal subject model into three parts: upper body, limb and foot model. We locate and label all markers by validating their camera space coordinates along with axes X,Y, and measure $H0^*$, $H7^*$, and $W4^*$ to $W8^*$ as sagittal model parameters shown in Fig. 2.

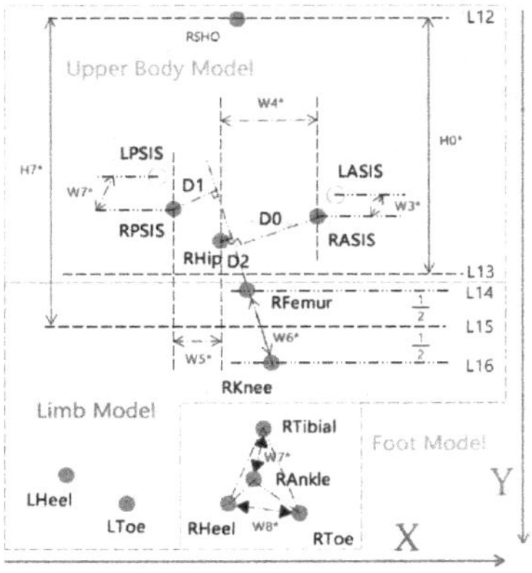

Fig. 2. Sagittal Model (Right Hand Side). 12 visible markers are marked with green circles. 2 partial invisible markers are shown in circle outlines.

2.2 Tracking

In this section, we introduce the proposed tracker for detecting and identifying the optical markers attached on the subject during the walking exercise, on a frame-by-frame basis using both IR and depth images.

In each frame, each marker is detected using: (1) Blob Detector - detecting centre of each blob. (2) Contour Finder [15] - finding valid contours. (3) Ellipse And Minimum Area Rectangle Fitter [16][17] - extracting blob information. (4) Our Kernel Cluster Filter - marking valid blobs.

The blob detector converts the acquired IR images into binary images using threshold T following 4 steps: (a) Adopt the contour extraction method of [15] and ellipse and minimum area rectangle fitter of [16][17] to detect each blob's centroid. (b) Remove redundant blobs (due to reflection phenomenon) by forming concentric cycles around each blob centroid. Let R_{Marker} be the radius of the marker in pixels, and $Centre$ as blob centroid. Let $C(R_n)$ be the pixel values forming an imaginary circle centred at $Centre$ with radius R_n [in pixels], where $R_n = 1, \ldots, R_{Marker}$ pixels. (c) Apply a histogram filter on all $C(R_n)$ to obtain the significant pixel values κ_n for each concentric cycle. Let κ^m be the mean of κ_n for Marker m. Then, for Marker m find the smallest index i^m such that $\frac{\kappa_i^m}{\kappa_{i+1}^m} > 2$. (d) Let $A^m = \sum_{j=1,i^m} R_j$ and obtain the marker detection threshold T as the mean of all κ^m weighted by $\frac{A^m}{\sum_{l=1}^M A^l}$ where M is the total number of visible markers in the floor square.

During marker detection, we apply the contour algorithm from [15] to locate concentric contours $\boldsymbol{\Omega} = \omega_0, \omega_1, \ldots$ for each blob in the binary image using threshold T. Let $|\boldsymbol{\Omega}|$ be the number contours in the set $\boldsymbol{\Omega}$. Then, each marker centroid is located by:

$$Centroid = \begin{cases} Fit_{Ellipse}(\boldsymbol{\Omega}) & \text{if } |\boldsymbol{\Omega}| > 5 \\ Fit_{MinRect}(\boldsymbol{\Omega}) & \text{if } |\boldsymbol{\Omega}| \in (2,5) \\ \frac{\omega_0 + \omega_1}{2} & \text{if } |\boldsymbol{\Omega}| = 2 \text{ and } Fit_{Depth}[Grow(\boldsymbol{\Omega}, \delta)] = 1 \\ \omega_0 & \text{if } |\boldsymbol{\Omega}| = 1 \text{ and } Fit_{Depth}[Grow(\boldsymbol{\Omega}, \delta)] = 0 \end{cases} \quad (1)$$

where $Fit_{Ellipse}$ and $Fit_{MinRect}$ uses the algorithm of [16], [17] to locate the centroid given each blob's contours $\boldsymbol{\Omega}$. In order to deal with extreme cases that $|\boldsymbol{\Omega}| < 3$, we adopt function $Grow$ given by (2) to generate a new rectangular window by applying kernel increment δ on pixels $P_{i,j}$ from contours ω_0 (and ω_1).

$$G = Grow(P_{i,j}, \delta) = \underbrace{Min_{i, P_{i,j} \in \boldsymbol{\Omega}}(P_{i,j}) - \delta}_{\text{left}}, \underbrace{Min_{j, P_{i,j} \in \boldsymbol{\Omega}}(P_{i,j}) - \delta}_{\text{top}},$$
$$\underbrace{Max_{i, P_{i,j} \in \boldsymbol{\Omega}}(P_{i,j}) + \delta}_{\text{right}}, \underbrace{Max_{j, P_{i,j} \in \boldsymbol{\Omega}}(P_{i,j}) + \delta}_{\text{bottom}} \quad (2)$$

where δ is set to 3 and 2 for the case $|\boldsymbol{\Omega}| = 2$ and $|\boldsymbol{\Omega}| = 1$, respectively. Function Fit_{Depth} in (1) determines the validity of each $Centroid$ by scanning a new window G grown by (2) as:

$$Fit_{Depth} = \begin{cases} 1, & \text{for } N > \tau \\ 0, & \text{for } N = \tau \end{cases} \quad (3)$$

where we set $\tau = 0$ and N as the number of pixels in G whose corresponding depth value is in the Kinect's reliable range of $(500, 4500]$ mm. As a result, we regard all blobs centred at $Centroid$ as the final detected markers.

To label the detected marker, we introduce a model-based identifier by restoring the depth value using our histogram clustering algorithm, described next. Since optical markers reflect the IR emission, the marker region is full of zero depth values in the depth image and the spatially collocated regions in the IR image will have very high values. Therefore, the task can be simplified into calculating the weighted mean depth from depth-map histogram statistics with our proposed clustering algorithm, reducing the noise from sensors as well as uncertain overlap conditions. We set the recovery radius $\delta = 3$ for growing the high IR $P_{i,j}$ region by Eq.2 and calculate the weight value as the significant mean relative distance between depth pixels to the centroid in each histogram bin.

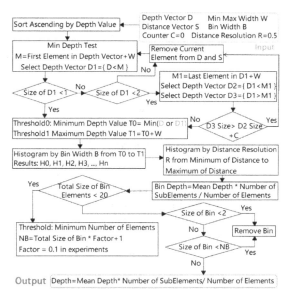

Fig. 3. Histogram Clustering Workflow.

In Fig. 3, we provide the flowchart of the proposed histogram clustering algorithm applied on knee, ankle, heel, and toe markers. Two situations are analyzed based on histogram bin width: (1) Bottom of the nearest pixels with occlusion (such as hip, femur) - using $T_0 = Min(D)$, $T_1 = Max(D_1)$ and $T_0 = T_0 - W$, where D, W, and D_1 are distances shown in Fig. 2. (2) Top of surrounding pixels (such as shoulder), in which case set $T_0 = Min(D_1)$.

We use the subject model defined in Sec. 2.1 to inspect all potential groups for upper body, limb and foot models (see Fig. 2). In particular, we order all markers between L12 and L13 by X-coordinate and validate the distances D0, D1, D2 for obtaining the most likely groups as the first look-up table. Then for the upper limb, we sort markers under L13 by Y-coordinate and X-coordinate and evaluate the nearest six markers to the ground by splitting them up into two groups with the triangular foot model shown in Fig. 2. Finally, we categorize the remaining left markers in the upper limb region by Y-coordinates and solve foot position by examining relative position to the right knee marker and histories over time.

3   Visual Analysis

We design a user-friendly interface for kinematics reconstruction with an interactive multi-view scene manager. For testing, we adopt relative knee angle (based on hip, knee and ankle trajectories) and gait phases (detecting local extremum

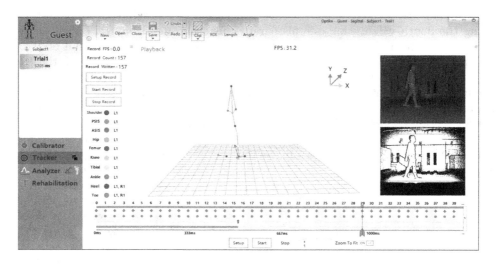

Fig. 4. Multi-view Tracker Snapshot

and inflection ranges) defined in [12] for kinematics analysis. The multi-view tracking snapshot of the software is shown in Fig. 4.

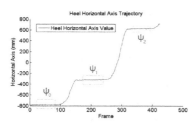

Fig. 5. Heel Horizontal Axis

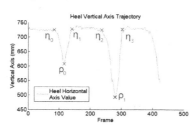

Fig. 6. Heel Vertical Axis

As it can be seen from the snapshot, it is convenient to access the recorded trials or streaming by selecting the tracker tab page. Users can also view the automatic reconstruction process within our multimedia application or manually playback the whole trial. After autonomous analysis and user authentication, the kinematics results (including joint angles, movement patterns, gait phases, measure step and stride length, swing and stance phases) will be generated and dispatched to cloud servers. The designed multimedia system provides a platform service for online/offline analysis, interaction and rehabilitation. Therefore, users can easily share all authorized local measurements across platforms with provided high quality multimedia content analysis and visualization as local and remote interaction services for tele-rehabilitation.

For analyzing a gait cycle, we follow the gait phases definitions from [12] and adopt trajectories (100 fps) of heel, ankle, knee and hip markers to calculate step and stride length, stance and swing phases. The main task is to calculate vertical thigh segment angle, tibia segment angle, and find inflection points and local peaks of heel markers' horizontal and vertical axis values shown in Figs. 5 and 6.

The task of measuring step and stride length can be simplified into examining the stable values ψ_0, ψ_1, ψ_2 using window matching for the region between inflection points in Fig. 5. Once the left and right heels horizontal stable values are found, the step and stride length can be calculated using the adjacent stable values over time.

Stance and swing phases are separated by the following two gait events: heel strike and toe off. This can be solved by searching inflection points η_0, η_1, η_2, η_3 and local extremum ρ_0, ρ_1 in Fig. 6 by searching the region between the inflection points from a global minimum to maximum by regrouping iteratively.

4 Experimental Results and Discussion

We tested the system using 40 independent trials for 5 subjects by measuring knee angle α, step length ζ, stride length ξ, stance and swing phases defined in [12], as shown in Fig. 7.

Fig. 7. Knee Angle, Step and Stride Length

Four typical trials from 4 different subjects are shown in Fig. 8

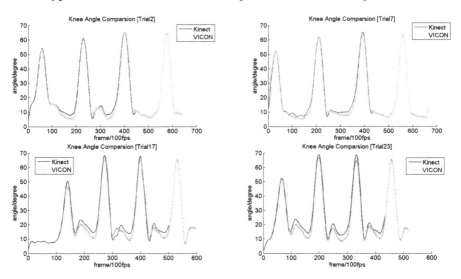

Fig. 8. Relative Knee Angle Comparison with VICON

It is obvious that our sagittal plane knee angle results have high accuracy benchmarked to the state-of-the-art industrial standard VICON. Furthermore, we closely followed the definitions of each gait event [12], and manually selected the key frames from the recorded IR and depth sequences as gait cycle references. Then we validated the step and stride lengths, and stance and swing phases with manually measured values that are based on [12]. The mean percentage error and standard derivation of the error [in percentage] on 40 sets of results are listed in Table 1.

Table 1. Performance of the proposed method for measuring step and stride length, and stance and swing phases

Error	Step	Stride	Stance	Swing
Mean(%)	1.05	1.17	1.82	1.10
Std(%)	5.33	4.76	5.83	4.37

5   Conclusion

The proposed system provides a mature solution for building up a mobile multimedia interactive service for visualization, presentation and tele-rehabilitation. It is more attractive than typical optical motion capture systems since it is portable and cheaper for clinic and home use. As a convenient indoors kinematics diagnosis system, it only uses single MS Kinect v2 and needs low operational expertise within a user-friendly application. Validation results indicate good agreement for the sagittal plane gait analysis benchmarked with the commercial industry standard VICON.

References

1. Yang, C., Ugbolue, U., Carse, B., Stankovic, V., Stankovic, L., Rowe, P.: Multiple marker tracking in a single-camera system for gait analysis. In: ICIP IEEE Int. Conf. Image Processing, pp. 3128–3131. IEEE, October 2013
2. VICON: Gait Analysis (2015). http://www.vicon.com
3. Ugbolue, U.C., et al.: The evaluation of an inexpensive, 2d, video based gait assessment system for clinical use. Gait & Posture **38**, 483–489 (2013)
4. Leu, A., Ristic-Durrant, D., Graser, A.: A robust markerless vision-based human gait analysis system. In: 2011 6th IEEE International Symposium on Applied Computational Intelligence and Informatics (SACI), pp. 415–420, May 2011
5. Liao, T.Y., Miaou, S.G., Li, Y.R.: A vision-based walking posture analysis system without markers. In: 2010 2nd International Conference on Signal Processing Systems (ICSPS), vol. 3, pp. V3-254–V3-258, July 2010
6. Li, Y.R., Miaou, S.G., Hung, C., Sese, J.: A gait analysis system using two cameras with orthogonal view. In: 2011 International Conference on Multimedia Technology (ICMT), pp. 2841–2844, July 2011
7. Kinect for Window software development kit, May 2015. http://www.microsoft.com/en-us/kinectforwindowsdev

8. Kook Jun, S., Zhou, X., Ramsey, D.K., Krovi, V.N.: A comparative study of human motion capture and analysis tools. http://citeseerx.ist.psu.edu/viewdoc/summary?doi=10.1.1.391.73

9. Nguyen, H.A., Meunier, J.: Gait analysis from video: camcorders vs. kinect. In: Campilho, A., Kamel, M. (eds.) ICIAR 2014, Part II. LNCS, vol. 8815, pp. 66–74. Springer, Heidelberg (2014)

10. Clark, R., Vernon, S., Mentiplay, B., Miller, K., McGinley, J., Pua, Y., Paterson, K., Bower, K.: Instrumenting gait assessment using the kinect in people living with stroke: reliability and association with balance tests. Journal of NeuroEngineering and Rehabilitation **12**(1), 15 (2015)

11. Agosto, M.K.: Bezier curves. In: Computer Graphics and Geometric Modelling: Implementation & Algorithms, pp. 396–404 (2005)

12. Casey Kerrigan, D., Schaufele, M., Wen, M.: Gait analysis. In: Rehabilitation Medicine: Principles and Practice, pp. 167–174 (1998)

13. Lachat, E., Macher, H., Mittet, M.A., Landes, T., Grussenmeyer, P.: First experiences with kinect v2 sensor for close range 3d modelling. In: ISPRS - Int. Archives of the Photogr., Remote Sens. Spatial Inform. Sciences XL-5/W4, pp. 93–100 (2015)

14. Kinect for Windows features: Kinect sensor key features and benefits, May 2015. https://www.microsoft.com/en-us/kinectforwindows/meetkinect/features.aspx

15. Suzuki, S., Be, K.: Topological structural analysis of digitized binary images by border following. Comp. Vision, Graphics and Image Proc. **30**(1), 32–46 (1985)

16. Fitzgibbon, A.W., Fisher, R.B.: A buyer's guide to conic fitting. In: Proc. of the 6th British Conf. Machine Vision, vol. 2, pp. 513–522. BMVC, BMVA Press (1995)

17. Toussaint, G.: Solving geometric problems with the rotating calipers. In: IEEE MELECON 1983, May 1983

Evaluation of Signal Processing Methods for Attention Assessment in Visual Content Interaction

Georgia Elafoudi[1]([✉]), Vladimir Stankovic[1], Lina Stankovic[1],
Deepti Pappusetti[2], and Hari Kalva[2]

[1] Department of Electronic and Electrical Engineering,
University of Strathclyde, Glasgow, UK
{georgia.elafoudi,vladimir.stankovic,lina.stankovic}@strath.ac.uk
[2] Department of Computer and Electrical Engineering and Computer Science,
Florida Atlantic University, Boca Raton, FL, USA
{dpappuse,hari.kalva}@fau.edu

Abstract. Eye movements and changes in pupil dilation are known to provide information about viewer's attention and interaction with visual content. This paper evaluates different statistical and signal processing methods for autonomously analysing pupil dilation signals and extracting information about viewer's attention when perceiving visual information. In particular, using a commercial video-based eye tracker to estimate pupil dilation and gaze fixation, we demonstrate that wavelet-based signal processing provides an effective tool for pupil dilation analysis and discuss the effect that different image content has on pupil dilation and viewer's attention.

1 Introduction

Objectively assessing users' experience when interacting with visual content is gaining increased research interest due to its relevance for numerous applications ranging from video compression, Human Computer Interaction (HCI)-based decision support tools design, web-site design, and Internet visual searches, to those related to marketing, science and medicine. Eye trackers that use high-resolution, high-speed video cameras to record eye movements and corneal reflections are cost-effective tools for high-precision measurement of the size of the pupil, gaze locations and the time length of fixation. They consist of a video camera and infrared illuminators, positioned in front of an eye, used to track the movement of the eyes which are then mapped into real-world coordinates by camera calibration.

The gaze location and the time length of fixation obviously show which features of the image the user is looking at and can reveal, for example, which features attract "the eye", which features are missed, and identify the point of

---

We would like to thank all participants in the study. The work was supported by FP7 QoSTREAM project, http://www.qostream.org.

V. Murino et al. (Eds.): ICIAP 2015 Workshops, LNCS 9281, pp. 580–588, 2015.
DOI: 10.1007/978-3-319-23222-5_70

visual fixation. However, since purely looking at an image feature does not necessarily mean that the feature attracted attention and caused the desired cognitive reaction, relating pupil dilation to cognition is a promising research direction. Numerous studies in psychology have demonstrated that changes in pupil dilation consistently occurs during the cognition process, including reading, visual search, and problem solving, as well as valence, arousal, pain, etc. (see [1]-[10]).

Extracting useful information from raw pupil dilation signals is not a trivial task due to high measurement noise of the commercial camera-based eye trackers, distortion due to gaze angle [1], frequent eye blinking, effects of illumination changes, irregular time delays in pupil response to stimuli, as well as the fact that pupil reaction is caused by different factors, which are hard to separate. In this paper, we designed a set of simple experiments based on a commercially available eye tracker, and use them to evaluate several statistical and signal processing tools for extracting useful information from pupil dilation signal when a user is presented with a sequence of coloured images. We demonstrate that mean, peak and variance are insufficient to capture the dynamics of pupil dilation change and propose frequency-based and wavelet-based analysis, for defining and extracting features that can be further used for clustering or pattern matching.

2   Background

Pupils respond to different stimuli, including pain, emotional reaction, mental workload, and arousal with a very uneven reaction time delay and intensity that depends on the intensity and type of stimuli. The reaction delay can range from 0.1sec (mainly in the case of pain) to 2-7 seconds for emotional stimuli [1]. For example, [2] investigated reaction to sound stimuli, and observed that only after 400ms the pupil starts to sharply dilate, reaching a peak 2-3sec after the stimuli.

Beatty [3] concluded that pupil dilation is a good representation of the difficulty and amount of mental workload across tested subjects and cognitive tasks. For example, calculating 16×23 causes 10% larger pupil dilation than 7×8, or memorizing a 3-digit number and 7-digit number caused 0.1mm and 0.55mm of pupil dilation, respectively (see [1]).

Different measures, such as mean dilation, peak dilation, variance, as in [4], and response time, have been proposed to quantify pupil dilation as a response to cognitive tasks (see [1] and references therein). However, these measures are not very robust and often not informative enough.

The key challenge in extracting meaningful information from pupil dilation lies in distinguishing the exact cause of pupil reaction. The preprocessing task needs to remove distortion and camera noise as well as natural blinking and pupillary light reflex. Indeed, as a reaction to brightness change, pupils naturally dilate, which can significantly affect measurements. To mitigate this problem, in [5] and [6], principal component analysis (PCA) is used on the pupil dilation data. Another approach can be found in [7], where a Hilbert transform method was used in order to study cognitive overload and cognitive dissonance. Though the initial results show potential, they are not conclusive, according to the authors, requiring further studies.

[8] proposed a measure called *Index of cognitive activity* (ICA), that represents the average number of "abrupt" changes in pupil size per second. This was estimated using wavelet decomposition, a technique that proved capable of filtering out the change of brightness effect. Building on this work, Marshall [9] compared pupil dilation with other measures such as blink rates, fixation time, saccade distance and speed, during different tasks, such as driving a car and visual search, in order to identify the best combination of measures for assessing the cognitive state of a subject. This research has proposed a combination of seven "eye metrics", left and right index, left and right blink, left and right movement, and divergence.

All these methods are either limited in conclusions they can make due to a restricted extracted feature space, or require additional measurands. Despite the fact that the pupil dilation signal has been studied for long (see [1] and references therein), there are still many unknowns w.r.t exploiting pupil dilation analysis for assessing multimedia experience, and appropriate signal processing and machine learning tools are needed to make the information extraction process fast and automated, to open the door for real-time visual feedback design mechanisms.

3 Methods

Experiments were designed to examine the gaze position and pupil responses to different, "neutral-content" images (indoors and outdoors) with and without searching for a specific target. The "neutral-content" images were selected as we want to examine pupil activity that is not a product of emotional triggering (pleasant/unpleasant), which is expected to create a more intense response. Additionally, we want to assess the effect of "busy" indoor images versus less busy outdoor images.

The eye tracker used during all our experiments is the Tobii X2-60 Eye Tracker, which provides pupil dilation and gaze fixation data with a 60Hz sampling rate. Data collection and stimuli presentation were obtained using Ogama.

Experimental Setup. Experiments were performed in a laboratory using moderate artificial light conditions, which were kept constant for the duration of all trials. Ten subjects who participated in the experiment ranged between 25 and 50 years old, both male and female, either with normal or corrected-to normal vision. The subjects were sitting in front of a screen with a resolution of 1920x1080 pixels, at a ∼ 70 cm distance (35° angle from the eye tracker). Calibration was performed using Ogama's calibration process, where a coloured dot was moving in the corners and centre of the screen and the subjects were asked to gaze at the dot. This process was performed before each trial.

Stimuli. The stimuli for this experiment were four high quality images that were acquired from Flickr under Creativity Commons Licences and are shown in Fig. 1. Two of the images represent the outside of residential properties and the other two are indoor bedroom images. Outdoor images did not resemble the architecture of the area where the test subjects reside. Between each image, and

(a) Content Image 1

(b) Content Image 2

(c) Content Image 3

(d) Content Image 4

Fig. 1. Content images used as a stimuli during the experiments.[1]

at the beginning and end of the presentation, a whole grey-coloured blank image of the same size was used to separate each different stimuli. Each image (stimuli or grey) was shown for 10 sec.

For each subject, the experiment comprised three trials, which took place at the same time and place, with a gap of less than a minute between the two trials. During the first trial (Trial 1), the subjects were shown the stimuli presentation, and were asked to watch the presentation with no further instructions. After the end of the trial, the same stimuli was shown for the second time (Trial 2), with no further instructions. During the final trial (Trial 3), all subjects were requested verbally to locate the flower(s) in the images at the beginning of the trial, without doing any task when this occurred or without verbally suggesting that they had identified the target.

Preprocessing. Pupil dilation and gaze data were cleaned during the preprocessing by removing all eye blink artifacts, as in [4,6]. All missing data were replaced using data interpolation from both right and left pupil data using linear interpolation. We perform three types of signal processing analysis on the processed data: (1) statistical analysis using dilation mean, variance, and peak; (2) frequency analysis; and (3) wavelet-based analysis.

Harmonic Analysis is performed using Welch Method [12] which is a commonly used method for estimating the *power spectral density* (PSD) of a signal in the presence of noise. It splits the data into overlapping segments, computes modified periodograms of the overlapping segments and then averages them in order to estimate the PSD and mitigate effects of random noise. In the applied procedure, the signal is segmented into eight sections of equal length, each with 50% overlap. All remaining signal parts that cannot be included into these eight

---

[1] Image 1 was taken from Billy Wilson under CC BY-NC 2.0, Image 2 and 4 from Kay Gaensler and Marketing Deluxe, respectively, under CC BY-NC-SA 2.0, and Image 3 from Les Haines under CC BY 2.0.

segments are discarded. Each segment is windowed with a Hamming window of the same length as the segment.

Wavelet-based Analysis. After interpolation and prior to wavelet-based analysis, to mitigate the effect of random measurement noise, the pupil dilation signal was filtered by a 5th order low-pass Butterworth filter with a cutoff frequency of $f_c = 4$Hz, which was selected as in [4] and [6], since the pupil servomechanism's break frequency is roughly 2Hz (see [6] and references therein).

After filtering, we performed *Discrete Wavelet Transform* (DWT) decomposition of the signal and wavelet denoising using soft thresholding [11]. This is done by passing the signal through a low-pass and a high-pass filter, and then down-sampling the filtered signals in order to remove the over-completeness of the transform coefficients. Due to the properties of DWT, the energy of the transformed signal is concentrated in only few DWT coefficients that have high magnitudes, and the energy of the noise is spread across a large number of DWT coefficients that have low magnitudes. Wavelet Denoising by Soft Thresholding [11] can be applied to remove the remaining noise in the 0-4Hz band, by minimizing mean square error (MSE) of the reconstructed signal compared to the original signal under the constraint that with high probability the reconstruction is at least as smooth as the original. This allows for the removal of undesirable noise ripples or oscillations that would not be removed with a simple MSE minimization. The idea of wavelet denoising by soft thresholding is to first decompose the noisy signal into N levels using a pyramidal wavelet filter, and then apply thresholding on the wavelet coefficients coordinate-wise with a specially selected threshold. All DWT coefficients whose absolute value is less than the predefined threshold are set to zeros and all remaining coefficients will have magnitude reduced by the applied threshold. In the proposed method, we use *Minimax thresholding* and estimate the level of noise based on the first level coefficients. Finally, the inverse transform is applied to recover the original signal. We note that a similar wavelet denoising procedure was used in [8] to evaluate the level of cognitive activity based on pupil dilation.

4   Results and Discussion

We separated the filtered pupil dilation signal into image segments and then concatenated all content image segments and all grey image segments, forming in this way two signals: a signal carrying four content images and a signal carrying grey images. Fig. 2 shows the filtered pupil dilation signal for Subject 5 and 10 during all three trials for the content images. Each vertical line represents the temporal transition between images. These subjects were selected as a representative example of all subjects. The pupil dilation range was around 1mm for both subjects and it dynamically changed during the experiments. From these graphs it is apparent that the dilation on average is higher during Trial 3, compared to the other two trials.

In Fig. 3 we show the gaze fixation for Subjects 5 and 10 during Trial 3, where the subjects were asked to locate "flower(s)" in the images. Figs. 3 (a)

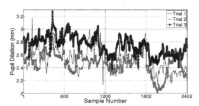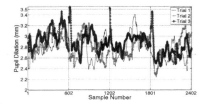

Fig. 2. Filtered Pupil Dilation for Subjects 5 and 10 respectively during all three trials

and (d) show Gaze Position (X,Y) versus Time, i.e., the sample number. Figs. 3 (b)-(c) and (e)-(f) illustrate the gaze position for both subjects for each content image. It is apparent by looking at the original images in Fig 1 that clusters of gaze points are located in the image areas with flowers. Indeed, for Image 2, in Fig. 3(c), we can observe that Subject 5 was able to target the living flowers. On the other hand, Subject 10 noticed many artificial flowers in the image. Note that there was no specification about the type of flower(s) the subjects should locate. Similarly, Images 1 and 3 have multiple flowers, hence the multiple clusters of gaze fixation points. In Image 4, both subjects were able to locate the vase on the table. The 3D graphs provide extra information of when the different targets were identified, spread out across the period the image(s) were shown.

Table 1 shows the Mean values of pupil dilation when viewing the Content Images, after filtering. From Table 1, we can see that predominately the highest values (bold) of mean pupil dilation were during Trial 3, which is expected.

In general though, mean, variance and number of peaks (not shown here due to space restrictions) rather irregularly change across the images and subjects, failing to capture signal transients. Thus, time averaging over the images do not, in this case, provide information that can be used to assess user's attention and experience, since the signal transition information is lost.

Harmonic Analysis. Next, we performed harmonic analysis by estimating the PSD of the signal in the range of interest (0-2Hz) using the Welch method described above. We separately estimated PSD for each grey image and each content image. The results for all content images are shown in Table 2. Frequency analysis shows the distribution of the power indicating in which frequency sub-band most of signal's energy is concentrated. It could potentially indicate increased mental activity, if small enough time windows are applied. This can be seen from Table 2 as on average Trial 3 shows increased power values per image, when compared with other trials. For example, Subject 5 in Image 1 shows 564.4W, which is higher compared to 477.6W and 468.5W for Trials 1 and 2, respectively. This pattern is similar to the case of mean values in Table 1 and generally power values are higher for Trial 3 when the subjects were asked to perform a target search task. This is mostly pronounced for Image 3 where all subjects show higher energy at Trial 3 (see bold values in Table 2).

Table 1. Mean of the Filtered Pupil Dilation Signal of the Content Images [in mm]. S stands for Subject and **Bold** represents the highest mean value per image

S$	Image1 Trial1	Trial2	Trial3	Image 2 Trial1	Trial2	Trial3	Image 3 Trial1	Trial2	Trial3	Image 4 Trial1	Trial2	Trial3
1	2.180	**2.193**	2.123	2.215	**2.236**	2.213	2.135	2.227	**2.315**	2.111	**2.258**	2.246
2	**2.576**	2.500	2.546	2.606	2.751	**2.795**	2.479	2.583	**2.745**	2.458	**2.481**	2.417
3	3.104	**3.241**	3.215	3.312	3.103	**3.429**	3.091	2.991	**3.097**	**3.038**	2.849	2.958
4	**3.109**	2.631	2.749	**3.157**	2.823	2.843	2.779	2.699	**2.808**	2.642	2.644	**2.703**
5	2.550	2.520	**2.771**	2.528	2.442	**2.765**	2.477	2.428	**2.640**	2.275	2.270	**2.530**
6	2.578	**2.689**	2.673	2.645	2.665	**2.833**	2.609	2.683	**2.781**	2.499	**2.608**	2.586
7	2.614	2.544	**2.657**	**3.023**	2.653	2.872	**2.680**	2.627	2.668	**2.830**	2.612	2.542
8	**3.402**	3.204	3.374	3.481	3.185	**3.500**	3.209	3.050	**3.350**	**3.265**	3.139	3.221
9	3.131	3.059	**3.134**	**3.186**	3.159	3.032	2.929	3.029	**3.163**	2.804	**2.829**	2.707
10	2.757	2.873	**2.925**	2.639	2.739	**2.828**	2.770	2.743	**2.828**	2.546	**2.690**	2.653

Fig. 3. Gaze Position for Subject 5 and 10 for all images (3D) during Trial 3, and individually per content image.

As frequency analysis loses time information and makes it difficult to conclude which time stimuli caused the reaction, we propose next wavelet-based analysis.

Wavelet-based Signal Processing. Fig. 4 shows the wavelet-based analysis for Subjects 5 and 10 for all trials. Similar results are obtained for other subjects. Horizontal axis again shows the sample number with vertical lines pointing to the image transition moments; vertical axis denotes the right eye pupil dilation in mm. We used Daubechies-4 wavelet filter which is one of the most popular orthogonal wavelet filter with fast wavelet transform. In contrast to the Fourier analysis, DWT can tradeoff frequency and time resolution allowing for detection of time interval when specific frequency component occurred. We used a 4-level wavelet decomposition, decomposing the signal into 4 frequency bands, to maintain high frequency resolution. The areas around the image transitions should be ignored as they are caused by signal stitching. We can clearly observe

Table 2. Signal Power in the 0-2Hz Band in [W] per content image. **Bold** represents the highest power per image.

S	Image1 Trial1	Trial2	Trial3	Image 2 Trial1	Trial2	Trial3	Image 3 Trial1	Trial2	Trial3	Image 4 Trial1	Trial2	Trial3
1	348.8	**355.4**	335.1	362.2	**367.7**	359.5	336.4	365.5	**392.2**	329.8	**373.2**	373.2
2	490.2	461.8	**506.9**	502.6	**557.4**	520.4	451.1	490.2	**491.1**	447.0	**451.9**	428.9
3	707.9	**772.9**	763.1	802.5	708.6	**863.1**	701.6	663.8	**703.2**	**677.3**	596.9	642.6
4	**710.8**	510.2	554.5	**731.0**	585.7	592.4	567.6	538.0	**580.0**	512.7	516.2	**538.9**
5	477.6	468.5	**564.4**	470.0	436.5	**559.0**	451.8	432.9	**512.6**	379.1	379.8	**470.9**
6	490.2	**530.6**	523.5	513.5	521.3	**585.3**	500.6	529.3	**567.0**	458.0	**498.6**	491.9
7	502.2	476.9	**523.2**	**672.6**	516.4	602.9	528.8	507.2	**531.7**	**620.3**	502.1	474.5
8	**855.8**	756.3	852.0	891.8	749.3	**910.0**	757.0	687.1	**823.2**	**782.6**	721.4	771.4
9	**726.8**	695.3	722.2	**746.2**	742.2	676.3	636.3	678.7	**736.3**	579.8	**590.6**	540.5
10	561.0	605.3	**624.4**	517.0	551.2	**588.4**	567.6	554.4	**587.6**	477.4	**539.6**	519.6

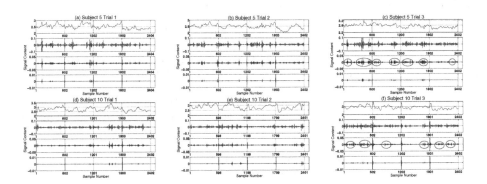

Fig. 4. Wavelet Analysis of Content Images for Subject 5 and 10 for all three trials.

increased activity in the band of interest. Trial 3 is characterised by significant pupil dilation activity in the beginning (until the task is solved, bearing in mind delayed reaction) and then reduction, while the other two trials have more evenly spread activity. Trial 1 has evidently more activity than Trial 2, since new content was presented in Trial 1. This activity has been marked for both subjects in Figs. 4(c) and (f) with red circles, where activity is more clear. In Trial 3, the pupil dilation activity indicates that Image 2 was most challenging, which is true since the flower position is not so obvious.

Conclusion. The paper discussed different signal processing methods for analyzing pupil dilation signals with applications to multimedia experience assessment. Our main goal was to review and test different methods, in order to evaluate their future use for feature definition and extraction for autonomous pattern matching and event detection. As in [8], our findings show that clearly wavelets provide a clearer view of activity on pupil dilation and can be essentially used as a helping tool for extracting signatures from the pupil dilation signal in order to relate each segment to image information/task for automated pattern matching. In addition to the wavelets, mean, variance, and power spectral density using Welch method, can be used in order to provide a more accurate activity recognition process.

References

1. Wang, J.Y.-Y.: Pupil dilation and eye-tracking. In: Schulte-Mecklenbeck, M., Kuhberger, A., Ranyard, R. (eds.) A Handbook of Process Tracing Methods for Decision Research: A Critical Review and User's Guide. Psychology Press (2010)
2. Partala, T., Surakka, V.: Pupil size variation as an indication of affective processing. International Journal of Human-Computer Studies **59**(1), 185–198 (2003)
3. Beatty, J.: Task-Evoked Pupillary Responses, Processing 19, and the Structure of Processing Resources. Psychological Bulletin **91**(2), 276–292 (1982)
4. Privitera, C.M., Renninger, L.W., Carney, T., Klein, S., Aguilar, M.: The pupil dilation response to visual detection. In: Human Vision and Electronic Imaging (2008)
5. Oliveira, F.T.P., Aula, A., Russell, D.M.: Discriminating the relevance of web search results with measures of pupil size. In: Proc. 27th ACM CHI'2009 (2009)
6. Privitera, C.M., Renninger, L.W., Carney, T., Klein, S., Aguilar, M.: Pupil dilation during visual target detection. Journal of Vision **10**(10), 3 (2010)
7. Hossain, G., Yeasin, M.: Understanding effects of cognitive load from pupillary responses using hilbert analytic phase. In: CVPRW 2014, pp. 381–386 (2014)
8. Marshall, S.P.: Method and apparatus for eye tracking and monitoring pupil dilation to evaluate cognitive activity. Google Patents, US6090051 (2000)
9. Marshall, S.P.: Identifying cognitive state from eye metrics. Aviation, Space, & Environmental Medicine **78**(5), 165–175 (2007)
10. Klingner, J., Kumar, R., Hanrahan, P.: Measuring the task-evoked pupillary response with a remote eye tracker. In: Proc. ETRA 2008 (2008)
11. Donoho, D.L.: Denoising by soft-thresholding. IEEE Transactions on Information Theory **41**(3), 613–627 (1995)
12. Welch, P.D.: The Use of Fast Fourier Transform for the Estimation of Power Spectra: A Method Based on Time Averaging Over Short, Modified Periodograms. IEEE Trans. Audio Electroacoustics **AU–15**, 70–73 (1967)

Why You Trust in Visual Saliency

Edoardo Ardizzone, Alessandro Bruno$^{(\boxtimes)}$, Luca Greco, and Marco La Cascia

DICGIM, Università degli Studi di Palermo, Viale delle Scienze bd.6 90128, Palermo, Italy
{edoardo.ardizzone,alessandro.bruno15,luca.greco,
marco.lacascia}@unipa.it

Abstract. Image understanding is a simple task for a human observer. Visual attention is automatically pointed to interesting regions by a natural objective stimulus in a first step and by prior knowledge in a second step. Saliency maps try to simulate human response and use actual eye-movements measurements as ground truth. An interesting question is: how much corruption in a digital image can affect saliency detection respect to the original image? One of the contributions of this work is to compare the performances of standard approaches with respect to different type of image corruptions and different threshold values on saliency maps. If the corruption can be estimated and/or the threshold is fixed, the results of this work can also be used to help in the selection of a method with best performance.

Keywords: Saliency maps · Image corruption · Image compression

1 Introduction

The problems of automatic categorization and understanding of digital images is still open even tough for a human observer are quite simple problems to solve. Humans use both purely visual features (pre-attentive) and prior knowledge on the world to assign a sense to a picture.

The term saliency refers to visual characteristic of interest for a human observer. The aim of visual saliency detection methods is to build a saliency map that tries to replicate the human visual system (HVS) behavior in the visual attention process. Salient parts of a scene are those regions that create a strong visual response and polarize attention. Human attention is the sum of factors coming from two different stimuli: the first one depends exclusively on the characteristics of the image, the second one is subjective for the observer and is related to his will (it is task-dependent). The objective stimulus (pre-attentive) is excited by the physical characteristics such as brightness, color, shape and has a bottom-up activation. In many situations, however, the largest contribution is given by the top-down process, because the focus of the attention is largely influenced by the knowledge obtained by learning the probabilistic structure of the scene.

Methods of the state of the art observe the actual behavior of human eye tracking its movements with special glasses (eye-tracker) and use observed movements as benchmark for proposed approaches. In most cases, the image quality is not mentioned in saliency map generation.

© Springer International Publishing Switzerland 2015
V. Murino et al. (Eds.): ICIAP 2015 Workshops, LNCS 9281, pp. 589–596, 2015.
DOI: 10.1007/978-3-319-23222-5_71

In this paper we want to investigate the robustness of some popular visual saliency methods against image degradation, such as jpeg compression and noise. In the next sections of the paper we try to answer this question by analyzing the performances of some saliency map generation algorithms with respect several kind of image corruptions. A similar work is [10], that focus on the performances of several saliency models on a corrupted database [11] for the quality assessment of digital images. Authors performed the analysis of the ROC and other metrics using five different saliency extraction methods in blurred, compressed (JPEG) and noisy images. In this case the benchmark dataset is formed by the results of eye-tracking both in original than in distorted images. The remainder of the paper is organized as follows: Section 2 shows related works in this field both in saliency extraction than in methods comparison; Section 3 describes which metrics can be used in saliency performance evaluation; Section 4 gives the result of different methods on original and corrupted images. Section 5 contains conclusions.

2   Visual Saliency Estimation

Models for visual saliency detection and extraction are inspired by human visual system and tend to reproduce the dynamic modifications of cortical connectivity for scene perception. Generally Saliency approaches can be divided in three main groups: Bottom-up, Top-down, Hybrid.

In Bottom-up methods, human attention is considered a cognitive process that selects most unusual part (i.e. distinct objects, contours) of an environment while ignoring most common aspects (i.e. uniform background).

A fundamental bottom-up and stimulus driven approach, proposed by [1], for Saliency detection adopted multi-scale analysis of the image. Multi-scale image features are combined into a single topographical saliency map. A dynamical neural network selects attended locations in order of decreasing saliency.

Harel [2] saliency method is based on a biologically plausible graph based model, consists of two steps: activation maps on certain feature channels and normalization which highlights conspicuity. The method proposed in [3] is based on parallel extraction of different feature maps using center-surround differences.

In Top-down approaches [4,5] the visual attention process is considered task dependent, and the observer's expectations and wills analyzing the scene are the reason why a point is fixed rather than others.

Generally Hybrid systems for saliency use the combination of bottom-up and top-down stimulus. In many hybrid approaches [6,7] Top-down layer is used to refine the noisy map extracted from Bottom-up layer. For example the top-down component in [6] is face detection. Chen et al. [7] used a combination of face and text detection and they found the optimal solutions through branch and bound technique.

A state of the art well known hybrid approach was proposed by Judd et al. [8] in addition to database [9] of eye tracking data from 15 viewers. Low, middle and high-level features of this data have been used to learn a model of saliency.

A comparative study that evaluates the performances of 13 state-of-the-art saliency maps has been reported in [12]. Test images are composed of a target object and a cluttered background and the conspicuity of the image is assumed to rely in the target area. A new metric is also proposed and compared with previous models.

The work [13] is a short survey on current state of the art. It contains some formal definitions on three different type of approaches (bottom-up, top-down, hybrid) and an overview on existing methods. Then, authors offer a description of publicly available datasets and the performance metrics used. Finally there is a description of the computational methods used in previous described literature of saliency extraction.

3   Metrics

Benchmarks in saliency extraction are formed by a list of fixation points and a continue map representing how much a pixel is salient. Generally, this map is obtained convolving a gaussian filter across the real points. On the other hand, saliency extraction methods give as result a map showing the value of the saliency for each pixel of the image. Using the continue ground truth as the reference one permits only an approximate comparison. A deeper investigation include the analysis using several thresholds on the map, so appreciating the similarity of the results centering on blobs corresponding to real fixation points. In experimental results section a deeper analysis about the robustness of saliency extraction methods against image degradation is given. We performed several experiments using different approaches of saliency computation.

3.1   Considered Metrics

There are many ways to compare two, normalized, saliency maps. Assuming that a pixel shows "positive" result if his value is over a threshold and a "negative" result otherwise, the classical information retrieval can be used.

Most known metrics are:

- Precision (P): the ratio of true positives (TP) and the sum of true positives and false positives (FP). It measure how much the pixels considered as salient in the computed map are salient also in the ground truth.

$$P = \frac{(TP)}{(TP+FP)} \tag{1}$$

- Recall (R):the ratio of true positives and the sum of true positives and false negatives (FN). It measure how much the regions considered as salient in the ground truth are present in the compared map.

$$R = \frac{(TP)}{(TP+FN)} \tag{2}$$

- Detection Measure (DM): the product of P and R. It prevents incorrect cases of high precision (i.e. a few of small blobs) with a low recall and the inverse situation of a high recall (i.e. considering salient the entire image)

$$DM = P \times R \qquad (3)$$

- F-Measure (F): the harmonic mean of P and R. It uses a different approach in limiting the problems also addressed by DM.

$$F = 2 \times \frac{(P \times R)}{(P + R)} \qquad (4)$$

4   Results

The contribution of this work is mostly a comparative evaluation of three well-known method ITTI [1], GBVS [2], and TORRALBA [8]. The attention is focused on the results obtained using a corrupted version of the test images. We used the dataset provided in [8], where benchmark fixation maps are created tracking the real movements of the eye. In our test we used these maps to see how different approaches can simulate the real response of the eye with or without corruption in the images. In particular, we considered the effect of compression and two common type of noise.

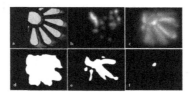

Fig. 1. Original Image (a), Ground truth (b), Saliency map (c), Resulting maps with thresholds 0.1 (d), 0.5 (e) and 0.75 (f)

4.1   Saliency Map Accuracy

A first evaluation of the methods is done analyzing how much resulting maps are similar to real fixation maps. Continue maps of the benchmark are generated from fixation maps by convolving gaussian filters on the fixation points, so approximating the result for a unknown observer. The perfect fitting is not very important in continue maps, a best way to compare maps is looking at the regions of concentration of saliency and seeing how much these regions are corresponding. Assuming a saliency normalized map in range 0-1 this can be done thresholding the map and obtaining a binary version, for example assigning the value 0 to original values under the threshold and 1 otherwise. An example of this is shown in Fig. 1.

First comparison is done calculating P,R,DM and FM for the methods using 4 values of threshold: 0.1, 0.25, 0.5, 0.75. Results are shown in Fig. 2.

Observing this values, it is possible to notice that Bottom-up methods (GBVS, ITTI) show better performances with lower level of thresholding (0.1 to 0.50) in P, DM and FM metrics and TORRALBA exceed others only in R. On the other hand, TORRALBA method normally gives a more sparse map (covering a large part of the image) so high values of recall is an expected result. TORRALBA method outperforms ITTI and GVBS with high values of thresholding. Its resulting map, using various low- mid- and high- level features, covers a large part of the image but contains high concentrated saliency values in blobs close to the actual fixation points.

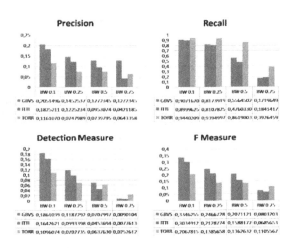

Fig. 2. Graphs of P, R, DM and FM for different thresholds

4.2   Effect of Noise

In this section we study the effect of additive noise in saliency calculation. The saliency map of the original image of [8] is compared with the one extracted from eight noisy versions: four with Gaussian noise and four with salt and pepper noise having variance 0.01, 0.1, 0,5 and 1 respectively. Larger is the variance, stronger is the corruption of the image.

In Table 1 P, R and FM values are shown for GBVS, ITTI and TORRALBA methods. The results show that R of all methods increases with noise because the resulting maps are more sparse and cover a larger part of the image. Results for TORRALBA are the best ones. On the other hand, P has better results with bottom-up approach for low thresholds (and best performer GBVS) but TORRALBA is preferable for higher values and is generally more stable with noise, leading to a P value similar to the original in noisy images. GBVS shows the best result for low thresholds and always outperforms ITTI;TORRALBA is less affected by noise, giving best results only for high thresholding.

Table 1. Performances of GBVS, ITTI and TORRALBA with noise introduction

GBVS	Precision				Recall				F-measure			
	TH 0.1	TH 0.25	TH 0.5	TH 0.75	TH 0.1	TH 0.25	TH 0.5	TH 0.75	TH 0.1	TH 0.25	TH 0.5	TH 0.75
original	0,176	0,123	0,087	0,051	0,976	0,928	0,582	0,233	0,287	0,206	0,148	0,074
gauss 0.01	0,174	0,121	0,086	0,054	0,976	0,926	0,583	0,244	0,275	0,191	0,133	0,075
gauss 0.1	0,165	0,111	0,079	0,048	0,979	0,947	0,606	0,266	0,253	0,162	0,114	0,066
gauss 0.5	0,152	0,097	0,071	0,045	0,983	0,959	0,635	0,311	0,259	0,171	0,122	0,074
gauss 1	0,147	0,090	0,065	0,039	0,985	0,965	0,647	0,318	0,290	0,204	0,142	0,075
S&P 0.01	0,175	0,122	0,087	0,051	0,976	0,978	0,581	0,233	0,289	0,208	0,142	0,076
S&P 0.1	0,169	0,115	0,083	0,051	0,977	0,935	0,589	0,243	0,281	0,198	0,137	0,076
S&P 0.5	0,153	0,098	0,069	0,039	0,983	0,955	0,605	0,254	0,226	0,131	0,088	0,030
S&P 1	0,130	0,071	0,044	0,016	0,991	0,980	0,643	0,306	0,259	0,173	0,118	0,062

ITTI	Precision				Recall				F-measure			
	TH 0.1	TH 0.25	TH 0.5	TH 0.75	TH 0.1	TH 0.25	TH 0.5	TH 0.75	TH 0.1	TH 0.25	TH 0.5	TH 0.75
original	0,156	0,110	0,074	0,038	0,978	0,872	0,520	0,164	0,248	0,183	0,243	0,059
gauss 0.01	0,146	0,106	0,072	0,038	0,984	0,891	0,530	0,164	0,216	0,148	0,201	0,053
gauss 0.1	0,123	0,083	0,057	0,032	0,996	0,948	0,568	0,187	0,194	0,102	0,126	0,024
gauss 0.5	0,111	0,060	0,041	0,022	1,000	0,980	0,585	0,191	0,196	0,111	0,149	0,038
gauss 1	0,109	0,052	0,034	0,013	1,000	0,994	0,581	0,164	0,262	0,187	0,247	0,059
S&P 0.01	0,147	0,103	0,071	0,038	0,979	0,875	0,570	0,166	0,250	0,178	0,238	0,060
S&P 0.1	0,133	0,088	0,061	0,034	0,990	0,903	0,533	0,164	0,238	0,156	0,209	0,053
S&P 0.5	0,111	0,067	0,038	0,014	1,000	0,985	0,567	0,148	0,191	0,095	0,108	0,013
S&P 1	0,107	0,050	0,028	0,007	1,000	0,999	0,668	0,336	0,197	0,115	0,139	0,024

TORRALBA	Precision				Recall				F-measure			
	TH 0.1	TH 0.25	TH 0.5	TH 0.75	TH 0.1	TH 0.25	TH 0.5	TH 0.75	TH 0.1	TH 0.25	TH 0.5	TH 0.75
original	0,109	0,059	0,060	0,062	1,000	0,998	0,744	0,489	0,193	0,108	0,102	0,095
gauss 0.01	0,109	0,058	0,060	0,061	1,000	0,999	0,745	0,491	0,193	0,106	0,098	0,090
gauss 0.1	0,108	0,057	0,057	0,058	1,000	0,998	0,743	0,487	0,192	0,102	0,091	0,081
gauss 0.5	0,108	0,055	0,053	0,054	1,000	0,999	0,748	0,497	0,192	0,103	0,094	0,085
gauss 1	0,108	0,054	0,051	0,047	1,000	0,998	0,762	0,525	0,194	0,110	0,103	0,095
S&P 0.01	0,109	0,058	0,060	0,062	1,000	0,998	0,741	0,484	0,194	0,109	0,102	0,096
S&P 0.1	0,108	0,057	0,058	0,060	1,000	0,999	0,738	0,478	0,193	0,107	0,099	0,090
S&P 0.5	0,108	0,055	0,054	0,054	1,000	0,998	0,746	0,493	0,191	0,095	0,077	0,060
S&P 1	0,107	0,050	0,039	0,022	1,000	0,998	0,740	0,483	0,192	0,103	0,096	0,089

4.3   Effect of Compression

In this section are presented the performances using compressed (JPEG) images. The maps are calculated using the compressed version of the original image with different quality factors. Results of P for GBVS and TORRALBA methods are shown in following figures. Results for ITTI are not shown because similar to GVBS. The visual effects of compression depend on morphological surface of the images, for this reason we analyzed several effects on images with very different morphological surfaces. The testset we used consists of a lot of images with very different background and foreground compositions: a simple object in the foreground and a homogenous background, many object in the foreground and a chaotic background.

The results show that, in terms of P and R, saliency methods are robust against different compression rates. In practical terms this means that substantially the jpeg compression do not affect the performance of saliency detection methods. In greater details, GBVS approach overcomes the others method Precision results, while

TORRALBA shows the lower Precision values. On the other side, TORRALBA shows the higher values of Recall (because, generally the resulting saliency maps cover larger regions of the image) that, however, are close to GBVS and ITTI ones.

Furthermore, observing preliminary experimental results, we notice that, for every methods, Precision values of saliency maps with several thresholds are really close to each other.

Table 2. Performances of GBVS and TORRALBA with compressed images

GBVS	Precision				Recall				F-measure			
	TH 01	TH 0.25	TH 0.5	TH 0.75	TH 01	TH 0.25	TH 0.5	TH 0.75	TH 01	TH 0.25	TH 0.5	TH 0.75
JPEG 1%	0,186	0,137	0,099	0,052	0,959	0,846	0,517	0,180	0,298	0,212	0,147	0,071
JPEG 5%	0,182	0,133	0,100	0,061	0,958	0,879	0,551	0,206	0,294	0,212	0,147	0,083
JPEG 10%	0,185	0,134	0,107	0,057	0,958	0,880	0,590	0,188	0,295	0,217	0,157	0,073
JPEG 20%	0,186	0,137	0,054	0,049	0,959	0,872	0,904	0,181	0,297	0,215	0,094	0,068
JPEG 40%	0,187	0,138	0,110	0,050	0,959	0,872	0,588	0,186	0,298	0,217	0,160	0,070
JPEG 60%	0,186	0,136	0,109	0,050	0,958	0,870	0,593	0,185	0,297	0,215	0,159	0,069
JPEG 80%	0,187	0,137	0,110	0,050	0,958	0,869	0,589	0,184	0,298	0,216	0,160	0,069
original	0,187	0,138	0,110	0,050	0,958	0,869	0,589	0,185	0,298	0,216	0,160	0,069

TORRALBA	Precision				Recall				F-measure			
	TH 01	TH 0.25	TH 0.5	TH 0.75	TH 01	TH 0.25	TH 0.5	TH 0.75	TH 01	TH 0.25	TH 0.5	TH 0.75
JPEG 1%	0,111	0,058	0,052	0,050	1,000	0,998	0,916	0,370	0,196	0,108	0,095	0,081
JPEG 5%	0,111	0,058	0,053	0,055	1,000	0,998	0,920	0,402	0,196	0,109	0,095	0,086
JPEG 10%	0,111	0,058	0,050	0,060	1,000	0,998	0,928	0,457	0,196	0,108	0,090	0,096
JPEG 20%	0,111	0,059	0,071	0,068	1,000	0,997	1,000	0,453	0,197	0,109	0,041	0,103
JPEG 40%	0,111	0,059	0,051	0,064	1,000	0,998	0,925	0,446	0,197	0,109	0,091	0,099
JPEG 60%	0,111	0,059	0,051	0,064	1,000	0,997	0,926	0,449	0,197	0,109	0,091	0,101
JPEG 80%	0,111	0,059	0,051	0,066	1,000	0,998	0,924	0,441	0,197	0,109	0,092	0,102
original	0,111	0,059	0,051	0,064	1,000	0,998	0,924	0,445	0,197	0,109	0,097	0,101

5   Conclusions and Future Works

In this paper we investigated the robustness of visual saliency methods against image corruption (additive noise and image compression). We compared the results of three popular saliency estimation methods with a ground truth that consists of real fixation maps. Several experiments have been conducted in order to analyze the effect of image corruptions in the resulting saliency maps, we focus our attention on additive noise (salt & pepper, gaussian noise) and jpeg compression.

As we expected, statistical accuracy measures of saliency maps decreases with respect to increasing global spatial distribution of noise into the images, GBVS method outperforms the other approaches showing accuracy values very close to the original values (i.e. the comparison between the real fixation maps and the saliency maps of the original images). Otherwise, the effects of jpeg compression depend on some features, such as the morphological surface of the image and the level of complexity of the scene. For this reasons we investigated on the performances of saliency detection methods and the rate of image compression: by observing preliminary results we noticed that jpeg compression substantially do not affect the performance of saliency detection methods.

It also would be interesting to analyze the relationship between the color quantization and the single steps of image compressions and the visual perception. In future works, we also want to extend this analysis to a larger set of images under varying conditions.

References

1. Itti, L., Koch, C., Niebur, E.: A model of saliency-based visual attention for rapidscene analysis. IEEE Transactions on Pattern Analysis and Machine Intelligence **20**(11), 1254–1259 (1998)
2. Harel, J., Koch, C., Perona, P.: Graph-based visual saliency. In: Advances in NeuralInformation Processing Systems, vol. 19, pp. 545–552. MIT Press (2007)
3. Koch, C., Ullman, S.: Shifts in selective visual attention: towards the underlying neural circuitry. Human Neurobiology **4**, 219–227 (1985)
4. Luo, J.: Subject content-based intelligent cropping of digital photos. In: IEEE International Conference on Multimedia and Expo (2007)
5. Sundstedt, V., Chalmers, A., Cater, K., Debattista, K.: Topdown visual attention for efficient rendering of task related scenes. In: Vision, Modeling and Visualization, pp. 209–216 (2004)
6. Itti, L., Koch, C.: Computational modeling of visual attention. Nature Reviews Neuroscience **2**(3) (2001)
7. Chen, L.-Q., Xie, X., Fan, X., Ma, W.-Y., Zhang, H.-J., Zhou, H.-Q.: A visual attention model for adapting images on small displays. ACM Multimedia Systems Journal **9**(4) (2003)
8. Judd, Y., Ehinger, K., Durand, F., Torralba, A.: Learning to predict where humans look. In: IEEE 12th International Conference on Computer Vision, pp. 2106–2133 (2009)
9. http://people.csail.mit.edu/tjudd/WherePeopleLook/index.html
10. Gide, M.S., Karam, L.J.: Comparative evaluation of visual saliency models for quality assessment task. In: International Workshop on Video Processing and Quality Metrics for Consumer Electronics (VPQM) (2012)
11. Redi, J., Liu, H., Zunino, R., Heynderickx, I.: Interactionsof visual attention and quality perception. Proceedings of SPIE, Human Vision and ElectronicImaging XVI **7865**(1), 1–11 (2011)
12. Toet, A.: Computational versus psychophysical bottom-up image saliency: A comparative evaluation study. IEEE Transactions on Pattern Analysis and Machine Intelligence **33**(11), 2131–2146 (2011)
13. Duncan, K., Sarkar, S.: Saliency in images and video: a brief survey. IET Computer Vision **6**(6), 514–523 (2012)
14. Simoncelli, E.P., Freeman, W.T.: The steerable pyramid: A flexible architecture for multiscale derivative computation, pp. 444–447 (1995)
15. Oliva, A., Torralba, A.: Modeling the shape of the scene: A holistic representation of the spatial envelope. International Journal of Computer Vision **42**, 145–175 (2001)
16. Rosenholtz, R.: A simple saliency model predicts a numberof motion popout phenomena. Vision Research **39**(19), 3157–3163 (1999)
17. Treisman, A.M., Gelade, G.: A Feature-Integration Theory of Attention. Cognitive Psychology **12**(1), 97–136 (1980)

Author Index

Printed in the United States
By Bookmasters